Psychotherapy Relationships That Work

Psychotherapy Relationships That Work

Evidence-Based Responsiveness

Second Edition

Edited by

John C. Norcross

OXFORD
UNIVERSITY PRESS

OXFORD
UNIVERSITY PRESS

Published in the United States of America by Oxford University Press, Inc.,
198 Madison Avenue, New York, NY, 10016
United States of America

Oxford University Press, Inc., publishes works that further Oxford University's
objective of excellence in research, scholarship, and education.

Oxford is a registered trade mark of Oxford University Press
in the UK and in certain other countries

Library of Congress Cataloging-in-Publication Data

Psychotherapy relationships that work : evidence-based
responsiveness / edited by John C. Norcross. — 2nd ed.
    p. ; cm.
  Includes bibliographical references.
  ISBN 978-0-19-973720-8 (alk. paper)
  1. Psychotherapist and patient. 2. Evidence-based psychotherapy.
I. Norcross, John C., 1957-
  [DNLM: 1. Professional-Patient Relations—Meta-Analysis.
2. Psychotherapy—methods—Meta-Analysis. 3. Evidence-Based
Practice—Meta-Analysis. WM 420]
  RC480.8.P78 2011
  616.89'14—dc22
                                        2010037228

978-0-19-973720-8

Dedicated to

Emma and Owen
Daily reminders of the healing power of nurturing relationships

Arnold A. Lazarus, Ph.D.
Lifelong champion of adapting psychotherapy to the individual patient

PREFACE

A cordial welcome to the second edition of *Psychotherapy Relationships That Work*. This volume seeks, like its predecessor, to identify effective elements of the psychotherapy relationship and to determine effective methods of adapting or tailoring that relationship to the individual patient. That is, we summarize the empirical research and clinical practice on what works in general as well as what works in particular. This dual focus has been characterized as "two books in one": one book on relationship elements and one book on adaptation methods.

My hope in this book, as with the first edition, is to advance a rapprochement between the warring factions in the culture wars of psychotherapy and to demonstrate that the best available research clearly demonstrates the healing qualities of the therapy relationship. The first edition brought renewed and corrective attention to the substantial research behind the therapy relationship and, in the words of one reviewer (*Psychotherapy Research*, 2003, p. 532), "will convince most psychotherapists of the rightful place of ESRs (empirically supported relationships) alongside ESTs in the treatments they provide." Note the desired emphasis on "alongside" treatments, not "instead of" or "better than."

Changes in the New Edition

The aims of this edition of *Psychotherapy Relationships That Work* remain the same as its predecessor, but its sponsorship, methodology, and scope differ. First, the inaugural edition of the book was sponsored by a single professional association (Division of Psychotherapy), but this second edition was sponsorship by both the American Psychological Association (APA) Division of Clinical Psychology and the APA Division of Psychotherapy. Second, we retitled the focus *evidence-based psychotherapy relationships* instead of *empirically supported (therapy) relationships* to parallel the contemporary movement to the newer terminology. This title change, in addition, properly emphasizes the confluence of the best research, clinical expertise, and patient characteristics in a quality treatment relationship. Third, we expanded the breadth of coverage. New reviews were commissioned on the alliance with children and adolescents, the alliance in couple and family therapy, collection of real-time feedback from clients, patient preferences, culture, and attachment style. Fourth, we decided to insist on meta-analyses for all research reviews. These original meta-analyses enable direct estimates of the magnitude of association and the ability to search for moderators. Unfortunately, that also meant that several relationship elements and adaptation methods in the first edition (self-disclosure, transference interpretations, anaclitic vs. introjective styles, assimilation of problematic experiences) were excluded due to their insufficient number of studies. Fifth, we improved the process for determining whether a particular relationship element—say, the alliance or empathy—could be classified as demonstrably effective, probably effective, or promising but insufficient research to judge. We constituted expert panels to establish a consensus on the evidentiary strength of the relationship elements and adaptation methods. Experts independently reviewed and rated the meta-analyses on several objective criteria, thus adding a modicum of rigor and consensus to the process, which was admittedly less so in the first edition of the book.

The net result is a compilation of two dozen, cutting-edge meta-analyses devoted to what works in the therapy relationship and what works in adapting that relationship to the individual client and his/her singular situation. This new edition, appearing 10 years after the first incarnation, presents a slightly slimmer book offering more practical, bulleted information on clinical practice at the end of each chapter.

Probable Audiences

One of our earliest considerations in planning the first edition of the book concerned the intended audiences. Each of psychotherapy's stakeholders—patients, practitioners, researchers, trainers, students, organizations, insurance companies, and policymakers—expressed different preferences for the content and length of the volume.

We prepared the book for multiple audiences but in a definite order of priority. First came clinical practitioners and trainees of diverse theoretical orientations and professional disciplines. They need to address urgent pragmatic questions: What do we know from the empirical research about cultivating and maintaining the therapeutic relationship? What are the research-supported means of adapting that relationship to the patient beyond his/her diagnosis? Our second priority was accorded to the mental health disciplines themselves, specifically those committees, task forces, and organizations promulgating lists of

evidence-based practices or treatment guidelines. We hope our work will inform and balance any efforts to focus exclusively on techniques or treatments to the neglect of the humans involved in the enterprise. Our third priority was insurance carriers and accreditation organizations, many of which have unintentionally devalued the person of the therapist and the centrality of the relationship by virtue of reimbursement decisions. Although supportive of the recent thrust toward science informing practice, we must remind all parties to the therapy relationship that healing cannot be replaced with treating, caring cannot be supplanted by managing. Finally, *Psychotherapy Relationships That Work* is intended for psychotherapy researchers seeking a central resource on the empirical status of the multiple, interdependent qualities of the therapy relationship.

Organization of the Book

The opening chapter introduces the book by outlining the purpose and history of the interdivisional Task Force and its relation to previous efforts to identify evidence-based practices in psychotherapy. This chapter also presents the key limitations of our work.

The heart of the book is composed of research reviews on the therapist's relational contributions and recommended therapeutic practices predicated on that research. Section II—Effective Elements of the Therapy Relationship: What Works in General—features eleven chapters on relationship elements primarily provided by the psychotherapist. Chapters 2–5 report on broader, more inclusive relationship elements. The therapy alliance and group cohesion are composed, in fact, of multiple elements. Chapters 6–9 feature more specific elements of the therapy relationship, and Chapters 10–12 review specific therapist behaviors that promote the relationship and favorable treatment results. Section III—Tailoring the Therapy Relationship to the Individual Patient: What Works in Particular—features eight chapters on adaptation methods. They feature probably and demonstrably effective means of tailoring psychotherapy to the entire person beyond diagnosis alone.

The final section of the book consists of a single chapter. It presents the Task Force conclusions, including a list of evidence-based relationship elements and adaptation methods, and our recommendations, divided into general, practice, training, research, and policy recommendations.

Chapter Guidelines

With the exception of the bookends (Chapters 1 and 21), all chapters use the same section headings and adhere to a consistent structure, as follows:

• *Introduction* (untitled). Introduce the relationship element or the adaptation method and its historical context.

• *Definitions and Measures*. Define in theoretically neutral language the relationship element or adaptation method. Identify any highly similar or equivalent constructs from diverse theoretical traditions. Review the popular measures used in the research and included in the ensuing meta-analysis.

• *Clinical Example*. Provide several concrete examples of the relationship behavior being reviewed. Portions of psychotherapy transcripts are encouraged.

• *Meta-Analytic Review*. Compile all available empirical studies linking the relationship behavior to treatment outcome in the English language. Use the Meta-Analysis Reporting Standards (MARS) as a general guide for the information included in the chapter.

Report the effect size as weighted r (in Section II) or d (in Section III).

• *Moderators*. Present the results of the moderator analyses on the association between the relationship element and treatment outcome. If available in the studies, examine the possible moderating effects of (1) rater perspective (assessed by therapist, patient, or external raters), (2) therapist variables, (3) patient factors, (4) different measures, (5) time of assessment (when in the course of therapy), and (6) type of psychotherapy/theoretical orientation.

• *Patient Contribution*. The meta-analyses pertain largely to the psychotherapist's contribution to the relationship; by contrast, this section will address the patient's contribution to that relationship and the distinctive perspective he/she brings to the interaction.

• *Limitations of the Research*. Point to the major limitations of both the meta-analysis and the available studies.

• *Therapeutic Practices*. Emphasize what works. Bullet the practice implications from the foregoing research, primarily in terms of the therapist's contribution and secondarily in terms of the patient's perspective.

These research reviews are based on the results of empirical research linking the relationship element or adaptation method to psychotherapy outcome. Outcome was inclusively defined but consisted largely of distal posttreatment outcomes. Authors were asked to specify the outcome criterion when a particular study did not employ a typical end-of-treatment measure of symptom or functioning. Indeed, the type of outcome measure was frequently analyzed as a possible moderator of the overall effect size.

Acknowledgments

Psychotherapy Relationships That Work would not have been possible without a decade of organizational and individual support. On the organizational front, the board of directors of the APA Division of Psychotherapy and the APA Division of Clinical Psychology commissioned and supported the Task Force. In particular, I am indebted to the presidents of the respective divisions: Drs. Jeffrey Barnett, Nadine Kaslow, and Jeffrey Magnavita of the psychotherapy division, and Drs. Marsha Linehan, Irving Weiner, and Marvin Goldfried of the clinical division. At Oxford University Press, Joan Bossert shepherded both books through the publishing process and recognized early on that they would compliment Oxford's landmark *Treatments That Work*. This second edition has been improved by the OUP book team of Sarah Harrington, Jodi Nardi, and Tony Orrantia.

On the individual front, many people modeled and manifested the ideal therapeutic relationship throughout the course of the project. The authors of the respective chapters, of course, were indispensible in generating the research reviews and in sharing their expertise. Dr. Bruce Wampold expertly reviewed each meta-analysis and provided valuable guidance on the entire project. Members of the expert consensus panels critiqued each meta-analysis and rated the evidentiary strength of the results; I appreciate the generosity of Drs. Guillermo Bernal, Franz Caspar, Louis Castonguay, Charles Gelso, Mark Hilsenroth, Michael Lambert, and Bruce Wampold. The Steering Committee of the first Task Force assisted in canvassing the literature, defining the parameters of the project, selecting the contributors, and writing the initial conclusions. I am grateful to them all: Steven J. Ackerman, Lorna Smith Benjamin, Larry E. Beutler, Charles J. Gelso, Marvin R. Goldfried, Clara E. Hill, Michael J. Lambert, David E. Orlinsky, and Jackson P. Rainer. Last but never least, my immediate family—Nancy, Jonathon, and Rebecca—tolerated my absences, preoccupations, and irritabilities associated with editing this book with a combination of empathy and patience that would do any seasoned psychotherapist proud.

John C. Norcross, PhD
Clarks Summit, Pennsylvania

CONTRIBUTORS

Jennifer Alonso, B.S.
Department of Psychology,
Brigham Young University

Rebecca M. Ametrano, B.A.
Department of Psychology,
University of Massachusetts Amherst

Diane B. Arnkoff, Ph.D.
Department of Psychology,
Catholic University of America

Sara B. Austin, B.S.
Department of Psychology, University of
Wisconsin–Madison

Guillermo Bernal, Ph.D.
Institute for Psychological Research,
University of Puerto Rico

Samantha L. Bernecker, B.S.
Department of Psychology,
Pennsylvania State University

Larry E. Beutler, Ph.D.
Pacific Graduate School of Psychology,
Palo Alto University

Kathy Blau, M.S.
Pacific Graduate School of Psychology,
Palo Alto University

Arthur C. Bohart, Ph.D.
Department of Psychology, California
State University–Dominguez Hills and
Graduate College of Psychology and
Humanistic Studies, Saybrook University

Gary M. Burlingame, Ph.D.
Department of Psychology,
Brigham Young University

Jennifer L. Callahan, Ph.D.
Department of Psychology,
University of North Texas

Michael J. Constantino, Ph.D.
Department of Psychology,
University of Massachusetts-Amherst

Don E. Davis, M.S.
Department of Psychology,
Virginia Commonwealth University

AC Del Re, M.A.
Department of Counseling Psychology,
University of Wisconsin–Madison

Gary M. Diamond, Ph.D.
Department of Psychology,
Ben-Gurion University of the Negev

Erin M. Doolin, M.Ed.
Department of Counseling Psychology,
University of Wisconsin–Madison

Robert Elliott, Ph.D.
School of Psychological Sciences and
Health, University of Strathclyde

William D. Ellison, M.S.
Department of Psychology,
Pennsylvania State University

Valentín Escudero, Ph.D.
Departamento de Psicología,
Universidad de A Coruña

Catherine Eubanks-Carter, Ph.D.
Ferkauf Graduate School of Psychology,
Yeshiva University

Barry A. Farber, Ph.D.
Department of Counseling and Clinical
Psychology, Teachers College
Columbia University

Christoph Flückiger, Ph.D.
Department of Clinical Psychology and
Psychotherapy, University of Bern

Myrna L. Friedlander, Ph.D.
Department of Educational and
Counseling Psychology, University at
Albany/State University of New York

Charles J. Gelso, Ph.D.
Department of Psychology,
University of Maryland-College Park

Carol R. Glass, Ph.D.
Department of Psychology,
Catholic University of America

Leslie S. Greenberg, Ph.D.
Department of Psychology,
York University

T. Mark Harwood, Ph.D.
Private Practice
Chicago, Illinois

Jeffrey A. Hayes, Ph.D.
Counseling Psychology Program,
Pennsylvania State University

Laurie Heatherington, Ph.D.
Department of Psychology,
Williams College

John Holman, M.S.
Pacific Graduate School of Psychology,
Palo Alto University

Joshua N. Hook, Ph.D.
Department of Psychology,
University of North Texas

Adam O. Horvath, Ed.D.
Faculty of Education & Department of
Psychology, Simon Fraser University

Ann M. Hummel, M.S.
Department of Psychology,
University of Maryland-College Park

Marc S. Karver, Ph.D.
Department of Psychology,
University of South Florida

Satoko Kimpara, Ph.D.
Pacific Graduate School of Psychology,
Asian American Community Involvement
(AACI) and Palo Alto University

Marjorie H. Klein, Ph.D.
Department of Psychiatry,
University of Wisconsin–Madison

Gregory G. Kolden, Ph.D.
Department of Psychiatry and
Psychology, University of
Wisconsin–Madison

Paul M. Krebs, Ph.D.
Department of General Internal
Medicine, New York University
Medical Center

Michael J. Lambert, Ph.D.
Department of Psychology,
Brigham Young University

Kenneth N. Levy, Ph.D.
Department of Psychology,
Pennsylvania State University

Debra Theobald McClendon, Ph.D.
Department of Psychology,
Brigham Young University

Michael A. McDaniel, Ph.D.
Department of Management,
Virginia Commonwealth University

Aaron Michelson, M.S.
Pacific Graduate School of Psychology,
Palo Alto University

J. Christopher Muran, Ph.D.
Derner Institute of Advanced
Psychological Studies,
Adelphi University

John C. Norcross, Ph.D.
Department of Psychology,
University of Scranton

James O. Prochaska, Ph.D.
Cancer Prevention Research Consortium,
University of Rhode Island

Melanie M. Domenech Rodríguez, Ph.D.
Department of Psychology,
Utah State University

Jeremy D. Safran, Ph.D.
Department of Psychology,
New School for Social Research

Lori N. Scott, M.S.
Department of Psychology,
Pennsylvania State University

Kenichi Shimokawa, Ph.D.
Family Institute,
Northwestern University

Stephen R. Shirk, Ph.D.
Department of Psychology,
University of Denver

JuliAnna Z. Smith, M.A.
Center for Research on Families,
University of Massachusetts Amherst

Timothy B. Smith, Ph.D.
Department of Counseling
Psychology and Special Education,
Brigham Young University

Xiaoxia Song, Ph.D.
Department of Psychology,
Ohio University

Joshua K. Swift, Ph.D.
Department of Psychology,
University of Alaska Anchorage

Dianne Symonds, Ph.D.
Faculty of Community and
Health Studies, Kwantlen
Polytechnic University

Georgiana Shick Tryon, Ph.D.
Ph.D. Program in Educational
Psychology, The Graduate Center,
City University of New York

David Verdirame, M.S.
Pacific Graduate School of
Psychology, Palo Alto University

Barbara M. Vollmer, Ph.D.
Department of Counseling
Psychology, University of
Denver

Bruce E. Wampold, Ph.D.
Department of Counseling
Psychology, University of
Wisconsin–Madison

Chia-Chiang Wang, M.Ed.
Department of Rehabilitation
Psychology and Special Education,
University of Wisconsin–Madison

Jeanne C. Watson, Ph.D.
Department of Adult Education,
University of Toronto

Greta Winograd, Ph.D.
Psychology Department,
State University of
New York-New Paltz

Everett L. Worthington, Jr., Ph.D.
Department of Psychology,
Virginia Commonwealth
University

TABLE OF CONTENTS

PART 1

Introduction

1   Evidence-Based Therapy Relationships

John C. Norcross *and* Michael J. Lambert

The culture wars in psychotherapy dramatically pit the treatment method against the therapy relationship. Do treatments cure disorders or do relationships heal people? Which is the most accurate vision for practicing, researching, and teaching psychotherapy?

Like most dichotomies, this one is misleading and unproductive on multiple counts. For starters, the patient's contribution to psychotherapy outcome is vastly greater than that of either the particular treatment method or the therapy relationship (Lambert, 1992). The empirical evidence should keep us mindful and a bit humble about our collective tendency toward therapist centricity (Bohart & Tallman, 1999). For another, decades of psychotherapy research consistently attest that the patient, the therapist, their relationship, the treatment method, and the context all contribute to treatment success (and failure). We should be looking at all of these determinants and their optimal combinations (Norcross, Beutler, & Levant, 2006).

But perhaps the most pernicious and insidious consequence of the false dichotomy of treatment versus relationship has been its polarizing effect on the discipline. Rival camps have developed, and countless critiques have been published on each side of the culture war. Are you on the side of the treatment method, the RCT (randomized controlled/clinical trial), and the scientific-medical model? Or do you belong to the side of the therapy relationship, the effectiveness and process-outcome studies, and the relational-contextual model? Such polarizations not only impede psychotherapists from working together but also hinder attempts to provide the most efficacious psychological services to our patients.

We hoped that a balanced perspective would be achieved by the adoption of an inclusive, neutral definition of evidence-based practice. The American Psychological Association (2006, p. 273) did endorse just such a definition: "Evidence-based practice in psychology (EBPP) is the integration of the best available research with clinical expertise in the context of patient characteristics, culture, and preferences." However, even that definition has been commandeered by the rival camps as polarizing devices. On the one side, some erroneously equate EBP solely with the best available research and particularly the results of RCTs on treatment methods, while on the other side, some mistakenly exaggerate the primacy of clinical or relational expertise while neglecting research support.

Within this polarizing context, in 1999, the American Psychological Association (APA) Division of Psychotherapy commissioned a task force to identify, operationalize, and disseminate information on empirically supported therapy relationships. That task force summarized its findings and detailed its recommendations in the first edition of this book (Norcross, 2002). In 2009, the Division of Psychotherapy along with the Division of Clinical Psychology commissioned a second task force on evidence-based therapy relationships to update the research base and clinical practices on the psychotherapist–patient relationship. This second edition, appearing 10 years after its predecessor, does just that.

Our hope now, as then, is to advance a rapprochement between the warring factions and to demonstrate that the best available research clearly supports the healing qualities of the therapy relationship and the beneficial value of adapting that relationship to patient characteristics beyond diagnosis. The bulk of the book summarizes the best available research and clinical practices on numerous elements of the therapy relationship and on several methods of treatment adaptation. In doing so, our grander goal is to repair some of the damage incurred by the culture wars in psychotherapy and to promote integration between science and practice.

In this chapter, we begin by tracing the purpose and processes of the interdivisional Task Force. We explicate the need for identifying evidence-based elements of the therapy relationship and means of matching or adapting treatment to the individual. In a tentative way, we offer two models to account for psychotherapy outcome as a function of various therapeutic factors (e.g., patient, relationship, technique). The latter part of the chapter features the limitations of the Task Force's work and responds to frequently asked questions.

The Interdivisional Task Force

The dual purposes of the interdivisional Task Force were to identify effective elements of the therapy relationship and to determine effective methods of adapting or tailoring therapy to the individual patient on the basis of his/her (transdiagnostic) characteristics. In other words, we were interested in both what works in general and what works for particular patients. This twin focus has been characterized as "two books in one": one book on relationship elements and one book on adaptation methods under the same cover.

For the purposes of our work, we again adopted Gelso and Carter's (1985, 1994) operational definition of the therapy relationship: The relationship is the feelings and attitudes that therapist and client have toward one another, and the manner in which these are expressed. This definition is quite general, and the phrase "the manner in which it is expressed" potentially opens the relationship to include everything under the therapeutic sun (see Gelso & Hayes, 1998, for an extended discussion). Nonetheless, it serves as a concise, consensual, theoretically neutral, and sufficiently precise definition.

We acknowledge the deep synergy between treatment methods and the therapeutic relationship. They constantly shape and inform each other. Both clinical experience and research evidence (e.g., Rector, Zuroff, & Segal, 1999; Barber et al., 2006) point to a complex, reciprocal interaction between the interpersonal relationship and the instrumental methods. Consider this finding from a large collaborative study: For patients with a strong therapeutic alliance, adherence to the treatment manual was irrelevant for treatment outcome, but for patients with a weak alliance, a moderate level of therapist adherence was associated with the best outcome (Barber et al., 2006). The relationship does not exist apart from what the therapist does in terms of method, and we cannot imagine any treatment methods that would not have some relational impact. Put differently, treatment methods are relational acts (Safran & Muran, 2000).

For historical and research convenience, the field has distinguished between relationships and techniques. Words like "relating" and "interpersonal behavior" are used to describe *how* therapists and clients behave toward each other. By contrast, terms like "technique" or "intervention" are used to describe *what* is done by the therapist. In research and theory, we often treat the how and the what—the relationship and the intervention, the interpersonal and the instrumental—as separate categories. In reality, of course, what one does and how one does it are complementary and inseparable. To remove the interpersonal from the instrumental may be acceptable in research, but it is a fatal flaw when the aim is to extrapolate research results to clinical practice (see Orlinsky, 2000; 2005 special issue of *Psychotherapy* on the interplay of techniques and therapeutic relationship).

In other words, the value of a treatment method is inextricably bound to the relational context in which it is applied. Hans Strupp, one of our first research mentors, offered an analogy to illustrate the inseparability of these constituent elements. Suppose you want your teenager to clean his or her room. Two methods for achieving this are to establish clear standards and to impose consequences. A reasonable approach, but the effectiveness of these two evidence-based methods will vary on whether the relationship between you and the teenager is characterized by warmth and mutual respect or by anger and mistrust. This is not to say that the methods are useless, merely that how well they work depends upon the context in which they are used (Norcross, 2010).

The work of the Task Force applies psychological science to the identification and promulgation of effective psychotherapy. It does so by expanding or enlarging the typical focus of evidence-based practice to therapy relationships. Focusing on one area—in this case, the therapy relationship—may unfortunately convey the impression that this is the only area of importance. We review the scientific literature on the therapy relationship and provide clinical recommendations based on that literature without, we trust, degrading the simultaneous contributions of the treatments, patients, or therapists to outcome. Indeed, we wish that more psychotherapists would acknowledge the inseparable context and practical interdependence of the relationship and the treatment. That can prove a crucial step in reducing the polarizing strife of the culture wars and in improving the effectiveness of psychotherapy (Lambert, 2010).

An immediate challenge to the Task Force was to establish the inclusion and exclusion criteria for the elements of the therapy relationship. We readily agreed that the traditional features of the therapeutic relationship—the alliance in individual therapy and cohesion in group therapy, for example—and the Rogerian facilitative conditions would constitute core elements. We further agreed that discrete, relatively nonrelational techniques were not part of our purview, but that a few relational methods would be included. Therapy methods were considered for inclusion if their content, goal, and context were inextricably interwoven into the emergent therapy relationship. We settled on three relationship behaviors (collecting real-time client feedback, repairing alliance ruptures, and managing countertransference) because these methods are deeply embedded in the interpersonal character of the relationship itself. But which relational behaviors to include and which to exclude under the rubric of the *therapy relationship* bexeviled us, as it has the field.

How does one divide the indivisible relationship? For example, is *support* similar enough to *positive regard* or *validation* to be considered in the same meta-analysis, or is it distinct enough to deserve a separate research review? We struggled on how finely to slice the therapy relationship. As David Orlinsky opined in one of his e-mail messages, "It's okay to slice bologna that thin, but I doubt that it can be meaningfully done to the relationship." We agreed, as a group, to place the research on support in the positive regard chapter, but we understand that some practitioners may understandably take exception to collapsing these relationship elements. As a rule, we opted to divide the research reviews into smaller chunks so that the research conclusions were more specific and the practice implications more concrete.

In our deliberations, several members of the Steering Committee advanced a favorite analogy: the therapy relationship is like a diamond, a diamond composed of multiple, interconnected facets. The diamond is a complex, reciprocal, and multidimensional entity. The Task Force endeavored to separate and examine many of these facets.

Once these decisions were finalized, we commissioned original meta-analyses on the relationship elements and the adaptation methods. The chapters and the meta-analyses therein were reviewed and subsequently underwent at least one revision. Once revised, two consensus panels (each composed of five experts) were established to review the evidentiary strength of the relationship element or adaptation method according to the following criteria: number of empirical studies, consistency of empirical results, independence of supportive studies, magnitude of association between the relationship element and outcome, evidence for causal link between relationship element and outcome, and the ecological or external validity of research.

Their respective ratings of demonstrably effective, probably effective, or promising but insufficient research to judge were then combined to render a consensus. These conclusions are presented in the last chapter of this book.

The deliberations of the Steering Committee and the expert panels were not easy or unanimous. Democracy is messy and inefficient; science is even slower and painstaking. We debated and, in most instances, voted on our decisions. We relied on expert opinion, professional consensus, and most importantly, reviews of the empirical evidence. But these were all human decisions—open to cavil, contention, and future revision.

Therapy Relationship

Recent years have witnessed the controversial compilation of practice guidelines and evidence-based treatments in mental health. In the United States and other countries, the introduction of such guidelines has provoked practice modifications, training refinements, and organizational conflicts. Insurance carriers and government policymakers are increasingly turning to such guidelines to determine which psychotherapies to approve and fund. Indeed, along with the negative influence of managed care, there is probably issue no more central to clinicians than the evolution of evidence-based practice in psychotherapy (Barlow, 2000).

All of the efforts to promulgate evidence-based psychotherapies have been noble in intent and timely in distribution. They are praiseworthy efforts to distill scientific research into clinical applications and to guide practice and training. They wisely demonstrate that, in a climate of accountability, psychotherapy stands up to empirical scrutiny with the best of health care interventions. And within psychology, these have proactively counterbalanced documents that accord primacy to biomedical treatments for mental disorders and largely ignore the outcome data for psychological therapies. On many accounts, then, the extant EBP efforts have addressed the realpolitik of the socioeconomic situation (Messer, 2001; Nathan, 1998).

At the same time, many practitioners and researchers have found these recent efforts to codify evidence-based treatments seriously incomplete. While scientifically laudable in their intent, these efforts have largely ignored the therapy relationship and the person of the therapist. If one were to read previous efforts literally, disembodied therapists apply manualized interventions to discrete DSM disorders. Not only is the language offensive on clinical grounds to some practitioners, but the research evidence is weak for validating treatment methods in isolation from the therapy relationship and the individual patient.

Suppose we asked a neutral scientific panel from outside the field to review the corpus of psychotherapy research to determine what is the most powerful phenomenon we should be studying, practicing, and teaching. Henry (1998, p. 128) concludes that the panel

> would find the answer obvious, and *empirically validated*. As a general trend across studies, the largest chunk of outcome variance not attributable to preexisting patient characteristics involves individual therapist differences and the emergent therapeutic relationship between patient and therapist, regardless of technique or school of therapy. This is the main thrust of three decades of empirical research.

What's missing, in short, are the person of the therapist and elements of the therapeutic relationship.

Person of the Therapist

Most practice guidelines and evidence-based practice compilations depict disembodied psychotherapists performing procedures on DSM disorders. This stands in marked contrast to the clinician's experience of psychotherapy as an intensely interpersonal and deeply emotional experience. Although efficacy research has gone to considerable lengths to eliminate the individual therapist as a variable that might account for patient improvement, the inescapable fact is that it's simply not possible to mask the person and the contribution of the therapist (Orlinsky & Howard, 1977). The curative contribution of the person of the therapist is, arguably, as empirically validated as manualized treatments or psychotherapy methods (Duncan, Miller, Wampold, & Hubble, 2010).

Multiple and converging sources of evidence indicate that the *person* of the psychotherapist is inextricably intertwined with the outcome of psychotherapy. A large, naturalistic study estimated the outcomes attributable to 581 psychotherapists treating 6,146 patients in a managed care setting. About 5% of the outcome variation was due to therapist effects and 0% due to specific treatment methods (Wampold & Brown, 2005). Quantitative reviews of therapist effects in psychotherapy outcome studies show consistent and robust effects—probably 5% to 9% of psychotherapy outcome (Crits-Christoph et al., 1991). In reviewing the research, Wampold (2001, p. 200) concluded that "a preponderance of evidence indicates that there are large therapist effects . . . and that the effects greatly exceed treatment effects."

Two controlled studies examining therapist variables in the outcomes of cognitive-behavioral therapy are instructive (Huppert et al., 2001; Project MATCH Research Group, 1998). In the Multicenter Collaborative Study for the Treatment of Panic

Disorder, considerable care was taken to standardize the treatment, the therapist, and the patients in order to increase the experimental rigor of the study and in order to minimize therapist effects. The treatment was manualized and structured, the therapists were identically trained and monitored for adherence, and the patients rigorously evaluated and relatively uniform. Nonetheless, the therapists significantly differed in the magnitude of change among caseloads. Effect sizes for therapist impact on outcome measures ranged from 0% to 18%. In the similarly controlled multi-site study on alcohol abuse conducted by Project MATCH, the therapists were carefully selected, trained, supervised, and monitored in their respective treatment approaches. Although there were few outcome differences among the treatments, over 6% of the outcome variance (1%–12% range) was due to therapists. Despite impressive attempts to experimentally render individual practitioners as controlled variables, it is simply not possible to mask the person and the contribution of the therapist.

Further evidence comes from naturalistic studies of clinical practice rather than research settings where attempts are made to reduce individual therapist's contribution to patient outcomes. Okiishi, Lambert, Nielsen, and Ogles (2003) examined the outcomes of clients seen by 56 therapists practicing a variety of treatment methods. Despite the fact that the psychotherapists had similarly disturbed clients, there were dramatic differences in client outcome as a function of seeing a top-rated therapist or one at the bottom. On average, clients seeing a top-rated therapist achieved reliable improvement, while those clients seen by bottom-ranked therapists were unchanged or slightly worse off after treatment. Client deterioration for the low performers included one therapist who had 21% of his/her clients deteriorate while the

average at the center was about 8%. In a related study of many of the same therapists (Anderson, Ogles, Patterson, Lambert, & Vermeersch, 2009), the strongest predictor of patient outcome was these therapists' interpersonal skills.

Relationship Elements

A second omission from most evidence-based practice guidelines has been the decision to validate only the efficacy of treatments or technical interventions, as opposed to the therapy relationship or therapist interpersonal skills. This decision both reflects and reinforces the ongoing movement toward high-quality comparative effectiveness research (CER) on brand-name psychotherapies. "This trend of putting all of the eggs in the "technique" basket began in the late 1970s and is now reaching the peak of influence" (Bergin, 1997, p. 83).

Both clinical experience and research findings underscore that the therapy relationship accounts for as much of the outcome variance as particular treatment methods (Lambert & Barley, 2002), especially after the effects of researcher allegiance to treatment are accounted for (Luborsky et al., 1999). An early and influential review by Bergin and Lambert (1978, p. 180) anticipated the contemporary research consensus: "The largest variation in therapy outcome is accounted for by pre-existing client factors, such as motivation for change, and the like. Therapist personal factors account for the second largest proportion of change, with technique variables coming in a distant third."

Even those practice guidelines enjoining practitioners to attend to the therapy relationship do not provide specific, evidence-based means of doing so. The APA Template for Developing Guidelines (Task Force on Psychological Intervention Guidelines, 1995, pp. 5–6), for example, sagely recognizes that factors common to all therapies, "such as the clinician's ability to form a therapeutic alliance or to generate a mutual framework for change, are powerful determinants of success across interventions" but only vaguely addresses how research protocols or individual practitioners should do so. For another example, the scholarly and comprehensive review on treatment choice from Great Britain (Department of Health, 2001) devotes a single paragraph to the therapeutic relationship. Its recommended principle is that "Effectiveness of all types of therapy depends on the patient and the therapist forming a good working relationship" (p. 35), but no evidence-based guidance is offered on which therapist behaviors contribute to that relationship. Likewise, although most treatment manuals mention the importance of the therapy relationship, few specify which therapist qualities or in-session behaviors lead to a curative relationship.

All of this is to say that extant lists of EBPs and best practices in mental health give short shrift—some would say lip service—to the person of the therapist and the emergent therapeutic relationship. The vast majority of current attempts are thus seriously incomplete and potentially misleading, both on clinical and empirical grounds.

Treatment Adaptation

Since the earliest days of modern psychotherapy, practitioners have realized that treatment should be tailored to the individuality of the patient and the singularity of his/her context. As early as 1919, Freud introduced psychoanalytic psychotherapy as an alternative to classical analysis on the recognition that the more rarified approach lacked universal applicability (Wolitzky, 2011). The mandate for individualizing psychotherapy was embodied in Gordon

Paul's (1967) iconic question: "*What* treatment, by *whom*, is most effective for *this* individual with *that* specific problem, and under which set of circumstances?" Every psychotherapist recognizes that what works for one person may not work for another; we seek "different strokes for different folks."

To many, the means of such matching was to tailor the psychotherapy to the patient's disorder or presenting problem—that is, to find the best treatment for a particular disorder. The research suggests that it is certainly useful for select disorders; some psychotherapies make better marriages with some mental health disorders (e.g., Barlow, 2007; Nathan & Gorman, 2007; Roth & Fonagy, 2004). Indeed, the overwhelming majority of randomized clinical trials in psychotherapy compare the efficacy of specific treatments for specific disorders (Lambert, 2011).

However, only matching psychotherapy to a disorder is incomplete and not always effective (Wampold, 2001). Particularly absent from much of the research has been the person of the patient, beyond his/her disorder. As Sir William Osler, father of modern medicine, said: "It is sometimes much more important to know what sort of a patient has a disease than what sort of disease a patient has."

Most practice guidelines and evidence-based compilations unintentionally reduce our clients to a static diagnosis or problem. The impressive American Psychiatric Association *Practice Guidelines for the Treatment of Psychiatric Disorders* (2006), to take one prominent example, is organized exclusively around diagnoses. Virtually all practice guidelines are directed toward categorical disorders. DSM diagnoses have ruled the evidence-based roost to date.

This choice flies in the face of clinical practice and research findings that a categorical, nonpsychotic Axis I diagnosis exercises only a modest impact on treatment outcome (Beutler, 2000). While the research indicates that certain psychotherapies make better marriages for certain disorders, psychological therapies will be increasingly matched to people, not simply diagnoses.

The process of creating the optimal match in psychotherapy has been accorded multiple names: adaptation, responsiveness, attunement, matchmaking, customizing, prescriptionism, treatment selection, specificity factor, differential therapeutics, tailoring, treatment fit, and individualizing. By whatever name, the goal is to enhance treatment effectiveness by tailoring it to the individual and his/her singular situation. In other words, psychotherapists endeavor to create a new therapy for each patient.

This position can be easily misunderstood as an authority figure therapist prescribing a specific form of psychotherapy for a passive client. Far from it: the goal is for an empathic therapist to arrange for an optimal relationship collaboratively with an active client on the basis of the client's personality, culture, and preferences. If a client frequently resists, for example, then the therapist considers whether he or she is pushing something that the client finds incompatible (preferences), or the client is not ready to make those changes (stage of change) or is uncomfortable with a directive style (reactance).

As every clinician knows, different types of patients respond more effectively to different types of treatments and relationships. Clinicians strive to offer or select a therapy that accords with the patient's personal characteristics, proclivities, and worldviews—in addition to diagnosis. Any differential effectiveness of different therapies may well prove to be a function of cross-diagnostic patient characteristics, such as patient preferences, coping styles, stages of change, personality dimensions, and culture.

Research studies problematically collapse numerous patients under a single diagnosis. It is a false and, at times, misleading presupposition in randomized clinical trials that the patient sample is homogenous. Perhaps the patients are diagnostically homogeneous, but nondiagnostic variability is the rule, as every clinician also knows. It is precisely the unique individual and the singular context that many psychotherapists attempt to treat.

Moreover, most practice and EBP guidelines do little for those psychotherapists whose patients and theoretical conceptualizations do not fall into discrete disorders (Messer, 2001). Consider the client who seeks more joy in his/her life, but who does not meet diagnostic criteria for any disorder, whose psychotherapy stretches beyond 20 sessions, and whose treatment objectives are not easily specified in measurable, symptom-based outcomes. Current evidence-based compilations have little to contribute to this kind of treatment (see O'Donohue, Buchanan, & Fisher, 2000, for general characteristics of ESTs).

The upshot of these considerations is that a truly evidence-based psychotherapy will necessarily consider the person of the psychotherapist, the therapy relationship, and means to adapt or tailor that relationship to the individual patient—in addition to diagnosis. Otherwise, evidence-based practice will prove clinically incomplete as well as scientifically suspect.

Effect Sizes

The second edition of this book endeavors to systemically appraise the empirical research performed on elements of the therapy relationship and means of treatment adaptation in order to identify what works. The subsequent chapters feature original meta-analyses on the link between the relationship elements (Section II) and adaptation methods (Section III) to psychotherapy outcome. Insisting on meta-analyses for all these chapters enables direct estimates of the magnitude of association in the form of effect sizes. And conducting these meta-analytic tests with random effects models permits generalization to studies outside the samples, although the random effects model is slightly less powerful than the fixed effect model (Rosenthal, 1995).

The meta-analyses in Section II of the book all employed the weighted r. This decision improved the consistency among the meta-analyses, enhanced their interpretability among the readers (square r for the amount of variance accounted for), and enabled direct comparisons of the meta-analytic results to one another as well as to d (the ES typically used when comparing the relative effects of two treatments). In all of these analyses, the larger the magnitude of r, the higher the probability of patient success in psychotherapy. By convention (Cohen, 1988), an r of .10 in the behavioral sciences is considered a small effect, .30 a medium effect, and .50 a large effect.

The meta-analyses presented in Section III of the book, by contrast, employed the weighted d. That is the common indicator of a difference between two treatments or conditions: in this case, the difference between the conventional or unadapted therapy and the adapted therapy. In all of these analyses, the larger the value of d, the higher the effectiveness of the specific adaptation or tailoring. By convention (Cohen, 1988), a d of .30 in the behavioral sciences is considered a small effect, .50 a medium effect, and .80 a large effect.

Table 1.1 presents several concrete ways to interpret r and d in health care. For example, the authors of Chapter 6 conducted a meta-analysis of 57 studies that investigated the link between therapist empathy and patient success at the end of treatment. Their meta-analysis, involving a total of 3,599 clients, found a weighted mean r of .30. As shown in Table 1.1, this is a medium effect size. That translates into happier and healthier clients: patients with empathic therapists tend to progress more in treatment and experience a higher probability of eventual improvement.

Consider another example, this one involving the effectiveness of tailoring therapy. The authors of Chapter 16 conducted a meta-analysis on 65 experimental and quasi-experimental studies, involving 8,620 patients, which evaluated the impact of culturally adapted treatments versus traditional (nonadapted) treatments. The resultant d of .46 favored those clients receiving a culturally adapted therapy. As seen in Table 1.1, this effect size also represents a medium, beneficial effect; incorporating clients' culture into treatment typically enhances the effectiveness of psychotherapy.

Given the large number of factors contributing to such success, and the inherent complexity of psychotherapy, we do not expect large, overpowering effects of any one of its facets. Instead, we expect to find a number of helpful facets. And that is exactly what we find in the following chapters—beneficial, medium-sized effects of several elements of the complex therapy relationship.

Accounting for Psychotherapy Outcome

What, then, accounts for psychotherapy success (and failure)? This question represents an understandable desire for clarity and guidance, but we answer with trepidation. Our collective ability to answer in meaningful ways is limited by the huge variation in methodological designs, theoretical orientations, treatment settings, and patient presentations. Of the dozens of variables that contribute to patient outcome, only a few can be included in any given study. How can we divide the indivisible complexity of psychotherapy outcome?

Table 1.1 Interpretation of Effect Size (ES) Statistics

d	r	Cohen's Benchmark	Type of effect	Percentile of treated patients[a]	Success rate of treated patients[b]	Number needed to treat[c]
1.00			Beneficial	84	72%	2.2
.90			Beneficial	82	70%	2.4
.80	.50	Large	Beneficial	79	69%	2.7
.70			Beneficial	76	66%	3.0
.60			Beneficial	73	64%	3.5
.50	.30	Medium	Beneficial	69	62%	4.1
.40			Beneficial	66	60%	5.1
.30			Beneficial	62	57%	6.7
.20	.10	Small	Beneficial	58	55%	10.0
.10			No effect	54	52%	20.0
.00	0		No effect	50	50%	
−.10			No effect	46	48%	
−.20	−.10		Detrimental	42	45%	
−.30			Detrimental	38	43%	

Sources: Adapted from Cohen (1988); Norcross, Hogan, & Koocher (2008); and Wampold (2001)

[a] Each ES can be conceptualized as reflecting a corresponding percentile value: in this case, the percentile standing of the average treated patient after psychotherapy relative to untreated patients.

[b] Each ES can also be translated into a success rate of treated patients relative to untreated patients; a d of .70, for example, would translate into approximately 66% of patients being treated successfully compared with 50% of untreated patients.

[c] Number needed to treat (NNT) refers to the number of patients who need to receive the experimental treatment vis-à-vis the comparison to achieve one success. An effect size of .70 approximates an NNT of 3: three patients need to receive psychotherapy to achieve a success relative to untreated patients (Wampold, 2001).

Nonetheless, psychotherapy research has made tremendous strides in clarifying the question and addressing the uncertainty. Thus, we tentatively advance two models that account for psychotherapy outcome, averaging across thousands of outcome studies and hundreds of meta-analyses, and acknowledging that this matter has been vigorously debated for over six decades. We implore readers to consider the following percentages as crude estimates, not as exact numbers.

The first model estimates the percentage of explained psychotherapy outcome variance as a function of therapeutic factors. This comparative importance of each of these factors is summarized in Figure 1.1. The percentages presented in Figure 1.1 are based on decades of research, but not formally derived from meta-analytic methods (see Lambert & Barley, 2002, for details). The patient's extratherapeutic change—self-change, spontaneous remission, social support, fortuitous events—accounts for roughly 40% of success. Common factors, variables found in most therapies regardless of theoretical orientation, probably account for another 30%. The therapy relationship represents the sine qua non of common factors, along with client and therapist factors. Technique factors, explaining approximately 15% of the variance, are those treatment methods fairly specific to the prescribed therapy, such as biofeedback, transference interpretations, desensitization, or two-chair work. Finally, playing

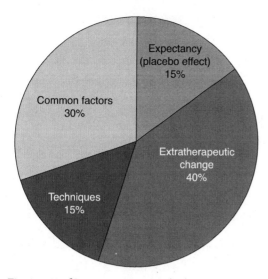

Fig. 1.1 % of Improvement in Psychotherapy Patients as a Function of Therapeutic Factors.

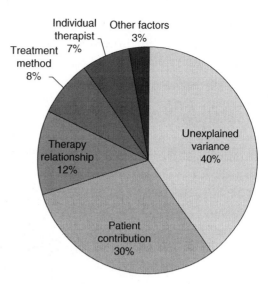

Fig. 1.2 % of Total Psychotherapy Outcome Variance Atrributable to Therapeutic Factors.

an important role is expectancy—the placebo effect, the client's knowledge that he/she is being treated and his/her conviction in the treatment rationale and methods. These four broad factors account for the *explained* outcome variance.

The second model begins with the *unexplained* variance in psychotherapy outcome, which necessarily decreases the amount of variance attributable to the therapeutic factors. As summarized in Figure 1.2, psychotherapy research cannot explain all of the variation in psychotherapy success. To be sure, some of this is attributable to measurement error and fallible research methods, but some is also attributable to the complexity of human behavior. Thereafter, we estimate that the patient (including severity of disorder) accounts for approximately 30% of the total variance, the therapy relationship for 12%, the specific treatment method for 8%, and the therapist for 7% (when not confounded with treatment effects). In this model, we assume that common factors are spread across the therapeutic factors—some pertain to the patient, some to the therapy method, some to the treatment method, and some to the therapist him/herself.

How to improve psychotherapy outcome? Follow the evidence; follow what contributes to psychotherapy outcome. Begin by leveraging the patient's resources and self-healing capacities; emphasize the therapy relationship and so-called common factors; employ research-supported treatment methods; select interpersonally skilled and clinically motivated practitioners; and adapt all of them to the patient's characteristics, personality, and worldviews. This, not simply matching a treatment method to a particular disorder, will maximize success.

The differences between the two models help explain the rampant confusion in the field regarding the relative percentages accounted for by relationships and techniques. The first model (Figure 1.1) presents only the explained variance and separates common factors and specific factors, whereas the second model (Figure 1.2) presents the total variance and assigns common factors to each of the constituent elements. Hence, it is essential to inquire whether the percentages attributable to particular therapeutic factors are based on total or explained variance and how common factors are conceptualized in a particular model.

Despite the differing percentages, both models converge mightily on several take-home points. One: patients contribute the lion's share of psychotherapy success (and failure). Simply consider the probable outcome of psychotherapy with an adjustment disorder in a healthy person in the action stage versus a chronically mentally ill person presenting in precontemplation/denial. Two: the therapeutic relationship generally accounts for as much psychotherapy success as the treatment method. Three: particular treatment methods do matter in some cases, especially with severe anxiety disorders treated via systematic exposure (Lambert & Ogles, 2004). Four: Adapting or customizing therapy to the patient enhances the effectiveness of psychotherapy probably by innervating multiple pathways—the patient, the relationship, the method, and the expectancy. Fifth: psychotherapists need to consider multiple factors and their optimal combinations, not only one or two of their favorites.

Limitations of the Task Force

A single task force can accomplish only so much work and cover only so much content. As such, we wish to acknowledge several necessary omissions and unfortunate truncations in our work.

The products of the Task Force probably suffer from content overlap. We may have cut the "diamond" of the therapy relationship too thin at times, leading to a profusion of highly related and possibly redundant constructs. Goal consensus, for example, correlates highly with parts of the therapeutic alliance, but these are reviewed in separate chapters. Collecting client feedback and repairing alliance ruptures, for another example, may represent different sides of the same therapist behavior, but these too are covered in separate meta-analyses. Thus, to some, the content may appear swollen; to others, the Task

Force may have failed to make necessary distinctions.

Another lacuna in the Task Force work is that we may have neglected, relatively speaking, the productive contribution of the client to the therapy relationship. We decided not to commission a separate chapter on the client's contributions; instead, we asked the authors of each chapter to address them. We encouraged authors to pay attention to the chain of events among the therapist's contributions, the patient processes, and eventual treatment outcomes. This, we hoped, would maintain the focus on what is effective in patient change. Further, all of the chapters in Section III examine patient contributions directly in terms of specific patient characteristics. Nonetheless, by omitting separate chapters on the client, we may be understandably accused of an omission akin to the error of leaving the relationship out at the expense of method. This book may be "therapist centric" in minimizing the client's relational contribution and self-healing processes.

Another prominent limitation across these research reviews is the difficulty of establishing causal connections between the relationship behavior and treatment outcome. The only meta-analysis in Section II that contains randomized clinical trials (RCTs) capable of demonstrating a causal effect is collecting client feedback. (Note that most of the meta-analyses in Section III were conducted on RCTs and are capable of causal conclusions.) Causal inferences are always difficult to make concerning process variables, such as the therapy relationship. Does the relationship cause improvement or simply reflect it? The interpretation problems of correlational studies (third variables, reverse causation) render such studies less convincing than RCTs. It is methodologically difficult to meet the three conditions to make a causal claim: nonspuriousness, covariation between the process variable and the outcome measure, and temporal precedence of the process variable (Feeley, DeRubeis, & Gelfand, 1999). We still need to determine whether and when the therapeutic relationship is a mediator, moderator, or mechanism of change in psychotherapy (Kazdin, 2007).

At the same time as we acknowledge this central limitation, let's remain mindful of several considerations. First, the establishment of temporal ordering is essential for causal inference, but it is not sufficient. In showing that these facets of a therapy relationship precede positive treatment outcome, we can certainly state that the therapy relationship is, at a minimum, an important predictor and antecedent of that outcome. Second, within these reality constraints, dozens of lagged correlational, unconfounded regression, structural equation, and growth curve studies suggest that the therapy relationship probably causally contributes to outcome (e.g., Barber et al., 2000). For example, using growth curve analyses and controlling for prior improvement and eight prognostically relevant client characteristics, Klein and colleagues (2003) found that the early alliance significantly predicted later improvement in 367 chronically depressed clients. Although we need to continue to parse out the causal linkages, the therapy relationship has probably been shown to exercise a causal association to outcome. Third, some of the most precious behaviors in life are incapable on ethical grounds of random assignment and experimental manipulation. Take parental love as an exemplar. Not a single randomized clinical trial has ever been conducted to conclusively determine the causal benefit of a parental love on children's functioning, yet virtually all humans aspire to it and practice it. Nor can we envision an institutional review board (IRB) ever approving a grant proposal to randomize patients in a psychotherapy study to an empathic, collaborative, and supportive therapist versus a nonempathic, authoritarian, disrespectful, and unsupportive therapist.

A final interesting drawback to the present work, and psychotherapy research as a whole, is the paucity of attention paid to the disorder-specific and treatment-specific nature of the therapy relationship. It is premature to aggregate the research on how the patient's primary disorder or the type of treatment impacts the therapy relationship, but there are early links. For example, in the National Institute on Drug Abuse Collaborative Cocaine Treatment Study, higher levels of the working alliance were associated with increased retention in supportive-expressive therapy, but in cognitive therapy, higher levels of alliance were associated with decreased retention (Barber et al., 2001). In the treatment of severe anxiety disorders, the specific treatments seem to exert a larger effect than the therapy relationship, but in depression, the relationship appears more powerful. The therapeutic alliance in the NIMH Treatment of Depression Collaborative Research Program, in both psychotherapy *and* pharmacotherapy, emerged as the leading force in reducing a patient's depression (Krupnick et al., 1996). The therapeutic relationship probably exhibits more impact in some disorders and in some therapies than others (Beckner, Vella, Howard, & Mohr, 2007). As with research on specific treatments, it may no longer suffice to ask "Does the relationship work?" but "How does the relationship work for this disorder and this treatment?"

Frequently Asked Questions

The interdivisional Task Force on Evidence-Based Therapy Relationships has generated considerable enthusiasm in the professional community, but it has also provoked misunderstandings and reservations. Here we address frequently asked questions (FAQs) about the Task Force's objectives and results.

♦ *What is the relationship of this task force to the Division 12 Task Force on Research-Supported Treatments (now the standing Committee on Science and Practice)?*

Questions abound regarding the connection of the task forces, probably because they are both associated with the same division of the American Psychological Association. Organizationally, the Task Forces are separate creatures. Their respective foci obviously diverge: one looking at therapist contributions to the relationship and patient responsiveness, the other looking at treatment methods for specific disorders. However, both task forces share the same book publisher (Oxford University Press) and overarching goals (to identify and promulgate evidence-based practices).

♦ *Are you saying that treatment methods are immaterial to psychotherapy outcome?*

Absolutely not. The empirical research shows that both the therapy relationship and the treatment method make frequent contributions to treatment outcome. It remains a matter of judgment and methodology on how much each contributes, but there is virtual unanimity that both the relationship and the method (insofar as we can separate them) "work." Looking at either treatment methods or therapy relationships alone is incomplete. We encourage practitioners and researchers to look at multiple determinants of outcome, particularly client contributions.

♦ *But are you not exaggerating the effects of relationship factors and/or minimizing the effects of treatments in order to set up the importance of your work?*

We think not and hope not. With the guidance of Task Force members and external consultants, we have tried to avoid dichotomies and polarizations. Focusing on one area—the psychotherapy relationship—in this volume may unfortunately convey the impression that it is the only area of importance. This is certainly not our intention. Relationship factors are important, and we need to review the scientific literature and provide clinical and training recommendations based upon that literature. This can be done without trivializing or degrading the effects of specific treatments.

♦ *Isn't your report just warmed-over Carl Rogers?*

No. While Rogers' (1957) facilitative conditions are represented in this book, they comprise only about 15% of the research critically reviewed. More fundamentally, we have moved beyond a limited and invariant set of necessary relationship conditions. Monolithic theories of change and one-size-fits-all therapy relationships are out; adapting the therapy to the unique patient is in.

♦ *An interpersonal view of psychotherapy seems at odds with what managed care and bean counters ask of me in my clinical practice. How do you reconcile these?*

It is true that a dominant image of modern psychotherapy, among both researchers and reimbursers, is as a mental health treatment. This "treatment" or "medical" model inclines people to define process in terms of method, therapists as providers trained in the application of techniques, treatment in terms of number of contact hours, patients as embodiments of psychiatric disorders, and outcome as the end result of a treatment episode (Orlinsky, 1989).

It is also true that the Task Force members believe this model to be restricted and inaccurate. The psychotherapy enterprise is far more complex and interactive than the linear "Treatment operates on patients to produce effects" (Bohart & Tallman, 1999). We would prefer a broader, integrative model that incorporates the relational and educational features of psychotherapy, one that recognizes both the interpersonal and instrumental components of psychotherapy, one that appreciates the bidirectional process of therapy, and one in which the therapist and patient cocreate an optimal process and outcome.

♦ *Won't these results contribute further to deprofessionalizing psychotherapy? Aren't you unwittingly supporting efforts to have any warm, empathic person perform psychotherapy?*

Perhaps some will misuse our conclusions in this way, but that is neither our intent nor commensurate with our meta-analyses. It trivializes psychotherapy to characterize it as simply "a good relationship with a caring person." The research shows that an effective psychotherapist is one who employs specific methods, who offers strong relationships, and who customizes both treatment methods and relationship stances to the individual person and condition. That requires considerable training and experience, the antithesis of "anyone can do psychotherapy."

♦ *Are psychotherapists really able to adapt their relational style to fit the proclivities and personalities of their patients? Where is the evidence we can do this?*

Relational flexibility conjures up many concerns, but two of particular import in this question: the limits of human capacity and the possibility of capricious posturing (Norcross & Beutler, 1997). Although the psychotherapist can, with training and experience, learn to relate in a number of different ways, there are limits to our human capacity to modify relationship stances. It may be difficult to change interaction styles from client to client and session to session, assuming one is both aware and in control of one's styles of relating (Lazarus, 1993)

Can psychotherapists authentically differ from their preferred or habitual style of relating? There is some research supporting this assertion. Experienced therapists are capable of more malleability and "mood transcendence" than might be expected. In Gurman's (1973) research, for example, expert therapists appeared to be less handicapped by their own "bad moods" than were their less skilled peers. From the literature on the cognitive psychology of expertise (Schacht, 1991), experienced psychotherapists are disciplined improvisationalists who have stronger self-regulating skills and more flexible repertoires than novices. The research on the therapist's level of experience suggests that experience begets heightened attention to the client (less self-preoccupation), an innovative perspective, and in general, more endorsement of an "eclectic" orientation predicated on client need (Auerbach & Johnson, 1977). Indeed, several research studies (see Beutler, Machado, & Neufeldt, 1994) have demonstrated that therapists can consistently use different treatment models in a discriminative fashion.

Thus, our clinical experience and the modest amount of research attest that seasoned practitioners can shift back and forth among different relationship styles for a given case. Whether inexperienced psychotherapists can do so is still unanswered. And we caution therapists to be careful that the blending of stances and strategies never deteriorates into playacting or capricious posturing.

♦ *What should we do if we are unable or unwilling to adapt our therapy to the patient in the manner that research indicates is likely to enhance psychotherapy outcome?*

Five avenues spring to mind. First, address the matter forthrightly with the patient as part of the evolving therapeutic contract and the creation of respective tasks, in much the same way one would with patients requesting a form of therapy or a type of medication that research has indicated would fit particularly well in their case but which is not in your repertoire.

Second, treatment decisions are the result of multiple, interacting, and recursive considerations on the part of the patient, the therapist, and the context. A single evidence-based guideline should be seriously considered, but only as one of many determinants of treatment itself. Third, formal tracking of patient functioning during the course of psychotherapy provides a systematic way of assessing the consequences of treatment as it unfolds. Determine if, in this particular case, the treatment is helping. Fourth, an alternative to the one-therapist-fits-most-patients perspective is practice limits. Without a willingness and ability to engage in a range of interpersonal stances, the therapist may limit his or her practice to clients who fit that practice. Psychotherapists need not offer all services to all patients. Finally, consider a judicious referral to a colleague who can offer the relationship stance (or treatment method or medication) indicated for a particular patient.

♦ *Are the Task Force's conclusions and recommendations intended as practice standards?*

No. These are research-based conclusions that can lead, inform, and guide practitioners toward evidence-based therapy relationships and responsiveness to patient needs. They are not legal, ethical, or professional mandates.

♦ *Well, don't these represent the official positions of Division 12 (Clinical), Division 29 (Psychotherapy), or the American Psychological Association?*

No. No. No.

♦ *Isn't it premature to launch a set of research-based conclusions on the therapy relationship and patient matching?*

Science is not a set of answers; science is a series of processes and steps by which we arrive closer and closer to elusive answers. A vast amount of sophisticated research over the past five decades has been conducted on both the general elements of the therapy relationship and the particular means of adapting it to individual patients. It is premature to proffer the last word, but it is time to codify and disseminate what we do know. We look forward to regular updates on our research conclusions and practice recommendations.

♦ *So, are you saying that the therapy relationship (in addition to the treatment method) is crucial to outcome, that it can be improved by certain therapist contributions, and that it can be effectively tailored to the individual patient?*

Precisely. And this book, on the basis of the empirical research, suggests important directions for practitioners, trainers, researchers, and policymakers.

Concluding Reflections

The future of psychotherapy portends the integration of science and service, of the instrumental and the interpersonal, of the technical and the relational in the tradition of evidence-based practice (Norcross, Freedheim, & VandenBos, 2011). *Evidence-based therapy relationships* align with this future and embody a crucial part of evidence-based practice, when properly conceptualized. We can imagine few practices in all of psychotherapy that can confidently boast that they integrate "the best available research with clinical expertise in the context of patient characteristics, culture, and preferences" (American Psychological Association Task Force on Evidence-Based Practice, 2006) as well as the relational behaviors and treatment adaptations presented in this book. We are reminded daily that research can guide how we create, cultivate, and customize that powerful human relationship.

Moreover, we fervently hope this book will indirectly serve another master: to heal the damage incurred by the culture wars in psychotherapy. If our Task Force is even a little bit successful, then the pervasive gap between the science and practice communities will be narrowed, and the insidious dichotomy between the therapy relationship and the treatment method will be lessened. Phrased more positively, psychotherapists from all camps and communities will increasingly collaborate, and our patients will benefit from the most efficacious treatments *and* relationships available.

References

American Psychiatric Association. (2006). Practice guidelines for the treatment of psychiatric disorders: Compendium 2006. Washington, DC: Author.

American Psychological Association Task Force on Evidence-Based Practice. (2006). Evidence-based practice in psychology. *American Psychologist, 61,* 271–285.

Anderson, T., Ogles, B. M., Patterson, C. L., Lambert, M. J., & Vermeersch, D. A. (2009). Therapist effects: Facilitative interpersonal skills as a predictor of therapist success. *Journal of Clinical Psychology, 65,* 755–768.

Auerbach, A. H., & Johnson, M. (1977). In A. S. Gurman & A. M. Razin (Eds.), *Effective psychotherapy: A handbook of research.* New York: Pergamon.

Barber, J. P., Connolly, M. B., Crits-Christoph, P., Gladis, L., & Siqueland, L. (2000). Alliance predicts patients' outcomes beyond in-treatment change in symptoms. *Journal of Consulting and Clinical Psychology, 68,* 1027–1032.

Barber, J. P., Gallop, R., Crits-Christoph, P., Frank, A., Thase, M. E., Weiss, R. D., et al. (2006). The role of therapist adherence, therapist competence, and alliance in predicting outcome of individual drug counseling: Results from the National Institute on Drug Abuse Collaborative Cocaine Treatment Study. *Psychotherapy Research, 16,* 229–240.

Barber, J. P., Luborsky, L., Gallop, R., Crits-Christoph, P., Frank, A., Weiss, R. D., et al. (2001). Therapeutic alliance as a predictor of outcome and retention in the National Institute on Drug Abuse Collaborative Cocaine Treatment Study. *Journal of Consulting & Clinical Psychology, 69,* 119–124.

Barlow, D. H. (2000). Evidence-based practice: A world view. *Clinical Psychology: Science and Practice, 7,* 241–242.

Barlow, D. H. (Ed.). (2007). *Clinical handbook of psychological disorders: A step-by-step treatment manual (4th ed.).* New York: Guilford.

Beckner, V., Vella, L., Howard, I., & Mohr, D. C. (2007). Alliance in two telephone-administered treatments: Relationship with depression and health outcomes. *Journal of Consulting and Clinical Psychology, 75,* 508–512.

Bergin, A. E. (1997). Neglect of the therapist and the human dimensions of change: A commentary. *Clinical Psychology: Science and Practice, 4,* 83–89.

Bergin, A. E., & Lambert, M. J. (1978). The evaluation of outcomes in psychotherapy. In S. L. Garfield & A. E. Bergin (Eds.), *Handbook of psychotherapy and behavior change* (pp. 139–189). New York: Wiley.

Beutler, L. E. (2000). David and Goliath: When empirical and clinical standards of practice meet. *American Psychologist, 55,* 997–1007.

Beutler, L.E., Machado, P. P. P., & Neufeldt, S.A. (1994). Therapist variables. In A. E. Bergin & S. L. Garfield (Eds.), *Handbook of psychotherapy and behavior change* (4th ed., pp. 229–269). New York: Wiley.

Bohart, A. C., & Tallman, K. (1999). *How clients make therapy work: The process of active self-healing.* Washington, DC: American Psychological Association.

Cohen, J. (1988). *Statistical power analysis for the behavioral sciences* (2nd ed.). Hillsdale, NJ: Erlbaum.

Crits-Christoph, P., Baranackie, K., Kurcias, J. S., Beck, A. T., Carroll, K., Perry, K., et al. (1991). Meta-analysis of therapist effects in psychotherapy outcome studies. *Psychotherapy Research, 1,* 281–91.

Department of Health. (2001). *Treatment choice in psychological therapies and counseling.* London: Department of Health Publications.

Duncan, B. L., Miller, S. D., Wampold, B. E., & Hubble, M. A. (Eds.). (2010). *The heart and soul of change (2nd ed.).* Washington, DC: American Psychological Association.

Feeley, M., DeRubeis, R. J., & Gelfand, L. A. (1999). The temporal relation of adherence and alliance to symptom change in cognitive therapy for depression. *Journal of Consulting and Clinical Psychology, 67,* 578–582.

Gelso, C. J. (Ed.). (2005). The interplay of techniques and the therapeutic relationship in psychotherapy. *Psychotherapy, 42(4),* whole.

Gelso, C. J., & Carter, J. A. (1985). The relationship in counseling and psychotherapy: Components, consequences, and theoretical antecedents. *The Counseling Psychologist, 13*, 155–243.

Gelso, C. J., & Carter, J. A. (1994). Components of the psychotherapy relationship: Their interaction and unfolding during treatment. *Journal of Counseling Psychology, 41*, 296–306.

Gelso, C. J., & Hayes, J. A. (1998). *The psychotherapy research: Theory, research, and practice.* New York: Wiley.

Gurman, A. S. (1973). Effects of therapist and patient mood on the therapeutic functioning of high- and low-facilitative therapists. *Journal of Consulting and Clinical Psychology, 40*, 48–58.

Henry, W. P. (1998). Science, politics, and the politics of science: The use and misuse of empirically validated treatment research. *Psychotherapy Research, 8*, 126–140.

Huppert, J. D., Bufka, L. F., Barlow, D. H., Gorman, J. M., Shear, M. K., & Woods, S. W. (2001). Therapists, therapist variables, and cognitive–behavioral therapy outcome in a multicenter trial for panic disorder. *Journal of Consulting and Clinical Psychology, 69*, 747–755.

Kazdin, A. E. (2007). Mediators and mechanism of change in psychotherapy research. In S. Nolen-Hoeksema, T. D. Cannon, & T. Widiger (Eds.), *Annual Review of Clinical Psychology, 3*, 1–27.

Klein, D. N., Schwartz, J. E., Santiago, N. J., Vivian, D., Vocisano, C., Castonguay, L. G., et al. (2003). Therapeutic alliance in depression treatment: Controlling for prior change and patient characteristics. *Journal of Consulting and Clinical Psychology, 71*, 997–1006.

Krupnick, J. L., Sotsky, S. M., Simmens, S., Moyer, J., Elkin, I., Watkins, J., et al. (1996). The role of the therapeutic alliance in psychotherapy and pharmacotherapy. *Journal of Consulting and Clinical Psychology, 64*, 532–539.

Lambert, M. J. (1992). Psychotherapy outcome research: Implications for integrative and eclectic therapists. In J. C. Norcross and M. R. Goldfried (Eds.), *Handbook of psychotherapy integration* (pp. 94–129). New York: Basic Books.

Lambert, M. J. (2010). *Prevention of treatment failure: The use of measuring, monitoring, & feedback in clinical practice.* Washington, DC: American Psychological Association.

Lambert, M. J. (2011). Psychotherapy research and its achievements. In J. C. Norcross, G. R. VandenBos, & D. K. Freedheim (Eds.), *History of psychotherapy* (2nd ed.). Washington, DC: American Psychological Association.

Lambert, M. J., & Barley, D. E. (2002). Research summary on the therapeutic relationship and psychotherapy outcome. In J. C. Norcross (Ed.), *Psychotherapy relationships that work* (pp. 17–32). New York: Oxford University Press.

Lambert, M. J., & Ogles, B. M. (2004). The efficacy and effectiveness of psychotherapy. In M. J. Lambert (Ed.), *Begin and Garfield's handbook of psychotherapy and behavior change* (5th ed., pp. 139 – 193). New York: Wiley.

Lazarus, A. A. (1993). Tailoring the therapeutic relationship, or being an authentic chameleon. *Psychotherapy, 30*, 404–407.

Luborsky, L., Diguer, L., Seligman, D. A., Rosenthal, R., Krause, E.D., Johnson, S., et al. (1999). The researcher's own therapy allegiances: A "wild card" in comparisons of treatment efficacy. *Clinical Psychology: Science and Practice, 6*, 95–106.

Messer, S. B. (2001). Empirically supported treatments: What's a nonbehaviorist to do?. In B. D. Slife, R. N. Williams, & S. H. Barlow (Eds.), *Critical issues in psychotherapy.* Thousand Oaks, CA: Sage.

Nathan, P. E. (1998). Practice guidelines: Not yet ideal. *American Psychologist, 53*, 290–299.

Nathan, P. E., & Gorman, J. M. (Eds.). (2007). *A guide to treatments that work* (3rd ed.). New York: Oxford University Press.

Norcross, J. C. (Ed.). (2002). *Psychotherapy relationships that work: Therapist contributions and responsiveness to patient needs.* New York: Oxford University Press.

Norcross, J. C. (2010). The therapeutic relationship. In B. L. Duncan, S. D. Miller, B. E. Wampold, & M. A. Hubble (Eds.), *Heart & soul of change in psychotherapy* (2nd ed.). Washington, DC: American Psychological Association.

Norcross, J. C., & Beutler, L. E. (1997). Determining the therapeutic relationship of choice in brief therapy. In J. N. Butcher (Ed.), *Personality assessment in managed health care: A practitioner's guide.* New York: Oxford University Press.

Norcross, J. C., Beutler, L. E., & Levant, R. F. (Eds.). (2006). *Evidence-based practices in mental health: Debate and dialogue on the fundamental questions.* Washington, DC: American Psychological Association.

Norcross, J. C., Hogan, T. P., & Koocher, G. P. (2008). *Clinician's guide to evidence-based practices: Mental health and the addictions.* New York: Oxford University Press.

Norcross, J. C., Freedheim, D. K., & VandenBos, G. R. (2011). Into the future: Retrospect and prospect in psychotherapy. In J. C. Norcross, G. R. VandenBos, & D. K. Freedheim (Eds.). (2011). *History of psychotherapy* (2nd ed.). Washington, DC: American Psychological Association.

O'Donohue, W., Buchanan, J. A., & Fisher, J. E. (2000). Characteristics of empirically supported treatments. *Journal of Psychotherapy Practice and Research, 9,* 69–74.

Okiishi J., Lambert, M. J., Nielsen, S. L., & Ogles, B. M. (2003). In search of supershrink: Using patient outcome to identify effective and ineffective therapists. *Clinical Psychology and Psychotherapy, 10,* 361–373.

Orlinsky, D. E. (1989). Researchers' images of psychotherapy: Their origins and influence on research. *Clinical Psychology Review, 9,* 413–441.

Orlinsky, D. E. (2000, August). *Therapist interpersonal behaviors that have consistently shown positive correlations with outcome.* Paper presented at the 108th annual convention of the American Psychological Association, Washington, DC.

Orlinsky, D., & Howard, K. E. (1977). The therapist's experience of psychotherapy. In A. S. Gurman & A. M. Razin (Eds.), *Effective psychotherapy: A handbook of research.* New York: Pergamon.

Paul, G. L. (1967). Strategy of outcome research in psychotherapy. *Journal of Consulting Psychology, 31,* 109–118.

Project MATCH Research Group. (1998). Therapist effects in three treatments for alcohol problems. *Psychotherapy Research, 8,* 455–474.

Rector, N. A., Zuroff, D. C., & Segal, Z. V. (1999). Cognitive change and the therapeutic alliance: The role of technical and nontechnical factors in cognitive therapy. *Psychotherapy, 36,* 320–328.

Rogers, C. R. (1957). The necessary and sufficient conditions of therapeutic personality change. *Journal of Consulting Psychology, 22,* 95–103.

Rosenthal, R. (1995). Writing meta-analytic reviews. *Psychological Bulletin, 118,* 183–192.

Roth, A., & Fonagy, P. (2004). *What works for whom? A critical review of psychotherapy research* (2nd ed.). New York: Guilford.

Safran, J. D., & Muran, J. C. (2000). *Negotiating the therapeutic alliance.* New York: Guilford.

Schacht, T. E. (1991). Can psychotherapy education advance psychotherapy integration? A view from the cognitive psychology of expertise. *Journal of Psychotherapy Integration, 1,* 305–320.

Task Force on Psychological Intervention Guidelines. (1995). *Template for developing guidelines: Interventions for mental disorders and psychosocial aspects of physical disorders.* Washington, DC: American Psychological Association.

Wampold, B. E. (2001). *The great psychotherapy debate: Models, methods, and findings.* Mahwah, NJ: Lawrence Erlbaum.

Wampold, B. E., & Brown, G. S. (2005). Estimating variability in outcomes attributable to therapists: A naturalistic study of outcomes in managed care. *Journal of Consulting and Clinical Psychology, 73,* 914–923.

Wolitzky, D. L. (2011). Psychoanalytic theories of psychotherapy. In J. C. Norcross, G. R. VandenBos, & D. K. Freedheim (Eds.), *History of psychotherapy* (2nd ed.). Washington, DC: American Psychological Association.

PART 2

Effective Elements of the Therapy Relationship: What Works in General

2   Alliance in Individual Psychotherapy

Adam O. Horvath, AC Del Re, Christoph Flückiger, *and* Dianne Symonds

Since our last review of the literature in 2002, research on the alliance in psychotherapy has continued to flourish. By searching the electronic databases at the end of 2000, we located just over 2,000 references using the keywords *alliance, helping alliance, working alliance*, and *therapeutic alliance*. The same search in early 2010 yielded over 7,000 items. The growing attraction of the alliance concept appears to be the result of a number of related sources:

One reason is the convergence of evidence, staring in the '70s, that different psychotherapies typically produce similar beneficial effect for clients (e.g., Luborsky, Singer, & Luborsky, 1975; Smith & Glass, 1977; Stiles, Shapiro, & Elliot, 1986). Although the "Dodo bird interpretation" (All have won and all must have their prizes. . .) of these meta-analyses of psychotherapy effectiveness has proven somewhat controversial (Chambless, 2002), most therapists and researchers alike have accepted the notion that a large part of what is helpful for clients receiving psychotherapy is shared across diverse treatments. The quality of the therapeutic relationship in general, and the alliance in particular, are obvious "common factors" shared by most if not all psychotherapies.

Another important precursor of the alliance concept, and a pioneering force in the development of therapy process research,

was the work of Carl Rogers and his colleagues. By applying rigorous empirical methods to the examination of person-centered treatment, they not only proved that the therapy process can be explored beyond anecdotal records, but also moved the concept of the therapeutic relationship to the center of the healing process. Rogers and colleagues generated an important body of literature exploring the interpersonal interior of psychotherapy (Rogers, Gendlin, Kiesler, & Truax, 1967).

A third important precursor can be traced back to the 1930s: A growing curiosity and interest in the integration of diverse theories of psychotherapies (Frank & Frank, 1991; Rosenzweig, 1936). The desire to reconcile some conflicting therapeutic methods and their underlying theories eventually led to the founding of the Society for the Exploration of Psychotherapy Integration (SEPI) in 1983. On the practice side, psychotherapists in North America started to reject the strict boundaries of classical theories and became increasingly interested in utilizing a variety of effective methods irrespective of their "school;" the field was moving from theoretical monism to an eclectic pragmatism. The value of aspects of therapist–client relatedness (e.g., alliance) found ready acceptance among those committed to psychotherapy integration (Goldfried, 1980).

But perhaps the most potent force responsible for the sustained growth of interest in the alliance was the consistent finding of a moderate but robust relationship between the alliance and treatment outcome across a broad spectrum of treatments in a variety of client/problem contexts (Horvath & Bedi, 2002; Horvath & Symonds, 1991; Martin, Ganske, & Davis, 2000).

In this chapter, we reexamine the empirical evidence linking the alliance to outcome in individual psychotherapy with adults. But the relation between alliance and therapy is only the first level of interest. Beyond the strength of the overall alliance–outcome link, it was our intent to use the accumulated data to examine the role of several potential moderators and mediators that impact this relationship, with particular attention to issues that help us better understand the way alliance and treatment results are linked.

Definitions and Measures

The term *alliance* (also *therapeutic alliance*, *working alliance*, and *helping alliance*) as it is used in the research literature, can refer to a number of related constructs; at this time we do not have a single, consensually accepted definition of the concept (Horvath & Luborsky, 1993; Saketopoulou, 1999). While there are important shared aspects in the way researchers use the construct in the literature (e.g., Bordin, 1980, 1989; Gaston et al., 1995; Hatcher & Barends, 2006; Horvath & Luborsky, 1993), there are also nontrivial differences among authors about the precise meaning of the term (*Psychotherapy*, 43(3), whole). The best way to grasp the complexity of the current status of this concept is by briefly reviewing its history.

Definitions

The concept of the alliance (though not the term itself) originated with Freud (1910/1913). His basic premise was that all relationships were transference based (Freud, 1912/1958). Early in his writings, he struggled with the question of what keeps the analysand in therapy in the face of the psyche's unconscious fear and rejection of exploring repressed material. His first formulation suggested that he thought that there was an "analyst" within the patient supporting the healing journey (Freud, 1912/1958). Later he speculated about the reality-based *collaboration* between therapist and client, a conjoint effort to conquer the client's pain. He also referred to this process as the unobjectionable or positive transference (Freud, 1913/1940). Both the wisdom of recognizing the client's attachment to the therapist, and his ambiguity about the status of this attachment (reality based and conscious versus transferential and unconscious) has echoed throughout the evolution of the concept.

The term *ego alliance* was coined by Sterba (1934), who conceptualized it as part of the client's ego-observing process that alternated with the experiencing (transferential) process. Zetzel (1956) used the term *therapeutic alliance* to refer to the patient's ability to use the healthy part of her/his ego to link up or join with the analyst to accomplish the therapeutic tasks. Greenson (1965, 1967) made a distinction between the *working alliance*, the client's ability to align with the tasks of analysis, and the *therapeutic alliance*, which refers to the capacity of therapist and client to form a personal bond.

During the 1970s efforts were made to extrapolate and extend the concept of the alliance from its psychodynamic roots to encompass components of the relational elements of all helping endeavors: Luborsky (1976) proposed an extension of Zetzel's (1956) and Stone's (1961) concept. He suggested that the alliance between therapist and client developed in two phases: The first phase, Type I alliance, involved the client's belief in the therapist as a potent source of help, and the therapist providing a warm, supporting, and caring relationship. This level of alliance results in a secure holding relationship within which the work of the therapy can begin. The second phase, Type II alliance, involved the client's investment and faith in the therapeutic process itself, a commitment to the core concepts undergirding the therapy (e.g., nature of the problem, value of the exploratory process), as well as a willing investment of her or himself, to share the ownership for the therapy process. While Luborsky's (1976, 1994) assumptions about the therapy process itself were grounded in psychodynamic theory, his description of the alliance as a therapeutic process was quite general. Luborsky and his team also pioneered an alliance assessment method for raters, using transcripts or audio recordings, to count signs of in-session events indicative of the presence of either type of alliance.

Bordin (1975, 1976, 1989, 1994) proposed a somewhat different pan-theoretical alliance concept he called the *working alliance*. His concepts of the alliance were based on Greenson's' (1965) ideas as a starting point but departed from the psychodynamic premises even more clearly than Luborsky did. For Bordin, the alliance was centrally the achievement of collaborative stance in therapy and was built on three components: agreements on the therapeutic goals, consensus on the tasks that make up therapy, and a bond between the client and the therapist. He predicted that different therapies would place different demands on the relationship, thus the "profile" of the ideal working alliance would be different across theoretical orientations. Bordin also proposed that as therapy progresses, the strength of the working alliance would build and ebb in the normal course of events, and that the repair of these stresses in the alliance would constitute the core task of any helping relationship.

The most distinguishing feature of the modern pantheoretical reconceptualization of the alliance is its emphasis on collaboration and consensus (Bordin, 1980; Hatcher, Barends, Hansel, & Gutfreund, 1995; Luborsky, 1976). In contrast to previous conceptualizations that emphasized either the therapist's contributions to the relationship (i.e., Rogers & Wood, 1974) or the unconscious distortions of the relation between therapist and client, the revised alliance theory emphasized the active collaboration between the participants.

An equally significant consequence of the way the alliance concept was reintroduced is that there were two different voices theorizing about the concept. Each wanting to separate the idea from its long history within the psychodynamic framework and operationalize the concept in a way in which it would be compatible with most, if not all, theoretical approaches. But neither of these theorists (Bordin or Luborsky) offered a precise definition of how this new conceptualization of the alliance related to (or was different from) other concepts that are parts of the therapeutic relationship. This theoretical ambiguity created a void which was filled by a number of alliance measures developed in parallel between 1978 and 1986. What we know about the alliance and its relation to outcome and other therapy variables has been gleaned from studies that, in practice, define the alliance by the instrument used to measure it. In this sense, the instrumentation defines the construct. In the following section we review the alliance instruments and discuss the differences and similarities of their undergirding conceptualizations.

Measures

In this chapter we refer to the *alliance* in the singular. However, in the database of 201 studies we have assembled for this meta-analysis, over 30 different alliance measures were used, not counting different versions of the same instrument. Similar to previous reports, the four core measures: California Psychotherapy Alliance Scale (CALPAS, Gaston & Marmar, 1994), Helping Alliance Questionnaires (HAq, Alexander & Luborsky, 1987), Vanderbilt Psychotherapy Process Scale (VPPS, O'Mally, Suh & Stupp, 1983), and Working Alliance Inventory (WAI, Horvath & Greenberg, 1986) accounted for approximately two thirds of the data. In examinations of the shared factor structure of the WAI, CALPAS, and HAq, the concept of "confident collaborative relationship" was the central common theme (Hatcher et al., 1995; Hatcher & Barends, 1996). Each of these four instruments has been in use for over 20 years and has demonstrated an acceptable levels of internal consistency. The methods of reporting reliability of measures were somewhat inconsistent, but we estimated that clients' and therapists' rating of the alliance using these core measures were in the range of 0.81–0.87 (Cronbach's alpha). Rated (observer) measures tended to report interrater reliability indexes of similar values. However, the shared variance, even among these well-established measures, has been shown to be less than 50% (Horvath, 2009).

Fifty four of the research reports in our data set used less-well-validated instruments or assessment procedures; the relation of most of these measures to the core instruments, or to each other, are not well documented, and sometimes nonexistent. Relatively little data are available with respect to their psychometric properties, but when this information was provided,

the numbers were similar to those reported for the core measures. In Table 2.1, each instrument is identified using the label or identification the authors provided. However, in the moderator analyses we discuss later in this chapter, the less often used measures ($n \ of \ use \le 3$) were merged into one category: "Other." In this "Other" category are: some newer alliance measures with relatively few administrations, measures developed for the specific investigation, and instruments originally developed for relationship constructs other than the alliance.

Adding to the diversity of measures is the fact that, over time, the four core instruments have evolved as well and currently exist in a number of different forms (e.g., short versions, observer versions, versions specific to context and/or application, translations). The relation of these modified instruments to the original is not always well documented. As we noted, the diversity in the definition of the alliance via the use of a variety of assessment measures has become an important issue. The consequences of these differences will be discussed in the section evaluating the interpretation of this corpus of research.

Clinical Examples

The alliance represents an emergent quality of partnership and mutual collaboration between therapist and client. As such, it is not the outcome of a particular intervention; its development can take different forms and may be achieved almost instantly or nurtured over a longer period of time depending on the kind of therapy and the stage of treatment (Bordin, 1994). The following is an excerpt from an early session that illustrates the challenges of negotiating the clients' whole-hearted participation in the therapy process:

> Client (C): Well aren't you going to ask me what this reminds me of?

Table 2.1   Research Reports included in the Meta Analysis

	Treatment		Alliance			Outcome			
Study	Sessions	Type	Rater	Measure	Time	Measure	Rater	ES	N
Adler (1988)	12	Various	C.T	WAI, HAq, CIS	E, L	TC, SCL/BSI, RSE, IIP, PTQ	C, T	0.28	44
Allen et al. (1985)[a]	*	Inpatient	T	ITAS	E, L, A	Overall Outcome, GAS, Outcome Composite	T	0.54	37
Allen et al. (1986)[a]	*	Inpatient	T	ITAS	E, L	Premature Termination	C	0.54	37
Andreoli et al. (1993)[b]	6	Crisis intervention	T	ITAS	E	Overall Outcome, Interpersonal Functioning, Specific Outcomes	T	0.57	16
Ankuta (1993)	6	Crisis intervention	T	ITAS	E	Overall Outcome	T	0.02	44
Arnow et al. (2003)	20	CBT	C	WAI-S	E	Premature Termination	O	0.10	681
Baldwin (2007)	*	Various	C	WAI	M	OQ-45	C	0.24	331
Barber et al. (2006)	20	Various	C, T	HAq-II, CALPAS	E, M	SCL/BSI, Addiction Severity Index, BDI	C	0.10	121
Barber et al. (1999)[a]	40	Various	C, O	HAq-II, CALPAS	E, M	SCL/BSI, Addiction Severity Index, BDI	C	0.13	83
Barber et al. (2000)	*	Dynamic	C	CALPAS	E, M, L	BDI	C	0.37	83
Barber et al. (2001)[a]	40	Various	C	CALPAS	E, M	Addiction Severity Index	C	0.08	265
Barber et al. (2008)	36	Dynamic	C	HAq, CALPAS	E	Addiction Severity Index	C	0.10	89
Barkham et al. (1993)	12	Interpersonal	O	CALPAS	E	Overall Outcome	C	0.41	12
Bassler et al. (1995)	14 w	Various	C	HAq	E	Overall Outcome	C	0.16	237
Bethea et al. (2008)	8	CBT	C, T, O	HAq II	E, M, L, A	Drug Use, Functioning Adherence, Pain Rating	C, O	0.21	25
Bieschke et al. (1995)	7	Various	C	WAI	L	Change in Distress	C	0.38	90
Biscoglio (2005)	*	CBT	C, T	WAI-S	E	GAS, IIP, SCL/BSI, TC	C, O	0.21	32
Botella (2008)	*	Various	C	WAI-S	E	Premature Termination	O	0.16	190

(Continued)

Table 2.1   Continued

	Treatment		Alliance			Outcome			
Study	Sessions	Type	Rater	Measure	Time	Measure	Rater	ES	N
Bredel et al. (2004)	*	Various	C	NSI	E	Satisfaction	C, O	0.44	78
Broome (1996)[b]	46	Drug Counseling, Methodone	C	3-item NSI	M	Premature Termination	C	0.11	167
Brotman (2004)	16	Various	C, O	WAI, HA(r)	E	HRSD	O	0.31	51
Burns et al. (2007)	12 w	Rehabilitation	C	WAI-S	E	Cardiac Depression Scale, Diet Progress, Exercise and Diet Self-Efficacy, General Health Survey	C	0.12	79
Busseri et al. (2003)	*	Eclectic	C, T	WAI	E, M	SCL/BSI, TC	C, T	0.36	54
Busseri et al. (2004)	8	Eclectic	C, T	WAI	E	PTQ, TC, SCL	C, T	0.35	50
Card (1991)	6	Cognitive-behavior	O	CALPAS	E, M, L	STAI, BDI, HRSD, SCL/BSI	C, O	0.07	55
Castonguay et al. (1996)	15	Cognitive, Medication	O	WAI	M	BDI, HRSD, GAS	C, O	0.57	30
Chilly (2004)[b]	16	Interpersonal	C	WAI	E	BDI	C	0.52	9
Cislo (1998)	10	Various	C	HAq	A	Session Impact	C	0.30	47
Clarkin et al. (1987)	*	Inpatient Psychiatric Unit	O	ITAS	A	GAS	O	0.39	96
Cloitre et al. (2004)	16	Various	C	WAI-S	E	Premature Termination, PTSD Symptoms	C, O	0.27	30
Coleman (2006)	*	Eclectic	C	WAI-S	C	SCL/BSI, SWLS		0.12	102
Connors et al. (1997)[a]	12 w	Various	C, T	WAI	E	DpD, Abstinence	C	0.11	579
Constantino et al. (2005)[b]	19	CBT, Interpersonal	C	HAq	E, M	Purge Frequency		0.29	75
Crits-Cristoph et al. (1988)	54	Dynamic	O	HAq(cs)	E	Composite Outcome, Residual Gain	C, T, O	0.39	43
Davis et al. (2007)	26 w	CBT	O	WAI-S	A	PANSS, WBI		0.43	26
de Roten et al. (2004)	4	Dynamic	C	HAq	M, E, A	SCL/BSI, Evaluation Questionnaire, SAS	C	0.45	70

(*Continued*)

Table 2.1 **Continued**

Study	Treatment		Alliance			Outcome			
	Sessions	Type	Rater	Measure	Time	Measure	Rater	ES	*N*
Dearing et al. (2005)	12	CBT	C	WAI	E	DpD, Abstinence, Drinking Related Consequences, Satisfaction with Treatment	C	0.29	208
Deu et al. (2009)	10 w	Interpersonal	C	HAq	E	Depressive Symptoms	O	0.18	17
Dorsch et al. (2002)	*	Various	C	HAq II	E	ACQ, BDI, BSQ, Clinical Improvement, SCL/BSI, STAI	C	0.61	30
Dundon et al. (2008)	*	Various	C, T	WAI	E	Abstinence, Sessions Attended	O	0.08	194
Dunn et al. (2006)	18 w	CBT	C	CALPAS	E	PANSS	O	-0.11	29
Eaton et al. (1988)	*	Various	O	TARS	A	Overall Outcome, SCL/BSI	C, T	0.00	40
Emmerling et al. (2009)	*	Eclectic	C	WAI-S	E	GHQ	C	0.42	56
Fakhoury et al. (2007)	*	Various	T	HA	E	Rehospitalization	O	0.14	223
Feeley (1993)	12	Cognitive	O	HAr	A	BDI	C	0.40	25
Ferleger (1993)	41	Dynamic	O	CALPAS	E	SCL/BSI, TC, Social Adjustment	C	0.09	40
Florsheim et al. (2000)	90–100 days	Various (residential program)	C, O	WAI	E, M	Drug Use, Teachers and Youths Report Form, Recidivism	C, O	0.22	78
Flückiger et al. (2005)	*	CBT	C	BPSR	E, M, L	SCL/BSI, IIP, Satisfaction, Improvement, Goal attainment	C, T	0.58	47
Forbes et al. (2008)	NS	Counseling	C	WAI-S	E	PTSD symptoms	C	0.10	84
Forman (1990)	6	Rehabilitation	C, T	WAI	M, L	Global Outcome	C, T	0.48	29
Frank et al. (1990)	56	Various	T	ITAS	M	Premature Termination, Specific Symptoms, Overall Outcome, Symptom Severity, Social Relations	C, O	0.32	46

(*Continued*)

Table 2.1   Continued

	Treatment		Alliance			Outcome			
Study	Sessions	Type	Rater	Measure	Time	Measure	Rater	ES	N
Freitas (2001)	*	Therapeutic Community	C, T	WAI	E	Lengths of Treatment, Neuropsychological Status	T, O	0.00	80
Fries et al. (2003)[b]	25 w	Various	C	BPSR	A	PANSS	C, O	0.32	30
Gaiton (2004)	24	CBT	T, O	CALPAS	E	Composite Outcome	C, O	0.14	38
Gallop et al. (1994)	10	Inpatient Eating Disorders Unit	C, T	WAI	E	Premature Termination	C	0.16	31
Gaston et al. (1991)[a, b]	18	Various	C, T	CALPAS	E, M, L	BDI, HRSD	C	0.21	18
Gaston et al. (1994)[a, b]	18	Dynamic	C, T	CALPAS	A	Depression-Anxiety, Interpersonal Behavior Scale	C	0.15	32
Gaston et al. (1998)	18	Various	O	CALPAS	A	BDI, HRSD	C	0.34	88
Geider (1997)	*	Experiential	O	CALPAS	A	Global Outcome	C	0.48	10
Geiser et al. (2002)	*	Various	C	HAq II	E	ACQ, BDI, BSQ, GAF	C, T	0.55	231
Gerstley et al. (1989)	48	Various	C, T	HAq	E	Addictive Severity Index	O	0.36	30
Godfrey et al. (2007)	6w	CBT	O	OAS	E	Chronic Fatique	C	0.10	71
Gomes-Swartz (1978)[a]	18	Various	O	VPPS	A	Overall Ratings, MMPI Maladjustment, TC	C, T, O	0.46	35
Greenberg et al. (1982)	6	Gestalt	C	WAI	E	Scale of Indecision, STAI, TC	C, T	0.62	31
Greenberg et al. (2002)	32	Experiential	C	WAI	A	SCL/BSI, IIP, Intrex, TC	C	0.14	32
Grob et al. (1989)	19w	Inpatient	O	ITAS	E, M, L	Overall Improvement	T	0.41	60
Gunderson et al. (1997)	*	Various	C, T	HAq	E, M, L	SCL/BSI, SAS, GAS	C	0.22	28
Gunther (1991)	15	Various	O	CALPAS	E, L	SCL/BSI	C	0.25	41
Gutfreund (1992)	29	Various	O	CALPAS	A	SCL/BSI, Dynamic Outcome	C	0.16	46

(*Continued*)

Table 2.1   Continued

Study	Treatment		Alliance			Outcome			
	Sessions	Type	Rater	Measure	Time	Measure	Rater	ES	N
Hansson et al. (1992)	4 w	Inpatient	C	ITAS	E, L	SCL/BSI, CPRS, DTES, TC	C	0.19	106
Hardy et al. (2001)	16 w	CBT	C	CALPAS	A	BDI	C	0.71	24
Hartley et al. (1983)	18	Various	O	VTAS	A	Composite Gain Scale	C, T, O	0.27	28
Hartmann (2001)	12	Dynamic	O	CS	E, M, L	SCL/BSI, IIP	C	0.46	10
Hatcher et al. (1996)	51	Dynamic	C	CALPAS	Various	Improvement to Date	C	0.10	230
Hawley et al. (2006)[a]	16	Various	O	VTAS	A	HRSD	O	0.27	162
Hayes et al. (2007)	NS	CBT	C, O	WAI		Severity Rating	O	0.26	18
Hays (1994)	6	Various	C, T	WAI	E	Global Outcome, Personal Growth, Relations with Others	C, T	0.30	29
Hervé et al. (2008)	*	Mother–infant Consultation	O	WAI	E	Growth	C	0.35	58
Hilliard et al. (2000)	25	Dynamic	C,T,O	SASB Intrex	M	Interject-best/worst, SCL/BSI, Global Outcome	C, T, O	0.21	64
Hopkins (1988)	12	Various	C, T	WAI	E	SCL/BSI	C	0.25	15
Hopkins et al. (2006)	30	Case Management	T	WAI-S	C	MCAS	T	0.24	28
Horowitz et al. (1984)	12	Dynamic	O	TARS	A	SCL/BSI, PCS	C, O	0.11	52
Horvath (1981)	10	Various	C, T	WAI	E	PTQ	C, T	0.49	29
Howard (2003)	16	Various	C	WAI	E	BDI, HRSD, IIP	C, O	0.57	47
Howard et al. (2006)	16	CBT	C	WAI	M	BDI	C,	0.67	19
Huber et al. (2003)	*	Various	C, T	TRS	E	BDI, Contentment, Premature Termination	C, T	0.28	275
Ilgen et al. (2006a)[a]	*	Alcohol and drug Abstinence Program	C, T	WAI	E	Alcohol Abstincence Self-Efficacy, DpD	O	0.11	785

(*Continued*)

Table 2.1 Continued

	Treatment		Alliance			Outcome			
Study	Sessions	Type	Rater	Measure	Time	Measure	Rater	ES	N
Ilgen et al. (2006b)[a]	*	Alcohol and Drug Abstinence Program	C, T	WAI	E	Alcohol Abstincence Self-Efficacy, DpD	O	0.11	785
Irelan (2004)	*	Various	C	WAI	E	Premature Termination	O	0.35	40
Jacob (2003)	13	Various	C	WAI	E	OQ-45, Panic Severity	C	0.16	80
Janecke (2003)	38 w	Various	C	HAq	E	IIP, Satisfaction, Symptom Reduction	C	0.00	50
Johansson et al. (2006)	*	Various	C, T	HAq II	E	SCL/BSI, IIP	O	0.23	122
Joyce et al. (1998)	20	Dynamic	C, T	NSI	A	General Symptoms, Individual Objectives, Social-sexual Adjustment	C, T, O	0.29	64
Joyce et al. (2003)a	18	Various	C, T	AAS	A	Improvement, Severity of Disturbance	C, T, O	0.27	144
Jumes (1995)	28 w	Inpatient, Medication	C	WAI	E	BPRS, GAS	O	0.28	121
Kabuth et al. (2005)	*	Hospital	O	HAq	E, L	Social Development, Symptom Reduction	O	0.41	33
Karver et al. (2008)[a]	12 w	CBT	C, T, O	WAI-S, AOCS	E	CES-D	C	0.12	12
Katz (1999)	5	Dynamic	C	WAI-S	E	Premature Termination	O	0.03	100
Kech (2008)	16	IPT	C	NSI	A	Depression Composite	C	0.56	20
Kelly et al. (2009)	*	Various	C, T	WAI-S	A	SCL/BSI	C	0.28	83
Kivlighan et al. (1995)	12	Various	C, T	WAI	E, M, L	Interpersonal Problems	C	0.17	21
Kivlighan et al. (2000)	4	Various	C	WAI	E	IIP, BIC	O	0.55	38
Klee et al. (1990)	29	Various	O	TARS	E	SCL/BSI, Global Outcome	C	0.23	32
Klein et al. (2003)	12	CBT	T	WAI-S	E, M	HRSD	O	0.31	367

(*Continued*)

Table 2.1 Continued

Study	Sessions	Type	Rater	Measure	Time	Measure	Rater	ES	N
		Treatment		Alliance			Outcome		
Knaevelsrud et al. (2007)	5 w	CBT	C	WAI-S	L	SCL/BSI, IES	C	0.48	41
Kokotovic et al. (1990)	4	Various	C, T	WAI	E	Premature Termination	C	0.13	105
Kolden (1996)	4	Dynamic	C	TBS	E	Mental Health Index	C	0.30	60
Konzag et al. (2004)	12 w	Various	C, T	HAq	E	SCL/BSI	C	0.21	225
Kramer et al. (2008)[a]	*	Various	C	HAq	A	SCL/BSI	C	0.25	50
Kramer et al. (2009)[a]	*	Various	C	HAq	A	SCL/BSI	C	0.80	50
Krupnick et al. (1994)[a]	16	Various	O	VTAS	E, A	Global Outcome	C, O	0.46	206
Krupnick et al. (1996)	16	Various	O	VTAS	E, A	HRSD, BDI	O	0.46	206
Kukla et al. (2009)	*	Vocational Program	C	WASc	A	Job Tenure, Working Duration	O	-0.18	91
Lansford (1986)	12	Dynamic	O	AWR	A	Global Outcome	C, T, O	0.89	6
Lieberman et al. (1992)	*	Acute Inpatient	C, T	ITGA, EH	E	Symptom Improvement, GAS, Premature Termination, Defense Style, RSE	C	0.30	63
Liebler et al. (2004)	*	Various	C	BPSR	M	SCL/BSI	C	0.07	87
Loneck et al. (2002)	*	Intake Interview	O	VPPS	E	Referral Appointment	O	0.23	39
Luborsky et al. (1983)	52	Dynamic	O	HAq(cs), HAq(r)	E, L, A	Rated Benefits, Residual Gain, Success, Satisfaction, Improvement	C, T, O	0.54	20
Luborsky et al. (1985)[a]								0.79	77
Mallinckrodt (1993)	12	Various	C, T	WAI	E	Global Outcome	C, T	0.63	40
Mallinckrodt (1996)	15	Brief Interpersonal	C	WAI	E	SCL/BSI, Social Support, BDI	C	0.54	34

(Continued)

Table 2.1 Continued

	Treatment		Alliance			Outcome			
Study	Sessions	Type	Rater	Measure	Time	Measure	Rater	ES	N
Marmar et al. (1989a)[b]	18	Various	C, T	CALPAS	E	BDI	C	0.18	18
Marmar et al. (1989b)	12	Dynamic	O	CALTARS	A	Patterns of Individual Change Scores, SCL	C	0.39	52
Marmarosh et al. (2009)	*	Various	C, T	WAI-S	E	SCL/BSI	C	0.30	48
Marshel (1986)	50	Dynamic	C	HAq, TARS,	E	Premature Termination	C	-0.06	101
Marziali et al. (1981)	12	Dynamic	O	TARS	A	Composite Outcome	C, O	0.35	10
Marziali (1984)	20	Dynamic	C, T, O	TARS	A	Behavioral Symptom Index, SAS, Global Outcome	C, T, O	0.24	42
Marziali et al. (1999)[b]	30	Dynamic	C	TAS[†]	E, L	SAS, Objective Behavior Index, SCL/BSI	C	0.79	17
McNeil (2006)	12	Various	C, T, O	AQ	A	General Symptoms	O	0.22	99
McLeod et al. (2005)	*	Various	O	TPOCS	A	Trait and Stait Anxiety	C	0.50	22
Meier et al. (2006a)[a]	*	Alcohol and Drug Abstinence Program	C, T	WAI-S	E	Premature Termination	O	0.01	187
Meier et al. (2006b)[b]	*	Alcohol and Drug Abstinence Program	C, O	WAI-S	E	Premature Termination	O	0.01	187
Meyer et al. (2002)[a]	16	Various	O	VTAS	E	HRSD, BDI	C, O	0.49	151
Missirlian et al. (2005)	16	Experiential	C	WAI-S	E, M, L	SCL/BSI, BDI, IIP, RSE	C	0.37	32
Mohl et al. (1991)	*	Various	C	HAq	E	Premature Termination	C	0.30	80
Moleiro (2003)[a]	20	Alcohol and Drug Abstinence Program	C	STS, TPRS	A	BDI, Composite Outcome	C, O	0.48	186

(*Continued*)

Table 2.1   Continued

	Treatment		Alliance			Outcome			
Study	Sessions	Type	Rater	Measure	Time	Measure	Rater	ES	N
Morgan et al. (1982)[a]	52	Dynamic	O	HAr	E, A	Composite Outcome, Rated Benefits	C, T, O	0.59	20
Moseley (1983)	14	Various	C	WAI	E	State-Trait Anxiety, Self-Concept, TC, PTQ	C	0.28	25
Multon et al. (2001)	7	Career Counseling	C	WAI-S	E	SCL/GSI, Instability	C	0.14	42
Muran et al. (1995)	20	Cognitive	C	CALPAS	A	SCL/BSI, Interpersonal Problems, GAS, TC, Overall Outcome	C, T	0.38	37
Muran et al. (2009)	30 w	Various	C, T	WAI-S	E	Premature Termination, Interpersonal Functioning	O	0.38	99
O'Malley et al. (1983)[a]	*	Various	O	VPPS	E	Overall Outcome, TC	C, T, O	0.55	38
Ogrodniczuk et al. (2000)	20	Interpretive, Supportive	C, T	NSI	A	General Symptoms, Individual Objectives, Social-Sexual Adjustment	C, T, O	0.35	67
Pantalon et al. (2004)	19 w	CBT	C	IVRS	A	Abstinence, Premature Termination	O	0.46	16
Pavio et al. (1998)	12	Experiential	C	WAI	E, L	SCL/BSI, SASB Introject, Unfinished Business Schale	C	0.24	33
Piper et al. (1991)	19	Dynamic	C, T	AAS	A	Composite Outcome	C, T, O	0.52	64
Piper et al. (1995)	19	Dynamic	C, T	AAS	A	State-Trait Anxiety, BDI, SCL/BSI, Overall Usefulness	C, T	0.54	30
Piper et al. (2004)[a]	20	Dynamic	C, T	NSI	A	Composite Outcome	C, O	0.10	144
Pos (2007)	18	Experiential	C	WAI	M	SCL/BSI, BDI	C	0.34	74
Pos et al. (2009)	18	Experiential	C	WAI	M	SCL/BSI, BDI	C	0.34	74

(*Continued*)

Table 2.1 Continued

Study	Treatment			Alliance			Outcome			
	Sessions	Type	Rater	Measure	Time	Measure	Rater	ES	N
Priebe et al. (1993)	20 months	Case management	C	BAS	E	Hospitalization Index, Work Axis, Accommodation	O	0.28	58
Prigatano et al. (1994)	6 months	Neuropsychology Rehabilitation	T	NAS	L	Productivity	O	0.40	35
Pugh (1991)	12	Various	C, T	WAI	E	SCL/BSI, TC	C, T	0.18	55
Pyne (1991)	6	Various	T, O	HAq(r), VPPS	A	Global Outcome, Premature Termination	C, T, O	0.34	29
Ramnerö et al. (2007)	16	CBT	T	WAI-S	M	Outcome Composite	O	-0.06	59
Reiner (1987)	*	Dynamic	C	TBS	E	Overall Outcome	O	0.40	82
Reis et al. (2004)	16	Dynamic	C	WAI	E	HRSD	O	0.07	58
Riley (1992)	8	Various	C, T	WAI, CALPAS	E, L	SCL/BSI, TC, GAS	C, T, O	0.17	61
Rogers et al. (2008)	*	Case Management	C, T	WAI-S	E	Depressive Symptoms	O	0.27	64
Rounsaville et al. (1987)[a]	14	Interpersonal	O	VPPS	E	Schedule for Affective Disorders, SAS, Patient Self-Assessment	O, C	0.25	35
Rudolf et al. (1993)	*	Dynamic	C, T	TRS	E, L	Composite Outcome	C, T	0.44	238
Safran et al. (1991)	20	Cognitive	C	WAI, CALPAS	E	SCL/BSI, MCMI, BDI, Global Success, TC	C, T	0.53	22
Sammet et al. (2004)	*	Various	C	HAq	A	SCL/BSI, IIP	C	0.16	213
Samstag et al. (2008)	30	Various	C, T	WAI-S	A	SCL/BSI, IIP	C	0.55	48
Santiago et al. (2005)	12	CBT	C	WAI-S	E	HRSD	O	0.22	324
Saunders (2000)[a]	26	Dynamic	C	TSR	E	Mental Health Index	C	0.16	114
Saunders et al. (1989)[a]	26	Dynamic	C	TBS	E	Session Quality, Termination Outcome	C, O	0.20	113

(Continued)

Table 2.1 Continued

Study	Treatment Sessions	Type	Alliance Rater	Measure	Time	Outcome Measure	Rater	ES	N
Schauenburg et al. (2005)	11	Dynamic	C, T	HAq	L	SCL/BSI, Severity Rating	C	0.23	284
Schleussner (2005)	*	Dynamic	C	HAq	E	Satisfaction	C	0.13	57
Schönberger et al. (2006a)[a]	14	Rehabilitation	C, T	WAI-S	E	EBIQ	C, T	0.14	59
Schönberger et al. (2006b)[a]	14	Rehabilitation	C, T	WAI-S†	E	EBIQ	C, T	0.31	103
Schönberger et al. (2006c)[a]	14	Rehabilitation	C, T	WAI-S	E	Composite Outcome	C, T	0.14	59
Schönberger et al. (2007)[a]	14	Rehabilitation	C, T	WAI-S	E	Cognitive Functioning	C, T	0.14	104
Sexton (1996)	10	Various	C	WAI-S	E	BOPS, Beck Anxiety Scale, SAS, GAS, BSO, Zung, Global Problem Rating	C, O	0.40	27
Sherer et al. (2007)	*	Rehabilitation	C, O, T	CALPAS, NAS	E	Premature Termination, Productivity, Functional Status	O	0.18	56
Shirk et al. (2008)[a]	12 w	CBT	C, T, O	AOCS	A	BDI, Depressive Symptoms	C, T	0.25	50
Solomon et al. (1995)	2 years	Case Management	C, T	WAI	L	Quality of Life, Compliance, Satisfaction with Treatment, other Variables	C, O	0.28	82
Sonnenberg (1996)	11	Inpatient	C, T	ITAS	E	SCL/BSI	C	0.03	63
Spinhoven et al. (2007)	*	Various	C, T	WAI	E	Symptom Status	O	0.25	70
Stevens et al. (2007)	30	30	C	WAI	E, M, L	Outcome Composite	C, T	0.37	44
Stiles et al. (2004)	12	Various	C	ARM	A	SCL/BSI, BDI, IIP, SAS, RSE	C	0.25	76

(Continued)

Table 2.1 Continued

	Treatment		Alliance			Outcome			
Study	Sessions	Type	Rater	Measure	Time	Measure	Rater	ES	N
Strauser et al. [*] (2004)[b]		Mental Retardation	C	WAS	A	Employment Prospects, Job Satisfaction	C	0.41	97
Strauss (2001)	[*]	CBT	C	CALPAS	A	WISPI	C	0.41	25
Strauss et al. (2006)	[*]	CBT	C	CALPAS	A	WISPI, SCID-II, BDI	C, O	0.45	30
Svartberg et al. (1994)	20	Dynamic	C	FAI	M	SCL/BSI, DAS	C	0.38	11
Tichenor (1989)	16	Various	C, T, O	WAI, CALPAS, HAq(r), VTAS	A	SCL/BSI, Self Concept, TC, HRSD, HRSA	C, T, O	0.16	8
Trepka et al. (2004)	16	CBT	C	CALPAS, ARM	A	BDI	C	0.50	30
Tryon et al. (1990)	19	Various	C, T	HAq	M	Premature Termination	C	0.20	74
Tryon et al. (1993)	13	Various	C, T	WAI-S	E	Premature Termination	C	0.25	86
Tryon et al. (1995)	10	Various	C, T	WAI-S	E	Premature Termination	C	0.25	71
Tunis et al. (1995)	180 days	Methadone Detox.	C	CALPAS	E, M, L, A	Premature Termination, Opioid Use, HIV Risk Behavior	C	0.34	20
Van et al. (2008)	16	Various	C	HAq	M	Depressive Symptoms	C	0.24	62
Vogel et al. (2006)	12	CBT	C	HAq	M	Y-BOCS	O	0.36	37
Vronmans (2007)	8	Narrative Therapy	C	WAI	E, M, L	BDI, OQ-45	C	0.48	34
Wettersten (2000)	12	Various	C	WAI	A	SCL/BSI, Satisfaction	C	0.27	32
Wettersten et al. (2005)[b]	12	Various	C	WAI	A	SCL/BSI, Satisfaction	C	0.27	32
Wilson et al. (2002)	19	Various	C	HRQ	E	Frequency of Vomiting	C	0.00	154
Windholtz et al. (1988)	16	Dynamic	O	VPPS	M	SCL/BSI, Overall Change, TC, GAS	C, T, O	0.20	38

(*Continued*)

Table 2.1 Continued

Study	Treatment			Alliance			Outcome			
	Sessions	Type	Rater	Measure	Time	Measure	Rater	ES	N
Yeomans et al. (1994)	230	Dynamic	O	CALPAS	E	Premature Termination	C	0.05	20
Zuroff et al. (2000)	16	Various	O	VTAS	L	DAS, Maladjustment Composite	C	0.10	149
Zuroff et al. (2006)	16	CBT	O	BLRI	E	Maladjustment Composite	C, O	0.18	48

Notes:

Raters:	C = client, T = therapist, O = other/observer
Time	E = early, M = middle, L = late, A = averaged alliance
	RG = residual gain score
Alliance Measures:	AAS = Alberta Alliance Scale
	AE = Active Engagement
	AOCS = Alliance Observation Coding System
	AQ = Alliance Questions
	ARM = Agnew Relationship Measure
	AWR = Alliance Weakenings and Repairs
	BAS = Berlin Alliance Scale
	BLRI = Barrett-Lennard Relationship Inventory
	BPSR = Bern Post Session Report
	CALPAS = California Psychotherapy Alliance Scale
	CALTARS = California Therapeutic Alliance Rating Scale
	CIS = Client Involvement Scale
	CS = Coordination Scale
	EH = Patient expectation of helpfulness
	FAI = Facilitative Alliance Inventory
	HA(r) = Penn Helping Alliance Scale - Rated
	HAq = Helping Alliance Questionnaire - Self-Rated
	HA(cs) = Helping Alliance Counting Signs
	HRQ = Helping Relationship Questionnaire
	ITAS = Various Inpatient Therapeutic Alliance Scales
	ITGA = Inpatient Task and Goal Agreement
	IVRS = Interpersonal Variables Rating Scale
	NAS = Neuropsychology Alliance Scale, Prigatano Alliance Scale
	NSI = Non Standard Instrument (Measure developed for the specific research project)
	OAS = Observer Alliance Scale
	SASB = Structural Analysis of Social Behavior
	STS TPRS = Systematic Treatment Selection Therapy Process Rating Scale
	TARS = Therapeutic Alliance Rating Scale
	TBS = Therapeutic Bond Scale
	TRS = Therapeutic Relationship Scale
	VTAS = Vanderbilt Therapeutic Alliance Rating Scale,
	VPPS = Vanderbilt Psychotherapy Process Scale,
	WAI = Working Alliance Inventory,
	WAI-S = Working Alliance Inventory - Short version
	WASu = Working Alliance Survey
	WASc = Working Alliance Scale

(*Continued*)

Table 2.1   Continued

Outcome measures:	ACQ = Agoraphobic Cognitions Questionnaire
	BDI = Beck Depression Inventory
	BIC = Battery of Interpersonal Capabilities
	BOPS = Brief Outpatient Psychopathology Scale
	BPRS = Brief Psychiatric Rating Scale
	BSQ = Body Sensation Questionnaire
	CES-D = Center of Epidemiologic Studies Depression Scale
	CPRS = Comprehensive Psychopathological Rating Scale
	DAS = Dysfunctional Attitudes Scale
	DpD = Drinking per Day
	DTES = Drug Taking Evaluation Scale
	EBIQ = European Brain Injury Questionnaire
	GAS = Global Assessment Scale
	GHQ = General Health Questionnaire
	HRSA = Hamilton Rating Scale for Anxiety
	HRSD = Hamilton Rating Scale for Depression,
	IES = Impact of Event Scale
	MCAS = Multnomah Community Ability Scale
	PANSS = Positive and Negative Syndrome Scale
	PICS = Pattern of Individual Change Scores
	PTQ = Post Therapy Questionnaire
	RSE = Rosenberg Self-Esteem Index
	SCL/BSI = Symptom Checklist 90, Brief Symptom Inventory
	SEQ = Session Evaluation Questionnaire
	STAI = State-Trait Anxiety Inventory
	SWLS = Satisfaction with Life Scale
	TC = Target Complaints
	WBI = Working Behavior Inventory
	WISPI = Wisconsin Personality Disorder Inventory
	Y-BOCS = Yale-Brown Obsessive-Compulsive Scale
	Zung = Zung's Self-Rating of Depression
Treatment:	* = various length
	w = weeks of treatment

†Partial Scale
ªStudies that share data with other report(s).
ᵇStudies that contributed multiple independent alliance–outcome relations.

Therapist (T): You think I should?

C: You do; always.

T: Because we agreed that looking at connection between past relationship patterns and how you and [name] are getting on is . . .

C: {voice over} Yes, unfinished business . . . And all that.

T: It may be that there is a pattern here, which would be useful to explore and understand better. Once we understand it, we can recognize it, and perhaps prevent a re-play of the same old grooves . . . [pause 10 sec]

T: I said that "we agreed" that this is the way to go, but I get the sense that you may not be convinced that's so . . . it is such a good idea.

C: Look, I mean . . . you are the therapist and I keep fucking up with my "old lady." So I guess I better start thinking & talking about these patterns . . . I wish there was a pill or electric shock therapy to . . ., it would be faster.

T: Maybe we better take a step back. I am a therapist, but I can't give you a pill or shock you to fix you. And looking for these unfinished patterns don't seem to make an awful lot of sense to you . . . right now. But I hear you are willing to be a "good client"

C: But this not what it is about, about me being good, I mean, right?

T: What would you say if you were not a "good patient"? Would you rebel?

C: I guess I might . . . It's crazy you know, before I got married I was a pretty wild dog . . . long hair, motorcycles, some pretty crazy stuff.

T: So, what happened? Where did the "crazy you" go? What did you do with him?

C: Married, good job, slick house, nice kids, you know . . .

T: You think I might meet this character? He seems to have been shut up but not forgotten . . . He might have something interesting to say . . .

C: I might be a little afraid of my old self . . . But [with different voice]: Doc, I'm trash, my old man was trash, but he put his money in good booze; not in psychiatrists' pockets!

T: He did not have much faith in this therapy business

C: Yeah, Of course you should not let him write the cheque for the session; it would for sure bounce . . . [both laugh]

In the above excerpt the therapist starts off defending his "modus operandi," but when he becomes aware of the client's ambivalent feelings about dealing with the past—and possibly about being in therapy—he drops his previous agenda and demonstrates his commitment to find a way of working collaboratively with his patient. Clients frequently have a mixture of hopes and worries about discussing long suppressed feelings and memories of deep significance. The therapist's challenge in building the alliance is to recognize, legitimize, and work through these issues and engage the client in a joint exploration of these obstacles.

The following excerpt provides another brief example of such a process:

C: "[topic discussed last week]" . . . was interesting . . . But sometimes I can't remember what I talked about from one week to the next.

T: . . . I think we ended up last talking about how difficult it is to imagine how things would be different.

C: <overlap> I sometimes wonder . . . what do therapists do after the session? I mean . . . Do you walk around the block to forget all this craziness . . .? Do you go home and dream about it?

T: Hmm, I . . .

C: [overlap] I mean, it is not like having a discussion with a friend; though goodness knows, I sometimes forget about those too. I think to myself, does he (T) need to hear all this? How often did I tell you that stuff? I read that Freud sometimes napped behind the couch . . . Not, mind you, that I think you nap! But sometimes you look tired <Laughs>. Oh, don't mind; this was a useful session. <looks at the clock> Are we done? <Stands up>

T: So I guess sometimes you wonder "what is it in it for him (T)"?

C: I knew you'd say that!

T: Well . . . I am not "really a friend." It is a strange thing to pour one's heart out to someone and then wonder: Did it mean anything to him? What am I to him?

C: Yeah, I guess . . . That's therapy, for you! <stand up again as to go>

T: Not sure if you want to talk about this or go?

C: Well it is late . . .

T: Interesting that this came up to-day. And . . . kind of left hanging . . . between us.

C: You mean "Hit & Run" . . .? when I don't . . . get . . . something . . . [I want] I don't wait for an answer.

T: There was something you wanted . . . from me . . .?

C: Doesn't take a rocket scientist to figure out . . . When you where asking "does it (therapy) work for you" {reference to last week's discussion} I thought here it comes . . .

T: You mean I'll quit on you?

C: I know you would not do that. I know you wouldn't. But, I mean, we are talking about this all this time, and I think . . . I talk about it to others too {relates an incident of talking about his marriage to a colleague} Now I know she {colleague} feels sorry for me, but of course this doesn't help either. But that's different. Kind of . . .it's not sympathy I need, but sometimes feels . . . <voice goes shallow, eyes moist>

T: You want from me . . . how I as person feel . . . about . . .

C: <Change of expression; sarcastic> Good fucking time to bring it up!

T: Does this; like this . . . remind . . .

C: You mean do I do this Hit & Run with B (wife), yeah. I've been thinking about that. Kind of stupid but interesting; I felt we were really . . . I was telling you something

in a way I have not been able to talk about it before. Last week, I mean . . . But kind of pulled back and felt mixed up when we started . . .I don't like risking myself much do I? . . . Hmm, I guess I went to the right school: "The hit and run academy of motherly love" . . . I am so tired of it [pause] . . . I think I am making the connection . . . [pause] We got someplace today.

It is important to note that clients, especially in the beginning of treatment, may appear to be hostile, rejecting, or fearful of treatment or the therapist. The therapist's ability to respond with acceptance and an openness to discuss these challenges is an important asset in establishing the alliance. There is some research evidence to show that therapists who respond with their own negativity to client's hostile remarks will likely damage the alliance (Henry, 1994).

The last excerpt offers a brief illustration of what the concept that we psychologists call alliance feels like from the client's perspective.

C: Yeah, I am more comfortable working with you . . . After finishing with Dr. "K" I was not too sure about getting into therapy again for two years. My previous therapist— I went to him for about a year—he was great at listening . . . I mean he had a good reputation and I think he was older than you. He must have heard of these things before. But I thought he was afraid that if he told me something I'll do it like a robot or something. I mean, I know these are my decisions and I got to get my own answers and sometimes you tell me that I'm trying to get around busting my own ass by getting you to tell me what you think . . .

Th: I . . .

C: [Chuckle]. It's OK, you do it quite nicely. But I can tell. [Pause] But you respect an honest question and seem to try to work with me the way I want to, not always out of the book . . .

I mean the other day, last week I mean, I was . . . I just could not let go of that anger. I guess I was not very well behaved here, as a patient I mean. But it was important for me to hear when you said "you will not let go without taking a piece of me." Then we talked . . . I talked like a normal client. But I needed to get a foot into you and hear "ouch" for me to look at what is happening. I needed your "ouch" to see into me, and not a finger from on high.

These brief excerpts were selected to illustrate how different therapy contexts draw on diverse therapist resources, and also the fact that the concept of the alliance unites the notions of interventions and the development of the relationship in therapy. Alliance is built by doing the work of therapy collaboratively.

Meta-Analytic Review
Sources of Data

To locate research published between 1973 and 2000, we relied on the three previously published meta-analyses (Horvath & Bedi, 2002; Horvath & Symonds, 1991; Martin, Garske, & Davis, 2000). However, most of the previously published effect sizes (ESs) were recomputed for this analysis, using a more detailed coding system to take account of added features and to better identify interdependencies in the underlying data when more than one research report shared the same client sample. We also applied more sensitive statistical analyses to the previously published data to

account for correlations of the outcome measures within studies. In addition, we extracted some alliance–outcome relations not available previously, and adjusted for variations in the number of participants used to calculate alliance–outcome relations within studies. As a result, both the ES and sample size (k) associated with some studies in this report are not identical to the values reported in previous meta-analyses.

To locate research with data on the relation between alliance and outcome from 2000 to 2009, we searched the PsycINFO database using the same search parameters as the Horvath and Bedi (2002) meta-analysis published in the previous edition of this book. In addition, we had access to a list of e-mail address for persons with whom the first author corresponded on the subject of the alliance; these individuals were invited to identify studies meeting the selection criteria.

The criteria for inclusion in this report were: (1) the study author referred to the therapy process variable as *alliance* (including variants of the term), (2) the research was based on clinical as opposed to analog data, (3) five or more patients participated in the study, and (4) the data reported was such that we could extract or estimate a value indicating the relation between alliance and outcome.

In reviewing the retrieved material, we discovered that there is a growing literature linking alliance to the effectiveness of medical interventions as well as a variety of social and even legal services. However, it was decided that this literature was outside the scope of this report. We chose to focus more narrowly on the relation between the quality of the alliance and outcome in the context of psychological treatments. Alliance research conducted on couples and family therapy and alliance research on children were also excluded as these topics are covered by other chapters in this volume. However, treatments for substance abuse as well as psychological problems that involve psychoactive medications are included.

In contrast to previous meta-analyses, we attempted to include research published in languages other than English. Our literature search was extended to material published in Italian, German, and French. A search was conducted of the German language database (PSYNDEX) using the same inclusion criteria as for the English language searches. One hundred and fifty- two German abstracts were retrieved. Of these, 17 manuscripts contained usable alliance–outcome data and were included in the analysis. For the French and Italian literature, we searched in PsycINFO with the additional keywords *French OR Francais OR Italian OR Italiano*. We accessed the search platforms EBSCO (USA) and OVID (Europe). Of the 87 French articles located, 73 manuscripts were written in English and published in English journals; of the remaining 14 items, 2 had usable alliance–outcome data; these are included in the analyses. Twenty-six Italian manuscripts were located; of these 14 were published in English journals, and none of the Italian-only papers had usable data. In total, 19 research reports unavailable in English were included in the analysis.

The 201 research reports included in the meta-analysis are listed in Table 2.1. Thirty-nine of these manuscripts were based on a shared data; that is, two or more reports provided alliance–outcome information derived from a common pool of clients. Thus, some of these reported effect sizes were not independent. In addition, 10 research publications listed in the table reported multiple alliance–outcome relations based on two or more independent samples.

The data on which our analysis is based includes both published (158) and unpublished (53) research. The published research appeared overwhelmingly (153) in peer-reviewed journals, with some (5) in book chapters, while 43 items came from unpublished (mostly dissertations) sources. The later represent a significant increase in the proportion of unpublished research in the current data compared to previous meta-analyses. In total, the data captures information based on over 14,000 treatments. (In Table 2.1, we provide ESs associated with each *manuscript*, but the aggregated effect sizes, and all of the calculations presented below, were adjusted for shared (nonindependent) data and are based on the 190 independent effects sizes.)

The number of eligible studies included in this chapter is roughly double the size of the data that were available in the previous chapter. The growth in the literature over the past decade means not only that there are more studies available for analysis, but also that there is a significant increase in the types of therapies, treatment contexts, client problems, and research designs captured by the current analysis.

Even with an effort to include non-English publications, the geographic distribution of research in our data is strongly biased: 153 manuscripts came from North America (134 USA, 19 Canada), 45 from Europe (22 from German-speaking countries, 10 from Scandinavia, 8 from UK, and 8 from other countries in Europe), and three research reports came from Australia. Notwithstanding these limitations, it is reasonable to claim that the data we present closely mirrors the universe of alliance research, since it appears that most foreign-speaking researchers who do this kind of work publish in English language journals.

Methods of Analysis

For our numerical estimates, we used the random-effects model. The reasons for this were twofold. First, given the broad range of applications, research designs, and measurement approaches within our data, we could not assume the existence of an underlying, homogeneous, singular, alliance–outcome index of alliance–outcome relations. By using a fixed-effects model, we would ". . . assume homogeneity of underlying treatment effects across studies [and this] may lead to substantial understatement of uncertainty" (National Research Council, 1992, p. 187). Second, the random-effects model, apart from requiring fewer assumptions, yields a more conservative estimate and hence leads to safer, more trustworthy, conclusions (Cooper, Hedges, & Valentine, 2009; Hunter & Schmidt, 2004). A random-effects model assumes that the studies analyzed are selected from a population of studies and thus the results are generalizable to the larger universe of studies.

In many studies, there were a number of different outcome measures and hence multiple effect sizes were reported. In order to account for the dependencies among outcome measures, due to multiple within-study ESs, we employed Hunter & Schmidt's (2004) aggregation procedures to obtain one correlation effect size per study. These procedures take into account the correlation among within-study outcome measures and thus yield a more precise estimate of the population parameter. In cases where the primary studies did not provide actual correlations among outcome measures, the estimate of between-outcome measure correlation was set to 0.50 (Wampold, 1997).

When conducting categorical and continuous moderator analyses, all correlations were transformed to a Fisher's z (Fisher, 1924) and then transformed back to r for interpretive purposes. The correlation coefficient is known to be nonnormally distributed, particularly with high values of correlation (which has a negative skew), and the Fisher's z transformation results in an approximately normal distribution.

In cases where the primary study reported more than one level of a categorical variable (e.g., both clients' and therapists' alliance scores), dependencies at the moderator level were accounted for by randomly selecting one within-study level per study. This procedure allowed for a fully independent analysis at the moderator level. This random selection procedure provided a safeguard from violating the assumption of independence in testing differences among levels of moderators; however, using this procedure also reduced the sample size and thus the power of the analysis. All procedures for this meta-analysis were conducted using the MAc (Del Re & Hoyt, 2010) and RcmdrPlugin.MAc (Del Re, 2010) meta-analysis packages for the R statistical software program (R Development Core Team, 2009).

Results

The aggregate effect size, for the 190 independent alliance–outcome relations representing over 14,000 treatments was $r = 0.275$. The 95% confidence interval of this aggregated ES ranged from 0.249 to 0.301. The aggregated value is adjusted for sample size, as well as the intercorrelation among outcome measures. The magnitude of the relationship in the current meta-analysis is a little larger but similar to the values reported in previous research (Horvath & Bedi, 2002, $r = 0.21$, $k = 100$; Horvath & Symonds, 1991, $r = 0.26$, $k = 26$; Martin, Garske, & Davis, 2000, $r = 0.22$, $k = 79$). The median effect size of ESs of the current data set is 0.28 (not adjusted for sample size), suggesting that the group of effect sizes we collected are not strongly skewed. The overall effect size of 0.275 is statistically significant at p < 0.0001 level, indicating a moderate but highly reliable relation between alliance and psychotherapy outcome.

This effect size of 0.275 was estimated based on studies located using electronic databases. Therefore, this estimate is potentially vulnerable to the file drawer bias (Sutton, 2009): the possibility that the research literature we accessed represents a biased sample, as there might be a number of studies with smaller or null ESs languishing in file drawers and unlisted in databases (possibly rejected by journals because they report nonsignificant results). The consequence of such a scenario can be evaluated by computing the fail-safe N. This is the number of studies with ES = 0 that would make the aggregate ES in the database statistically nonsignificant ($p > 0.05$). We have calculated the fail-safe value (Rosenthal, 1979): there would have to be over one thousand ES = 0 (null) additional studies hidden in dusty file drawers to generate an aggregate ES that was no longer statistically significant.

Another way to explore the question of whether there is a sampling bias effecting the data is by inspecting the funnel plot of the collection of ES in our set. A funnel plot is a diagram of standard error on the vertical axis as a function of effect size on the horizontal axis. In the presence of bias, we would expect the plot to show a higher concentration of studies on one side of the mean than the other. Typically, smaller sample size studies (having larger standard errors) are more likely to be published if they have larger-than-average effects. In the absence of publication bias, we would expect the studies to be distributed relatively symmetrically around the aggregated ES. The funnel plot in Figure 2.1 does not indicate a strongly biased set of data, but

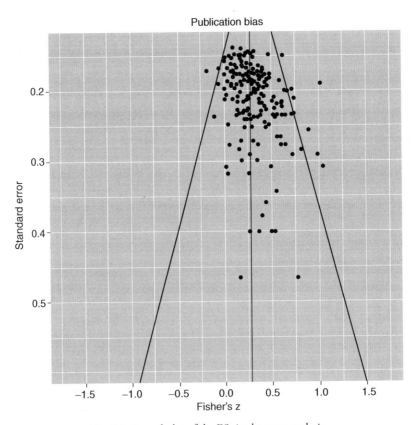

Fig. 2.1 Funnel plot of the ESs in the meta analysis.

neither is it perfectly symmetrical about the vertical axes.

We investigated two possible sources of systemic bias in the distribution of ESs: date of publication and study sample size. There was a small and statistically nonsignificant negative time trend observed ($p = 0.082$). Over time (1972–2009) researchers were reporting slightly decreasing ESs. This makes intuitive sense because recent studies use more sophisticated methods for controlling for pre-therapy effects that might impact the strength of the alliance. There are also more studies published recently involving client populations with more severe psychological problems. Both of these factors would likely exert a downward pressure on the correlation between alliance and outcome.

More surprisingly, we found a significant relation between sample size and ES ($r = -.25$ $p < 0.01$). The best fitting regression line for this puzzling association is quadratic, nonlinear; the studies with sample sizes between 100 to 200 appear to report lower ESs compared to studies with both smaller and larger sample size. This effect may be an artifact of some sort but will require further investigation.

In sum, the overall relation between alliance and outcome in individual psychotherapy is robust, is not effected by the file drawer problem, and accounts for approximately 7.5% of the variance in treatment outcomes.

Variability of Effect Sizes

There is a great deal of variability in the alliance–outcome relations across the 190 ESs in the current data set. Similar to what we found in the previous meta-analysis (Horvath & Bedi, 2002), the group of alliance–outcome relations in this data set are not homogenous ($Q = 498.42$, $df = 189$, $p < 0.00001$). If all the alliance–outcome research in our data were sampling the same

relation, we would expect the reported research results to cluster around a population parameter with deviations from the true value due only to random errors. We computed the I^2 statistic, which provides an estimate of the percentage of variance of ESs over and above the amount of variability that can be accounted for by random (chance) variation. The I^2 of 0.56 we obtained indicates that the variance in our data is approximately 56% greater than one would expect if all the studies were measuring the same relation. This finding, in and of itself, is not surprising; researchers assessed alliance at different points of therapy, in a variety of therapy contexts, using therapists, clients, or observers for their evaluations. In addition, outcomes were measured from a variety of perspectives, sometimes immediately after treatments, at other times at follow-up points. Heterogeneity in the data encouraged us to investigate the possible moderators effecting the alliance outcome correlations.

Moderators and Mediators
Alliance Measures

In our meta-analysis, over 30 different alliance instruments were employed, but only the four core instruments (CALPAS, HAq, VPPS, WAI) were used in three or more studies. (The HAq family is composed of two quite different instruments: the original [1983] versions coded as HAq, and the [1996] revision coded as HAqII). Therefore, for the current study, we compared the aggregated ES of each of the four core instruments plus a residual category called "other." The box and whisker plot (Figure 2.2) displays the ESs associated with these measures (range $r = 0.23–0.39$). The differences among them were not significant ($Q = 1.851$, $df = 5$). However, it should be noted that within the four core instruments, only the ES associated with the CALPAS and the VPPS were homogeneous. Effect sizes reported

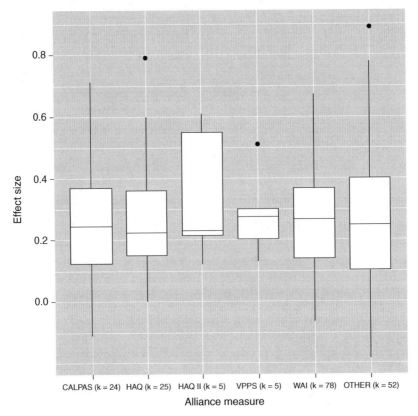

Fig. 2.2 Box-and-Whisker plot of Effect Sizes (ES) associated with different alliance measures.

within each of the other measures were more variable than one would expect from chance or random error alone. A likely reason for the homogeneity of the the CALPAS and the VPPS measures are available in fewer versions than the WAI and the HAq.

Time-of-Alliance Assessment

The time-of-alliance assessment was grouped into four categories: *Early:* Sessions 1–5; *Mid:* after the fifth, but four or more sessions before end-of-treatment; *Late:* within three sessions of end-of-treatment; and *Averaged* a combination of assessment points. A number of researchers provided information on multiple assessment times within the same study. In most of our analyses, one ES was randomly selected if multiple ESs were available in order to ensure independence of the data. However, for reasons of clinical relevance, in this analysis only, if multiple assessments were available in a study, we chose the earliest assessment available for the computations. Figure 2.3 shows the results of this analysis graphically. As one would anticipate, the relation between alliance and outcome grew in magnitude as the alliance and outcome became closer in time. The omnibus Q statistic for the overall contrast among these time categories was highly significant (Q 17.42, df = 3, p <0.001), but the post-hoc pairwise multiple comparisons were not statistically significant (p > 0.05), due to the large within-category heterogeneity.

Sources-of-Alliance Assessment

The alliance can be rated from three perspectives: Clients, therapists, and observers. Client and observer ratings are similar [Clients r = 0.282 (k = 109); Observer r = 0.295 (k = 47)], and both of these

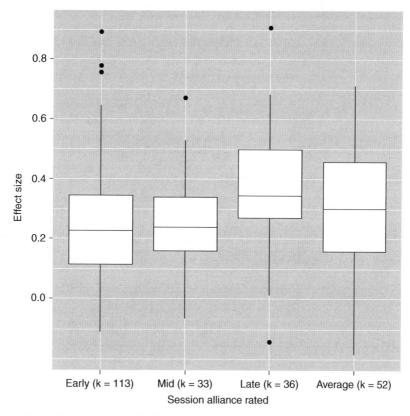

Fig. 2.3 Box-and-Whisker plot of Effect Sizes between alliance and outcome measured at different phases of treatment.

perspectives of the alliance provided better prediction of therapy outcome than therapist evaluations ($r = 0.196$, $k = 40$). These findings are consistent with previous research (Horvath & Bedi 2002; Horvath & Symonds, 1991). However, the differences among these categories were not statistically significant ($Qb = 5.16$, $df = 2$, $p = 0.076$). An examination of the distribution of ESs within these categories indicated that the variability of the ESs in the client and therapist ratings was over 50% greater than expected by chance. That is, the ESs in the set were heterogeneous, likely due to the variety of measuring instruments used. Such a high degree of variability within these categories made it less likely that the differences between the categories of raters would reach statistical significance.

Outcome Measures

As was the case with the alliance measures, a broad range of therapy outcome measures were utilized in the studies in our meta-analysis. Of the over 35 outcome assessments, only three measures — Beck Depression Inventory (Beck et al., 1961, BDI), SCL (Derogatis, Lippman, & Covi, 1973), and premature termination or "dropout"— were utilized in sufficient frequency (5 ESs or more) to permit analysis. As a result, only a subset of 60 ESs that utilized these three outcome measures could be included in this analysis. Table 2.2 displays the results of this analysis. The Q statistics for this set of moderators is significant (Q 10.98, $df = 2$, $p = 0.004$). Post-hoc analysis indicated a statistically significant difference between studies using dropout (or premature termination) and

Table 2.2 Relation between the Alliance and Outcome Measures

	K	ES	95% CI (Lower)	95% CI (Upper)	p
Dropout	15	0.164	0.062	0.262	.001
SCL	28	0.276	0.195	0.353	.000
BDI	17	0.409	0.304	0.505	.000

BDI as an outcome measure. In considering these results, it is helpful to keep in mind that the BDI is most often used as a symptom-specific outcome measure for clients receiving treatment for depression. The relation between alliance and therapy outcome for the treatment for depression tends to be relatively high. Dropout as a treatment outcome was almost exclusively utilized in studies of clients with substance abuse problems. While unilateral termination represents, in one sense, "hard" outcome data, the substance abuse treatments included in our data were highly varied, and clients in these treatments were often volatile and multidisordered. This being the case, individuals might have terminated therapy for a variety of reasons, apart from lack of progress in treatment. The observed differences among these studies are consistent with this hypothesis; the 15 ESs within the dropout group were highly variable ($p = 0.37$).

Types of Treatments

Bordin (1976, 1994) argued that the alliance is a significant factor in all types of helping relationships. We explored the evidence for this claim by contrasting the averaged effect sizes associated with CBT, IPT, psychodynamic, and substance abuse treatments. The ESs for each type of treatment, reflecting the strength of the association between alliance and outcome, were highly significant ($p < 0.001$). But an analysis of the contrast between the treatment categories indicated that the differences in

the alliance–outcome relation among them were not statistically significant ($Qb = 4.85$, $df = 3$, $p = 0.183$)[*]. These results support the claim that the alliance is a pantheoretical factor in diverse types of treatments. However, it should be noted that only 93 out of the total of 190 ES in the data set could be fitted into the four categories used for this analysis.

Raters of Outcome Data

Similar to the measurement of alliance, researchers used outcome evaluations obtained from clients, therapists, independent observers, or some combination of these sources. In the data set, 109 ESs were based on clients, 47 ESs on observers, 12 ESs on therapists, and 22 ESs were generated by other sources (e.g., dropouts, days of sobriety, rehospitalization). The difference among the alliance–outcome ES obtained by these disparate raters was statistically significant ($Q = 8.34$. $df = 3$, $p < 0.05$), but the post-hoc test of pairwise contrast of differences was not statistically significant. Again, this result is likely due to the large variability within these rater categories.

Halo Effect

We examined the question of whether ESs were inflated when the alliance and outcome information came from the same (e.g., client rates both alliance and outcome) or different sources (e.g., client rated alliance and observer rated outcome).

---

[*]Qb = between-group statistic

Table 2.3 Alliance outcome correlations disaggregated by raters of assessment.

Alliance rater	Outcome rater			
	Client	Therapist	Observer	Other
Client	**0.30 (98)**	0.27 (14)	0.21 (40)	0.34 (13)
Therapist	0.18 (31)	**0.29 (20)**	0.13 (20)	0.30 (12)
Observer	0.24 (28)	0.39 (10)	**0.27 (17)**	0.58 (7)
Other	0.16 (9)	N/A	0.16 (2)	**0.22 (8)**

Note: Numbers in parentheses (k); Diagonal values represent data generated when the alliance and outcome were rated by the same source. Data in this table are not independent; some studies provided data from more than one source.

Table 2.3 shows that ESs from studies in which the same raters completed both the outcome, and alliance measures were indeed higher on average than those coming from different rater categories, but the difference between these values fell slightly below the critical level for statistical significance ($p = 0.079$). It is notable that the difference between same source versus independent source ESs has increased progressively since this effect was first analyzed in 1991 using 27 data points (Horvath & Symonds, 1991). Keeping in mind this apparent trend, the possibility that same-source evaluations might be inflated may be a concern of clinical significance in the future.

Publication Sources

The lion's share of the ESs in our data was published in refereed journals (153), followed by unpublished studies (43), and 5 extracted from books. The effect sizes associated with these sources were $r = 0.287$, 0.237, and 0.399, respectively. The differences among these ESs were not significant.

Interaction among Moderators

We examined a number of categorical variables that potentially moderate the alliance–outcome relation, but within most of these moderators, the range of ESs was quite broad; most levels of moderator categories were themselves heterogeneous. One possible reason for such heterogeneity is that the categories we coded were not pure factors, but variables that interact with one another. To better understand the influence of these variables on the relation between alliance and outcome, one needs to examine the complexities of these variables acting together.

Modeling the full complement of potential moderator interactions is statistically unmanageable even with a large data set such as the one we collected. Not all the levels of these categorical variables intersect, and there are computational difficulties because many of the joint values are not independent (i.e., are based on the same data). Taking these limits into consideration, a random effects multipredictor meta-regression was computed to explore the joint impact of a subset of the clinically most interesting categorical moderators: The alliance raters (client, therapist, observer), the alliance measurements (using only the core instruments WAI, HAq, HAq II, VPPS, and CALPAS), and the three major outcome indexes (BDI, SCL, and dropout). The effects of the year of publication and sample size were controlled in this analysis.

Because of the restrictions in the data, only 54 ESs could be entered into this analysis. However, almost half of the total variance among these alliance–outcome relations were explained by the individual and joint effects of these variables ($R^2 = 0.46$).

It was particularly interesting that the addition of the joint effect of the alliance measure × alliance rater alone contributed an R^2 change of 0.23. While the results of this analysis cannot be generalized to the alliance–outcome literature, since only about 25% of the studies could be used for these calculations, the findings strongly suggest that the abundant heterogeneity in the research findings is due in large part to the range of methods used to measure the alliance combined with the variety of means used to assess outcome.

The cost of inclusivity in defining both the outcome and especially the process (alliance) variable in research praxis is the difficulty in arriving at a focused conclusion. An exemplar of the how this broad conceptualization of variables both enriches the alliance research literature and at the same time creates challenges in generating convergence toward clinically useful conclusion, we will briefly review one of the most dynamic strands of the current research agenda: the investigation of the dynamics of the alliance over the span of treatment.

Patterns of Alliance over Time

The patterns of growth and development of the alliance over the course of psychotherapy associated with a good outcome have been of continued interest to researchers. Bordin (1985, 1989) suggested that the repairs of stresses or tears in the alliance will make an important contribution toward therapeutic gains. Gelso and Carter (1994) predicted that a rise in early alliance followed by a decline in the quality of the alliance, followed again by an increase, would be associated with positive outcomes in therapy. There have been a number of research projects aimed at investigating these and other predictions in order to document the relation between the various alliance patterns and outcome.

The results of these research studies defies easy summary. Multiple studies found some support for the existence of quadratic alliance patterns and their relation to positive outcome in short-term therapy (e.g., Horvath & Marx, 1991; Kivlighan & Shaughnessy, 2000; Man, 1973; Miller et al., 1983). But several other studies (e.g., Piper et al., 2004; Stevens et al., 2007; Stiles et al., 2004) were unable to replicate their results and confirm this hypothesis. There is some support for the prediction that linear and increasing levels of the quality of alliance over the length of treatment are associated with better outcome than flat-linear and decreasing-linear patterns (de Roten et al., 2004; Kramer et al., 2009; Piper et al., 2004). However, the association of linear-increasing pattern with outcome is problematic: some researchers analyzed data that was collected close to the end of therapy; these "late" alliance measures are difficult to disentangle from outcome (Horvath & Luborsky, 1993). Kivlighan and Shaughnessy (2000) have also identified "U" and reverse or inverted "U" patterns in brief therapy. However, there are number of reports confirming the existence of these patterns but the number of published reports unable to confirm the pattern (e.g., Kramer et al., 2009; Piper et al., 2004; Stiles et al., 2004; Stevens et al., 2007) were about equally divided.

The diversity among these findings is almost certainly related to a number of research design and measurment issues. The different length of therapies is one: researchers have examined treatments ranging from as few as 6 to over 30 sessions. Some studies explored the change in the level and the shape of alliance patterns over time independently (Stiles, et al., 2004; Strauss, 2001), but others choose not to make those distinctions (e.g., Kivlighan & Shaughnessy, 2000). In addition, a number different alliance measures and a variety of statistical approaches, have been used by different researchers, (e.g., regression models, HLM, and cluster analysis), and there is no consistency across studies in terms of the length of time in the course of psychotherapy over which patterns were examined. As well, researchers used different criteria for the identification of growth patterns and curve shape. As a result, it is not yet clear if the lack of convergence in this literature signals that the hypothesized good alliance development patterns are local to specific contexts (e.g., type of treatment or client problems), and thus cannot be generalized, or that the broad diversity of research methods obscure a yet-to-be discovered general pattern of good alliance development.

There are a couple of hypotheses, however, with promise of convergence: The most consistent finding appears to be the proposition that some fluctuation, that is, change over time, particularly in the mid-phase of therapy, is associated with positive outcome when contrasted with a linear or stable alliance pattern. It is also safe to conclude that no single pattern of alliance development or growth has been consistently documented as better or more predictive of good outcome than alternative shapes, across different kinds of therapies in different lengths of treatments. There is mounting evidence that in treatments where the quality of alliance is steadily declining over time, the outcome is usually poor (Stiles, 2004). There is also convergence that some variability in the quality of the alliance is likely an indication of superior outcome compared to a situation where the alliance is level and stable, so long as the overall quality of the alliance does not decline over time (Safran, 1993; Safran, Crocker, McMain, & Murray, 1990; Safran & Muran, 1996, 2000; Strauss et al., 2006). But, the amount of variation that is optimal for outcome, or indeed the period over which the fluctuation (i.e., growth or growth-decay-and-growth pattern) may be most beneficial is not yet resolved.

Limitations of the Research

This chapter is based on a numerical synthesis of the research results. While our team has made a sustained effort to seek out all the available research on alliance–outcome relation, no meta-analysis is comprehensive, and this one is no exception. At the very least, by the time the chapter goes to press, there will be, no doubt, a number of new studies available.

A more significant challenge is the "apples and oranges" problem (Hunter & Schmidt, 1990, p. 521). In including all research in which the authors refer to the process variable as *alliance*, we might have collected and summarized a number of different kinds of things. This is a serious concern, especially in light of the fact that the ESs in this data set are quite diverse. A practical response to this conceptual problem is to assert that this chapter reports the results of alliance–outcome relation *as it is researched*.

There are also some technical constraints to the analyses we reported. We chose to use independent data whenever possible. To achieve this, on many occasions we needed to randomly discard some data (ES) in order to make sure that only one result from a particular data pool was used in each analysis. As a result, we lost power to detect differences in a number of analyses. In the long run, the use of independent data is statistically well justified, but the resulting constraints put on the computations are also important to consider.

Therapeutic Practices

The positive relation between the quality of the alliance and treatment outcomes for many different types of psychotherapies is confirmed in this meta-analysis. The question of whether alliance contributes to outcome beyond early therapy gains (e.g., Feeley, DeRubeis, & Gelfand, 1999) has also been largely resolved: a number of studies that controlled for this factor found that alliance is predictive of outcome above and beyond early gains (e.g., Barber, et al., 2001; Brotman, 2004; Constantino, Arnow, Blasey & Agras, 2005; Gaston, et al., 1991; Klein, et al., 2003; Strauss, et al., 2006). While the overall ES of $r = 0.275$ accounts for a relatively modest proportion of the total variance in treatment outcome, the magnitude of this correlation makes it one of the strongest and most robust predictors of treatment success that research has been able to document (Wampold, 2001). In the following section, we condense some of the most salient points for practicing therapists.

• The alliance is not the same as the therapeutic relationship. The relationship is made of several interlocking elements (empathy, responsiveness, creating a safe secure environment, etc.) The alliance is one way of conceptualizing what has been achieved by the appropriate use of these elements.

• The fostering of the alliance is not separate from the interventions therapists implement to help their clients; it is influenced by, and is an essential and inseparable part of, everything that happens in therapy. In this sense, the therapist does not "build alliance" but rather does the work of treatment in such a way that the process forges an alliance with the client.

• The development of a "good enough" alliance early in therapy is vital for therapy success. The sense of collaboration creates a working space, room to introduce new ways of addressing the clients concerns.

• The alliance matters in all forms of therapy, including treatments mediated through some media (e.g., Internet, telephone). Different forms of therapy call on diverse relational resources and different levels of intimacy and intensity. The therapist and client must find the level of collaboration suited to achieve the work of therapy—even if they do not have face-to-face contact.

• In the early phases of therapy, modulating the methods of therapy (tasks) to suit the specific client's needs, expectations, and capacities is important in building the alliance. Clients are often naïve in their expectation of what therapy entails, how they have to participate in the process, and unaware of the links between what is happening moment to moment during the session and the changes they desire. Bridging the client's expectations and what the therapist believes to be the most appropriate interventions is an important and delicate task. Alliance emerges, in part, as a result of the smooth coordination of these elements.

• Therapists need to closely monitor the client's perspective on the alliance throughout treatment. It is frequently the case that therapists' and clients' perceptions of the alliance, particularly early in treatment, do not converge. Misjudging the client's experience of the alliance (i.e., believing that it is in good shape when the client does not share this perception) could render therapeutic interventions less effective.

• The strength of the alliance, within or between sessions, often fluctuates in response to a variety of in-therapy factors, such as the therapist challenging clients to grapple with difficult conflicts, misunderstandings, and transference. These "normal" variations —as long as they are attended to and resolved— are associated with good treatment outcomes.

• Therapists' non-defensive response to client negativity or hostility is critical for maintaining a good alliance. Therapists ought to neither internalize nor to ignore client's negative responses.

• Clients presenting with high interpersonal anxiety or with personality disorders tend to be particularly challenging in terms of alliance development and maintenance.

References

Asterisk indicates works used in meta-analysis.

*Adler, J. V. (1988). *A study of the working alliance in psychotherapy.* Unpublished doctoral dissertation, University of British Columbia.

Alexander, L. B., & Luborsky, L. (1987). The Penn Helping Alliance Scales. In L. S. Greenberg & W. M. Pinsoff (Eds.), *The psychotherapeutic process: A research handbook* (pp. 325–356). New-York: Guilford.

*Allen, J. G., Tarnoff, G., & Coyne, L. (1985). Therapeutic alliance and long-term hospital treatment outcome. *Comprehensive Psychiatry, 26*, 187–194.

*Allen, J. G., Tarnoff, G., Coyne, L., Spohn, H. E., Buskirk, J. R., & Keller, M. W. (1986). An innovative approach to assessing outcome of long-term psychiatric hospitalization. *Hospital and Community Psychiatry, 37*, 376–380.

*Andreoli, A., Frances, A., Gex-Mabry, M., Aapro, N., Gerin, P., & Dazord, A. (1993). Crisis intervention in depressed patients with and without DSM-II-R personality disorders. *Journal of Nervous and Mental Disease, 181*, 732–737.

*Ankuta, G. Y. (1993). *Initial and later therapeutic alliance and psychotherapy outcome.* Unpublished doctoral dissertation, Michigan State University, East Lansing.

*Arnow, B. A., Manber, R., Blasey, C., Blalock, J. A., Rothbaum, B. O., Thase, M. E., et al. (2003). Therapeutic reactance as a predictor of outcome in the treatment of chronic depression. *Journal of Consulting and Clinical Psychology, 71*, 1025–1035.

*Baldwin, S. A., Wampold, B. E., & Imel, Z. E. (2007). Untangling the alliance-outcome correlation: Exploring the relative importance of therapist and patient variability in the alliance. *Journal of Consulting and Clinical Psychology, 75*(6), 842–852.

*Barber, J. P., Connolly, M. B., Crits-Christoph, P., Gladis, L., & Siqueland, L. (2000). Alliance predicts patients' outcome beyond in-treatment change in symptoms. *Journal of Consulting and Clinical Psychology, 68*(6), 1027–1032.

*Barber, J. P., Gallop, R., Crits-Christoph, P., Barrett, M. S., Klostermann, S., McCarthy, K. S., et al. (2008). The role of the alliance and techniques in predicting outcome of supportive-expressive dynamic therapy for cocaine dependence. *Psychoanalytic Psychology, 25*(3), 461–482.

*Barber, J. P., Gallop, R., Crits-Christoph, P., Frank, A., Thase, M. E., Weiss, R. D., et al. (2006). The role of therapist adherence, therapist competence, and alliance in predicting outcome of individual drug counseling: Results from the National Institute Drug Abuse Collaborative Cocaine Treatment Study. *Psychotherapy Research, 16*(2), 229–240.

*Barber, J. P., Luborsky, L., Crits-Cristoph, P., Thase, M. E., Weiss, R., Frank, A., et al. (1999). Therapeutic alliance as predictor of outcome in treatment of cocaine dependence. *Psychotherapy Research, 9*, 54–73.

*Barber, J. P., Luborsky, L., Gallop, R., Crits-Christoph, P., Frank, A., Weiss, R. D., et al. (2001). Therapeutic alliance as a predictor of outcome and retention in the National Institute on Drug Abuse Collaborative Cocaine Treatment Study. *Journal of Consulting and Clinical Psychology, 69*(1), 119–124.

*Barkham, M., Agnew, R. M., & Culverwell, A. (1993). The California Psychotherapy Alliance Scales: A pilot study of dimensions and elements. *British Journal of Medical Psychology, 66*, 157–165.

*Bassler, M., Potratz, B., & Krauthauser, H. (1995). Der "Helping Alliance Questionnaire" (HAQ) von Luborsky [The Helping Alliance Questionnaire (HAQ) by Luborsky]. *Psychotherapeut, 40*(1), 23–32.

Beck, A. T., Ward, C. H., Mendelson, M., Mock, J., & Erbaugh, J. (1961). An inventory for measuring depression. *Archives of General Psychiatry, 4*, 561–571.

*Bethea, A. R., Acosta, M. C., & Haller, D. L. (2008). Patient versus therapist alliance: whose perception matters? *Journal of Substance Abuse Treatment, 35*(2), 174–183.

*Bieschke, K. J., Bowman, G. D., Hopkins, M., Levine, H., & McFadden. (1995). Improvement and satisfaction in short-term therapy at a university counseling center. *Journal of College Student Development, 36,* 553–559.

*Biscoglio, R. L. (2005). *Patient and therapist personality, therapeutic alliance, and overall outcome in Brief Relational Therapy.* Unpublished doctoral dissertation, City University, New York, NY.

Bordin, E. S. (1975, September). *The working alliance: Basis for a general theory of psychotherapy.* Paper presented at the Society for Psychotherapy Research, Washington, DC.

Bordin, E. S. (1976). The generalizability of the psychoanalytic concept of the working alliance. *Psychotherapy: Theory, Research, and Practice, 16,* 252–260.

Bordin, E. S. (1980, June). *Of human bonds that bind or free.* Paper presented at the Society for Psychotherapy Research, Pacific Grove, CA.

Bordin, E. S. (1989, June). *Building therapeutic alliances: The base for integration.* Paper presented at the Society for Psychotherapy Research, Berkley, CA.

Bordin, E. S. (1994). Theory and research on the therapeutic working alliance: New directions. In A. O. Horvath & L. S. Greenberg (Eds.), *The working alliance: Theory, research, and practice.* (pp. 13–37). New York: Wiley.

*Botella, L., Corbella, S., Belles, L., Pacheco, M., Maria Gomez, A., Herrero, O., et al. (2008). Predictors of therapeutic outcome and process. *Psychotherapy Research, 18*(5), 535–542.

*Bredel, S., Brunner, R., Haffner, J., & Resch, F. (2004) Behandlungserfolg, Behandlungserleben und Behandlungszufriedenheit aus der Sicht von Patienten, Eltern und Therapeuten - Ergebnisse einer evaluativen Studie aus der stationären Kinder- und Jugendpsychiatrie [Treatment success, experience of treatment, and treatment satisfaction from the viewpoint of patients, parents, and therapists]. *Praxis der Kinderpsychologie und Kinderpsychiatrie.* 53(4), 256–276.

*Broome, K.M. (1996). *Antisocial personality and drug abuse treatment process.* Unpublished doctoral dissertation. Texas Christian University, Fort Worth.

*Brotman, M. A. (2004). *Therapeutic alliance and adherence in cognitive therapy for depression.* Unpublished doctoral dissertation, University of Pennsylvania, Philadelphia.

*Burns, J. W., & Evon, D. (2007). Common and specific process factors in cardiac rehabilitation: Independent and interactive effects of the working alliance and self-efficacy. *Health Psychology, 26*(6), 684–692.

*Busseri, M. A., & Tyler, J. D. (2003). Interchangeability of the Working Alliance Inventory and Working Alliance Inventory, Short Form. *Psychological Assessment, 15*(2), 193–197.

*Busseri, M. A., & Tyler, J. D. (2004). Client-therapist agreement on target problems, working alliance, and counselling outcome. *Psychotherapy Research, 14*(1), 77–88.

*Card, C. A. (1991). *Therapeutic alliance, complementarity, and distress during stress prevention training after HIV testing.* Unpublished doctoral dissertation, New School for Social Research, New York.

*Castonguay, L. G., Goldfried, M. R., Wiser, S., Raue, P. J., & Hayes, A. M. (1996). Predicting the effect of cognitive therapy for depression: A study of unique and common factors. *Journal of Clinical and Consulting Psychology, 64,* 497–504.

Chambless, D. L. (2002). Beware the dodo bird: The dangers of overgeneralization. *Clinical Psychology: Science and Practice, 9*(1), 13–16.

*Chilly, C. (2004). *The effects of the interpersonal framework of intervention on therapeutic compliance, alliance, and outcome.* Unpublished doctoral dissertation, York University, Toronto, Canada.

*Cislo, D. A. (1988). *Client perceptions of the therapeutic alliance and session outcome.* Unpublished doctoral dissertation, University of Toledo, Toledo, OH.

*Clarkin, J. F., & Crilly, J. L. (1987). Therapeutic alliance and hospital treatment outcome. *Hospital and Community Psychiatry, 38,* 871–875.

*Cloitre, M., Chase Stovall-McClough, K., Miranda, R., & Chemtob, C. M. (2004). Therapeutic alliance, negative mood regulation, and treatment outcome in child abuse-related posttraumatic stress disorder. *Journal of Consulting and Clinical Psychology, 72*(3), 411–416.

*Coleman, D. (2006). Client personality, working alliance and outcome: A pilot study. *Social Work in Mental Health, 4*(4), 83–98.

*Connors, G. J., Carroll, K. M., DiClemente, C. C., Longabaugh, R., & Donovan, D. M. (1997). The therapeutic alliance and its relationship to alcoholism treatment participation and outcome. Journal of Consulting and Clinical Psychology, 65(4), 588–598.

*Constantino, M. J., Arnow, B. A., Blasey, C., & Agras, W. S. (2005). The association between patient characteristics and the therapeutic alliance in cognitive-behavioral and interpersonal therapy for bulimia nervosa. *Journal of Consulting and Clinical Psychology, 73*(2), 203–211.

Cooper, H., Hedges, L.V., & Valentine, J. C. (2009). *The handbook of research synthesis and meta-analysis* (2nd edition). New York, Russell Sage Foundation.

*Crits-Cristoph, P., Cooper, A., & Luborsky, L. (1988). The accuracy of therapists' interpretations and the outcome of dynamic psychotherapy. *Archives of General Psychiatry, 56*, 490–495.

*Davis, L. W., & Lysaker, P. H. (2007). Therapeutic alliance and improvements in work performance over time in patients with schizophrenia. *The Journal of Nervous and Mental Disease, 195*(4), 353–357.

*Dearing, R. L., Barrick, C., Dermen, K. H., & Walitzer, K. S. (2005). Indicators of client engagement: Influences on alcohol treatment satisfaction and outcomes. *Psychology of Addictive Behaviors, 19*(1), 71–78.

Del Re., A. C. (2010). *RcmdrPlugin.MAc: Meta-Analysis with Correlations (MAc) Rcmdr Plug-in.* R package version 1.0.5. http://CRAN.Rproject.org/package=RcmdrPlugin.MAc

Del Re., A. C., & Hoyt, W. T. (2010). MAc: Meta-Analysis with Correlations. R package version 1.0.5. http://CRAN.R-project.org/package=MAc

*de Roten, Y., Fischer, M., Drapeau, M., Beretta, V., Kramer, U., Favre, N., et al. (2004). Is one assessment enough? Patterns of helping alliance development and outcome. *Clinical Psychology & Psychotherapy, 11*(5), 324–331.

*Deu, A., Heimbrock, F., & Röhrle B. (2009). Der Zusammenhang zwischen Merkmalen Sozialer Netzwerke und der therapeutischen Beziehung. Eine kombinierte Prozess-Outcome-Studie [The relation between social network attributes and the therapeutic relationship - A combined process-outcome study]. In Röhrle, B., & Laireiter, A. R. (Eds.). *Soziale Unterstützung und Psychotherapie* (pp. 227–253). Tübingen, Germany: dgvt Verlag.

*Dorsch, B., & Joraschky, P. (2002). *Katamnestische Untersuchung an Patienten mit einer Angststörung nach stationärer Therapie* [Follow-up study of patients with anxiety disorders after inpatient therapy]. Lage, Germany: Verlag Hans Jacobs.

*Dundon, W. D., Pettinati, H. M., Lynch, K. G., Xie, H., Varillo, K. M., Makadon, C., et al. (2008). The therapeutic alliance in medical-based interventions impacts outcome in treating alcohol dependence. *Drug & Alcohol Dependence, 95*(3), 230–236.

*Dunn, H., Morrison, A. P., & Bentall, R. P. (2006). The relationship between patient suitability, therapeutic alliance, homework compliance and outcome in cognitive therapy for psychosis. *Clinical Psychology & Psychotherapy, 13*(3), 145–152.

*Eaton, T. T., Abeles, N., & Gutfreund, M. J. (1988). Therapeutic alliance and outcome: Impact of treatment length and pretreatment symptomology. *Psychotherapy: Theory, Research, Practice and Training, 25*, 536–542.

*Emmerling, M. E., & Whelton, W. J. (2009). Stages of change and the working alliance in psychotherapy. *Psychotherapy Research, 19*(6), 687–698.

*Fakhoury, W. K. H., White, I., Priebe, S., & PLAO Study Group (2007). Be good to your patient: How the therapeutic relationship in the treatment of patients admitted to assertive outreach affects rehospitalization. *Journal of Nervous and Mental Disease, 195*, 789–791.

*Feeley, W. M. (1993). *Treatment components of cognitive therapy for major depression: The good, the bad, and the inert.* Unpublished doctoral dissertation. University of Pennsylvania, Philadelphia.

Feeley, M., DeRubeis, R. J., & Gelfand, L. A. (1999). The temporal relation of adherence and alliance to symptom change in cognitive therapy for depression. Journal of Consulting and Clinical Psychology, *67*(4), 578–582.

*Ferleger, N. A. (1993). *The relationship of dependency and self-criticism to alliance, complementarity and outcome in short-term dynamic psychotherapy.* Unpublished doctoral dissertation, Fordham University, Bronx, NY.

Fisher, R. A. (1924) On a distribution yielding the error functions of several well known statistics. *Proceedings of the International Congress of Mathematics, Toronto, 2*, 805–813.

*Florsheim, P., Shotorbani, S., Guest-Warnick, G., Barratt, T., & Hwang, W. (2000). Role of the working alliance in treatment of delinquent boys in community-based programs. *Journal of Clinical Child Psychology, 29*, 94–107.

*Flückiger, C., Regli, D., & Grawe, K. (2005). Allgemeine Psychotherapie im Gruppensetting: Das Zusammenspiel von gruppen- und interventionsspezifischen Wirkfaktoren [General psychotherapy in the group setting: Interaction between group- and intervention-specific factors].

Gruppenpsychotherapie und Gruppendynamik, 41(3), 306–322.

*Forbes, D., Parslow, R., Creamer, M., Allen, N., McHugh, T., & Hopwood, M. (2008). Mechanisms of anger and treatment outcome in combat veterans with posttraumatic stress disorder. *Journal of Traumatic Stress*, 21(2), 142–149.

*Forman, N.W. (1990). *The nature of trait empathy in clients with chronic pain and their counselors and its impact on the development of the working alliance and outcome*. Unpublished doctoral dissertation, Ohio State University, Columbus.

*Frank, A. F., & Gunderson, J. G. (1990). The role of the therapeutic alliance in the treatment of schizophrenia. *Archives of General Psychiatry*, 47, 228–236.

Frank, J. D., & Frank, J. B. (1991). *Persuasion and healing: A comparative study of psychotherapy* (3rd ed.). Baltimore: Johns Hopkins University Press.

*Freitas, T. T. (2001). *The relationship between neurocognitive impairment, working alliance, and length of stay in a therapeutic community*. Unpublished doctoral dissertation, Norfolk State University, Virginia.

Freud, S. (1912/1958). The dynamics of transference [Zur Dynamik der Übertragung]. In J. Strachey (Ed. & Trans.), *The standard edition of the complete psychological works of Sigmund Freud* (Vol. 12, pp. 99–108). London: Hogarth Press.

Freud, S. (1913). On the beginning of treatment: Further recommendations on the technique of psychoanalysis [Zur Einleitung der Behandlung–Weitere Ratschläge zur Technik der Psychoanalyse]. In J. Strachey (Ed.), *Standard edition of the complete psychological works of Sigmund Freud* (Vol. 12, pp. 122–144). London: Hogarth.

Freud, S. (1913/1940). The technique of psychoanalysis. In J. Strachey (Ed.), *Standard edition of the complete psychological works of Sigmund Freud* (Vol. 23, pp. 172–182). London: Hogarth.

*Fries, A., Pfammatter, M., Andres, K., & Brenner, H. D. (2003). Wirksamkeit und Prozessmerkmale einer psychoedukativen und bewältigungsorientierten Gruppentherapie für schizophren und schizoaffektiv Erkrankte [Outcome and process characteristics of a psychoeducational and coping-oriented group therapy for patients with schizophrenia and schizoaffective disorder]. *Verhaltenstherapie*, 13(4), 237–243.

*Gaiton, L. R. (2004). Investigation of therapeutic alliance in a treatment study with substance-abusing women with Ptsd. *Dissertation Abstracts International. Section B: Physical Sciences and Engineering*, 65(09), 4828.

*Gallop, R., Kennedy, S. H., & Stern, S. D. (1994). Therapeutic alliance on an inpatient unit for eating disorders. *International Journal of Eating Disorders*, 16, 405–410.

Gaston, L., Goldfried, M. R., Greenberg, L. S., Horvath, A. O., Raue, P. J., & Watson, J. (1995). The therapeutic alliance in psychodynamic, cognitive-behavioral and experiential therapies. *Journal of Psychotherapy Integration*, 15, 1–26.

Gaston, L., & Marmar, C. (1994). The California Psychotherapy Alliance Scales. In A. O. Horvath & L. S. Greenberg (Eds.), *The working alliance: Theory, research and practice*. New York: Wiley.

*Gaston, L., Marmar, C. R., Thompson, L. W., & Gallager, D. (1991). Alliance prediction of outcome beyond in-treatment symptomatic change as psychotherapy progresses. *Psychotherapy Research*, 1, 104–112.

*Gaston, L., Piper, W. E., Debbane, E. G., Bienvenu, J. P., & Garant, J. (1994). Alliance and technique for predicting outcome in short- and long-term analytic psychotherapy. *Psychotherapy Research*, 4, 121–135.

*Gaston, L., Thompson, L., Gallager, D., Cournoyer, L. G., & Gagnon, R. (1998). Alliance, technique and their interactions in predicting outcome of behavioral, cognitive and brief dynamic therapy. *Psychotherapy Research*, 8, 190–209.

*Geider, F. J. (1997). *Die Messung therapeutischer Allianz: Dimensionierung und Konstruktvalidierung einer deutschen Version der California Psychotherapeutic Alliance Scales (CALPAS)* [The measurement of therapeutic alliance: Dimensionality and construct validation of a German version of the California Psychotherapeutic Alliance Scales (CALPAS)]. Unpublished doctoral dissertation, University of Ruprecht-Karls-University, Heidelberg, Germany.

*Geiser, F., Bassler, M., Bents, H., Carls, W., Joraschky, P., Michelitsch, B., et al. (2002). Bewertung des Therapieerfolgs durch Patienten mit Angststörungen nach stationärer Psychotherapie [Patient's subjective assessment of therapy outcome after inpatient psychotherapy for anxiety disorders.] *Der Nervenarzt*, 73(1), 59–64.

Gelso, C. J., & Carter, J. A. (1994). Components of the psychotherapy relationship: Their interaction and unfolding during treatment. *Journal of Counseling Psychology*, 41, 296–306.

*Gerstley, L., McLellan, A.T., Alterman, A.I., Woody, G.E., Luborsky, L., & Prout, M. (1989). Ability to form an alliance with the therapist: A possible marker of prognosis for patients with antisocial personality disorder. *American Journal of Psychiatry, 146,* 508–512.

*Godfrey, E., Chalder, T., Ridsdale, L., Seed, P., & Ogden, J. (2007). Investigating the 'active ingredients' of cognitive behaviour therapy and counselling for patients with chronic fatigue in primary care: Developing a new process measure to assess treatment fidelity and predict outcome. *British Journal of Clinical Psychology, 46*(3), 253–272.

Goldfried, M. R. (1980). Toward the delineation of therapeutic change principles. *American Psychologist, 35,* 991–999.

*Gomes-Schwartz, B. (1978). Effective ingredients in psychotherapy: Prediction of outcome from process variables. *Journal of Consulting and Clinical Psychology, 46,* 1023–1035.

*Greenberg, L. S., & Malcolm, W. (2002). Resolving unfinished business: Relating process to outcome. *Journal of Consulting and Clinical Psychology, 70*(2), 406–416.

*Greenberg, L. S., & Webster, M. C. (1982). Resolving decisional conflict by Gestalt two-chair dialogue: Relating process to outcome. *Journal of Counseling Psychology, 29,* 468–477.

Greenson, R. R. (1965). The working alliance and the transference neuroses. *Psychoanalysis Quarterly, 34,* 155–181.

Greenson, R. R. (1967). *Technique and practice of psychoanalysis.* New York: International University Press.

*Grob, M. C., & Eisen, S. V. (1989). Most likely to succeed: Correlates of good versus poor hospital outcome in young adult inpatients. *Psychiatric Hospital, 20,* 23–30.

*Gunderson, J. G., Najavits, L. M., Leonhard, C., Sullivan, C. N., & Sabo, A. N. (1997). Ontogeny of the therapeutic alliance in borderline patients. *Psychotherapy Research, 7,* 301–309.

*Gunther, G. J. (1992). *Therapeutic alliance, patient object relations and outcome in psychotherapy.* Unpublished doctoral dissertation, Michigan State University, East Lansing.

*Gutfreund, M. J. (1992). *Therapist interventions: Their relation to therapeutic alliance and outcome in dynamic psychotherapy.* Unpublished doctoral dissertation, Michigan State University, East Lansing.

*Hansson, L., & Berglund (1992). Stability of therapeutic alliance and its relationship to outcome in short-term inpatient psychiatric care. *Scandinavian Journal of Social Medicine, 20,* 45–50.

*Hardy, G. E., Cahill, J., Shapiro, D. A., Barkham, M., Rees, A., & Macaskill, N. (2001). Client interpersonal and cognitive styles as predictors of response to time-limited cognitive therapy for depression. *Journal of Consulting and Clinical Psychology, 69*(5), 841–845.

*Hartley, D. E., & Strupp, H. H. (1983). The therapeutic alliance: Its relationship to outcome in brief psychotherapy. In J. Masling (Ed.), *Empirical studies in analytic theories.* (Vol. 1, pp. 1–37). Hillside, NJ: Erlbaum.

*Hartmann, H. A. (2001). *Clients' contribution to the alliance and the role it plays in outcome.* Unpublished doctoral dissertation, Adelphi University. New York, NY.

*Hatcher, R. L., & Barends, A. W. (1996). Patient's view of the alliance in psychotherapy: Exploratory factor analysis of three alliance measures. *Journal of Clinical and Consulting Psychology, 64,* 1326–1336.

Hatcher, R. L., & Barends, A. W. (2006). How a return to theory could help alliance research. *Psychotherapy: Theory, Research, Practice, Training, 43*(3), 292–299.

Hatcher, R. L., Barends, A., Hansell, J., & Gutfreund, M. J. (1995). Patient's and therapist's shared and unique views of the therapeutic alliance: An investigation using confirmatory factor analysis in a nested design. *Psychoanalysis Quarterly, 63,* 636–643.

*Hawley, L. L., & Moon-Ho Ringo, H. (2006). The relationship of perfectionism, depression, and therapeutic alliance during treatment for depression: Latent difference score analysis. *Journal of Consulting & Clinical Psychology, 74*(5), 930–942.

*Hayes, S. A., Hope, D. A., VanDyke, M. M., & Heimberg, R. G. (2007). Working alliance for clients with social anxiety disorder: Relationship with session helpfulness and within-session habituation. *Cognitive Behaviour Therapy, 36*(1), 34–42.

*Hays, V.L. (1994). *The effects of the therapeutic alliance and social support on therapy outcome and mental health of women.* Unpublished doctoral dissertation, University of Wisconsin, Madison.

Henry, W. P., & Strupp, H. H. (1994). The therapeutic alliance as interpersonal process. In A. O. Horvath & L. S. Greenberg (Eds.), *The working alliance: Theory, research and practice.* New York: Wiley.

*Hervé, M.-J., White-Koning, M., Paradis-Guennou, M., Guiraud, A., Picot, M.-C., Grandjean, H., et al. (2008). Adaptation d'une echelle d'alliance therapeutique au contexte des consultations mere-nourrisson. Etude preliminaire [Adaptation of a therapeutic alliance scale in mother-infant consultations. A preliminary study]. *Devenir, 20*(1), 65–85.

*Hilliard, R. B., Henry, W. P., & Strupp, H. H. (2000). An interpersonal model of psychotherapy: Linking patient and therapist developmental history, therapeutic process, and types of outcome. *Journal of Consulting and Clinical Psychology, 68*(1), 125–133.

*Hopkins, M., & Ramsundar, N. (2006). Which factors predict case management services and how do these services relate to client outcomes? *Psychiatric Rehabilitation Journal, 29*(3), 219–222.

*Hopkins, W. E. (1988). *The effects of conceptual level matching on the working alliance and outcome in time-limited counseling.* Unpublished doctoral dissertation, University of Maryland, College Park.

*Horowitz, M. J., Marmar, C., Weiss, D. S., DeWitt, K. N., & Rosenbaum, R. (1984). Brief psychotherapy of bereavement reactions: The relationship of process to outcome. *Archives of General Psychiatry, 41*, 438–448.

*Horvath, A. O. (1981). *An exploratory study of the working alliance: Its measurement and relationship to outcome.* Unpublished doctoral dissertation, Vancouver, Canada.

Horvath, A. O. (2009). *Conceptual and methodological challenges in alliance research: Is it time for a change.* Paper presented at the European Society for Psychotherapy Research Conference. Bolzano, Italy.

Horvath, A. O., & Bedi, R. P. (2002). The alliance. In J. C. Norcross (Ed.), *Psychotherapy relationships that work: Therapist contributions responsiveness to patients* (pp. 37–70). New York: Oxford University Press.

Horvath, A. O., Gaston, L., & Luborsky, L. (1993). The role of alliance in psychotherapy. In N. E. Miller, L. Luborsky, J. P. Barber, & J. P. Docherty (Eds.), *Psychodynamic treatment research: A handbook for clinical practice.* (pp. 247–274). New York: Basic Books.

Horvath, A. O., & Greenberg, L. S. (1986). Development of the working alliance Inventory. In L. S. Greenberg & W. M. Pinsof (Eds.), *The psychotherapeutic process: A research handbook* (pp. 529–556). New York: Guilford.

Horvath, A. O., & Luborsky, L. (1993). The role of the therapeutic alliance in psychotherapy. *Journal of Consulting and Clinical Psychology, 61,* 561–573.

Horvath, A. O., & Marx, R. W. (1991). The development and decay of the working alliance during time-limited counselling. *Canadian Journal of Counselling, 24,* 240–259.

Horvath, A. O., & Symonds, B. D. (1991). Relation between working alliance and outcome in psychotherapy: A meta-analysis. *Journal of Counseling Psychology, 38,* 139–149.

*Howard, I. (2003). *Interpersonal factors in relationship to therapy outcome and therapeutic alliance in a cohort of multiple sclerosis patients.* Unpublished doctoral dissertation, Alliant International University, San Francisco.

*Howard, I., Turner, R., Olkin, R., & Mohr, D. C. (2006). Therapeutic alliance mediates the relationship between interpersonal problems and depression outcome in a cohort of multiple sclerosis patients. *Journal of Clinical Psychology, 62*(9), 1197–1204.

*Huber, D., Brandl, T., Henrich, G., & von Rad, M. (2003). Interaktive Beziehungsmuster und ihre Bedeutung für psychotherapeutische Veränderungen [Satisfaction and compliance after a psychosomatic-psychotherapeutic consultation session]. *Zeitschrift für Klinische Psychologie und Psychotherapie, 32*(2), 85–93.

Hunter, J. E., & Smith, F. L. (1990). *Methods of Meta-analysis: Correcting error and bias in research findings.* London: Sage.

Hunter, J. E., & Schmidt, F. L. (2004). *Methods of meta-analysis* (2nd edition). Thousand Oaks, CA: Sage.

*Ilgen, M. A., McKellar, J., Moos, R., & Finney, J. W. (2006a). Therapeutic alliance and the relationship between motivation and treatment outcomes in patients with alcohol use disorder. *Journal of Substance Abuse Treatment, 31*(2), 157–162.

*Ilgen, M., Tiet, Q., Finney, J., & Moos, R. H. (2006b). Self-efficacy, therapeutic alliance, and alcohol-use disorder treatment outcomes. *Journal of Studies on Alcohol, 67*(3), 465.

*Irelan, C. S. (2004). *The therapeutic alliance, resolution of alliance ruptures and termination outcome.* Central Michigan University, Michigan.

*Jacob, K. L. (2003). Toward understanding change in psychotherapy: A closer look at the *relationship between client-therapist match and treatment outcome.* Unpublished doctoral dissertation, Clark University, Worchester, MA.

*Janecke, N. (2003). *Bedeutung der Motivation und therapeutischen Beziehung in der Psychotherapie* [The importance of motivation and therapeutic alliance in psychotherapy]. Unpublished doctoral dissertation, University of Innsbruck, Innsbruck, Austria.

*Johansson, H. K., & Eklund, M. (2006). Helping alliance and early dropout from psychiatric outpatient care: The influence of patient factors. *Social Psychiatry and Psychiatric Epidemiology*, *41*(2), 140–147.

*Joyce, A. S., & Piper, W. E. (1998). Expectancy, the therapeutic alliance, and treatment outcome in short-term individual psychotherapy. *Journal of Psychotherapy Practice and Research*, *7*, 236–248.

*Joyce, A. S., Ogrodniczuk, J. S., Piper, W. E., & McCallum, M. (2003). The alliance as mediator of expectancy effects in short-term individual therapy. *Journal of Consulting and Clinical Psychology*, *71*(4), 672–679.

*Jumes, M. T. (1995). *The developmental course of the inpatient working alliance in state psychiatric hospital clients.* Unpublished doctoral dissertation, University of Texas Southwestern Medical Center, Dallas.

*Kabuth, B., De Tychey, C., & Vidailhet, C. (2005). Alliance therapeutique avec les mères et evolution clinique des enfants d'un hôpital de jour [Mothers' therapeutic alliance and children outcome in a day hospital]. *Annales Médico Psychologiques*, *163*(6), 486–492.

*Karver, M., Shirk, S., Handelsman, J. B., Fields, S., Crisp, H., Gudmundsen, G., et al. (2008). Relationship processes in youth psychotherapy: Measuring alliance, alliance-building behaviors, and client involvement. *Journal of Emotional & Behavioral Disorders*, *16*(1), 15–28.

*Katz, J. (1999). *Self-handicapping, the working alliance, interpersonal tendencies and the prediction of drop-out.* Unpublished doctoral dissertation, New School for Social Research, New York.

*Kech, S. (2008). *Einflussfaktoren auf den Behandlungserfolg der Interpersonellen Psychotherapie bei stationären Depressionspatienten: Analyse der Wirkmechanismen* [Determinats of success of interpersonal psychotherapy with depressive inpatients: Analysis of effective factors.] Published doctoral dissertation, University of Freiburg, Freiburg, Germany. http://www.freidok.uni-freiburg.de/volltexte/5318/

*Kelly, A. E., & Yuan, K.-H. (2009). Clients' secret keeping and the working alliance in adult outpatient therapy. *Psychotherapy: Theory, Research, Practice, Training*, *46*(2), 193–202.

*Kivilighan, D. M., & Shaugnessy, P. (1995). Analysis of the development of the working alliance using hierarchical linear modeling. *Journal of Counseling Psychology*, *42*, 338–349.

*Kivlighan, D. M, Jr., & Shaughnessy, P. (2000). Patterns of working alliance development: A typology of client's working alliance ratings. *Journal of Counseling Psychology*, *47*(3), 362–371.

*Klee, M. R., Abeles, N., & Mullere, R. T. (1990). Therapeutic alliance: Early indicators, course, and outcome. *Psychotherapy*, *27*, 166–174.

*Klein, D. N., Schwartz, J. E., Santiago, N. J., Vivian, D., Vocisano, C., Castonguay, L. G., et al. (2003). Therapeutic alliance in depression treatment: Controlling for prior change and patient characteristics. *Journal of Consulting and Clinical Psychology*, *71*(6), 997–1006.

*Knaevelsrud, C., & Maercker, A. (2007). Internet-based treatment for PTSD reduces distress and facilitates the development of a strong therapeutic alliance: A randomized controlled clinical trial. *BMC Psychiatry*, *7*, 13–10.

*Kokotovic, A. M., & Tracey, T. J. (1990). *Working alliance in the early phase of counseling.* Journal of Counseling Psychology, *37*, 16–21.

*Kolden, G. G. (1996). Change in early sessions of dynamic therapy: Universal processes and the generic model of psychotherapy. *Journal of Clinical and Consulting Psychology*, *64*, 489–496.

*Konzag, T., Bademer-Greulich, U., Bahreke, U., & Fikentscher, E. (2004). Therapeutische Beziehung und Therapieerfolg bei der stationären Psychotherapie von Persönlichkeitsstörungen [Therapeutic relationship and outcome in psychotherapy for personality disorders]. *Zeitschrift für Psychosomatische Medizin und Psychotherapie*, *50*(4), 394–405.

*Kramer, U., de Roten, Y., Beretta, V., Michel, L., & Despland, J.-N. (2009). Alliance patterns over the course of short-term dynamic psychotherapy: The shape of productive relationships. *Psychotherapy Research*, *19*(6), 699–706.

*Kramer, U., de Roten, Y., Beretta, V., Michel, L., & Despland, J.-N. (2008). Patient's and therapist's views of early alliance building in dynamic psychotherapy: Patterns and relation to outcome. *Journal of Counseling Psychology*, *55*(1), 89–95.

Kramer, U., de Roten, Y., Beretta, V., Michel, L., & Despland, J.-N. (2009). Alliance patterns over the course of short-term dynamic psychother-apy: The shape of productive relationships. *Psychotherapy Research, 19*(6), 669–706.

*Krupnick, J. L., Elkin, I., Collins, J., Simmens, S., Sotsky, S. M., Pilkonis, A., & Watkings, J. T. (1994). Therapeutic alliance and clinical out-come in the NIMH Treatment of Depression Collaborattive Research Program: Preliminary findings. *Psychotherapy, 31*, 28–35.

*Krupnick, J. L., Sotsky, S. M., Simmens, A., Moyer, J., Elkin, I., Watkins, J., et al. (1996). The role of the alliance in psychotherapy and pharmacotherapy outcome: Findings in the National Institute of Mental Health treatment of depression collaborative research program. *Journal of Clinical and Consulting Psychology, 64*, 532–539.

*Kukla, M., & Bond, G. R. (2009). The working alliance and employment outcomes for people with severe mental illness enrolled in voca-tional programs. *Rehabilitation Psychology, 54*(2), 157–163.

*Lansford, E. (1986). Weakenings and repairs of the working alliance in short-term psychotherapy. *Professional Psychology: Research and Practice, 17*, 364–366.

*Lieberman, P. B., von Rehn, S., Dickie, E., & Elliott, B. (1992). Therapeutic effects of brief hospitalization: The role of a therapeutic alli-ance. *Journal of Psychotherapy Practice & Research, 1*(1), 56–63.

*Liebler, A., Biella, M., Schulz, W., & Hartmann, U. (2004). Differenzielle Therapieverläufe und Behandlungserfolg in der stationären Grup-penpsychotherapie [Differential courses of treat-ment and their relation to outcome in inpatient group psychotherapy]. *Gruppenpsychotherapie und Gruppendynamik. 40*(1), 1–21.

*Loncek, B., Banks, S., Way, B., & Bonaparte, E. (2002). An empirical model of therapeutic pro-cess for psychiatric emergency room clients with dual disorders. *Social Work Research, 26*(3), 132.

Luborsky, L. (1976). Helping alliances in psycho-therapy. In J. L. Cleghhorn (Ed.), *Successful psy-chotherapy* (pp. 92–116). New York: Brunner/Mazel.

Luborsky, L. (1994). Therapeutic alliance measures as predictors of future benefits of psychotherapy. In A. O. Horvath & L. S. Greenberg (Eds.), *The working alliance: Theory, research and practice*. New York: Wiley.

*Luborsky, L., Crits-Cristoph, P., Alexander, L., Margolis, M., & Cohen, M. (1983). Two helping

alliance methods for predicting outcomes of psy-chotherapy: A counting signs vs. a global rating method. *Journal of Nervous and Mental Disease 171*, 480–491.

*Luborsky, L., McLellan, A. T., Woody, G. E., O'Brien, C. P., & Auerbach, A. (1985). Therapist success and its determinants. *Archives of General Psychiatry, 42*, 602–611.

Luborsky, L., Singer, B., & Luborsky, L. (1975). Comparative studies of psychotherapies; "Is it true that everybody has won and all must have prizes"? *Archives of General Psychiatry, 32*, 995–1008.

*Mallinckrodt, B. (1993). Session impact, work-ing alliance, and treatment outcome in brief counseling. *Journal of Counseling Psychology, 40*, 25–32.

*Mallinckrodt, B. (1996). Change in working alliance, social support and psychological symp-toms in brief therapy. *Journal of Counseling Psychology, 43*, 448–455.

*Marmar, C. R., Gaston, L., Gallager, D., & Thompson, L. W. (1989b). Therapeutic alli-ance and outcome in behavioral, cognitive, and brief dynamic psychotherapy in late-life depres-sion. *Journal of Nervous and Mental Disease 177*, 464–472.

*Marmar, C., Weiss, D. S., & Gaston, L. (1989a). Toward the validation of the California Therapeutic Alliance Rating System. *Psychological Assessment: A Journal of Consulting and Clinical Psychology, 1*, 46–52.

*Marmarosh, C. L., Gelso, C. J., Markin, R. D., Majors, R., Mallery, C., & Choi, J. (2009). The real relationship in psychotherapy: Relationships to adult attachments, working alliance, transfer-ence, and therapy outcome. *Journal of Counseling Psychology, 56*(3), 337–350.

*Marshel, R. L. (1986). *An exploration of the relationship between the therapeutic alliance and premature termination*. Unpublished doc-toral dissertation, Northwestern University, Evanston, IL.

Martin, D. J., Garske, J. P., & Davis, K. M. (2000). Relation of the therapeutic alliance with out-come and other variables: A meta analytic review. *Journal of Clinical and Consulting Psychology, 68*, 438–450.

*Marziali, E. (1984). Three viewpoints on the therapeutic alliance scales: Similarities, differ-ences and associations with psychotherapy out-come. *Journa*l of Nervous and Mental Disease *172*, 417–423.

*Marziali, E., Marmar, C., & Krupnick, J. (1981). Therapeutic alliance scales: Development and relationship to psychotherapy outcome. *American Journal of Psychiatry, 138*, 361–364.

*Marziali, E., Munroe-Blum, H., & McClery, L. (1999). The effects of the therapeutic alliance on the outcomes of individual and group psychotherapy with borderline personality disorder. *Psychotherapy Research, 9*, 452–467.

*McLeod, B. D., & Weisz, J. R. (2005). The Therapy Process Observational Coding System-Alliance Scale: Measure characteristics and prediction of outcome in usual clinical practice. *Journal of Consulting and Clinical Psychology, 73*(2), 323–333.

*McNeil, D. C., (2006). *Patient, therapist, and observer perspectives on cohesion and alliance and their relationship to outcome in psychodynamic group psychotherapy for persons experiencing complicated grief.* Unpublished doctoral dissertation, University of Alberta, Edmonton, Canada.

*Meier, P. S., & Donmall, M. C. (2006). Differences in client and therapist views of the working alliance in drug treatment. *Journal of Substance Use, 11*(1), 73–80.

*Meier, P. S., Donmall, M. C., McElduff, P., Barrowclough, C., & Heller, R. F. (2006). The role of the early therapeutic alliance in predicting drug treatment dropout. *Drug & Alcohol Dependence, 83*(1), 57–64.

*Meyer, B., Pilkonis, P. A., Krupnick, J. L., Egan, M. K., Simmens, S. J., & Sotsky, S. M. (2002). Treatment expectancies, patient alliance and outcome: Further analyses from the National Institute of Mental Health Treatment of Depression Collaborative Research Program. *Journal of Consulting and Clinical Psychology, 70*(4), 1051–1055.

Miller, N. E., Luborsky, L., Barber, J. P., & Docherty, J. P. (1993). *Psychodynamic treatment research: A handbook for clinical practice.* New York, NY US: Basic Books.

*Missirlian, T. M., Toukmanian, S. G., Warwar, S. H., & Greenberg, L. S. (2005). Emotional arousal, client perceptual processing, and the working alliance in experiential psychotherapy for depression. *Journal of Consulting and Clinical Psychology, 73*(5), 861–871.

*Mohl, P. C., Martinez, D., Ticknor, C., Huang, M., & Cordell, L. (1991). Early dropouts from psychotherapy. *Journal of Nervous and Mental Disease, 179*(8), 478–481.

*Moleiro, C. M. D. M. (2003). *Change in therapy: A model of the effects of systematic treatment selection variables and quality of alliance on individual growth.* Unpublished doctoral dissertation, University of California, Santa Barbara.

*Morgan, R., Luborsky, L., Crits-Christoph, P., Curtis, H., & Solomon, J. (1982). Predicting the outcomes of psychotherapy by the Penn Helping Alliance Rating Method. *Archives of General Psychiatry, 39*, 397–402.

*Moseley, D. (1983). *The therapeutic relationship and its association with outcome.* Unpublished thesis, University of British Columbia, Vancouver, Canada.

*Multon, K. D., Heppner, M. J., Gsybers, N. C., Zook, C., & Ellis-Kalton, C. A. (2001). Client psychological distress: An important factor in career counseling. *The Career Development Quarterly, 49*, 324–335.

*Muran, J. C., Gorman, B. S., Safran, J. D., Twining, L, Samstag, I. W., & Winston, A. (1995). Linking in-session change to overall outcome in short term cognitive therapy. *Journal of Consulting and Clinical Psychology, 63*, 651–657.

*Muran, J. C., Safran, J. D., Gorman, B. S., Samstag, L. W., Eubanks-Carter, C., & Winston, A. (2009). The relationship of early alliance ruptures and their resolution to process and outcome in three time-limited psychotherapies for personality disorders. *Psychotherapy: Theory, Research, Practice, Training, 46*(2), 233–248.

National Research Council (1992). Combining information: Statistical issues and opportunities for research. Washington DC: National Academy Press.

*Ogrodniczuk, J. S., Piper, W. E., Joyce, A. S., & McCallum, M. (2000). Different perspectives of the therapeutic alliance and therapist technique in 2 forms of dynamically oriented psychotherapy. *Canadian Journal of Psychiatry, 45*, 452–458.

*O'Malley, S. S., Suh, C. S., & Strupp, H. H. (1983). The Vanderbilt Psychotherapy Process Scale: A report on the scale development and a process-outcome study. *Journal of Clinical and Consulting Psychology, 51*, 581–586.

*Pantalon, M. V., Chawarski, M. C., Falcioni, J., Pakes, J., & Schottenfeld, R. S. (2004). Linking process and outcome in the community reinforcement approach for treating cocaine dependence: A preliminary report. *American Journal of Drug & Alcohol Abuse, 30*(2), 353–367.

*Pavio, S. C., & Bahr, L. B. (1998). Interpersonal problems, working alliance, and outcome in short-term experiential therapy. *Psychotherapy Research*, 8, 392–406.

*Piper, W. E., Azim, H. F. A., Joyce, A. S., MacCallum, M., Nixon, G. W. H., & Segal, P. S. (1991). Quality of object relations vs. interpersonal functioning as predictor of therapeutic alliance and psychotherapy outcome. *Journal of Nervous and Mental Disease 179*, 432–438.

*Piper, W. E., Boroto, D. R., Joyce, A. S., McCallum, M., & Azim, H. F. A. (1995). Pattern of alliance and outcome in short-term individual psychotherapy. *Psychotherapy, 32*, 639–647.

*Piper, W. E., Ogrodniczuk, J. S., & Joyce, A. S. (2004). Quality of object relations as a moderator of the relationship between pattern of alliance and outcome in short-term individual psychotherapy. *Journal of Personality Assessment, 83*(3), 345–356.

*Pos, A. E., & B. (2007). *Experiential treatment for depression: A test of the experiential theory of change, differential effectiveness, and predictors of maintenance of gains.* Unpublished dissertation, York University. Toronto, Canada.

*Pos, A. E., Greenberg, L. S., & Warwar, S. H. (2009). Testing a model of change in the experiential treatment of depression. *Journal of Consulting and Clinical Psychology, 77*(6), 1055–1066.

*Priebe, S., & Gruyters, T. (1993). The role of helping alliance in psychiatric community care: A prospective study. *Journal of Nervous and Mental Disease, 181*, 552–557.

*Prigatano, G. P., Klonoff, P. S., O'Brien, K. P., Altman, I. M., Amin, K., Chiapello, D., Shepherd, J., Cunningham, M., & Mora, M. (1994). Productivity after neuropsychologically oriented milieu rehabilitation. *Journal of Head Trauma Rehabilitation, 9*, 91–102.

*Pugh, M. A. (1991). *The working alliance, pretherapy interpersonal relationships and therapeutic outcome.* Unpublished doctoral dissertation, Virginia Commonwealth University, Richmond.

*Pyne, S. C. (1991). *Therapist's use of countertransference in short-term psychotherapy: A focus on rescuing and counterhostility.* Unpublished doctoral dissertation, University of Colorado, Boulder.

R Development Core Team (2009). *R: A language and environment for statistical computing.* R Foundation for Statistical Computing, Vienna, Austria. ISBN 3-900051-07-0, http://www.R-project.org.

*Ramnerö, J., & Öst, L.-G. (2007). Therapists' and clients' perception of each other and working alliance in the behavioral treatment of panic disorder and agoraphobia. *Psychotherapy Research, 17*(3), 328–337.

*Reiner, P. A. (1987). *The development of the therapeutic alliance.* Unpublished doctoral dissertation, University of North Carolina, Chapel Hill.

*Reis, S., & Grenyer, B. F. S. (2004). Fearful attachment, working alliance and treatment response for individuals with major depression. *Clinical Psychology & Psychotherapy, 11*(6), 414–424.

*Riley, J. D. (1992). *The impact of pre-therapy and extra-therapy role preparation on the development of therapeutic alliance and outcome.* Unpublished doctoral dissertation, Pacific Graduate School of Psychology, Palo Alto, CA.

Rogers, C. R., Gendlin, G. T., Kiesler, D. V., & Truax, L. B. (1967). *The therapeutic relationship and its impact: A study of psychotherapy with schizophrenics.* Madison: University of Wisconsin Press.

Rogers, C. R., & Wood, J. K. (1974). Client-centered theory: Carl R. Rogers. . In A. Burton (Ed.), Operational theories of personality (pp. 211–258.). New York: Bruner/Mazel.

*Rogers, N., Lubman, D. I., & Allen, N. B. (2008). Therapeutic alliance and change in psychiatric symptoms in adolescents and young adults receiving drug treatment. *Journal of Substance Use, 13*(5), 325–339.

Rosenthal, R. (1979). The file drawer problem and tolerance for null results. *Psychological Bulletin, 86*, 638–41.

Rosenzweig, S. (1936). Some implicit common factors in diverse methods of psychotherapy. *American Journal of Orthopsychiatry, 6*, 412–415.

*Rounsaville, B. J., Chevron, E. S., Prusoff, B. A., Elkin, I., Imber, S., Sotsky, S., (1987). The relation between specific and general dimensions of the psychotherapy process in interpersonal psychotherapy of depression. *Journal of Clinical and Consulting Psychology, 55*, 379–384.

*Rudolf, G., & Manz, R. (1993). Zur prognostischen Bedeutung der therapeutischen Arbeitsbeziehung aus der Perspektive von Patienten und Therapeuten [The prognostic relevance of a therapeutic working alliance as seen by patients and therapists]. *Psychotherapie, Psychosomatik, Medizinische Psychologie. 43*(6), 193–199.

Safran, J. D. (1993). The therapeutic alliance rupture as a transtheoretical phenomenon: Definitional and conceptual issues. *Journal of Psychotherapy Integration, 3*(1), 33–49.

Safran, J. D., Crocker, P., McMain, S., & Murray, P. (1990). The therapeutic alliance rapture as a therapy event for emperical investigation. *Psychotherapy: Theory, Research, Practice and Training, 27*, 154–165.

Safran, J. D., & Muran, C. (2000). *Negotiating the therapeutic alliance: A relational treatment guide.* New York: Guilford.

*Safran, J. D., & Wallner, L. K. (1991). The relative predictive validity of two therapeutic alliance measures in cognitive therapy. *Psychological Assessment, 3*, 188–195.

Saketopoulou, A. (1999). The psychotherapeutic alliance in psychodynamic psychotherapy: Theoretical conceptualizations and research findings. *Psychotherapy, 36*, 329–342.

*Sammet, V. I., Staats, H., & Schauenburg, H. (2004). Beziehungserleben und Therapieergebnis in stationärer Psychotherapie [Relationship experiences and therapeutic outcome in inpatient psychotherapy]. *Zeitschrift für Psychosomatische Medizin und Psychotherapie, 50*(4), 376–393.

*Samstag, L. W., Muran, J. C., Wachtel, P. L., Slade, A., Safran, J. D., & Winston, A. (2008). Evaluating negative process: A comparison of working alliance, interpersonal behavior, and narrative coherency among three psychotherapy outcome conditions. *American Journal of Psychotherapy, 62*(2), 165–194.

*Santiago, N. J., Klein, D. N., Vivian, D., Arnow, B. A., Blalock, J. A., Kocis, J. H., et al. (2005). The therapeutic alliance and CBASP-specific skill acquisition in the treatment of chronic depression. *Cognitive Therapy and Research, 29*, 803–817.

*Saunders, S. M. (2000). Examining the relationship between the therapeutic bond and the phases of treatment outcome. *Psychotherapy: Theory, Research, Practice, Training, 37*(3), 206–218.

*Saunders, S. M., Howard, K. I., & Orlinsky, D. E. (1989). The therapeutic bond scales: Psychometric characteristics and relationship to treatment effectiveness. *Psychological Assessment, 1*, 323–330.

*Schauenburg, H., Dinger, U., & Starck, M. (2005). Zur Bedeutung der Einzeltherapeuten für das Therapieergebnis in der stationären Psychotherapie - eine Pilotstudie [The significance of individual psychotherapists for psychotherapeutic outcomes in inpatient psychotherapy. A pilot study]. *Psychotherapie, Psychosomatik, Medizinische Psychologie, 55*(7), 339–346.

*Schleussner, D. (2005). Wirksamkeit individualpsychologisch-psychoanalytischer Psychotherapie - Eine Langzeitstudie zur Psychotherapieforschung [Effectiveness of individual psychological psychoanalytic psychotherapy - A longitudinal study on psychotherapy research]. *Zeitschrift für individualpsychologie, 30*(1), 51–77.

*Schönberger, M., Humle, F., & Teasdale, T. W. (2006a). Subjective outcome of brain injury rehabilitation in relation to the therapeutic working alliance, client compliance and awareness. *Brain Injury, 20*(12), 1271–1282.

*Schönberger, M., Humle, F., & Teasdale, T. W. (2006b). The development of the therapeutic working alliance, patients' awareness and their compliance during the process of brain injury rehabilitation. *Brain Injury, 20*(4), 445–454.

*Schönberger, M., Humle, F., & Teasdale, T. W. (2007). The relationship between clients' cognitive functioning and the therapeutic working alliance in post-acute brain injury rehabilitation. *Brain Injury, 21*(8), 825–836.

*Schönberger, M., Humle, F., Zeeman, P., & Teasdale, T. (2006c). Working alliance and patient compliance in brain injury rehabilitation and their relation to psychosocial outcome. *Neuropsychological Rehabilitation, 16*(3), 298–314.

*Sexton, H. (1996). Process, life events, and symptomatic change in brief eclectic psychotherapy. *Journal of Consulting and Clinical Psychology, 64*, 1358–1365.

*Sherer, M., Evans, C. C., Leverenz, J., Stouter, J., Irby, J. W., Jae Eun, L., et al. (2007). Therapeutic alliance in post-acute brain injury rehabilitation: Predictors of strength of alliance and impact of alliance on outcome. *Brain Injury, 21*(7), 663–672.

*Shirk, S. R., Gudmundsen, G., Kaplinski, H. C., & McMakin, D. L. (2008). Alliance and outcome in cognitive-behavioral therapy for adolescent depression. *Journal of Clinical Child & Adolescent Psychology, 37*(3), 631–639.

Smith, M. L., & Glass, G. V. (1977). Meta-analysis of psychotherapy outcome studies. *American Psychologist, 32*, 752–760.

*Solomon, P., Draine, J., & Delaney, M. A. (1995). The working alliance and consumer case management. *Journal of Mental Health Adminstration, 22*, 126–134.

*Sonnenberg, R. T. (1996). *An examination of the outcome of a brief psychiatric hospitalization with particular reference to the therapeutic alliance and select patient characteristics*, Unpublished doctoral dissertation, University of Nebraska, Lincoln.

*Spinhoven, P., Giesen-Bloo, J., van Dyck, R., Kooiman, K., & Arntz, A. (2007). The therapeutic alliance in schema-focused therapy and transference- focused psychotherapy for borderline personality disorder. *Journal of Consulting & Clinical Psychology, 75*(1), 104–115.

Sterba, R. F. (1934). The fate of the ego in analytic therapy. *International Journal of Psychoanalysis, 115,* 117–126.

*Stevens, C. L., Muran, J. C., Safran, J. D., Gorman, B. S., & Winston, A. (2007). Levels and patterns of the therapeutic alliance in brief psychotherapy. *American Journal of Psychotherapy, 61*(2), 109–129.

*Stiles, W. B., Glick, M. J., Osatuke, K., Hardy, G. E., Shapiro, D. A., Agnew-Davies, R., et al. (2004). Patterns of alliance development and the rupture-repair hypothesis: Are productive relationships U-shaped or V-shaped? *Journal of Counseling Psychology, 51*(1), 81–92.

Stiles, W. B., Shapiro, D., & Elliot, R. (1986). Are all psychotherapies equivalent? *American Psychologist, 41,* 165–180.

Stone, L. (1961). *The Psychoanalytic Situation: An Examination of Its Development and Essential nature.* New York: International Universities Press.

*Strauser, D. R., Lustig, D. C., & Donnell, C. (2004). The relationship between working alliance and therapeutic outcomes for individuals with mild mental retardation. *Rehabilitation Counseling Bulletin, 47*(4), 215–223.

*Strauss, J. L. (2001). *Patterns and impact of the alliance and affective arousal in psychotherapy: An application to cognitive therapy for avoidant and obsessive-compulsive personality disorders.* Unpublished doctoral dissertation, University of Miami, Coral Gables, FL.

*Strauss, J. L., Hayes, A. M., Johnson, S. L., Newman, C. F., Brown, G. K., Barber, J. P., et al. (2006). Early alliance, alliance ruptures, and symptom change in a nonrandomized trial of cognitive therapy for avoidant and obsessive-compulsive personality disorders. *Journal of Consulting and Clinical Psychology, 74*(2), 337–345.

Sutton, A. J. (2009). Publication bias. In H. Cooper, L. V. Hedges, & J. C. Valentine (Eds.), *The handbook of research synthesis and meta-analysis (2nd ed.).* New York: Russell Sage Foundation.

*Svartberg, M., & Stiles, T. C. (1994). Therapeutic alliance, therapist competence and client change in short-term anxiety-provoking psychotherapy. *Psychotherapy Research, 4,* 20–33.

*Tichenor, V. (1989). *Working alliance: A measure comparison.* Unpublished doctoral dissertation, University of Maryland, Chapel Hill, MD.

Tichenor, V., & Hill, C. E. (1989). A comparison of six measures of working alliance. *Psychotherapy: Theory, Research, and Practice, 26,* 195–199.

*Trepka, C., Rees, A., Shapiro, D. A., Hardy, G. E., & Barkham, M. (2004). Therapist competence and outcome of cognitive therapy for depression. *Cognitive Therapy & Research, 28*(2), 143–157.

*Tryon, G., & Kane, A. S. (1990). The helping alliance and premature termination. *Canadian Psychologist, 3,* 223–238.

*Tryon, G. S., & Kane, A. S. (1993). Relationship of working alliance to mutual and unilateral termination. *Journal of Counseling Psychology, 40,* 33–36.

*Tryon, G. S., & Kane, A. S. (1995). Client involvement, working alliance and type of psychotherapy termination. *Psychotherapy Research, 5,* 189–198.

*Tunis, S. L., Deluchi, K. L., Schwartz, K., Banys, P., & Sees, K. L. (1995). The relationship of counselor and peer alliance to drug use and HIV risk behaviors in a six-month methadone detoxification program. *Addictive Behaviors, 20,* 395–405.

*Van, H. L., Hendriksen, M., Schoevers, R. A., Peen, J., Abraham, R. A., & Dekker, J. (2008). Predictive value of object relations for therapeutic alliance and outcome in psychotherapy for depression: An exploratory study. *Journal of Nervous & Mental Disease, 196*(9), 655–662.

*Vogel, P. A., Hansen, B., Stiles, T. C., & Gotestam, K. G. (2006). Treatment motivation, treatment expectancy, and helping alliance as predictors of outcome in cognitive behavioral treatment of OCD. *Journal of Behavior Therapy and Experimental Psychiatry, 37*(3), 247–255.

*Vronmans, L. P. (2007). *Process and outcome of narrative therapy for major depressive disorder in adults: Narrative reflexivity, working alliance and improved symptom and interpersonal outcomes.* Unpublished doctoral dissertation, Queensland University of Technology, Brisbane, Australia.

Wampold, B. E. (2001). *The great psychotherapy debate: Models, methods, and findings.* Mahwah, NJ: Erlbaum.

Wampold, B. E., Mondin, G. W., Moody, M., Stich, F., Benson, K., & Ahn, H. (1997). A meta-analysis of outcome studies comparing bona fide psychotherapies: Empiricially, 'all must have prizes.' *Psychological Bulletin, 122*(3), 203–215.

*Wettersten, K. B. (2000). *Solution-focused brief therapy, the working alliance, and outcome: A comparative analysis.* Unpublished doctoral dissertation, University of Kansas, Lawrence.

*Wettersten, K. B., Lichtenberg, J. W., & Mallinckrodt, B. (2005). Associations between working alliance and outcome in solution-focused brief therapy and brief interpersonal therapy. *Psychotherapy Research, 15*(1–2), 35–43.

*Wilson, G. T., Fairburn, C. C., Agras, W. S., Walsh, B. T., & Kraemer, H. (2002). Cognitive-behavioral therapy for bulimia nervosa: Time course and mechanisms of change. *Journal of Consulting and Clinical Psychology, 70*(2), 267–274.

*Windholtz, M. J., & Silbershatz, G. (1988). Vanderbilt psychotherapy process scale: A replication with adult outpatients. *Journal of Clinical & Consulting Psychology, 56*, 56–60.

*Yeomans, F. E., Gutfreund, J., Selzer, M. A., Clarkin, J., Hull, J. W., & Smith, T. E. (1994). Factors related to drop-outs by borderline patients: Treatment contract and therapeutic alliance. *Journal of Psychotherapy Practice and Research, 3*, 16–24.

Zetzel, E. R. (1956). Current concepts of transference. *International Journal of Psychoanalysis, 37*, 369–376.

*Zuroff, D. C., & Blatt, S. J. (2006). The therapeutic relationship in the brief treatment of depression: Contributions to clinical improvement and enhanced adaptive capacities. *Journal of Consulting and Clinical Psychology, 74*(1), 130–140.

*Zuroff, D. C., Blatt, S. J., Sotsky, S. M., Krupnick, J. L., Martin, D. J., Sanislow, C. A., et al. (2000). Relation of therapeutic alliance and perfectionism to outcome in brief outpatient treatment for depression. *Journal of Clinical & Consulting Psychology, 68*, 114–124.

CHAPTER 3

Alliance in Child and Adolescent Psychotherapy

Stephen R. Shirk *and* Marc S. Karver

The therapeutic alliance has a long history in the child and adolescent psychotherapy literature dating to the work of Anna Freud (1946). In contrast, research on the alliance in youth treatment is relatively new. In their 2003 meta-analysis of relationship predictors of child and adolescent treatment outcomes, Shirk and Karver (2003) identified only one study that met the inclusion criteria used in adult alliance meta-analyses. Fortunately, the last decade has produced a substantial increase in research on the alliance in child and adolescent treatment, but the total number of studies still pales in comparison to the adult literature (see Chapter 2).

The discrepancy between the adult and youth alliance research is not surprising. In general, research on child and adolescent therapy has lagged behind its adult counterpart in many areas. Yet, developmental differences between children and adults make the alliance especially important in youth treatment. Children and adolescents rarely refer themselves for treatment (Shirk & Saiz, 1992). Often young clients fail to acknowledge the existence of psychological problems, and when they do, they attribute their cause to environmental factors. Children, like persons with severe mental illness, lack both awareness of their problems and interest in self-exploration that facilitate involvement in therapy (Wright, Everett, & Roisman, 1986). Consequently,

engaging children and adolescents in a working relationship is a major challenge for those who treat young clients.

Relationship processes, including the alliance, have been neglected in the child and adolescent literature for other reasons. In contrast to the adult literature, where treatment equivalence has prompted the search for common factors, the development of specific treatment methods has remained the focal point of youth therapy research. This difference in focus is not just another example of child research lagging behind its adult counterpart but, rather, reflects the absence of a "Dodo Bird verdict" for treatment equivalence in youth outcomes. Broad-band meta-analyses of youth treatment outcomes indicate that behavioral treatments tend to produce significantly better results than nonbehavioral therapies across many childhood disorders (Weisz, Weiss, Alicke, & Klotz, 1987; Weisz, Weiss, Han, & Granger, 1995), a finding that holds up even after controlling for differences in methodological quality (Weiss & Weisz, 1995). Although this perspective has its critics (Miller, Wampold, & Varhely, 2008; Spielmans, Gatlin, & McFall, 2010), the focus on specific treatment procedures has dislocated research on common factors in the child and adolescent literature. Despite this trend, research on the alliance in youth therapy has expanded in recent years (Shirk & Karver, 2006; Zack, Castonguay,

& Boswell, 2007), partially in response to growing recognition of within-treatment variability in outcomes.

The aims of this chapter are threefold. First, we review definitions, measures, and clinical examples of the alliance in the child and adolescent literature. Of particular importance are developmental issues that distinguish youth and adult alliances. Second, we provide a meta-analytic review of alliance–outcome associations in child and adolescent therapy. Third, we summarize the research on client factors and therapist strategies that facilitate alliance formation with children and adolescents.

Definitions and Measures

Two views of the therapeutic relationship were prominent in the early history of child therapy. Anna Freud (1946) observed that an "affectionate attachment" between child and therapist is a "prerequisite for all later work" in child therapy (p. 31). In this early statement, we find an enduring distinction in the alliance literature, the distinction between bond and work, between the emotional relationship and the collaborative relationship (Estrada & Russell, 1999; Shirk & Saiz, 1992). Of equal importance, the link between bond and collaboration is framed functionally; the emotional bond enables the child to work purposefully on the tasks of therapy. The bond itself is not posited as curative, but rather as a catalyst for promoting therapeutic work. Interestingly, this view is revived in later cognitive-behavioral formulations of the therapy relationship. The alliance serves specific technical procedures and can facilitate child involvement in tasks ranging from exposure to homework completion (Kendall, Comer, Marker, Creed, & Puliafico, 2009; Shirk & Karver, 2006). In the area of parent management training, where parents rather than children are the focus of treatment, the alliance is hypothesized to improve parent attendance and adherence to adaptive parenting strategies (Kazdin & Wassell, 2000). Although the content of therapeutic work varies across treatments, the association between alliance and outcome is presumed to be mediated through involvement in treatment tasks.

In contrast to this perspective, play therapists have long emphasized the curative nature of the therapy relationship (Axline, 1947). In this tradition, the child's *experience* of the therapist as supportive, attuned, and nonjudgmental was essential for therapeutic change (Shirk & Russell, 1996; Wright, Everett, & Roisman, 1986). Drawing on the work of Rogers (1957), therapy was not conceptualized as *treatment*, as something you do to the child, but rather as an *opportunity* for growth. The relational conditions of empathy, genuineness, and positive regard are posited as the active ingredients of therapy. The development and maintenance of an emotional bond facilitates emotional and behavioral change. Associations between bond and outcome in this tradition are direct rather than mediated through therapeutic work.

Common to the foregoing perspectives is an emphasis on an emotional connection between child and therapist. Emotional bond, then, appears to be a core component of alliance with children. This view has taken root in recent approaches to assessing the alliance in child and adolescent therapy (e.g., Shirk, Gudmundsen, Kaplinski, & McMakin, 2008; Shirk & Russell, 1996; Shirk & Saiz, 1992).

In contrast, some have criticized this perspective for failing to acknowledge the *social contractual* features of the therapeutic alliance. "Traditional theories of child and adolescent psychotherapy appear to have overly focused on the *bond* as necessary and sufficient for change" (DiGiuseppe, Linscott, & Jilton, 1996, p. 87). From this perspective, the central component of alliance, especially with older children and adolescents, consists of *agreements* regarding treatment goals and the methods for accomplishing them. The fact that youth are typically referred by others makes the establishment of agreements both difficult and essential for treatment collaboration. Given the press toward autonomy in adolescence, this issue takes on added importance. At present, however, it is not clear if goal agreement is equally relevant for younger child clients as with adolescents.

As these clinical perspectives suggest, there are important parallels between adult and youth models of alliance. Consistent with Bordin's (1979) pantheoretical model, three facets of alliance—emotional bond, task collaboration (work), and agreements (goal consensus)—are prominent in the youth literature. Although it is tempting to view this convergence as evidence for configural invariance in the alliance construct across age groups, at least two studies have failed to fully support the three-factor model with youth. These studies produced a single-factor solution, thus suggesting that features of the alliance may be less differentiated at younger ages (DiGiuseppe et al., 1996; Faw, Hogue, Johnson, Diamond, & Liddle, 2005).

Of equal importance, a number of developmental issues contribute to differences across youth and adults in the nature of bond, task, and goal dimensions of alliance. Consider first the therapy bond. Anna Freud (1946) noted some time ago that a child's relationship with the therapist could arise from a number of sources, not all of them developmentally equivalent. For many children, the relationship with a therapist is an opportunity to obtain gratifications not available in other contexts. As A. Freud observed, "if no one at home plays games with the child, for example, he might like to come to treatment because there a grown-up pays attention to him" (Sandler, Kennedy, & Tyson, 1980, p.47). For children who lack sustaining relationships with

adults, the relationship with a therapist fills a need for such connection. Indeed, this type of relationship might be quite therapeutic for relationship-deprived children. However, other children may anchor their positive feelings for their therapists on features not typically regarded as therapeutic, for example, how fun, stimulating, or rewarding the therapist might be. In such cases it is unclear if the "bond" reflects an experience of the therapist as an "ally," or as a valued playmate. In fact, A. Freud (1946) distinguished this type of relationship from the alliance. In the latter, the therapeutic bond is based on experiencing the therapist as *someone who can be counted on for help with emotional or behavioral problems.* This is a rather tall order for many children and adolescents, and possibly for some adults. But it draws attention to the potential developmental differences and the multiplicity of meanings in the emotional bond in child versus adult therapy.

A second developmental issue concerns the task dimension of the alliance. In the adult literature, tasks are framed in terms of *agreements* about the content and methods of therapy; in essence, whether there is consensus between client and therapist on the substance of therapy (Bordin, 1979). Such judgments may exceed the cognitive capacities of many child and adolescent clients. For example, studies of children's understanding of therapy have shown important developmental progressions in their recognition of therapy processes and parameters (e.g., Shirk & Russell, 1998, for a review). For example, children's causal reasoning may limit their ability to understand links between specific therapy tasks and subsequent therapy goals (Shirk, 1988). Perhaps it should not be surprising that research finds little agreement between child and therapist ratings of task collaboration, but greater convergence for therapy bond (Shirk & Saiz, 1992). Such developmental concerns have prompted some investigators to suggest that task collaboration with children is best assessed through observation (Karver et al., 2008; Shirk & Karver, 2006). In essence, the task dimension of alliance in youth therapy, especially with children, should be operationalized as observed participation in therapy tasks and not as agreements about such tasks.

Developmental issues complicate the goal dimension of the alliance as well. An important difference between adult and youth therapy is the involvement of other family members aside from the identified client. Minimally, parents or guardians are involved in transportation to and payment of therapy. Quite often, however, parents are more actively involved as informants about client functioning, collateral participants, or even as therapeutic collaborators who help with treatment implementation outside sessions. Consequently, the therapist is faced with multiple sets of goals, and often the goals of parents and youth diverge. Agreement on goals, then, is complicated by whose goals are considered. A study of clinic-referred children (Hawley & Weisz, 2003) examined therapist, child, and parent agreement about the most important problems to be addressed in therapy. Amazingly, more than 75% of child, parent, and therapist triads began treatment without agreement on even one target problem. Nearly half failed to agree on one broad problem domain such as aggression versus depression. It is interesting to note that therapists agreed with parents more often than with children. Such evidence suggests that agreement on goals may mean something quite different in youth therapy than in adult therapy At present, it is not clear if agreement between parent and therapist or child and therapist is a better predictor of treatment outcome.

A related issue involves the presence of multiple alliances in youth treatment even when it is child focused. Unlike with adults,

therapists are faced with establishing and maintaining an alliance with the youth and his or her parent(s). Most research on alliance–outcome relations with children and adolescents has focused on the youth–therapist relationship. A notable exception is in the area of parent management training where parents are the primary focus of child therapy. It is possible that alliances with parents and youth may relate to different sets of outcomes. For example, Hawley and Weisz (2005) found that parent, but not youth, alliance predicted better therapy participation. Youth alliance, but not parent alliance, predicted symptom change. These findings suggest that a strong alliance with parents is important for treatment continuation, whereas the youth alliance may be more critical for treatment outcomes.

At present, a unified definition of alliance has yet to emerge in the youth literature. In fact, our review of the research literature reveals 10 different alliance measures for children and adolescents. No study has examined the concurrent validity of the most frequently used measures. Thus, it is not clear if different measures with similar names are assessing the same facets of the alliance.

The two most frequently used patient and therapist report instruments in youth research are the *Working Alliance Inventory* (WAI; Horvath & Greenberg, 1989) and the *Therapeutic Alliance Scale for Children* (TASC; Shirk & Saiz, 1992). The WAI has been used primarily with adolescents and the TASC with children and young adolescents. Although the WAI, originally developed for adult therapy, has been modified for use with adolescents (Linscott, DiGuiseppe, & Jilton, 1993), the original or short version has been employed most frequently. The WAI measures the quality of the therapeutic relationship across three subscales: bonds, tasks, and goals. The final item pool for the measure was generated on the basis of content analysis of

Bordin's (1979) model of working alliance. Expert raters evaluated items for goodness of fit with the working alliance construct.

The TASC was developed specifically for child therapy and also was based on Bordin's model (1979). Two dimensions are assessed: bond between child and therapist, and level of task collaboration. Unlike the WAI, task collaboration does not refer to agreements on tasks, but to ratings of actual collaboration on tasks such as "talking about feelings" and "trying to solve problems." The therapist version of the TASC involves ratings of the *child's* bond and task involvement rather than the therapist's own. Although items on the bond subscale remain constant, items on the task collaboration scale vary with type of treatment in order to be consistent with CBT (cognitive-behavioral therapy) or psychodynamic tasks. The subscales show good internal consistency and relatively high levels of stability over a 4- to 7-week period (Shirk et al., 2008). Although therapist and child agreement on bond ratings are medium to strong, agreement is substantially lower for task collaboration.

A number of observational measures have appeared in the youth literature but none have become the "gold standard." One measure that was developed specifically for child and adolescent therapy and that has been used in more than one study is the *Therapy Process Observation Coding System–Alliance Scale* (McLeod & Weisz, 2005). This observation scale took as its starting point the distinction between bond and task collaboration found in factor analyses of child and therapist reports of alliance (Shirk & Saiz, 1992) and factor analyses of process codes (Estrada & Russell, 1999). Items from a broad range of measures that mapped onto the bond and task dimensions were initially included in the item pool, and redundant items reduced. Expert raters then sorted items into bond

or task categories and consistently sorted items were retained. The resulting coding system includes eight bond items and six task collaboration items. Interrater reliability has been shown to be good across items. Bond and task dimensions are highly correlated, consistent with what has been found with youth self-reports of alliance dimensions, suggesting that alliance may be a unitary construct in youth therapy.

Clinical Examples

The following verbal interactions derived from a composite of cases reflect different features of the therapeutic alliance with young clients. The first example illustrates a strong emotional bond between a young adolescent and her therapist:

> Therapist: So, what is it like when you're feeling really down?
> Client: I get like I don't want to talk to anyone. I'm like get away, leave me alone. My dad asks me how I'm doing and I just say nothing or walk away.
> Therapist: You just want some space. You don't want to be pushed.
> Client: Exactly.
> Therapist: In here, I'm going to ask you a lot about how you are feeling. If you feel like I'm pushing you, is it possible you will not want to talk with me.
> Client: I don't think that'll happen because you're not in my face. Talking gets my stress out. When I'm in a bad mood on the day of our meetings, I look forward to our talking . . . it helps keep me going because I know you get me.

In the next example, the goal dimension of the alliance is prominent. Here the therapist explores the adolescent's goals for therapy.

> Therapist: I know what your parents are hoping for from our therapy, but what are your goals?

Client: I want to stop worrying that I'll say something wrong, so I won't just feel all stuck.

Therapist: It sounds like you'd like to shift your focus away from all the things that make you worry and feel trapped.

Client: Yeah, when I think about what could happen, I become so nervous I just avoid everyone. I want to go walk up to the ins (popular girls) and just be right there talking and not all what if.

Therapist: So, if we could change how much you worry and think about all the negatives that would be a good result?

Client: Definitely, I'm tired of worrying all the time.

In the final example, an older child talks with his therapist about dealing with anger. The client's statements reflect the collaborative aspect of the alliance:

Client: I feel better since we last talked. That stuff we worked on was pretty helpful.

Therapist: That's cool. Great. What did you do?

Client: Like . . . I forgot what it is called . . . like . . . I controlled my temper . . . when I got angry . . . I was like OK like take a deep breath . . . then I walked away.

Therapist: Great. It helped bring your anger down.

Client: mmhmm.

Therapist: You made a good decision. Some people get angry and are like, hey, I'm right, I'm not backing down.

Client: If I get up in their face when I'm mad, I end up losing anyway.

Therapist: Losing anyway?

Client: Yeah, I pay for it later. Get in trouble and stuff.

Therapist: So using what we've worked on might have a payoff?

Client: Yeah, like what we practiced in here.

It should be noted that other features of interactions can reflect the condition of the alliance. For example, a child who is unresponsive to therapist questions or who is only willing to talk about topics unrelated to problems or issues that prompted therapy demonstrates behaviorally low levels of collaboration. Similarly, many children will actively participate in games and unstructured play but will avoid talking about concerns or practicing relevant skills in session. Though such children appear to like their therapist, it is not evident that the therapist is viewed as someone who could help with emotional or behavioral problems.

Prior Reviews

In their 2003 meta-analysis of associations between relationship variables and treatment outcomes, Shirk and Karver found only 23 studies with quantifiable relationships published over the previous 27 years. The majority of these studies did not assess alliance per se but evaluated various dimensions of relationship quality such as therapist warmth, therapeutic climate, or treatment participation. Only nine studies examined the alliance, and of these nine only one evaluated the alliance prospectively in individual therapy. Overall, Shirk and Karver (2003) found that relationship variables are related to youth treatment outcomes with a weighted mean correlation of 0.20, slightly smaller than, but similar to, estimates from the adult literature (see Chapter 2).

Although Shirk and Karver (2003) did not report results for alliance studies alone, a reanalysis of the data indicates that the weighted mean alliance–outcome association in the sample of nine studies was $r = 0.25$. It should be noted, however, that this estimate includes both prospective and concurrent measurement of alliance and outcome, and the assessment of alliance in individual and family therapy.

In a subsequent meta-analysis, Karver, Handelsman, Fields, & Bickman (2006) specifically examined alliance–outcome relations for child and adolescent clients. These estimates did not include parent and family alliance data. Karver et al. (2006) identified 10 studies that assessed youth alliance in relation to outcome. Correlations varied widely across studies and ranged from 0.05 to 0.49 with a weighted mean correlation of 0.21. Like the original meta-analysis by Shirk and Karver (2003), these results indicate a moderate association between alliance and outcome in child and adolescent therapy.

Meta-Analytic Review

In recent years, there has been significant growth in the number of studies evaluating alliance–outcome relations in child and adolescent therapy. In order to provide an estimate of this association based on a larger sample of studies than previously reported, we conducted a meta-analysis of current evidence on alliance–outcome relationships in child and adolescent therapy. Our meta-analysis is restricted to child- and adolescent-focused treatments and does not include studies of family therapy (which are reviewed in Chapter 4). Consistent with prior youth meta-analyses, we included both prospective and concurrent assessments of alliance and outcome because of the limited number of studies in the literature. However, we provide separate estimates of association for each design. Because parents are often included in child and adolescent therapy, and in fact, they may be the focus of behavioral treatments, we also provide an estimate of association between parent alliance and outcome.

Our analyses were guided by a number of hypotheses based on prior findings in the child and adolescent literature. First, consistent with earlier meta-analyses, we expected alliance to predict outcomes and hypothesized that this association might be moderated by timing of alliance assessment. Prior research on relationship processes in child and adolescent treatment has been criticized for the inclusion of studies involving the concurrent measurement of alliance and outcome (Shirk & Karver, 2003). It has been suggested that concurrent measurement inflates estimates of association. In order to address this possibility, we examined associations by timing of alliance measurement. Second, some evidence suggests that parent alliance may be more strongly associated with treatment continuation and attendance than treatment outcome. (Hawley & Weisz, 2005), thus we examined this possibility by comparing correlations by type of alliance (parent vs. youth). Third, consistent with prior results (Shirk & Karver, 2003), we did not expect a difference in the strength of alliance–outcome relations by treatment type; instead, we expected comparable associations across behavioral and nonbehavioral therapies. We did, however, predict differences in alliance–outcome relations as a function of type of problem treated, as previous research (Shirk & Karver, 2003) found somewhat stronger alliance–outcome relations for youth with externalizing (disruptive) problems than with internalizing (emotional) problems. Therefore, we examined outcomes by type of problem. Finally, we did not expect age-related differences in alliance–outcome relations. Comparisons were made between studies with child samples and those with adolescent samples.

Alliance–Outcome Studies

To identify applicable studies that measured the relationship between alliance and outcome, a three-pronged approach was used. First, prior reviews of the alliance-to-outcome relationship were examined for qualifying manuscripts (Karver et al., 2006; Shirk & Karver, 2003). Citations of these articles were then examined as a means to identify additional manuscripts. Second, the PsycINFO database was searched from 2004 forward to identify articles that have been published since the last major meta-analytic review of the therapeutic alliance in child and adolescent therapy. Finally, Google Scholar was used to search for studies that may have been missed and for unpublished manuscripts. For both searches, *child* and *adolescent* were used in conjunction with the terms *alliance* or *relationship* and *therapeutic* or *therapy*.

To be included in the current meta-analysis, studies had to meet the following criteria: (1) the study had to include a specific measure explicitly described in the manuscript as an alliance measure; (2) the alliance had to be related to some indicator or measure of posttreatment outcome and not another process variable; (3) the study had to be of individual or group mental health treatment delivered to a youth under age 18 or a parent; (4) the study could not be an analog study; (5) the study needed to be available in English; (6) the study must have included at least 10 participants; and (7) if the study did not directly report a correlation between alliance and outcome, enough information had to be available in the manuscript to calculate the effect size.

The resulting sample consisted of 29 studies with 2,202 youth clients and 892 parents. Studies were coded for type of alliance (youth vs. parent), timing of alliance measurement (early- or middle- during first two thirds of therapy sessions, late- during the last third of therapy sessions, at termination, or posttreatment, or combined), type of treatment (cognitive-behavioral/behavioral, nonbehavioral, or mixed), type of problem (internalizing, externalizing, mixed, or substance abuse), and mean age of youth (child = less than 12; adolescent = ages 12–18).

Calculation of Effect Sizes

Because most studies reported results (alliance-to-outcome relationships) as correlations, the product-moment correlation coefficient r was used as our effect size estimate. All results (typically product-moment correlation coefficient rs) in each study were converted to Fisher's Z in order to normalize the r distribution (Hedges & Olkin, 1985). For all studies it was possible to compute effect sizes, thus no effects were imputed as zero. In most studies, more than one alliance–outcome relationship was reported. In order to correct for bias due to correlated effects within studies and an unequal number of associations reported in different studies, we averaged (simple mean) the Fisher's Z's for each study. In order to calculate a more precise estimate of the overall relationship between alliance and outcome, we weighted the average effect size (Z) for each study by the number of participants in the study. We weighted each effect size so that the final estimate of the alliance-to-outcome relationship properly accounts for the fact that more precise estimates should be given more weight in the aggregate. The weighted effect sizes for each study were aggregated, and then this sum was divided by the sum of the weights (number of participants per study minus 3) for each study, resulting in an estimate of the overall alliance-to-outcome relationship. This weighted effect size Z was then converted back to the product-moment correlation coefficient r. We then analyzed effect size estimates by the type of alliance, timing of alliance measurement, type of therapy, type of problem treated, and child age.

Results of the Meta-Analysis

The 29 studies that met inclusion criteria are displayed in Table 3.1. The sample includes 26 published studies and 3 doctoral dissertations. Twenty-eight studies evaluated the child or adolescent alliance, and 10 studies

Table 3.1 Reviewed Studies, Alliance Measures, Classifications, and Effect Sizes

Study	N	Alliance measure	Classifications	Wt. mean r
Adler (1998)	92	Parent Evaluation Questionnaire	Both ages Mixed problems Nonbehavioral	0.24
Auerbach et al. (2008)	39	Working Alliance Inventory - Short	Adolescent Substance Abuse Nonbehavioral	0.12
Champion (1998)	19	Child Behavior in Therapy Scale	Child Mixed problems Nonbehavioral	0.18
Chiu et al. (2009)	34	Therapy Process Observation System - Alliance	Child Internalizing Behavioral	0.21
Colson et al. (1991)	69	Therapeutic Alliance Difficulty Scale	Adolescent Mixed problems Nonbehavioral	0.28
Creed & Kendall (2005)	68	Therapeutic Alliance Scale for Children	Adolescent Internalizing Behavioral	0.30
Darchuck (2007)	40	Working Alliance Inventory - Short	Adolescent Substance Abuse Nonbehavioral	0.25
Diamond et al. (2006)	353	Working Alliance Inventory - Short	Adolescent Substance abuse Behavioral	0.20
Eltz et al. (1995)	38	Penn Helping Alliance Questionnaire	Adolescent Mixed problems Nonbehavioral	0.32
Florsheim et al. (2000)	78	Working Alliance Inventory	Adolescent Externalizing Nonbehavioral	0.12
Gavin et al. (1999)	60	Treatment Alliance Scale	Adolescent Mixed problems Nonbehavioral	0.03
Green (1996)	25	Family Engagement Scale Empathy and Understanding Scale	Child Mixed problems Nonbehavioral	0.58
Green	20	Family Engagement Scale Empathy and Understanding Scale	Adolescent Mixed problems Nonbehavioral	−0.04
Handwerk et al. (2008)	71	Working Relationship Scale	Adolescent Mixed problems Behavioral	0.25
Hawley & Garland (2008)	78	Working Alliance Inventory - Short	Adolescent Mixed problems Nonbehavioral	0.29

(Continued)

Table 3.1. Continued

Study	N	Alliance measure	Classifications	Wt. mean r
Hawley & Weisz (2005)	81	Therapeutic Alliance Scale for Children	Both Mixed problems Nonbehavioral	0.13
Hintikka (2006)	45	Working Alliance Inventory	Adolescent Mixed problems Nonbehavioral	0.07
Hogue et al. (2006)	56	Vanderbilt Therapeutic Alliance Scale	Adolescent Substance abuse Behavioral	−0.02
Holmqvist et al. (2007)	59	Penn Helping Alliance Questionnaire	Adolescent Externalizing Combined	0.13
Karver et al. (2008)	23	Alliance Observation Coding System Working Alliance Inventory	Adolescent Internalizing Combined	0.08
Kaufman et al. (2005)	45	Working Alliance Inventory - Short	Adolescent Mixed problems Behavioral	0.00
Kazdin et al. (2006)	310	Working Alliance Inventory Therapeutic Alliance Scale for Children	Child Externalizing Behavioral	0.29
Kazdin et al. (2005)	185	Working Alliance Inventory	Child Externalizing Behavioral	0.21
Kazdin & Whitley (2006)	218	Working Alliance Inventory Therapeutic Alliance Scale for Children	Child Externalizing Behavioral	0.30
McLeod & Weisz (2005)	22	Therapy Process Observation System - Alliance	Child Internalizing Nonbehavioral	0.25
Shirk et al. (2008)	50	Therapeutic Alliance Scale for Adolescents	Adolescent Internalizing Behavioral	0.26
Smith et al. (2008)	55	Penn Helping Alliance Questionnaire	Adolescents Mixed problems Nonbehavioral	0.36
Tetzlaff et al. (2005)	434	Working Alliance Inventory - Short	Adolescent Substance abuse Combined	0.24
Zaitsoff et al. (8)	36	Penn Helping Alliance Questionnaire	Adolescent Eating Disorders Nonbehavioral	0.48

examined the parent alliance. In terms of timing of alliance measurement, 15 studies assessed the alliance early or in the middle of treatment, 8 studies measured alliance late or posttreatment, and 8 studies assessed alliance over time as an average and 2 assessed alliance as a slope or change score. In terms of types of treatment, 20 studies involved nonbehavioral therapy, 14 involved behavioral or cognitive-behavioral therapy, and 4 involved mixed therapies, usually the inclusion of family therapy with individual therapy. Eleven studies included child samples, 12 included only adolescents, and 5 studies included both children and adolescents. One study could not be classified. Finally, 9 studies focused on internalizing problems, 7 on externalizing problems, 5 on substance abuse, 6 on mixed problems, and 1 on eating disorders. As shown in Table 3.1, weighted correlations averaged 0.19 with a confidence interval of +/− 0.04 (range = −.09 to 0.59). This estimate is very similar to earlier results for the association between relationship variables and outcomes (r_w = 0.20), but slightly lower than the estimate based on studies that measured alliance and outcome (r_w = 0.25). The current meta-analysis includes over three times as many alliance studies and excluded studies of family therapy.

Mediators and Moderators

A number of variables were expected to moderate the strength of association between alliance and outcome. One methodological variable was timing of alliance assessment. It was hypothesized that concurrent measurements would show stronger associations than prospective designs. Studies that assessed alliance early produced an r_w = 0.15 (CI = +/− 0.06), those that measured it late or posttreatment resulted in an r_w = 0.24 (CI = +/− 0.09), those that used an average resulted in an r_w = 0.21 (CI = +/− 0.07), and the two that used a slope or a change score across early and late alliances yielded

an r_w = 0.38 (CI = +/− 0.24). As predicted, studies that included a measure of alliance later in treatment, either as part of an average, change score, or slope, or simply as a late measure of alliance, yielded larger effects ($p < 0.05$) than studies that measured alliance early in treatment (See Figure 3.1).

With regard to client characteristics, age and type of problem were examined as potential moderators. Studies with child samples (under age 12) yielded significantly larger weighted mean correlations (r = 0.27; CI = +/− 0.08) than studies with adolescent samples (r = 0.17; CI = +/− 0.05). A number of studies included both children and adolescents and produced a mean correlation of 0.12 (CI= +/− 0.10), also significantly different from the child estimate ($p < 0.05$). Previous research (e.g, Shirk & Karver, 2003) did not find age-related differences in alliance–outcome associations, and this finding is somewhat surprising given the clinical focus on alliance difficulties with adolescents (Castro-Blanco & Karver, 2010).

Effect sizes did not differ across types of treatment. The weighted mean correlations for behavioral/cognitive behavioral, nonbehavioral, and mixed therapies were 0.18 (CI = +/− 0.05), 0.19 (CI = +/− 0.06), and 0.20 (CI = +/− 0.08), respectively. These results are consistent with earlier findings reported by Shirk and Karver (2003). Nor was there a difference in the weighted mean correlation for therapist–parent and therapist–youth alliance. Both associations averaged r_w=19.

Consistent with earlier findings (Shirk & Karver, 2003), strength of alliance–outcome relations varied as a function of type of treated problem. The weighted mean correlation for externalizing problems was 0.24 (CI = +/− 0.07). In contrast, internalizing problems, substance abuse, and mixed problems showed weighted mean correlations of 0.17 (CI = +/− 0.11), 0.14 (CI = +/− 0.07), and 0.20 (CI = +/− .07), respectively. One study evaluated youth with eating disorders and produced a mean correlation of 0.53 (CI = +/− 0.34). The strength of alliance–outcome relations differed between studies with externalizing samples and those with substance abuse samples ($p < 0.05$). Other differences were not reliable. The difference in alliance–outcome effect size for youth with externalizing versus internalizing problems was in the same direction as previous research, but it did not attain statistical significance.

Despite theoretical models that posit a mediated relation between alliance and outcome, no study examined mediation through involvement in specific treatment tasks. Only one study (Karver et al., 2008) demonstrated a strong link between early alliance and later task involvement.

Summary of Meta-Analytic Findings

Results from our meta-analysis indicate a small-to-medium association between alliance and outcome in child and adolescent therapy. Estimates of alliance–outcome relations in the child and adolescent literature may be slightly inflated by the inclusion of studies that only measure alliance late in treatment. However, studies that assessed alliance with methods that included early measures of alliance—through averaged scores, slopes, or change scores—produced effects that were slightly larger than the overall estimate for all studies. Thus, results support the view that the therapeutic alliance is an important predictor of outcome in youth therapy.

The strength of alliance–outcome relations did not vary with type of treatment. The alliance thus appears to be important for therapies that vary widely in terms of specific treatment procedures, including therapies that focus on teaching contingency management to parents. The alliance is an important component of broad classes of child and adolescent therapy, and it appears

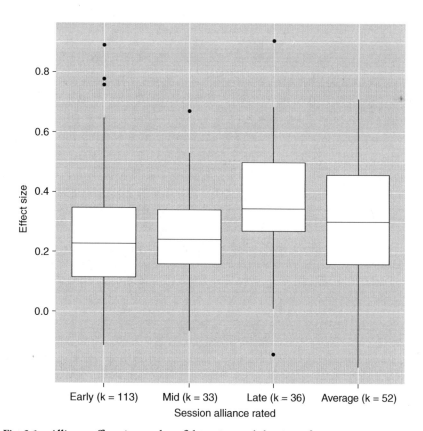

Fig. 3.1   Alliance effect sizes and confidence intervals by time of measurement

to contribute to outcomes in treatments as different as manual-guided CBT and non-directive, play therapy. It is noteworthy that alliance also is predictive of outcome in parent-focused therapies.

The strength of association between alliance and outcome varied as a function of several variables. Our results showed a slightly stronger association between alliance and outcome among children compared with adolescents. A prior meta-analysis did not find such a difference (Shirk & Karver, 2003). It is possible that age-related differences in alliance–outcome associations are confounded with the typical problems treated in these two age groups. Specifically, child studies often include samples of disruptive children and adolescent studies include substance abuse samples. Given that correlations were stronger for externalizing samples than substance abuse samples, the age differences in alliance–outcome associations could be due to age differences in problem types.

It is not clear why stronger associations between alliance and outcome are found with externalizing youth, as they were in our earlier meta-analysis (Shirk & Karver, 2003). We have speculated that the challenge of engaging oppositional and disruptive youth increases variability in alliance, and thus increases the possibility of larger correlations than those obtained in samples with a more attenuated range of alliance scores. It is also possible that alliance plays an especially critical role in the treatment of disruptive problems, possibly by facilitating the internalization of skills or an empathic attitude toward others.

The question of *how* important the alliance is to youth outcomes deserves some comment. When viewed in terms of explained variance, the estimate of less than 4% of total outcome variance seems rather small. However, an important question is how does this compare with the contribution of specific treatment methods to youth

therapy outcomes? One way of thinking about this issue is to use a common metric and to benchmark effects from comparative outcome studies with the results of the current meta-analysis. The mean correlation obtained in this study, $r_w = 0.19$, converts to an effect size, d, of approximately 0.39. How does this compare with effect sizes obtained by comparing two or more youth treatments involving different procedures?

Two recent estimates are relevant. In a comparison of evidence-based treatments (EBTs) with usual-care (UC) therapy, Weisz, Jensen-Dose, and Hawley (2006) found EBTs to be superior to UC with an effect size of 0.25 for direct comparisons of psychotherapies. In an effort to estimate the impact of specific treatment methods on outcome, Miller et al. (2008) conducted a meta-analysis of youth comparative outcome studies in which two or more bona fide treatments were evaluated. Although they found some evidence for method effects, the total outcome variance explained by treatment method was 0.037, or when converted to a correlation, an r of 0.19, identical to the mean correlation obtained in our current meta-analysis. Thus, when benchmarked to findings from comparisons of treatment methods, the contribution of alliance to outcome appears similar to the contribution of specific methods. Of course, it is possible that differences in specific methods are more critical for some disorders than others, for example, obsessive-compulsive disorder versus depression, just as alliance appears to be more strongly related to outcome for externalizing compared to internalizing disorders.

A critical question, then, is the relation between the alliance and specific treatment factors in child and adolescent therapy. Are these factors complementary and do they contribute to outcome in an additive manner, or might alliance actually account for differences in outcome currently attributed to specific methods? Only one published study in the child and adolescent literature has attempted to evaluate the latter possibility. Kaufman and colleagues (2005) examined the alliance as a potential mediator of treatment effects obtained in a comparison of group CBT and a Life Skills group for adjudicated, depressed adolescents. These investigators found more positive alliances in the group CBT condition than in the Life Skills condition, but this difference in alliance did not account for significant variance in depression outcomes. Unfortunately, few comparative outcome studies have assessed the alliance in the youth literature; consequently, the relative contribution of alliance and specific factors cannot be readily addressed.

Client and Therapist Contributions

A small but growing number of studies have examined predictors of the therapeutic alliance in child and adolescent therapy. Emerging evidence points to a number of client characteristics and therapist behaviors associated with alliance formation.

Pretreatment Predictors of Child and Adolescent Alliance

Numerous clinical accounts have highlighted some of the potential challenges to engaging children and adolescents in a working alliance (Castro-Blanco & Karver, 2010; A. Freud, 1946; Meeks, 1971). Among the obstacles to alliance formation are the limited problem recognition and acknowledgement, the tendency to attribute problems to external sources, low motivation for change, absence of self-referral (or the presence of coaxed or coerced referral), and a lack of understanding of the therapy processes. Although some of these factors could be indicative of psychopathology, most are simply a consequence of developmental level. Surprisingly few studies have examined direct links between these developmental factors and youth alliance.

One exception is motivation for change. Consistent with the adult literature (see Chapter 2), results generally show that youth with greater motivation, more problem recognition, and more stated reasons for changing their behavior form more positive alliances (Christensen & Skogstad, 2009; Estrada & Russell, 1999; Fitzpatrick & Irannejad, 2008), though one study failed to find these associations (Garner, Godley, & Funk, 2008).

Within the youth clinical literature, adolescence is viewed as one of the most difficult periods for alliance formation (Castro-Blanco & Karver, 2010; Meeks, 1971). The developmental press toward autonomy, the increasing centrality of peer relationships, and growing doubts about adults' capacity for understanding youth experiences can contribute to alliance difficulties. One might expect, then, relatively clear evidence for more positive alliances among children than adolescents. Yet, the limited evidence is mixed with two studies showing more positive alliances among older youth (Garner, Godley, & Funk, 2008; Gavin, Wamboldt, Sorokin, Levy, & Wamboldt, 1999), and two studies reporting younger children forming better alliances (Creed & Kendall, 2005; DeVet, Kim, Charlot-Swilly, & Ireys, 2003). It is certainly possible that adolescents' greater capacity for understanding therapy rationale and tasks might contribute to better alliances among older than younger youth. However, the paucity of research evidence on this issue pales in comparison with practice-based observations of alliance difficulties with adolescents. Given that most treatment studies focus on either children or adolescents, direct comparisons of alliance processes are likely to remain limited.

Two other pretreatment factors have attracted some attention in the research literature: type and severity of psychopathology and interpersonal functioning. Research on symptom severity and alliance formation has produced mixed results. Three studies found no relationship between initial symptom severity and subsequent alliance (Bickman et al., 2004; DeVet et al., 2003; Eltz et al., 1995), one found a negative relationship between overall level of maladaptive functioning and alliance (Green, Kroll, Imrie, Frances, Begum et al., 2001), and two actually showed a positive relationship between initial severity and alliance (Christensen & Skogstad, 2009; Shirk et al., 2008). It is likely that greater clarity will be attained by examining specific symptoms (e.g., depressive symptoms) and alliance rather than overall symptom severity. For example, clinical accounts have highlighted the unique challenges of engaging youth with high levels of oppositional and rule-breaking behavior (Gallager, Kurtz, & Blackwell, 2010). High levels of defiance, distrust of adult authority, and externalization of problems have been found to make alliance formation especially difficult with this group. (Bickman et al., 2004; Garcia & Weisz, 2002)

In contrast to symptom severity, interpersonal variables appear associated with youth alliance. A recurrent finding in the adult literature is that quality of past and present relationships predict alliance quality (e.g., Hersoug, Monsen, Havik, & Hoglend, 2002; Mallinckrodt, Coble, & Gantt, 1995). One study (Eltz, Shirk, & Sarlin, 1995) found that youth with more interpersonal problems, but not greater overall problem severity, had more alliance difficulties, and another (Fields et al., 2010) found social competence to be related to alliance. In the former study, a history of child maltreatment predicted early alliance difficulties even after controlling for problem severity. Perhaps it should not be surprising that youth with interpersonal trauma histories, especially abuse in the context of the family, would be cautious forming a close relationship with an adult caregiver (therapist).

Some studies have taken a more indirect approach to looking at the contribution of pretreatment relationship factors to alliance formation. The idea behind the indirect approach is that if youth have poor family relationships or low levels of social support, these factors might indicate poor interpersonal skills or poor prior experiences of healthy relationships. Consistent with this perspective, a number of studies have found social support—both youth and parent reported—to be related to youth and/or parent alliances (DeVet et al., 2003; Fields et al., 2010; Garner, Godley, & Funk, 2008; Hawley & Garland, 2008; Kazdin & Whitley, 2006). As these results suggest, alliance formation is a social process, and youth relational experiences and competencies appear to impact the alliance.

Finally, it should be noted that gender and race have been considered in a small number of studies. The evidence is split on the role of gender; two studies showed no association between gender and alliance (Creed & Kendall, 2005; Fitzpatrick & Irannejad, 2008), but three showed females to rate the alliance more positively than male youth (Christensen & Skogstad, 2009; Eltz, Shirk, & Sarlin, 1995; Wintersteen, Mensinger, & Diamond, 2005). One study showed the opposite with males rating the alliance more positively than females (Hawke, Hennen & Gallione, 2005). Given that the majority of child and adolescent therapists are female, it would be useful to know if gender matching has an impact on alliance, and if so, for whom. The evidence with regard to race effects is extremely limited. Hawke and colleagues (2005) found Hispanic and African-American youth to have stronger youth–therapist alliances than European-American youth, but Wintersteen et al. (2005) found no race effects. The impact of therapist–youth matching on race has not been examined. The reality is that we know very little about whether gender, race, or matching on these variables is related to the alliance in youth therapy.

Therapist Strategies for Strengthening the Youth Alliance

Despite the importance of the alliance in youth therapy, research on therapist behaviors that contribute to alliance formation has only recently emerged. With the exception of research on family therapy (Diamond, Liddle, Hogue, & Dakof, 1999), all of these studies have been conducted with children and adolescents in individual CBT. Although generalizations to other forms of child therapy would be premature, some patterns have emerged across these initial studies and deserve consideration.

Two studies address therapist strategies with children. Creed and Kendall (2005) examined a set of therapist behaviors hypothesized to promote or interfere with alliance formation during the first three sessions of CBT with anxious children. Child and therapist reports were used to assess the alliance at Sessions 3 and 7. Child-reported alliance at Session 3 was positively associated with therapist collaboration strategies, including presenting therapy as a team effort, building a sense of togetherness by using words like "we," "us," and "let's," and by helping the child set goals for therapy. In contrast, two therapist verbal behaviors predicted a weaker alliance at Session 3. Not surprisingly, "pushing the child to talk" about anxiety and anxious situations was negatively associated with early child alliance. Similarly, therapist efforts to "emphasize common ground," that is, therapists' comments like "Me, too!" in response to children's statements about interests and activities were predictive of weaker alliances. For therapist-reported alliance, none of the therapist behaviors predicted alliance scores at Session 3, but collaborative strategies predicted better alliances at Session 7. Talking to the child in an overly formal manner, that is, being too didactic or patronizing, predicted weaker therapist reported alliance at Session 7.

Two findings seem especially important. First, therapist collaborative behavior, including the establishment of treatment goals with the child, may be critical for alliance formation. Recognition and validation of the child's perspective on this critical issue may help differentiate the therapist from parents, and help the child view the therapist as an ally. Second, therapists need to balance their approach between setting a collaborative tone without being either too formal or overly familiar with the child. Similarly, therapists need to balance their focus on problems with the maintenance of rapport. Too little focus on problems can amount to supporting avoidance, and too great a focus can undermine alliance. Therapists must be mindful of the child's level of tolerance and work to gradually facilitate the child's ability to talk about anxiety. Therapist flexibility about the pace of treatment may be critical for alliance formation.

Chu and Kendall (2009) evaluated therapist flexibility as a strategy for promoting client involvement in CBT for child anxiety disorders. In this context, flexibility is conceptualized as treatment adaptation occurring within the parameters of treatment fidelity: this is a way of individualizing manual-guided therapy. In fact, therapist flexibility was significantly associated with increases in child involvement over the course of therapy. Later child involvement predicted treatment improvement and lower levels of impairment. Results from this study, in conjunction with findings reported by Creed and Kendall (2005), suggest that therapists who provide CBT in a flexible manner, who are less didactic, less pressing, and better able to integrate client needs within the treatment protocol are more likely to facilitate better alliances and greater treatment involvement.

In addition to the foregoing research on child anxiety, Shirk and colleagues have published a series of studies on engagement of depressed adolescents. Their work has focused on the evaluation of three clusters of therapist engagement strategies—motivational strategies that focus on goal setting and mobilizing clients' intention to change, socialization strategies that focus on clarifying roles and tasks in therapy, and experiential strategies that focus on eliciting the client's experience and the provision of support. In addition, alliance-impeding behaviors (therapist lapses) were examined, including therapists' failure to acknowledge client emotion, therapists misunderstanding client's statements, and therapist criticism.

In their first study, Karver et al. (2008) examined engagement strategies in relation to early alliance in a small sample of adolescents who had attempted suicide and were treated with either problem-solving therapy or nondirective, supportive therapy. Results showed that therapist lapses were the most robust predictor of subsequent alliance across both conditions. Failure to respond to expressed emotion was one of the most characteristic problems.

In a second study, Russell, Shirk, and Jungbluth (2008) examined the same set of engagement strategies in a school-based trial of CBT for adolescent depression.

A unique feature of this study was the prediction of subsequent alliance from temporal patterns in therapist behavior rather than from overall frequency of behavior. Reliable temporal *patterns* in therapist engagement behavior were identified. Therapists who steadily increased their focus on being responsive and remoralizing the adolescent after the first 10 minutes of their sessions, but who then dampened the rate of increase over the rest of the session, reported more positive alliances two sessions later. These results suggest that more positive alliances are associated with a *shift* in therapist

focus in the first session. After initially socializing the adolescent to treatment, therapists who reported more positive alliances later turned their attention to responding to adolescent concerns while providing some hope for change. In a complementary manner, therapists who opened and closed the first session with a focus on treatment socialization were more likely to have adolescents report positive alliances than therapists who did not follow this pattern.

Finally, Jungbluth and Shirk (2009) uncovered an interesting pattern in their analysis of first-session engagement behavior and subsequent adolescent involvement in CBT for depression. Therapists who provided *less* structure in the first session were more likely to have adolescents who were highly involved in CBT tasks in later sessions than therapists who initiated therapy with high structure. Low structure is not equivalent to therapist inactivity but, rather, indicates greater exploration of adolescents' experiences and motives as well as greater provision of support.

Although the foregoing results are promising, they also must be considered preliminary. At present only five studies have been published that address the contribution of therapist behaviors and strategies to alliance formation and therapy involvement. All of these studies have been conducted in the context of CBT, and only two childhood disorders, anxiety and depression, have been considered. Nevertheless, some initial patterns can be discerned.

Results with children suggest that "pushing" child clients, especially in a more formal, didactic manner, is counterproductive for alliance formation. With adolescents there is evidence that greater attention to the teen's experience, especially in a way that acknowledges the adolescent's perspective and expressions of emotion, is associated with more positive alliance and involvement. Taken together, these results suggest that a less directive and less task-focused approach to therapy is critical at the start of treatment. Subsequent alliance and involvement appear to benefit from therapists taking the time to attend to their client's experiences and life stories. Efforts to engage the client by pushing or praising are contraindicated. This pattern is somewhat inconsistent with the emphasis on psycho-education as a method of treatment socialization and suggests that client-centered strategies at the start of therapy may be more effective for alliance formation.

Limitations of the Research

As indicated in our review of definitions and measures, the field has yet to reach consensus about the crucial features of the therapeutic alliance with youth. We were not surprised to find a large number of alliance measures in a relatively small number of studies. One way to advance the field would be to conduct a study in which multiple measures of alliance are administered in order to derive core underlying dimensions. Such an empirical approach could anchor future development of the alliance construct with youth.

Our meta-analysis revealed some important progress in research on alliance–outcome relations with children and adolescents. First, the number of studies has more than tripled since the first meta-analysis of relationship predictors of child outcomes. Many new studies do not measure alliance and outcome concurrently, as was found in the earlier meta-analysis, but examine associations prospectively. And there is clearly a trend toward assessing alliance at multiple points in treatment and evaluating alliance trajectories in relation to outcomes. Finally, a growing number of studies assess alliance from multiple perspectives—client, therapist, parent, and observer. Despite this progress, areas for improvement remain.

First, too many studies still rely on outcome assessments from a single source. As a result, alliance–outcome relations can be inflated by shared source variance. Second, studies that include multiple outcome measures from multiple sources often fail to distinguish among primary and secondary outcomes. Although it makes sense at this early stage of research to explore a wide range of outcomes, too few associations are based on specific hypotheses. It is possible that the alliance as an interpersonal construct will predict interpersonal outcomes like changes in relational schema, social engagement, or support-seeking behaviors.

Third, research must evaluate the temporal relationship between alliance and outcomes. Research has revealed early gains in child and adolescent therapy, yet no study has examined early alliance in relation to early symptom changes. This last issue is particularly important, as no study in the youth literature has ruled out the possibility that alliance is actually predicted *from* early improvement. Designs that account for possible symptom changes prior to the measure of alliance are clearly needed. And finally, no study in the youth literature has evaluated the contribution of alliance to outcome while controlling for client adherence to specific treatment tasks. Alliance may very well predict involvement in specific therapy components (Karver et al., 2008), but too few studies assess alliance in relation to other important process variables.

In conclusion, the alliance has a long history in the child and adolescent literature. Recent research progress on alliance–outcome relations indicates that this long-standing interest is clearly justified. Alliance is a predictor of youth therapy outcomes and may very well be an essential ingredient that makes diverse child and adolescent therapies work. Future research on the relative contribution of alliance and specific factors to youth outcomes, as well as the contribution of alliance to child and adolescent utilization of specific treatment procedures, will surely clarify its clinical importance.

Therapeutic Practices

- Alliances with both youth and their parents are predictive of treatment outcomes. Consequently, psychotherapists need to attend to the development of multiple alliances, not just to the alliance with the youth. A solid alliance with the parent may be particularly important for treatment continuation.

- Parents and youth often have divergent views about treatment goals. Formation of a therapeutic alliance with both youth and parent requires the therapist to attend to multiple perspectives and to develop a treatment plan that accommodates both youth and parent perspectives.

- The maintenance of a positive alliance over time predicts successful outcomes with youth. Therapists are advised to monitor alliance over the course of treatment. Alliance formation is not simply an early treatment task, it is a recurrent task.

- Youth are likely to have a limited understanding of therapy. Initial results suggest that early alliance formation with youth requires the therapist to balance active listening to the youth with providing an explicit framework for understanding therapy processes (roles, tasks, relevance). Overemphasizing the latter to the exclusion of the former appears to interfere with alliance formation, at least with adolescents.

- "Pushing" youth to talk about emotionally sensitive material appears to undermine alliance, at least among younger clients. Therapists can "scaffold" young clients' emotional disclosures by initially focusing on emotional experiences of low intensity and gradually attending to emotions of higher intensity.

- Although it can be tempting to try to connect with young clients by finding shared interests and activities, initial evidence suggests that such efforts may be counterproductive. Alliance formation appears to be better served by emphasizing the collaborative nature of therapy.

- Attending to client's experiences and acknowledging their expressed emotion are crucial for alliance formation, especially with adolescents. Providing an opportunity for client-directed interaction at the start of psychotherapy appears to set the stage for subsequent treatment involvement.

References

An asterisk (*) indicates studies included in the meta-analysis.

*Adler, A. G. (1998). *The alliance between child therapist and parent: How it predicts treatment outcome and reflects parent characteristics.* Unpublished dissertation.

*Auerbach, S., May, J., Stevens, M., & Kiesler, D. (2008). The interactive role of working alliance and counselor-client interpersonal behaviors in adolescent substance abuse treatment. *International Journal of Clinical and Health Psychology, 8*(3), 617–629.

Axline, V. (1947). *Play therapy.* Boston: Houghton Mifflin.

Bickman, L., Andrade, A., Lambert, E., Doucette, A., Sapyta, J., Boyd A., et al. (2004). Youth therapeutic alliance intensive treatment settings. *The Journal of Behavioral Health Services and Research. 31*(2), 134–148.

Bordin, E. S. (1979). The generalizability of the psychoanalytic concept of the working alliance. *Psychotherapy: Theory, Research, and Practice, 16,* 252–260.

Castro-Blanco, D., & Karver, M. (2010). *The elusive alliance: Treatment engagement strategies with with high-risk adolescents.* Washington, DC: APA Books.

*Champion, K. M. P. (1998). The change process in therapeutic programs for children. (ProQuest Information & Learning). *Dissertation Abstracts International: Section B: The Sciences and Engineering, 59,* 90.

*Chiu, A. W., McLeod, B. D., Har, K., & Wood, J. J. (2009). Child-therapist alliance and clinical outcomes in cognitive behavioral therapy for child anxiety disorders. *Journal of Child Psychology and Psychiatry, 50*, 751–758.

Chu, B., & Kendall, P. (2009). Therapist responsiveness to child engagement: Flexibility within manual-based CBT for anxious youth. *Journal of Clinical Psychology, 65*(7), 736–754.

Christensen, M., & Skogstad, R. (2009). What predicts quality of the therapeutic alliance in a cognitive behavioral treatment for children with anxiety disorders? Therapeutic alliance measured from the patient, therapist and observer perspective. Unpublished manuscript. *Det Psykologiske Facultet.*

*Colson, D.B., Cornsweet, C., Murphy, T., O'Malley, F., Hyland, P.S., McParland, M., Coyne, L. (1991). Perceived treatment difficulty and the therapeutic alliance in an adolescent psychiatric hospital, *American Journal of Orthopsychiatry, 61*, 221–229.

*Creed, T., & Kendall, P. (2005). Therapist alliance-building behavior within a cognitive-behavioral treatment for anxiety in youth. *Journal of Consulting and Clinical Psychology, 73*(3), 498–505.

*Darchuk, A. J. (2007). The role of the therapeutic alliance and its relationship to treatment outcome and client motivation in an adolescent substance abuse treatment setting. (ProQuest Information & Learning). *Dissertation Abstracts International: Section B: The Sciences and Engineering, 68*, 5, 195.

DeVet, K., Kim, Y., Charlot-Swilley, D., & Ireys H. (2003). The therapeutic relationship in child therapy: Perspectives of children and mothers. *The Journal of Clinical Child & Adolescent Psychology, 32* (2), 277–283.

Diamond, G., Liddle, H., Hogue, A., & Dakof, G. (1999). Alliance-building interventions with adolescents in family therapy: A process study. *Psychotherapy: Theory, Research, Practice, Training, 36*(4), 355–368.

*Diamond, G.S., Liddle, H.A., Wintersteen, M.B., Dennis, M.L., Godley, S.H., & Tims, F. (2006). Early therapeutic alliance as a predictor of treatment outcome for adolescent cannabis users in outpstient treatment. *The American Journal of Addictions, 15*, 26–33.

DiGiuseppe, R., Linscott, J., & Jilton, R. (1996), Developing the therapeutic alliance in child-adolescent psychotherapy. *Applied and Preventive Psychology, 5*, 85–100.

*Eltz, M., Shirk, S., & Sarlin, N. (1995). Alliance formation and treatment outcome among maltreated adolescents. *Child Abuse & Neglect, 19*(4), 419–431.

Estrada, A., & Russell, R. (1999). The development of the child psychotherapy process scales (CPPS). *Psychotherapy Research, 9*(2), 154–166.

Faw, L., Hogue, A., Johnson, S., Diamond, G. M., & Liddle, H. A. (2005). The Adolescent Therapeutic Alliance Scale (ATAS): Initial psychometrics and prediction of outcome in family-based substance abuse prevention counseling. *Psychotherapy Research, 15*(1–2), 141–154.

Fields, S., Handelsman, J., Karver, M. S., & Bickman, L. (2010). *Youth and parent predictors of the therapeutic alliance.* Manuscript submitted.

Fitzpatrick, M., & Irannejad, S. (2008). Adolescent readiness for change and the working alliance in counseling. *Journal of Counseling & Development. 86*(4), 438–445.

*Florsheim, P., Shotorbani, S., Guest-Warnick, G., Barratt, T., & Hwang, W. (2000). Role of the working alliance in the treatment of delinquent boys in community-based programs. *Journal of Clinical Child Psychology, 29*, 94–10.

Freud, A. (1946). *The psychoanalytic treatment of children.* New York: International Universities Press.

Garcia, J., & Weisz, J. (2002). When youth mental health care stops: Therapeutic relationship problems and other reasons for ending youth outpatient treatment. *Journal of Consulting and Clinical Psychology, 70*(2), 439–443.

Garner, B., Godley, S., & Funk, R. (2008). Predictors of early therapeutic alliance among adolescents in substance abuse treatment. Journal of Psychoactive Drugs, 40(1) 55–65.

*Gavin, L. A., Wamboldt, M. Z., Sorokin, N., Levy, S. Y., & Wamboldt, F. S. (1999). Treatment alliance and its association with family functioning, adherence, and medical outcome in adolescents with severe, chronic asthma. *Journal of Pediatric Psychology, 24*(4), 355–365.

*Green, J.M. (1996) Engagement and empathy: A pilot study of the therapeutic alliance in outpatient child psychiatry, *Child Psychology and Psychiatry Review, 1*, 130–138.

*Green, J., Kroll, L., Imrie, D., Frances, F., Begum, K., Harrison, L., et al. (2001). Health gain and outcome predictors during inpatient and related day treatment in child and adolescent psychiatry. *Journal of the American Academy of Child & Adolescent Psychiatry, 40*(3), 325–332.

*Handwerk, M., Smith, G., Thompson, R., Spellman, D., & Daly, D. (2008). Psychotropic medication utilization at a group-home residential facility for children and adolescents. *Journal of Child and Adolescent Psychopharmacology, 18*(5), 517–525.

Hawke, J., Hennen, J., & Gallione, P. (2005). Correlates of therapeutic involvement among adolescents in residential drug treatment. *The American Journal of Drug and Alcohol Abuse, 31*(1), 163–177.

*Hawley, K., & Garland, A. (2008). Working alliance in adolescent outpatient therapy: Youth, parent and therapist reports and associations with therapy outcomes. *Child and Youth Care Forum, 37*(2), 59–74.

Hawley, K., & Weisz, J. (2003). Child, parent and therapist (dis)agreement on target problems in outpatient therapy: The therapist's dilemma and its implications. *Journal of Consulting and Clinical Psychology, 71*(1), 62–70.

*Hawley, K. M., & Weisz, J. R. (2005). Youth versus parent working alliance in usual clinical care: Distinctive association with retention, satisfaction, and treatment. *Journal of Clinical Child and Adolescent Psychology, 34*, 117–128.

Hedges, L. V., & Olkin, I. (1985). *Statistical methods for meta-analysis*. New York: Academic Press.

Hersoug, A., Monsen, J., Havik, O., & Hoglen, P. (2002). Quality of early working alliance in psychotherapy: Diagnoses, relationship and intrapsychic variables as predictors. *Psychotherapy and Psychosomatics, 71*(1), 18–27.

*Hintikka, U., Laukkanen, E., Marttunen, M., & Lehtonen, J. (2006). Good working alliance and psychotherapy are associated with positive changes in cognitive performance among adolescent psychiatric inpatients. *Bulletin of the Menninger Clinic, 70*, 316–335.

*Hogue, A., Dauber, S., Stambaugh, L., Cecero, C., & Liddle, H. (2006). Early therapeutic alliance and treatment outcome in individual and family therapy for adolescent behavior problems. *Journal of Consulting and Clinical Psychology, 74*(1) 121–129.

*Holmqvist, R., Hill, T., & Lang, A. (2007). Treatment alliance in residential treatment of criminal adolescents. *Child and Youth Care Forum, 36*(4), 163–178.

Horvath, A. O., & Greenberg, L. S. (1989). Development and validation of the Working Alliance Inventory. *Journal of Counseling Psychology, 36*(2), 223–233.

Jungbluth, N., & Shirk, S. (2009). Therapist strategies for building involvement in cognitive–behavioral therapy for adolescent depression. *Journal of Consulting and Clinical Psychology, 77*(6), 1179–1184.

Karver, M., Handelsman, J., Fields, S., & Bickman, L. (2006). Meta-analysis of relationship variables in youth and family therapy: Evidence for different relationship variables in the child and adolescent treatment literature. *Clinical Psychology Review, 26*, 50–65.

*Karver, M., Shirk, S., Handelsman, J. B., Fields, S., Crisp, H., Gudmundsen, G., et al. (2008). Relationship processes in youth psychotherapy: Measuring alliance, alliance-building behaviors, and client involvement. *Journal of Emotional and Behavioral Disorders, 16*(1), 15–28.

*Kaufman, N., Rohde, P., Seeley, J., Clarke, G., & Stice, E. (2005). Potential mediators of cognitive-behavioral therapy for adolescents with comorbid major depression and conduct disorder. *Journal of Consulting and Clinical Psychology, 73*(1), 38–46.

*Kazdin, A. E., Marciano, P. L., & Whitley, M. K. (2005). Therapeutic alliance in cognitive-behavioral treatment of children referred for oppositional, aggressive, and antisocial behavior. *Journal of Consulting and Clinical Psychology, 73*, 726–730.

Kazdin, A., & Wassell, G. (2000). Predictors of barriers to treatment and therapeutic change in outpatient therapy for antisocial children and their families. *Mental Health Services Research, 2*, 27–40.

*Kazdin, A. E., & Whitley, M. K. (2006). Pretreatment social relations, therapeutic alliance, and improvements in parenting practices in parent management training. *Journal of Consulting and Clinical Psychology, 74*(2), 346–355.

*Kazdin, A. E., Whitley, M., & Marciano, P. L. (2006). Child-therapist and parent-therapist alliance and therapeutic change in the treatment of children referred for oppositional, aggressive, and antisocial behavior. *Journal of Child Psychology and Psychiatry, 47*, 436–445.

Kendall, P., Comer, J., Marker, C., Creed, T., Puliafico, A., Hughes, A., et al. (2009). In-session exposure tasks and therapeutic alliance across the treatment of childhood anxiety disorders. *Journal of Consulting and Clinical Psychology, 77*(3), 517–525.

Linscott, J., DiGiuseppe, R., & Jilton, R. (1993). *A measure of TA in adolescent psychotherapy*. Poster presented at the 101st Annual Convention of the American Psychological Association, Toronto, Canada.

Mallinckrodt, B., Coble, H., & Gantt, D. (1995). Working alliance, attachment memories, and social competencies of women in brief therapy. *Journal of Counseling Psychology, 42*(1), 79–84.

*McLeod, B., & Weisz, J. (2005). The therapy process observational coding system-alliance scale: Measure characteristics and prediction of outcome in usual clinical practice. *Journal of Consulting and Clinical Psychology, 73*(3), 323–333.

Meeks, J. (1971). *The fragile alliance: An orientation to the outpatient psychotherapy of the adolescent.* Oxford England: Williams & Wilkins.

Miller, S., Wampold, B., & Varhely, K. (2008). Direct comparisons of treatment modalities for youth disorders: A meta-analysis. *Psychotherapy Research, 18*(1), 5–14.

Rogers, C. (1957). The necessary and sufficient conditions for therapeutic personality change. *Journal of Consulting Psychology, 21*, 95–103.

Russell, R., Shirk, S., & Jungbluth, N. (2008). First-session pathways to the working alliance in cognitive-behavioral therapy for adolescent depression. *Psychotherapy Research, 18*(1), 15–27.

Sandler, J., Kennedy, H., & Tyson, R. (1980). *The techniques of child psychoanalysis: Discussions with Anna Freud.* Cambridge, MA: Harvard University Press.

Shirk, S. (Ed.). (1988). *Cognitive development and child psychotherapy.* New York: Plenum.

*Shirk, S., Gudmundsen, G., Kaplinski, H., & McMakin, D. (2008). Alliance and outcome in cognitive-behavioral therapy for adolescent depression. *Journal of Clinical Child and Adolescent Psychology, 37*(3), 631–639.

Shirk, S., & Karver, M. (2003). Prediction of treatment outcome from relationship variables in child and adolescent therapy: A meta-analytic review. *Journal of Consulting and Clinical Psychology, 71*, 462–471.

Shirk, S., & Karver, M. (2006). Process issues in cognitive-behavioral therapy for youth. In P. C. Kendall (Ed.), *Child and adolescent therapy: Cognitive-behavioral procedures* (pp. 465–491). New York: Guilford Press.

Shirk, S., & Russell, R. L. (1996). *Change processes in child psychotherapy: Revitalizing treatment and research.* New York: Guilford Press.

Shirk, S., & Russell, R. L. (1998). Process issues in child psychotherapy. In A. Bellack & M. Hersen (Eds.), *Comprehensive clinical psychology.* London: Pergamon.

Shirk, S., & Saiz, C. (1992). Clinical, empirical, and developmental perspectives on the therapeutic relationship in child psychotherapy. *Development and Psychopathology, 4*, 713–728.

*Smith, B., Duffee, D., Steinke, C., Haung, Y., & Larkin, H. (2008). Outcomes in residential treatment for youth: The role of early engagement. *Children and Youth Services Review, 30*(12), 1425–1436.

Spielman, G., Gatlin, E., & McFall, J. (2010). The efficacy of evidence-based psychotherapy versus usual care for youths: Controlling confounds in a meta-analysis. *Psychotherapy Research, 20*, 234–246.

*Tetzlaff, B. T., Kahn, J. H., Godley, S. H., Godley, M. D., Diamond, G. S., & Funk, R. R. (2005). Working alliance, treatment satisfaction, and patterns of post-treatment use among adolescent substance users. *Psychology of Addictive Behavior, 19*, 199–207.

Weiss, B., & Weisz, J. (1995). Relative effectiveness of behavioral versus nonbehavioral child psychotherapy. *Journal of Consulting and Clinical Psychology, 63*(2), 317–320.

Weisz, J., Jensen-Doss, A., & Hawley, K. (2006). Evidence-based youth psychotherapy versus usual clinical care: A meta-analysis of direct comparisons. *American Psychologist, 61*, 671–689.

Weisz, J., Weiss, B., Han, S., Granger, D., & Morton, T. (1995). Effects of psychotherapy with children and adolescents revisited: A meta-analysis of treatment outcome studies. *Psychological Bulletin, 117*(3), 450–468.

Weisz, J. R., Weiss, B., Alicke, M. D., & Klotz, M. L. (1987). Effectiveness of psychotherapy with children and adolescents: A meta-analysis for clinicians. *Journal of Consulting and Clinical Psychology, 55*, 542–549.

Wintersteen, M., Mensinger, J., & Diamond, G. (2005). Do gender and racial differences between patient and therapist affect therapeutic alliance and treatment retention in adolescents? *Professional Psychology: Research and Practice, 36*(4), 400–408.

Wright, L., Everett, F., & Roisman, L. (1986). *Experiential psychotherapy with children.* Baltimore: Johns Hopkins University Press.

Zack, S., Castonguay, L., & Boswell, J. (2007). Youth working alliance: A core clinical construct in need of empirical maturity. *Harvard Review of Psychiatry, 15*, 278–285.

*Zaitsoff, S., Doyle, A., Hoste, R., & le Grange, D. (2008). How do adolescents with bulimia nervosa rate the acceptability and therapeutic relationship in family-based treatment? *International Journal of Eating Disorders, 41*(5), 390–398.

4 Alliance in Couple and Family Therapy

Myrna L. Friedlander, Valentín Escudero, Laurie Heatherington, *and* Gary M. Diamond

Although the salience of the working alliance in couple and family therapy (CFT) was recognized over 20 years ago, it has received far less theoretical and empirical attention than has the alliance in individual psychotherapy. In their seminal work on CFT alliances, Pinsof and Catherall (1986; Catherall, 1984) took Bordin's (1979) conceptualization of the alliance as a point of departure and applied the goal, task, and bond constructs to three interpersonal facets of the alliance in family treatment (self-with-therapist, other-with-therapist, and group-with-therapist). The rationale was that not only do family members vary in the degree to which they form a personal bond and agree with the therapist about treatment goals and tasks, but also each person observes, can report on, and is influenced by how others in the family feel about the therapy and by how the couple or family unit as a whole is responding to what is taking place in treatment (Pinsof & Catherall, 1986). Thus, from its first introduction into the literature, the CFT alliance was described as unique, complex, and multilayered. It is no longer in question that, as a treatment format, CFT demands a unique conceptualization of the alliance.

In this chapter we define CFT alliances, summarize the major observational and self-report measures, and offer an extended clinical example. We then report the results of our original meta-analysis of the CFT alliance outcome studies published through 2008. We summarize the literature on moderators, mediators, and client contributions to CFT alliances, discuss the limitations of the research, and conclude with recommended clinical practices on the basis of the meta-analysis.

Definitions and Measures

Creating and sustaining CFT alliances are complicated by the fact that family members often seek psychotherapy as a last resort, when the conflicts among them seem irreconcilable. Moreover, it is common for family members to have different motives and motivational levels for treatment, and sometimes disagree about whether there even exists a problem that requires professional attention. Even when a problem is jointly acknowledged, for example, "We fight all the time," therapy may not be seen as the solution, or individuals' goals may differ ("You need to stop drinking" versus "We need to be a couple—it's like we're living parallel lives") (Friedlander, Escudero, & Heatherington, 2006; Lambert, Skinner, & Friedlander, in press). Consequently, family members' willingness to engage in various therapy tasks may also differ ("Why should we argue about my drinking if you don't even want to stay married to me?"). Indeed, it is not uncommon for one partner or family member to feel like a therapy hostage ("Come to therapy with me or else …") or expect the therapist to take sides, particularly if the problem is defined in zero-sum terms (e.g., to divorce or not, to have a baby or not, to relocate or not) (Friedlander, Escudero, & Heatherington, 2006).

CFT alliances develop simultaneously on an individual level (self-with-therapist) and a group level (group-with-therapist). Just as in individual therapy, alliances in CFT involve the creation of a strong emotional bond as well as negotiation of goals and tasks with the therapist. A unique characteristic of CFT, though, is that at any point in treatment there are multiple alliances that interact systemically. For example, the degree to which a mother likes the psychotherapist and is engaged in the treatment may have a facilitating (or hindering) effect on her son's willingness to trust the therapist. The son's involvement also depends on the mother–son bond and whether he agrees with his mother about the nature of the problems, goals, or need for treatment. Moreover, the family members' degree of comfort with one another affects each person's willingness to negotiate goals with the others and with the therapist. In other words, every individual simultaneously creates a personal alliance with the therapist, and each person's alliance with the therapist can negatively or positively affect the others'.

An important aspect of CFT alliances is the degree to which family members feel safe and comfortable with each other in the therapeutic context. The revelation of secrets and in-session exploration of conflicts are not easily left behind in the consulting room at the end of the session. Family members go home together, and therapy can only progress if they feel that the material discussed in-session is not used against them during the course of the week

(Friedlander, 2000). Breaches of safety can severely undermine a client's trust in the therapist and the therapeutic process. Moreover, the degree of safety felt by family members can change as new problems are revealed and explored and as different family members join or leave treatment (Beck, Friedlander, & Escudero, 2006). What feels safe to the children when only their father is there, for example, might feel quite unsafe when their stepmother is present. Likewise, it may seem safer in couples therapy to discuss conflicts over parenting than to explore expectations about intimacy or sexuality. In CFT, the conjoint nature of the treatment and ever-changing composition of sessions makes creating a safe environment both complicated and critical.

A related construct is the group aspect of the alliance, which has alternately been conceptualized as *allegiance* (Symonds & Horvath, 2004), *within-family alliance* (Pinsof, 1994), and *shared sense of purpose* (Friedlander, Escudero, & Heatherington, 2006). A complex part of the conjoint therapy process, this "we-ness" refers not only to a willingness to collaborate in treatment but also to a strong emotional bond between and among family members. In other words, the within-family alliance has more to do with family members' thoughts, feelings, and behavior toward one another than it does with any one person's alliance with the therapist considered in isolation.

Moreover, the within-family alliance develops simultaneously and in interaction with all of the individual alliances. Indeed, research shows that family members often see their personal relationships with the therapist differently from their allegiance with each other (e.g., Beck et al., 2006; Friedlander, Lambert, Escudero, & Cragun, 2008; Lambert et al., in press). For this reason, a complete picture of the alliance requires some accounting of how well the family works together in therapy as well as how similarly individuals feel about the therapist.

When alliances are "split" (Heatherington & Friedlander, 1990; Pinsof & Catherall, 1986) or "unbalanced" (Robbins, Turner, Alexander, & Perez, 2003), at least one family member has a stronger bond with the therapist than do other family members. There is ample evidence that, in both couples and family therapy, split alliances occur frequently and vary in severity (Heatherington & Friedlander, 1990; Mamodhoussen, Wright, Tremblay, & Poitras-Wright, 2005; Muñiz de la Peña, Friedlander, & Escudero, 2009). In family therapy, although we might expect parents to feel a greater connection with the therapist than do their adolescents, and indeed such a split alliance pattern has been found in several studies, in at least one study several of the adolescents felt closer to the therapist than did their parents (Muñiz de la Peña et al., 2009). Although severely split alliances often lead to premature termination, this is not invariably the case (Muñiz de la Peña et al., 2009), and splits may occur in reverse as new topics or are explored or secrets are revealed.

To assess CFT alliances, the most widely used self-report measures are the Couple Therapy Alliance Scale (CTAS; Pinsof & Catherall, 1986) and the Family Therapy Alliance Scale (FTAS), which were revised to include the Within Alliance, "My partner and I…." (couple) and "Some of the other members of my family and I …" (family). Like the couple version of the Working Alliance Inventory (WAI-Co; Symonds, 1999), the CTAS and FTAS reflect Bordin's (1979) concept of goals, tasks, and bonds. However, unlike the 63-item WAI-Co, which also has a therapist version and yields a total alliance score as well as 9 subscale scores (Goals, Tasks, and Bonds crossed with Self, Partner, and Group), the shortened CTAS-r and FTAS-r

(Pinsof, Zinbarg, & Knobloch-Fedders, 2008) only has 12 items in 3 subscales: Self/Group, Other, and Within. Self and Group were combined because these subscales were indistinguishable both statistically and experientially, and factor analyses did not support the independence of the original Goals, Tasks, and Bonds subscales.

Only one measure of the alliance includes the element of safety. In the System for Observing Family Therapy Alliances (SOFTA; Friedlander, Escudero, & Heatherington, 2006; Friedlander, Escudero, Horvath et al., 2006) or Sistema de la Observación de la Alianza en Terapia Familiar (SOATIF; Escudero & Friedlander, 2003), Safety is one of four alliance dimensions. In brief, *Safety within the Therapeutic System* reflects each client's degree of comfort taking risks, being vulnerable, and exploring conflicts with a therapist and other family members, *Engagement in the Therapeutic Process* reflects Bordin's (1979) agreement with the therapist on tasks and goals, *Emotional Connection with the Therapist* is similar to Bordin's concept of client–therapist bond, and *Shared Sense of Purpose within the Family* refers to productive family collaboration (the within-family alliance).

The pantheoretical SOFTA contains observational (SOFTA-o; Friedlander, Escudero, & Heatherington, 2006; Friedlander, Escudero, Horvath, et al., 2006; Friedlander, Lambert, & Muñiz de la Peña, 2008) and 16-item self-report (SOFTA-s; Friedlander, Escudero, & Heatherington, 2006; Friedlander, Lambert et al., 2008; Lambert & Friedlander, 2008) measures from both client and therapist perspectives. Whereas the client version reflects the strength of the alliance, the therapist version assesses alliance-related interventions. Using the SOFTA-o, trained raters observe a videotaped or live session, tallying the frequency of specific positive behaviors, for example, "Client introduces a problem for discussion"

(Engagement), and negative behaviors, for example, "Family members try to align with the therapist against each other" (Shared Purpose), and using these tallies to make a global rating for each alliance dimension. To date there has only been one published study with the therapist version (Friedlander, Lambert et al., 2008), a comparison of good and poor outcome cases with the same therapist.

CFT alliances have also been studied using the Vanderbilt Therapeutic Alliance Scale (Hartley & Strupp, 1983), an observational measure developed for individual psychotherapy and subsequently revised for CFT (VTAS-R; Diamond, Liddle, Dakof, & Hogue, 1996). Recently, the 26 Patient Contribution items in the VTAS-R were pared down through factor and item analyses to a 5-item scale (Shelef & Diamond, 2008) that includes three client behaviors reflecting bonds and tasks and two client + therapist behaviors reflecting goals and tasks. The VTAS-R requires raters to provide global judgments of each client's overall behavior and therapist–client interactions across an entire session, for example, "To what extent did the patient indicate that she experiences the therapist as understanding and supporting her?" (Shelef & Diamond, 2008, p. 439).

Case Example
A middle-aged couple brought their reluctant 15-year-old son and 13-year-old daughter to psychotherapy. The girl, who exhibited anxiety and an eating disorder (only at home), refused to speak in the session, as did the boy, who had vandalized a neighbor's car and was failing in school. While the parents barely glanced at each other, both adamantly insisted that their children were in desperate need of help. Thus ended the first session, which clearly evidenced a lack of safety all around and an exceedingly poor within-family alliance.

Because it was obvious that conjoint sessions with the four family members would not be productive at this stage of treatment, the therapist proposed holding the next two sessions with the teens and the parents separately. Indeed, this seemed to be the only arrangement that could provide even a modest amount of safety. In the children's session, the boy willingly expressed concern about his sister, but he cavalierly dismissed his own problems. For her part, the girl denied being anxious or having eating problems and, instead, complained about how her brother constantly annoyed her. As siblings, they collaborated minimally, each one only willing to talk about the other's problems. When asked about relations with their parents, both teens remained silent. Finally, the son asked if the therapist thought he could help their parents, but the boy refused to clarify the basis for this request. Notably, the alliance seemed split: The boy was visibly more involved and connected with the (male) therapist than was his sister, whose sense of safety appeared to be quite fragile.

In their conjoint session, mother and father demonstrated even greater unease with each other. Not only did they not make eye contact or confer with one another, but they also sat on either end of the couch, their bodies positioned in opposing directions. Although both parents cooperatively described the children's problems, they refused to discuss their own relationship. Finally, the husband haltingly explained that "after something happened," he and his wife had agreed that the marriage was finished. This "emotional divorce" was unknown to the children, however. Because neither parent was willing to leave the home, they planned to continue living together until both children grew up and moved out. After that, they would separate. Neither client was willing to consider couples work, as they were in agreement that their marriage was a "lost cause." They were, however, willing to come for sessions if it would help their children.

Interestingly, within each subsystem there was a shared sense of purpose, at least about why they would continue coming to therapy: The children agreed to be seen so that the therapist would help their parents, and the parents agreed to come in order to help their children.

Given this curious arrangement and everyone's clear fear of taking emotional risks, the therapist continued to see each subsystem weekly. He found it relatively easier to develop a personal bond with the son and the mother. By working hard to enhance his connection with the daughter and father, the therapist gradually became a trusted figure, and slowly everyone began to engage more freely in the therapeutic work. Because the adolescents adamantly refused to acknowledge their own problems and were clearly protecting their parents— never criticizing them or even acknowledging their parents' overt hostility—the therapist focused solely on improving the sibling bond. In one homework assignment, for example, the girl was asked to choose a set of digital family photos that held happy memories for her, and her brother was asked to arrange these pictures into a slideshow that he would set to music.

As brother and sister began fighting less at home and cautiously started to enjoy each other's company, both parents began to trust the therapist more. However, they rarely looked at one another in session, and the chasm between them remained as deep as ever.

Alone with the parents in Week 5, the therapist made some strategic moves. Focusing first on the within-system alliance, he praised their mutual dedication to their children, pointing out how they were both willing to "sacrifice [their] personal happiness to keep the family together." For the first time, the spouses looked at and spoke directly to one another. When the husband made a joke that his wife smiled at, the therapist commented that they both seemed to be experiencing "deep hurts" that they were afraid to express. He said that he wanted it to "see if there was another way for [their marital] relationship to improve, if only to keep on helping the children."

The mother, who seemed to trust the therapist a great deal, admitted thinking that the children were "reacting" to the emotional divorce. Moving closer to her, the therapist softly commented that, "As a parent myself, I know it's extremely hard to realize that something I've done has hurt my children." The mother responded with tears, and at the end of the session admitted that the children "deserved to be told" about the status of the marriage. The husband agreed, albeit reluctantly.

The parents chose to reveal the secret at home rather than in a family session. In their next session (alone) with the therapist, the teens no longer felt the need to protect their parents. They responded positively to the therapist's empathic response to their expressions of resentment and sadness. When the daughter burst out, "But we're not a real family!," the therapist replied by proposing a new shared sense of purpose, in other words, a common goal: "I disagree. Both of your parents care for you and want the best for you, and both of you feel the same for your parents. I'm sure you can learn to work together so that everyone has a happier life."

Over the next month, the teens pushed their parents into committing to couples therapy, with the goal of either working out their differences or deciding to separate. Although the son's grades in school did not improve substantially, he had no further delinquent offenses. The daughter remained highly stressed but ate normally and began spending more time with friends.

This case illustrates how an alliance-empowering approach can potentially repair seriously broken within-family attachments. By strategically focusing on different alliances and different aspects of each alliance, this therapist moved a stalled treatment forward. He began by separating the parents and children to enhance safety and negotiate different problem definitions and goals within each subsystem. With the adolescents, the therapist relied heavily on five interventions that have been shown to improve poor alliances with teens (Diamond et al., 1999): He emphasized trust, honesty and confidentiality; he explained the importance of collaborating in therapy; he defined personally meaningful goals for each child; and, most importantly, he presented himself as an ally in the one thing the children agreed on—helping their parents. Then, by encouraging engagement in therapy tasks through his personal bond with each family member, the therapist eventually redefined the family's problem and the treatment goals in a way that was both respectful and challenging. The success of this process goal, to create a within-family shared sense of purpose, seemed largely due to the therapist's attending to and emphasizing the strong parent–child bonds.

Meta-Analysis

Table 4.1 summarizes 24 studies in which CFT alliances, self-reported and observed, were used to predict treatment retention, improvement midtreatment, and/or final outcomes. To obtain as comprehensive a sample as possible, we cross-referenced articles known to us and searched electronically (PsycINFO, PubMed, Social Sciences Citation Index) for additional alliance-related studies in CFT. Unpublished dissertations were excluded, as were analog studies. Only articles published in English with validated measures of the alliance were included.

Seven of the 24 were studies of couples therapy (2 of which were conducted in groups), and the remaining 17 were family studies in which at least a portion of the treatment was conducted conjointly. The total number of clients who participated in these 24 studies is 1,461. Studies examined both treatment as usual as well as specifically defined approaches, including cognitive-behavioral therapy, functional family therapy, family-based therapy, systemic and ecosystemic-oriented therapy, emotion-focused therapy, integrative problem-centered therapy, multidimensional family therapy, brief strategic family therapy, parent management training, and psycho-educative family therapy. Most of the treatments were no more than 20 sessions in length, and the majority (65%) described the therapy as manualized treatment, although only a few studies provided information about treatment integrity.

The problems targeted in these treatments ranged from parent–adolescent communication difficulties to substance abuse, child abuse or neglect, and schizophrenia. Some studies were highly specific in defining the presenting problems or disorders, but many other studies identified the clients' problems in a general way. The samples in the more naturalistic studies tended to have a variety of presenting issues.

The instruments and methods used to evaluate outcome reflect the variability in problems treated. In terms of measures, roughly 50% of the studies used an observational methodology. Most evaluated the alliance early in the therapy, and only a few studies assessed the alliance at different stages of treatment (early, middle, and late). The observational instruments were primarily the SOFTA-o and the VTAS; the WAI and CTAS/FTAS were most often used to measure self-reported alliance. Five of the 24 studies did not measure

Table 4.1   Summary of Alliance Outcome Studies in CFT

Study	Treatment		Alliance			Outcome	Overall effect size	
	Therapy model	Format	Rater	Measure	Time	Measure	Wt. Ave. r	Ave. N
Bourgeois et al. (1990)	CSP	Couples group	C, T	CTAS	E	Dyadic Adjustment Scale, Marital Happiness Scale, Potential Problem Checklist	0.43	63
Brown & O'Leary (2000)	CBT, PE	Couples group	O	WAI	E	Psychological Maltreatment of Women Scale, Modified Conflict Tactics Scale	0.53	70
Escudero et al. (2008)	BFT	Family	O	SOFTA	E, L	Perceived therapeutic improvement	0.22	68
Flicker et al. (2008)	FFT	Family	O	VTAS-R	E	Completion vs. dropout	0.25	86
Friedlander et al. (2008)	FS	Family	O	SOFTA	E	Perceived improvement-so-far	0.35	33
Greenberg et al. (2010)	EFT	Couple	C	CTAS	E	Enright Forgiveness Inventory	0.35	40
Hawley & Garland (2008)	FS	Family	C, T	WAI	E, L	Youth Symptom Self-Report	0.33	36.7
Hogue et al. (2006)	MDFT	Family	O	VTAS-R	E	Child Behavior Checklist (internalizing, externalizing), Timeline Follow-Back interview for substance use	0.05	44
Johnson et al. (2006)	EcoS	Family, home based	C	FTAS (tasks)	L	Outcome Questionnaire, Inventory of Parent and Peer Attachment	0.46	32
Johnson & Ketring (2006)	EcoS	Family, home based	C	FTAS (bond)	L	Outcome Questionnaire 45.2 -Symptom Distress subscale, Conflict Tactics Scale - Physical Aggression Subscale	0.10	430
Johnson & Talitman (1997)	EFT	Couple	C	CTAS	E	Dyadic Adjustment Scale, Miller Social Intimacy Scale	0.54	23
Kazdin et al. (2005)	PE	Family	T, C	WAI, CTAS	E, L	Treatment Improvement Scale, Marital Satisfaction Scale	0.32	49
Knobloch et al. (2007)	IPCT	Couple	C	CTAS	E, L	Marital Satisfaction Inventory Revised	0.39	37
Pereira et al. (2006)	FBT	Family	O	WAI	E, L	Eating Disorders Examination	0.32	31.4

(Continued)

Table 4.1   Continued

Study	Treatment		Alliance			Outcome	Overall effect size	
	Therapy model	Format	Rater	Measure	Time	Measure	Wt. Ave. r	Ave. N
Pinsof et al. (2008)	IPCT	Couple	C	CTAS-R	E, L	COMPASS Treatment Assessment System, Marital Satisfaction Inventory Revised	0.31	80
Quinn et al. (1997)	FS	Family	C	FTAS	E	Goal achievement and expectation of maintenance	0.53	19
Raytek et al. (1999)	CBT	Marital	O	VTAS-R	E	Attrition status (completers, partial completers, vs. early dropouts)	0.37	66
Robbins et al. (2003)	FFT	Family	O	VTAS-R	E	Completion vs. dropout	0.29	34
Robbins et al. (2006)	MDFT	Family	O	VTAS-R	E	Completion vs. dropout	0.35	30
Robbins et al. (2008)	BSFT	Family	O	VTAS-R	E	Completion vs. dropout	0.36	31
Shelef et al. (2005)	MDFT	Family	C, O	WAI	E	Global Appraisal of Individual Needs, Substance Problem Index	0.24	59
Shelef & Diamond (2008)	MDFT	Family	O	VTAS-R	E, L	Completion vs. dropout, days of cannabis use	0.41	45
Smerud & Rosenfarb (2008)	PE	Family	O	SOFTA	L	Brief Psychiatric Rating Scale, Social Adjustment Scale-II, days until first rehospitalization, days until first use of rescue medication, Patient Rejection Scale	0.54	28
Symonds & Horvath (2004)	NS	Couple	C	WAI-Co	E	Marital Satisfaction Scale (female)	0.37	22.4

Note: N refers to the average sample size for the various correlations used in the within-study meta-analysis, i.e., not the *N* in the entire study. CSP = Couple Survival Program; CBT = cognitive-behavioral therapy; PE = psycho-educative; BFT = brief family therapy; FFT = functional family therapy; FS = family systems; EFT = emotion-focused therapy; MDFT = multidimensional family therapy; EcoS = ecosystemic therapy; FBT = family-based therapy; IPCT= integrative problem-centered therapy; BMT = behavioral marital therapy; BSFT = brief strategic family therapy; NS = not specified. C = client self-report; T = therapist self-report; O= external observer. CTAS = Couple Therapy Alliance Scale (Pinsof & Catherall, 1986); CTAS-r = Couple Therapy Alliance Scale-Revised (Pinsof et al., 2008); FTAS = Family Therapy Alliance Scale (Pinsof & Catherall, 1986); SOFTA-o: System for Observing Family Therapy Alliances - observer (Friedlander, Escudero, & Heatherington, 2006); VTAS-R = Vanderbilt Therapeutic Alliance Scale - Revised (Diamond et al., 1996); WAI = Working Alliance Inventory (Horvath & Greenberg, 1986); WAI-Co = Working Alliance Inventory - couple (Symonds & Horvath, 2004). E = early; L = late.

client outcome but, rather, only explored associations between alliance and treatment retention.

For the meta-analysis of correlation coefficients, we used the recommendations and computation program of Diener, Hilsenroth, and Weinberger (2009), which are based on Hunter and Schmidt's (1990) random-effects approach. For studies that reported statistics other than correlation coefficients (e.g., a *t* test to compare the alliance in families that completed therapy versus those that dropped out), we calculated the corresponding conversions to r (using Diener et al.'s (2009) computation program).

Because of the complex structure of alliance in family therapy (multiple participants generating multiple levels of analysis), most of the 24 studies reported more than a single alliance–outcome correlation. In these cases, we calculated a meta-analytic statistic within each study in order to maintain statistical assumption of independence. These calculations were conducted in the same way as the meta-analytic calculations for the entire group of 24 studies. That is, the effect sizes listed in the far right column of Table 4.1 were calculated from aggregated correlations within each study (Diener et al., 2009; Hunter & Schmidt, 1990). We also calculated the weighted average effect size of the 24 studies, minimizing sampling error by weighting each study by its sample size.

The resulting weighted average effect size for the 24 studies was $r = 0.26$. The standardized normal test for determining whether an aggregate r is statistically significant yielded $z = 8.13$, which is sufficiently large to reject the null hypothesis ($p < 0.005$). The upper and lower limits of the weighted average effect size calculated for a 95% confidence interval were 0.33 and 0.20, respectively.

These results indicate that the association between alliance and outcome in couple and family therapy was statistically significant. According to conventional benchmarks, an r of 0.26 ($d = 0.53$), which is a medium effect size in the behavioral sciences, is quite similar to the $r = 0.275$ reported in Chapter 2 of this book for the alliance–outcome relation in individual therapy.

In addition to statistical significance, the meta-analytic results demonstrated that alliance accounted for a substantial proportion of variance in CFT retention and/or outcome. At the same time, evident differences in the designs, measures, treatment formats, and problems treated in the group of 24 studies made it essential to test for variables that may moderate the average effect size. We performed a chi-square test to examine the homogeneity of various subsamples.

The resulting $\chi^2 = 43.52$, $p < 0.005$, indicated that the null hypothesis of homogeneity was rejected. In other words, there was unaccounted-for variability among the effects produced by the various studies. Consequently, we explored various moderators that might explain the heterogeneity.

Moderators and Mediators

We computed a series of moderator analyses with various subsamples. First, analysis of the 17 family studies showed a similar average weighted effect size ($r = 0.24$; $z = 6.55$, $p < 0.005$), and the null hypothesis of homogeneity was rejected ($\chi^2 = 27.77$, $p < 0.05$). In other words, the group of studies with a family therapy format had significant unexplained variability in the relation between alliance and outcome. (The subsample of seven couple studies was too small to test for either effect size or homogeneity.)

Second, we analyzed the 13 studies that used observational (rather than self-report) measures of the alliance. This result showed a somewhat higher global effect size (weighted average $r = 0.33$; $z = 8.85$, $p < 0.001$), and the variability in these studies was not large enough to reject the null hypothesis of homogeneity ($\chi^2 = 16.48$, ns). By contrast, the 11 studies that used self-reported alliances had a slightly lower effect size (weighted average $r = 0.22$; $z = 4.46$, $p < 0.01$). In this analysis, the homogeneity hypothesis was rejected ($\chi^2 = 22.39$, $p < 0.02$), possibly due to the diversity of perspectives (parents', children's, partners' and therapists') in self-report studies of alliance.

Taken together, these results mean that in every subsample tested, the alliance in CFT accounted for a substantial proportion of variance in treatment retention and/or outcome. However, the most homogeneous studies were the observational ones, likely due to the fact that trained external observers use well-defined behavioral criteria to assess the alliance. By contrast, in the family studies and in the studies that relied on self-report to assess alliance, the alliance–outcome relation was more variable.

These divergences in effect sizes across the outcome studies, as well as complex findings *within* these studies, raise questions about the circumstances under which the alliance figures more or less strongly in outcomes. Because very few direct tests of moderators and mediators have been conducted, a meta-analysis was not possible. In this section, we summarize what is known and what has been suggested about moderators and mediators of the alliance–outcome relation in CFT.

Alliance and Treatment Retention

Good outcomes depend on treatment attendance, and retention in family therapy is particularly challenging, as any one person's strong negative feelings can lead to premature termination for the entire family. For this reason there has been significant work in CFT on strategies for engaging and retaining families, especially families with drug-using adolescents (cf. Liddle et al., 1992; Szapoznick et al., 1988).

Regarding retention, the only clear moderator is *family role*—parent, spouse, child. First, we note that the composite index of CFT alliance, that is, an average of all family members' alliances, is not predictive of retention (or outcome). Rather, more nuanced indices of alliance matter: (a) the interplay of each individual family member's alliance with the therapist, and (b) unbalanced alliances, in various

permutations (mother–child, father–mother, etc.). For example, with adolescents who have externalizing problems (Shelef & Diamond, 2008) or anorexia (Pereira, Lock, & Oggins, 2006), research has found that the parents' (but not the youths') alliances predicted treatment completion. Further, in other studies with externalizing adolescents (Robbins et al., 2006, 2008), both the children's and the parents' alliances with the therapist discriminated dropout from completer families. Unbalanced alliances tend to be negatively related to retention, and this relation is also moderated in complex ways by family role. Unbalanced father-adolescent alliances (where the first person in the pair is the one with the higher alliance) discriminated dropout from completer families in functional family therapy (FFT; Robbins, Turner, Alexander, & Perez, 2003), and increasingly unbalanced mother–adolescent alliances and unbalanced mother–father alliances characterized families who dropped out of brief strategic family therapy (Robbins et al., 2008). Further, unbalanced parent–adolescent alliances in FFT discriminated dropout from completer Hispanic families but not Anglo families (Flicker, Turner et al., 2008).

Therapist experience has not been systematically manipulated in any study, although experience did differ across studies, prompting some thoughtful speculation (Flicker & Turner, 2008) about how it might account for differing results. Therapist experience was positively associated with the alliance (as measured by observer ratings of therapist behavior and errors in technique) in conjoint alcoholism treatment for couples (Raytek, McCready, Epstein, & Hirsch, 1999). A qualitative analysis revealed that experienced therapists were relatively more active, more responsive to topics initiated by clients, more flexible in following manualized treatment guidelines, and better at managing the couples' negativity. The authors suggested that such responsiveness and flexibility strengthened the emotional bond with the therapist and the clients' involvement in treatment, which in turn facilitated retention in therapy.

Couples Therapy Outcomes

In general, with respect to *gender*, the man's alliance tends to be more strongly associated with outcome in both group marital therapy (Bourgeois, Sabourin, Wright, 1990; Brown & O'Leary, 2000) and couples therapy (Symonds & Horvath, 2004). Less frequently, the woman's alliance is the stronger predictor of outcome (Knobloch-Fedders, Pinsof, & Mann, 2007). Explanations for the gender difference focus on the documented greater reluctance of men to engage in treatment, as well as their relative power in some couples (especially where there is abuse), and women's relatively higher commitment and "ability to work toward positive outcomes regardless of the relative strength of their relationship with the therapist" (Symonds & Horvath, 2004, p. 453).

Family Therapy Outcomes

In outcome studies of conjoint family therapy, *family role* emerged as the most consistent (albeit complex) potential moderator; its effects vary depending on the measures used and the treatment administered. A study of family treatment for anorexia nervosa (Pereira et al., 2006), for example, found that adolescents' (but not parents') observed alliance with the therapist predicted early weight gain, whereas parents' alliance later in therapy was associated with teens' overall weight gain.

Similarly, in a study of family treatment for adolescent substance abuse (Shelef et al., 2005), observer measures (but not self-report measures) of adolescents' alliance predicted posttreatment outcomes, whereas

parent measures did not. Moreover, adolescent alliance predicted outcome only in cases in which the parent–therapist alliance was moderate to strong. In a study of outpatient psychotherapy "as usual" that combined individual and conjoint parent–teen sessions, youths' alliance predicted outcomes (youth symptom improvement, family functioning) as reported by all family members, whereas parents' alliance predicted fewer outcomes and only their own (i.e., not their childrens') ratings of treatment success (Hawley & Garland 2008).

Interestingly, there is no evidence that therapist gender, race/ethnicity, or therapist–family ethnic match are significant factors in the strength of alliance. Nor have they been found to moderate the CFT alliance–outcome relation.

Type of treatment may moderate the alliance–outcome relation, given the differences in findings across studies that employed different kinds of treatment. In a study of behavioral family management treatment for schizophrenia (Smerud & Rosenfarb, 2008), only the relatives' observed alliances predicted the patient's reoccurrence of symptoms, a finding that underscores the importance of family environment in preventing relapse in major mental illness. Interestingly, patients' alliance predicted less rejection by relatives and less care burden, suggesting that alliances in one subsystem may have positive effects on others. Another study (Hogue et al., 2006) that compared cognitive-behavior therapy (CBT) and multidimensional family therapy (MDFT) for adolescent substance abuse found that in CBT, the adolescents' alliance was not associated with outcome, whereas in MDFT both the youths' and the parents' alliances were associated with outcomes, albeit in different ways. Finally, in a study of home-based family therapy, the youths' *attachment*, as measured by trust in each parent, in tandem with the "tasks" dimension of the alliance, predicted symptom reduction (Johnson, Ketring, Rohacs, & Brewer, 2006). The quality of parents' attachment relationships with their children was not a significant moderator, however.

We located only one study that specifically tested a mediating model (Friedlander et al., 2008). In this study, the within-family alliance (shared sense of purpose within the family) mediated the relationship between the parents' observed sense of safety in Session 1 and their ratings of improvement-so-far in Session 3. In other words, parents who felt comfortable in the first session were more likely to exhibit a strong within-family alliance that, in turn, predicted their perceptions of improvement after the third session. In another study (Escudero et al., 2008), within-family alliance was the only observed alliance dimension to increase over time; this dimension predicted therapists' perceptions of the alliance and ratings of improvement-so-far after Session 6. Although within-family alliance was not tested as a mediator, the latter findings suggest that a stronger shared sense of purpose may indeed be an important step along the way to treatment success.

Client Contributions

By its very definition, the alliance construct implies interaction and collaboration. For this reason, isolation of family members' contributions to the alliance is somewhat artificial. On the other hand, considering client contributions is essential as, during the session, therapists must gauge clients' receptivity and reactions to therapeutic change attempts.

The clinical CFT literature focuses almost exclusively on therapist behavior, with far less emphasis on client participation in treatment. One could well argue that *all* client behavior contributes to (or detracts from)

the alliance, just as some authors have claimed that all therapeutic interventions are indistinguishable from alliance building and maintenance (e.g., Hatcher & Barends, 2006). To some extent, clients' collaboration in therapy depends on the therapist's theoretical approach. Couples in behavioral therapy, for example, spend less time accessing primary emotions than do couples in emotion-focused therapy. Yet, on a different process level, clients' alliance-related behaviors cut across therapy approaches and formats. That is, like successful clients in individual therapy, successful family members form a close, trusting bond with their therapists and negotiate (and renegotiate) treatment goals and tasks. Regardless of the kinds of in-session or out-of-session tasks, clients who have a shared sense of purpose listen respectfully to one another, validate each other's perspective (even when they disagree), offer to compromise, and avoid excessive cross-blaming, hostility, and sarcasm. Family members who feel safe and comfortable in therapy are emotionally expressive, ask each other for feedback, encourage one another to open up and speak frankly, and share thoughts and feelings, even painful ones, that have never been expressed at home (Friedlander, Escudero, & Heatherington, 2006).

Couples Therapy

While scant, the literature offers some evidence about the personal characteristics and in-session behaviors of clients who develop strong working relationships in couples therapy. Research suggests that whereas psychiatric symptoms are not associated with alliance formation (Knobloch-Fedders, Pinsof, & Mann, 2004; Mamodhoussen et al., 2005), greater trust in the couple relationship (Johnson & Talitman, 1997) and less marital distress (Johnson & Talitman, 1997; Knobloch-Fedders et al., 2004) are predictive of more favorable alliances. In one study (Knobloch-Fedders et al., 2004), alliance development differed for men and women. For men, recalling positive experiences in the family of origin was most critical for early alliance development, whereas marital distress had a negative impact on the alliance later on. For women, sexual dissatisfaction was negatively associated with the alliance throughout therapy, and women's family-of-origin distress contributed to a split alliance early in the process.

With respect to in-session behavior, the findings from one study (Thomas et al., 2005) reflect the complexity of CFT alliances. Results showed that men were less likely to agree with the therapist on the goals for treatment when their partners made negative statements about them, whereas women tended to feel more negative about therapy tasks when they were challenged by their partners. Both men and women had a stronger bond with the therapist when their partners self-disclosed, and they felt more distant from the therapist when their partners challenged or made negative comments about them.

Family Therapy

In community-based family therapy, parental differentiation of self, assessed prior to the beginning of treatment, predicted stronger perceived alliances after Session 3 (Lambert & Friedlander, 2008). Well-differentiated individuals are able to balance thinking and feeling, autonomy and togetherness (Bowen, 1978). The most closely associated aspects of these two constructs were emotional reactivity and safety. That is, parents who reported being generally less emotionally reactive tended to feel safer and more comfortable in conjoint family therapy.

There is some evidence to suggest that diagnosis or presenting problem maybe associated with the alliance. For example,

a study of family-based therapy for anorexia nervosa found that teens with relatively more weight and eating concerns found it particularly difficult to establish an alliance with the therapist (Pereira et al., 2006). On the other hand, the nature of adolescents' emotional problems played no role in alliance development in a study of MDFT for drug-using adolescents (Shelef & Diamond, 2008). That study showed no variability in teens' alliance-related behavior based on pretreatment externalizing or internalizing behaviors.

Not surprisingly, alliances are stronger when family members respond favorably to therapists' alliance-building interventions. In a comparison of two families treated by the same experienced therapist (Friedlander, Lambert et al., 2008), clients in the poor-outcome case were less likely than those in the good-outcome case to respond positively to the therapist's alliance-related behaviors. Another small sample study, although not directly assessing the alliance, has implications for client contributions to a shared sense of purpose. In this study, family members moved from disengagement with each other to productive in-session collaboration when, with the therapist's help, they were willing and able to explore the underlying basis for their disengagement and recognize some motivation for breaking through the impasse (Friedlander, Heatherington, Johnson, & Skowron, 1994).

Limitations of the Research

The body of research covered in the meta-analysis is small but solid. Diverse client populations and therapy approaches have been sampled, and many of the treatments studied have strong empirical support and/or have been delivered by experienced therapists. Under these conditions, the finding that alliances predict treatment retention and outcome over and above specific therapy methods strengthens the case for the unique contribution of relationship variables in CFT. Nonetheless, there are limitations in this body of work that require caution in interpreting the findings and applying them to practice.

Considerable variation across studies in alliance instruments and in timing and rating source of the measurement make it challenging to interpret results. Understandably but unfortunately, sample sizes in many of the studies are small, rendering it difficult to test more than one or two moderators with confidence. Thus, much of what we know about moderators is speculative, based on results across different studies.

The bulk of the research to date focuses on drug-abusing, externalizing adolescents. The alliance–outcome associations found, as well as the kinds of therapist behaviors shown to strengthen the alliance, may largely be specific to these kinds of families. For this reason, it is unwise to generalize from these results to families with younger children or to families whose children have internalizing problems (depression, anxiety, eating disorders). The effects of unbalanced alliances, for example, may be weaker or nonexistent in families in which, by virtue of the child's age, symptoms, or psychological dynamics, the children are less inclined to resist treatment. Moreover, there are few studies of the alliance in family treatments for adults with major mental disorders, such as family psychoeducation for bipolar disorder and schizophrenia, despite the demonstrated efficacy of these treatments. Finally, little research to date has examined individual psychodynamics (e.g., attachment styles) as moderators. Attachment, in particular, has been a fruitful area of inquiry in the alliance research on individual therapy (see Chapter 19 by Levy et al., this volume). Given the importance of attachment for a couple's level of intimacy and for a family's level of cohesion, attachment may well mediate or moderate the relationship between alliance and treatment outcomes.

Although alliances develop and change over the course of psychotherapy, as several studies have shown, we have little knowledge about how multiple alliances develop over time and interact with each other. Furthermore, we have little information about how therapists behave in order to best nurture and sustain working alliances with multiple clients over time. Finally, we still have not fully answered the question of whether early symptom improvement in CFT actually prompts alliance development or is the consequence of a strong alliance.

Therapeutic Practices

- The first, perhaps most important practice implication is that the therapeutic alliance is a critical factor in the process and outcome of CFT. Our meta-analysis underscores the necessity to be aware of what is going within the system itself as well as to monitor the personal bond and agreement on goals and tasks with each individual family member.

- Knowing the importance of the alliance in CFT, practitioners are encouraged to systematically evaluate their alliances with clients. One option is periodically to ask clients to complete brief self-report measures of the alliance. Doing so would not only provide the therapist with crucial information regarding each client's private experience but also would provide the impetus for directly addressing the quality of the relationship and the therapy process and, if necessary, for focusing specifically on improving safety or repairing a seriously split alliance.

- Our findings suggest that evaluating the alliance based on observation is a skill that can be taught. Observationally measured alliances were as predictive of outcome and more homogeneous in their effect size than alliances measured using self-report. These findings suggest that therapists may be taught, or alternatively may train themselves, to validly assess the strength of their alliance with different family members by reviewing videotaped sessions (as was shown to be effective in the exploratory training study of Carpenter, Escudero, & Rivett, 2008).

- The meta-analytic findings also underscore the need to develop alliances with *all* family members. Therapists frequently identify more easily with, or feel a greater affinity to, one family member than another. However, the studies we reviewed indicate that each and every alliance exerts both a direct and an interactive effect on the course of treatment. For example, whereas a woman may feel connected to and aligned with the therapist from the outset of treatment, it may be the degree to which her disenfranchised partner develops a connection with the therapist that determines outcome. Findings from studies examining unbalanced alliances underscore this point, in that couples and families that experienced disparate alliances with the therapist tended to fare more poorly in treatment.

- One approach to developing multiple alliances is to establish overarching systemic goals (e.g., "It sounds like what the two of you want is a relationship in which you feel both connected and that you can sometimes do your own thing") that resonate for all family members rather than focusing on first-order, individual goals (i.e., "I want him to stop watching sports on TV every Sunday" or "I want her

to give me more space") that compete with one another. In this manner, therapists can facilitate a shared sense of purpose between family members regarding the goals of treatment and how they can productively collaborate to achieve these goals.

- Indeed, shared sense of purpose, a whole system aspect of the alliance, seems to be a particularly important dimension of the alliance. Creating a safe space, which is critical early on in therapy, is important for all therapy participants. A therapist who allies too strongly with an adolescent may unwittingly damage his or her alliance with the parents, particularly when the latter are expecting the child to change but are not expecting to be personally challenged by the therapist.

- In short, each person's alliance matters and alliances are not interchangeable. Thus, clinicians should build and maintain strong alliances with each party and be cognizant of the ways in which, depending on the couple or family dynamics, the whole alliance is not equal to the sum of its parts.

References

Beck, M., Friedlander, M. L., & Escudero, V. (2006). Three perspectives on clients' experiences of the therapeutic alliance: A discovery-oriented investigation. *Journal of Marital and Family Therapy, 32,* 355–68.

Bordin, E. S. (1979). The generalizability of the psychoanalytic concept of the working alliance. *Psychotherapy, 16,* 252–60.

Bourgeois, L., Sabourin, S., & Wright, J. (1990). Predictive validity of therapeutic alliance in group marital therapy. *Journal of Consulting and Clinical Psychology, 58,* 608–613.

Bowen, M. (1978). *Family therapy in clinical practice.* NY: Jason Aronson.

Brown, P. D., & O'Leary, K. D. (2000). Therapeutic alliance: Predicting continuance and success in group treatment for spouse abuse. *Journal of Consulting and Clinical Psychology, 68,* 340–45.

Carpenter, J., Escudero, V., & Rivett, M. (2008). Training family therapy students in conceptual and observation skills relating to the therapeutic alliance: An evaluation. *Journal of Family Therapy, 30*, 409–22.

Catherall, D. (1984). *The therapeutic alliance in individual, couple, and family therapy*. Unpublished doctoral dissertation, Northwestern University, Chicago, IL.

Diamond, G. M., Liddle, H. A., Dakof, G. A., & Hogue, A. (1996). *Revised version of the Vanderbilt Therapeutic Alliance Scale*. Unpublished manuscript, Temple University, Philadelphia, PA.

Diamond, G. M., Liddle, H. A., Hogue, A., & Dakof, G. A. (1999). Alliance-building interventions with adolescents in family therapy: A process study. *Psychotherapy, 36*, 355–68.

Diener, M. J., Hilsenroth, M. J., & Weinberger, J. (2009). A primer on meta-analysis of correlation coefficients: The relationship between patient-reported therapeutic alliance and adult attachment style as an illustration. *Psychotherapy Research, 19*, 519–26.

Escudero, V., & Friedlander, M. L. (2003). El sistema de observación de la alianza terapeutica en intervención familiar (SOATIF): Desarrollo trans-cultural, fiabilidad, y aplicaciones del instrumento. *Mosaico (Journal of the Spanish Federation of Family Therapy Associations), 25*, 32–36.

Escudero, V., Friedlander, M. L., Varela, N., & Abascal, A. (2008). Observing the therapeutic alliance in family therapy: Associations with participants' perceptions and therapeutic outcomes. *Journal of Family Therapy, 30*, 194–214.

Feeley, M., DeRubeis, R. J., & Gelfand, L. A. (1999). The temporal relation of adherence and alliance to symptom change in cognitive therapy for depression. *Journal of Consulting and Clinical Psychology, 67*, 578–82.

Flicker, S. M., Turner, C. W., Waldron, H. B., Ozechowski, T. J., & Brody, J. L. (2008). Ethnic background, therapeutic alliance, and treatment retention in functional family therapy with adolescents who abuse substances. *Journal of Family Psychology, 22*, 167–70.

Friedlander, M. L. (2000). Observational coding of family therapy processes: State of the art. In A. P. Beck & C. M. Lewis (Eds.), *The process of group psychotherapy: Systems for analyzing change* (pp. 67–84). Washington, DC: American Psychological Association.

Friedlander, M. L., Bernardi, S., & Lee, H. (2010). Better versus worse family therapy sessions as reflected in clients' alliance-related behavior. *Journal of Counseling Psychology, 57*, 198–204.

Friedlander, M. L., Escudero, V., & Heatherington, L. (2006). *Therapeutic alliances with couples and families: An empirically-informed guide to practice*. Washington, DC: American Psychological Association.

Friedlander, M. L., Escudero, V., Horvath, A., Heatherington, L., Cabero, A., & Martens, M. (2006). System for Observing Family Therapy Alliances: A tool for research and practice. *Journal of Counseling Psychology, 53*, 214–25.

Friedlander, M. L., Heatherington, L., Johnson, B., & Skowron, B. (1994). "Commitment to engage:" A change event in family therapy. *Journal of Counseling Psychology, 41*, 1–11.

Friedlander, M. L., Lambert, J. E., Escudero, V., & Cragun, C. (2008). How do therapists enhance family alliances? Sequential analyses of therapist–client behavior in two contrasting cases. *Psychotherapy: Theory, Research, Practice, Training, 45*, 75–87.

Friedlander, M. L., Lambert, J. E., & Muñiz de la Peña, C. (2008). A step toward disentangling the alliance/improvement cycle in family therapy. *Journal of Counseling Psychology, 55*, 118–24.

Greenberg, L. S., Warwar, S., & Malcolm, W. (2010). Emotion-focused couples therapy and facilitation of forgiveness. *Journal of Marital and Family Therapy, 36*, 28–42.

Hartley, D., & Strupp, H. H. (1983). The therapeutic alliance: Its relationship to outcome in brief psychotherapy. In J. Masling (Ed.)., *Empirical studies of psychoanalytic theories* (Vol. 1, pp. 1–37). Hillsdale, NJ: Erlbaum.

Hatcher, R. L., & Barends, A. W. (2006). How a return to theory could help alliance research. *Psychotherapy: Theory, Research, Practice, & Training, 43*, 292–99.

Hawley, K. M., & Garland, A. F. (2008). Working alliance in adolescent outpatient therapy: Youth, parent, & therapist reports and association with therapy outcomes. *Child and Youth Care Forum, 27*, 59–74.

Heatherington, L., & Friedlander, M. L. (1990). Couple and family therapy alliance scales: Empirical considerations. *Journal of Marital and Family Therapy, 16*, 299–306.

Hogue, A., Dauber, S., Stambaugh, L. F., Cecero, J. J., & Liddle, H. A. (2006). Early therapeutic alliance and treatment outcome in individual and family therapy for adolescent behavior problems. *Journal of Consulting and Clinical Psychology*, *74*, 121–29.

Horvath, A. O., & Greenberg, L. S. (1986). The development of the Working Alliance Inventory. In L. S. Greenberg & W. M. Pinsof (Eds.), *The psychotherapeutic process: A research handbook.* (pp. 529–56). New York: Guilford Press.

Hunter, J. E., & Schmidt, F. L. (1990). *Methods of meta-analysis: Correcting error and bias in research findings.* Newbury Park, CA: Sage.

Johnson, L. N., & Ketring, S. A. (2006). The therapy alliance: A moderator in therapy outcome for families dealing with child abuse and neglect. *Journal of Marital and Family Therapy*, *32*, 345–54.

Johnson, L. N., Ketring, S. A., Rohacs, J., & Brewer, A. L. (2006). Attachment and the therapeutic alliance in family therapy. *American Journal of Family Therapy*, *34*, 205–218.

Johnson, S. M., & Talitman, E. (1997). Predictors of success in emotionally focused marital therapy. *Journal of Marital and Family Therapy*, *23*, 135–53.

Kazdin, A. E., Marciano, P. L., & Whitley, M. K. (2005). The therapeutic alliance in cognitive-behavioral treatment of children referred for oppositional, aggressive, and antisocial behavior. *Journal of Consulting and Clinical Psychology*, *73*, 726–30.

Knobloch-Fedders, L. M., Pinsof, W. M., & Mann, B. J. (2007). Therapeutic alliance and treatment progress in couple psychotherapy. *Journal of Marital & Family Therapy*, *33*, 245–57.

Lambert, J. E., & Friedlander, M. L. (2008). Relationship of differentiation of self to adult clients' perceptions of the alliance in brief family therapy. *Psychotherapy Research*, *43*, 160–66.

Lambert, J., Skinner, A., & Friedlander, M. L. (in press). Problematic within-family alliances in conjoint family therapy: A close look at five cases. *Journal of Marital and Family Therapy*.

Liddle, H. A., Dakof, G., Diamond, G., Holt, M., Aroyo, J., & Watson, M. (1992). The adolescent module in multidimensional family therapy. Adolescent substance abuse: Etiology, treatment, and prevention. In G. W. Lawson & A. W. Lawson (Eds.), *Adolescent substance abuse: Etiology, treatment, and prevention* (pp. 165–86). Gaithersburg, MD: Aspen Publishers.

Mamodhoussen, S., Wright, J., Tremblay, N., & Poitras-Wright, H. (2005). Impact of marital and psychological distress on therapeutic alliance in couples undergoing couple therapy. *Journal of Marital and Family Therapy*, *31*, 159–69.

Muñiz de la Peña, C., Friedlander, M. L., & Escudero, V. (2009). Frequency, severity, and evolution of split family alliances: How observable are they? *Psychotherapy Research*, *19*, 133–42.

Pandyaa, K., & Herlhyb, J. (2009). An exploratory study into how a sample of a British South Asian population perceive the therapeutic alliances in family therapy. *Journal of Family Therapy*, *31*, 384–404.

Pereira, T., Lock, J., & Oggins, J. (2006). Role of therapeutic alliance in family therapy for adolescent anorexia nervosa. *International Journal of Eating Disorders*, *39*, 677–84.

Pinsof, W. B. (1994). An integrative systems perspective on the therapeutic alliance: Theoretical, clinical, and research implications. In A. O. Horvath & L. S. Greenberg (Eds.), *The working alliance: Theory, research, and practice* (pp. 173–95). New York: Wiley & Sons.

Pinsof, W. B., & Catherall, D. (1986). The integrative psychotherapy alliance: Family, couple, and individual therapy scales. *Journal of Marital and Family Therapy*, *12*, 137–51.

Pinsof, W. B., Zinbarg, R., & Knobloch-Fedders, L. M. (2008). Factorial and construct validity of the revised short form Integrative Psychotherapy Alliance Scales for family, couple, and individual therapy. *Family Process*, *47*, 281–301.

Quinn, W. H., Dotson, D., & Jordan, K. (1997). Dimensions of therapeutic alliance and their associations with outcome in family therapy. *Psychotherapy Research*, *7*, 429–38.

Rait, D. S. (1998). Perspectives on the therapeutic alliance in brief couples and family therapy. In J. D. Safran & J. C. Muran (Eds.), *The therapeutic alliance in brief psychotherapy* (pp. 171–91). Washington, DC: American Psychological Association.

Raytek, H. S., McCready, B. S., Epstein, E. E., & Hirsch, L. S. (1999). Therapeutic alliance and the retention of couples in conjoint alcoholism treatment. *Addictive Behaviors*, *24*, 317–30.

Robbins, M. S., Liddle, H. A., Turner, C. W., Dakof, G. A., Alexander, J. F., & Kogan, S. M. (2006). Adolescent and parent therapeutic alliances as predictors of dropout in multidimensional family therapy. *Journal of Family Psychology*, *20*, 108–116.

Robbins, M. S., Mayorga, C. C., Mitrani, V. B., Turner, C. W., Alexander, J. F., & Szapocznik, J. (2008).

Adolescent and parent alliances with therapists in brief strategic family therapy with drug-using Hispanic adolescents. *Journal of Marital & Family Therapy, 34*, 316–28.

Robbins, M. S., Turner, C. W., Alexander, J. F., & Perez, G.A. (2003). Alliance and dropout in family therapy for adolescents with behavior problems: Individual and systemic effects. *Journal of Family Psychology, 17*, 534–44.

Shelef, K., & Diamond, G. M. (2008). Short form of the Vanderbilt Therapeutic Alliance Scale: Development, reliability, and validity. *Psychotherapy Research, 18*, 433–43.

Shelef, K., Diamond, G. M., Diamond, G. S., & Liddle, H. A. (2005). Adolescent and parent alliance and treatment outcome in multidimensional family therapy. *Journal of Consulting and Clinical Psychology, 73*, 689–98.

Smerud, P. E., & Rosenfarb, I. S. (2008). The therapeutic alliance and family psychoeducation in the treatment of schizophrenia: An exploratory prospective change process study. *Journal of Consulting and Clinical Psychology, 76*, 505–510.

Symonds, B. D. (1999). *The measurement of alliance in short term couples therapy.* Unpublished doctoral dissertation, Simon Fraser University, Burnaby, British Columbia, Canada.

Symonds, B. D., & Horvath, A. O. (2004). Optimizing the alliance in couple therapy. *Family Process, 43*, 443–55.

Szapocznik, J., Perez-Vidal, A., Brickman, A., Foote, F. H., Santisteban, D. A., Hervis, O., et al. (1988). Engaging adolescent drug users and their families into treatment: A strategic structural approach. *Journal of Consulting and Clinical Psychology, 56*, 552–57.

Thomas, S. E. G., Werner-Wilson, R. J., & Murphy, M. J. (2005). Influence of therapist and client behaviors on therapy alliance. *Contemporary Family Therapy: An International Journal, 27*, 19–35.

5   Cohesion in Group Therapy

Gary M. Burlingame, Debra Theobald McClendon, *and* Jennifer Alonso

Cohesion is the most popular of several relationship constructs (e.g., alliance, group climate, group atmosphere) in the clinical and empirical literature on groups. Over time it has become synonymous with the therapeutic relationship in group psychotherapy (Burlingame, Fuhriman, & Johnson, 2002). From the perspective of a group member, relationships are comprised of three structural components: member–member, member–group, and member–leader. From the perspective of the therapist, relationships include the same three components as well as two additional ones: leader–group and, in the case of a cotherapy, leader–leader. The complexity of these multilevel structural definitions coupled with the dynamic interplay among them has created an array of competing cohesion instruments and an absence of a consensual definition.

In this chapter, we review the multiple measures of group cohesion and then discuss a new measure that elucidates group relationships by suggesting two latent factors that explain common variance among these group therapy relationship instruments—quality and structure. We provide clinical examples to illustrate the multiple facets of cohesion in group work. We then present an original meta-analytic review of cohesion's relation with treatment outcome and discuss potential moderators. We conclude

by providing a tabular summary of therapeutic practices that have been linked to increased cohesion. Our intent in this chapter is to illuminate the coherence in the cohesion literature, present the meta-analytic conclusions, and offer group leaders the measures and practices to improve treatment outcomes.

Definitions and Measures

Definitions of cohesion have traveled a serpentine trail (Bednar & Kaul, 1994; Crouch, Bloch, & Wanlass, 1994; Kivlighan, Coleman, & Anderson, 2000) ranging from broad and diffuse (e.g., forces that cause members to remain in the group, "sticking-togetherness") to focused (e.g., attractiveness, alliance) and structurally coherent (e.g., tripartite relationship; Yalom & Leszcz, 2005). At different times, reviewers have pleaded for definitional clarity with two noting that "there is little cohesion in the cohesion research" (Bednar & Kaul, 1978, p. 800). Indeed, instruments tapping group acceptance, emotional well-being, self-disclosure, interpersonal liking, and tolerance for personal space have been used as measures of cohesion (Burlingame et al., 2002). Behavioral definitions have included attendance, verbal content, early termination, physical seating distance, amount of eye contact, and the length of time group members engaged in a group hug

(Hornsey, Dwyer, & Oei, 2007). The definitional challenges of cohesion are reflected by one team's observation that "just about anything that has a positive valence [with outcome] has been interpreted at some point as an index of cohesion" (Hornsey, Dwyer, Oei, & Dingle, 2009, p. 272).

Empirical investigations examining the multidimensional structure of cohesion have reported as few as two and as many as five dimensions (Braaten, 1991; Cattell & Wispe, 1948; Griffith, 1988; Selvin & Hagstrom, 1963) with common factors including vertical and horizontal cohesion as well as task and social/affective cohesion. After reviewing the literature, we believe there is ample evidence to support two fundamental definitional dimensions of cohesion. The first dimension relates to the structure of the therapeutic relationship in groups and is most often referred to as vertical and horizontal cohesion (Dion, 2000). Vertical cohesion represents a member–leader relationship and refers to a group member's perception of the group leader's competence, genuineness, and warmth. Horizontal cohesion describes a group member's relationship with other group members and with the group as a whole. The second dimension contrasts task cohesion (task performance) or the work of the group with affective or emotional cohesion (interpersonal/emotional support; Griffith, 1988). In task cohesion, members are drawn to the group to accomplish a given task, while in affective cohesion members feel connected because of the emotional support the group experience affords.

The measures of cohesion that have been most frequently studied are summarized in Table 5.1. All but the Harvard measure (Budman et al., 1989) are self-report,

Table 5.1 Cohesion measures that appear two or more times in the literature

Cohesion Measure	Description of Measure Scales	Dimensions: Direction & Function
Group Climate Questionnaire (GCQ; MacKenzie, 1981, 1983)	• *Engaged* measures the degree of self-disclosure, cohesion, and work orientation in the group. • *Avoiding* examines the degree to which individuals rely on the other group members or leaders, avoiding responsibility for their own change process. • *Conflict* examines interpersonal conflict and distrust.	• Horizontal • Affective
Group Atmosphere Scale (GAS; Silbergeld et al., 1975)	• *Group Cohesion* includes: Autonomy, Affiliation, Involvement, Insight, Spontaneity, Support, and Clarity. • *Submission* examines group conformity. • *Aggression, Order, Practicality,* and *Variety* contribute to other aspects of perceived environment. Authors did not define these scales.	• Horizontal & Vertical • Affective
Feelings about group (Lieberman, Yalom & Miles, 1973)	• Modified from Schutz (1957) Cohesiveness Questionnaire; 13-item Likert scale • No subscales; items ask members to reflect on group participation, liking of group, inclusion in the group and feelings about leader • Designed to measure attractiveness of a group for its members and perceived belonging or acceptance by other members in the group.	• Horizontal & Vertical • Affective

(Continued)

Table 5.1 Continued

Cohesion Measure	Description of Measure Scales	Dimensions: Direction & Function
Gross (1957) Cohesion Scale Revised (Lieberman et al., 1973)	• No subscales reported • Questions examine: group fit, perceived inclusion, attraction to group activities, likability of members, how well the group works together, and the like.	• Horizontal • Affective & Task
Group Cohesion (Piper et al., 1983)	Member–member: • *Positive qualities* examines likability, trust, and ease of communication. • *Personal compatibility* examines attraction, similarity, and desire for personal friendship. • *Significance as a group member* examines personal importance. Member–leader: • *Positive qualities* examines likability, trust, attraction, and ease of communication. • *Dissatisfaction with leader's role* examines discontent with style, communication, and level of personal disclosure. • *Personal compatibility* examines similarity and desire for friendship. Member–group: • *Mutual stimulation and effect* examines engagement, inclusion, and influence. • *Commitment to group* examines attending the group and desire for the group to continue. • *Compatibility of the group* examines fit and attractiveness to the group.	• Horizontal & Vertical • Affective & Task
Group Environment Scale (GES; Moos, 1986; Moos & Humphrey, 1974)	• *Relationship* examines cohesion, leader support, and the amount of freedom of action and expression of feelings encouraged in the group. • *Personal Growth* examines independent action and expression among members, the degree of the group's task orientation, the group's encouragement of discussion of personal problems, and anger and disagreement. • *System Maintenance and Change* measures the degree of organization, structure and rules in the group, role of the leader in making decisions and enforcing rules, and how much the group promotes diversity and change in its own process.	• Horizontal & Vertical • Affective & task
Group Attitude Scale (Evans & Jarvis, 1986)	• 20-items no subscales reported, measures attraction to group. • Illustrative items: "I feel involved in what is happening in my group", "If I were told my group would not meet today I would feel bad" & "I feel it would make a difference to the group if I were not here". • Initially validated against the Moos and Humphrey 1974 version of GES.	• Horizontal • Affective

(Continued)

Table 5.1   Continued

Cohesion Measure	Description of Measure Scales	Dimensions: Direction & Function
Group cohesion questionnaire (GCQ23: van Andel et al., 2003; Trijsburg et al., 2004).	• 23-items based on combining selected items from the Group Attitude Questionnaire and Stokes (1983) 3-factor questionnaire; no subscales reported. • Illustrative items: "The group is honest and straightforward", "I feel involved in what is happening in my group" & "There are people in the group I would enjoy spending time with outside the group session".	• Horizontal • Affective
Harvard Group Cohesiveness Scale (Budman et al., 1987, 1989)	• Behavioral process scale rated by clinicians from videotapes • Five subscales and a global score: (1) withdrawal and self-absorption vs. interest and involvement, (2) mistrust vs. trust, (3) disruption vs. cooperation, (4) abusiveness vs. expressed caring and (5) unfocused vs. focused • Global scale called fragmentation vs. global cohesiveness	• Horizontal • Affective & Task

and several were developed by modifying previous measures. We have classified each measure in Table 5.1 by its use of the structural and affective/task definitions of cohesion. All assess horizontal cohesion between members and their group, while fewer than half focus on a member's relationship with the leader (vertical). Similarly, affective bond is universally assessed by all measures while the task cohesion is assessed by a third of the measures.

A different relation with outcome might result from using different cohesion measures. In fact, we have proposed a two-factor definition of the therapeutic relationship in groups to potentially clarify mixed results in the literature: (1) belonging and acceptance factors—cohesion and member–leader alliance; and (2) interpersonal work factors—group working alliance, individual working alliance, and group climate (Burlingame, Mackenzie, & Strauss, 2004). We undertook a series of studies to evaluate a toolkit containing several therapeutic relationship measures (Strauss, Burlingame, & Bormann, 2008). The first study (Johnson, Burlingame, Davies, & Gleave, 2005) estimated the empirical overlap of

four commonly used relationship measures by having 662 members from 111 different groups complete a copy of each. This study found that a two-dimensional model (quality & structure) explained a majority of the common variance across the four measures. Specifically, *positive bond, positive work,* and *negative relationship* factors explained how members perceived the *quality* of the relationship in both non-clinical and clinical groups. *Positive bond* described the affective relationship members felt with their leader (vertical cohesion) and in member-to-member relationships (horizontal cohesion). *Positive work* equally captured the tasks and goals of the group while *negative relationship* captured empathic failure with the leader and conflict in the group. Interestingly, members were unable to distinguish member-to-group from member-to-member relationships yielding a two-factor structural dimension: member–leader/–member.

The three relationship qualities (*positive bond, positive work, & negative relationship*) and two structural factors (*member–leader & member–member*) stimulated subsequent studies that attempted to replicate these findings across clinical settings and countries. One study (Bormann & Strauss, 2007) collected data from 67 inpatient psychodynamic groups drawn from 15 hospitals in Germany and Switzerland. Both the relationship quality and structure dimensions emerged, but unlike the first study, these authors found support for three structural components (member–member, member–leader, & member–group). The next study (Lorentzen, Høglend, & Ruud, 2008) tested the same four measures and reported a similar two-dimensional model that varied by stage of treatment (Bakali, Baldwin, & Lorentzen, 2009). More specifically, early sessions produced a strong member–leader positive bond while later sessions (10–11 & 17–18 sessions) included positive bonds with both other members and the group.

Findings from these studies led to an item reduction process to determine if a subset of "practice friendly" items could be identified from the original measures that contained over 80 items. A four-person team with 75 collective years of clinical experience used both empirical (statistical fit with two-dimensional model) and clinical criteria (does it provide actionable clinical information?) to produce a 40-item instrument called the Group Questionnaire that measured the three quality and structural factors (Burlingame, 2010). After item consensus was achieved, data was collected from counseling centers and nonclinical process groups replicating the first study (Johnson et al., 2005). Another population was added (seriously mentally ill inpatients; SMI) to determine if the model could be used with seriously ill members; groups were primarily psycho-educational (Krogel, 2009; Krogel & Burlingame, 2009). Using a sample of 485 group members, they found the same two-dimensional relationship quality and structure model based on a 30-item solution.

These studies improve our consensual definition of cohesion. Table 5.2a weds the past definition of affective and task cohesion dimensions from Table 5.1 with the relationship quality and structure model. As can be seen, affective cohesion is split by the emotional valence of the item loading either on the positive bond or negative relationship dimensions. Table 5.2b depicts how horizontal and vertical cohesion load on the relationship structure dimension. Specifically, horizontal cohesion captures the quality of member-to-member relationships and vertical cohesion captures the quality of member-to-leader relationships. Interestingly, the member–group dimension has been the most elusive theoretical construct to empirically detect with mixed findings from preceding studies. The positive and negative valence items that consistently load on the member–group factor across the five studies were principally drawn from MacKenzie's

Table 5.2a   Modified Framework for Understanding Cohesion Using Relationship Quality

	Relationship Structure		
Relationship Quality	Member–member	Member–leader	Member–group
Positive Bond	Affective cohesion—positive feelings & belonging		
Positive Work	Task cohesion		
Negative	Affective cohesion—empathic failure & conflict		

Table 5.2b   Modified Framework for Understanding Cohesion Using Relationship Structure

	Relationship Structure		
Relationship Quality	Member–member	Member–leader	Member–group
Positive Bond			
Positive Work	Horizontal Cohesion	Vertical Cohesion	Group-as-a-whole Cohesion (Climate)[a]
Negative			

[a]cf. McClendon & Burlingame (in press)

(1983) Group Climate Questionnaire (see Table 5.1).

Clinical Examples

The multidimensional complexity of group cohesion makes it impossible to provide a single, concrete example. However, the relationship quality and structure model (Tables 5.2a, 5.2b) provide a practice-friendly framework to recognize group behavior that might facilitate cohesion. We selected a transcript from Session 14 of a 15-session group therapy (Burlingame & Barlow, 1996). The segment begins with a leader acknowledging that the next session will be the last and then probes regarding the work achieved over the course of the group. Group members don't respond to the work probe but instead focus on the positive bond. The quality and structure categories from Table 5.2 are identified by italics.

> Leader to group: This is our next-to-last session. In thinking about our group, I wondered if anyone would care to speak to how they met their goals over the past 14 weeks? *Leader–group positive work probe*
> Mary to leader/group: Well … I think we've all had fun, I know I have. In fact, we talked after you left last night. We're gonna keep our group

going after the last session (smiles at leader). *Member–group positive work*
> Pete to group: I've had this rotten headache all day … it would have been real easy to stay home from almost anything … but not from our group. *Member–group positive bond*
> Mary to group: Yeah, today as I thought about coming to group I knew that Steve was going to make me laugh, everybody else in the group is so good to give me their advice and support, and I enjoy everybody so much. *Member–member/group positive bond*
> Leader to group: That's great. I really think every single person needs this kind of a positive association, maybe not in a formal setting like this, but somehow or another like this, we need it. We really do. Every human being needs it. *Leader–member/group positive bond*

The relationship quality/structure model also accounts for the multiplicity of relationships in the group. This allows a leader to consider multiple aspects of the therapeutic relationship as they plan interventions. The following dialogue includes all three relationship structures (member–member, member–leader, and member–group) and begins with a leader probe regarding a conflictual event that happened at the end of the last group.

Leader to Steve: Steve, you OK? You seemed upset at the end of our last group meeting. *Leader–member, negative relationship probe*

Steve: I need to apologize to you because I was a little bit abrupt with you last week and I ... thought that was kinda tacky, uh ... even though I said it was none of you damned business.

[Group laughs] ... But uh, what I meant was I'm not handling it well and, therefore, I can't share anything with you. I have nothing to give [laughs] because I ... uh, I'm not handling it well. *Member–leader negative relationship*

Leader: You've done a lot of good work over the past few months, but right now you feel like you've got nothing to give—that you're no longer handling it well. *Leader–member positive work*

Steve: I also feel badly that Susan is not here today, I miss her. *Member–member positive bond* [later interaction will reveal an underlying *member–member negative relationship* valence]

Steve: I've been thinking about her and her crisis a great deal, and I almost called you [leader] up to get her phone number. I know we're not supposed to interact outside ... [Steve goes on to tell the group what he has been thinking about Susan's situation. As they are talking Susan comes into the group and the whole group cheers when she enters]. *Group-member positive bond* toward Susan

Leader to Susan: We wanted you to be here so bad, some of us were thinking that you had a crisis and we were worried. *Leader–member positive bond* [Susan explains why she is late].

Steve to Susan: Well, I'm glad you're here ... because I've been worried about you [Steve goes on to inquire about Susan's situation and tell her all his thoughts about it. This goes on for quite a while.] *member–member positive bond*

Susan to Steve: Thank you. The reason I tore out of work so fast to get here is because I knew I'd get the reception I just got. [Susan starts to cry and group laughs lightly, leader pats Susan on the shoulder and Susan pats Mary on the knee] *member–group/member positive bond*

Steve to Susan: I apologize for being abrupt with you last week. That was tactless. I'm sorry. *Member–member negative relationship*

Susan to Steve: It didn't bother me, but I accept your apology. It means a lot to me that you'd check in with me on that. *Member–member positive bond*

In this dialogue we see Steve interacting with a notable level of interpersonal risk with the group leader. When Susan arrives we see multiple levels of positive bond, which undoubtedly supports Steve's ability to handle a second negative relationship concern from the last session with Susan.

The next segment reflects the end of the group session with continued evidence of member–group cohesion as another group member who reinitiates discussion about continuing to meet after the group has formally ended:

Mary to group: I would like to see us work more on what we discussed last week, and that's to continue it all until it finishes. I really am very interested in that ... for your information ... sort of a, you know, forming after the group ... *Member–group positive work/bond*

Susan to Mary, leaning on her
   shoulder: I don't know if we can live
   without each other [dramatically].
   [Group laughs.] *Member–member
   positive bond*
Mary to group: Uh, yeah . . . uh once
   a month or something like that or
   whatever . . . I'm easy . . . but just to
   get together and see how we're doing
   and talk it over and support each
   other. *Member–group positive bond*

Meta-Analytic Review

Before undertaking this meta-analysis,
we reviewed the literature for similar or
related meta-analyses. Three cohesion meta-
analyses were located (Evans & Dion, 1991;
Gully, Devine, & Whitney, 1995; Mullen
& Copper, 1994), but none focused on
cohesion in group psychotherapy; all
examined cohesion's relationship to task
performance in nontherapeutic settings.
Thus, we relied upon five published group
therapy meta-analyses to develop inclusion
criteria herein (Burlingame, Fuhriman, &
Mosier, 2003; Hoag & Burlingame, 1997;
Kosters, Burlingame, Nachitgall, & Strauss,
2006; Lipsey & Wilson, 2001; McRoberts,
Burlingame, & Hoag, 1998). To be included
in our meta-analysis, studies must have
included: (a) a group that was comprised of
at least three members, (b) groups meeting
for the purpose of counseling, psychotherapy, or personal growth, (c) at least one
quantitative measure of both cohesion and
outcome, (d) data that allowed the calculation of effect sizes as weighted correlations,
and (e) English text.

Search Strategy

Articles were obtained by searching
PsycINFO, MedLine, and Google Scholar
for publications between January 1969
and May 2009. A total of 1,506 abstracts
were retrieved using the following search
terms: *group psychotherapy, group therapy,
support groups, group counseling, cohesion,
group cohesion, cohesiveness,* and *group climate.* Each abstract was reviewed for fit
with the above inclusion criteria and, if
deemed promising, the article was retrieved
and again reviewed for fit. A total of 24
articles were included using this method.
Next, the reference sections of obtained
articles were reviewed, and 42 unduplicated
studies were identified and reviewed resulting in 6 studies being included. Finally, six
of the most frequently used cohesion measures (Group Environment Scale, Piper's
Cohesion Questionnaire Scale, Group
Climate Questionnaire, Group Atmosphere
Scale, Shulz's Cohesion Questionnaire,
Gross Cohesion Scale; cf. Table 5.1) across
the 30 identified studies were searched using
Google Scholar, yielding 1,027 abstracts.
Ten additional studies were added, yielding
a final data set of 40 studies.

Coding and Analysis

We selected and coded 19 variables, many
of which had been found to moderate
outcome in previous group therapy meta-
analyses. Five variables that assessed study
characteristics were coded: year of publication, type of cohesion, outcome measure,
and time when cohesion was assessed. Three
leader (experience, orientation, single leader
vs. co-led groups) and three member
characteristics (gender, diagnosis, treatment
setting) were examined. The largest numbers
of variables were associated with the group
itself. Specifically, we were interested in
the degree of structure associated with the
group treatment given the recent emphasis
on manual-based treatments. We coded for
specific practices in the studies that were
used to increase cohesion. We also coded
for groups that allowed greater interaction
among members, believing this might lead
to higher levels of cohesion than those that
are more problem focused.

Group treatments varied from psycho-educational through psychotherapy/counseling to personal growth groups, so we also coded this variable. In an earlier meta-analysis (McRoberts et al., 1998), homogeneous groups were associated with greater improvements. Thus, we coded for identical or similar diagnoses and presenting problems (homogeneous) contrasted with heterogeneous member composition to determine if the correlation between cohesion and outcome might be greater for homogeneous groups.

The task group literature has suggested that group size may moderate the cohesion–outcome link, so we coded for small, medium, and large groups. Finally, since dose of therapy has been shown to moderate overall outcome, we coded for both session length and number of group sessions.

Eight raters (one graduate student and seven undergraduate students) were trained on a codebook to rate articles unrelated to the studies herein using an 85% criterion level of agreement with interrater reliability being high (kappa = 0.73). After achieving this criterion, raters were paired and independently coded the same article contained in our meta-analysis. Complete agreement was required with discrepancies resolved by the graduate student. In a few instances, the first and second authors met with the graduate student (third author) to clarify discrepancies.

A number of studies used several outcome and cohesion measures, thus creating multiple cohesion–outcome correlations from a single study. When this occurred, we averaged the several values (weighted by n) so that only one correlation per study was included in subsequent analyses. Following calculation of the aggregate correlation, we examined the degree of heterogeneity in the results across studies using the Q-statistic (Berkeljon & Baldwin, 2009).

If heterogeneity is found, variability among the study's effect size mean would be higher than what would be expected from sampling error. Moderator results are ultimately interpreted with more confidence when heterogeneity exists.

A random-effects model was used to determine whether differences in the cohesion–outcome relationship existed across the 19 variables. Random effects assume that studies are selected from a population of studies and that variability between studies is the result of sampling error. This analytic model is recommended as a more conservative test (Hedges & Vevea, 1998; Lipsey & Wilson, 2001).

Results

A summary of study characteristics is provided in Table 5.3. As one might expect, most of the groups (80%) had a therapy focus. The majority (58%) of studies were published after 2000, although over a fourth were published prior to 1990, capturing several classic papers (e.g., Braaten, 1989; Budman et al., 1989; Roether & Peters, 1972; Yalom, Houts, Zimerberg, & Rand, 1967). We elected to include a few personal growth group studies that met our criteria and used a task format (e.g., Flowers, Booraem, & Hartman 1981; Hurley, 1989; Kivlighan & Lilly, 1997) since all are frequently cited in cohesion–outcome literature.

Past reviewers have concluded that cohesion has shown a positive relation with patient improvement in nearly every published report (Tschuschke & Dies, 1994). Our own previous, narrative review concluded that approximately 80% of published studies demonstrated a positive association between group cohesion and treatment outcome (Burlingame et al., 2002).

The results from our meta-analysis with each study depicted in Figure 5.1 show

Table 5.3 Study Characteristics

Variable	%	N
Number of Studies		40
Year of publication (median)		1,997.7
Overall number of clients		3,323
Average age of clients		36.4
Average number of sessions		23.5
Theoretical orientation of group		
Cognitive/behavioral	33	13
Psychodynamic/Existential	25	10
Humanistic/Interpersonal/Supportive	20	8
Eclectic	8	3
Unknown[1]	20	8
Primary Diagnosis		
Informal	35	14
Anxiety Disorder	13	5
Mood Disorder	18	7
Substance Disorder	3	1
Eating Disorder	5	2
Personality Disorder	13	5
Medical Condition (not Somatic disorder)	5	2
Unknown	18	7
Country		
North America	50	20
Europe	23	9
Canada	18	7
Australia	5	2
Role of Group		
Only group/group as primary treatment	10	4
Part of milieu of treatment (e.g. medication, individual therapy)	23	9
Unknown	68	27
Setting		
Inpatient	15	6
Outpatient	68	27
Unknown	18	7

(Continued)

Table 5.3   Continued

Variable	%	N
Location		
University Counseling Center	3	1
Clinic or Private Practice	13	5
Hospital	45	18
Community Mental Health Center	05	2
Community Location	3	1
Classroom Setting	13	5
Unknown	20	8
Type of Outcome Measure		
General psychological distress	38	15
Depression	30	12
Anxiety	15	6
Quality of Life/General well being	20	8
Interpersonal Problems / Relationships	23	9
Self Esteem	13	5
Other	45	18
Unknown[1]	8	3
Number of Cohesion Measure administrations		
Once	10	4
Twice	20	8
Three times	20	8
Four times	0	0
Five or more times	48	19
Unknown	3	1

Note: 1. Values don't add up to 40 because some studies used multiples

a less glowing picture than past reviews, including our own. Only 43% of the studies posted a statistically significant correlation between cohesion and patient improvement. Nonetheless, the weighted aggregate correlation for the 40 studies was a statistically significant $r = 0.25$ with a 95% confidence interval of .17 to .32 (SE = .04) which is considered to be a moderate effect. Thus, the overall conclusion from 40 studies published across a 4-decade span is a positive relation between cohesion and outcome.

Moderators and Mediators

Until recently, there have been few empirical studies examining moderator or mediator variables for the cohesion–outcome link (Hornsey et al., 2007). Mediators have

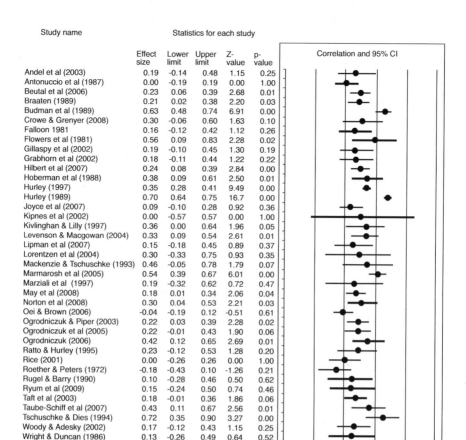

Study name	Statistics for each study					Correlation and 95% CI
	Effect size	Lower limit	Upper limit	Z-value	p-value	
Andel et al (2003)	0.19	-0.14	0.48	1.15	0.25	
Antonuccio et al (1987)	0.00	-0.19	0.19	0.00	1.00	
Beutal et al (2006)	0.23	0.06	0.39	2.68	0.01	
Braaten (1989)	0.21	0.02	0.38	2.20	0.03	
Budman et al (1989)	0.63	0.48	0.74	6.91	0.00	
Crowe & Grenyer (2008)	0.30	-0.06	0.60	1.63	0.10	
Falloon 1981	0.16	-0.12	0.42	1.12	0.26	
Flowers et al (1981)	0.56	0.09	0.83	2.28	0.02	
Gillaspy et al (2002)	0.19	-0.10	0.45	1.30	0.19	
Grabhorn et al (2002)	0.18	-0.11	0.44	1.22	0.22	
Hilbert et al (2007)	0.24	0.08	0.39	2.84	0.00	
Hoberman et al (1988)	0.38	0.09	0.61	2.50	0.01	
Hurley (1997)	0.35	0.28	0.41	9.49	0.00	
Hurley (1989)	0.70	0.64	0.75	16.7	0.00	
Joyce et al (2007)	0.09	-0.10	0.28	0.92	0.36	
Kipnes et al (2002)	0.00	-0.57	0.57	0.00	1.00	
Kivlinghan & Lilly (1997)	0.36	0.00	0.64	1.96	0.05	
Levenson & Macgowan (2004)	0.33	0.09	0.54	2.61	0.01	
Lipman et al (2007)	0.15	-0.18	0.45	0.89	0.37	
Lorentzen et al (2004)	0.30	-0.33	0.75	0.93	0.35	
Mackenzie & Tschuschke (1993)	0.46	-0.05	0.78	1.79	0.07	
Marmarosh et al (2005)	0.54	0.39	0.67	6.01	0.00	
Marziali et al (1997)	0.19	-0.32	0.62	0.72	0.47	
May et al (2008)	0.18	0.01	0.34	2.06	0.04	
Norton et al (2008)	0.30	0.04	0.53	2.21	0.03	
Oei & Brown (2006)	-0.04	-0.19	0.12	-0.51	0.61	
Ogrodniczuk & Piper (2003)	0.22	0.03	0.39	2.28	0.02	
Ogrodniczuk et al (2005)	0.22	-0.01	0.43	1.90	0.06	
Ogrodniczuk (2006)	0.42	0.12	0.65	2.69	0.01	
Ratto & Hurley (1995)	0.23	-0.12	0.53	1.28	0.20	
Rice (2001)	0.00	-0.26	0.26	0.00	1.00	
Roether & Peters (1972)	-0.18	-0.43	0.10	-1.26	0.21	
Rugel & Barry (1990)	0.10	-0.28	0.46	0.50	0.62	
Ryum et al (2009)	0.15	-0.24	0.50	0.74	0.46	
Taft et al (2003)	0.18	-0.01	0.36	1.86	0.06	
Taube-Schiff et al (2007)	0.43	0.11	0.67	2.56	0.01	
Tschuschke & Dies (1994)	0.72	0.35	0.90	3.27	0.00	
Woody & Adesky (2002)	0.17	-0.12	0.43	1.15	0.25	
Wright & Duncan (1986)	0.13	-0.26	0.49	0.64	0.52	
Yalom et al (1967)	0.11	-0.30	0.48	0.52	0.60	

Favors negative relationship   Favors positive relationship

Fig. 5.1 Weighted effect size for cohesion-outcome relationship

been proposed (e.g., member acceptance, support, self-disclosure, and feedback), but there has been little progress due to the varied definitions and confounds with group cohesion (Hornsey et al., 2007). Our analysis of the studies found only a handful of moderators among the 19 coded variables.

Study Characteristics

None of the study characteristics (publication year, outcome or cohesion measure, or time of assessment) explained variability among the studies. However, there were a number of cohesion measures that were used two or more times, and their weighted averages are depicted in Figure 5.2. The most frequently used was the engaged scale

from the Group Climate Questionnaire (MacKenzie, 1983), which posted the second highest weighted correlation (0.35). Interestingly, one of the oldest cohesion measures (Group Environment Scale) posted the lowest *r* value.

The cohesion–outcome relationship was explored to see if it varied by outcome measure. As with the cohesion instrument analysis, most measures were used too infrequently to test for reliable differences. However, two measures (SCL-90, BDI) that assess general psychiatric and depressive symptoms, respectively, were each used in a dozen studies posting reliable values that were at or above the meta-analytic average. Higher weighted averages were found on both interpersonal and self-esteem

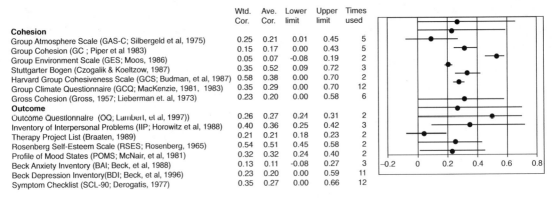

	Wtd. Cor.	Ave. Cor.	Lower limit	Upper limit	Times used
Cohesion					
Group Atmosphere Scale (GAS-C; Silbergeld et al, 1975)	0.25	0.21	0.01	0.45	5
Group Cohesion (GC ; Piper et al 1983)	0.15	0.17	0.00	0.43	5
Group Environment Scale (GES; Moos, 1986)	0.05	0.07	-0.08	0.19	2
Stuttgarter Bogen (Czogalik & Koeltzow, 1987)	0.35	0.52	0.09	0.72	3
Harvard Group Cohesiveness Scale (GCS; Budman, et al, 1987)	0.58	0.38	0.00	0.70	2
Group Climate Questionnaire (GCQ; MacKenzie, 1981, 1983)	0.35	0.29	0.00	0.70	12
Gross Cohesion (Gross, 1957; Lieberman et. al, 1973)	0.23	0.20	0.00	0.58	6
Outcome					
Outcome Questionnaire (OQ; Lambert, et al, 1997))	0.26	0.27	0.24	0.31	2
Inventory of Interpersonal Problems (IIP; Horowitz et al, 1988)	0.40	0.36	0.25	0.42	3
Therapy Project List (Braaten, 1989)	0.21	0.21	0.18	0.23	2
Rosenberg Self-Esteem Scale (RSES; Rosenberg, 1965)	0.54	0.51	0.45	0.58	2
Profile of Mood States (POMS; McNair, et al, 1981)	0.32	0.32	0.24	0.40	2
Beck Anxiety Inventory (BAI; Beck, et al, 1988)	0.13	0.11	-0.08	0.27	3
Beck Depression Inventory(BDI; Beck, et al, 1996)	0.23	0.20	0.00	0.59	11
Symptom Checklist (SCL-90; Derogatis, 1977)	0.35	0.27	0.00	0.66	12

Fig. 5.2 Weighted Correlations and range by cohesion and outcome measure

measures (IIP, RSES), but these results are heavily influenced by the two student growth group studies (Hurley, 1989; Kivlighan & Lilly, 1997). Thus, it remains unclear how these outcome measures might operate in clinical populations. A conclusion that seems warranted is that the cohesion–outcome relationship is well supported when outcome is defined by general psychiatric and depressive symptoms. Moreover, since the SCL-90 and BDI are also two of the most frequently used instruments to evaluate the effectiveness of group psychotherapy, the generalizability to outcome appears sound.

Member Variables
Of the member variables, only one explained differences in the cohesion–outcome link. The average age of participants was negatively associated with effect size magnitude within studies ($r = -.63$; $p < 0.0001$). Studies with relatively younger group members tended to yield effect sizes of higher magnitude than studies with relatively older group members; $Q = 14.92$, $df = 1$, $p < 0.05$. This finding was not explained by client symptom severity; cohesion was reliably related to outcome in both inpatient and outpatient settings ($r = 0.29$ and 0.24, respectively). Furthermore, the positive association of group cohesion and client outcome was

demonstrated across all three major diagnostic classifications; Axis I ($r = 0.17$), Axis II ($r = 0.41$), and V-code ($r = 0.26$).

Leader Variables
No evidence was found to support that leader experience or single versus co-led groups explained differences in the cohesion–outcome correlations. However, there was a difference in the cohesion–outcome relation when one considered the differences across the theoretical orientation of the group leader; $Q = 23.56$, $df = 9$, $p < 0.05$. Leaders espousing an interpersonal orientation posted the highest cohesion–outcome relation ($r = 0.58$), with psychodynamic ($r = 0.25$) and cognitive-behavioral ($r = 0.18$) orientations posting the lowest values. The remaining orientations posted either statistical trends (humanistic, $r = 0.21$) or no reliable relationship (behavioral, eclectic). This argues for cohesion being considered as an evidence-based relationship factor for groups using a cognitive-behavioral, psychodynamic, and interpersonal orientation.

Group Variables
Four group variables proved useful in explaining differences in the cohesion–outcome association. In the past, we (Burlingame et al., 2004; Fuhriman &

Burlingame, 1994) have suggested that the best test of the cohesion–outcome relation would be to examine studies that emphasized the importance of cohesion as a therapeutic strategy. If group cohesion is undervalued or neglected by a group leader, its presence would likely be diminished and perhaps attenuate its relationship with outcome. Two previous studies which included cognitive pre-training to enhance cohesion showed higher cohesion for the pre-trained groups (Santarsiero, Baker & McGee, 1995; Palmer, Baker & McGee, 1997). The one study herein that described procedures for enhancing cohesion in their methods section (Kivlighan & Lilly 1997) pre-trained participants using videotapes and produced a cohesion–outcome correlation (r = .36) that was slightly higher yet not statistically different from the weighted average.

Another significant group variable (group focus) found a difference between problem specific and interactive groups; $Q = 4.75$, $df = 1$, $p < 0.05$. Problem specific groups were comprised of members with similar diagnoses, and group time appeared to be principally focused on this common theme. Interactive groups had members who were more interactive, and group time appeared to be less structured. Interactive groups posted a higher cohesion–outcome correlation than problem-specific groups ($r = 0.38$ and $r = 0.21$, respectively).

The cohesion–outcome relationship proved to be statistically significant when examining the size of the group, $Q = 4.54$, $df = 1$, $p < 0.05$. Groups comprised of 5–9 members in each session posted the strongest cohesion–outcome relationship ($r = 0.35$) whereas groups of any other size (fewer than 5 members present or more than 9 members) were much weaker ($r = 0.16$). Finally, there were differences in the cohesion–outcome correlations by number of sessions; $Q = 6.87$, $df = 2$, $p < 0.05$. Groups lasting more than 12 sessions posted

higher cohesion–outcome correlations than did groups lasting 12 or fewer sessions ($r = 0.17$). Interestingly, there was no statistically significant difference between groups lasting 13–19 sessions ($r = 0.36$) and for 20 or more sessions ($r = 0.31$).

Other Potential Moderators

Two studies that fell outside our meta-analytic review parameters—because they were recently published or the text is in German—suggest a potential patient moderator variable. In the first study, members' interpersonal style moderated the relationship between cohesion and outcome with 73 depressed German inpatients (Schauenburg, Sammet, Rabung & Strack, 2001). Specifically, patients with interpersonal problems described as "too friendly" improved more when their cohesion decreased during therapy, whereas patients with cold or hostile interpersonal problems improved most when their experience of cohesion increased during the group.

A recent replication of that study involved 327 mixed-diagnosis adults treated on a psychodynamically oriented inpatient psychotherapy unit in Germany (Dinger & Schauenburg, 2010). Higher levels of cohesion as well as an increase in cohesion over the life of the group were associated with greater symptom improvement, replicating the findings of our meta-analysis. Once again patients who described themselves as too cold and who reported increased cohesion posted the greatest improvement; the opposite was evident for those who described themselves as too friendly. The value of this study is that it offers one theory-driven explanation of both the positive and neutral relationship findings in this meta-analysis. Could a member's interpersonal style explain past mixed cohesion–outcome findings? Unfortunately, the "jury is out" on this question since the primary measure assessing cohesion in both studies falls short on psychometric support, thus attenuating our confidence in its conclusions.

Limitations of the Research

One of the clear challenges in understanding and utilizing cohesion as an evidence-based principle has been the variability in definition and measurement. The two-dimensional model (structure and quality) offers a promising, parsimonious, and empirically based definition of the latent structure inherent in measures of group relationship. It suggests that leaders pay attention to the "who" (member, group, & leader), "what" (are we getting work done?), and "how" (positive and negative emotional valence) of group relationships.

A second challenge in the literature has been the mixed findings regarding cohesion's relation with treatment outcome. Some studies support its relationship with outcome; others show no association. The meta-analysis clarifies this confusion by pointing out differences between measures, theoretical orientations, group length, and group focus. For instance, cognitive-behavioral groups make up 80% of the recent group literature (Burlingame & Baldwin, in press), and it's clear that a cohesion–outcome link exists for these groups. Similarly, longer and more interactive groups produce larger cohesion–outcome correlations, but even short groups (fewer than 12 sessions) still show a cohesion–outcome link.

There are several specific limitations to the findings herein. First, it is virtually impossible to assess potential member or leader moderators because of the absence of research on this topic in the group therapy literature. For instance, low psychological mindedness and more severe symptoms have been linked to early dropout (Burlingame et al., 2004), but to our knowledge, these have never been formally tested as moderators of cohesion–outcome. Additionally, there is no consensus on leader moderators due to the scant number of studies that focus on the leader (Burlingame et al., 2004). Even if one were to uncover a handful of studies testing the same member or leader moderator, it is highly likely that different measures of cohesion would be used.

We believe the biggest limitation to our findings and the research in general is the heterogeneity of study characteristics that is often hidden in meta-analyses. Even though we used 40 studies, when one considers the possible interactions among different diagnoses, settings, orientations, and type of groups, considerable caution must be invoked in interpreting our results. There are simply too few studies to adequately test for potential interactions between the characteristics tested herein. For example, the larger relation between cohesion and outcome makes sense for groups that last longer than 12 sessions. However, what we don't know is how this plays out for different theoretical orientations and clinical settings.

Finally, the question of causality cannot be addressed in these correlational studies. Perhaps the strongest evidence to support a causal relationship was the finding from studies that intentionally used interventions to enhance cohesion that resulted in a stronger cohesion–outcome relation. However, as pointed out above, these studies were not based on groups comprised of members having a formal psychiatric diagnosis.

Therapeutic Practices

We see the following therapeutic practices supported by our meta-analysis:

- Cohesion is reliably associated ($r = 0.25$) with group outcome when outcome is defined as reduction in symptom distress or improvement in interpersonal functioning. All group leaders should foster cohesion in its multiple manifestations.

- Cohesion is certainly involved with patient improvement in groups using a cognitive-behavioral, psychodynamic, or interpersonal orientation.
- Group leaders emphasizing member interaction, irrespective of theoretical orientation, post higher cohesion–outcome links than problem-focused groups. Thus, it is important to encourage member interaction.
- Cohesion explains outcome regardless of the length of the group, but is strongest when a group lasts more than 12 sessions and is comprised of 5–9 members. Group cohesion obviously requires the correct balance of member interaction and time to build.
- Younger group members experience the largest outcome gains when cohesion is present within their groups. Fostering cohesion may be particularly useful for those working with young people (e.g., counseling centers and adolescents).
- Cohesion contributes to group outcome across different settings (inpatient and outpatient) and diagnostic classifications. Thus, all leaders should actively engage in interventions that foster and maintain cohesion.

In this regard, we would point to therapist behaviors that can enhance group cohesion. These specific interventions are depicted in Table 5.4. These behaviors track onto a behavioral rating scale (Group Psychotherapy Interventions Rating Scale; GPIRS) developed from interventions suggested in our first cohesion chapter (Burlingame et al., 2002). In two studies (Sternberg & Trijsburg, 2005; Snijders, Trijsburg, De Groot, & Duivenvoorden, 2005), *group structure, verbal interaction,* and *emotional climate* interventions were positively correlated with member-reported cohesion. A recent North American study (Chapman, Baker, Porter, Thayer & Burlingame, 2010) translated the Dutch GPIRS into English and replicated these findings. Small-to-moderate correlations were found with each GPIRS subscale, suggesting that leader interventions intended to affect *emotional climate,* manage *verbal interaction,* and maintain *group structure* were moderately correlated with member-reported levels of cohesion. Leader interventions facilitating structure, emotional climate, and managing verbal interaction were positively related to cohesion and negatively related to interpersonal distrust and conflict, replicating the Dutch findings on a different measure of cohesion.

Cohesion is integrally related to the success of group therapy, and the research has identified specific behaviors that enhance cohesion. For these reasons, we recommend the behaviors in Table 5.4 to group practitioners.

Table 5.4 Group Psychotherapy Intervention Rating Scale (GPIRS)

	Group Structuring
Setting treatment expectation	Set group agendas (such as discussion topics or group activities) Described rationale underlying treatment
Establishing group procedures	Discussed group rules (such as time, attendance, absences, tardiness, confidentiality, participation) Identified and discussed fears/concerns regarding self disclosure Structured exercises that focus on emotional expression and exchange

(Continued)

Table 5.4 Continued

| Role preparation | Discussed member roles and responsibility |
| | Discussed leader roles and responsibility |

	Verbal Interaction
Verbal style and interaction	Modeled giving personal information in the "here and now"
	Modeled appropriate member-member behavior
	Modeled appropriate self disclosure
	Modeled appropriate feeling disclosure
	Maintained moderate control
	Facilitated appropriate member-member interaction
Self disclosure	Encouraged self disclosure without "forcing it"
	Encouraged self disclosure relevant to the current group agenda
	Helped members understand that disclosed issues achieve more resolution than undisclosed issues
	Encouraged here-and-now vs. story-telling disclosure
	Interrupted ill-timed or excessive member disclosure
	Elicited member-member feeling disclosure (versus informational disclosures)
	Leader shared relevant personal experience from outside of therapy (without being judgmental or overly-intellectual)
Feedback	Reframed injurious feedback (interrupting, if necessary)
	Restated corrective feedback by member
	Used consensus to reinforce feedback (toward therapist or group member)
	Balanced positive and corrective leader-to-member feedback
	Encouraged positive feedback
	Gave structured feedback exercise
	Helped balance positive and corrective member-to-member feedback
	Therapist helped members apply in-group feedback to out-of-group situations

	Creating and Maintaining a Therapeutic Emotional Climate
Leader contribution	Maintained balance in expressions of emotional support and confrontation
	Showed understanding of the members and their concerns
	Refrained from conveying personal feelings of hostility and anger in response to negative member behavior
	Leader was not defensive when interventions failed
	Leader was not defensive when confronted by a member
	Maintained an active engagement with the group and its work
	Used nonjudgmental language with members
	Modeled expressions of open and genuine warmth
	Encouraged active emotional engagement between group members
	Fostered a climate of both support and challenge
	Responded at an emotional level
	Developed and/or facilitated relationships with and among group members
	Helped members recognize why they feel a certain way (identifying underlying concerns or motives)
Member contribution	Prevented or stopped attacking and judgmental expressions between members
	Assisted members in describing their emotions
	Recognized and responded to the meaning of groups members' comments
	Prevented situations in which members felt discounted, misunderstood, attacked, or disconnected
	Involved members in describing and resolving conflict (instead of avoiding conflict)
	Elicited verbal expressions of support among group members
	Encouraged members to respond to other members' emotional expression (such as acceptance, belonging, empathy)

References

An asterisk (*) indicates studies included in the meta-analysis.

*Antonuccio, D. O., Davis, C., Lewinsohn, P. M., & Breckenridge, J. S. (1987). Therapist variables related to cohesiveness in a group treatment for depression. *Small Group Research, 18*, 557–64.

Bakali, J., Baldwin, S., & Lorentzen, S. (2009). Modeling group process constructs at three stages in group psychotherapy. *Psychotherapy Research, 19*, 332–43.

Beck, A. T., Epstein, N., Brown, G., & Steer, R. A. (1988). An inventory for measuring clinical anxiety: Psychometric properties. *Journal of Consulting and Clinical Psychology, 56*, 893–97.

Beck, A. T., Steer, R. A., & Brown, G. K. (1996). *Manual for the Beck Depression Inventory-II.* San Antonio, TX: Psychological Corporation.

Bednar, R. L., & Kaul, T. J. (1978). Experiential group research: Current Perspectives. In S. L. Garfield & A. E. Bergin (Eds.), *Handbook of psychotherapy and behavior change* (2th ed., pp. 769–815). New York: Wiley.

Bednar, R. L., & Kaul, T. J. (1994). Experiential group research: Can the canon fire? In A. E. Bergin & S. L. Garfield (Eds.), *Handbook of psychotherapy and behavior change* (4th ed., pp. 631–63). New York: Wiley.

Berkeljon, A., & Baldwin, S. A. (2009). An introduction to meta-analysis for psychotherapy outcome research. *Psychotherapy Research, 19*(4), 511–518.

*Beutal, M. E., Knickenberg, R. J., Krug, B., Mund, S., Schattenburg, L., & Zwerenz, R. (2006). Psychodynamic focal group treatment for psychosomatic inpatients—with an emphasis on work-related conflicts. *International Journal of Group Psychotherapy, 56*(3), 285–305.

Bormann, B., & Strauß, B. (2007). Gruppenklima, Kohäsion, Allianz und Empathie als Komponenten der therapeutischen Beziehung in Gruppenpsychotherapien–Überprüfung eines Mehrebenen-Modells. [Group climate, cohesion, alliance, and empathy as components of the therapeutic relationship within group psychotherapy–Test of a multilevel model]. *Gruppenpsychotherapie und Gruppendynamik, 43*, 1–20.

Bormann, B., & Strauß, B. (2009, June). *The German Group Questionnaire: A multi-site validation study.* Paper presented at the annual meeting of the Society for Psychotherapy Research, Santiago, Chile.

Braaten, L. (1991). Group cohesion: A new multi-dimensional model. *Group, 15*, 39–55.

*Braaten, L. J. (1989). Predicting positive goal attainment and symptom reduction from early group climate dimensions. *International Journal of Group Psychotherapy, 39*(3), 377–87.

Broker, M., Rohricht, F., & Priebe, F. (1995). Initial assessment of hospital treatment by patients with paranoid schizophrenia: A predictor of outcome. *Psychiatry Research, 58*(1), 77–81.

Budman, S. H., Demby, A., Feldstein, M., Redondo, J., Scherz, B., Bennett, M. J., et al. (1987). Preliminary findings on a new instrument to measure cohesion in group psychotherapy. *International Journal of Group Psychotherapy, 37*, 75–94.

*Budman, S. H., Soldz, S., Demby, A., Feldstein, M., Springer, T., & Davis, M. S. (1989). Cohesion, alliance and outcome in group psychotherapy. *Psychiatry, 52*(3), 339–50.

Burlingame, G. (2010). Small group treatments: Introduction to special section. *Psychotherapy Research, 20*(1), 1–7.

Burlingame, G., & Baldwin, S. (2010). History of group psychotherapy. In *History of Psychotherapy* (2nd ed.), J. Norcross, G. VandenBos, & D. Freedheim. (Eds). (pp. 505–515), Washington DC: American Psychological Association.

Burlingame, G. M., & Barlow, S. (1996). Outcome and process differences between professional and nonprofessional therapists in time-limited group psychotherapy. *International Journal of Group Psychotherapy, 46*, 455–78.

Burlingame, G. M., MacKenzie, K. R., & Strauß, B. (2004). Evidence-based small group treatments. In M. Lambert, A. E. Bergin, & S. L. Garfield (Eds.), *Handbook of psychotherapy and behavior change* (5th ed.). New York: Wiley & Sons.

Burlingame, G. M., & Fuhriman, A. (1994). Epilogue. In A. Fuhriman & G. M. Burlingame (Eds.), *Handbook of group psychotherapy: An empirical and clinical synthesis* (pp. 559–62). New York: Wiley & Sons.

Burlingame, G., Fuhriman, A., & Johnson, J. (2002). Cohesion in group psychotherapy. In J. C. Norcross (Ed). *Psychotherapy Relationships That Work* (pp. 71–87). New York: Oxford University Press.

Burlingame, G. M., Fuhriman, A. F., & Mosier, J. (2003). The differentiated effectiveness of group psychotherapy: A meta-analytic review. *Group Dynamics: Theory, Research, and Practice, 7*(1), 3–12.

Cattell, R. B., & Wispe, L. G. (1948). The dimensions of syntality in small groups. *Journal of Social Psychology, 28*, 57–78.

Chapman, C., Baker, E., Porter, G., Thayer, S., & Burlingame, G. (2010). Rating group therapist interventions: The validation of the Group Psychotherapy Rating Scale. *Group Dynamics: Theory, Research, & Practice, 14*(1), 15–31.

Crouch, E. C., Bloch, S., & Wanlass, J. (1994). Therapeutic factors: Interpersonal and intrapersonal mechanisms. In A. Fuhriman & G. M. Burlingame (Eds.), *Handbook of group psychotherapy* (pp. 269–315). New York: Wiley.

*Crowe, T. P., & Grenyer, B. F. S. (2008). Is therapist alliance or whole group cohesion more influential in group psychotherapy outcomes? *Clinical Psychology and Psychotherapy, 15*, 239–46.

Czogalik, D., & Koltzow, R. (1987). Zur Normierung des Stuttgarter Bogens. *Gruppenpsychotherapie und Gruppendynamik, 23*, 36–45.

Derogatis, L. R. (1977). *SCL-90: Administration, scoring, and procedures manual-R* (revised). Baltimore: John Hopkins University School of Medicine, Clinical Psychometrics Research Unit.

Dinger, U., & Schauenburg, H. (2010). Effects of individual cohesion and patient interpersonal style on outcome in psychodynamically oriented inpatient group psychotherapy. *Psychotherapy Research, 20*(1), 22–29.

Dion, K. L. (2000). Group cohesion: From "field of forces" to multidimensional construct. *Group Dynamics, 4*, 7–26.

Evans, C. R., & Dion, K. L. (1991). Group cohesion and performance: A meta-analysis. *Small Group Research, 22*, 175–86.

Evans, N. J., & Jarvis, P. A. (1986). The Group Attitude Scale: A measure of attraction to group. *Small Group Behavior, 17*, 203–216.

*Falloon, I. R. H. (1981). Interpersonal variables in behavioural group therapy. *British Journal of Medical Psychology, 54*, 133–41.

*Flowers, J. V., Booraem, C. D., & Hartman, K. A. (1981). Client improvement on higher and lower intensity problems as a function of group cohesiveness. *Psychotherapy: Theory, Research, and Practice, 18*, 246–251.

Fuhriman, A., & Burlingame, G., (Eds.). (1994). *Handbook of group psychotherapy: An empirical and clinical synthesis.* New York: John Wiley & Sons.

*Gillaspy, J. A., Jr., Wright, A. R., Campbell, C., Stokes, S., & Adinoff, B. (2002). Group alliance and cohesion as predictors of drug and alcohol abuse treatment outcomes. *Psychotherapy Research, 12*(2), 213–29.

*Grabhorn, R., Kaufhold, J., & Overbeck, G. (2002). The role of differentiated group experience in the course of inpatient psychotherapy. In Serge P. Shohov (Ed.), *Advance in psychology research, Volume 12*, (pp. 141–54). Hauppauge, NY: Nova Science Publishers.

Griffith, J. (1988). Measurement of group cohesion in U.S. Army units. *Basic and Applied Social Psychology, 9*, 149–71.

Gross, E. F. (1957). *An empirical study of the concepts of cohesiveness and compatibility.* Honors thesis, Harvard University, Cambridge, MA.

Gully, S. M., Devine, D. J., & Whitney, D. J. (1995). A meta-analysis of cohesion and performance: Effects of level of analysis and task interdependence. *Small Group Research, 26*, 497–520.

Hedges, L. V., & Vevea, J. L. (1998). Fixed- and random-effects models in meta-analysis. *Psychological Methods, 3*, 486–504.

*Hilbert, A., Saelens, B. E., Stein, R. I., Mockus, D. S., Welch, R. R., Matt, G. E., et al. (2007). Pretreatment and process predictors of outcome in interpersonal and cognitive behavioral psychotherapy for binge eating disorder. *Journal of Consulting and Clinical Psychology, 75*(4), 645–51.

Hoag, M. J., & Burlingame, G. M. (1997). Evaluating the effectiveness of child and adolescent group treatment. *Journal of Clinical Child Psychology, 26*, 234–46.

*Hoberman, H. M., Lewinsohn, P. M., & Tilson, M. (1988). Group treatment of depression: Individual predictors of outcome. *Journal of Consulting and Clinical Psychology, 56*(3), 393–98.

Hornsey, M., Dwyer, L., & Oei, T. (2007). Beyond cohesiveness: Reconceptualizing the link between group processes and outcomes in group psychotherapy. *Small Group Research, 38*, 567–92.

Hornsey, M., Dwyer, L., Oei, T., & Dingle, G. A. (2009). Group processes and outcomes in group therapy: Is it time to let go of cohesiveness? *International Journal of Group Psychotherapy, 59*(2), 267–78.

Horowitz, L., Rosenberg, S., Baer, B., Ureno, F., & Villasenor, V. (1988). Inventory of interpersonal problems: Psychometric properties and clinical applications. *Journal of Consulting and Clinical Psychology, 56*(6), 885–92.

*Hurley, J. R. (1989). Affiliativeness and outcome in interpersonal groups: Member and leader perspectives. *Psychotherapy, 26*(4), 520–23.

*Hurley, J. R. (1997). Interpersonal theory and measures of outcome and emotional climate in 111 personal development groups. *Group Dynamics: Theory, Research, and Practice, 1*(1), 86–97.

Johnson, J. E., Burlingame, G. M., Olsen, J. A., Davies, D. R., & Gleave, R. L. (2005). Group climate, cohesion, alliance, and empathy in group psychotherapy: Multilevel structural equation models. *Journal of Counseling Psychology, 52*, 310–21.

*Joyce, A. S., Piper, W. E., & Ogrodniczuk, J. S. (2007). Therapeutic alliance and cohesion variables as predictors of outcome in short-term group therapy. *International Journal of Group Psychotherapy, 57*(3), 269–96.

*Kipnes, D. R., Piper, W. E., & Joyce, A. S. (2002). Cohesion and outcome in short-term psychodynamic groups for complicated grief. *International Journal of Group Psychotherapy, 52*(4), 483–509.

Kivlighan, D. M., Coleman, M. N., & Anderson, D. C. (2000). Process, outcome, and methodology in group counseling research. In S. D. Brown & R. W. Lent (Eds.), *Handbook of counseling psychology* (3rd ed., pp. 767–96). New York: Wiley.

*Kivlighan, D. M., & Lilly, R. L. (1997). Developmental changes in group climate as they relate to therapeutic gain. *Group Dynamics: Theory*, Research, and Practice, *1*, 208–21.

Kosters, M., Burlingame, G., Nachtigall, C., & Strauss, B. (2006). A meta-analytic review of the effectiveness of inpatient group psychotherapy. *Group Dynamics: Theory, Research, & Practice. 10*(2), 143–63.

Krogel, J. (2009). *The Group Questionnaire: A new measure of the group relationship*. Provo, UT: Brigham Young University.

Krogel, J., & Burlingame, G. (2009). The group questionnaire: A new measure of the therapeutic group relationship. Paper presented at the annual meeting of the *Society for Psychotherapy Research*. Santiago, Chile.

Lambert, M. J., Hansen, N. B., Umpress, V., Lunnen, K., Okiiski, J., & Burlingame, G. M. (1997). *Administration and scoring manual for the OQ-45.2*. Stevenson, MD: American Professional Credentialing Services.

*Levenson, J. S., & Macgowan, M. J. (2004). Engagement, denial, and treatment progress among sex offenders in group therapy. *Sexual Abuse: A Journal of Research and Treatment, 16*(1), 49–63.

Lieberman, M., Yalom, I., & Miles, M. (1973). *Encounter groups: First facts*. New York: Basic Books.

*Lipman, E. L., Waymouth, M., Gammon, T., Carter, P., Secord, M., Leung, O., Mills, B., & Hicks, F. (2007). Influence of group cohesion on maternal well-being among participants in a support/education group program for single mothers. *American Journal of Orthopsychiatry, 77*(4), 543–49.

Lipsey, M. W., & Wilson, D. B. (2001). *Practical meta-analysis*. Applied Social Research Methods Series, Vol. 49). Thousand Oaks, CA: Sage.

Lorentzen, S., Høglend, P., & Ruud, T. (2008, June). *The efficacy of short- and long-term psychodynamic group psychotherapy: A Norwegian multi-center study*. Panel presentation at the annual meeting of the Society for Psychotherapy Research, Barcelona, Spain.

*Lorentzen, S., Sexton, H. C., & Hoglend, P. (2004). Therapeutic alliance, cohesion and outcome in a long-term analytic group. A preliminary study. *Nordic Journal of Psychiatry, 58*, 33–40.

MacKenzie, K. R. (1981). Measurement of group climate. *International Journal of Group Psychotherapy, 31*, 287–95.

MacKenzie, K. R. (1983). The clinical application of a group climate measure. In R. R. Dies & K. R. MacKenzie (Eds), *Advances in group psychotherapy: Integrating research and practice* (pp. 159–70). New York: International Universities Press.

*Mackenzie, R. K., & Tschuschke, V. (1993). Relatedness, group work, and outcome in long-term inpatient psychotherapy groups. *Journal of Psychotherapy Practice and Research, 2*, 147–56.

*Marmarosh, C., Holtz, A., & Schottenbauer, M. (2005). Group cohesiveness, group-derived collective self-esteem, group-derived hope, and the well-being of group therapy members. *Group Dynamics: Theory, Research, and Practice, 9*(1), 32–44.

*Marziali, E., Munroe-Blum, H., & McCleary, L. (1997). The contribution of group cohesion and group alliance to the outcome of group psychotherapy. *International Journal of Group Psychotherapy, 47*(4), 475–97.

*May, A. M., Duivenvoorden, H. J., Korstjens, I., Weert, E. V., Hoekstra-Weebers, J. E., Borne, B. V. D., et al. (2008). The effect of group cohesion on rehabilitation outcome in cancer survivors. *Psycho-Oncology, 17*, 917–25.

McClendon-Theobald, D., & Burlingame, G. (in press). Group climate: Construct in search of clarity. In R. Conyne (Ed.), *Oxford handbook of group counseling*. New York: Oxford University Press.

McNair, D. M., Lorr, M., & Droppleman, L. F. (1981). *Profile of mood states manual*. San Diego, CA: Educational and Industrial Testing Services.

McRoberts, C., Burlingame, G. M., & Hoag, M. J. (1998). Comparative efficacy of individual and group psychotherapy: A meta-analytic perspective. *Group Dynamics, 2*(2), 101–117.

Moos, R. H. (1986). *Group Environment Scale manual* (2nd ed.). Palo Alto, CA: Consulting Psychologists Press.

Moos, R., & Humphrey, B. (1974). *Group environment scale*, Palo Alto, CA: Consulting Psychologists Press.

Mullen, B., & Copper, C. (1994). The relationship between group cohesiveness and performance: An integration. *Psychological Bulletin, 115*, 210–27.

*Norton, P. J., Hayes, S. A., & Springer, J. R. (2008). Transdiagnostic cognitive-behavioral group therapy for anxiety: Outcome and process. *International Journal of Cognitive Therapy, 1*(3), 266–79.

*Oei, T. P. S., & Browne, A. (2006). Components of group processes: Have they contributed to the outcome of mood and anxiety disorder patients in a group cognitive-behaviour therapy program? *American Journal of Psychotherapy, 60*(1), 53–70.

*Ogrodniczuk, J., & Piper, W. (2003). The effect of group climate on outcome in two forms of short-term group therapy. *Group Dynamics: Theory, Research, and Practice, 7*, 64–76.

*Ogrodniczuk, J. S., Piper, W. E., & Joyce, A. S. (2005). The negative effect of alexithymia on the outcome of group therapy for complicated grief: What role might the therapist play? *Comprehensive Psychiatry, 46*, 206–213.

*Ogrodniczuk, J. S., Piper, W. E., & Joyce, A. S. (2006). Treatment compliance among patients with personality disorders receiving group psychotherapy: What are the roles of interpersonal distress and cohesion? *Psychiatry: Interpersonal and Biological Processes, 69*(3), 249–61.

Palmer, K. D., Baker, R. C., & McGee, T. F. (1997). The effects of pretraining on group psychotherapy for incest-related issues. *International Group Psychotherapy, 47*(1), 71–89.

Piper, W. E., Marrache, M., Lacroix, R., Richardsen, A. M., & Jones, B. D. (1983). Cohesion as a basic bond in groups. *Human Relations, 36*, 93–108.

*Ratto, R., & Hurley, J. R. (1995). Outcomes of inpatient group psychotherapy associated with dispositional and situational affiliativeness. *Group, 19*(3), 163–72.

*Rice, A. H. (2001). Evaluating brief structured group treatment for depression. *Research on Social Work Practice, 11*(1), 53–78.

*Roether, H. A., & Peters, J. J. (1972). Cohesiveness and hostility in group psychotherapy. *American Journal of Psychiatry, 128*(8), 1014–1017.

Rosenberg, M. (1965). *Society and the adolescent self-image*. Princeton, NJ: Princeton University Press.

*Rugel, R. P., & Barry, B. (1990). Overcoming denial through the group: A test of acceptance theory. *Small Group Research, 21*(1), 45–58.

*Ryum, T., Hagen, R., Nordahl, H. M., Vogel, P. A., & Stiles, T. C. (2009). Perceived group climate as a predictor of long-term outcome in randomized controlled trial of cognitive-behavioral group therapy for patients with comorbid psychiatric disorders. *Behavioural and Cognitive Psychotherapy, 37*, 497–510.

Santarsiero, L. J., Baker, R. C., & McGee, T. F. (1995). The effects of cognitive pretraining on cohesion and self-disclosure in small groups: An analog study. *Journal of Clinical Psychology, 51*(3), 403–409.

Schauenburg, H., Sammet, I., Rabung, S., & Strack, M. (2001). Zur differentiellen Bedeutung des Gruppenerlebens in der stationaren Psychotherapie depressiver Patienten [On the differential importance of group experience in inpatient psychotherapy of depressive patients]. *Gruppenpsychotherapie und Gruppendynamik, 37*, 349–64.

Selvin, H. C., & Hagstrom, W. O. (1963). The empirical classification of formal groups. *American Sociological Review, 28*, 399–411.

Silbergeld, S., Koenig, G. R., Manderscheid, R. W., Meeker, B. F., & Hornung, C. A. (1975). Assessment of environment-therapy systems: The Group Atmosphere Scale. *Journal of Consulting and Clinical Psychology, 43*, 460–69.

Snijders, J. A., Trijsburg, R. W., De Groot, M. H., & Duivenvoorden, H. J. (2005, March). Group cohesion, working alliance, and therapeutic interventions as factors predicting outcome in group psychotherapy for personality disorders: First results of a follow-along study (2003–2006).

Presented at AGPA Research Symposium, New York).

Sternburg, S., & Trijburg, W. (2005). *The relationship between therapeutic interventions and therapeutic outcome.* Unpublished manuscript.

Stokes, J. (1983). Components of Group Cohesion: Intermember attraction, instrumental value and risk taking. *Small Group Research, 14* (2), 163-173.

Strauss, B., Burlingame, G., & Bormann, B (2008). Using the CORE-R batter in group psychotherapy. *Journal of Clinical Psychology, 64*(11), 1225–37.

*Taft, C. T., Murphy, C. M., King, D. W., Musser, P. H., & DeDeyn, J. M. (2003). Process and treatment adherence factors in group cognitive-behavioral therapy for partner violent men. *Journal of Consulting and Clinical Psychology, 71*(4), 812–20.

*Taube-Schiff, M., Suvak, M. K., Antony, M. M., Bieling, P. J., & McCabe, R. E. (2007). Group cohesion in cognitive-behavioral group therapy for social phobia. *Behaviour Research and Therapy, 45,* 687–98.

Trijsburg, R. W., Bogaerds, H., Letiche, M., Bidzjel, L., & Duivenvoorden, H. J. (2004). *De ontwikkeling van de Group Cohesion Questionnaire (GCQ).* The Netherlands: University of Amsterdam/Rotterdam.

*Tschuschke, V., & Dies, R. R. (1994) Intensive analysis of therapeutic factors and outcome in long-term inpatient groups. *International Journal of Group Psychotherapy, 44*(2), 185–208.

*van Andel, P., Erdman, R. A. M., Karsdorp, P. A., Appels, A., & Trijsburg, R. W. (2003). Group cohesion and working alliance: Prediction of treatment outcome in cardiac patients receiving cognitive behavioral group psychotherapy. *Psychotherapy and Psychosomatics, 72,* 141–49.

*Woody, S. R., & Adessky, R. S. (2002). Therapeutic alliance, group cohesion, and homework compliance during cognitive-behavioral group treatment of social phobia. *Behavior Therapy, 33,* 5–27.

*Wright, T. L., & Duncan, D. (1986). Attraction to group, group cohesiveness, and individual outcome: A study of training groups. *Small Group Research, 17*(4), 487–92.

*Yalom, I., Houts, P. S., Zimerberg, S. M., & Rand, K. H. (1967). Prediction of improvement in group therapy: An exploratory study. *Archives of General Psychiatry, 17,* 159–68.

Yalom, I. D., & Leszcz, M. (2005). *The theory and practice of group psychotherapy* (5th ed.). New York: Basic Books.

6

Empathy

Robert Elliott, Arthur C. Bohart, Jeanne C. Watson, *and* Leslie S. Greenberg

Psychotherapist empathy has had a long and sometimes stormy history in psychotherapy. Proposed and codified by Rogers and his followers in the 1940s and 1950s, it was put forward as the foundation of helping skills training popularized in the 1960s and early 1970s. Claims concerning its universal effectiveness were treated with skepticism and came under intense scrutiny by psychotherapy researchers in the late 1970s and early 1980s. After that, research on empathy went into relative eclipse, resulting in a dearth of research between 1975 and 1995 (Duan & Hill, 1996; Watson, 2001).

Since the mid-1990s, however, empathy has once again become a topic of scientific interest in developmental and social psychology (e.g., Bohart & Greenberg, 1997; Ickes, 1997), particularly because empathy came to be seen as a major part of "emotional intelligence" (Goleman, 1995). We believe the time is ripe for the reexamination and rehabilitation of therapist empathy as a key change process in psychotherapy (Bohart & Greenberg, 1997). Indeed, the meta-analytic results we will present clearly support such a conclusion. The most important development in the past 10 years, however, is the emergence of active scientific research on the biological basis of empathy, as part of the new field of social neuroscience

(Decety & Ickes, 2009), which we will address briefly in the next section.

Definitions and Measures
Defining Empathy

The first problem with researching empathy in psychotherapy is that there is no consensual definition (Batson, 2009; Bohart & Greenberg, 1997; Duan & Hill, 1996). Recent neuroscience research on empathy begins to clarify some of the conceptual confusion, as a result of the concerted efforts of researchers using a variety of methods ranging from performance tasks, self-report, and neuropsychological assessment to fMRI and transcranial stimulation. Research examining the brain correlates of different component subprocesses of empathy (Decety & Ickes, 2009) has extended the initial discovery of "mirror neurons" in the motor cortex of macaque monkeys (e.g., Gallese, Fadiga, Fogassi, & Rizzolatti, 1996) to a broader range of affective and perspective-taking components of empathy in humans (Decety & Lamm, 2009). The result of this research has been to deepen and clarify our understanding of therapist empathic processes (Watson & Greenberg, 2009), resulting in a growing consensus (e.g., Eisenberg & Eggum, 2009) that it consists of three major subprocesses, each with specific sets of neuroanatomical correlates. First, there is an *emotional simulation* process that mirrors the emotional elements of the other's bodily experience with brain activation centering in the limbic system (amygdala, insula, anterior cingulate cortex) and elsewhere (Decety & Lamm, 2009; Goubert, Craig, & Buysse, 2009). Second, a conceptual, *perspective-taking* process operates, particularly localized in medial and ventromedial areas of prefrontal cortex as well as the temporal cortex (Shamay-Tsoory, 2009). Third, there is an *emotion-regulation* process that people use to reappraise or soothe their personal distress at the other person's pain or discomfort, allowing them to mobilize compassion and helping behavior for the other (probably based in orbitofrontal cortex, as well as in the prefrontal and right inferior parietal cortex).

Interestingly, the two therapeutic approaches that have most focused on empathy—client-centered therapy and psychoanalytic—have emphasized its cognitive or perspective-taking (Selman, 1980) aspects, as well as its feeling aspects. That is, they have focused on empathy as connected knowing (Belenky et al., 1986), understanding the client's frame of reference or way of experiencing the world. By some accounts, 70% or more of Carl Rogers' responses were to meaning rather than to feeling, despite the fact that his mode of responding is typically called "reflection of feeling" (Brodley & Brody, 1990; Hayes & Goldfried, 1996; Tausch, 1988). However, understanding clients' frames of reference does include understanding their affective experiences. In addition, empathy and sympathy have typically been sharply differentiated, with therapists such as Rogers disdaining sympathy but prizing empathy (Shlien, 1997). In affective neuroscience terms, this means that therapists in this tradition have often emphasized conscious perspective-taking processes over the more automatic, bodily-based emotional simulation processes.

Nevertheless, it is easy to see both processes in Rogers' (1980) definition of empathy:

> "the therapist's sensitive ability and willingness to understand the client's thoughts, feelings and struggles from the client's point of view. [It is] this ability to see completely through the client's eyes, to adopt his frame of reference . . ." (p. 85) . . . "It means entering the private perceptual world of the other . . . being sensitive, moment by moment, to the changing felt meanings which flow in this other person . . . It means sensing meanings of which he or she is scarcely aware. . . ." (p. 142).

Defined this way, empathy is a higher-order category, under which different subtypes, aspects, expressions, and modes can be nested. There are different ways one can put oneself into the shoes of the other: emotionally, cognitively, on a moment-to-moment basis, or by trying to grasp an overall sense of what it is like to be that person. Within these subtypes different aspects of the client's experience can become the focus of empathy (Bohart & Greenberg, 1997). Similarly, there are many different ways of expressing empathy, including empathic reflections, empathic questions, experience-near interpretations, empathic conjectures, as well as the responsive use of other therapeutic procedures. Accordingly, empathy is best understood as a complex construct consisting of a variety of different acts used in different ways.

We distinguish between three main modes of therapeutic empathy: empathic rapport, communicative attunement, and person empathy. First, for some therapists empathy is primarily the establishment of empathic rapport and support. The therapist exhibits a compassionate attitude toward the client and tries to demonstrate that he or she understands the client's experience, often in order to set the context for effective treatment. A second mode of empathy consists of an active, ongoing effort to stay attuned on a moment-to-moment basis with the client's communications and unfolding experience. Client-centered and experiential therapists are most likely to emphasize this form of empathy. The therapist's attunement may be expressed in many different ways, but most likely in empathic responses. The third mode, person empathy (Elliott, Watson, Goldman, & Greenberg, 2003) or experience-near understanding of the client's world, consists of a sustained effort to understand the kinds of experiences the client has had, both historically and presently, that form the background of the client's current experiencing. The question is: How have the client's experiences led him or her to see/feel/think and act as he or she does? This is the type of empathic understanding emphasized by psychodynamic therapists. However, empathic rapport, communicative attunement, and person empathy are not mutually exclusive, and the differences are a matter of emphasis.

Many other definitions for empathy have been advanced: as a trait or response skill (Egan, 1982; Truax & Carkhuff, 1967), as an identification process of "becoming" the experience of the client (Mahrer, 1997), and as a hermeneutic interpretive process (Watson, 2001). Perhaps the most practical conception, and one that we will draw on in our meta-analysis, is Barrett-Lennard's (1981) operational definition of empathy in terms of three different perspectives: that of the therapist (empathic resonance), the observer (expressed empathy), and the client (received empathy).

Measuring Empathy
Reflecting the complex, multidimensional nature of empathy, a confusing welter of measures have been developed. Within psychotherapy, the measures of therapist empathy fall into four categories: empathy rated by nonparticipant raters; client-rated empathy; therapists rating their own empathy; and empathic accuracy (congruence between therapist and client perceptions of the client).

Observer-Rated Empathy. Some of the earliest observer measures of empathy were those of Truax and Carkhuff (1967) and Carkhuff and Berenson (1967). These scales asked raters to decide if the content of the therapist's response detracts from the client's response, is interchangeable with it, or adds to or carries it forward. Typically, trained raters listened to 2–5 minute samples from session tapes. Samples are usually drawn from the beginning, middle, and/or the end of therapy. Scales such as these do not adequately reflect the client-centered conception of empathy as an attitude because they focus narrowly on a particular kind of response, often empathic reflections. Furthermore, the equation of a particular response with empathy has also made these scales less appropriate for measuring empathy in approaches other than client centered (Lambert, De Julio, & Stein, 1978).

More recent observer empathy measures are based on broader understandings of forms of empathic responding. Elliott and colleagues' (1982) measure breaks empathy down into component elements and has shown good psychometric properties, but it has not been widely used. Watson and Prosser (2002) developed a promising new observer-rated measure of empathy that assesses therapists' verbal and nonverbal behavior and shows convergent validity with client ratings on the Barrett-Lennard Relationship Inventory.

In addition, the therapist's general empathy can also be rated by others who know or have supervised the therapist. For instance, therapists' empathic capacities can be rated by their supervisors (Gelso, Latts, Gomez, & Fassinger, 2002). For purposes of our meta-analysis, we lumped together all observer perspective measures of empathy.

Client Ratings. The most widely used client-rated measure of empathy is the empathy scale of the Barrett-Lennard Relationship Inventory (BLRI). Other client rating measures have been developed (e.g., Hamilton, 2000; Lorr, 1965; Persons & Burns, 1985; Truax & Carkhuff, 1967). Rogers (1957) hypothesized that clients' *perceptions* of therapists' facilitative conditions (positive regard, empathy, and congruence) predict therapeutic outcome. Accordingly, the BLRI, which measures clients' perceptions, is an operational definition of Rogers' hypothesis. In several earlier reviews, including our meta-analysis in the previous edition of this book, client-perceived empathy predicted outcome better than observer- or therapist-rated empathy (Barrett-Lennard, 1981; Gurman, 1977; Bohart, Elliott, Greenberg, & Watson, 2002; Orlinsky, Grawe, & Parks, 1994; Orlinsky & Howard, 1978, 1987).

Therapist Ratings. Therapist empathy self-rating scales are not so common, but the BLRI does have one. Earlier reviews (Barrett-Lennard, 1981; Gurman, 1977) found that therapist-rated empathy neither predicted outcome nor correlated with client-rated or observer-rated empathy. However, we previously found that therapist-rated empathy did predict outcome, but at a lower level than client or observer ratings (Bohart et al., 2002).

Empathic Accuracy. Several studies use measures of therapist–client perceptual congruence, commonly referred to as "empathic accuracy" (Ickes, 1997, 2003). These typically consist of therapists rating clients as they think the clients would rate themselves on various measures, such as personality scales or lists of symptoms, and then comparing these ratings to how clients actually rated themselves. For instance, one study compared how therapists rated clients on Kelly's REP grid with how clients rated themselves (Landfield, 1971). The measure of empathy is the degree of congruence between therapist and client ratings. This can be referred to as predictive empathy, because the therapist is trying to predict how clients will rate themselves. This is closer to a measure of the therapist's ability to form a global understanding of what it is like to be the client (person empathy) than it is to a process measure of ongoing communicative attunement.

Recent work on empathic accuracy, however, does provide a predictive measure of communicative attunement (Ickes, 1997, 2003). This line of research typically employs a tape-assisted recall procedure in which therapists or observers' moment-to-moment empathy is measured by comparing their perceptions of client experiences to clients' reports of those experiences. Unfortunately, no process–outcome studies using this promising but time-consuming method have yet been carried out.

Correlations among Different Empathy Measures. Intercorrelations of different empathy measures have generally been weak. Low correlations have been reported between cognitive and affective measures (Gladstein et al., 1987) and between predictive measures and the BLRI (Kurtz & Grummon, 1972). Other research has found that tape-rated measures correlate only moderately with client-perceived empathy (Gurman, 1977). These weak correlations are not surprising when one considers what the different instruments are supposed to be measuring. Trying to predict how a client will fill out a symptom check list is very different from responding sensitively and tentatively in a way that demonstrates subtle understanding of what the client is trying to communicate, while checking and adjusting one's emerging understanding with that of the client. Similarly, client ratings of therapist understanding may be based on many other things than the therapists' particular skill in empathic reflection. Accordingly, we should not expect different measures of this complex construct to correlate (Gladstein et al., 1987).

Confounding between Empathy and Other Relationship Variables. A related concern is the distinctiveness of empathy from other relationship constructs. One early review of more than 20 studies primarily using the BLRI found that, on average, empathy correlated 0.62 with congruence and 0.53 with positive regard, and 0.28 with unconditionality (Gurman, 1977). Factor analysis of scale scores found that one global factor typically emerged, with empathy loading on it along with congruence and positive regard (Gurman, 1977). Others have reported that the empathy scale loaded 0.93 on a global BLRI factor, with Positive Regard loading 0.87 and Congruence loading 0.92 (Blatt et al., 1996). Such results suggest that clients' perceptions of empathy are not clearly differentiated from their perceptions of other relationship factors.

On the other hand, reviews of several factor analytic studies where, instead of using scale scores, specific items were used have found empathy emerging as a separate factor (Gurman, 1977). In addition, empathy tends to correlate more highly with the bond component of the therapeutic alliance than with the task and goal components (Horvath & Greenberg, 1986).

Thus, there is evidence both for and against the hypothesis that the Rogerian triad of empathy, unconditional positive regard, and congruence are separate and distinct variables. We view empathy as a relationship component that is both conceptually distinct and part of a higher-order relationship construct.

Clinical Example

Mark presented to psychotherapy complaining of pervasive anxiety. He was a 30-year-old unmarried man who had been struggling since his early 20s to break into the movie business. When he entered therapy, he was working as a waiter. He came from a traditional family, living in the southern United States. His brothers and sisters all had successful careers and were married, with children. His parents were constantly pestering him about his not being married and not having a stable career. His anxiety attacks had begun a few weeks after a visit home for the Christmas holidays. When Mark came to his first appointment, he was clearly agitated. He had previously called and had sounded desperate over the phone. The therapist initially was concerned that Mark might be in a state of crisis.

The therapist's orientation was integrative experiential/humanistic, based in the principles of person-centered therapy. The therapist tried to understand the client's point of view actively and empathically and to share that understanding, using her attunement to the client's experience to identify effective interventions, and to stay responsively attuned so that therapeutic procedures could be adjusted to maximize learning. The following are two examples of the therapist's utilization of empathic responding during the first session:

C1: I'm really in a panic (anxious, looking plaintively at the therapist). I feel anxious all the time. Sometimes it seems so bad I really worry that I'm on the verge of a psychotic break. I'm actually afraid of completely falling apart. Nothing like this has ever happened to me before. I always felt in charge of myself before, but now I can't seem to get any control over myself at all.

T1: So a real sense of vulnerability—kind of like you don't even know yourself anymore.

C2: Yes! That's it. I don't know myself anymore. I feel totally lost. The anxiety feels like a big cloud that just takes me over, and I can't even find myself in it anymore. I don't even know what I want, what I trust . . . I'm lost.

T2: Totally lost, like, "Where did Mark go? I can't find myself anymore."

C3: No, I can't (sadly, and thoughtfully).

The dialogue continued like this, and soon the therapist's empathic recognition provided the client with a sense of being understood. This fostered a sense of safety, and gradually the client moved from agitation into reflective sadness. The client then began to reflect on his experience in a more productive, exploratory manner. He talked about the basic conflict in his life: over whether to continue to pursue an acting career or to find a "real job" and life partner, given that he was now 30 and had shown no signs of making a breakthrough in acting.

Later, the client role-played a dialogue between two sides of himself. One side, his critic or "should" side, said that he should get a stable job and get married and criticized him for not being married. The other side was the "want" side—or in this case, the "don't want" side—which said "I don't want to live an ordinary life; I want to live a creative life." This side came out in the form of defensive rebellion. Empathic sensitivity was used to help the therapist tune into the client's point of view and to focus the client's exploratory activities during the role-play. What emerged from this role-play was that there was a longing for a "normal" lifestyle underlying Mark's defensive rebellion, in conflict with a desire to do something creative.

During the first few sessions, the client had repeatedly expressed the suspicion that something about his early relationships with his parents played an important role in his current problems. Initially, the therapist had not taken this too seriously, since progress was apparently being made through the collaborative use of other procedures. Because the therapist was not psychogenetic and past oriented, she had not tuned into this. The therapist's lack of person empathy (i.e., grasping of how figural this was for the client within the client's frame of reference) for the larger meaning of the client's interest in this topic had effectively shut off this avenue of exploration.

Eventually, the therapist listened, responded in an invitational way to the client, and the client began to explore his childhood. This illustrates how empathy not only gives permission, but also provides active support for exploration. It also illustrates how sensitive empathic understanding of the *client's* way of seeing the problem is sometimes crucial for therapeutic progress (Hubble, Duncan, & Miller, 1999). This led to a breakthrough moment. In reviewing his childhood, Mark became emotionally aware of how neglected he had felt as a child by his high-achieving parents, who were not mean and cruel, but who were not themselves highly empathic. As a child, the client had always been unusually interested in fantasy activities, and was a rather "inner" person, in contrast to his siblings, who were more conventional and high-achievers at school. The parents had not known what to make of their unique child and were unable to respond in an empathic and supportive way to his emerging uniqueness.

The result was that he had had to adopt a defensive "I have a right to be different" attitude. He was rarely able to genuinely consider whether he wanted to be conventional or not. Underlying this was a longing for conventionality. Accessing this in the context of his family life helped him accept that he was different and to mourn the fact that he was not conventional (and, in effect, mourn that he might never be what his family wanted him to be). Over the course of this work, Mark's anxiety decreased. Eventually he made a decision to continue to pursue an acting career, for a while at least; and his crisis abated.

Meta-Analytic Review

In this section we report the results of an original meta-analysis conducted on available research relating empathy to psychotherapy outcome. We addressed the following questions: (a) What is the association between therapist empathy and client outcome? (b) Do different forms of psychotherapy yield different levels of association between empathy and outcome? (c) Does the type of empathy measure predict the level of association between empathy and outcome? (d) What other study and sample characteristics predict an association between empathy and outcome (i.e., sample size, treatment setting, therapy format and length, level of client severity, therapist experience, type of outcome measure, unit of process)?

Search Strategy

Articles were culled from previous reviews (Beutler, Crago, & Arizmendi, 1986; Gurman, 1977; Lambert, DeJulio & Stein, 1978; Mitchell, Bozarth, & Krauft, 1977; Orlinsky & Howard, 1986; Orlinsky, Grawe, & Parks, 1994; Parloff et al., 1978; Truax and Mitchell, 1971; N. Watson, 1984). We also searched PsycINFO and PsycLIT forward from 1992 (2 years before the publication of the last major review of empathy research in Orlinsky et al., 1994), using the search terms, "empathy" or "empathic" and "psychotherapy,"

"counseling," or "counselling". Additionally, we consulted the tables of contents of relevant journals such as: *Psychotherapy*, *Person-Centered Journal*, *Psychotherapy Research*, *Journal of Counseling Psychology*, and *Person-Centered and Experiential Psychotherapies*.

Inclusion Criteria

Our inclusion criteria were as follows: (a) a specific measure of empathy was used, (b) empathy was related to some measure of therapy outcome, (c) the client sample involved genuine clinical problems, (d) the average number of sessions was three or more, (e) the study was available in English, (f) the study included at least five clients, (g) the study was available in published form, and (h) the study contained sufficient information to calculate a weighted effect size.

Characteristics of the Studies

To examine variables that might moderate the empathy–outcome association, we evaluated the studies on a wide range of sample and methodological features. For measures of outcome, we included a study as long as there was some assessment of the effects of therapy, even if only at the session level (immediate outcome). For example, we included abstinence from drinking (Miller et al., 1980), level of depression (Burns & Nolen-Hoeksema, 1992), MMPI scores (Kiesler et al., 1967), client satisfaction (Lorr, 1965), supervisors' ratings of client improvement (Gelso et al., 2002), client and therapist posttherapy ratings of amount of change (Hamilton, 2000), and postsession ratings of progress (Orlinsky & Howard, 1967). There is some conceptual overlap between feeling understood and client satisfaction, but this one outcome measure represented only 6% of effects; we subsequently examined type of outcome measure as a moderator variable. The resulting sample consisted of 224 separate tests of the empathy–outcome association, aggregated into 59 different samples of clients (from 57 studies) and encompassing a total of 3,599 clients. Table 6.1 summarizes relevant study characteristics.

Estimation of Effect Size

For effect sizes, we used Pearson correlations if available. Our strategy was to extract all possible effects. Therefore, we used the following conventions (extensions of those used in Smith, Glass, & Miller, 1980) to estimate r: First, if we had a significance level, we converted it to r. If the result was nonsignificant, but we had enough information to calculate a t and then convert, we did so. If we had no other information than that the effect was nonsignificant, we set r at 0. If the authors indicated a "nonsignificant trend" but did not report a correlation (for instance, a key study, Kiesler et al., 1967, indicated several trends on MMPI scales), we estimated the trend by assigning an ES of half the size of a significant r.

Coding Procedure

The following variables were coded: therapy format (individual or group); theoretical orientation; experience level of therapists; treatment setting (inpatient, outpatient); number of sessions (typically the mean); type of problems (mixed neurotic, depression, anxiety, severe problems such as psychosis); source of outcome measure (therapist rating, client rating, objective, and other measures); when outcome was measured (e.g., postsession, posttherapy, followup); type of outcome measured (symptom change, improvement, global); source of empathy measure (objective ratings, therapist, client, therapist/client congruence, trait measure); and unit of measure (2–5 minute samples, session, therapy to date).

We conducted two sets of analyses: by effects and by studies. First, we analyzed the 224 separate effects in order to examine the impact of perspective of empathy measurement and type of outcome. Second, study-level analyses used averaged individual effects within client samples using

Table 6.1   Study Characteristics

Parametric characteristics:	M	SD	Range	
Sample size:	61	59.6	6–320	
Length of therapy (sessions)	24	42.4	3–228	
Effects per study	3.8	5.7	1–42	
Categorical characteristics:	**Modal categories**		**%**	
Time period (range: 1961–2008)	Before 1980		49	
Theoretical orientation	Mixed, eclectic, or unknown		40	
Modality	Individual		74	
Client presenting problem	Mixed neurotic (mixed anxiety/depression)		40	
Therapist experience level	Recent PhD or M.D.		36	
Outcome assessment time point	Posttreatment		60	
Empathy perspective	Client (mostly Barrett-Lennard) (Observer, mostly Truax-Carkhuff: 34%)		39	
Empathy measurement unit	Therapy to date		60	

Fisher r-to-Z conversions to correct for distributional biases before further analysis, thus avoiding problems of nonindependence and eliminating bias due to variable numbers of effects reported in different studies (Lipsey & Wilson, 2001; e.g., one study, Kurtz & Grummon, 1972, contributed 42 effects). For analyses across studies, we weighted studies by inverse error and analyzed for heterogeneity of effects using Cochrane's Q (following the Hunter-Schmidt method, using the program in Diener, Hilsenroth, & Weinberger, 2009), and also I^2, an estimate of the proportion of variation due to true variability as opposed to random error (Higgins, Thompson, Deeks, & Altman, 2003). Finally, where necessary in the correlational analyses of moderator variables to correct for nonindependence, we used effects weighted by the inverse of number of analyses per study.

Results

The single best summary value, as shown in Table 6.2, is the study-level, weighted r of 0.30, a medium effect size. Average effects were 0.22 for analyses of the 224 nonindependent separate effects, probably an underestimate due to smaller effects found in one study (Kurtz & Grummon, 1972). These values were very similar to our previous review (Bohart et al., 2002) and mean that in general empathy accounts for about 9% of the variance in therapy outcome. This effect size is on the same order of magnitude as, or slightly larger than, previous analyses of the relationship between the alliance in individual therapy and treatment outcome (i.e., Horvath, Flückiger, & Symonds, this volume, Chapter 2: 0.275; Martin, Garske, & Davis, 2000: 0.22). Overall, empathy typically accounts for more outcome variance than do specific treatment methods (compare Wampold's, 2001, estimate of 1% to 8% for intervention effects).

However, the 0.30 figure conceals statistically significant variability in effects, as indicated by a study-level Cochrane's Q of 205.8 ($p < 0.001$); in addition, I^2 was 67%, considered to be a large value. This means that a further examination of possible moderators of the empathy–outcome association is not only justified but is in fact necessary (Lipsey & Wilson, 2001).

Moderators and Mediators

We divide this section on moderators and mediators into two parts: meta-analytic analyses of moderator variables and therapist-mediating factors.

Meta-Analytic Moderator Analyses

The significant Q and large I^2 statistics point to the existence of important moderator variables or sources of heterogeneity but do not specify what those are. We began our search by testing the hypothesis that

Table 6.2 Empathy–Outcome Correlations: Overall Summary Statistics

N	Effect level (N = 224)		Study level (N = 59)	
	M	SD	M	SD
Weighted mean r	0.22*	0.33	0.30*	0.13
Cochrane's Q		646.22*		174.65*
I^2		65.49		66.79

* $p < 0.001$.

Note: Fisher's r-to-z transformation used to calculate means and SDs. Weighted rs use inverse variance (i.e., n–3) as weights and are tested against mean r = 0 following the Hunter-Schmidt method using Deiner's (2010) program.

different empathy–outcome correlations might be obtained for different theoretical orientations. For example, one might expect the association to be larger in those therapies for which empathy is held to be a key change process, such as person-centered therapies. However, our analyses, summarized in Table 6.3, turned up little evidence of such a trend, but significant, large amounts of nonchance heterogeneity within the CBT and Other/Unspecified therapy samples. This finding contrasts with our previous meta-analysis (Bohart et al., 2002), where we found tantalizing evidence that empathy might be more important to outcome in cognitive-behavioral therapies than in others. However, our present analysis failed to confirm that conjecture but points to important sources of variability that need to be explored

In Table 6.4 we chart relations between specific types of empathy measures and outcome, using effect-level analyses aggregated within studies (n = 82). As we expected, and has been noted by previous reviewers (e.g., Barrett-Lennard, 1981; Parloff, Waskow & Wolfe, 1978), the perspective of the empathy rater made a difference for empathy–outcome correlations. Specifically, client measures predicted outcome the best (mean corrected r = 0.32; n = 38), slightly but not significantly better than observer-rated measures (0.25; n = 27) and therapist measures (0.20; n = 11); each of these mean effects was significantly greater than zero (p < 0.001). In contrast, empathy accuracy measures were unrelated to outcome (0.08; n = 5, ns). Although the overall Q value for between-group heterogeneity was not significant, comparison of confidence intervals indicated that client-perceived empathy significantly predicted outcome better than accuracy measures (p < 0.05). A word of caution: All perspectives except empathic accuracy are characterized by large (>50%), statistically significant amounts of nonchance heterogeneity. Clarification of the source of this heterogeneity awaits further research; however, for now it seems fair to say that clients' feelings of being understood and observer ratings (and to a lesser extent, therapist impressions) appear to carry significant weight as far as outcome goes, but that empathic accuracy measures do not, in spite of their intuitive appeal.

Finally, in Table 6.5, we examine several other variables that might account for some of the heterogeneity of the effect sizes: year of publication, sample size, outpatient versus inpatient treatment, treatment format (individual vs. group), length of therapy, client severity, therapist experience level, globalness of outcome measures

Table 6.3 Mean Effects across Theoretical Orientation

Theoretical orientation	n	Mean weighted r	Within group Q	I^2
Experiential/ humanistic	8	0.26**	7.68	8.91
Cognitive-behavioral	10	0.31**	24.55*	63.34
Psychodynamic	4	0.19**	2.01	0
Other/unspecified	37	0.31**	138.01**	74.64
Between groups Q	2.39 (df = 3, 55, ns)			

*p < 0.01; **p < 0.001.

Note: Mean correlations calculated using Fisher's z-scores. Significance tests for mean correlations are against the null hypothesis of mean r = 0. Q tests for heterogeneity are evaluated as a chi-square test, using Diener et al.'s (2009) program and the Hunter-Schmidt method. Within-groups Q is analogous to a one-way ANOVA with study samples as levels; between-groups Q calculated as difference between total sample Q and within-group Q, following Lipsey and Wilson (2001).

Table 6.4   Mean Effects across Empathy Measurement Perspectives

Measurement perspective	n	Mean weighted r	Within group Q	I^2
Observer	27	0.25**	93.14**	72.09
Client	38	0.32**	119.35**	69.00
Therapist	11	0.20**	21.05*	52.50
Empathic accuracy	5	0.08	5.91	32.35
Total	82	0.27	258.08**	68.61
Between-groups Q	2.39 (df = 3, 78, ns)			

$*p < 0.05; **p < 0.001.$
Note: See note for Table 6.3.

(individualized to satisfaction ratings), and size of empathy unit (5 min segment to whole therapy). Using ordinary (that is, unweighted correlations), none of these were statistically significant. On the other hand, analyses using weighting for inverse error (i.e., sample size minus 3) were significant for all variables except outcome globality and size of empathy unit; however, these suffer from nonindependence within studies and will require a substantially larger set of studies or more sophisticated, multilevel meta-analytic methods to verify. Briefly, these analyses point to the

possibility that empathy is slightly more predictive of positive outcome in group therapy, with more severely distressed clients, in more recent studies, and with more global outcome measures (i.e., satisfaction ratings, which begin to overlap conceptually with empathy).

On the other hand, it may be that the empathy relationship is slightly less predictive of positive outcome in inpatient settings, and with more experienced therapists (study level mean $r = -0.19$; effect level = -0.29); the latter is the largest of this set of correlations and is consistent with our 2002

Table 6.5   Correlations between Empathy–Outcome Effect Size and Selected Moderator Variables

Predictor	Unweighted		Weighted	
	r	n	r	n
Year of publication	0.14	59	0.12*	3422
No. of clients in study	0.06	59	0.15*	3422
Setting (1 = outpatient; 2 = inpatient)	−0.13	58	−0.08*	3305
Format (1 = individual; 2 = group)	0.12	54	0.15*	2807
Length of therapy (in sessions)	0.04	41	−0.08*	2074
Client severity (3-point scale)	0.10	41	0.14*	2320
Therapist experience level (6-point scale)	−0.19	51	−0.29*	2820
Outcome globality (6-point scale: individualized to satisfaction ratings)	0.17	59	0.00	3360
Size of empathy unit (4-point scale)	−0.06	59	-0.02	3443

$*p < 0.001.$
Note: Weighted analyses used inverse error (i.e., degrees of freedom) but are not corrected for nonindependence of participants within studies; analyses of outcome globality and size of empathy unit analyses were also inverse weighted by number of effects per study to correct for nonindependence of effects within studies.

meta-analysis. As we previously speculated, there are at least two possible reasons for this: To begin with, inexperienced therapists may vary more in empathy, while smaller correlations for experienced therapists may reflect a restriction of range or ceiling effect. Alternatively, experienced therapists may have developed additional skills such as effective problem solving, so that clients are more likely to forgive empathic misattunements.

Therapist-Mediating Factors

As noted earlier, affective neuroscience researchers have proposed that empathy involves three interlinked skills or processes: affective simulation, perspective taking, and regulation of one's own emotions (Decety & Jackson, 2004). Supporting this, research has found a relationship between various measures of cognitive complexity, such as those of perspective taking or abstract ability, and empathy in both developmental psychology and in psychotherapy (Eisenberg & Fabes, 1990; Henschel & Bohart, 1981; Watson, 2001). With respect to affective simulation and emotion regulation, therapists who were open to conflictual, countertransferential feelings were perceived as more empathic by clients (Peabody & Gelso, 1982).

The degree of similarity between therapist and client (Duan & Hill, 1996; Gladstein & Associates, 1987; Watson, 2001) also influences the level of empathy. Similarity and familiarity between the target of empathy and the empathizer have been found to be important modulators of empathy in neuroscientific studies of mirror neurons (Watson & Greenberg, 2009). Another important factor is therapist nonlinguistic and paralinguistic behavior. This encompasses therapists' posture, vocal quality, ability to encourage exploration using emotion words, and the relative infrequency of talking too much, giving advice, and interrupting

(Duan & Hill, 1996; Watson, 2001). Other research has shown that responses that are just ahead of the client seem to be more effective than responses that are either at the same level as the client, or at a more global level (Sachse, 1990a, 1990b; Tallman et al., 1994; Truax & Carkhuff, 1967). And a qualitative study of clients' experience of empathy, interrupting, failing to maintain eye contact, and dismissing the client's position while imposing the therapist's own position were all perceived as unempathic (Myers, 2000). Conversely, being nonjudgmental, attentive, open to discussing any topic, and paying attention to details were perceived as empathic.

Client Contributions

Clinical and research experience suggest that the amount of therapist empathy varies as a function of the client. Early studies (Kiesler et al.,1967), for example, found that levels of empathy were higher with clients who had less pathology, who were brighter, but yet who were lower in self-esteem. Therefore, the client him or herself almost certainly influences therapist empathy. As Barrett-Lennard (1981) pointed out, the client's revealing of their experiencing is an essential link in the cycle of empathy. Clients who are more open to and able to communicate their inner experiencing will be easier to empathize with. Empathy truly appears to be a mutual process of shared communicative attunement (Orlinsky et al., 1994).

On the other hand, not all clients respond favorably to explicit empathic expressions. In their review, Beutler, Crago, and Arizmendi (1986, p. 279) cite evidence that suggests that "patients who are highly sensitive, suspicious, poorly motivated, and reactive against authority perform relatively poorly with therapists who are particularly empathic, involved, and accepting." Another study (Mohr & Woodhouse, 2000) found that some clients prefer businesslike rather than warm, empathic therapists. It is worth noting, however, that when therapists are truly empathic they attune to their clients' needs and accordingly adjust how and how much they express empathy.

More broadly, Duan and Hill (1996) speculated that different types of empathy may be hindering or helpful to clients at different times. Hill and her colleagues (Hill et al., 1992; Thompson & Hill, 1991) found that when clients had negative in-session reactions to their therapists, the therapist's awareness or understanding of the reaction "led to interventions that were perceived as less helpful than when the awareness was absent" (p. 269). In such relational ruptures, it is probably useful for therapist empathy to be accompanied and deepened by genuine warmth, openness, and concern for the clients' feelings, rather than defending oneself and blaming the client (also see Safran, Muran, & Eubanks-Carter, this volume, Chapter 11).

Keeping in mind the notion of empathy as not only getting inside the skin of the client, but getting inside the skin of the relationship (O'Hara, 1984), it may be that in some cases the therapist is more empathic by not expressing empathy. Martin (2000, pp. 184–185) notes: "Think of the insensitive irony of a therapist who says, 'I sense the sadness you want to hide. It seems like you don't want to be alone right now but you also don't want somebody talking to you about your sadness . . .'" This response might technically seem empathic, but in fact at a higher level, it is unempathic, controlling, and intrusive, because it violates the client's need for interpersonal distance. Variations among clients in desire for and receptivity to different expressions of empathy need further research.

Limitations of the Research

Many reviewers (e.g., Watson, 2001; Patterson, 1984) have discussed problems with the research on empathy. In addition to the well-known difficulty of inferring causality from correlational data, these entail: (a) the questionable validity of some outcome measures (e.g., client satisfaction); (b) lack of appropriate, sensitive outcome measures; (c) restricted range of predictor and criterion variables; (d) confounds among variations in time of assessment, experience of raters, and sampling methods; (e) reliance on obsolete diagnostic categories; and (f) incomplete reporting of methods and results. In fact, these and other problems are not restricted to empathy research but are common to all process–outcome research (Elliott, 2010).

The restricted range of predictor and criterion variables is particularly a problem. In the Mitchell, Truax, Bozarth, and Krauft (1973) study, for instance, most of the therapists scored below the minimum considered to be effective, and outcome was only modest to moderate in the study. It is not surprising that no significant correlations were found. Furthermore, in a few cases, results were reported as either significant in the positive direction or nonsignificant, possibly disguising weak negative effects. This is particularly a problem for calculating effect sizes based on limited information, thus introducing error into the process.

The key question of whether empathy is causally related to therapeutic outcome—as opposed to being merely a correlate of it—cannot be answered definitively from our meta-analysis. This is the central limitation of the process–outcome research reviewed here. However, data from several studies shed light on the question. First, Burns and Nolen-Hoeksema (1992) and Cramer and Takens (1992) have used causal modeling (structural equation modeling, path analysis) to explore the relationship between empathy and outcome. Second, in another study (Miller et al., 1980), ratings of therapist empathy were made by supervisors before and independent of knowing about outcome data. Yet empathy showed a strong ($r = 0.82$) relationship to outcome in a cognitive-behavioral program for drinking. Third, Anderson (1999) measured therapists' facilitative interpersonal skills, including accurate empathy, before therapy, by having them respond to videotapes of clients who presented in difficult interpersonal ways. Anderson found statistically significant relationships between this prior measure of therapist interpersonal skills and client outcome in subsequent psychotherapy, a finding recently replicated with a larger, practice-based sample of therapists and clients (Anderson, Ogles, Patterson, Lambert, & Vermeersch, 2009).

On the other hand, Burns and Nolen-Hoeksema (1992) note that structural equation modeling cannot definitely show causality but only explore and elaborate particular causal models. Miller et al. (1980) had supervisors rate supervisees' levels of empathy, but it is possible that these ratings were influenced by supervisees' reports of how well therapy was going with the clients. In Anderson et al.'s (2009) study in which empathy was measured independently of therapy, empathy is confounded with other facilitative interpersonal skills. Even though empathy is the predominant process in client-centered and related therapy, it is not the only process.

The evidence we have presented is clearly compatible with a causal model implicating therapist empathy as a mediating process leading to client change. It is true that correlational studies can only probe into or lend support for or against causal models of therapeutic change. As is the case for much of the behavioral sciences, establishing conclusive evidence for particular hypothesized causal processes is notoriously difficult and may ultimately prove elusive. Insofar as codes of professional ethics stipulate a caring, transparent, empathic stance in all professional contacts, it is therefore both impractical and unethical to randomize clients to demonstrably empathic versus unempathic therapists. In such cases, meta-analyses can provide a valid alternative to randomized clinical trials (Berman & Parker, 2002), providing that the identification and analysis of observational studies has been done carefully and systematically.

Therapeutic Practices

The most consistent and robust evidence is that clients' perceptions of feeling understood by their therapists relate favorably to outcome. As we have shown, empathy is a medium-sized predictor of outcome in psychotherapy. It also appears to be a general predictor across theoretical orientations, treatment formats, and client severity levels. This repeated finding, in both dozens of individual studies and now in multiple meta-analyses, leads to a series of clinical recommendations.

• It is important for psychotherapists to make efforts to understand their clients, and to demonstrate this understanding through responses that address the needs of the client as the client perceives them on an ongoing basis. The empathic therapist's primary task is to understand experiences rather than words.

• Empathic therapists do not parrot clients' words back or reflect only the content of those words; instead, they understand overall goals as well as moment-to-moment experiences, both explicit and implicit. Empathy entails capturing the nuances and implications of what people say, and reflecting this back to them for their consideration.

• Empathic responses follow the "moving point" of the focus of the client's concerns as therapy progresses.

• Research has identified a range of useful types of empathic responses, several of which we illustrate here with a running example. *Empathic understanding responses* convey understanding of client experience. For example:

Client: I have been trying to push things away, but every time I sit down to do something it is like I forget what I am doing.
Therapist: Somehow you are not in a space to work, it's hard for you to concentrate.

Empathic affirmations are attempts by the therapist to validate the client's perspective:

C: And my cat is still lost, so we have been staying up at night in case he returns, so last night was another night without sleep . . . and work has been so busy and I have been so tired and P needs my attention. I have been going around in circles and, oh, everything is just a big mess, you know?
T: Yeah, really hard, being pulled in a million different directions and there hasn't been time for you, no wonder it feels like things are a mess.

Empathic evocations try to bring the clients' experience alive using rich, evocative, concrete, connotative language and often have a probing, tentative quality:

C: I don't know what I'm going to do. I have two hundred dollars this month, everything's behind, there isn't enough work, and I have been doing other things, and then my Dad was here. Things are just swirling around me. I don't know how to keep my stuff together enough for me even to survive.
T: It's like being caught in a whirlpool as if it is hard to keep your boat from being sucked in or capsizing.

Empathic explorations are attempts by therapists to get at that which is implicit in clients' narratives and focus on information that has been in the background but not yet articulated:

C: I keep responding to him, like it's against what I want to do.
T: Somehow you can't let go. It is just so hard to walk away.

• Empathic therapists assist clients to symbolize their experience in words and track their emotional responses, so that clients can deepen their experience and reflexively examine their feelings, values, and goals. To this end they need to attend to that which is not said, or that which is at the periphery of awareness as well as that which is said and is in focal awareness (Watson, 2001).

• Empathy entails individualizing responses to particular patients. For example, certain fragile clients may find the usual expressions of empathy too intrusive, while hostile clients may find empathy too directive; still other clients may find an empathic focus on feelings too foreign (Kennedy-Moore & Watson, 1999). Therapists therefore need to know when—and when not—to respond empathically. When clients do not want therapists to be explicitly empathic, truly empathic therapists will use their perspective-taking skills to provide an optimal therapeutic distance (Leitner, 1995) in order to respect their clients' boundaries.

• There is no evidence that accurately predicting clients' own views of their problems or self-perceptions is effective. Therapists should neither assume that they are mind readers nor that their experience of understanding the client will be matched by the client feeling understood. Empathy should always be offered with humility and held lightly, ready to be corrected.

• Finally, because research has shown empathy to be inseparable from the other relational conditions, therapists should seek to offer empathy in the context of positive regard and genuineness. Empathy will not be effective unless it is grounded in authentic caring for the client. We encourage psychotherapists to value empathy as both an "ingredient" of a healthy therapeutic relationship as well as a specific, effective response that strengthens the self and deeper exploration.

References

An asterisk (*) indicates studies included in the meta-analysis.

Anderson, T. (1999). *Specifying non-'specifics' in therapists: The effect of facilitative interpersonal skills in outcome and alliance formation.* Paper presented at the 30th annual meeting of the International Society for Psychotherapy Research, Braga, Portugal.

Anderson, T., Ogles, B. M., Patterson, C. L., Lambert, M. J., & Vermeersch, D. V. (2009). Therapist effects: Facilitative interpersonal skills as a predictor of therapist success. *Journal of Clinical Psychology, 65,* 755–68.

*Barrett-Lennard, G. (1962). Dimensions of therapist response as causal factors in therapeutic change. *Psychological Monographs, 76,* 1–33, Whole Number 562.

Barrett-Lennard, G. T. (1981). The empathy cycle: Refinement of a nuclear concept. *Journal of Counseling Psychology, 28,* 91–100.

*Barrington, B. L. (1967). The differential effectiveness of therapy as measured by the Thematic Apperception Test. In C. R. Rogers, et al. (Eds.), *The therapeutic relationship and its impact* (pp. 337–52). Madison: University of Wisconsin Press. [combined with Kiesler, Mathieu, Klein & Schoeninger, 1967, and Van der Veen, 1967]

Batson, C. D. (2009). These things called empathy: Eight related but distinct phenomena. In J. Decety & W. Ickes (Eds.) (2009). *The social neuroscience of empathy* (pp. 3–15). Cambridge, MA: MIT Press.

Belenky, M. F., Clinchy, B. M., Goldberger, N. R., & Tarule, J. M. (1986). *Women's ways of knowing: The development of self, voice, and mind.* New York: Basic Books.

*Bergin, A. E., & Jasper, L. G. (1969). Correlates of empathy in psychotherapy: A replication. *Journal of Abnormal Psychology, 74,* 477–81.

Berman, N.G., & Parker, R. (2002). Meta-analysis: Neither quick nor easy. BMC Medical Research Methodology, 2(10). Accessed online on June 19, 2010 at http://www.biomedcentral.com/1471-2288/2/10

Beutler, L. E., Crago, M., & Arizmendi, T. G. (1986). Research on therapist variables in psychotherapy. In S. L. Garfield & A. E. Bergin (Eds.), *Handbook of psychotherapy and behavior change* (3rd ed., pp. 257–310). New York: Wiley.

*Beutler, L. E., Johnson, D. T., Neville, C. W., & Workman, S. N. (1972). "Accurate empathy" and the AB dichotomy. *Journal of Consulting and Clinical Psychology, 38,* 372–75.

Blatt, S. J., Zuroff, D. C., Quinlan, D. M., & Pilkonis, P. A. (1996). Interpersonal factors in brief treatment of depression: Further analyses of the National Institute of Mental Health Treatment of Depression Collaborative Research Program. *Journal of Consulting and Clinical Psychology, 64,* 162–71.

Bohart, A. C., Elliott, R., Greenberg, L. S., & Watson, J. C. (2002). Empathy. In J. Norcross (Ed.), *Psychotherapy relationships that work* (pp. 89–108). New York: Oxford University Press.

Bohart, A. C., & Greenberg, L. S. (1997). Empathy: Where are we and where do we go from here? In A. C. Bohart & L. S. Greenberg (Eds.), *Empathy reconsidered: New directions in psychotherapy* (pp. 419–50). Washington, DC: American Psychological Association.

Brodley, B. T., & Brody, A. F. (1990, August). *Understanding client-centered therapy through interviews conducted by Carl Rogers.* Paper presented at the annual convention of the American Psychological Association, Boston, MA.

*Buckley, P., Karasu, T. B., & Charles, E. (1981). Psychotherapists view their personal therapy. *Psychotherapy: Theory, Research, and Practice, 18,* 299–305.

*Bugge, I., Hendel, D. D., & Moen, R. (1985). Client evaluations of therapeutic processes and outcomes in a university mental health center. *Journal of American College Health, 33,* 141–46.

*Bullmann, F., Horlacher, K. D., & Kieser, B. (2004). *Clarifying as a mediator-variable in person-centered psychotherapy and therapists' gender and therapy-school differences in empathy and positive regard.* Unpublished study, Psychological Institute, University of Heidelberg, Germany.

*Burns, D. D., & Nolen-Hoeksma, S. (1992). Therapeutic empathy and recovery from depression in cognitive-behavioral therapy: A structural equation model. *Journal of Consulting and Clinical Psychology, 60,* 441–49.

Carkhuff, R. R., & Berenson, B. (1967). *Beyond counseling and therapy.* New York: Holt, Rinehart, & Winston.

*Cartwright, R. D., & Lerner, B. (1965). Empathy, need to change, and improvement in psychotherapy. *Journal of Consulting Psychology, 27,* 138–44.

*Clark, J. V., & Culbert, S. A. (1965). Mutually therapeutic perception and self-awareness in a T-group. *Journal of Applied Behavioral Science, 1,* 180–94.

*Cooley, E. J., & Lajoy, R. (1980). Therapeutic relationship and improvement as perceived by clients and therapists. *Journal of Clinical Psychology, 36,* 562–70.

*Cramer, D., & Takens, R. (1992). Therapeutic relationship and progress in the first six sessions of individual psychotherapy: A panel analysis. *Counselling Psychology Quarterly, 5,* 25–36.

Decety, J., & Ickes, W. (Eds.) (2009). *The social neuroscience of empathy.* Cambridge, MA: MIT Press.

Decety, J., & Jackson, P. L. (2004). The functional architecture of human empathy. *Behavioral and Cognitive Neuroscience Reviews, 3,* 71–100.

Decety, J., & Lamm, C. (2009). Empathy versus personal distress: Recent evidence from social neuroscience. In J. Decety & W. Ickes (Eds.) (2009). *The Social Neuroscience of Empathy* (pp. 199–213). Cambridge, MA: MIT Press.

Diener, M. J., Hilsenroth, M. J. & Weinberger, J. (2009). A primer on meta-analysis of correlation coefficients: The relationship between patient-reported therapeutic alliance and adult attachment style as an illustration. *Psychotherapy Research, 19,* 519–26.

*Dormaar, J. M., Dijkman, C. I., & de Vries, M. W. (1989). Consensus in patient-therapist interactions: A measure of the therapeutic relationship related to outcome. *Psychotherapy and Psychosomatics, 51,* 69–76.

Duan, C., & Hill, C. E. (1996). A critical review of empathy research. *Journal of Counseling Psychology, 43,* 261–74.

Egan, G. (1982). *The skilled helper* (2nd ed.). Monterey, CA: Brooks/Cole.

Eisenberg, N., & Eggum, N. D. (2009). Empathic responding: Sympathy and personal distress. In J. Decety & W. Ickes (Eds.) (2009). *The Social Neuroscience of Empathy* (pp. 71–83). Cambridge, MA: MIT Press.

Eisenberg, N., & Fabes, R. A. (1990). Empathy: Conceptualization, assessment, and relations to prosocial behavior. *Motivation and Emotion, 14,* 131–49.

Elliott, R. (2010). Psychotherapy change process research: Realizing the promise. *Psychotherapy Research, 20,* 123–35.

Elliott, R., Filipovich, H., Harrigan, L., Gaynor, J., Reimschuessel, C., & Zapadka, J. K. (1982). Measuring response empathy: The development of a multi-component rating scale. *Journal of Counseling Psychology, 29,* 379–87.

Elliott, R., Watson, J., Goldman, R., Greenberg, & L. S. (2003). *Learning emotion-focused therapy: The process-experiential approach to change.* Washington, DC: APA.

*Filak, J., & Abeles, N. (1984). Posttherapy congruence on client symptoms and therapy outcome. *Professional Psychology: Research & Practice, 15,* 846–55.

*Fretz, B. R. (1966). Postural movements in a counseling dyad. *Journal of Counseling Psychology, 13,* 335–43.

*Fuertes, J. N., Mislowack, A., Brown, S., Gur-Arie, S., Wilkinson, S., & Gelso, C. J. (2007). Correlates of the real relationship in psychotherapy: A study of dyads. *Psychotherapy Research, 17,* 423–30.

*Fuertes, J. N., Stracuzzi, T. I., Bennett, J., Scheinholtz, J., Mislowack, A., Hersh, M., et al. (2006). Therapist multicultural competency: A study of therapy dyads. *Psychotherapy: Theory, Research, Practice, Training, 43,* 480–490.

*Gabbard, C. E., Howard, G. S., & Dunfee, E. J. (1986). Reliability, sensitivity to measuring change, and construct validity of a measure of counselor adaptability. *Journal of Counseling Psychology, 33,* 377–86.

Gallese, V., Fadiga, L., Fogassi, L., & Rizzolatti, G., (1996). Action recognition in the premotor cortex. *Brain, 119,* 593–609.

*Garfield, S. L., & Bergin, A. E. (1971). Therapeutic conditions and outcome. *Journal of Abnormal Psychology, 77,* 108–114.

*Gelso, C. J., Latts, M. G., Gomez, M. J., & Fassinger, R. E. (2002). Countertransference management and therapy outcome: An initial evaluation. *Journal of Clinical Psychology, 58,* 861–67.

*Gillispie, R., Williams, E., & Gillispie, C. (2005). Hospitalized African American mental health consumers: Some antecedents to service satisfaction and intent to comply with aftercare. *American Journal of Orthopsychiatry, 75,* 254–61.

Gladstein, G. A., & Associates (1987). *Empathy and counseling: Explorations in theory and research.* New York: Springer-Verlag.

*Goldman, R., Greenberg, L., & Angus, L. (June, 2000). *The York II Psychotherapy Study on Experiential Therapy of Depression.* Paper presented at Society for Psychotherapy Research, Chicago, IL.

Goleman, D. (1995). *Emotional intelligence.* New York: Bantam.

Goubert, L., Craig, K. D., & Buysee, A. (2009). Perceiving others in pain: Experimental and clinical evidence of the role of empathy. In J. Decety & W. Ickes (Eds.) (2009). *The Social Neuroscience of Empathy* (pp. 153–65). Cambridge, MA: MIT Press.

*Greenberg, L. S., & Webster, M. (1982). Resolving decisional conflict by means of two-chair dialogue: Relating process to outcome. *Journal of Counseling Psychology, 29,* 468–77.

*Gross, W. F., & DeRidder, L. M. (1966). Significant movement in comparatively short-term counseling. *Journal of Counseling Psychology, 13,* 98–99.

Gurman, A.S. (1977). The patient's perception of the therapeutic relationship. In A. S. Gurman & A. M. Razin (Eds.), *Effective psychotherapy: A handbook of research* (pp. 503–43). New York: Pergamon.

*Hall, J. A., & Davis, M. H. (2000). Dispositional empathy in scientist and practitioner psychologists: Group differences and relationship to self-reported professional effectiveness. *Psychotherapy, 37,* 45–56.

*Hamilton, J. C. (2000). Construct validity of the core conditions and factor structure of the Client Evaluation of Counselor Scale. *The Person-Centered Journal, 7,* 40–51.

*Hansen, J. C., Moore, G. D., & Carkhuff, R. R. (1968). The differential relationships of objective and client perceptions of counseling. *Journal of Clinical Psychology, 24,* 244–46.

Hayes, A. M., & Goldfried, M. R. (1996). Rogers' work with Mark: An empirical analysis and cognitive-behavioral perspective. In B. A. Farber,

D. C. Brink, & P. M. Raskin (Eds.), *The psychotherapy of Carl Rogers* (pp. 357–74). New York: Guilford.

Henschel, D. N., & Bohart, A. C. (1981, August). *The relationship between the effectiveness of a course in paraprofessional training and level of cognitive functioning.* Paper presented at the American Psychological Association, Los Angeles, CA.

Higgins, J. P. T., Thompson, S. G., Deeks, J. J., & Altman, D. G. (2003). Measuring inconsistency in meta-analyses, *British Journal of Medicine, 327,* 557–60.

Hill, C. E., Thompson, B. J., & Corbett, M. (1992). The impact of therapist ability to perceive displayed and hidden client reactions on immediate outcome in first sessions of brief therapy. *Psychotherapy Research, 2,* 143–55.

*Hoffart, A., Versland, S., & Sexton, H. (2002). Self-understanding, empathy, guided discovery, and schema belief in schema-focused cognitive therapy of personality problems: A process-outcome study. *Cognitive Therapy and Research, 26,* 199–219.

Horvath, A. O., & Greenberg, L. S. (1986). The development of the Working Alliance Inventory. In L. S. Greenberg & W. M. Pinsof (Eds.), *The psychotherapeutic process: A research handbook* (pp. 529–56). New York: Guilford.

*Horvath, A. O., & Greenberg, L. S. (1989). Development and validation of the working alliance inventory. *Journal of Counseling Psychology, 36,* 223–33.

Hubble, M. A., Duncan, B. L., & Miller, S. D. (1999). Directing attention to what works. In M. A. Hubble, M. A. Duncan, & S. D. Miller (Eds.), *The heart and soul of change: What works in therapy* (pp. 407–48). Washington, DC: American Psychological Association.

Ickes, W. (Ed.). (1997). *Empathic accuracy.* New York: Guilford.

Ickes, W. (2003). *Everyday mind reading: Understanding what other people think and feel.* Amherst, NY: Prometheus Books.

Kennedy-Moore, E., & Watson, J. C. (1999). *Expressing emotion: Myths, realities, and therapeutic strategies.* New York: Guilford.

*Kiesler, D. J., Klein, M. H., Mathieu, P. L., & Schoeninger, D. (1967). Constructive personality change for therapy and control patients. In C. R. Rogers, et al. (Eds.), *The therapeutic relationship and its impact* (pp. 251–94), Madison: University of Wisconsin Press. (Combined with Barrington, 1967, and Van Der Veen, 1967)

*Kurtz, R. R., & Grummon, D. L. (1972). Different approaches to the measurement of therapist empathy and their relationship to therapy outcomes. *Journal of Consulting and Clinical Psychology, 39,* 106–115.

*Lafferty, P., Beutler, L. E., & Crago, M. (1989). Differences between more and less effective psychotherapists: A study of select therapist variables. *Journal of Consulting and Clinical Psychology, 57,* 76–80.

Lambert, M. J., DeJulio, S. J., & Stein, D. M. (1978). Therapist interpersonal skills: Process, outcome, methodological considerations, and recommendations for future research. *Psychological Bulletin, 85,* 467–89.

Landfield, A. W. (1971). *Personal construct systems in psychotherapy.* Chicago: Rand McNally.

*Langhoff, C., Baer, T., Zubraegel, D., & Linden, M. (2008). Therapist-patient alliance, patient-therapist alliance, mutual therapeutic alliance, therapist-patient concordance, and outcome of CBT in GAD. *Journal of Cognitive Psychotherapy, 22,* 68–79.

Leitner, L. M. (1995). Optimal therapeutic distance: A therapist's experience of personal construct psychotherapy. In R. A. Neimeyer & M. J. Mahoney (Eds.), *Constructivism in psychotherapy* (pp. 70). Washington, DC: American Psychological Association.

*Lerner, B. (1972). *Therapy in the ghetto.* Baltimore: Johns Hopkins University Press.

*Lesser, W. M. (1961). The relationship between counseling progress and empathic understanding. *Journal of Counseling Psychology, 8,* 330–36.

Lipsey, M. W., & Wilson, D. B. (2001). Practical meta-analysis. Thousand Oaks, CA: Sage.

*Lorr, M. (1965). Client perceptions of therapists: A study of therapeutic relation. *Journal of Consulting Psychology, 29,* 146–49.

Mahrer, A. R. (1997). Empathy as therapist-client alignment. In A. C. Bohart & L. S. Greenberg (Eds.), *Empathy reconsidered: New directions in psychotherapy* (pp. 187–216). Washington, DC: American Psychological Association.

*Marshall, W. L., Serran, G. A., Fernandez, Y. M., Mulloy, R., Mann, R. E., & Thornton, D. (2003). Therapist characteristics in the treatment of sexual offenders: Tentative data on their relationship with indices of behaviour change. *Journal of Sexual Aggression, 9,* 25–30.

*Marshall, W. L., Serran, G. A., Moulden, H., Mulloy, R., Fernandez, Y. M., Mann, R. E., et al. (2002). Therapist features in sexual offender treatment: Their reliable identification and influence on behaviour change. *Clinical Psychology and Psychotherapy, 9,* 395–405.

Martin, D. G. (2000). *Counseling and therapy skills* (*2nd ed.*). Prospect Heights, IL: Waveland Press.

Martin, D. J., Garske, J. P., & Davis, M. D. (2000). Relation of the therapeutic alliance with outcome and other variables: A meta-analytic review. *Journal of Consulting and Clinical Psychology, 68,* 438–50.

*Martin, P. J., & Sterne, A. L. (1976). Post-hospital adjustment as related to therapist's in-therapy behavior. *Psychotherapy: Theory, Research, and Practice, 13,* 267–273.

*Melnick, B., & Pierce, R. M. (1971). Client evaluation of therapist strength and positive-negative evaluation as related to client dynamics, objective ratings of competence and outcome. *Journal of Clinical Psychology, 27,* 408–410.

*Miller, W., Taylor, C., & West, J. (1980). Focused versus broad spectrum behavior therapy for problem drinkers. *Journal of Consulting and Clinical Psychology, 48,* 590–601.

Mitchell, K. M., Bozarth, J. D., & Krauft, C. C. (1977). A reappraisal of the therapeutic effectiveness of accurate empathy, nonpossessive warmth, and genuineness. In A. S. Gurman & A. N. Razin (Eds.), *Effective psychotherapy.* New York: Pergamon.

*Mitchell, K. M., Truax, C. B., Bozarth, J. D., & Krauft, C. C. (1973, March). *Antecedents to psychotherapeutic outcome.* NIMH Grant Report (12306). Arkansas Rehabilitation Research and Training Center, Arkansas Rehabilitation Services, Hot Springs, Arkansas.

Mohr, J. J., & Woodhouse, S. S. (2000, June). *Clients' visions of helpful and harmful psychotherapy: An approach to measuring individual differences in therapy priorities.* Paper presented at the 31st Annual Meeting of the Society for Psychotherapy Research, Chicago, IL.

*Muller, J., & Abeles, N. (1971). Relationship of liking, empathy and therapists' experience to outcome in psychotherapy. *Journal of Counseling Psychology, 18,* 39–43.

Myers, S. (2000). Empathic listening: Reports on the experience of being heard. *Journal of Humanistic Psychology, 40,* 148–73.

O'Hara, M. M. (1984). Person-centered gestalt: Towards a holistic synthesis. In R. F. Levant & J. M. Shlien (Eds.), *Client-centered therapy and the person-centered approach: New directions in theory, research and practice* (pp. 203–21). New York: Praeger.

Orlinsky, D. E., Grawe, K., & Parks, B. K. (1994). Process and outcome in psychotherapy—noch einmal. In A. E. Bergin & S. L. Garfield (Eds.), *Handbook of psychotherapy and behavior change* (4th ed., pp. 270–378). New York: Wiley.

*Orlinsky, D. E., & Howard, K. I. (1967). The good therapy hour: Experiential correlates of patients' and therapists' evaluations of therapy sessions. *Archives of General Psychiatry, 12,* 621–32.

Orlinsky, D. E., & Howard, K. I. (1978). The relation of process to outcome in psychotherapy. In Garfield, S. L., & Bergin, A. E. (Eds.), *Handbook of psychotherapy and behavior change* (2nd ed., pp. 283–330). New York: Wiley.

Orlinsky, D. E., & Howard, K. I. (1986). Process and outcome in psychotherapy, In S. L. Garfield & A. E. Bergin (Eds.), *Handbook of psychotherapy and behavior change* (3rd ed., pp. 311–84). New York: Wiley.

*Pantalon, M. V., Chawarski, M. C., Falcioni, J., Pakes, J., & Schottenfeld, R. S. (2004). Linking process and outcome in the community reinforcement approach for treating cocaine dependence: A preliminary report. *American Journal of Drug and Alcohol Abuse, 30,* 353–67.

Parloff, M. B., Waskow, I. E., & Wolfe, B. E. (1978). Research on therapist variables in relation to process and outcome. In Garfield, S. L., & Bergin, A. E. (Eds.), *Handbook of psychotherapy and behavior change* (2nd ed., pp. 233–82). New York: Wiley.

Patterson, C. H. (1984). Empathy, warmth, and genuineness: A review of reviews. *Psychotherapy, 21,* 431–38.

*Payne, A., Liebling-Kalifani, H., & Joseph, S. (2007). Client-centred group therapy for survivors of interpersonal trauma: A pilot investigation. *Counselling & Psychotherapy Research, 7,* 100–105.

Peabody, S. A., & Gelso, C. J. (1982). Countertransference and empathy: The complex relationship between two divergent concepts in counseling. *Journal of Counseling Psychology, 29,* 240–45.

*Peake, T. H. (1979). Therapist-patient agreement and outcome in group therapy. *Journal of Clinical Psychology, 35(3),* 637–46.

Persons, J. B., & Burns, D. D. (1985). Mechanisms of action of cognitive therapy: Relative contribution of technical and interpersonal intervention. *Cognitive Therapy and Research, 9,* 539–51.

*Rabavilas, A. D., Boulougouris, J. C., & Perissaki, C. (1979). Therapist qualities related to outcome with exposure in vivo in neurotic patients. *Journal of Behaviour Therapy and Experimental Psychiatry, 410,* 293–94.

*Roback, H. B., & Strassberg, D. S. (1975). Relationship between perceived therapist-offered conditions and therapeutic movement in group psychotherapy with hospitalized mental patients. *Small Group Behavior, 6,* 345–52.

Rogers, C. R. (1957). The necessary and sufficient conditions of therapeutic personality change. *Journal of Consulting Psychology, 21,* 95–103.

Rogers, C. R. (1980). *A way of being.* Boston: Houghton Mifflin.

Sachse, R. (1990a). Concrete interventions are crucial: The influence of the therapist's processing proposals on the client's intrapersonal exploration in client-centered therapy. In G. Lietaer, J. Rombauts, & R. Van Balen (Eds.), *Client-centered and experiential psychotherapy in the nineties* (pp. 295–308). Leuven, Belgium: Leuven University Press.

Sachse, R. (1990b). The influence of therapist processing proposals on the explication process of the client. *Person-Centered Review, 5,* 321–44.

*Saltzman, C., Leutgert, M. J., Roth, C. H., Creaser, J., & Howard, L. (1976). Formation of a therapeutic relationship: Experiences during the initial phase of psychotherapy as predictors of treatment duration and outcome. *Journal of Consulting and Clinical Psychology, 44,* 546–55.

*Sapolsky, A. (1965). Relationship between patient-doctor compatibility, mutual perceptions, and outcome of treatment. *Journal of Abnormal Psychology, 70,* 70–76.

*Saunders, S. M. (2000). Examining the relationship between the therapeutic bond and the phases of treatment outcome. *Psychotherapy, 37,* 206–218.

Selman, R. I. (1980). *The growth of interpersonal understanding.* Orlando, FL: Academic Press.

Shamay-Tsoory, S. (2009). Empathic processing: Its cognitive and affective dimensions and neuroanatomical basis. In J. Decety & W. Ickes (Eds.), *The social neuroscience of empathy* (pp. 215–32). Cambridge, MA: MIT Press.

Shlien, J. (1997). Empathy in psychotherapy: A vital mechanism? Yes. Therapist's conceit? All too often. In A. C. Bohart & L. S. Greenberg (Eds.), *Empathy reconsidered: New directions in psychotherapy* (pp. 63–80). Washington, DC: American Psychological Association.

Smith, M. L., Glass, G. V., & Miller, T. I. (1980). *The benefits of psychotherapy*. Baltimore: The Johns Hopkins University Press.

*Staples, F. R., Sloane, R. D., Whipple, K., Cristol, A. H., & Yorkston, N. (1976). Process and outcome in psychotherapy and behavior therapy. *Journal of Consulting and Clinical Psychology, 44,* 340–50.

*Strupp, H. H., Fox, R. E., & Lessler, K. (1969). *Patients view their psychotherapy*. Baltimore: Johns Hopkins Press.

Tallman, K., Robinson, E., Kay, D., Harvey, S., & Bohart, A. (1994, August). *Experiential and non-experiential Rogerian therapy: An analogue study*. Paper presented at the American Psychological Association Convention, Los Angeles.

Tausch, R. (1988). The relationship between emotions and cognitions: Implications for therapist empathy. *Person-Centered Review, 3,* 277–91.

Thompson, B., & Hill, C. (1991). Therapist perception of client reactions. *Journal of Counseling and Development, 69,* 261–65.

*Truax, C. B. (1966). Therapist empathy, warmth, and genuineness and patient personality change in group psychotherapy: A comparison between interaction unit measures, time sample measures, and patient perception measures. *Journal of Clinical Psychology, 22,* 225–29.

Truax, C. B., & Carkhuff, R. R. (1967). *Toward effective counseling and psychotherapy: Training and practice*. Chicago: Aldine.

*Truax, C. B., Carkhuff, R. R., & Kodman, F., Jr. (1965). Relationships between therapist-offered conditions and patient change in group psychotherapy. *Journal of Clinical Psychology, 21,* 327–29.

Truax, C. B., & Mitchell, K. M. (1971). Research on certain therapist interpersonal skills in relation to process and outcome. In A. E. Bergin & S. L. Garfield (Eds.), *Handbook of psychotherapy and behavior change* (1st ed., pp. 299–344). New York: Wiley.

*Truax, C. B., Wargo, D. G., Frank, J. D. Imber, S. D., Battle, C. C., Hoehn-Saric, R., et al. (1966). Therapist empathy, genuineness and warmth and patient therapeutic outcome. *Journal of Consulting Psychology, 30,* 395–401.

*Truax, C. B., & Wittmer, J. (1971). The effects of therapist focus on patient anxiety source and the interaction with therapist level of accurate empathy. *Journal of Clinical Psychology, 27,* 297–99.

*Truax, C. B., Wittmer, J., & Wargo, D. G. (1971). Effects of the therapeutic conditions of accurate empathy, nonpossessive warmth, and genuineness on hospitalized mental patients during group therapy. *Journal of Clinical Psychology, 27,* 137–42.

*Van der Veen, F. (1967). Basic elements in the process of psychotherapy: A research study. *Journal of Consulting Psychology, 31,* 295–303. (Combined with Barrington, 1967, and Kiesler, Mathieu, Klein & Schoeninger, 1967)

Wampold, B. E. (2001). *The great psychotherapy debate: Models, methods, and findings*. Mahwah, NJ: Erlbaum.

Watson, J. C. (2001). Re-visioning empathy. In D. Cain & J. Seeman (Eds.), Humanistic psychotherapies: Handbook of research and practice (pp. 445–71). Washington, DC: APA.

*Watson, J. C., & Geller, S. M. (2005). The relation among the relationship conditions, working alliance, and outcome in both process-experiential and cognitive-behavioral psychotherapy. *Psychotherapy Research, 15,* 25–33.

Watson, J. C., & Greenberg, L. S. (2009). Empathic resonance: A neuroscience perspective. In J. Decety & W. Ickes (Eds.) (2009). *The social neuroscience of empathy* (pp. 125–38). Cambridge, MA: MIT Press.

Watson, J. C., & Prosser, M. (2002). Development of an observer rated measure of therapist empathy. In J. C. Watson, R. Goldman, & M Warner (Eds.), *Client-centered and experiential psychotherapy in the 21st century: Advances in theory, research and practice* (pp. 303–314). Ross on Wye, UK: PCCS Books.

Watson, N. (1984). The empirical status of Rogers' hypotheses of the necessary and sufficient conditions for effective psychotherapy. In R. F. Levant & J. M. Shlien (Eds.), *Client-centered therapy and the person-centered approach* (pp. 17–40). New York: Praeger.

7   Goal Consensus and Collaboration

Georgiana Shick Tryon *and* Greta Winograd

This chapter focuses on one element of the therapeutic contract between patient and psychotherapist—goal consensus—that sets the parameters of treatment and one therapeutic operation—collaboration—that implements the contract that should contribute to a satisfactory treatment outcome. In support of this statement, our chapter in the first edition of this volume (Tryon & Winograd, 2002) presented evidence that goal consensus and collaboration were positively associated with measures of adult patient psychotherapy outcome. The current chapter updates and improves upon this work by examining via meta-analyses results of more recent studies, published from 2000 through 2009, that relate goal consensus and collaboration to therapy outcome.

Our chapter begins with definitions of terms followed by a clinical example of goal consensus and collaboration. We then describe and present results of two meta-analyses (one on goal consensus and one on collaboration). We also present results of a small meta-analysis using data from studies that relate goal consensus and collaboration to each other. Following this, we discuss the patients' contributions and the perspectives that they bring to these elements of the therapeutic relationship. We also discuss the limitations of the research reviewed. The chapter concludes with suggestions for therapeutic practice.

Definitions and Measures
Goal Consensus

At the beginning of treatment, psychotherapists effect a contract with their patients that outlines the conditions of their work together. This "... therapeutic contract is their 'understanding' about their goals and conditions for engaging each other as patient and therapist" (Orlinsky, Grawe, & Parks, 1994, p. 279). Agreement about treatment goals and the processes by which patient and therapist will achieve these goals is the essence of goal consensus. Goal consensus is part of the pantheoretical working alliance that includes patient–therapist agreement on the therapy goals and the tasks to reach those goals as well as formation of a bond between the members of the therapeutic dyad (Bordin, 1979; Chapter 11 of this book).

As in our chapter in the first edition of this book, we define goal consensus as:

(a) patient therapist agreement on goals; (b) the extent to which a therapist explains the nature and expectations of therapy, and the patient's understanding of this information; (c) the extent to which goals are discussed, and the patient's belief that goals are clearly specified; (d) patient commitment to goals; and (e) patient–therapist congruence on the origin of the patient's problem, and congruence on who or what is responsible for problem solution (Tryon & Winograd, 2001, pp. 385–386).

The third column of Table 7.1 shows that the studies included in the goal consensus meta-analysis for this chapter measured goal consensus using several different instruments. These studies were published between 2000 and 2009. Our earlier chapter (Tryon & Winograd, 2002) covered the goal consensus literature prior to 2000. The instruments comprised scales of measures that assess the working alliance, such as the Working Strategy Consensus scale of the California Psychotherapy Alliance Scale (CALPAS; Marmar, Gaston, Gallagher, & Thompson, 1989); the Goals and Tasks scale for patients, and the Shared Goals and Goal and Task

Table 7.1 Descriptions of Studies of Collaboration Outcome and Goal Consensus Outcome (2000–2009) with Effect Sizes

Study	N	Goal consensus measure(s)	Collaboration measure(s)	Outcome measure(s)	Effect Size (95% CI)	
					GC	C [b]
Ablon et al. (2006)	17		Psychotherapy Process Q-Set	Symptom Checklist 90 - R, Anxiety Sensitivity Index, Panic Disorder Severity Scale		.18 (−.33 − 0.62)
Abramowitz et al. (2002)	28	Therapy rationale acceptance rating	Treatment compliance, homework completion	Yale-Brown Obsessive Compulsive Scale	.65 (0.37 − 0.83)	.68 (0.42 − 0.84)
Ackerman et al. (2000)	128	Combined Alliance Short Form–Evaluation scales	Combined Alliance Short Form–Evaluation scales	Session Evaluation Questionnaire	.66 (0.56 − 0.76)	.55 (0.42 − 0.67)
Addis & Jacobson (2000)	150	Treatment acceptance rating	Homework completion rating	Beck Depression Inventory, Hamilton Rating Scale for Depression	.35 (0.20 − 0.49)	.29 (0.14 − 0.43)
Bogalo & Moss-Morris (2006)	30		Homework Assessment Tool	IBS-Symptom Severity Scale, Subject's Global Assessment of Relief		.16 (−.22 − 0.50)
Brocato & Wagner (2008)	124	Working Alliance Inventory		Stages of Change Readiness & Eagerness for Treatment Scale, treatment retention	.05 (−.13 − 0.23)	
Burns & Spangler (2000)	521		Homework completion	Beck Depression Inventory, Hopkins Symptom Checklist		.34 (0.27 − 0.42)
Busseri & Tyler (2004)	46	Patient & therapist goal agreement		Patient improvement ratings, Post Therapy Questionnaire	.14 (−.16–.42)	

(Continued)

Table 7.1 Continued

Study	N	Goal consensus measure(s)	Collaboration measure(s)	Outcome measure(s)	Effect Size (95% CI) GC	Effect Size (95% CI) C [b]
Caspar et al. (2005)	21		Plan Analysis	Beck Depression Inventory, Global Assessment of Functioning, Hamilton Rating Scale for Depression, Symptom Checklist 90 - R		.33 (−.12 − 0.66)
Clemence et al. (2005)	113	Combined Alliance Short Form	Combined Alliance Short Form	Help Received Scale, Patient's Estimate of Improvement to Date	.37 (0.20 − 0.53)	.44 (0.29 − 0.58)
Cowan et al. (2008)	576		Homework completion	Beck Depression Inventory, Hamilton Rating Scale for Depression, Perceived Social Support Scale, Social Support Instrument		.08 (0.00 − 0.16)
Dunn et al. (2006)	29		Rating of homework	Positive and Negative Signs of Schizophrenia		−.13 (−.48 −0.25)
Fitzpatrick et al. (2005)	48	Working Alliance Inventory		Session Impact Scale	.28 (0.00 − 0.53)	
Gabbay et al. (2003)	128	Problem agreement		Dropout	.02 (−.16 − 0.20)	
Gonzalez et al. (2006)	123		Homework completion rating	% positive urine, treatment retention		.12 (−.06 − 0.29)
Graf et al. (2008)	44		Post writing questionnaire	Satisfaction rating, insight rating		.45 (0.18 − 0.67)
Hegel et al. (2002)	179	Rating of patient understanding of therapy	Homework completion	Hamilton Rating Scale for Depression	.25 (0.11 − 0.38)	.21 (0.07 − 0.35)
Lingiardi et al. (2005)	47	California Psychotherapy Alliance Scale	California Psychotherapy Alliance Scale	Dropout	.42 (0.15 − 0.64)	.45 (0.19 - 0.66)
Long (2001)	24	Working Alliance Inventory, Goal Statement Inventory		Causal Dimension Scale II, Global Assessment of Functioning, Target Complaint questionnaire	.21 (−.21 − 0.57)	

(Continued)

Table 7.1 Continued

Study	N	Goal consensus measure(s)	Collaboration measure(s)	Outcome measure(s)	Effect Size (95% CI) GC	C[b]
Principe et al. (2006)	91	Working Alliance Inventory		Dropout	.12 (−.09 − 0.32)	
Schönberger et al. (2006, 2007)	45[c]	Working Alliance Inventory	Client's Compliance Scale	d2 Test of Concentration, European Brain Injury Questionnaire, Neurosensory Center Comprehensive Examination for Aphasia, Ravens Advanced Progressive Matrices, success ratings, Trail Making Test, WAIS-R, Wisconsin Card Sorting Test, word fluency	.18 (−.05 − 0.40)	.52 (0.27 − 0.71)
Stein et al. (2004)	53		Adherence to intervention checklist	Hamilton Rating Scale for Depression		.31 (0.04 − 0.54)
Wettersten et al. (2005)	64	Working Alliance Inventory		Brief Symptom Inventory, Counseling Center Follow-up Questionnaire	.18 (−.07 − 0.41)	
Whittal et al. (2004)	59		Homework Compliance	Yale-Brown Obsessive Compulsive Scale		.34 (0.09 − 0.56)
Woods et al. (2002)	82		Homework hours, homework completion	Behavioral Avoidance Test, target symptoms		.05 (−.17 − 0.27)
Yovel & Safren (2007)	15		Homework adherence, symptom change	AD/HD Rating Scale, Clinical Global Impression Scale, Global Assessment of Functioning, Hamilton Anxiety Scale, Hamilton Rating Scale for Depression		.39 (−.15 − 0.76)
Zane et al. (2005)	60	Goals measure, Perceptual Rating Scale		Global Assessment of Functioning, Session Evaluation Questionnaire	.24 (−.01 − 0.46)	

Note: Of the 15 goal consensus effect sizes reported in column 6, 11 were based on zero-order correlations, 3 were derived from partial beta coefficients (Abramowitz et al., 2002; Brocato & Wagner, 2008; Zane et al., 2005), and 1 originated from a combination of zero order correlations and partial beta coefficients (Wettersten et al., 2005). Of the 19 collaboration effect sizes reported in column 7, 15 were based on zero-order correlations, and 4 (Ablon et al., 2006; Abramowitz et al., 2002; Cowan et al., 2008; Woods et al., 2002) were derived from partial beta coefficients with two or more independent variables.
[a] GC = Goal Consensus. [b] C = Collaboration. [c] Both Schönberger et al. (2006) and Schönberger et al. (2007) used the same study sample. The 2006 paper assessed collaboration (N = 45). Both papers assessed goal consensus (N = 72).

Disagreement scales for therapists of the Combined Alliance Short Form (CASF; Hatcher, 1999; Hatcher & Barends, 1996); and the Goal and Task scales of the Working Alliance Inventory (WAI; Horvath & Greenberg, 1989). Other studies assessed goal consensus using rating scales specifically designed to assess actual patient–therapist goal agreement, such as the Goal Statement Inventory (GSI; McNair & Lorr, 1964) and the Causal Dimensions Scale II (CDS-II; McAuley, Duncan, & Russell, 1992). Still others (e.g., Gabbay et al., 2003; Hegel, Barrett, Cornell, & Oxman, 2002) used goal consensus measures unique to their studies.

Column 5 in Table 7.1 shows that the studies also used several measures of therapy outcome associated with goal consensus. Most outcome measures assessed patient improvement (e.g., as in Busseri & Tyler, 2004), while others examined treatment dropout (e.g., as in Gabbay et al., 2003), and others considered session impact (e.g., as in Fitzpatrick, Iwakabe, & Stalikas, 2005). In our previous review of the goal consensus literature (Tryon & Winograd, 2001), we found that 68% ($n = 17$) of the studies reviewed ($n = 25$) "revealed a positive relationship between goal consensus and outcome on at least one measure completed by patient, therapist, or observer" (p. 386).

Collaboration

To implement the therapeutic contract, patient and therapist must function as a team. Collaboration represents the active process of working together to fulfill treatment goals. As with goal consensus, collaboration is a pantheoretical concept that applies to all types of therapies. Collaboration ". . . is largely defined by the instruments devised to assess the concept" (Bachelor, Laverdière, Gamache, & Bordeleau, 2007, p. 175). These instruments assess (a) mutual involvement of patient and therapist in a helping relationship as well as (b) patient cooperation and (c) role involvement. Another indicator of, but not a measure of, collaboration is (d) patient completion of assigned homework.

The fourth column of Table 7.1 presents collaboration measures used by the studies in our meta-analysis. These studies were published between 2000 and 2009. Our earlier chapter (Tryon & Winograd, 2002) covered the collaboration literature prior to 2000. Collaboration measures include scales from working alliance measures such as the Therapist Understanding and Involvement scale of the CALPAS (Marmar et al., 1989); the Confident Collaboration scale of the patient CASF (Hatcher & Barends, 1996); and the Patient Working Engagement, Patient Confidence and Commitment, and Therapist Confident Collaboration scales of the therapist CASF (Hatcher, 1999). Other studies used ratings of patient treatment compliance (e.g., as in Abramowitz, Franklin, Zoellner, & DiBernardo, 2002), treatment acceptance (e.g., as in Addis & Jacobson, 2000), and patient adherence to the treatment (e.g., Stein et al., 2004) that were unique to the study. Studies that assessed homework compliance also generally used measures unique to their studies (e.g., as in Yovel & Safren, 2007).

The studies in the collaboration outcome meta-analysis used several types of outcome measures (see fifth column of Table 7.1). These ranged from patient symptom improvement (e.g., as in Ablon, Levy, & Katzenstein, 2006), session evaluation (e.g., as in Ackerman, Hilsenroth, Baity, & Blagys, 2000), treatment retention (e.g., as in Brocato & Wagner, 2008), and patient satisfaction (e.g., as in Graf, Gaudiano, & Geller, 2008). In our previous review of the collaboration outcome literature (Tryon & Winograd, 2001), "we combined results from 24 studies and found that 89% of the time, collaborative involvement and outcome were significantly positively related on at least one measure completed by patient, therapist, or observer" (p. 387).

Relationship of Goal Consensus and Collaboration

By definition, consensus implies an agreement based on the opinions of the parties involved.[1] Achievement of consensus requires that those involved work cooperatively, which is the definition of collaboration.[2] Since therapist and patient work together to establish agreement on the goals and tasks of psychotherapy, one might expect that measurements of goal consensus and collaboration would be related. Since 2000, however, only seven of the published studies that we found reported this relationship (Abramowitz et al., 2002; Ackerman et al., 2000; Addis & Jacobson, 2000; Clemence, Hilsenroth, Ackerman, Strassle, & Handler, 2005; Hegel et al., 2002; Lingiardi, Filippucci, & Baiocco, 2005; Schönberger, Humle, & Teasdale, 2006, 2007).

Clinical Example

Hope is a 21-year-old college senior and honors student who took a leave of absence from school last semester after being hospitalized for several weeks in a mental health crisis center. A psychotic episode—her first—led to Hope's hospitalization and to a diagnosis of bipolar disorder. Hope has recently returned to college on a part-time basis while she continues to work toward recovery.

The excerpt below is from Hope and her therapist's second session together. Elements of goal consensus and collaboration in their interaction are indicated in brackets.

Therapist: Last time we talked about the challenges you've been facing as you return to school and reconnect with friends and family members who know about your recent episode and hospitalization. I asked you to jot down some of the thoughts that have been running through your mind when you are around people at school, and some of the ways people act or the things they say that you find upsetting.

Hope: Yes, I did both of those things *[collaboration: homework completion]*. I realized that even with classmates I hardly know, I find myself worrying constantly about whether they know what happened, or if they can just tell by the way I act that I was in the hospital, that I have a mental illness. And when I'm thinking this way, I start to act nervous and insecure, and just find it hard to concentrate. But when I'm around friends and family members who know about my crisis, I feel even worse. They act so differently from the way they acted before my diagnosis. This is what I wrote down: "They either act like I'm made of glass and about to break, or they keep their distance." And I don't know how to get them to just treat me like a regular person again.

Therapist: It sounds to me like some of the people you are close to have disappointed you. You'd like to reconnect with them but aren't sure how to do this. It also sounds to me

---

1 consensus. (2010). In *Merriam-Webster Online Dictionary*. Retrieved June 6, 2010, from http://www.merriam-webster.com/dictionary/consensus

2 collaboration. (2010). In *Merriam-Webster Online Dictionary*. Retrieved June 6, 2010, from http://www.merriam-webster.com/dictionary/collaboration

as though even when other students don't necessarily act differently, you are worried that they are seeing you differently, or *would* see you differently if they knew about your recent life events. This makes it hard to relax around them and focus on your schoolwork.

Hope: Yes, I am quite uncomfortable around other people now, almost all of the time *[goal consensus: congruence on patient problem]*.

Therapist: I also recall that you mentioned being quite isolated.

Hope: Yes, that's true. Since I don't know what to say or how to act, I've started to avoid people. I basically just go directly to my classes and then straight home. But I don't think spending so much time alone is good for my mood. It doesn't even feel like me. I used to be a really social person *[goal consensus: further congruence on patient problem]*.

Therapist: I was thinking that over the next few sessions, we could work together to come up with ideas about how to talk about your hospitalization and recovery with your friends and family *[collaboration: mutual involvement of patient and therapist in a helping relationship]*. I was also thinking we might try out some relaxation and thought replacement strategies for when you get anxious around classmates in school.

Hope: I like the sound of that. And I'd also like you to help me experiment with gradually coming out of my shell as I work on getting healthy again *[goal consensus: discussion and specification of goals; covllaboration: patient role involvement]*.

Presuming Hope continued to experience her psychotherapy as a collaborative enterprise, she would likely strongly endorse collaboration items from the revised Helping Alliance Questionnaire (Haq-II; Luborsky et al., 1996) such as, "the therapist and I have meaningful exchanges" and "I feel I am working together with the therapist in a joint effort" (p. 271). Hope would also be likely to endorse consensus items from the Working Alliance Inventory such as, "we agree about what is important for me to work on" and "my therapist and I are working towards mutually agreed upon goals" (Horvath & Greenberg, 1989a, p. 226).

Meta-Analytic Review
Inclusion Criteria and Study Selection

We included goal consensus and collaboration studies in their respective meta-analysis if they used: (a) at least one measure of goal consensus and/or one measure of collaboration defined according to criteria listed above; (b) at least one psychotherapy outcome measure; (c) a group design; (d) individually conducted psychotherapy; (e) adult clients (aged 18 and older). Finally, each study (f) reported a correlation, its equivalent (standardized β weight), or other statistic (t, F, or d) that could be converted to a correlation between goal consensus and/or collaboration scores and outcome scores; and (g) was published in English in a refereed journal from 2000 through 2009.

We and our students (a psychology doctoral student, a psychology masters student, and an undergraduate psychology major) conducted advanced Google Scholar searches for articles from 2000 through 2009 using the following terms: *patient–therapist collaboration* (1,290 references), *patient–therapist goal consensus* (631 references), *homework compliance and psychotherapy outcome* (3,760 references), *patient–therapist goal consensus and psychotherapy outcome* (459 references), *patient–therapist agreement and psychotherapy outcome* (796 references), and *patient–therapist collaboration and psychotherapy outcome* (555 references).

We cross-tabulated the references, inspected the article abstracts, and identified 53 articles for in-depth examination by the two authors of this chapter. After reviewing each of the 53 studies independently, the authors were in perfect agreement in identifying 28 studies that met inclusion criteria and 25 studies that did not. The reasons for not meeting inclusion criteria were: other than individual therapy (*n* = 8), measure of collaboration or goal consensus not used in outcome analysis (*n* = 8), no measure of collaboration or goal consensus (*n* = 3), no outcome measure (*n* = 3), no treatment (*n* = 2), and results could not be converted to effect size (*n* = 1).

Table 7.1 describes the 28 studies that met inclusion criteria. Thirteen of the 28 studies (46%) provided effect sizes for collaboration and outcome only, 9 studies (32%) provided effect sizes for goal consensus and outcome only, and 7 studies (25%) provided effect sizes for both goal consensus and collaboration with outcome. Thus, the goal consensus meta-analysis included results from 15 studies, and the collaboration meta-analysis included results from 19 studies. We were also in perfect agreement in categorizing the studies into these two groups.

Coding of Study Characteristics

In keeping with editorial requirements for this chapter and similar to a prior meta-analysis by the first author and colleagues (Tryon, Blackwell, & Hammel, 2007), we independently recorded and coded the following information from each study: number of participants, severity of patient disturbance, therapist experience, treatment theoretical orientation, treatment length, measures of goal consensus and/or collaboration and outcome, time of measurement

in the course of therapy, and rater perspective. We also independently identified goal consensus, collaboration, and outcome data and calculated effect sizes for the relationships among these data. Our ratings and calculations were in agreement for 498 out of 512 items (97%). When we disagreed, we discussed the item until we reached agreement. Table 7.1 presents the coded information for the measures and effect sizes.

We classified patient disturbance as mild (volunteers from college classes, no formal diagnosis, or seen at university-based training clinics), moderate (formal diagnoses of nonpsychotic mood disorder, seen in outpatient settings other than university training clinics), and severe (seen in inpatient settings, diagnosed with a psychosis, identified by study authors as severely disturbed). Eight studies had patients with severe disturbances, 13 studies had patients with moderate disturbances, and 7 studies had patients with mild disturbances.

Psychotherapists were either experienced (16 studies), trainees (2 studies), or a combination of experienced therapists and trainees (7 studies). Three studies did not specify therapist experience. Four studies did not specify theoretical orientation. In studies using a single theoretical orientation, therapy was behavioral (2 studies), cognitive behavioral (9 studies), psychodynamic (2 studies), or eclectic, interpersonal, individualized, or solution focused (1 study each). The remaining 7 studies used therapies reflecting more than one orientation (e.g., cognitive behavioral). We divided treatment length into 1–10 sessions (7 studies), 11–20 sessions (12 studies), and 21 or more sessions (7 studies). Two studies did not specify treatment length.

Table 7.1 shows the instruments used in studies for goal consensus (Column 3), collaboration (Column 4), and outcome (Column 5). The majority (13 out of

15, 87%) of goal consensus studies used only one measure of goal consensus (M = 1.20, SD = 0.56), and the majority of collaboration studies (16 out of 19, 84%) used only one collaboration measure (M = 1.16, SD = 0.37). The studies tended to have more than one outcome measure (M = 2.14, SD = 1.53). Measures were often completed by more than one rater. In total, patients completed the most measures (n = 49), followed by therapists (n = 37), and observers (n = 32).

For each study, we coded the time in therapy that measures were completed by dividing the number of sessions in the study into thirds, and naming the thirds as early, middle, and end of therapy (in all cases, measures in the latter third were at the very end of treatment). Most measures were completed at the end (54 measures) of therapy, followed by early (17 measures) and in the middle (3 measures) of therapy. Twelve studies used at least one measure (18 measures) that was completed continuously (in each third, often after each session) during therapy, and one study contained three measures completed at follow-up only. Finally, two studies did not specify time of completion of measures (7 measures).

Estimation of Effect Sizes

To obtain the effect sizes listed in Table 7.1, for each study, we recorded correlations or standardized β weights between goal consensus measures and outcome measures and/or collaboration measures and outcome measures. We averaged correlations or standardized β weights in studies that had more than one measure of goal consensus and/or collaboration or outcome to obtain one effect size for the relationship of each therapeutic element (goal consensus, collaboration) to outcome for each study. Most effect sizes were based on zero-order correlations; however, a few effect sizes (three for goal consensus and four for collaboration) were derived from partial beta coefficients with two or more independent variables (see table note). Partial beta coefficients *underestimate* the zero-order correlation coefficient.

When measures within a study were completed or recorded by different numbers of participants or observers, we weighted each correlation by the number of patients for whom the measures were completed and divided by the total number of patients represented for each correlation.

The Meta-Analyses

We used a meta-analysis package (Schmidt & Le, 2005) that corrects for study artifacts (Hunter & Schmidt, 2004) such as the unreliability of measures used in each study. For the current meta-analyses, we corrected for unreliability using coefficient alphas for the studies' measures. Because each study did not provide alphas for all measures used in the meta-analyses (i.e., collaboration, goal consensus, and outcome measures), we used the artifact distribution option of the program that allowed us to enter the alphas that the studies provided as well as alphas from other studies that used the measures (contact corresponding author for a reference list of additional studies providing reliabilities). Effect sizes were weighted by sample size and reliability so that effects that were more precise (i.e., derived from studies with larger sample sizes and greater reliability) were given more weight.

Results: Goal Consensus

Fifteen studies with a total sample size of 1,302 provided goal consensus–psychotherapy outcome effect sizes for the meta-analysis (see Table 7.1). Weighting for sample size and unreliability of measures, the meta-analysis yielded a mean correlation of 0.34 (SD = 0.19) with a 95% confidence interval of 0.23 to 0.45. The variability between studies after removal of the effects of unreliability of the measures and variation in sample size was 0.02. Because this procedure left virtually no variability in effects due to differences between studies, there was no variability to be explained by moderators. Therefore, as recommended (Hunter & Schmidt, 2004), we did not conduct a moderator analysis. The results signify a medium (Cohen, 1992), unmoderated effect between goal consensus and psychotherapy outcome. Because an r of 0.34 is equivalent to a d of 0.72 (Lyons, 2003), a 1 standard deviation improvement in goal consensus predicts nearly a 3/4 standard deviation improvement in outcome. This is a substantial relationship, especially considering outcomes as meaningful as retention in treatment, symptom reduction, and adaptive functioning.

Results: Collaboration

Nineteen studies involving a total sample of 2,260 patients provided collaboration–psychotherapy outcome effect sizes for the meta-analysis (Table 7.1). Weighing for sample size and unreliability of measures, the meta-analysis yielded a mean correlation of 0.33 ($SD = 0.17$) with a 95% confidence interval of 0.25 to 0.42. The variability between studies after removal of the effects of unreliability of the measures and variation in sample size was 0.02. Because this procedure left virtually no variability in effects due to differences between studies, there was no variability to be explained by moderators. Therefore, as recommended (Hunter & Schmidt, 2004), we did not conduct a moderator analysis. The results denote a medium (Cohen, 1992), unmoderated effect between collaboration and psychotherapy outcome. Across outcomes including service use, satisfaction with services received, and patient improvement, this effect corresponds to a 2/3

standard deviation ($d = 0.68$; Lyons, 2003) improvement associated with a 1 standard deviation boost in collaboration. Thus, patient experience and well-being appear to be considerably enhanced with a better quality collaborative relationship between patient and therapist.

Results: Relation of Goal Consensus and Collaboration

Of the 7 studies that had measures of both goal consensus and collaboration, only 4 reported effect sizes, or information from which to calculate effect sizes, for the association between these two variables. Studies by Addis and Jacobson (2000; $r = 0.17$, $n = 150$), Abramowitz et al. (2002; $r = 0.17$, $n = 28$), Clemence et al. (2005; $r = 0.09$, $n = 125$), and Lingiardi et al. (2005, $r = 0.19$, $n = 37$) provided data for the goal consensus–collaboration relationship. Collectively, these four studies provided a sample of 340 patients. Weighing for sample size and unreliability of measures, the meta-analysis on these four studies yielded a mean correlation of 0.19 ($SD = 0$), which represents an effect size between small and medium (Cohen, 1992). Variability between studies after removal of the effects of unreliability of the measures and variation in sample size was 0.

File Drawer Analyses

It is possible that studies not included in the meta-analyses (e.g., unpublished papers, dissertations, book chapters) could have null results that, if included, would have reduced the effects we found. Thus, we conducted file drawer analyses to determine how many studies with null results would reduce the effect sizes substantially. For the goal consensus meta-analysis, we would need to have found 87 studies with null results to reduce the effect size to 0.05. For collaboration, the number of studies needed is 106. Thus, it is unlikely that we would find such large numbers of well-designed, unpublished studies.

For the goal consensus–collaboration meta-analysis, however, we would need to find only 11 studies with null effects to reduce the effect size to 0.05. Consequently, the results of the goal consensus–collaboration analysis should be interpreted cautiously.

Potential Moderators and Mediators

Although in meta-analyses there may be moderators or mediators of statistical relationships between variables, after removal of the effects of unreliability of the measures and variation in sample size, results of the current meta-analyses indicated unmoderated relationships between the therapy elements of collaboration and goal consensus and therapy outcome. We, therefore, did not analyze for moderators.

Patient Contribution

Patients, particularly those who are new to therapy, may have an inaccurate perception of the role they are expected to play in the treatment process. In their experiences with other health professionals, such as physicians, patients tend to play a relatively passive, submissive role, presenting their symptoms and receiving treatment. The goals of such treatment typically do not involve much discussion, and there may be little collaboration regarding treatment beyond patient compliance in following professional directives.

Psychotherapy, in contrast, requires active involvement by patients from initial goal setting to termination. The therapist cannot effect treatment alone. Patients bring their concerns to therapists, and together they conceptualize treatment goals and ways to achieve them. Although therapists frequently reconceptualize patients' problems, refine goals, and suggest ways to achieve those goals, they do so with patients'

input and feedback. The verbal interchanges involved in goal consensus reflect a negotiation in which patients and therapists together refine the goals and tasks of therapy.

In addition to completing homework, the patient's contribution to the ongoing collaborative work of therapy takes the form of offering information, insights, self-reflections, elaborations and explorations of important themes, and "work(ing) actively with the therapist's comments" (Colli & Lingiardi, 2009, p. 723). Patients may not recognize the importance of these behaviors and the role they play in goal consensus and collaboration (Hatcher & Barends, 2006). Indeed, they tend to emphasize the importance of what the therapist does, and even when prompted, downplay their contribution to the work of therapy (Bedi, Davis, & Williams, 2005). Perhaps some patients have so little confidence in their efficacy in relation to their problems (after all, they have been unable to solve their troubles on their own) that they do not acknowledge the importance of their part in collaborating with therapists toward a successful outcome.

Limitations of the Research

This chapter only included studies with adults that were published in English and in refereed journals, and it did not include studies with child or adolescent patients. Because goal consensus and collaboration are often considered to be part of the working alliance, articles included in this chapter may also have been included in the analysis presented in Chapter 2 of this volume concerning the working alliance in adult psychotherapy. In contrast to analyses reported in other chapters in this volume, which covered a more extensive time period, the meta-analyses in this chapter used studies that were published in the past 10 years. For a review of studies published prior to 2000, see our earlier chapter in the first edition of this volume (Tryon & Winograd, 2002).

Although we included a goal consensus–collaboration meta-analysis using data from articles in listed Table 7.1, we did not search for additional articles that included these two elements because their relationship was not the focus of the chapter. So, we advise readers to interpret the correlation between goal consensus and collaboration reported here cautiously.

While the studies in the current meta-analyses represent improvements over those included in our prior chapter, they were not without limitations. Although many studies reported results as effect sizes, several studies did not. Several studies also failed to report nonsignificant results. Statistical correction of this problem through file drawer analyses or assignment of arbitrary effect sizes is a poor substitute for having the actual effect sizes. Also, some studies reported results based on fewer participants than indicated in their procedure sections. Readers should bear these limitations, and those in the previous paragraph, in mind when interpreting results. The acceptance of journal article reporting standards (JARS; APA Publications and Communications Working Board Group, 2008) by editors should address these difficulties and allow for more precise meta-analytic syntheses of research data.

A glance at Table 7.1 shows the diversity of goal consensus and collaboration measures. These reflect the various definitions of these elements in the literature, and in the case of collaboration, the element itself is defined by the measures used to assess it (Bachelor et al., 2007). Instrumentation frequently evolves from theoretical advances, and we endorse continuing conceptualization of these elements. The goal should be to provide researchers and practitioners with clear definitions of goal

consensus and collaboration and measures that allow for their accurate assessment.

Finally, while the results of the meta-analyses in this chapter indicate positive relationships between goal consensus and outcome and between collaboration and outcome, they do not provide proof that either goal consensus or collaboration causes positive outcomes.

Therapeutic Practices

The results of the primary meta-analyses indicate strong links between patient–therapist goal consensus and positive therapy outcomes, as well as between their collaboration and outcome. The results point to a number of practices that psychotherapists can profitably effect.

- Begin work on client problems only after you and the patient agree on treatment goals and the ways you will go about reaching them.
- Rarely push your own agenda. Listen to what your patients tell you and formulate interventions with their input and understanding.
- Encourage patients' contributions throughout psychotherapy by asking for their feedback, insights, reflections, and elaborations. Regularly seek information from patients about their current functioning, motivation to change, and social support and provide them with feedback about their progress (Harmon et al., 2007; Whipple et al., 2003; also see Chapter 10 by Lambert & Shimokawa).
- Educate patients about the importance of their collaborative contribution to the success of therapy. Psychotherapists can do so by sharing with patients the results of research, such as those reviewed in this chapter, that link their collaborative contribution to successful outcomes.

- Encourage homework completion. To enhance homework completion, encourage patient collaboration in formulating homework assignments; assign homework that relates to treatment goals; begin with small, easily accomplished assignments and build to larger ones; define homework tasks clearly; give homework assignments in writing; provide written reminders to complete tasks; encourage and incorporate client feedback on homework (Detweiler & Whisman, 1999; Nelson, Castonguay, & Barwick, 2007).

- Be "on the same page" with patients. Check frequently with patients to make sure that you understand each other and are working toward the same ends.

- Modify your treatment methods and relational stance, if ethically and clinically appropriate, in response to patient feedback.

References

References marked with an asterisk (*) indicate studies included in the meta-analyses.

*Ablon, J. S., Levy, R. A., & Katzenstein, T. (2006). Beyond grand names of psychotherapy: Identifying empirically supported change processes. *Psychotherapy, Theory, Research, Practice, Training, 43*, 216–231.

*Abramowitz, J. S., Franklin, M. E., Zoellner, L. A., & DiBernardo, C. L. (2002). Treatment compliance and outcome in obsessive-compulsive disorder. *Behavior Modification, 26*, 447–463.

*Ackerman, S. J., Hilsenroth, M. J., Baity, M. R., & Blagys, M. D. (2000). Interaction of therapeutic process and alliance during psychological assessment. *Journal of Personality Assessment, 75*, 82–109.

*Addis, M. E., & Jacobson, N. S. (2000). A closer look at the treatment rationale and homework compliance in cognitive-behavioral therapy for depression. *Cognitive Therapy and Research, 24*, 313–326.

APA Publications and Communications Board Working Group on Journal Article Reporting Standards. (2008). Reporting standards for research in psychology. *American Psychologist, 63*, 839–51.

Bachelor, A., Laverdière, O., Gamache, D., & Bordeleau, V. (2007). Clients' collaboration in therapy: Self-perceptions and relationships with client psychological functioning, interpersonal relations, and motivation. *Psychotherapy: Theory, Research, Practice, Training, 44*, 175–192.

Bedi, R. P., Davis, M. D., & Williams, M. (2005). Critical incidents in the formation of the therapeutic alliance from the client's perspective. *Psychotherapy: Theory, Research, Practice, Training, 42*, 311–323.

*Bogalo, L., & Moss-Morris, R. (2006). The effectiveness of homework tasks in an irritable bowel syndrome self-management programme. *New Zealand Journal of Psychology, 35*, 120–125.

Bordin, E. S. (1979). The generalizability of the psychoanalytic concept of the working alliance. *Psychotherapy: Theory, Research, Practice, Training, 16*, 252–260.

*Brocato, J., & Wagner, E. F. (2008). Predictors of retention in an alternative-to-prison substance abuse treatment program. *Criminal Justice and Behavior, 35*, 99–119.

*Burns, D. D., & Spangler, D. L. (2000). Does psychotherapy homework lead to improvements in depression in cognitive-behavioral therapy or does improvement lead to increased homework compliance? *Journal of Consulting and Clinical Psychology, 68*, 46–56.

*Busseri, M. A., & Tyler, J. D. (2004). Client-therapist agreement on target problems, working alliance, and counseling outcome. *Psychotherapy Research, 14*, 77–88.

*Caspar, F., Grossmann, C., Unmüssig, C., & Schramm, E. (2005). Complementary therapeutic relationship: Therapist behavior, interpersonal patterns, and therapeutic effects. *Psychotherapy Research, 15*, 91–102.

*Clemence, A. J., Hilsenroth, M. J., Ackerman, S. J., Strassle, C. G., & Handler, L. (2005). Facets of the therapeutic alliance and perceived progress in psychotherapy: Relationship between patient and therapist perspectives. *Clinical Psychology and Psychotherapy, 12*, 443–454.

Cohen, J. (1992). A power primer. *Psychological Bulletin, 112*, 155–159.

Colli, A., & Lingiardi, V. (2009). The Collaborative Interactions Scale: A new transcript-based method for assessment of therapeutic alliance ruptures and resolutions in psychotherapy. *Psychotherapy Research, 19*, 718–734.

*Cowan, M. J., Freedland, K. E., Burg, M. M., Saab, P. G., Youngblood, M. E., Cornell, C. E., et al. (2008). Predictors of treatment response for depression and inadequate social support–The ENRICHD randomized clinical trial. *Psychotherapy and Psychosomatics, 77*, 27–37.

Detweiler, J. B., & Whisman, M. A. (1999). The role of homework assignments in cognitive therapy for depression: Potential methods for enhancing adherence. *Clinical Psychology: Science and Practice, 6*, 267–282.

*Dunn, H., Morrison, A. P., & Bentall, R. P. (2006). The relationship between patient suitability, therapeutic alliance, homework compliance, and outcome in cognitive therapy for psychosis. *Clinical Psychology and Psychotherapy, 13*, 145–152.

*Fitzpatrick, M. R., Iwakabe, S., & Stalikas, A. (2005). Perspective divergence in the working alliance. *Psychotherapy Research, 15*, 69–79.

*Gabbay, M., Shields, C., Bower, B., Sibbald, M., King, M., & Ward, E. (2003). Patient-practitioner agreement: Does it matter? *Psychological Medicine, 33*, 241–251.

*Gonzalez, V. M., Schmitz, J. M., & DeLaune, K. A. (2006). The role of homework in cognitive-behavioral therapy for cocaine dependence. *Journal of Consulting and Clinical Psychology, 74*, 633–637.

*Graf, M. C., Gaudiano, B. A., & Geller, P. A. (2008). Written emotional disclosure: A controlled study of expressive writing homework in outpatient psychotherapy. *Psychotherapy Research, 18*, 389–399.

Harmon, S. C., Lambert, M. J., Smart, D. M., Hawkins, E., Nielsen, S. L., Slade, K., et al. (2007). Enhancing outcome for potential treatment failures: Therapist-client feedback and clinical support tools. *Psychotherapy Research, 17*, 379–392.

Hatcher, R. L. (1999). Therapists' views of treatment alliance and collaboration in therapy. *Psychotherapy Research, 9*, 405–423.

Hatcher, R. L., & Barends, A. W. (1996). Patients' view of the alliance in psychotherapy: Exploratory factor analysis of three alliance measures. *Journal of Consulting and Clinical Psychology, 64*, 1326–1336.

Hatcher, R. L., & Barends, A. W. (2006). How a return to theory could help alliance research. *Psychotherapy: Theory, Research, Practice, Training, 43*, 292–299.

*Hegel, M. T., Barrett, J. E., Cornell, J. E., & Oxman, T. E. (2002). Predictors of response to problem-solving treatment of depression in primary care. *Behavior Therapy, 33*, 511–527.

Horvath, A. O., & Greenberg, L. S. (1989a). Development and validation of the Working Alliance Inventory. *Journal of Counseling Psychology, 36*, 223–233.

Horvath, A. O., & Greenberg, L. S. (1989b). The development of the Working Alliance Inventory. In L. S. Greenberg & W. M. Pinsof (Eds.), *The psychotherapeutic process: A research handbook* (pp. 529–556). New York: Guilford Press.

Hunter, J. E., & Schmidt, F. L. (2004). *Methods of meta-analysis: Correcting error and bias in research findings* (2nd ed.). Thousand Oaks, CA: Sage.

*Lingiardi, V., Filippucci, L., & Baiocco, R. (2005). Therapeutic alliance evaluation in personality disorders psychotherapy. *Psychotherapy Research, 15*, 45–53.

*Long, J. R. (2001). Goal agreement and early therapeutic change. *Psychotherapy, 38*, 219–232.

Luborsky, L., Barber, J. P., Siqueland, L., Johnson, S., Najavits, L. M., Frank, A., et al. (1996). The revised Helping Alliance Questionnaire (Haq-II): Psychometric properties. *Journal of Psychotherapy Practice and Research, 5*, 260–271.

Lyons, L. C. (2003, January 30). *Meta-analysis: Methods of accumulating results across research domains.* Retrieved from http://www.lyonsmorris.com/MetaA/studyfx1.htm

Marmar, C. R., Gaston, L., Gallagher, D., & Thompson, L. W. (1989). Alliance and outcome in late-life depression. *Journal of Nervous and Mental Disease, 177*, 464–472.

McAuley, E., Duncan, T. E., & Russell, D. W. (1992). Measuring causal attributions: The revised Causal Dimension Scale (CDS-II). *Personality and Social Psychology Bulletin, 18*, 566–573.

McNair, D., & Lorr, M. (1964). Three kinds of psychotherapy goals. *Journal of Clinical Psychology, 20*, 390–593.

Nelson, D. L., Castonguay, L. G., & Barwick, F. (2007). Directions for the integration of homework in practice. In N. Kazantzis & L. L' Abate (Eds.), *Handbook of homework assignments in psychotherapy: Research, practice, and prevention* (pp. 425–444). New York: Springer.

Orlinsky, D. E., Grawe, K., & Parks, B. K. (1994). Process and outcome in psychotherapy–Noch einmal. In A. E. Bergin & S. L. Garfield (Eds.),

Hanbook of psychotherapy and behavior change (4th ed., pp. 270–376). New York, NY: Wiley.

*Principe, J. M., Marci, C. D., Glick, D. M., & Ablon, J. S. (2006). The relationship among patient contemplation, early alliance, and continuation in psychotherapy. *Psychotherapy: Theory, Research, Practice, Training, 43*, 238–243.

*Schönberger, M., Humle, F., & Teasdale, T. (2006). Subjective outcome of brain injury rehabilitation in relation to the therapeutic working alliance, client compliance and awareness. *Brain Injury, 20*, 1271–1282.

*Schönberger, M., Humle, F., & Teasdale, T. (2007). The relationship between clients' cognitive functioning and the therapeutic working alliance in post-acute brain injury rehabilitation. *Brain Injury, 21*, 825–836.

Schmidt, F. L., & Le, H. (2005). *Software for the Hunter-Schmidt meta-analysis methods* (Version 1.1) [Computer software]. Iowa City: University of Iowa, Department of Management & Organization.

*Stein, M. D., Solomon, D. A., Herman, D. S., Anthony, J. L., Ramsey, S. E., Anderson, B. J., et al. (2004). Pharmacotherapy plus psychotherapy for treatment of depression in active injection drug users. *Archives of General Psychiatry, 61*, 152–159.

Tryon, G. S., Blackwell, S. C., & Hammel, E. F. (2007). A meta-analytic examination of client-therapist perspectives of the working alliance. *Psychotherapy Research, 17*, 629–642.

Tryon, G. S., & Winograd, G. (2001). Goal consensus and collaboration. *Psychotherapy: Theory, Research, Practice, Training, 38*, 385–389.

Tryon, G. S., & Winograd, G. (2002). Goal consensus and collaboration. In J. C. Norcross (Ed.), *Psychotherapy relationships that work: Therapist contributions and responsiveness to patients* (pp. 109–125). New York: Oxford University Press.

*Wettersten, K. B., Lichtenberg, J. W., & Mallinckrodt, B. (2005). Associations between working alliance and outcome in solution-focused brief therapy and brief interpersonal therapy. *Psychotherapy Research, 15*, 35–43.

Whipple, J. L., Lambert, M. J., Vermeersch, D. A., Smart, D. W., Nielsen, S. L., & Hawkins, E. J. (2003). Improving the effects of psychotherapy: The use of early identification of treatment failure and problem-solving strategies in routine practice. *Journal of Counseling Psychology, 50*, 59–68.

*Whittal, M. L., Thordarson, D. S., & McLean, P. D. (2004). Treatment of obsessive-compulsive disorder: Cognitive behavior therapy vs. exposure and response prevention. *Behaviour Research and Therapy, 43*, 1559–1576.

*Woods, C. M., Chambless, D. L., & Steketee, G. (2002). Homework compliance and behavior therapy outcome for panic with agoraphobia and obsessive compulsive disorder. *Cognitive Behaviour Therapy, 31*, 88–95.

*Yovel, I., & Safren, S. A. (2007). Measuring homework utility in psychotherapy: Cognitive-behavioral therapy for adult attention-deficit hyperactivity disorder as an example. *Cognitive Therapy and Research, 31*, 385–399.

*Zane, N., Sue, S., Chang, J., Huang, L., Huang, J., Lowe, S., et al. (2005). Beyond ethnic match: Effects of client-therapist cognitive match in problem perception, coping orientation, and therapy goals on treatment outcomes. *Journal of Community Psychology, 33*, 569–585.

8 Positive Regard and Affirmation

Barry A. Farber *and* Erin M. Doolin

Author Note. We gratefully acknowledge the invaluable research assistance provided by Alex Behn, Sarah Bellovin-Weiss, and Valery Hazanov.

> The book [*Client-Centered Therapy*] . . . expresses, I trust, our conviction that though scientists can never make therapists, it can help therapy; that though the scientific finding is cold and abstract, it may assist us in releasing forces that are warm, personal, and complex; and that though science is slow and fumbling, it represents the best road we know to the truth, even in so delicately intricate an area as that of human relationships.
>
> —Rogers, 1951, p. xi

Over 50 years ago, in what is now considered a classic paper, Carl Rogers (1957) posited that psychotherapists' provision of positive regard (nonpossessive warmth), congruence (genuineness), and empathy were the necessary and sufficient conditions for therapeutic change. Rogers had been developing these views for many years, some of which were expressed as early as 1942 in his seminal work, *Counseling and Psychotherapy*. Still, the publication of the 1957 article seems to have catalyzed a shift in the way that many thought about the putative mechanisms of psychotherapeutic change. The prevailing view at the time—and still an enormously influential one, though currently cast in somewhat different (e.g., more evidence-based) terms—was that technical expertise on the part of the therapist, especially in terms of choice and timing of interventions, is the essential discriminating element between effective and noneffective therapy. Under the sway of Rogers' burgeoning influence in the late 1950s and throughout the 1960s, the notion that the relationship per se was *the* critical factor in determining therapeutic success, took hold.

Over the years, a great many studies have attempted to investigate Rogers' claims regarding the necessary and sufficient conditions of therapy. There is, then, a substantial body of research to draw upon in looking at the association between the therapist's positive regard for his or her patients and therapeutic outcome. However, as detailed below, drawing firm conclusions from these efforts has been difficult. The problems that typically plague the investigation of complex psychological issues have been played out in this area as well: inconsistent findings, small sample sizes, lack of standardized measures, and lack of operational definitions of the concepts themselves. In addition, as the Rogerian influence on clinical practice has diminished in the last three decades—or, more accurately, has been incorporated into the psychotherapeutic mainstream with little awareness or explicit acknowledgment (Farber, 2007)—empirical studies based on Rogerian concepts have also waned. Similarly, the focus of research and theory has shifted away from the individual contributions of each of the participants in therapy toward a consideration of the alliance or therapeutic relationship—what each member of the dyad contributes to the ongoing, interactive process of the work.

Whereas consideration of the therapeutic relationship as mutative began with Rogers, therapists of varying persuasions, even those from theoretical camps that had traditionally emphasized more technical factors, have begun to acknowledge the importance of the relationship. Behaviorists and cognitive-behaviorists now suggest that a good relationship may facilitate the provision of their technical interventions (e.g., Beck, 1995), and many psychoanalysts have shifted their clinical perspective to emphasize "relational" factors (Mitchell & Aron, 1999; Wachtel, 2009). But even before these relatively recent developments, there is evidence to suggest that Freud's psychoanalytic cases were only successful when he was supportive and positively regarding. As Breger (2009) has noted:

When Freud followed these [psychoanalytic] rules his patients did not make progress. His well-known published cases are failures . . . in contrast are patients like Kardiner and others—cases he never wrote or publicly spoke about—all of whom found their analyses very helpful. With these patients, what was curative was not neutrality, abstinence, or interpretations of resistance, but a more open and supportive relationship, interpretations that fit their unique experiences, empathy, praise, and the feelings that they were liked by their analyst. (p. 105).

This observation suggests that Freud was unaware of, or at least underappreciated, what may well have been the most potent elements of his approach—that along with whatever positive effects accrue as a result of accurate interpretations, psychoanalytic success has arguably always been based substantially on the undervalued ability of the analyst to be empathic and, even more to the point of this chapter, to be supportive and positively regarding of his or her patients.

In this chapter, we review Rogers' ideas about the concept of positive regard and discuss how the use of multiple terms (including *positive regard, affirmation, respect, warmth, support,* and *prizing*) has led to conceptual confusion as well as empirical difficulties in determining the link between this phenomenon and therapeutic outcome. The emphasis of this chapter is on meta-analytically reviewing the findings of those empirical studies that have investigated the relation between therapist support and treatment outcome in individual psychotherapy. Most studies of positive regard are framed within a Rogerian (person-centered) paradigm; however, as noted above, nearly all schools of therapy now either explicitly or implicitly promote the value of this basic attitude toward patients. Thus, the results of these studies have implications for the conduct not only of person-centered therapists, but for virtually all psychotherapists.

Definitions and Measures

To the extent that the therapist finds himself experiencing a warm acceptance of each aspect of the client's experience as being a part of that client, he is experiencing unconditional positive regard . . . it means there are no conditions of acceptance . . . it means a 'prizing' of the person . . . it means a caring for the client as a separate person (Rogers, 1957, p. 101).

From the beginning of his efforts to explicate the essential elements of client-centered therapy, Rogers focused on positive regard and warmth: "Do we tend to treat individuals as persons of worth, or do we subtly devaluate them by our attitudes and behavior? Is our philosophy one in which respect for the individual is uppermost?" (1951, p. 20). Implicit in this statement is his disapproval of what he perceived as the arrogance of, and strict hierarchical distinctions between, psychotherapists and patients held by the psychoanalytic community at that time. Rogers did not believe that anyone, including a therapist, could be more expert or knowledgeable about a client than the client him or herself. He did not believe that a therapist's neutrality, dispassionate stance, or even intellectual understanding could facilitate a client's growth—no matter how astute the interpretations emanating from such a therapy might be. Instead, he believed that treating clients in a consistently warm, highly regarding manner would inevitably allow them to grow psychologically, to fulfill their potential.

To this day, agreeing on a single phrase to refer to this positive attitude remains problematic. It is most often termed *positive regard* but early studies and theoretical writings preferred the phrase *nonpossessive warmth*. In his famous filmed work with Gloria (Shostrom, 1965), Rogers struggled to find a single phrase to illuminate this concept: it is, he said, "real spontaneous praising; you can call that quality acceptance, you can call it caring, you can call it a non-possessive love. Any of those terms tend to describe it." Some reviews of "acceptance, nonpossessive warmth, or positive regard" (Orlinsky, Grawe, & Parks, 1994, p. 326) grouped them under the category of *therapist affirmation*. We will use the phrase *positive regard* to refer to the general constellation of attitudes encompassed by this and similar phrases.

Further confusing the conceptual issues at play here, Rogers' focus on accepting and affirming the client has, from the outset, been conflated with an emphasis on empathy and genuineness. The therapist's attempt to "provide deep understanding and acceptance of the attitudes consciously held at the moment by the client" could only be accomplished by the therapist's "struggle to achieve the client's internal frame of reference, to gain the center of his own perceptual field and see with him as perceiver" (1951, pp. 30–31). Rogers seems to be suggesting here that positive regard (including the component of acceptance) can best be achieved through empathic identification with one's client. In a similar vein, Rogers suggested that the therapist's genuineness or congruence was a prerequisite for his or her experience of positive regard and empathy (Rogers & Truax, 1967).

Further problems with the concept of positive regard have been identified (e.g., Lietaer, 1984). One is that there may be an inherent tension between this attitude and that of genuineness; that is, therapists' own conflicts inevitably affect what they can and cannot truly accept or praise in others. A second, related problem is that it is unlikely that any therapist can provide constant doses of unconditional positive regard in that we all reinforce selectively. As Rogers himself anticipated:

> The phrase 'unconditional positive regard'
> may be an unfortunate one, since it
> sounds like an absolute, an all-or-nothing
> dispositional concept . . . From a clinical
> and experiential point of view I believe
> the most accurate statement is that
> the effective therapist experiences
> unconditional positive regard for the

client during many moments of his contact with him, yet from time to time he experiences only a conditional positive regard—and perhaps at times a negative regard, though this is not likely in effective therapy. It is in this sense that unconditional positive regard exists as a matter of degree in any relationship. (p. 101).

How can one, then, assess a therapist's level of positive regard without implicitly measuring empathy or genuineness as well? In fact, reading transcripts of Rogers' work (e.g., Farber, Brink, & Raskin, 1996) makes clear how difficult it is to tease out pure examples of positive regard. Rogers is consistently "with" his clients, testing his understanding, clarifying, and intent on entering and grasping as much as possible the client's experiential world. For these reasons, most research focusing on the effects of therapist positive regard have used measures, typically either the Barrett-Lennard Relationship Inventory (BLRI; 1964, 1978) or the Truax Relationship Questionnaire (Truax & Carkhuff, 1967), that include items reflecting multiple, overlapping, relational elements.

The BLRI consists of 64 items across four domains (Level of Regard, Empathic Understanding, Unconditionality of Regard, Congruence). Eight items are worded positively, eight negatively in each domain; each item is answered on a +3 (yes, strongly felt agreement) to −3 (no, strongly felt disagreement) response format. This instrument can be used by the client, therapist, or both. Both Level of Regard and Unconditionality have been used in research studies to investigate the influence of positive regard. Level of Regard, according to Barrett-Lennard (1986, p. 440–441), "is concerned in various ways with warmth, liking/caring, and 'being drawn toward'." Positive items include "she respects me as a person," "I feel appreciated by her," and "she is friendly and warm toward me." Representative negative items include "I feel that she disapproves of me," "She is impatient with me," and "At times she feels contempt for me."

Unconditionality of Regard is explained by Barrett-Lennard (1986, p. 443) in terms of its stability, "in the sense that it is not experienced as varying with other or otherwise dependently linked to particular attributes of the person being regarded." Examples of positively worded items: "How much he likes or dislikes me is not altered by anything that I tell him about myself"; "I can (or could) be openly critical or appreciative of him without really making him feel any differently about me." Examples of negatively worded items: "Depending on my behavior, he has a better opinion of me sometimes than he has at other times"; "Sometimes I am more worthwhile in his eyes than I am at other times."

Truax developed two separate instruments for the measurement of Rogers' facilitative conditions. One was a set of scales to be used by raters in their assessment of these conditions as manifest in either live observations or through tape recordings of sessions. There are five stages on the scale that measures Nonpossessive Warmth. At Stage 1, the therapist is "actively offering advice or giving clear negative regard" (Truax & Carkhuff, 1967, p. 60); at Stage 5, the therapist "communicates warmth without restriction. There is a deep respect for the patient's worth as a person and his rights as a free individual" (p. 66).

The second instrument developed by Truax, The Relationship Questionnaire, was to be used by clients. This measure consists of 141 items marked "true" or "false" by the client. Of these items, 73 are keyed to the concept of nonpossessive warmth; it is noteworthy, however, that many of these items are also keyed to the other two facilitative conditions (genuineness and empathy). That is, a "true" response on one item may count toward a higher score on more than one subscale. Representative items on the Nonpossessive Warmth scale: "He seems to like me no matter what I say to him" (this item is also on the "genuineness" scale); "He almost always seems very concerned about me"; "He appreciates me"; "I feel that he really thinks I am worthwhile"; "even if I were to criticize him, he would still like me"; and "whatever I talk about is OK with him."

In addition to these scales, therapist positive regard has been assessed via instruments designed primarily to measure the strength of the alliance. In particular, the Vanderbilt Psychotherapy Process Scale (VPPS) has been used in this manner. The VPPS is "a general-purpose instrument designed to assess both positive and negative aspects of the patient's and the therapist's behavior and attitudes that are expected to facilitate or impede progress in therapy" (Suh, Strupp, & O'Malley, 1986, p. 287). Each of 80 items is rated by clinical observers on a 5-point, Likert-type scale, either from the actual therapy sessions or from video- or audiotapes of therapy. Factor analyses of these items have yielded eight subscales, one of which, Therapist Warmth and Friendliness, closely approximates the concept of positive regard. The specific therapist attributes rated in this subscale include "involvement" (the therapist's engagement in the patient's experience), "acceptance" (the therapist's ability to help the patient feel accepted), "warmth and friendliness," and "supportiveness" (the therapist's ability to bolster the patient's self-esteem, confidence, and hope). Therapist positive regard has also sometimes been measured through the use of Structural Analysis of Social Behavior (SASB; Benjamin, 1984), specifically through the dimension of Helping and Protecting.

High scores on this dimension reflect the therapist's ability to teach or encourage a patient in a kind or positive manner.

Whereas the "bond" component of various alliance measures (e.g., Horvath & Greenberg, 1989; Tracey & Kokotovic, 1989) contains aspects of positive regard phenomena that have been elucidated above, its items primarily assume an interaction between patient and therapist, one that reflects the contributions and characteristics of each. Thus, results from studies using alliance measures were not included in our meta-analysis.

Clinical Examples

The case examples below have been purposely drawn from disparate theoretical perspectives. Although the concept of positive regard originated with Rogers, the provision of this facilitative condition can and does occur in the work of practitioners of quite distinct therapeutic traditions.

Case Example 1

Client: I can outsmart people. I won't be taken advantage of. I call the shots.

Therapist: It seems important for you to be dominant in every relationship.

Client: Yes. I don't show emotion and I don't put up with it in anyone else. I don't want someone to get all hysterical and crying with me. I don't like it.

Therapist: How did you learn that being emotional is a sign of weakness?

Client: I don't know.

Therapist: What if you meet your intellectual match, if you can't "outsmart" them?

Client: (silence)

Therapist: Okay, what if someone got to you through your feelings?

Client: Last week you did. It bothered me all day.

Therapist: That you were weak?

Client: Yeah.

Therapist: I didn't see you as submissive or weak. In fact, since showing emotion is so difficult for you I saw it as quite the opposite.

In this example, the therapist, primarily psychodynamic in orientation, initially tries to get the patient to open up about his past and discuss his "faulty strategy" of dominating relationships. It appears as if they are about to discuss transference issues. However, the therapist shifts at the end, perhaps intuitively sensing that what would be most effective for this patient (at least at this moment) is a statement of true positive regard. Thus, the therapist is affirming, suggesting that she views the client not as weak or submissive but rather the opposite, as perhaps brave for doing something that was difficult for him.

Case Example 2

"You're reading me entirely wrong. I don't have any of those feelings. I've been pleased with our work. You've shown a lot of courage, you work hard, you've never missed a session, you've never been late, you've taken chances by sharing so many intimate things with me. In every way here, you do your job. But I do notice that whenever you venture a guess about how I feel about you, it often does not jibe with my inner experience, and the error is always in the same direction: You read me as caring for you much less than I do" (Yalom, 2002, p. 24).

In this example, Yalom, an existential therapist, not only offers assumedly accurate feedback to his patient on her interpersonal tendencies (much like a psychoanalytic therapist might do) but in doing so, explicitly conveys the fact that he cares for this patient far more than she imagines to be the case.

Case Example 3

Client: It really hurts when I think about the fact that it is over.

Therapist: Yes, of course it hurts. It hurts because you loved him and it did not work out. It shows, I think, your capacity to love and to care. But it also hurts to have that ability.

Client: I don't think I'll ever feel that way.

Therapist: Right now it may be important for you to protect yourself with that feeling. Perhaps we can look at what you have learned about yourself and your needs and the kind of man who would be right for you.

Client: What do you mean?

Therapist: I mean that you have a great ability to love. But what can you learn about what you need in a man that [Tom] lacked?

Client: I guess I learned not to get involved with a married man.

Therapist: What do you think led you to think you'd be able to handle being involved with a married man?

Client: Well, after my marriage ended, I guess I didn't want to get too attached. So I thought that being involved with someone who is married would keep me from being hurt.

Therapist: Perhaps you've learned that you have such a strong ability to love that you can't compartmentalize your feelings that way (Leahy, 2001, p. 82).

In this example, Leahy, a cognitive therapist, is not only consistently empathic ("of course it hurts") and not only attempting to teach his patient something about her-self and her needs and choices, but he also makes sure that he contextualizes his interventions in a supportive, caring way, emphasizing his patient's "strong ability to love."

Case Example 4

Client: (smiles) I think I'm having male menopause.

Therapist: (smiles) OK, but I think you'll need to explain that condition to me.

Client: (laughs) I met this great guy coming out of the supermarket. And we chatted right there on the street and we exchanged phone numbers. He probably won't call. He's a lot younger than I am so I don't think he's really interested, but, hey, I actually had a daylight conversation with an attractive man and he knows my name. Now that's something, huh?

Therapist: Yes, it is. And something different for you.

Client: Yeah, I'm feeling less creature-like. More human these days. Like coming out from under a rock. Oh, I finished my painting . . . the one with the lost boy. I thought about what you said about the boy feeling lost . . . When I was finishing the painting, I felt like . . . it's almost like you and I came up with that together.

Therapist: I feel that, too. I think that we each contribute to our work here together. The accomplishment of finishing the painting is all yours, though. And talking to a man you find attractive, giving him your name and phone number . . . Sounds well, something commonplace, but not for you. Not in a long time.

Client: I actually surprised myself. It didn't even feel so risky. I just "went with it." He smiled, I smiled back . . .

Therapist: Good. And that was so courageous of you . . . .

Client: Yeah, that's me, I guess. My mother used to say that my refusal to not give in irritated the hell out of my father. I'm sure I disappointed him as a son . . . But sometimes, I'm glad he's gone. I feel guilty thinking and saying it but if I had to choose which parent would go first, I'm not sorry it was him and glad it wasn't my mother. I really still need her.

Therapist: I know. And you know, I want to tell you how much I appreciate your honesty in allowing yourself to think about these things that are sometimes hard to think about.

Client: Thanks. (Pause.) I hope he calls me.

Therapist: I hope so too.

Here, a relationally oriented psychody-namic clinician banters somewhat ("you'll have to explain that condition to me") as a means to be connected and supportive. Moreover, she values her patient's efforts to change ("that was so courageous of you") and gives him credit for the work he's doing in the here-and-now of the clini-cal setting ("how much I appreciate your honesty").

Case Example 5

Client: Yeah, I don't feel like it's [filling out diary cards every day] for me. I don't want to wake up every day, and go "Oh I felt like suicide last Tuesday! Oh my god, I was sad last week!" I don't want to keep remembering!

Therapist: Oh, okay, so you want one of those therapies where you don't remember things?

Client: No, I just don't want to keep bringing it up all the time. "Oh, I was raped on so-and-so date, let me remember what I felt at the time."

Therapist: Yeah, it's so painful to bring up this stuff. Why would anyone want that?

Client: Yeah, exactly!

Therapist: Now here's the dilemma. We could not talk about your problems, and if this would take away your pain and misery, I'd be all for it. On the other hand, if we help you figure out how to tolerate your bad feelings, then you won't have to rely on your pain medicine or resort to thinking of killing yourself when these feelings come up.

Client: But the feelings are horrible! What am I supposed to do, just wave a magic wand to make them go away? You make it sound so easy.

Therapist: It's not easy at all. This is incredibly tough and painful for you, and I also believe you have what it takes to do it. (Adapted from McMain, Korman, & Dimeff, 2001, p. 196).

In this dialogue, a dialectical behavior therapist offers a supportive statement ("I believe you have what it takes to do it") that has much in common with the comments of the relationally oriented therapist in the previous example. Here, the therapist's empathic response ("it's not easy at all") is followed up by a more explicit statement of positive regard.

Case Example 6

Client: I feel like there are people who do care and accept me. I do, but.

Therapist: But the person that can't accept and value you, is actually you.

Client: Yes, mostly.

Therapist: It seems the person who is hardest on you is you.

Client: Yes. No one else would be as cruel to me as I am.

Therapist: And make such harsh judgments, you're pretty tough on yourself.

Client: Yes, I wouldn't judge my friends the way I judge myself.

Therapist: No, you're not a very good friend to yourself.

Client: No, I wouldn't treat anyone the way I treat me.

Therapist: Maybe because you can see what is lovable in them, but not in yourself. To you, you're unlovable.

Client: Maybe there are small pieces of me that are lovable.

Therapist: (pause) So there are parts of you that you see as OK, as worthy of being loved.

Client: Yes, I guess. The child in me, the child that struggled and survived. She, I, can still be playful and fun and warm.

Therapist: Those are very wonderful qualities.

Client: She's strong, a survivor.

Therapist: She's a part of you that you can hold on to.

Client: Yes.

Therapist: Do you think she'd judge you so harshly?

Client: No, she loves me.

Therapist: To this special child part of you, none of you is unforgivable.

Client: No, she loves all of me.

In this final example, the client-centered therapist is clearly conveying to the patient that she is worthy of respect and love. The therapist's positive regard for the patient may allow her to begin to view herself as the therapist does. These last few examples are prime illustrations of the multiple aspects of positive regard, including affirmation, trust, understanding, warmth, interest, and respect.

Previous Reviews

Before describing the results of our meta-analysis, we summarize several previous reviews of the association between positive regard and outcome. The first such effort was by Truax and Carkhuff (1967) in their book, *Toward Effective Counseling and Psychotherapy*. Many of the studies they cited failed to report the separate associations of each of Rogers' facilitative conditions to outcome, focusing instead on the aggregate results of all three conditions taken together. They did, however, review 10 studies from which conclusions could be drawn on the effects of positive regard alone on therapeutic outcome, finding that 8 of these supported the hypothesis that nonpossessive warmth (the preferred term at that time) is significantly associated with therapeutic improvement.

Next, Bergin and Garfield's first (1971) edition of *Handbook of Psychotherapy and Behavior Change* included a chapter by Truax and Mitchell that summarized the results of 12 studies (involving 925 clients) that included nonpossessive warmth. The authors contended that the evidence was quite positive in regard to the relationship between warmth and therapeutic outcome, noting that there was a statistically significant relationship between this variable and a total of 34 specific outcome measures. Nevertheless, it is important to reiterate what others (Mitchell, Bozarth, Truax, & Krauft, 1973; Parloff, Waskow, &

Wolfe, 1978) later pointed out—namely, that there are multiple ways of understanding such complex data. For example, of 108 correlations noted in Truax and Mitchell's report, only 34 were reported as significantly positive. While none of these correlations were significantly negative, relatively few were significantly positive.

In a follow-up review, Mitchell, Bozarth, and Krauft (1977) evaluated 11 studies that investigated the relationship between positive regard (here again termed nonpossessive warmth) and treatment outcome. According to these authors, at most four of these studies offered support for the proposition that higher levels of therapist-provided warmth lead to better outcome. The following year, Orlinsky and Howard (1978) reviewed 23 studies, concluding that approximately two thirds of these indicated a significant positive association between therapist warmth and therapeutic outcome, with the remaining one third showing mostly null results. However, they also added several caveats, notably that the uneven quality and methodological flaws in the research made any firm conclusions suspect. Their conclusion: "If they [warmth and empathy] do not by themselves guarantee a good outcome, their presence probably adds significantly to the mix of beneficial therapeutic ingredients, and almost surely does no harm" (p. 293).

As part of a comprehensive review of process and outcome in psychotherapy, Orlinsky and Howard (1986) conducted separate reviews of studies evaluating the effects of *therapist support* and *therapist affirmation*. They identified 11 studies that included a support/encouragement variable; within this group of studies they focused on 25 separate findings. Their conclusion: "Although 6 of the 25 are significantly positive findings and none are negative, more than three-quarters show a null association between specific therapist efforts to give support and patient outcome" (p. 326). In addition, the authors identified 94 findings on the association between therapist affirmation (essentially warmth, caring, and acceptance) and outcome, with more than half (53%) demonstrating a significant relationship between these sets of variables. Underscoring their emphasis on considering the perspective of raters, they noted that "the proportion of positive findings is highest across all outcome categories when therapist warmth and acceptance are observed from the patient's process perspective" (p. 348). That is, in 30 cases where the patient's ratings of therapist positive regard were used, 20 outcome scores were positively correlated with these ratings (aggregated over the outcome perspectives of patient, therapist, rater, and objective score), and no outcome scores (regardless of the source) were significantly negatively correlated with patient ratings of therapist positive regard.

In 1994 Orlinsky and colleagues studied this general phenomenon under the rubric of *therapist affirmation*, explained by the authors as a variable that includes aspects of acceptance, nonpossessive warmth, or positive regard. They found that 56% of the 154 results reviewed were positive, and that, again, the findings based on patients' process perspective (the patient's rating of the therapist's positive regard) yielded even a higher rate of positive therapeutic outcomes, 65%. "Overall," Orlinsky et al. (p. 326) concluded, "nearly 90 findings indicate that therapist affirmation is a significant factor, but considerable variation in ES [effect size] suggests that the contribution of this factor to outcome differs according to specific conditions."

Lastly, in the previous review of positive regard for this volume, the authors (Farber & Lane, 2002) highlighted several patterns. First, no post-1990 study reported a negative relationship between positive regard and outcome. Second, the results of the 16 studies analyzed in that chapter were essentially evenly split between positive and nonsignificant effects. That is, 49% (27/55) of all reported associations were significantly positive and 51% (28/55) were nonsignificant. However, the authors noted that the majority of nonsignificant findings occurred when an objective rater (rather than the therapist or patient) evaluated therapeutic outcome. Third, confirming the pattern noted by previous reviewers, Farber and Lane found that when the patient rated both the therapist's positive regard and treatment outcome, a positive association between these variables was especially likely. Lastly, the effect sizes for the significant results tended to be modest, with the larger effect sizes occurring when positive regard was assessed in terms of its association to length of stay in therapy rather than outcome per se (for example, Najavits & Strupp, 1994).

Meta-Analytic Review
Literature Search and Study Selection
To find studies that documented a relationship between positive regard and outcome in psychotherapy, we used the PsycINFO database. Main root terms searched in the title or the abstract were *positive regard, warmth, nonpossessive warmth, therapist affirmation, unconditional positive regard, affirmation, acceptance,* and *unconditional regard*. All these terms were crossed with *psychotherapy*, searching for the following root terms in the title or the abstract: *psychotherapy, therapy, counseling,* and *client-centered*. Additional studies were located by running a search with the root term "*Barrett-Lennard*" since this is the most widely used instrument to assess positive regard.

Our specific inclusion criteria were as follows: (a) the study identified positive regard as either unconditional regard, positive regard, warmth, nonpossessive warmth, affirmation, or acceptance; (b) positive regard (in any of these forms) was considered as a predictor of outcome in the study; (c) the study reported quantitative outcome data and relevant statistics (e.g., correlations between positive regard ratings and treatment outcome or mean outcome comparisons between groups with differential positive regard ratings) that could be used to calculate effect sizes; (d) patients were adults or adolescents; and (e) treatment was individual psychotherapy. In addition, studies that reported the contribution of positive regard to other process or relational variables and thus indirectly to treatment outcome were excluded from our analysis. For example, studies that looked at positive regard as a component of other predictor variables (e.g., empathy, therapeutic alliance) or were part of an aggregated factor associated with outcome were not included in the analysis. In fact, many early studies looked at positive regard in the context of the entire constellation of facilitative conditions posed by Rogers—congruence, empathy, positive regard—without explicitly reporting the impact of positive regard as an individual variable.

In addition to searching for relevant studies in this manner, we consulted the 2002 chapter to determine which of those 16 studies met our current criteria. Six potential articles (Gaston et al., 1990; Hynan, 1990; Klein, 2002; Meyer, 1990; Rothman, 2007; Schauble & Pierce, 1974; Schut, Castonguay, Flanagan, & Yamasaki, 2005) were excluded because there was not enough information presented in the results to compute the appropriate effect size, and any contact with the original authors yielded no assistance. One article (Russell, Bryant, & Estrada, 1996) included in our 2002 review was excluded because it did not explicitly examine the relationship between positive regard and therapeutic outcomes. Another article (Schindler,

1991) was excluded from the revised analysis because it could no longer be located.

After scanning the literature with these criteria in mind, 44 studies were selected for review of which 18 were found to be entirely consistent with these criteria and thus were included in the meta-analysis.

Coding Potential Moderators

The moderator variables were broken into three categories: study characteristics, characteristics of sample/treatment, and therapist factors. All studies were coded by the junior author; a coding manual is available upon request.

Study characteristics included: (a) publication status (e.g., published article, book chapter, or unpublished dissertation); (b) sampling (whether the sample was random or a convenience sample); (c) rater perspective for both the independent and dependent variables; and (d) total number of participants. Characteristics of the sample/treatment that were coded were: mean age, percentage of women, percentage of racial/ethnic minorities, frequency of treatment, average number of sessions involved in treatment, measure of relationship element, point in time that the relationship element was assessed, and the theoretical orientation that informed said treatment.

The specific therapist factors coded for this analysis involved mean age, percentage of women, number of therapists used, and composition of therapists (e.g., trainees; four years postgraduation).

Effect Size Coding

Because the purpose of this meta-analysis was to examine the relation between therapist positive regard and treatment outcome, a simple correlation, r, was obtained to measure the effect for each study. The effect sizes for several studies had to be recomputed using the data the authors provided and then converted to r (per Cooper,

Hedges, & Valentine, 2009). After each study was coded for the moderator variables, effect sizes were again computed for each of the 18 studies. Additionally, if there was more than one effect size per study, within-study aggregation was performed. A new statistical package available online aided in the statistical analysis for this project (see Del Re, 2010; Del Re & Hoyt, 2010).

Results

A total of 18 effect sizes were yielded (after aggregation) and were included in the analysis. A complete list of the studies included in the analysis, their authors, date of publication, total sample size, and 95% confidence limits are provided in Table 8.1. The aggregate effect size was 0.27, indicating that positive regard has a moderate association with psychotherapy outcomes; only two of the 18 studies had negative effect sizes. Additionally, the 95% confidence interval (CI) did not include zero (CI = 0.16, 0.38), which demonstrates that the effect of positive regard on outcome is significantly different from zero.

To assess whether there were differences between these 18 studies above and beyond sampling error, a homogeneity test was conducted. Using the homogeneity statistic, Q (Hedge, 1982), the assumption that

Table 8.1   Effect Sizes between Positive Regard and Outcome

Study	n	Study effect size (r)	95% Confidence limits for r [lower, upper]
Bachelor (1991)	47	.49	[.24, 0.68]
Chisholm (1998)	173	−.04	[−.19, 0.11]
Coady (1991)	9	.71	[.09, 0.93]
Conte, Ratto, Clutz, & Karasu (1995)	138	.29	[.13, 0.44]
Cramer & Takens (1992)	37	.37	[.05, 0.62]
Eckert, Abeles, & Graham (1988)	77	.35	[.14, 0.53]
Garfield & Bergin (1971)	38	−.15	[−.45, 0.18]
Green & Herget (1991)	11	.83	[.46, 0.96]
Hayes & Strauss (1998)	32	.31	[−.04, 0.59]
Henry, Schacht, & Strupp (1990)	14	0	[−.53, 0.53]
Keijsers, Hoogduin, & Schaap (1994)	40	.12	[−.20, 0.42]
Litter (2004)	8	.53	[.29, 0.71]
Najavits & Strupp (1994)	12	.75	[.32, 0.93]
Quintana & Meara (1990)	48	.02	[−.26, 0.31]
Rabavilas, Boulougouris, & Perissaki (1979)	36	.09	[−.25, 0.41]
Sells, Davidson, Jewell, Falzer, & Rowe (2006)	83	.33	[.12, 0.51]
Williams & Chambless (1990)	33	.20	[−.15, 0.51]
Zuroff & Blatt (2006)	191	.20	[.06, 0.33]
Overall n or r	1067	.27	[.16, 0.38]
n of studies/samples	18		

the studies selected were sampled from the same population (i.e., were homogenous) was rejected, $Q(17) = 50.52$, $p = 0.000$. This indicates that there is a large amount of heterogeneity in the studies due to differences among the studies. This degree of heterogeneity implies that the overall effect varies as a function of study characteristics.

Moderators
Categorical Moderator Analyses
In order to account for the systematic variance present in this sample of studies, we conducted several univariate categorical moderator analyses. As Table 8.2 indicates, the following moderators were significant (i.e., demonstrated significant heterogeneity in their aggregate effect sizes): publication status, rater perspective, origin of sample, measure used to assess positive regard, time in treatment when positive regard was measured, and type of treatment. These variables moderate the overall effect of positive regard on therapeutic outcome. In other words, each of these moderators accounts for some portion of the unaccounted-for variance discussed in the previous section on the overall effect. Most notably, as indicated in Table 8.2, the overall effect of positive regard on outcome tends to be higher when studies are published in journal articles, or when the type of treatment provided is psychoanalytic/psychodynamic. In regard to this last finding, our hypothesis is that patients engaged in traditional (rather than more contemporary, relational) psychodynamic treatment were particularly affected by their therapists' occasional and perhaps unexpected displays of support and positive regard. In a manner analogous to the power of relatively infrequent therapist disclosures wherein "less is more" (Knox & Hill, 2003), these patients' treatment outcomes may have been influenced significantly by their therapists' ability and

willingness to deviate from the conventions of psychodynamic treatment. However, given that all of these moderators were significant, they all contribute in some way to the large amount of heterogeneity in the overall effect of positive regard on therapeutic outcomes.

Continuous Moderator Variables
We also conducted several univariate continuous moderator analyses; none were significant at the .05 level However, because of its increasing importance in contemporary psychological research, we note that the percentage of racial-ethnic minorities as a patient characteristic ($R^2 = .42$, $F(1, 7) = 4.37$, $p = .08$) approached significance. The numbers indicated that as the percentage of racial/ethnic minorities increases in the patient sample, the overall effect size also increases. If this finding proves to be robust, it has implications for the field of therapist-client matching, as well as multicultural competence (see Smith, Rodriguez, & Bernal, Chapter 16, this volume).

Patient Contribution
Although no patient characteristics emerged as significant moderators in our analyses of the data, we hypothesize that some patient factors, not assessed in the studies we examined, are likely to affect the therapist's provision of positive regard and the extent to which this increases the likelihood of therapeutic success. First, most therapists' behavior is a function, among other things, of the characteristics of the patients they work with. Simply put, some patients are more easily liked and therefore elicit more affirmation than others. Patients who themselves are warm, empathic, and disclosing are more easily liked and affirmed. Just as disclosure begets disclosure (Jourard, 1971), it is quite likely that warmth begets warmth. Conversely, demanding, resistant, or angry patients can be difficult to like or

Table 8.2 Significant Moderators

Moderator	No. of studies (*k*)	Effect size (*r*)	95% Confidence limits for *r* [lower, upper]
Publication status			
Journal article	16	.26	[.20, 0.32]
Unpublished dissertation	2	.09	[−.05, 0.22]
Rater perspective			
Patient	7	.29	[.20, 0.37]
Non-participant rater	6	.05	[−.06, 0.17]
More than one perspective	4	.46	[.29, 0.60]
Not specified	1	.20	[.17, 0.28]
Origin of Sample			
University setting	4	.07	[−.04, 0.18]
Part of larger study	7	.27	[.17, 0.37]
Hospital setting	1	.29	[.13, 0.44]
General outpatient setting	4	.26	[.11, 0.40]
K–12 setting	1	.53	[.28, 0.70]
Not specified	1	.09	[−.25, 0.41]
Measure Used			
VPPS: TWFS	1	.49	[.24, 0.68]
SASB: H&P	3	.23	[.02, 0.42]
TSS	1	.29	[.13, 0.44]
VPPS	1	.53	[.28, 0.70]
Measure created for study	3	.30	[.08, 0.50]
RSTCP	1	.00	[−.53, 0.53]
TRS	1	.20	[.15, 0.51]
BLRI	2	.24	[.12, 0.35]
More than one measure	2	.01	[−.14, 0.15]
Relationship Inventory	1	.12	[−.20, 0.42]
Other	2	.20	[.01, 0.37]
Time when positive regard was measured			
Pre- to post-	3	.16	[−.02, 0.32]
Post-treatment	7	.37	[.27, 0.46]
After second and sixth sessions	1	.83	[.46, 0.96]
One month and three years	1	.31	[−.05, 0.59]
More than one of the above-listed time periods	3	.01	[−.11, 0.14]
Intake, four, eight, twelve, and sixteen weeks	1	.20	[.06, 0.33]
Six and twelve months	1	.33	[.12, 0.51]
Follow-up 1.4 years later	1	.09	[−.25, 0.41]
Theoretical orientation/Type of treatment			
Psychoanalytic/psychodynamic	4	.52	[.35, 0.65]
Combination/eclectic	7	.12	[.03, 0.20]
Not specified	3	.31	[.20, 0.42]
Peer-based	1	.33	[.12, 0.51]
In-vivo/exposure	3	.14	[−.06, 0.32]

VPPS: TWFS = Vanderbilt Psychotherapy Process Scale: Therapist Warmth and Friendliness; SASB: H&P = Structured Analysis of Social Behavior: Helping & Protecting; TSS = Therapist Satisfaction Scale; VPPS = Vanderbilt Psychotherapy Process Scale; RSTCP = The Rating Scale of Therapy Change Processes; TRS = Therapist Rating Scale; BLRI = Barrett-Lennard Relationship Inventory.

affirm (see Winnicott, 1949). Thus, we suspect that those with Axis II pathologies, especially individuals with borderline or narcissistic disorders, are less likely to consistently evoke positive regard from their therapists. Many difficult patients are testing their sense of the world (e.g., their lovableness), simultaneously desperate to have their worst fears unconfirmed but overdetermining through their behavior that they will be reconfirmed (Weiss & Sampson, 1986).

A related client characteristic that may influence a therapist's tendency to be positively regarding is the nature of the client's needs at a particular point in therapy. For example, patients suffering acutely from any of the many variants of depression, or dealing with the aftermath of a recently experienced trauma, may explicitly ask for or more subtly indicate their need for intensive doses of positive regard and affirmation. These requests may range from "please tell me I'm OK," to "I really need your support now," to "no one cares about me at all." A third possible factor here is motivational status—that is, a patient's current stage of change (see Norcross, Krebs, & Prochaska, Chapter 14, this volume). Patients who are more highly motivated to do the work, who appear to be courageous or risk taking, are more likely to evoke their therapist's positive regard.

A consideration of how various patient characteristics may contribute to the expression of positive regard in the therapeutic relationship also illuminates the relevance of the perspective from which positive regard is rated. Although Rogers (1957) believed that it is only the client's perspective that matters—that it is the client's experience of positive regard (or genuineness or empathy) that "counts" and that the therapist's belief as to whether he or she has been positively regarding is essentially moot in regard to positive outcome—our data indicate a greater overall treatment effect of positive regard when more than one perspective (e.g., patient, therapist, and nonparticipant rater) was assessed. These multiple perspectives may serve as reliability checks on the accuracy, including the potential underevaluation, of the patient's perspective on the provision of therapist positive regard.

Our data indicated that the effects of positive regard increased as a function of the racial-ethnic composition in a study, although this association was statistically weak. Thus, we tentatively hypothesize that therapists' provision of positive regard may be a salient factor in treatment outcome when non-minority therapists work with minority clients. In such cases, the possibility of mistrust and of related difficulties—stemming in large part from our nation's troubled racial history as well as traditional neglect of minority clients by the mental health community--may be attenuated by clear indications of the therapist's positive regard, in turn facilitating the likelihood of a positive outcome (Sue & Sue, 1999).

Limitations of the Research

Our database was restricted to 18 studies, a relatively small basis for conclusions about a variable that has been part of psychotherapeutic lore for more than 50 years. In part, this reflects the stringent criteria we used in deciding which studies were to be entered in the meta-analysis; in part, it represents the fact that positive regard has been studied primarily within the realm of client-centered therapy, an orientation that no longer attracts the attention of many prominent researchers. In this respect, there have been very few studies of positive regard within the past 20 years. We believe that the concept of positive regard hasn't so much gone away in recent years as it has been folded into newer concepts in the field, particularly measures of the therapeutic alliance (see Chapters 2, 3, and 4 in this volume).

The restricted range of theoretical orientations in which positive regard has been studied leads to another limitation: the possibility that the action of this variable is restricted to a specific form of therapy (person-centered) or interacts with a specific aspect of this therapy. Thus, Orlinsky and Howard (1978) raised the possibility that empathy and warmth "interact differentially with other aspects of therapist style" (p. 293). That is, they suggested that these qualities might be significantly associated with outcome only when therapist directiveness is low—as is usually true of person-centered or psychodynamic therapists—and may not be the case when therapists practice from a more heterogeneous or directive perspective that might reflect a CBT orientation. In fact, our data allow us to know only partially the answer to this question. Whereas we found a significant moderating effect for psychodynamic treatment—patients in this form of therapy tended to improve more than others as a function of receiving positive regard from their therapists—our database included no studies of patients in any CBT-related treatment. It is nevertheless noteworthy that meta-analytic results on the association between therapist empathy and treatment outcome reveal no differences in effect sizes for different forms of therapy (Elliott, Bohart, Watson, & Greenberg, Chapter 6, this volume). Nor were there any differential effect sizes as a function of the type of treatment in the relation between treatment outcome and the therapeutic alliance in individual therapy for adults (Horvath, Del Re, & Flückiger, Symonds, Chapter 2, this volume) or youth (Shirk & Karver, Chapter 3, this volume).

More generally, the extant research has not addressed the question of specificity: For which patients, presenting with which types of problems at which point in therapy, is the provision of therapist regard most important?

Therapeutic Practice

The psychotherapist's ability to provide positive regard is significantly associated with therapeutic success. However, our meta-analysis indicates a moderate relationship, suggestive of the fact that, like many other relational factors, it is a significant but not exhaustive part of the process–outcome equation. Extrapolating from the data, we offer the following recommendations for clinical practice:

• Therapists' provision of positive regard is strongly indicated in practice. At a minimum, it "sets the stage" for other mutative interventions and that, at least in some cases, it may be sufficient by itself to effect positive change.

• There is virtually no research-driven reason to withhold positive regard. We are reminded of the oft-heard sentiment in contemporary psychoanalytic circles that one of Kohut's major contributions was to provide a theoretical justification for being kind to one's patients.

• Positive regard serves many valuable functions across the major forms of psychotherapy. From a psychodynamic perspective, positive regard serves to strengthen the client's ego (sense of self or agency) and belief in his or her capacity to be engaged in an effective relationship; from a behavioral perspective, the therapist's positive regard functions as a positive reinforcer for clients' engagement in the therapeutic process, including difficult self-disclosures; and from a more purely humanistic perspective, the therapist's stance of caring and positive regard facilitates the client's natural tendency to grow and fulfill his or her potential.

• Positive regard may be especially indicated in situations wherein a non-minority therapist is working with a minority client.

• Therapists cannot be content with feeling good about their patients but instead should ensure that their positive feelings are communicated to them. This does not have to translate to a stream of compliments or to a gushing of positive sentiment that, in fact, may overwhelm or even terrify some clients; rather, it speaks to the need for therapists to communicate a caring, respectful, positive attitude that serves to affirm a client's basic sense of worth. To many, if not most, clients, the conviction that "my therapist really cares about me" likely serves a critical function, especially in times of stress.

• Therapists need to monitor their positive regard and adjust it as a function of the needs of particular patients and specific clinical situations. The research demonstrates that therapists vary in the extent to which they are able to convey positive regard to their patients, and clients vary in the extent to which they need, elicit, and/or benefit from a therapist's positive regard. In this regard, too, we suspect that the inevitable ruptures in the therapeutic alliance (Safran, Muran, & Eubanks-Carter, Chapter 11, this volume) that occur over the course of therapy are the result not only of a therapist's technical errors but also of the therapist's occasional inability to demonstrate minimally facilitative levels of positive regard and support.

References

An asterisk (*) indicates studies included in the meta-analysis.

Bachelor, A. (1991). Comparison and relationship to outcome of diverse dimensions of the helping alliance as seen by client and therapist. *Psychotherapy, 28,* 534–49.

Barrett-Lennard, G. T. (1964). *The Relationship Inventory. Form OS-M-64 and OS-F-64 Form MO-M-64 and MO-F-64.* Armidale, New South Wales, Australia: University of New England.

Barrett-Lennard, G. T. (1978). The Relationship Inventory: Later development and applications. *JSAS: Catalog of selected documents in psychology,* 8, 68 (Ms. No. 1732, p. 55).

Barrett-Lennard, G. (1986). The relationship inventory now: Issues and advances in theory, method and use. In L. S. Greenberg & W. M. Pinsof (Eds.), *The Psychotherapeutic process: A research handbook* (pp. 439–76). New York: Guilford.

Beck, J. S. (1995). *Cognitive therapy: Basics and beyond.* New York: Guilford.

Benjamin, L. (1984). Principles of prediction using Social Analysis of Structural Behavior (SASB). In R. A. Zucker, J. Aronoff, and A. J. Rabin (Eds.), *Personality and the prediction of behavior* (pp. 121–73). New York: Academic Press.

Bergin, A. E., & Garfield, S. L. (Eds.) (1971). *Handbook of psychotherapy and behavior change: An empirical analysis.* New York: Wiley.

Beutler, L. E., Machado, P. P. P., & Neufeldt, S. A. (1994). Therapist variables. In S. L. Garfield & A. E. Bergin (Eds.), *Handbook of psychotherapy and behavior change* (4th ed., pp. 229–69). New York: Wiley.

Chisholm, S. M. (1998). *A comparison of the therapeutic alliances of premature terminators versus therapy completers.* Unpublished doctoral dissertation, Kent State University, Kent, OH.

Coady, N. F. (1991). The association between client and therapist interpersonal processes and outcomes in psychodynamic psychotherapy. *Research on Social Work Practice, 1,* 122–38.

Conte, H. R., Ratto, R., Clutz, K., & Karasu, T. B. (1995). Determinants of outpatients' satisfaction with therapists. *Journal of Psychotherapy Practice and Research, 4,* 43–51.

Cooper, H., Hedges, L. V., & Valentine, J. C. (Eds.). (2009). *The handbook of research synthesis and meta-analysis* (2nd ed.). New York: Russell Sage Foundation.

Cramer, D., & Takens, R. J. (1992). Therapeutic relationship and progress in the first six sessions of individual psychotherapy: A panel analysis. *Counseling Psychology Quarterly, 5,* 25–36.

Del Re, A. C. (2010). RcmdrPlugin.MAc: Meta-Analysis with correlations (MAc) Rcmdr Plug-in.

R package version 1.0.7. http://CRAN.R-project. org/package=RcmdrPlugin.MAc

Del Re, A. C., & Hoyt, W. T. (2010). MAc: Meta-Analysis with correlations. R package version 1.0.6. http://Cran.R-project.org/package=Mac

Eckert, P. A., Abeles, N., & Graham, R. N. (1988). Symptom severity, psychotherapeutic process, and outcome. *Professional Psychology: Research and Practice, 19*, 560–64.

Farber, B. A. (2007). On the enduring and substantial influence of Carl Rogers' not-quite essential nor necessary conditions. *Psychotherapy: Theory, Research, Practice, Training, 44*, 289–294.

Farber, B. A., Brink, D. C., & Raskin, P. M. (1996). *The psychotherapy of Carl Rogers: Cases and commentary.* New York: Guilford.

Garfield, S. L., & Bergin, A. E. (1971). Therapeutic conditions and outcome. *Journal of Abnormal Psychology, 77*, 108–114.

Gaston, L., Marmar, C. R., Gallagher, D., & Thompson, L. W. (1991). Alliance prediction of outcome beyond in-treatment symptomatic change as psychotherapy processes. *Psychotherapy Research, 1*, 104–113.

Green, R. J., & Herget, M. (1991). Outcomes of systemic/strategic team consultation: The importance of therapist warmth and active structuring. *Family Process, 30*, 321–36.

Gurman, A. (1977). The patient's perception of the therapeutic relationship. In A. S. Gurman & A. M. Razin (Eds.), *Effective psychotherapy* (pp. 503–43). New York: Pergamon.

Hayes, A. M., & Strauss, J. L. (1998). Dynamic systems theory as a paradigm for the study of change in psychotherapy: An application to cognitive therapy for depression. *Journal of Consulting and Clinical Psychology, 66*, 939–47.

Hedges, L. V. (1982). Estimating effect sizes from a series of independent experiments. *Psychological Bulletin, 92*, 490–99.

Henry, W. P., Schacht, T. E., & Strupp, H. H. (1990). Patient and therapist introject, interpersonal process, and differential psychotherapy outcome. *Journal of Consulting and Clinical Psychology, 58*, 768–74.

Horvath, A. O., & Greenberg, A. (1989). Development and validation of the Working Alliance Inventory. *Journal of Counseling Psychology, 36*, 223–33.

Hynan, D. J. (1990). Client reasons and experiences in treatment that influence termination of psychotherapy. *Journal of Clinical Psychology, 46*, 891–95.

Jourard, S. M. (1971). *The transparent self.* New York: Van Nostrand.

Keijsers, G. P., Hoogduin, C. A., & Schaap, C. P. (1994). Predictors of treatment outcome in the behavioral treatment of obsessive-compulsive disorder. *The British Journal of Psychiatry, 165*, 781–86.

Knox, S., & Hill, C. E. (2003). Therapist self-disclosure: Research-based suggestions for practitioners. *Journal of Clinical Psychology/In Session, 59*, 529–40.

Leahy, R. L. (2001). *Overcoming resistance in cognitive therapy.* New York: Guilford.

Lietaer, G. (1984). Unconditional positive regard: A controversial basic attitude in client-centered therapy. In R. F. Levant & J. M. Shlien (Eds.), *Client-centered therapy and the person-centered approach: New directions in theory, research, and practice* (pp. 41–58). New York: Praeger.

Litter, M. (2004). Relationship-based psychotherapy with court-involved youth: The therapy relationship's effect on outcome. *Dissertation Abstracts International, 65* (12), 4474. (AAT no. 3156920).

McMain, S., Korman, L. M., & Dimeff, L. (2001). Dialectical behavior therapy and the treatment of emotion dysregulation. *Journal of Clinical Psychology, 57*(2), 183–96.

Meyer, A. E. (1990). *Nonspecific and common factors in treatment outcome: Another myth?* Paper presented at the Annual Meeting, Society for Psychotherapy Research, Wintergreen, VA.

Mitchell, S. A., & Aron, L. (1999). *Relational psychoanalysis.* New York: Analytic Press.

Mitchell, K., Bozarth, J., & Krauft, C. (1977). A reappraisal of the therapeutic effectiveness of accurate empathy, non-possessive warmth and genuineness. In A. S. Gurman & A. M. Razin (Eds.), *Effective psychotherapy* (pp. 482–502). New York: Pergamon.

Mitchell, K., Bozarth, J., Truax, C., & Krauft, C. (1973). *Antecedents to psychotherapeutic outcome.* Arkansas Rehabilitation Research and Training Center, University of Arkansas (NIMH Final Report, MH 12306).

Najavits, L. M., & Strupp, H. H. (1994). Differences in the effectiveness of psychodynamic therapists: A process-outcome study. *Psychotherapy, 31*, 114–23.

Orlinsky, D. E., Grawe, K., & Parks, B. K. (1994). Process and outcome in psychotherapy—noch einmal. In A. E. Bergin & S. L. Garfield (Eds.), *Handbook of psychotherapy and behavior change* (4th ed., pp. 27–376). New York: Wiley.

Orlinsky, D. E., & Howard, K. (1978). The relation of process to outcome in psychotherapy. In S. L. Garfield & A. E. Bergin (Eds.), *Handbook of psychotherapy and behavior change* (2nd ed., pp. 283–329). New York: Wiley.

Orlinsky, D. E., & Howard, K. (1986). Process and outcome in psychotherapy. In S. L. Garfield, & A. E. Bergin (Eds.), *Handbook of Psychological Behavior and Change* (pp. 311–81) New York: Wiley.

Parloff, M. B., Waskow, I. E., & Wolfe, B. E. (1978). Research on therapist variables in relation to process and outcome. In S. L. Garfield & A. E. Bergin (Eds.), *Handbook of psychotherapy and behavior change* (2nd ed., pp. 233–82). New York: Wiley.

Quintana, S. M., & Meara, N. M. (1990). Internalization of therapeutic relationships in short-term psychotherapy. *Journal of Counseling Psychology, 2,* 123–30.

Rabavilas, A. D., Boulougouris, J. C., & Perissaki, C. (1979). Therapist qualities related to outcome with exposure in vivo in neurotic patients. *Journal of Behavior Therapy and Experimental Psychiatry, 10,* 293–94.

Rogers, C. R. (1942). *Counseling and psychotherapy.* Boston: Houghton Mifflin.

Rogers, C. R. (1951). *Client-centered therapy.* Boston: Houghton Mifflin.

Rogers, C. R. (1957). The necessary and sufficient conditions of therapeutic personality change. *Journal of Consulting Psychology, 21,* 95–103.

Rogers, C. R. (1986). A client-centered/person-centered approach to therapy. In I. Kutash & A. Wolf (Eds.), *Psychotherapist's casebook* (pp. 197–208). San Francisco: Jossey-Bass.

Rogers, C. R., & Truax, C. B. (1967). The therapeutic conditions antecedent to change: A theoretical view. In C. R. Rogers, E. T. Gendlin, D. J. Kiesler, & C. B. Truax (Eds.), *The therapeutic relationship and its impact: A study of psychotherapy with schizophrenics.* Madison: University of Wisconsin Press.

Russell, R. L., Bryant, F. B., & Estrada, A. U. (1996). Confirmatory P-technique analysis of therapist discourse: High- versus low-quality child therapy sessions. *Journal of Consulting and Clinical Psychology, 64,* 1366–76.

Schindler, L. (1991). *Die empirische analyse der therapeutischen Beziehung. Beitrage zur prozessforschung in der verhaltenstherapie* [The empirical analysis of the therapeutic relation: Contribution to process research in behavior therapy]. Berlin, Heidelberg, Germany: Springer-Verlag.

Sells, D., Davidson, L., Jewell, C., Falzer, P., & Rowe, M. (2006). The treatment relationship in peer-based and regular case management for clients with severe mental illness. *Psychiatric services, 57,* 1179–84.

Sue, D. W., & Sue, D. (1999). *Counseling the culturally different: Theory and practice* (3rd edition). New York: Wiley.

Suh, C. S., Strupp, H. H., & O'Malley, S. S. (1986). The Vanderbilt Process Measures: The Psychotherapy Process Scale (VPPS) and the Negative Indicators Scale (VNIS). In L. S. Greenberg & W. M. Pinsof (Eds.), *The psychotherapeutic process: A research handbook* (pp. 285–323). New York: Guilford.

Tracey, T. J., & Kokotovic, A. M. (1989). Factor structure of the working alliance inventory. *Psychological Assessment, 1,* 207–210.

Truax, C. B., & Carkhuff, R. R. (1967). *Toward effective counseling and psychotherapy: Training and practice.* Chicago: Aldine.

Wachtel, P. L. (2008). *Relational theory and the practice of psychotherapy.* New York: Guilford.

Wampold, B. (2001). *The great psychotherapy debate.* Mahwah, NJ: Erlbaum.

Weiss, J., Sampson, H., and the Mt. Zion Psychotherapy Research Group. (1986). *The psychoanalytic process: Theory, clinical observations and empirical research.* New York: Guilford Press.

Williams, K. E., & Chambless, D. L. (1990). The relationship between therapist characteristics and outcome of in vivo exposure treatment for agoraphobia. *Behavior Therapy, 21,* 111–116.

Winnicott, D. W. (1949). Hate in the countertransference. *International Journal of Psycho-Analysis, 30,* 69–74.

Yalom, I. D. (2002). *The Gift of therapy: An Open letter to a new generation of therapists and their patients.* New York: HarperCollins.

Zuroff, D., & Blatt, S. J. (2006). The therapeutic relationship in the brief treatment of depression: Contributions to clinical improvement and enhanced adaptive capacities. *Journal of Consulting and Clinical psychology, 74,* 130–40.

CHAPTER

9 Congruence/Genuineness

Gregory G. Kolden, Marjorie H. Klein, Chia-Chiang Wang, *and* Sara B. Austin

Congruence or genuineness is a relational quality that has been highly prized throughout the history of psychotherapy but of diminished research interest in recent years. In this chapter, we offer definitions and examples of this attribute of the therapy relationship as well as an original meta-analytic review of the empirical literature showing its relation to improvement. Moderators of the association between congruence and treatment outcome are examined, and limitations of the extant research are discussed as well. In closing, we advance several therapist practices that are likely to foster congruence and thus improve psychotherapy outcomes.

Definitions and Measures
Definitions
In 1957 Carl Rogers characterized the necessary and sufficient conditions of therapeutic change as the client being in a "state of incongruence," the client and therapist in "psychological contact," and the therapist as "congruent or integrated in the relationship" and experiencing "positive regard for the client" and "an empathic understanding of the client's internal frame of reference" (p. 96). This characterization underscores two facets of congruence. The first refers to the therapist's personal integration in the relationship, that "he is freely and deeply himself, with his experience accurately represented by his awareness of himself" (Rogers, 1957, p. 97). These days we might say that the therapist is mindfully genuine in the therapy relationship, underscoring present personal awareness as well as genuineness or authenticity.

The second facet of congruence refers to the therapist's capacity to communicate his or her experience with the client to the client. This requires careful reflection and considered judgment on the part of the therapist. While the aim is not for the therapist to indulge in indiscriminate self-disclosure or ventilation of feelings, the therapist must not deceive the client about his or her feelings, especially if they stand in the way of progress. Neither empathy nor regard can be conveyed unless the therapist is perceived as genuine. As such, congruence occupies a central position in Rogers' conceptualization.

The concept of congruence can at times seem abstract and elusive. Consider how this relational quality might appear in everyday interactions with people in your world. Insurance agent Jones is quite formal and proper while appearing to be playing a prescribed role. Mr./Ms Jones interacts in a relationally incongruent manner. Coffee barista Brian warmly greets you by your first name, attentively asks after your family, and openly shares his opinion about a movie he recently took in. Brian engages you, makes contact, and sincerely expresses himself in the brief time it takes to pour and pay for a cup of coffee. Brian interacts in a relationally congruent fashion.

In psychotherapy, this means that the therapist is openly "being the feelings and attitudes which at the moment are flowing within him" (Rogers et al., 1967, p. 100) and not hiding behind a professional role or holding back feelings that are obvious in the encounter. Congruence thus involves mindful self-awareness and self-acceptance on the part of the therapist, as well as a willingness to engage and tactfully share perceptions. To quote Rogers, the congruent therapist "comes into a direct personal encounter with his client by meeting him on a person-to-person basis. It means that he is *being* himself, not denying himself" (p. 101).

One reason why congruence plays so central a role in Rogers' thinking is that he defines the problems that clients bring to therapy in terms of their incongruence and sees the therapy process as one of helping the client to become more congruent; that is, to develop the capacity to own and express thoughts and feelings without fear. Thus, therapist congruence can model for the client a "realness" and can facilitate the client becoming more open to his/her own experiencing; this makes the therapist–client relationship deeper and the psychological contact more immediate.

Although most fully developed with the client-centered tradition, therapist congruence is highly prized in many theoretical orientations. The notion of the *therapist real relationship* (Gelso & Carter, 1985; Gelso & Hayes, 1998), for example, is conceptually similar to congruence/genuineness and is consistent with ideas initially offered by psychoanalysts (e.g., Greenson, 1967). The real relationship is seen as primarily undistorted by transferential material and comprised of two defining features: genuineness and realistic perceptions. Genuineness is viewed as "the ability to and willingness to be what one truly is in the relationship . . ." (Gelso & Carter, 1994, p. 297). Genuineness is also related to other terms, such as authenticity, openness, honesty, and nonphoniness (Gelso & Hayes, 1998). Realistic experiences of the therapeutic relationship pertain to perceptions that are not distorted by transference alterations and defense mechanisms.

In the current literature, genuineness is frequently considered the most important of the three Rogerian facilitative conditions. Moreover, Lietaer (1993) has offered a conceptualization of genuineness with both an internal and external facet. The internal facet ". . . refers to therapists' own internal experiencing with their clients . . . To the extent that therapists are able to be in touch with their own experience they may be termed congruent" (Watson, Greenberg, & Lietaer, 1998, p. 9). The external facet ". . . refers to the therapists' ability to reveal their experience to their clients. This is termed transparency . . . it is not necessary to share every aspect of their experience but only those that they feel would be facilitative of their clients' work. Transparency is always used in an empathic climate" (Watson, Greenberg, & Lietaer, 1998, p. 9).

There has also been some broadening of the definitions of congruence to include *therapeutic presence* (Geller & Greenberg, 2002). In an interview, Carl Rogers said, "Over time, I think I have become more aware of the fact that in therapy I do use myself. I recognized that when I am intensely focused on a client, just my presence seems to be healing" (Baldwin, 1987, p. 45). In addition to the three basic conditions "perhaps it is something around the edges of those conditions that is really the most important element of therapy–when myself is very clearly, obviously present" (p. 30). In sum, presence implies a dual level of mindful awareness whereby the therapist balances contact with his or her own experience and contact with the client's experience to maintaining a "place of internal and external connection" (Geller & Greenberg, 2002, p. 83).

Authenticity and transparency are also components of congruence that involve the therapist's awareness of his or her internal experience and willingness to communicate this awareness to the client (Greenberg & Watson, 2005). "The communicative aspects of congruence involve the ability to translate intrapersonal experience into certain types of interpersonal responses" (p. 127). A congruent interactional response involves the conveyance of "attitudes or intentions of being helpful, understanding, valuing, respecting and being nonintrusive or nondominant" (p. 129). Thus, congruence is more than avoiding formality on the one hand or phoniness on the other; it entails the therapist's attentive recognition and nonjudgmental acceptance of feelings, perceptions, and thoughts, both positive and negative.

Measures

The first measures of Rogers' facilitative conditions were developed at the University of Chicago Counseling Center. Halkides (1958) designed separate scales for each condition for use by independent raters. This groundbreaking work was followed by numerous studies examining the relation between judge's ratings of the core conditions and patient outcomes (Barrett-Lennard, 1998).

Barrett-Lennard (1959) developed what has become the most recognized and validated therapist- or patient self-report assessment of the core conditions: the Barrett-Lennard Relationship Inventory (BLRI; see Barrett-Lennard, 1962). Parallel forms of the BLRI ask the therapist to describe his or her feelings toward the client while in session (e.g., " I am willing to tell him my own thoughts and feelings") or the patient to describe his or her experience of the therapist (e.g., "He is willing to tell me his own thoughts and feelings").

The original 92-item version of the BLRI included five scales: level of regard, empathic understanding, unconditionality, genuineness, and willingness to be known. This last scale was merged into the genuineness/congruence scale in the 64-item 1964 revision (Barrett-Lennard, 1978). Likert scaling ranging from −3 (I strongly feel that it is not true) to +3 (I strongly feel that it is true) is used to rate each question (see Table 9.1). A shortened, 30-item version of the BLRI was developed later (Gurman, 1973a, 1973b).

Truax also developed a version of the BLRI entitled the Truax Relationship Questionnaire (TRQ; see Truax & Carkuff, 1967) as a self-report assessment of the core conditions. While Truax (1968) stated that client self-report was less valid for assessing the core conditions and impractical with certain populations (such as psychotic patients), he argued that the economical and wide-ranging uses for the instrument justified its development.

As Barrett-Lennard was developing and revising the BLRI, Rogers' group at the University of Wisconsin was engaged in extensive development of scales for raters to assess the conditions from audiotape recordings of sessions. Early versions (Hart, 1960; Gendlin & Geist, 1962) were followed by Truax's development of the 1962 Self-Congruence Scale (Rogers et al., 1967) for use in the Wisconsin Schizophrenia Project. Independent observers rate how the therapist "appears" in tape-recorded session samples; Table 9.1 lists the descriptors for the five stages of the Truax (1966a) Self-Congruence Scale. Further revisions of the measure were made for the final ratings of the Wisconsin Schizophrenia Project

(Rogers et al., 1967) because of difficulties obtaining acceptable reliability with the Truax version. This modification consisted of a five-point scale ranging from "a point where there is obvious discrepancy between the therapist's feelings about the patient and his concurrent communication to the patient (stage 1) to a high point where the therapist communicates both his positive and negative feelings about the patient openly and freely, without traces of defensiveness or retreat into professionalism (stage 5)" (Kiesler, 1973, p. 229; Rogers et al., 1967, pp 581–583). In contrast to the Truax version, ratings of the Kiesler scale only applied to session segments in which the client either "explicitly or implicitly questioned the therapist's feelings or opinions about him" (Rogers et al., p. 140).

Carkhuff (1969) also developed a scale of genuineness derived from the Truax scale for broad application to interpersonal interactions beyond those occurring between a therapist and client. Aside from its broader application, the Carkhuff scale differs from Truax's version in that it includes more of an emphasis on negative reactions resulting from moderate to low levels of genuineness.

More recently, patient and therapist versions of a Real Relationship Inventory have been published (Gelso, et al., 2005). Items for the Real Relationship Inventory were solicited from professional therapists and graduate students. A pool of 130 items was reduced to 44 items, which was administered to randomly selected members of APA Divisions 29 (Psychotherapy) and 42 (Independent Practice) with instructions to rate if they had used that item in their last session with a client. This resulted in a final scale of 24 items, 12 for "Realism" and 12 for "Genuineness."

The reliability of the two most frequently used measures of the core conditions—the BLRI and the Truax scale—has generally been adequate. Most internal and test–retest reliability coefficients for the BLRI range between 0.75 and 0.95 with the majority exceeding 0.80 (Barrett-Lennard, 1998). An extensive review reported internal reliability coefficients for congruence ranging from 0.76 to 0.92 with a mean coefficient of 0.89 (Gurman, 1977). On the Truax scale, reliability coefficients for congruence/genuineness ranged from 0.34 to 0.85 with most over 0.65 (Mitchell, Bozrath, & Krauft, 1977). Internal reliabilities for the Real Relationship Inventory in the professional and graduate student samples were 0.79 for Realism and 0.83 for Genuineness (Gelso et al., 2005). Confirmatory factor analysis compared 1-factor and 2-factor solutions; results were slightly more supportive of a single factor, but it was decided to retain the two scales for further study because "the theory from which the measures emanated is embedded in this dual notion" (p. 647).

Clinical Examples
Therapist Perspectives

The following excerpts are examples of Rogers' description of how his work with individuals who are schizophrenic led him to refine the experiential component of client-centered therapy (Rogers et al., 1967). In the first example, Rogers explains how he may use his feelings about the difficulty ending a session to provide the "vehicle for therapeutic responding" (p. 389):

> Some of my feelings about him (the patient) in the situation are a good source of responses, if I tell them in a personal, detailed way. . . . . One whole set of feelings I have for others in situations comes at first as discomfort. As I look to see why I am uncomfortable I find content relevant to the person I am with, to what we just did or said. Often it is quite

personal. I was stupid, rude, hurrying, embarrassed, avoidant, on the spot: I wished I didn't have to go since he wants me to stay. I wish I hadn't hurried him out of the store in front of all those people. Or, "I guess you're mad at me because I'm leaving. I don't feel very good about it either. It just never feels right to me to go away and leave you in here [hospital ward]. I have to go, or else I'll be late for everything I have to do all day today, and I'll feel lousy about that." Silence. "In a way, I'm glad you don't want me to go. I wouldn't like it at all if you didn't care one way or the other." (p. 390).

In reflecting on these moments, Rogers explains that:

These . . . have in common that I express feelings of mine which are at first troublesome or difficult, the sort I would at first tend to ignore in myself. It requires a kind of *doubling back*. When I first notice it, I have *already* ignored, avoided, or belied my feelings - only now do I notice what it was or is. I must double back to express it. At first, this seems a sheer impossibility! How can I express this all-tied-up, troublesome, puzzling feeling? Never! But a moment later I see that it is only another perfectly human way to feel, and in fact includes much concern for the patient, and empathic sensitivity to him. It is him I feel unhappy about - or what I just did to him. (p. 390).

Another example shows how Rogers uses an "openness to what comes next" to increase his sensitivity, even to repair a breach in the interaction. He notes that by being open to what comes next, a positive feeling will usually emerge:

I used to ponder whether I was about to say a right or wrong thing. Then, if it was

wrong (as I could tell from the patient's reaction), I would not know what to do. Now I spend moments letting my feelings clarify themselves, but once they feel clear, I no longer wonder so much whether it is right or wrong to express them. Rather, I have open curiosity, sensitivity, and a readiness to meet whatever reaction I will get. This may tell me what I said was "wrong," but all will be well if *now* I respond sensitively to what I have stirred. I now say whatever I now sense which *makes* what I said before "wrong." (It is not my admission that I was wrong which matters here. I rarely make a point of having been wrong. That matters only to me. I am the only one who cares how often I am right or wrong. But whatever it is in him which I now sense and which *makes* what I said wrong - I now see it in his further reaction - *that* is what I have to respond to in the next moment.) (p. 391).

A final example illustrates the key role of the therapist's self-experiencing in building mutual congruence:

We tend to express the *outer* edges of our feelings. That leaves *us* protected and makes the other person unsafe. We say, "This and this (which *you* did) hurt me." We do not say, "This and this weakness of mine *made me* be hurt when you did this and this." To find this inward edge of my feelings, I need only ask myself, "Why?" When I find myself bored, angry, tense, hurt, at a loss, or worried, I ask myself, "Why?" Then, instead of "You bore me," or "This makes me mad," I find the "why" *in me* which makes it so. That is always more personal and positive, and much safer to express. Instead of "You bore me," I find, "I want to hear more personally from you," or, "You tell me what happened, but I want

Patient Perspectives

How is congruence offered by the therapist perceived by the patient? One way to capture this is to review the items that a patient might endorse in the BLRI, as shown in Table 9.1. The patient's experience of the highly self-congruent therapist is that the therapist is fully at ease within the relationship and is openly him or herself. Being attuned to his or her experience in the moment, the therapist is open to honestly sharing this experience with the patient and does not avoid sharing uncomfortable feelings and impressions that are important to treatment. Because of this personal attunement and genuineness, the therapist's words accurately capture his or her momentary experience.

Observer Perspectives

A third perspective on genuineness is provided by samples from session transcripts. The following example of Stage 5 high-congruence comes from the training material for the Truax (1966a) scale:

> C: I guess you realize that, too, don't you? Or do you? (Laughs)
>
> T: Do I realize that? You *bet* I do! Sure yeah—I always wanted somebody to take *care of me*, you know, but I also wanted them to let me do what I wanted to do! Well, if you have somebody taking care of you, then you've got to do what *they* want you to do.
>
> C: That's right. (Pause)
>
> T: So, I never could kind of get it so that I'd have both, you know, *both* things at once: either I'm doing what *I* want to do and taking care of myself or, you know, I used to have somebody taking care of me

and then I'd do what *they* wanted to do. And I'd think, "Aw, hell!" It just—never works out, you know.

> C: Always somebody there, isn't there? (Laughs)
>
> T: Yeah, just somebody goofing up the works all the time. (Pause) Yeah, if you're dependent on somebody else, you're under their control, sort of.
>
> C: To a certain extent . . .
>
> T: Yeah, that's what I was going to say—yeah, you're right. (Pause). So you just sit around the ward and you read a little bit, and then you go out and play horseshoes and—boy, that sounds like a *drag!* (p. 72).

The next example comes from the transcripts of Carl Rogers's filmed demonstration session with the client "Gloria" (Shostrum, 1966) where he clearly expresses his feeling of closeness to Gloria:

> Gloria: That is why I like substitutes. Like I like talking to you and I like men that I can respect. Doctors, and I keep sort of underneath feeling like we are real close, you know, sort of like a substitute father.
>
> Rogers: I don't feel that is pretending.
>
> Gloria: Well, you are not really my father.
>
> Rogers: No. I meant about the real close business.
>
> Gloria: Well, see, I sort of feel that's pretending too because I can't expect you to feel very close to me. You don't know me that well.
>
> Rogers: All I can know is what I am feeling and that is I feel close to you in this moment.

Three aspects of congruence are its communication, transparency (in a disciplined manner), and affirmation of the client's

Table 9.1   Rating Scales for Congruence

Congruence items on the BLRI [a]

Positively valenced items

He is comfortable and at ease in our relationship.

I feel that he is real and genuine with me.

I nearly always feel that what he says expresses exactly what he is feeling and thinking as he says it.

He does not avoid anything that is important for our relationship.

He expresses his true impressions and feelings with me.

He is willing to express whatever is actually in his mind with me, including any feelings about himself or about me.

He is openly himself in our relationship.

I have not felt he tries to hide anything from himself that he feels with me.

Negatively valenced items

I feel that he puts on a role or front with me.

It makes him uneasy when I ask or talk about certain things.

He wants me to think that he likes me or understands me more than he really does.

Sometimes he is not at all comfortable but we go on, outwardly ignoring it.

At times I sense that he is not aware of what he is really feeling with me.

There are times when I feel that his outward response to me is quite different from the way he feels underneath.

What he says to me often gives a wrong impression of his whole thought or feeling at the time.

I believe that he has feelings he does not tell me about that are causing difficulty in our relationship.

Stages of the Truax Self-Congruence Scale [b]

Stage 1

The therapist is clearly defensive in the interaction, and there is explicit evidence of a very considerable discrepancy between what he says and what he experiences. There may be striking contradictions in the therapist's statements, the content of his verbalization may contradict the voice qualities or nonverbal cues (i.e., the upset therapist stating in a strained voice that he is "not bothered at all" by the patient's anger).

Stage 2

The therapist responds appropriately but in a professional rather than in a personal manner, giving the impression that his responses are said because they sound good from a distance but do not express what he really feels or means. There is a somewhat contrived or rehearsed quality or an air of professionalism present.

Stage 3

The therapist is implicitly either defensive or professional, although there is no explicit evidence.

Stage 4

There is neither implicit nor explicit evidence of defensiveness or the presence of a façade. The therapist shows no self-incongruence.

(Continued)

Table 9.1 Continued

Stage 5

The therapist is freely and deeply himself in the relationship. He is open to experiences and feelings of all types—both pleasant and hurtful—without traces of defensiveness or retreat into professionalism. Although there may be contradictory feelings, these are accepted or recognized. The therapist is clearly being himself in all of his responses, whether they are personally meaningful or trite. At Stage 5 the therapist need not express personal feelings, but whether he is giving advice, reflecting, interpreting, or sharing experiences, it is clear that he is being very much himself, so that his verbalizations match his inner experiences.

[a] Barrett-Lennard (1962).
[b] Truax (1966a, pp. 68–72).

perspective (Greenberg & Watson, 2005). These are illustrated in a vignette where a therapist described being told by a client that she saw the therapist as phony and presumptuous. The therapist responded by telling the client that he felt afraid of her anger and how hurt he felt. This disclosure led to a change in their interactions.

Meta-Analytic Review

The empirical evidence for the relation between therapist congruence or genuineness and patient outcome has been previously reviewed by at least 10 sets of researchers (in chronological order): Meltzoff & Kornreich, 1970; Truax & Mitchell, 1971; Luborsky, Chandler, Auerbach, Cohen, & Bachrach, 1971; Kiesler, 1973; Lambert, DeJulio, & Stein, 1978; Mitchell, Bozarth, & Krauft, 1977; Parloff, Waskow, & Wolfe, 1978; Orlinsky & Howard, 1978, 1986; Watson, 1984; Orlinsky, Grawe, & Parks, 1994). The consensus of these reviews is that empirical support for the contribution of congruence to patient outcome is mixed but leaning toward the positive.

Search Strategy

In order to identify studies to include in the present review, we narrowed our focus to published studies (in English) and dissertation research on individual or group therapy with adults or adolescents (thereby excluding studies of psychotherapy with children and unpublished research reports).

As such, we conducted PsycINFO and MEDLINE searches using the keywords "congruence," "genuineness," and "psychotherapy." In our previous review (Klein et al., 2002), we identified 20 articles meeting the above criteria. For the present review, we identified five additional potential articles.

Inclusion Criteria

In order to be included in the meta-analysis, a study had to include quantitative information adequate to calculate an effect size (e.g., a correlation coefficient). This procedure resulted in 14 articles reporting 16 studies that were included in our meta-analysis (see Table 9.2). Eleven of the 25 identified articles were excluded due to insufficient information. Table 9.2 lists studies included in our meta-analytic review and provides summary information with respect to (a) aggregate effect size (for those studies that included multiple reports of congruence–outcome relations), (b) type and perspective of congruence measure, and (c) type and perspective of outcome measure.

Methodological Decisions

The effect size (ES) we used in this chapter is r, the correlation coefficient for the relation between congruence and outcome. Each study was reviewed and coded by two raters (coauthors Wang and Austin). Discrepancies in original coding were negotiated in a consensus discussion involving

Table 9.2   Studies Included in Meta-Analytic Review

Reference	Effect size (r)	CM	CP	OM	OP
Athay (1973)	0.24	2	1	4	1,2
Buckley et al. (1981)	0.06	3	1	1,2,5	1
Fretz (1966)	0.25	1	1,2	4	1,2
Fuertes et al. (2007)	0.34	3	1, 2	4	1,2
Garfield & Bergin (1971)	−0.26	3	3	1,4,5	1,2,3
Hansen et al. (1968)	0.69	1,3	1,3	5	1
Jones & Zoppel (1982)	−0.02	3	1	1,3,4	1
Marmarosh et al. (2009)	0.41	3	1, 2	1	1
Melnick & Pierce (1971)	0.42	3	3	5	1
Ritter et al. (2002)	0.21	1	1	1,2,5	1
Rothman (2007)	0.50	1	1	2,4	2
Staples et al. (1976)	0.16	3	3	4	3
Truax (1966a)	0.38	1,3	1,3	4	1
Truax (1971)	−0.02	2	1	1,5	1
Truax (1971)	0.28	2	1	1,5	1
Truax (1971)	0.11	2	1	5	1

Note: CM = congruence measure (1 = Barrett-Lennard Relationship Inventory [BLRI], 2 = Truax Relationship Questionnaire [TRQ], 3 = other scales/checklists); CP = congruence perspectives (1 = patient, 2 = therapist, 3 = observer); OM = outcome measure (1 = symptoms [e.g., anxiety, SCL-90-R], 2 = functioning [e.g., GAFS, adaptive skills/coping], 3 = well-being [e.g., overall success], 4 = global [a measure focusing on general change without any particular dimension], 5 = other [e.g., MMPI, satisfaction, self-concept, goal attainment, personality, Q-sort, self-efficacy, self-esteem]); OP = outcome perspectives (1 = patient, 2 = therapist, 3 = observer).

the first author. If r was not available or was nonsignificant (and not reported), we adopted the strategy of entering zero as the effect size (Lipsey & Wilson, 2001).

For studies reporting multiple correlations and using multiple measures, we aggregated within each study by accounting for the dependencies of measures. This aggregation used the correlation matrix among measures if reported. Otherwise, we assumed that the correlation was 0.50 when the same method was used (e.g., self-report congruence and self-report outcome) and a correlation of 0.25 when different methods were used (e.g., self-report vs. observation; Gleser & Olkin, 1994). Overall, the correlation from each study was used to calculate an aggregated correlation using a weighted average where the weights were the inverse of variance (Hedges & Olkin, 1985).

A test of homogeneity, using Hedges and Olkin's Q statistic, was conducted to determine if the effect sizes among studies were homogeneous. We adopted a random-effects model for determining overall effect size (ES) since the studies we identified were quite heterogeneous ($Q = 35.32$, p < 0.01), thus violating the assumptions required for fixed-effects ES modeling (e.g., homogeneity of sample, variation in study ES due only to sampling error; Hedges & Vevea, 1998). In addition, random-effects modeling allows for greater generalizability. Moreover, if the analysis showed between-study heterogeneity, weighted univariate regression or weighted between-group tests were used to examine moderator variables.

Results

Estimates of effect sizes (ESs) in the 16 studies representing 863 participants ranged from $-.26$ to 0.69. The weighted aggregate ES for congruence with psychotherapy outcome was 0.24 (95% CI = 0.12 to 0.36). The overall ES of 0.24 for congruence is considered a medium effect (Cohen, 1988) and accounts for approximately 6% of the variance in treatment outcome. This provides evidence for congruence as a noteworthy facet of the psychotherapy relationship. Yet, this finding must be cautiously interpreted, as publication bias favors significant results; thus, this ES may be an overestimation of the true congruence–outcome relation in psychotherapy. At the same time, this ES could also be an underestimation as we used the conservative assumption of treating unreported, nonsignificant results as zero.

Moderators

The finding of heterogeneity of ESs among studies led us to examine the extent to which potential moderators accounted for the variability in magnitude of the congruence–outcome association across the studies. As noted above, weighted univariate regression or weighted between-group tests were used to examine moderator variables. Specifically, we examined potential moderator influences in the form of measurement-related variables (rater perspective, congruence measurement, outcome measurement), therapist variables, patient variables, and treatment variables (duration, orientation, setting, and format).

Rater Perspective

We found no consistent pattern regarding the influence of rater perspective on the measurement of congruence on the congruence–outcome association. ESs ranged from 0.13 to 0.31 across perspectives and were relatively homogeneous. However, patient-rated outcome ($r = 0.29$) produced a significantly higher ES than therapist-rated outcome ($r = 0.07$) ($QB = 8.05$, $p < 0.05$). This may be due to the fact that both congruence and outcome were more often assessed from the patient perspective and is consistent with the observation that relations within perspective (patient-rated process and patient-rated outcome) are often more robust (Hill & Lambert, 2004). Of course, it is also important to consider that this is simply an artifact of method variance. At the same time, these constructs are highly phenomenological in nature, and relations like this are likely to be best captured by within-perspective self-report.

Measurement

The specific congruence instrument used did not influence the magnitude of the congruence–outcome relation, as ESs ranged from 0.19 to 0.24. In other words, congruence measures yielded similar results across studies.

Similarly, aggregate ESs did not differ across four types of outcome measures (symptoms, functioning, global, other) ranging from 0.14 to 0.25. Outcome measures produced similar results across studies.

Therapist Variables

This chapter highlights the importance of therapist-offered congruence as an important influence in effective psychotherapy. As such, therapist variables may emerge as moderators of the congruence–outcome link. Unfortunately, limited therapist-relevant information was available in the studies included in our analyses, although there was sufficient data to examine five therapist variables: age, experience, gender, race/ethnicity, and training status.

The mean number of years of therapist clinical experience across five studies was 7.2 years (clinical experience ranged from 0 years for trainees to 13.6 years with a median of 5.6 years). Results from a weighted univariate regression analysis indicated a positive relation between therapist clinical experience and the congruence–outcome ES ($B = 0.05$, p < 0.01). Age as well as gender of therapist (coded as percent female), therapist minority status, and therapist's training status did not significantly moderate the congruence–outcome relationship.

Patient Variables

Perhaps because most of the studies included in this meta-analytic review were published prior to 1990, patient descriptive information was seldom reported. We could code only four patient variables: education, age, gender, and minority status. Educational attainment for patients was 11.6 years on average across the studies included for this review. This is somewhat low (when compared with typical adult outpatient psychotherapy samples) due to the inclusion of three studies involving adolescent patients. The mean years of education was 9.2 for the adolescent studies and 14.5 for the adult studies, indicating that most of the adults had completed at least some college, which is consistent with the adult outpatient therapy research literature (cf. Vessey & Howard, 1993). According to the weighted univariate regression analysis, patient education moderated the magnitude of the congruence–outcome relation. As education decreased, the congruence–outcome relation increased ($B = -0.09$, p < 0.001). Patients with less education were more likely to demonstrate a greater congruence–outcome relation; in other words, therapist congruence is more important for outcome with less educated patients.

Patient age as a continuous variable was not a significant moderator, but we dichotomized age as adolescent versus adult in order to clarify the previous finding regarding education. Adolescent versus adult moderated the congruence–outcome relation.

Studies examining the congruence–outcome relation in adolescents ($r = 0.42$) attained a significantly higher ES that those using adult patients ($r = 0.19$) ($Q_B = 7.15$, p < 0.01). Thus, it appears that therapist congruence may be more important for outcome in adolescent patients.

Gender of patient (coded as percent female) and patient minority status (coded as percent minority) did not significantly moderate the congruence–outcome relationship.

Treatment Variables

We coded four potential moderators of the congruence–outcome association in terms of treatment parameters: duration, orientation, setting, and format. The number of sessions of therapy attended, an index of duration, did not moderate the congruence–outcome relationship.

In terms of theoretical orientation, studies in a mixed category (described as eclectic, client-centered, or interpersonal) ($r = 0.36$) attained significantly higher ESs than those characterized as psychodynamic ($r = 0.04$) ($QB = 8.76$, p < 0.01). One could speculate that congruence is more important for outcome in a more present-oriented, problem-focused therapy in contrast to psychodynamic approaches.

The ESs among therapeutic settings showed significant differences. School counseling centers ($r = .43$), inpatient settings ($r = .27$), and mixed settings (2 or more settings) ($r = .23$) had a significantly higher ES than outpatient mental health settings ($r = -.02$) ($QB = 16.47$, p < .01). School counseling centers also had a significantly higher ES than mixed settings. This finding is difficult to interpret without resorting to conjecture.

Finally, we examined the effect of psychotherapy format (group vs. individual) on the congruence–outcome association. Group therapy studies ($r = 0.36$) obtained a higher ES than those examining individual therapy ($r = 0.18$) ($QB = 5.55$, $p < 0.05$). Congruence may be more important for outcome in group therapy. However, this finding may have more to do with the characteristics of the patients involved than the format per se given that adolescents (see findings for age and education) and inpatients were highly represented in the group therapy condition.

Patient Contribution

Congruence/genuineness is both *intrapersonal* and *interpersonal*. It can be seen as a *personal characteristic* (intrapersonal) of the psychotherapist as well as a *mutual, experiential quality* of the relationship (interpersonal). Thus, the patient contribution to our understanding of congruence refers to the experiential, interpersonal quality of genuineness and authenticity (i.e., congruence) in the therapy relationship, modeled by the therapist and experienced by the patient.

All of us have needs, preferences, and expectations for relationships; patients bring these to the therapy relationship (see Chapters 15 and 16). One can assume that the need for congruence varies across patients as well. Some would like a more congruent therapist, some less. Cultural background may importantly influence patient predilection for congruence. Members of other cultures often approach psychotherapy in fundamentally different ways than their Westernized counterparts (Patterson, 1996). Culturally informed therapy considers patient qualities such as personality, values, political heritage, social structure, and communication style. For example, the value in Western psychotherapy for autonomy and independence may not hold true for interdependently oriented patients from Eastern cultures (Tseng, 1999). Personal autonomy and self-differentiation is often discouraged in such patients; instead, they may desire a more structured relationship in which the therapist takes on a more formal, directive, and authoritative (i.e., less congruent) role (Sue & Sue, 2003). Congruence match between patient and therapist (Zane et al., 2004) may be of great consequence for the therapy relationship.

A patient who has greater needs and expectations for congruence is likely to find comfort and satisfaction (an emotional bond) with a highly congruent therapist. These patients require a therapist to: be comfortable and at ease; be "real and genuine;" say tactfully what s/he is feeling and thinking; naturally express honest/authentic impressions; and not avoid, hide, hold back, or fail to be direct when the "elephant in the room" requires confrontation. Patients in a congruent therapy relationship learn that they are capable and worthy of time and attention, that they matter as a person with strengths and weaknesses, and regrets as well as hopes and dreams for the future. Therapist commitment to truthfulness promotes patient acceptance of the problems they face as well as efforts to change.

Limitations of the Research

Any inferences arising from our meta-analysis of congruence–outcome relations must be mindful of the methodological limitations of the studies included as well as the meta-analytic methods used. Previous researchers have noted limitations of studies included in our meta-analysis: studies not limited to clients in need of change; low levels or restricted ranges of congruence; different rating perspectives; use of ratings from audiotapes that do not allow nonverbal behaviors to be considered; varying qualifications and/or training of raters; inadequate and variable sampling methods; and small sample sizes; (see Lambert et al., 1978; Parloff et al., 1978; Patterson, 1984; Watson, 1984). It is also important to note the paucity of recent studies examining the congruence–outcome association and the lack of any randomized controlled trials investigating the causal impact of congruence. Caution is therefore warranted.

Moreover, it is important not to overgeneralize. Positive findings for congruence/genuineness have appeared primarily in studies investigating client-centered, eclectic, and interpersonal therapies. As such, researcher bias (an allegiance effect) is one possible explanation for our results. Additionally, congruence/genuineness may not be as potent a change process in all types of therapy nor with all kinds of patients. Finally, congruence may only be important for patient change in the context of the other facilitative conditions, for example, as a precondition for the impact of either empathy or positive regard.

While meta-analytic techniques hold great utility in quantitatively integrating and summarizing results across studies, careful consideration is also warranted. Concerns for the present review include: quality of studies, comparability of studies, and limited number of studies including the exclusion of 11 due to lack of information sufficient to calculate an ES. Given these limitations, the finding of a medium ES in the present quantitative review, and affirmative impressions from our previous qualitative review (Klein et al., 2002), leads us to reaffirm our previous conclusion that the evidence is likely to be more strongly supportive than appears at first glance of a positive relation between congruence and psychotherapy outcome. Orlinsky and Howard (1978, pp. 288–289) noted, "If study after flawed study seemed to point in the same general direction, we could not help believing that somewhere in all that variance there must be a reliable effect." A consistent pattern of positive findings is quite unlikely to be explained by study flaws.

Therapeutic Practices

In closing, we offer several recommendations for clinical practice to foster congruence:

• Therapists can strive for genuineness with their patients. This involves acceptance of and receptivity to experiencing with the patient as well as a willingness to use this information in discourse. The congruent therapist is responsible for his or her feelings and reactions, and this "ownership of feelings is specified" (Rogers et al., 1967, p. 377). This might include the therapist's thinking out loud about why he or she said or did something. This experiential stance serves an attachment function (i.e., bonding) as well as a role function (i.e., guides behavior) for the therapy relationship.

• Therapists can mindfully develop the *intrapersonal* quality of congruence. As with all complex skills, this will require discipline, practice, and effort. Solicitation of feedback from colleagues, supervisors, peers, and perhaps patients (when appropriate) might also enhance the development of the capacity for relational authenticity.

• What can therapists "do" to foster as well as augment the *interpersonal* experience of congruence? Therapists must model congruence. Congruent responding may well involve considered self-disclosure of personal information and life experiences. It could also entail articulation of thoughts and feelings, opinions, pointed questions, and feedback regarding patient behavior. Congruent responses are honest. Congruent responses are not disrespectful, overly intellectualized, or insincere, although they may involve irreverence. They are authentic and consistent with the therapist as a real person with likes, dislikes, beliefs, and opinions. Genuine therapist responses are cast in the language of personal pronouns (e.g., "I feel . . .," "My view is . . .," "This is how I experience . . .").

• The *maintenance* of congruence requires that therapists be aware of instances when congruence falters. Rogers and colleagues (1967) speak of feeling "twisted . . . perhaps I am responding socially, smiling, while actually I know we are avoiding something" (p. 396), and then using the twisted feeling as a cue for the need for self-examination and a return to a more genuine and direct way of relating.

• It is important for therapists to identify and become aware of their *congruence style* and to discern the differing needs, preferences, and expectations that patients have for congruence. Effective therapists will modify and tailor their congruence style according to patient presentation (e.g., culture, age, education).

• Congruence may be especially important in younger, less educated, and perhaps less sophisticated patients (e.g., adolescents, college students, young adults). The congruent therapist communicates acceptance and the possibility of engaging in an authentic relationship, something not easily expected from the often formal and authoritarian adults in the lives of these patients.

• Congruence appears to be especially apparent in psychotherapy with more experienced (often older) practitioners. Perhaps therapists come to relax the pretense of role-bound formality and give themselves permission to genuinely engage their patients as they gain experience and confidence. Moreover, experienced therapists may recognize and more carefully discern a patient's need for relational congruence.

References

An asterisk (*) indicates studies included in the meta-analysis.

*Athay, A. L. (1973/1974). The relationship between counselor self-concept, empathy, warmth, and genuineness, and client rated improvement. (Doctoral dissertation, University of Utah, 1973). *Dissertation Abstracts International, 34,* 3976A.

Baldwin, M. (1987). Interview with Carl Rogers on the use of self in therapy. *Journal of Psychotherapy and the Family* , *3,* 45–52.

Barrett-Lennard, G. T. (1959). *Dimensions of perceived therapist response related to therapeutic change. Doctoral dissertation* (psychology), University of Chicago.

Barrett-Lennard, G. T. (1962). Dimensions of therapist response as causal factors in therapeutic change. *Psychological Monographs: General and Applied, 76* (43, Whole No. 562).

Barrett-Lennard, G. T. (1978). The Relationship Inventory: Later development and adaptations. JSAS *Catalog of Selected Documents in Psychology, 8,* 68.

Barrett-Lennard, G. T. (1998). *Carl Rogers' helping system: Journey and substance.* Beverly Hills, CA: Sage.

*Buckley, P., Karasu, T. B., & Charles, E. (1981). Psychotherapists' view their personal therapy. *Psychotherapy: Theory, Research and Practice, 18,* 299–305.

Carkhuff, R. R. (1969). *Helping and human relations: A primer for lay and professional helpers* (2 vols.). New York: Holt, Rinehart & Winston.

Cohen, J. (1988). *Statistical power analysis for the behavioral sciences* (2nd ed.). Hillsdale, NJ: Lawrence Erlbaum.

*Fretz, B. R. (1966). Postural movements in a counseling dyad. *Journal of Counseling Psychology, 13,* 335–43.

*Fuertes, J. N., Mislowack, A., Brown, S., Gur-Arie, S., Wilkinson, S., & Gelso, C. J. (2007). Correlates of the real relationship in psychotherapy: A study of dyads. *Psychotherapy Research, 17,* 423–30.

*Garfield, S., & Bergin, A. E. (1971). Therapeutic conditions and outcome. *Journal of Abnormal Psychology, 77,* 108–114(a).

Geller, S., & Greenberg, L. (2002). Therapeutic presence: Therapists experience of presence in the psychotherapy encounter in psychotherapy. *Person Centered & Experiential Psychotherapies, 1,* 71–86.

Gelso, C. J., & Carter, J. A. (1985). The relationship in counseling and psychotherapy. *The Counseling Psychologist, 13,* 155–244.

Gelso, C. J., & Carter, J. A. (1994). Components of the psychotherapy relationship: Their interaction and unfolding during treatment. *Journal of Counseling Psychology, 41,* 296–306.

Gelso, C. J., & Hayes, J. A. (1998). *The psychotherapy relationship: Theory, research, and practice.* New York: Wiley.

Gelso, C. J., Kelley, F. A., Fuertes, J. N., Marmarosh, C., Holmes, S. E., & Costas, C. (2005). Measuring the real relationship in psychotherapy: Initial validation of the Therapist Form. *Journal of Counseling Psychology, 52,* 640–49.

Gendlin, E. T., & Geist, M. (1962). The relationship of therapist congruence to psychological test evaluations of personality change. Wisconsin Psychiatric Institute, *Brief Research Reports,* 24.

Gleser, L. J., & Olkin, I. (1994). Stochastically dependent effect sizes. In H. M. Cooper & L. V. Hedges (Eds), The Handbook of Research Synthesis (pp. 339–55). New York: Russell Sage Foundation.

Greenberg, L., & Watson, J. (2005). *Emotion-focused therapy of depression.* Washington, DC: APA Press.

Greenson R. R. (1967). *The technique and practice of psychoanalysis* (Vol. 1). Madison, CT: International Universities Press.

Gurman, A. S. (1973a). Effects of the therapist and patient mood on the therapeutic functioning of high and low-facilitative therapists. *Journal of Consulting and Clinical Psychology, 40,* 48–58.

Gurman, A. S. (1973b). Instability of the therapeutic conditions in psychotherapy. *Journal of Counseling Psychology, 20,* 16–24.

Gurman, A. S. (1977). The patient's perception of the therapeutic relationship. In A. S. Gurman & A. M. Razin (Eds.), *Effective psychotherapy: A handbook of research* (pp. 503–43). Oxford, UK: Pergamon.

Halkides, G. (1958). *An experimental study of four conditions necessary for therapeutic change.* Unpublished doctoral dissertation, University of Chicago.

*Hansen, J. C., Moore, G. D., & Carkhuff, R. R. (1968). The differential relationships objective and client perceptions of counseling. *Journal of Counseling Psychology, 24,* 244–46.

Hart, J. T. (1960). *A replication of the Halkides study.* Unpublished manuscript, University of Wisconsin. Madison, WI.

Hedges, L. V., & Olkin, I. (1985). *Statistical methods for meta-analysis.* Orlando, FL: Academic Press.

Hedges, L. V., & Vevea, J. L. (1998). Fixed- and random-effects models in meta-analysis. *Psychological Methods, 3,* 486–504.

Hill, C. E., & Lambert, M. J. (2004). Methodological issues in studying psychotherapy processes and outcomes. In J. M. Lambert (Ed.), *Bergin and Garfield's handbook of psychotherapy and behavior change* (pp. 84–135). New York: Wiley and Sons.

*Jones, E. E., & Zoppel, C. L. (1982). Impact of client and therapist gender on psychotherapy process and outcome. *Journal of Consulting and Clinical Psychology, 50,* 259–72.

Kiesler, D. J. (1973). *The process of psychotherapy: Empirical foundations and systems of analysis.* Chicago: Aldine.

Klein, M. H., Kolden, G. G., Michels, J., & Chisholm-Stockard, S. (2002). Congruence. In J. C. Norcross (Ed.), *Psychotherapy relationships that work: Therapist contributions and responsiveness to patients* (pp. 195–215). New York: Oxford University Press.

Lambert, M. J., DeJulio, S. S., & Stein, D. M. (1978). Therapist interpersonal skills: Process, outcome, methodological considerations, and recommendations for future research. *Psychological Bulletin, 85,* 467–89.

Lietaer, G. (1993). Authenticity, congruence, and transparency. In D. Brazier (Ed.), *Beyond Carl Rogers: Toward a psychotherapy for the twenty-first century* (pp. 17–46). London: Constable.

Lipsey, M. W., & Wilson, D. B. (2001). *Practical meta-analysis.* Thousand Oaks, CA: Sage.

Luborsky, L., Chandler, M., Auerbach, A. H., Cohen, J., & Bachrach, H. M. (1971). Factors influencing the outcome of psychotherapy: A review of quantitative research. *Psychological Bulletin, 75,* 145–85.

*Marmarosh, C., Gelso, C., Majors, R., Markin, R., Mallery, C., & Choi, J. (2009). The real relationship in psychotherapy: Relationships to adult attachments, working alliance, transference, and therapy outcome. *Journal of Counseling Psychology, 56,* 337–50.

*Melnick, B., & Pierce, R. M. (1971). Client evaluation of therapist strength and positive-negative evaluation as related to client dynamics, objective ratings of competency and outcome. *Journal of Clinical Psychology, 27,* 408–11.

Meltzoff, J., & Kornreich, M. (1970). *Research in psychotherapy.* New York: Atherton.

Mitchell, K. M., Bozrath, J. D., & Krauft, C. C. (1977). A reappraisal of the therapeutic effectiveness of accurate empathy, nonpossessive warmth, and genuineness. In A. S. Gurman & A. M. Razin (Eds), *Effective psychotherapy: A handbook of research.* (pp. 503–43). Oxford, UK: Pergamon.

Orlinsky, D. E., Grawe, K., & Parks, B. K. (1994). Process and outcome in psychotherapy–Noch einmal. In A. E. Bergin & S. L. Garfield (Eds), *Handbook of psychotherapy and behavior change* (4th ed.) (pp. 270–376). New York: Wiley.

Orlinsky, D. E., & Howard, K. I. (1978). The relation of process to outcome in psychotherapy. In S. L. Garfield & A. E. Bergin (Eds.), *Handbook of psychotherapy and behavior change* (2nd ed.) (pp. 283–329). New York: Wiley.

Orlinsky, D. E., & Howard, K. I. (1986). Process and outcome in psychotherapy. In S. L. Garfield & A. E. Bergin (Eds.), *Handbook of psychotherapy and behavior change* (3rd ed.) (pp. 311–84). New York: Wiley.

Parloff, M. B., Waskow, I. E., & Wolfe, B. E. (1978). Research on client variables in psychotherapy. In S. L. Garfield & A. E. Bergin (Eds.), *Handbook of psychotherapy and behavior change* (2nd ed., pp. 233–82). New York: Wiley.

Patterson, C. H. (1984). Empathy, warmth, and genuineness in psychotherapy: A review of reviews. *Psychotherapy, 21,* 431–38.

Patterson, C. H. (1996). Multicultural counseling: From diversity to universality. *Journal of Counseling & Development, 74,* 227–31.

*Ritter, A., Bowden, S., Murray, T., Ross, P., Greeley, J., & Pead, J. (2002). The influence of the therapeutic relationship in treatment for alcohol dependency. *Drug and Alcohol Review, 21,* 261–68.

Rogers, C. R. (1957). The necessary and sufficient conditions of therapeutic personality change. *Journal of Consulting Psychology, 21,* 95–103.

Rogers, C. R., Gendlin, E. T., Kiesler, D. J., & Truax, C. B. (Eds.). (1967). *The therapeutic relationship and its impact: A study of psychotherapy with schizophrenics.* Madison: University of Wisconsin Press.

*Rothman, D. B. (2007). *The role of the therapeutic alliance in psychotherapy with sexual offenders.* Unpublished doctoral dissertation, University of Manitoba, Canada.

Shostrum, E. L. (Producer). (1966). Three approaches to psychotherapy. [Film]. (Available from Psychological and Educational Files, Santa Ana, CA).

*Staples, F. R., & Sloane, R. B. (1976). Truax factors, speech characteristics, and therapeutic outcome. *Journal of Nervous and Mental Disease, 163,* 135–40.

Sue, D. W., & Sue, D. (2003). *Counseling the culturally diverse: Theory and practice, 4th edition.* New York: John Wiley & Sons.

Truax, C. B. (1966a). *Toward a tentative measurement of the central therapeutic ingredients.*: Arkansas Rehabilitation Research and Training Center and University of Arkansas, Fayetteville.

*Truax, C. B. (1966b). Therapist empathy, warmth and genuineness and patient personality change in group psychotherapy: A comparison between interaction unit measures, time sample measures, patient perception measures. *Journal of Clinical Psychology, 22,* 225–29.

Truax, C. B. (1968). Therapist interpersonal reinforcement of client self-exploration and therapeutic outcome in group psychotherapy. *Journal of Counseling Psychology, 15,* 225–31.

*Truax, C. B. (1971). Perceived therapeutic conditions and client outcome. *Comparative Group Studies, 2,* 301–10.

Truax, C. B., & Carkhuff, R. R. (1967). *Toward effective counseling and psychotherapy: Training and practice.* Chicago: Aldine.

Truax, C. B., & Mitchell, K. M. (1971). Research on certain therapist interpersonal skills in relation to process and outcome. In A. E. Bergin & S. L Garfield (Eds.), *Handbook of psychotherapy and behavior change* (pp. 299–344). New York: Wiley.

Tseng, W. S. (1999). Culture and psychotherapy: Review and suggested practical guidelines. *Transcultural Psychiatry, 36,* 131–79.

Vessey, J. T., & Howard, K. I. (1993). Who seeks psychotherapy? *Psychotherapy, 30,* 546–53.

Watson, J. C., Greenberg, L. S., & Lietaer, G. (1998). The experiential paradigm unfolding: Relationship and experiencing in therapy. In L. S. Greenberg, J. C. Watson, & G. Lietaer (Eds.), *Handbook of experiential psychotherapy* (pp. 3–27). New York: Guilford.

Watson, N. (1984). The empirical status of Rogers' hypotheses of the necessary and sufficient conditions for effective psychotherapy. In R. F. Levant & J. M. Schlein (Eds.), *Client-centered therapy and the person centered approach: New directions in theory, research, and practice* (pp. 17–40). New York: Praeger.

Zane, N., Hall, G. N., Sue, S., Young, K., & Nunez, J. (2004). Research on psychotherapy with culturally diverse populations. In M. J. Lambert (Ed.), *Bergin and Garfield's handbook of psychotherapy and behavior change,* 5th edition (pp. 767–804). New York: Wiley & Sons.

Collecting Client Feedback

Michael J. Lambert *and* Kenichi Shimokawa

Hundreds of studies have now been conducted on the effects of psychotherapy, including research on psychodynamic, humanistic, behavioral, cognitive, and variations and combinations of these approaches. Reviews of this research, both qualitative and quantitative, have shown that about 75% of those who enter treatment show some benefit (Lambert & Ogles, 2004). This finding generalizes across a wide range of disorders with the exception of severe biologically based disturbances, such as bipolar disorder and the schizophrenias, where the impact of psychological treatments is secondary to psychoactive medications.

Quantitative reviews (meta-analyses) of psychotherapy efficacy support these conclusions and provide a numerical index for treatment effects. Early applications of meta-analysis to psychotherapy efficacy (e.g., Smith, Glass, & Miller, 1980) addressed the broad question of the extent of benefit associated with psychotherapy. For example, an average effect size of 0.85 standard deviation units was found over 475 studies comparing treated and untreated groups. This indicates that, at the end of treatment, the average treated person is better off than 80% of the untreated control sample. Subsequent meta-analytic findings (e.g., Shadish et al., 1997; Wampold, 2008) have supported the consistent benefit of treatment over control for a broad variety

of disorders and have determined that some disorders (e.g., phobias, panic) yield to treatment more easily than others (e.g., obsessive-compulsive disorder).

An often ignored but critical consideration in psychotherapy and related interventions is the degree to which they have negative rather than positive consequences for clients. An estimated 5%–10% of adult clients participating in clinical trials leave treatment worse off than they began (Lambert & Ogles, 2004). In routine care the situation is more problematic. Outcomes for more than 6,000 patients treated in routine practice settings suggest that the clients did not fare nearly as well as those in clinical trials, with only about one third showing improvement or recovery (Hansen, Lambert, & Forman, 2002). The situation for child psychotherapy in routine care is even more sobering. The small body of outcome studies in community-based, usual-care settings has yielded a mean effect size near zero (Weisz, 2004; Weiss, Catron, Harris, & Phung, 1999; Weisz, Donenberg, Han, & Weiss, 1995), yet millions of youths are served each year in these systems of care (National Advisory Mental Health Council, 2001; Ringel & Sturm, 2001). In a comparison of children being treated in community mental health ($N = 936$) or through managed care ($N = 3075$), estimates of deterioration were

24% and 14%, respectively (Warren et al., 2010).

There is no doubt that all of the deterioration that occurs during the time a patient is in treatment cannot be causally linked to therapist activities. Certainly, a portion of patients are on a negative trajectory at the time they enter treatment and the deteriorating course cannot be stopped. Some patients are prevented from taking their own lives as a result of effective practices, even if they do not show overall progress.

Just as positive psychotherapy outcomes depend largely on patient characteristics, so do the negative changes that occur in patients who are undergoing psychological treatments. Even so, positive as well as negative patient change can be affected by therapist actions and inactions. Research reviews find that the major contribution of the therapist to negative change is usually found in the nature of the therapeutic relationship, with rejections of either a subtle or manifest nature being the root cause (e.g., Safran, Muran, Samstang, & Winston, 2005). In fact, the research on negative outcomes find very little negative change as a result of the misapplication of therapeutic techniques, while relationship factors loomed large across treatment formats (e.g., couple, family, group, individual) and theoretical orientation (Lambert, Bergin, & Collins, 1977).

A recent trend in clinical practice involves regularly monitoring and tracking client treatment responses with standardized scales throughout the course of treatment and then providing clinicians with this information (Lambert & Burlingame, 2007). The basic rationale behind collecting client feedback is based on common sense. If we get information about what seems to be working, and more importantly, what is not working, our responsiveness to clients will improve. In many situations, performance and feedback are intertwined and obvious; in others a certain degree of blinding occurs, such that the association is not so temporally connected and the effects of performance are harder to discern (such as in psychotherapy), making it much more difficult to learn and improve. In obvious as well as more subtle situations, providing feedback to improve performance has been studied quite extensively in a variety of areas and confirms our common sense expectations that it is helpful.

In this chapter, we examine the effects of feedback broadly and then present evidence of its effects in relation to two widely used feedback systems applied specifically in psychotherapy. Following presentation of the effects of feedback, we turn our attention to implications for clinical practice.

Previous Reviews of Feedback

In a meta-analysis of the effects of feedback on human performance published since the 1930s, Kluger and DeNisi (1996) found a small to medium effect size (d = .41) for interventions utilizing feedback, suggesting about two-thirds of individuals receiving feedback performed better than those who received no feedback. Unfortunately, most of the studies examined in this meta-analysis were analog situations involving motor performance, puzzle solutions, memory tasks, and the like, rather than based in clinical practice. Further, of the few that tested feedback to professionals, not one study provided feedback on patient's status to health professionals. Nevertheless, this review does suggest that a broad array of feedback interventions consistently improve performance and encourages the idea that feedback will enhance performance.

In a more comprehensive meta-analysis, Sapyta (quoted in Sapyta, Riemer, and Bickman, 2005) examined 30 randomized clinical trials conducted in community settings that assessed the effectiveness of client *health status* feedback to health professionals. The nature of feedback interventions and methods of their delivery varied from giving general practice physicians depression or anxiety screening information about their patients to repeatedly and routinely providing clinicians with their patients' mental health status feedback. The average client in the feedback group was better off than 58% of the control group (d = .21, a small effect).

In general, this research supports the conclusion that feedback in clinical practice improves patient outcome.

A recent meta-analysis that focused directly on mental health status feedback in psychotherapy (Knaup, Koesters, Becker, & Puschner, 2009) based on 12 studies also found a statistically significant, albeit small effect (d = 0.10) for progress feedback. This particular analysis suggested that the effects may be short lived, although few studies had a follow-up.

The Sapyta, Riemer, and Bickman (2005) review indicated that the effectiveness of feedback is likely to vary as a function of the *degree of discrepancy* between therapists' views of progress and measured progress, and that the greater the discrepancy, the more likely feedback will be helpful. This finding is consistent with feedback theories and the role of negative feedback in regulatory systems (e.g., Bandura, 1997; Lord & Hanges, 1987); feedback about poor progress is expected to have a greater impact than feedback indicating positive progress. A key element of effective feedback is bringing into the recipient's awareness the discrepancy between what is thought and what is reality, thereby prompting corrective action.

When comparing the effect of feedback on "flagged" clients who were not progressing well versus clients who were progressing through treatment as expected, flagged clients responded more favorably to the feedback intervention. Feedback to flagged samples in the Sapyta and Bickman (as quoted in Sapyta, et al., 2005) meta-analysis achieved an effect size (d) of 0.31, which indicates that the average client in the treatment group had better outcomes than 62% of the flagged control group. At the same time, it appears that the feedback of client's health status is mainly beneficial to clients who may require changes to their current treatment.

This finding is consistent with feedback theories that suggest feedback will only change behavior when the information provided indicates the *individual is not meeting up to an established standard* of practice (e.g., Riemer & Bickman, 2004). Riemer and Bickman (Riemer & Bickman, 2004; Riemer, Rosof-Williams, & Bickman, 2005) have developed a contextual feedback intervention theory to explain how feedback is interpreted and made useful. Basic tenets of this theory are that clinicians (and professionals, generally) will benefit from feedback if they are *committed to the goal* of improving their performance; they are *aware of a discrepancy* between the goal and reality (particularly *if the goal is attractive and the clinician believes it can be accomplished*); the feedback *source is credible*; and if *feedback is immediate, frequent, systematic, cognitively simple* (such as graphic in nature), *unambiguous,* and provides clinicians with *concrete suggestions of how to improve.*

If clinicians do not consider feedback as credible, valid, informative, or useful, they are more likely to dismiss it whenever it does not fit their own preferences. As we know from research on cognitive dissonance, people can change attitudes rather than persevere toward goals, thus regarding the goal as less important, or see a client as too resistant or injured to benefit from treatment (e.g., disown personal responsibility for meeting the goal of positive functioning; Riemer, Rosof-Williams, & Bickman, 2005). As feedback research suggests, the value of monitoring and systematic feedback through psychological assessments hinges on the degree to which the information provided goes beyond what a clinician can observe and understand about patient progress without such information. It is important for the information to add something to the psychotherapist's view of patients' well-being and future actions.

Unfortunately, clinicians may have an overly optimistic view of their patients' progress (Walfish et al., 2010). Clinicians overlook negative changes and have a limited capacity to make accurate predictions of the final benefit clients will receive during treatment, particularly with clients who are failing to improve. One study, for example, found that even when therapists were provided with the base rate of deterioration in the clinic where they worked (8%), and were asked to rate each client that they saw at the end of each session (with regards to the likelihood of treatment failure and if the client was worse off at the current session in relation to their intake level of functioning), they rated only 3 of 550 clients as predicted failures and seriously underestimated worse functioning for a significant portion of clients (Hannan et al., 2005). A retrospective review of case notes of clients who had deteriorated during treatment found infrequent mention of worsening even when its degree was dramatic (Hatfield et al., 2010).

Such results are not surprising, given psychotherapist optimism, the complexity of persons, and a treatment context that calls for considerable commitment and determination on the part of the therapist, who actually has very little control over the patient's life circumstances and personal characteristics. Patients' response to treatment is, especially in the case of a worsening state, a likely place where outside feedback might have the greatest chance of impact.

Helping the therapist become aware of negative change and discussing such progress in the therapeutic encounter are much more likely when formal feedback is provided to therapists. Such feedback helps the client communicate and helps the therapist to become aware of the possible need to adjust treatment or alter or addresses problematic aspects of the treatment as appropriate (e.g., problems in the therapeutic relationship or in the implementation of the goals of the treatment). By contrast, for clients who are progressing well in treatment, progress feedback delivered to therapists is not expected to help therapists be more responsive, a finding that is consistent with the meta-analysis by Knaup et al. (2009) previously mentioned.

Definitions and Feedback Systems

Clients can complete a brief measure of their psychological function by using standardized rating scales, and then this information can be delivered to psychotherapists in real time. In addition to alerting therapists to deviations from expected treatment response, the information gathered from patients provides novel information to therapists. Collecting this information from the client on a session-by-session basis provides the clinician with a systematic way of monitoring life functioning from the client's point of view. A brief formal assessment can provide a summary of life functioning that is not otherwise available to the therapist, unless the therapist spends time within the treatment hour to systematically inquire about all the areas of functioning covered by the self-report scale.

Several psychotherapy outcome management systems that provide progress feedback have been developed and implemented in clinical settings worldwide. Although the specific procedures employed in each of these systems vary, their common features involve the monitoring of client outcome throughout the course of treatment, sharing the client data with clinicians, and using these data to improve outcomes.

The first system to arrive was that developed by Howard and colleagues using the COMPASS Treatment Outcome Systems (Lueger et al., 2001). Kordy, Hannover, and Richard (2001) developed a computer-assisted, feedback-driven psychotherapy quality management system in Germany. Barkham and colleagues (2001) created the Clinical Outcomes in Routine Evaluation (CORE) system widely used in the United Kingdom, while Kraus and Horan (1997) developed the Treatment Outcome Package (TOPS) system in use in the USA. In general, these later two systems have emphasized the administrative use of data rather than feedback to therapists during the course of psychotherapy. Administrative use allows managers of mental health services to examine the periodic and final outcome of treatments and compare outcomes to appropriate benchmarks.

Two systems have gone beyond measuring progress and outcome, investing considerable energy in collecting and feeding back client ratings of their therapist in the hopes of maximizing final treatment outcome.

Partners for Change Outcome Management System

The Partners for Change Outcome Management System (PCOMS; Miller, Duncan, Sorrell, & Brown, 2005) is a psychotherapy assurance system that employs two brief scales (four items each). The Outcome Rating Scale (ORS; Miller, Duncan, Brown, Sparks, & Claud, 2003) focuses on mental health functioning, modeled after the domains of outcome measured by subscales of the Outcome Questionnaire-45 (Lambert et al., 2004). The Session Rating Scale (SRS; Duncan and Miller, 2008) is aimed at assessing the therapeutic alliance. Because of its brevity,

this system is clinician friendly and insures discussion of assessment results by the client and therapist in session because rating of mental health status and therapeutic alliance are normally collected in the presence of the therapist. The therapeutic relationship as measured by the SRS is based on the concept of the therapeutic alliance by Bordin (1979), a similar concept of therapeutic alliance by Gaston (1990), and the construct Duncan, Miller, and Sparks (2004) termed "client's theory of change." These interrelated alliance theories emphasize three aspects of the helping relationship: the affective bond, agreement on tasks during sessions, and agreement about the ultimate goals of the encounter.

Miller and colleagues (2005) developed three items to rate these constructs and a fourth item that provides an overall rating of the relationship. Figure 10.1 provides a hypothetical example of feedback to both clinician and client for a client falling under benchmark predictions. ORS scores are graphically portrayed compared with the 50th percentile trajectory based on the client's intake score. Verbal feedback messages interpret the scores, taking the alliance measure (SRS) into account, and encourage client and provider discussion about next possible steps to avert a negative outcome.

Clinical use of the ORS and the SRS is gaining in popularity, and a growing number of published studies have examined the psychometric properties of these measures. Given the emphasis of this report on treatment outcome, we summarize here the psychometric properties of the ORS. The ORS is a visual analog scale that requires clients to rate their functioning on four items (subjective well-being, interpersonal relations, social functioning, and overall sense of well-being). Miller and Duncan (2003) reported test–retest correlations among nonclinical samples ranging

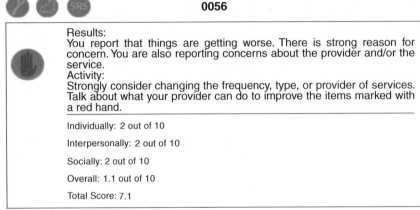

0056

Results:
You report that things are getting worse. There is strong reason for concern. You are also reporting concerns about the provider and/or the service.
Activity:
Strongly consider changing the frequency, type, or provider of services. Talk about what your provider can do to improve the items marked with a red hand.

Individually: 2 out of 10

Interpersonally: 2 out of 10

Socially: 2 out of 10

Overall: 1.1 out of 10

Total Score: 7.1

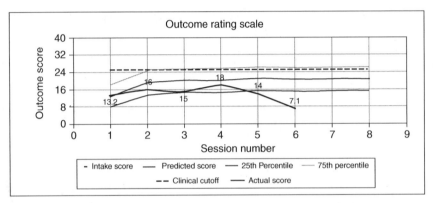

Fig. 10.1 Hypothetical example of feedback to both clinician and client for a client falling under benchmark predictions.

from 0.49 to 0.66 with Cronbach's alpha of 0.93. Miller and Duncan (2003) also tested correlations between the ORS and OQ-45 over four waves of repeated administrations among 86 nonclinical individuals and found correlations ranging from 0.53 to 0.69. When considering the intent of the ORS developers to create "a brief alternative" to the OQ-45 (Miller et al., 2003, p. 92), the modest degree of common variance among these two measures (i.e., $r^2 = 0.28$ to $r^2 = 0.48$) raises questions as to the extent to which the developers' intent was achieved.

The outcome studies reviewed in this chapter had the clients complete the ORS in the presence of the therapist in session. As Anker, Duncan, and Sparks (2009) noted, such an administrative protocol raises a

question as to the degree of potential influence exerted by therapists' presence on client response (e.g., demand characteristic).

The ORS incorporates expected trajectories of change based on the initial score and the change at a given session in relation to the initial score (Miller, Duncan, Sorrell, & Brown, 2005). Consistent with the recommendations given in the administration and scoring manual of the ORS, studies by Reese et al. (2009) classified clients as being at risk, or not progressing, if they failed to improve five ORS points or more by the third session. In the study, the identification of at-risk clients was generated by a different system, employing a web-based software that "calculates trajectories of change at the 25th, 50th, and 75th percentile levels" based on a large ORS database

(Anker et al., 2009, p. 697). Clients whose ORS score at the third session fell below the 50th percentile mark of expected trajectory of progress based on individual response were identified as at risk.

Concurrent validity of SRS and Helping Alliance Questionnaire-II (HAQ-II) correlate at 0.48, with each item ranging from 0.39 to 0.44. The SRS authors argue that it is essentially measuring the same thing as HAQ-II and other therapeutic alliance scales, although these moderate correlations suggest less overlap than would be hoped.

OQ Psychotherapy Quality Management System

Lambert and colleagues developed the OQ system, which emphasizes the measurement of mental health functioning and, like the PCOMS, includes a measure of the therapist-client relationship. In distinction to the PCOMS, the OQ system goes beyond feedback on the therapeutic alliance and includes additional assessments to aid problem solving. In addition, the relationship and problem-solving approach is only employed with specific patients who are experiencing a negative response to psychotherapy rather than with all persons who enter treatment. In the remainder of this chapter and our meta-analysis, the OQ psychotherapy system and to a lesser extent the PCOMS will be emphasized because of the evidence base surrounding these systems.

The Outcome Questionnaire-45 (OQ-45; Lambert et al., 2004) is a 45-item, self-report measure designed for repeated administration throughout the course of treatment and at termination with adult patients. In accordance with several reviews of the literature (e.g., Lambert, 1983), the OQ was conceptualized and designed to assess three domains of client functioning: symptoms of psychological disturbance (particularly anxiety and depression), interpersonal problems, and social role functioning. Consistent with this conceptualization of outcome, the OQ-45 provides a Total Score, based on all 45 items, as well as Symptom Distress, Interpersonal Relations, and Social Role subscale scores. Each of these subscales contains some items related to the positive quality of life of the individual. Higher scores on the OQ-45 are indicative of greater levels of psychological disturbance.

Research has indicated that the OQ-45 is a psychometrically sound instrument, with strong internal consistency (Cronbach's alpha = 0.93), adequate 3-week test–retest reliability ($r = 0.84$), and strong concurrent validity estimates ranging from 0.55 to 0.88 when the total score and the subscale scores were correlated with scores from the MMPI-2, SCL-90R, BDI, Zung Depression Scale, Taylor Manifest Anxiety Scale, State-Trait Anxiety Inventory, Inventory of Interpersonal Problems, and Social Adjustment Scale, among others (Lambert et al., 2004). Furthermore, the items that make up the OQ-45 have been shown to be sensitive to changes in multiple client populations over short periods of time while remaining relatively stable in untreated individuals (Vermeersch, Lambert, & Burlingame, 2002; Vermeersch et al., 2004). In addition, evidence from factor analytic studies suggests it measures an overall psychological distress factor as well as factors consistent with the three subscales (Bludworth, Tracey, & Glidden-Tracey, 2010; de Jong et al., 2007; Lo Coco et al., 2008). In short, the OQ-45 is a brief measure of psychological disturbance that is reliable, valid, and sensitive to changes clients make during psychotherapy. It provides clinicians with a *mental health vital sign*. Similar measures have been developed for use with children (www.oqmeasures.com).

A core element of outcome management systems is the prediction of treatment failure.

In order to improve outcomes of clients who are responding poorly to treatment, such clients must be identified before termination, and ideally, as early as possible in the course of treatment. The OQ system plots a statistically generated expected recovery curve for differing levels of pretreatment distress and uses this as a basis for identifying clients who are not making expected treatment gains and are at risk of having a poor outcome. The accuracy of this signal-alarm system has been evaluated in a number of empirical investigations (Ellsworth, Lambert, & Johnson, 2006; Lambert, Whipple, Bishop, et al., 2002; Lutz et al., 2006; Percevic, Lambert, & Kordy, 2006; Spielmans, Masters, & Lambert, 2006) and has been found to be highly sensitive. It accurately predicts deterioration in 85%–100% of cases that actually end with a negative outcome and far exceeds clinical judgment in its ability to identify clients who are at risk of having a negative treatment outcome (Hannan et al., 2005).

A sample feedback report for the OQ-45 is displayed in Figure 10.2. This report displays the client's progress at the ninth session of psychotherapy in relation to a horizontal line at a score of 64/63 marking normal functioning, and a solid dark line displaying the expected treatment response. Most important is the "Red" alert signal in the upper left hand corner which indicates the client is responding so poorly to therapy that he or she is predicted to leave therapy with a negative treatment response.

In conjunction with identifying *Alarm* status, an instrument *Assessment for signal cases* (ASC; Lambert, Whipple, et al., 2004) was developed to assist clinicians to problem-solve with the clients who backslide during treatment (i.e., when a therapist receives a warning message, indicating that the client is not responding or is deteriorating in treatment). This 40-item measure does not produce a total score but, rather, provides subscale score feedback and *item* feedback for therapists to consider in problem solving. The first 11 items of the ASC require the client to reflect on the therapeutic relationship and report his or her perceptions. In Figure 10.2 a sample feedback report is provided. Items that fall below an empirically based cutoff score (about one standard deviation from the mean rating on the item) are brought to the therapist's attention.

The ASC is central to the Clinical Support Tool (CST). The CST is composed of a problem-solving decision tree designed to systematically direct therapists' attention to certain factors that have been shown to be consistently related to client outcome in the empirical literature, such as the therapeutic alliance, social support, readiness to change, diagnostic formulation, and need for medication referral. The ASC provides the information necessary to go through the decision tree and focus the therapist's attention on the quality of the therapeutic alliance, client motivation, and client perceptions of social support as well as the possible need for medication. Furthermore, the CST provides specific intervention strategies that could be used by therapists if problems were detected in the aforementioned domains. Figure 10.3 depicts the CST problem-solving decision tree provided to therapists in cases in which their clients were predicted to have a poor outcome.

The signal-alarm system alerts clinicians to potential treatment failures and allows them to modify their treatment approach. Once a client takes the OQ-45, commences treatment, and completes a session of treatment, the signal-alarm system can be used to generate feedback regarding the client's progress.

Name:	12, case	ID:	12		Alert Status:	Red

Name:	12, case
Session Date:	12/21/2005
Clinician:	Maristany, Mariana
Diagnosis:	Unknown Diagnosis
Algorithm:	Empirical ▨

ID:	12	
Session:	9	
Clinic:	Aigle	

Alert Status:	Red
Most Recent Score:	79
Initial Score:	58
Change From Initial:	Reliably Worse
Current Distress Level:	Moderate

Most Recent Critical Item Status:

8. **Sucide** - I have thoughts of ending my life.	**Never**
11. **Substance Abuse** - After heavy drinking, I need a drink the next morning to get going.	**Never**
26. **Substance Abuse** - I feel annoyed by people who criticize my drinking.	**Never**
32. **Substance Abuse** - I have trouble at work/school because of drinking or drug use	**Never**
44. **Work Violence** - I feel angry enough at work/school to do something I might regret.	**Rarely**

Subscales	Current	Output. Norm	Comm. Norm
Symptom Distress:	45	49	25
Interpersonal Relations:	18	20	10
Social Role:	16	14	10
Total:	**79**	**83**	**45**

Total Score by Session Number

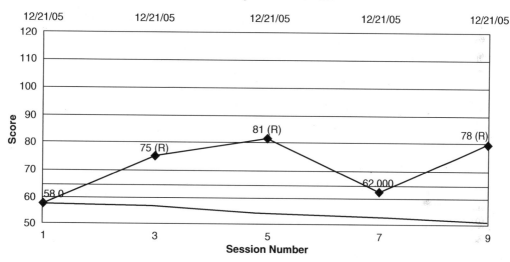

Graph Label Legend:

(R) = Red: High change of negative outcome   (Y) = Yellow: Some chance of negative outcome

(G) = Green: Making expected progress   (W) = White: Functioning in normal range

Feedback Message:

The patient is deviating from the expected response to treatment. They are not on track to realize substantial benefit from treatment. Chances are they may drop out of treatment prematurely or have a negative treatment outcome. Steps should be taken to carefully review this case and identify reasons for poor progress. It is recommended that you be alert to the possible need to improve the therapeutic alliance, reconsider the client's readiness for change and the need to renegotiate the therapeutic contact, intervene to strengthen social supports, or possibly alter your treatment plan by intensifying treatment, shifting intervention strategies, or decide upon a new course of action, such as referral for medication. Continuous monitoring of future progress is highly recommended.

Fig. 10.2 OQ-Analyst screen shot illustrating feedback report of client progress provided to therapist.

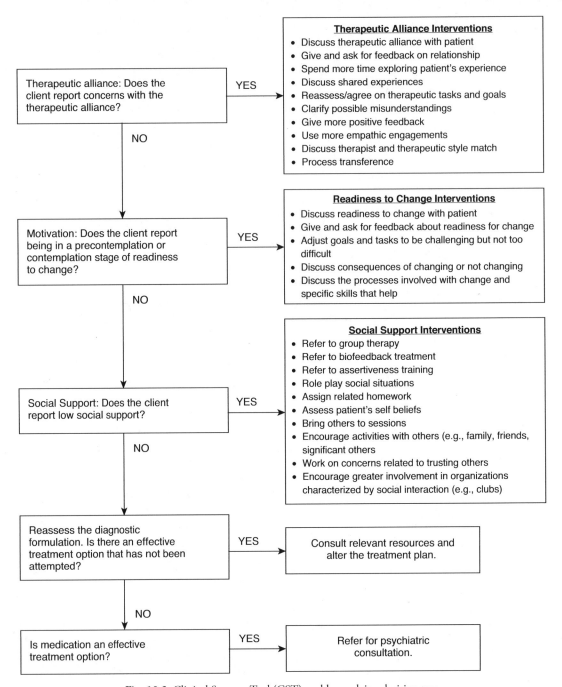

Fig. 10.3 Clinical Support Tool (CST) problem-solving decision tree.

Meta-Analytic Review
Inclusion Criteria and Search Strategy
In the following sections, we present a meta-analysis of the outcomes of two real-time feedback-based psychotherapy systems. Although studies utilizing the PCOMS provided some client-reported feedback to clinicians, several critical differences also existed. The OQ system was designed to enhance the outcome of clients predicted to experience treatment failure at termination. Accordingly, the studies examining the effects of the OQ systems conducted separate analyses for at-risk clients

and on-track clients. In contrast, while the PCOMS incorporates a method of identifying nonprogressing cases as at-risk clients, the studies employing the PCOMS, except for the study by Anker et al. (2009), did not investigate or report differential effects of the PCOMS feedback system on client outcome based on on-track versus not-on-track classification of client progress. Due to this difference in methodology, we present separate summaries of these two quality assurance systems.

Included in the meta-analysis were studies from just two well-developed systems that have published the effects of feedback. A few scattered efforts to examine feedback were not reviewed in this meta-analysis because they have yet to rise to the level of well-developed systems. For example, Brodey et al. (2005) examined the effect of providing feedback to clinicians on half of a total sample of 1,374 clients using 11 anxiety and depression items from the Symptom Checklist-90. Rather than provide mental health status (depressive & anxiety symptoms) at every session of care, thus allowing clinicians to track progress, the second administration (taken by 954 of the original sample; 69%) took place at a prespecified time and after many patients had completed treatment. Even the initial report was not provided in the most timely manner with only 14% of clinicians reporting they received it prior to the inception of treatment. Even so, the results suggested the intervention improved patient outcomes at a statistically significant level ($r = 0.05$; $d = 0.11$). Another example is provided by Berking, Orth, and Lutz (2006) who provided evidence that feedback enhanced outcome in a 30-day inpatient program.

Because a meta-analytic review of the OQ 45 was recently conducted (see Shimokawa, Lambert, & Smart, 2010), we provide here a summary of the meta-analytic findings. Only three well-designed

studies based on the PCOMS have been reported in two articles to date. To obtain overall estimates of the effects of the PCOMS, we meta-analytically aggregated the published results of those studies.

Dependent Measures and Computation of Effect Sizes

Because different effect size units were employed in original studies, we applied uniform units of effect size. For each comparison of mean posttreatment outcome measurement scores between an experimental condition and a treatment as usual (TAU), we employed Hedges' standard difference g (Hedges & Olkin, 1985) and correlation r, to be consistent with meta-analytic findings presented in other chapters of this book. Correlation r was obtained by converting the standardized mean difference d, utilizing a commonly used formula of $r = d/\sqrt{(d^2 + 4)}$ (e.g., Wolf, 1986).

A key element in psychotherapy research is operationalizing the concepts of positive and negative outcome for the individual client. Jacobson and Truax (1991) offered a methodology by which client changes on an outcome measure can be classified in the following categories: recovered, reliably improved, no change, deteriorated. There are two necessary pieces of information to make these client outcome classifications: a Reliable Change Index (RCI) and a normal functioning cutoff score.

Clinical and normative data were analyzed by Lambert and colleagues (2004) to establish an RCI and a cutoff score for the OQ-45. The RCI obtained on the OQ-45 was 14 points, indicating that client changes of 14 or more points on the OQ-45 can be considered reliable (i.e., not due to measurement error). The cutoff score for normal functioning on the OQ-45 was calculated to be 63, indicating that scores of 64 or higher are more likely to come from a dysfunctional population than a functional population, and scores of 63 or lower are more likely to come from a functional population than a dysfunctional population. Support for the validity of the OQ-45's reliable change and cutoff score has been reported by Lunnen and Ogles (1998) and Beckstead et al. (2003).

Similar to the OQ system, based on the same methods developed by Jacobson and Truax (1991), Miller and Duncan (2004) reported the RCI and clinical cutoff scores for the ORS. A change of five points or greater in either direction in comparison to the pretreatment ORS score is considered a reliable change. The clinical cutoff score used in studies examining the effects of the ORS was 25 points. Clinical significance classification of the ORS has not been cross-validated with that of OQ-45 or socially validated with other measures, thus empirical evidence on the meaning of clinical significance classification of the ORS is limited at this time.

To contrast the rates and odds of client deterioration and significant improvement between feedback groups and TAU, we calculated combined odds ratios (OR) as a measure of effect size. Specifically, when examining the odds of deterioration, we dichotomized clients into either the deterioration group or nondeterioration group and calculated the odds ratio of deterioration for a given comparison. Similarly, when comparing the odds of improvement in two groups, the odds ratio was calculated based on the odds of improvement versus those of nonimprovement.

Meta-Analytic Results

Results Based on the PCOMS. Three methodologically sound psychotherapy outcome studies investigating the effects of the PCOMS have been published in English to date (Anker, Duncan, & Sparks, 2009; Reese, Norsworthy, & Rowlands, 2009). Reese and colleagues (2009) conducted

two studies reported in a single article comparing the treatment outcome of clients receiving the PCOMS feedback intervention and those receiving no feedback. The first study, conducted at a university counseling center, was initially comprised of 131 clients of which 74 (56%) were included in the final analyses. Clients were randomly assigned to either a PCOMS-based feedback condition or no-feedback condition (TAU) to investigate the effects of the feedback intervention on client outcome. The authors reported the effect size of $d = 0.54$ when the feedback group and TAU were compared on the basis of pretreatment to posttreatment changes on the ORS total scale scores (using typical methods as applied to differences in means at posttest, the effect size was reduced to Hedges' g of 0.25). They further reported that 80% of clients in the feedback group experienced reliable change, while 54% of clients in TAU achieved the same criteria. Only 4% of those in the feedback group met the criteria for deterioration, while 13% of their TAU counterparts met the same.

The second study in the Reese et al. (2009) article, conducted at a graduate training clinic, was initially comprised of 96 clients of which 74 (77%) were included in the final analyses. In this study, 17 trainee therapists in graduate practicum, rather than clients, were randomly assigned to either a PCOMS-based feedback condition or TAU. The authors (Reese et al., 2009) reported an effect size of $d = 0.49$ when comparing the feedback group and TAU on the basis of the pre-post change in the ORS scores (the standard mean difference posttest comparison produced a Hedges' g of 0.58). The authors of the study reported that 16 clients (36%) in the feedback group and 11 clients (38%) in TAU were identified as "not progressing," therefore at risk of poor outcome. In terms of clinical significance, 67% of those in the feedback condition achieved reliable change status, while 4% deteriorated. This was contrasted to 41% of clients in TAU achieving reliable change, with 3% ($n = 1$) deteriorating.

Anker, Duncan, and Sparks (2009) conducted a randomized controlled trial investigating the effects of PCOMS-based feedback intervention on clients in couple therapy at a community family counseling clinic. Of the 906 Norwegian individuals who initially sought couple therapy, 410 individuals met the inclusion criteria ($n = 103$ in experimental and $n = 102$ in TAU). The authors of the study reported an effect size of $d = 0.50$ when comparing the posttreatment ORS scores. The authors reported posttreatment outcome classification (based on the notion of clinical significance) of couples at posttreatment. The reported n and percentage of outcome classification were based on couples where *both* individuals in the couple met the same outcome classification. Based on these inclusion criteria, 66% of couples in the feedback group and 50% of couples in the TAU were included in the analyses. The outcome classifications at the individual level were not reported. Of those included in the analysis, the authors reported 51% of couples in the feedback condition achieving either clinically significant change or reliable change, while 2% deteriorated. In contrast, 23% of couples in the TAU group reached either clinically significant change or reliable change and 4% experienced deterioration. Anker and colleagues (2009) reported the percentages of couples identified as being at risk at the third session. Among those in the feedback condition, 54% of couples were identified as being at risk, while 75% of couples in TAU were classified as the same. These results indicate that 54% of couples in the feedback group and 75% of couples in TAU were below the 50th percentile mark of expected progress for client progress based on individual

response. With regard to marital adjustment, feedback was found to be somewhat helpful. The posttreatment d between groups was 0.29 (an $r = 0.14$).

Findings from the three studies were aggregated to provide estimated weighted mean effect sizes. Because of the small number of studies ($k = 3$) included in the analyses, tests of moderators and mediators were not performed. Given the equivalence of pretreatment scores reported for each study in the original articles, we did not test for pretreatment score differences in this analysis. As shown in Table 10.1, when mean posttreatment ORS scores of the feedback group were compared to those of TAU, the combined effect size was $g = 0.48$, $p < 0.001$, 95% CI [0.31, 0.65]. The r equivalent of 0.23 favored the feedback group, suggesting that the average client in the feedback group was better off than approximately 68% of those in TAU. It should be noted that the type of effect size we report here is different from the effect sizes reported in the original article by Reese and colleagues (2003) in which the effect sizes were based on the group differences in pretreatment to posttreatment change.

As discussed earlier, the methods of classifying treatment outcome at posttreatment were different between the Reese et al. study and the Anker et al. study (i.e., outcome classification based on individuals' response or couples as a unit). However, given the consistency in the classification systems within studies, we calculated combined effect sizes for differential outcome classification between the feedback and TAU groups. When the odds of reliable improvement over the odds of not achieving reliable improvement were compared across groups, the results indicated that those in the feedback group had 3.5 times higher odds of experiencing reliable change, $OR = 3.52$, $p < 0.001$, 95% CI [2.08, 5.96],

$r = 0.32$, while having less than half the odds of experiencing deterioration, $OR = 0.44$, $p = 0.149$, 95% CI[0.14, 1.35], $r = -0.22$. The summary of these effect sizes in comparison to those found in the OQ system are presented in Table 10.1.

One aspect of the above studies based on the PCOMS system is worth noting in terms of comparative conclusions and implications for clinical practice. First, the rates of "at-risk" cases reported in the three PCOMS studies are considerably higher (36% to 75%) than studies based on the OQ system (11%–33%; Shimokawa et al., 2010). Although Anker et al. (2009) reported a higher percentage of at-risk couples responding favorably to treatment than those in TAU (29% vs. 9%), the meaning and clinical implication of this classification seem unclear because the majority of cases were identified as being at risk.

As Anker et al. (2009) pointed out, the differential rates of at risk cases suggest that the PCOMS may be effective in preventing poor outcome. Partial support for the social validity of the feedback effect was suggested in the authors' report that, among those who responded to 6-month follow-up (149 couples out of 205 couples), the feedback group had a lower rate of separation or divorce (18.4%) than TAU (34.2%), which indicates the couples in TAU had approximately 1.9 times higher probability of separation or divorce (relative risk = 1.86) than those in the feedback condition. These same outcomes, however, indicate that, despite the low deterioration rate at posttreatment (2% in feedback and 4% in TAU), a substantial number of couples experienced separation or divorce relatively shortly after terminating treatment. Although the occurrence of separation or

Table 10.1   Effect Sizes [a] of Client Feedback in Comparison with TAU (Efficacy Analysis)

Feedback system	k	Posttreatment score		Reliable improvement		Deterioration	
		Hedges' g [95% CI]	r	OR [95% CI]	r	OR [95% CI]	r[b]
OQ System							
NOT Fb	4	0.53*** [0.28, 0.78]	0.25	2.55*** [1.64, 3.98]	0.23	0.44* [0.23, 0.85]	−0.21
NOT P/ T Fb	3 [c]	0.55*** [0.36, 0.73]	0.25	2.87*** [1.93, 4.27]	0.27	0.68 [0.42, 1.13]	−0.10
CST Fb	3 [d]	0.70*** [0.52, 0.88]	0.33	3.85*** [2.65, 5.60]	0.34	0.23*** [0.12, 0.44]	−0.37
PCOMS							
Feedback	3	0.48*** [0.31, 0.65]	0.23	3.52*** [2.08, 5.96]	0.32	0.44* [0.14, 1.35]	−0.22

*$p < 0.05$. **$p < 0.01$. ***$p < 0.001$.
Note: k = number of studies; r = correlation r; CI = confidence interval; NOT Fb = not-on-track clients whose therapists received client progress feedback; NOT P/T Fb = not-on-track clients where both clients and therapists received client progress feedback. CST Fb = not-on-track clients whose therapists received client progress feedback and Clinical Support Tools feedback.
[a] Effect sizes (Hedges' g and *OR*) of OQ system-based feedback interventions were meta- and mega-analytically calculated and reported in Shimokawa. et al. (2010).
[b] Negative correlations indicate greater effect in reducing treatment failure at termination.
[c] Original data from three studies employing the P/T Fb groups were aggregated and compared with the aggregated TAU data from four studies, using a mega-analytic approach.
[d] Original data from three studies employing the CST Fb groups were aggregated and compared with the aggregated TAU data from four studies, using a mega-analytic approach.

divorce alone should not be used to assume the quality of treatment outcome (some couples sought treatment to "[end] their relationship in the best possible way" or to "seek clarification regarding whether the relationship should continue"; Anker et al., 2009, p. 695), the discrepancy between the proportion of clients classified as deterioration cases and the actual occurrences of separation/divorce raises a general question about the suitability of the clinically significant classification in addressing this dimension of treatment outcome.

Results Based on the OQ System. In the most recent meta-analytic review of the OQ system, Shimokawa et al. (2010) reanalyzed the combined data set ($N = 6,151$) from all six OQ feedback studies published to date (Harmon et al., 2007; Hawkins, Lambert, Vermeersch, Slade, & Tuttle, 2004; Lambert, Whipple, et al., 2001; Lambert, Whipple, Vermeersch, et al., 2002; Slade, Lambert, Harmon, Smart, & Bailey, 2008; Whipple et al., 2003). Each of the studies required about 1 year of daily data collection and evaluated the effects of providing feedback about each client's improvement through the use of progress graphs and warnings about clients who were not demonstrating expected treatment responses (signal-alarm cases). A primary question in each of these studies was: Does feedback to psychotherapists about their clients' progress improve psychotherapy outcomes compared with progress feedback only, and treatment without feedback (e.g., treatment as usual)? The hypothesis in each of these studies was: Clients identified as signal-alarm cases (those predicted to have a poor final treatment response) whose therapists received feedback will show better outcomes than similar clients whose therapists did not receive feedback.

The six studies shared many design and methodological features: (a) consecutive cases seen in routine care regardless of client diagnosis or comorbid conditions (rather than being disorder specific); (b) random assignment of clients to experimental conditions (various feedback interventions) and treatment-as-usual conditions (no feedback) was made in 4 of the 6 studies, while reasonable measures were taken in two studies to ensure equivalence in experimental and control conditions at pretreatment; (c) psychotherapists provided a variety of theoretically guided treatments, with most adhering to cognitive-behavioral and eclectic orientations and fewer representing psychodynamic and experiential orientations; (d) a variety of therapist experience—postgraduate therapists and graduate students each accounted for about 50% of clients seen; (e) therapists saw both experimental (feedback) and no-feedback cases, thus limiting the likelihood that outcome differences between conditions could be due to therapist effects; (f) the outcome measure as well as the methodology rules/standards for identifying signal-alarm clients (failing cases) remained constant; (g) the length of therapy (dosage) was determined by client and therapist rather than by research design or arbitrary insurance limits; and (h) client characteristics such as gender, age, and ethnicity were generally similar across studies and came from the same university counseling center, with the exception of Hawkins et al. study (2004).

The meta-analysis involved both intent-to-treat (ITT) and efficacy analyses on the effects of various feedback interventions in relation to TAU. These two distinct sets of analyses were performed to investigate the amount of effects expected for each feedback intervention based on treatment assignment alone, including clients who left treatments before the effects of feedback interventions could be experienced or measured (ITT analysis) and the amount of effects expected among clients who were beneficiaries of treatments (efficacy analysis). Furthermore, we investigated the incremental benefits of two newer feedback interventions: provision of formal progress feedback directly to both clients and therapists (patient/therapist feedback; P/F Fb), and provision of formal progress feedback to therapists combined with Clinical Support Tools feedback (CST Fb).

Because the PCOMS studies resembled the efficacy analyses, we present here the results of the efficacy analyses. In these analyses, only those clients who received and completed the treatments were compared to treatment as usual. Based on these inclusion criteria, the following percentage of clients out of those initially assigned to treatment conditions were included in the meta-analyses by Shimokawa and colleagues (2010): not-on-track feedback (61.6%); not-on-track feedback to therapists and patients, (79.7%); and not-on-track feedback plus the use of Clinical Support Tools, (52.2%). It should be noted, as expected in any comparison between efficacy analysis and ITT analysis, the ITT effect sizes were generally smaller than those of efficacy analyses. The summary of effect sizes are presented in Table 10.1.

Effects of OQ Progress Feedback (Fb) on at-risk Clients. When the at-risk clients whose therapists received feedback were compared with not-on-track clients whose therapist did not receive feedback, the effect size for posttreatment OQ score difference averaged $g = 0.53$, $p < 0.001$, 95% CI[0.28, 0.78], equivalent of $r = 0.25$. These results suggest that the average client whose therapist received feedback was better off than approximately 70% of clients in the no-feedback condition (routine care). In terms of the clinical significance at termination, 9% of those receiving feedback deteriorated while 38% achieved clinically significant improvement. In contrast, among clients whose therapists did not receive

feedback, 20% deteriorated while 22% clinically significantly improved. When the odds of deterioration and clinically significant improvement were compared, results indicated that those in the feedback group had less than half the odds of experiencing deterioration ($OR = 0.44$, $p < 0.05$, 95% CI[0.23, 0.85], $r = -.21$), while having approximately 2.6 times higher odds of experiencing reliable improvement ($OR = 2.55$, $p < 0.001$, 95% CI[1.64, 3.98], $r = 0.23$).

Effects of Patient/Therapist Feedback (P/T Fb) on at-risk Clients. The effect size of posttreatment OQ score averaged $g = 0.55$, $p < 0.001$, 95% CI[0.36, 0.73], equivalent of $r = 0.25$—effects very similar to that of the therapist-only feedback group. However, direct feedback to both psychotherapists and clients appeared to have had polarizing effects, resulting in deterioration rates and odds comparable to treatment-as-usual clients. The rates of deterioration and clinically significant improvement when both participants received feedback were 15% and 45%, respectively. The results suggest that clients who received feedback along with their therapist had approximately 0.7 times the odds of deterioration, $OR = 0.68$, $p = 0.134$, 95% CI[0.42, 1.13], $r = -0.10$, while having approximately three times higher odds of achieving clinically significant improvement, $OR = 2.87$, $p < 0.001$, 95% CI[1.93, 4.27], $r = 0.27$. These results suggest that, although the average client who received feedback along with his or her therapist was better off than 71% of clients in treatment as usual, there may have been moderators that facilitated outcome enhancement in some clients while failing to prevent, or possibly contributing to, outcome worsening.

Effects of Clinical Support Tools Feedback (CST Fb) on at-risk Clients. When the outcome of clients whose therapist received the Clinical Support Tool feedback was compared with that of the treatment-as-usual clients, the effect size for the difference in mean posttreatment OQ scores was $g = 0.70$, $p < 0.001$, 95% CI[0.52, 0.88], $r = 0.33$. These results indicate that the average client in the Clinical Support Tool feedback group, who stay in treatment to experience the benefit of this intervention, are better off than 76% of clients in treatment as usual. The rates of deterioration and clinically significant improvement among those receiving Clinical Support Tools were 6% and 53%, respectively. The results suggest that clients whose therapists used Clinical Support Tools have less than a fourth the odds of deterioration, $OR = 0.23$, $p < 0.001$, 95% CI[0.12, 0.44], $r = -0.37$, while having approximately 3.9 times higher odds of achieving clinically significant improvement, $OR = 3.85$, $p < 0.001$, 95% CI [2.65, 5.60].

The above findings from the OQ-based feedback studies indicate that three forms of feedback interventions in the OQ system are effective in enhancing the treatment effects of clients who are at risk of leaving therapy worse off than when they came in. Table 10.2 displays clinically significant change and reliable change in order to make the impact of feedback more clear.

As can be seen, reduction of deterioration and increases in positive outcomes are rather dramatic in relation to treatment as usual even though the same therapists offered both interventions.

Limitations of the Research

Major limitations of feedback research are the small number of studies evaluating effectiveness, the limited number of researchers responsible for the findings reviewed here, and the sole reliance on self-report measures. It is likely that future research will be done across a wider range of treatment settings and patient populations, thus illuminating the limits of these procedures and clarifying the factors that maximize patient gains.

The research reviewed here utilized two self-report measures of improvement and therefore provides only one view of the impact of therapy. Decisions regarding the continued provision of treatment, modification of ongoing treatment, and the like, cannot be made on the basis of a single questionnaire or independently from clinical judgment.

Therapeutic Practices

These two meta-analyses demonstrate the effectiveness of two well-developed feedback systems. In this closing section, we

Table 10.2   Percent of Not-on-Track (Signal-Alarm) Cases Meeting Criteria for Clinically Significant Change at Termination Summed across Six Studies (Efficacy Sample)

Outcome classification	CST Fb[a]	P/T Fb[b]	Fb[c]	TAU[d]
	n (%)	n (%)	n (%)	n (%)
Deteriorated [e]	12 (5.5%)	26 (14.7%)	24 (9.1%)	64 (20.1%)
No change	91 (41.9%)	71 (40.1%)	140 (53.2%)	183 (57.5%)
Reliable/Clinically significant change [f]	114 (52.5%)	80 (45.2%)	99 (37.6%)	71 (22.3%)

[a] CST Fb = patients who were not on track and whose therapist received feedback and used clinical support tools.
[b] P/T Fb = patients who were not on track and both patients and their therapist received feedback.
[c] Fb = patients who were not on track and whose therapist received feedback.
[d] TAU = patients who were not on track and whose therapist was not given feedback.
[e] Worsened by at least 14 points on the OQ from pretreatment to posttreatment.
[f] Improved by at least 14 points on the OQ or improved and passed the cutoff between dysfunctional and functional populations.

offer practice suggestions based on our findings.

- Routine use of a feedback system to augment clinical decision making—a "lab test" to be used by clinicians, rather than a replacement for the clinician's judgment. Feedback systems can be used with adults, adolescents, and children and in individual as well as couples therapy.

- Beware of those situations in which clients feel it may be in their interest to understate (or overstate) their problems and produce inaccurate ratings on feedback systems. The systems are predicated on accurate self-reporting of levels of disturbance and corresponding changes.

- Supplement with clinical support tools. As suggested by the general literature on feedback and the evidence presented here, problem-solving and decision-enhancement tools prove helpful to clinicians and, most importantly, clients. Brief assessment of the therapeutic alliance and suggestions for its modification, along with assessment of outside forces such as life events and the strength of social supports, can make a substantial impact on routine care for individuals whose treatment response is in doubt.

- For some patients, it is preferable to provide feedback to both patient and therapist. As yet we are uncertain of the necessity of sharing progress feedback directly with clients. In the PCOMS system, progress and relationship information is gathered within session and discussed routinely. Since both are a part of the session, either may account for the therapeutic effects that have occurred. In contrast, the OQ system has examined therapist feedback and direct client feedback separately with inconclusive results about additive effectiveness of direct client feedback. In addition, even when progress feedback was provided only to clinicians, they were left free to discuss progress reports with clients or to problem-solve on their own. We know that clinicians received feedback, but we do not know if or how it was provided to clients.

- Employ real-time client feedback to compensate for therapist's limited ability to accurately detect client worsening in psychotherapy. Despite considerable evidence that psychotherapists are not alert to treatment failure (e.g., Hannan et al., 2005; Hatfield, et al., 2010), and strong evidence that clinical judgments are usually inferior to actuarial methods (Meehl, 1954), therapists' confidence in their clinical judgment stands as a barrier to implementation of monitoring and feedback systems.

- Consider using electronic versions of feedback systems that expedite and ease practical difficulties. Adding monitoring measures to busy practices can also be a barrier to implementation. Fortunately, the brevity of the PCOMs and the recent software for the OQ can provide instantaneous feedback to clinicians. The electronic PCOMs takes only a few minutes in sessions, while if the client takes the OQ immediately prior to the scheduled psychotherapy session, electronic feedback is available to the therapist prior to beginning that session.

References

An asterisk (*) indicates studies included in the meta-analysis.

*Anker, M. G., Duncan, B. L., & Sparks, J. A. (2009). Using client feedback to improve couple therapy outcomes: A randomized clinical trial in a naturalistic treatment setting. *Journal of Consulting & Clinical Psychology, 77,* 693–704.

Bandura, A. (1997). Social cognitive theory of self regulation. *Organizational Behavior and Human Decision Processes, 50,* 248–87.

Barkham, M., Margison, F., Leach, C., Lucock, M., Mellor-Clark, J., Evans, C., et al. (2001). Service profiling and outcomes benchmarking using the CORE_OM: Toward practice-based evidence in the psychological therapies. *Journal of Consulting and Clinical Psychology, 69,* 184–96.

Beckstead, D. J., Hatch, A. L., Lambert, M. J., Eggett, D. L., Goates, M. K., & Vermeersch, D. A. (2003). Clinical significance of the Outcome Questionnaire (OQ-45.2). *The Behavior Analyst Today, 4,* 79–90.

Berking, M., Orth, U., & Lutz, W. (2006). Wie effekiv sind systematische Ruckmeldungen des therapieverlaufs an den therapeuten? Eine empirishe studie in einem stationar-verhalten-stherapeutischen setting, *Zeitchrift fur Klinishe Psychologie und Psychotherapie, 35,* 21–29.

Bludworth, J., Tracey, T. J. G., & Glidden-Tracey, C. (2010). The bi-level structure of the Outcome Questionnaire-45. *Psychological Assessment, 22,* 350–355.

Bordin, E. S. (1979). The generalizability of the psychoanalytic concept of the working alliance. *Psychotherapy, 16,* 252–60.

Brodey, B. B., Cuffel, B., McCulloch, J., Tani, S., Maruish, M., Brodey, I., et al. (2005). The acceptability and effectiveness of patient-reported assessments and feedback in managed behavioral healthcare setting. *The American Journal of Managed Care, 11,* 774–80.

de Jong, K., Nugter, M. A., Polak, M. G., Wagenborg, J. E. A., Spinhoven, P., & Heiser, W. J. (2007). The Outcome Questionnaire (OQ-45) in a Dutch population: A cross-cultural validation. *Clinical Psychology & Psychotherapy, 14,* 288–401.

Duncan, B. L., & Miller, S. D. (2008). *The Outcome and Session Rating Scales: The revised administration and scoring manual, including the Child Outcome Rating Scale.* Chicago: Institute for the Study of Therapeutic Change.

Ellsworth, J. R., Lambert, M. J., & Johnson, J. (2006). A comparison of the Outcome Questionnaire-45 and Outcome Questionnaire-30 in classification and prediction of treatment outcome. *Clinical Psychology and Psychotherapy, 13,* 380–91.

Gaston, L. (1990). The concept of the alliance and its role in psychotherapy: Theoretical and empirical considerations. *Psychotherapy, 27,* 143–53.

Hannan, C., Lambert, M. J., Harmon, C., Nielsen, S. L., Smart, D. W., Shimokawa, K., et al. (2005). A lab test and algorithms for identifying clients at risk for treatment failure. *Journal of Clinical Psychology: In Session, 61,* 155–63.

Hansen, N. B., Lambert, M. J., & Forman, E. V. (2002). The psychotherapy dose-response effect and its implications for treatment delivery services. *Clinical Psychology: Science and Practice, 9,* 329–43.

*Harmon, S. C., Lambert, M. J., Smart, D. W., Hawkins, E. J., Nielsen, S. L., Slade, K., et al. (2007). Enhancing outcome for potential treatment failures: Therapist/client feedback and clinical support tools. Psychotherapy Research, 17, 379–92.

Hatfield, D., McCullough, L., Plucinski, A., & Krieger, K. (2010). Do we know when our clients get worse? An investigation of therapists' ability to detect negative client change. *Clinical Psychology & Psychotherapy, 17,* 25–32.

*Hawkins, E. J., Lambert, M. J., Vermeersch, D. A., Slade, K., & Tuttle, K. (2004). The effects of providing patient progress information to therapists and patients. *Psychotherapy Research, 14,* 308–27.

Hedges, L. V., & Olkin, I. (1985). *Statistical methods for meta-analysis.* New York: Academic Press.

Jacobson, N. S., & Truax, P. (1991). Clinical significance: A statistical approach to defining meaningful change in psychotherapy research. *Journal of Consulting and Clinical Psychology, 59,* 12–19.

Kluger, A. N., & DeNisi, A. (1996). The effects of feedback interventions on performance: A historical review, a meta-analysis, and a preliminary feedback intervention theory. *Psychological Bulletin, 119,* 254–84.

Knaup, C., Koesters, M., Schoefer, D., Becker, T., & Puschner, B. (2009). Effect of feedback of treatment outcome in specialist mental healthcare: Meta-analysis. *The British Journal of Psychiatry, 195,* 15–22.

Kordy, H., Hannöver, W., & Richard, M. (2001). Computer-assisted feedback-driven quality management for psychotherapy: The Stuttgart-Heidelberg model. *Journal of Consulting and Clinical Psychology, 69,* 173–83.

Kraus D. R., & Horan, F. P. (1997). Outcomes roadblocks: Problems and solutions. *Behavioral Health Management, 17,* 22–26.

Lambert, M. J. (1983). Introduction to assessment of psychotherapy outcome: Historical perspective and current issues. In M. J. Lambert,

E. R. Christensen, & S. S. DeJulio (Eds), *The assessment of psychotherapy outcome*. New York: Wiley.

Lambert, M. J., Bergin, A. E., & Collins, J. L. (1977). Therapist induced deterioration in psychotherapy patients. In A. S. Gurman, & A. M. Razin (Eds.), *Effective psychotherapy: A handbook of research* (pp. 452–81). New York: Pergamon Press.

Lambert, M. J., & Burlingame, G. M. (2007). Measuring outcomes in the State of Utah: Practice-based evidence. *Behavioral Healthcare, 27*, 16–20.

Lambert, M. J., Morton, J. J., Hatfield, D., Harmon, C., Hamilton, S., Reid, R. C., et al. (2004). *Administration and scoring manual for the Outcome Questionnaire -45*. Salt Lake City, UT: OQ Measures.

Lambert, M. J., & Ogles, B. M. (2004). The efficacy and effectiveness of psychotherapy. In M. J. Lambert (Ed.), *Bergin and Garfield's handbook of psychotherapy and behavior change* (5th ed., pp. 139–93). New York: Wiley.

Lambert, M. J., Whipple, J. L., Bishop, M. J., Vermeersch, D. A., Gray, G. V., & Finch, A. E. (2002). Comparison of empirically derived and rationally derived methods for identifying clients at risk for treatment failure. *Clinical Psychology and Psychotherapy, 9*, 149–64.

Lambert, M. J., Whipple, J. L., Harmon, C., Shimokawa, K., Slade, K., & Christofferson, C. (2004). *Clinical support tools manual*. Provo, UT: Department of Psychology, Brigham Young University,.

*Lambert, M. J., Whipple, J. L., Smart, D. W., Vermeersch, D. A., Nielsen, S. L., & Hawkins, E. J. (2001). The effects of providing therapists with feedback on client progress during psychotherapy: Are outcomes enhanced? *Psychotherapy Research, 11*, 49–68.

*Lambert, M. J., Whipple, J. L., Vermeersch, D. A., Smart, D. W., Hawkins, E. J., Nielsen, S. L., et al. (2002). Enhancing psychotherapy outcomes via providing feedback on client progress: A replication. *Clinical Psychology and Psychotherapy, 9*, 91–103.

Lo Coco, G., Chiappelli, M., Bensi, L., Gullo, S., Prestano, C., & Lambert, M. J. (2008). The factorial structure of the Outcome Questionnaire-45: A study with an Italian sample. *Clinical Psychology & Psychotherapy, 15*, 418–23.

Lord, R. G., & Hanges, P. J. (1987). A control system model of organizational motivation: Theoretical development and applied implications. *Behavioral Science, 32*, 161–78.

Lueger, R. J., Howard, K. I., Martinovich Z., Lutz, W., Anderson, E. E., & Grissom, G. (2001). Assessing treatment progress of individual clients using expected treatment response models. *Journal of Consulting and Clinical Psychology, 69*, 150–58.

Lunnen, K. M., & Ogles, B. M. (1998). A multi-perspective, multivariable evaluation of reliable change. *Journal of Consulting and Clinical Psychology, 66*, 400–410.

Lutz, W., Lambert, M. J., Harmon, S. C., Tschitsaz, A., Schurch, E., & Stulz, N. (2006). The probability of treatment success, failure and duration- what can be learned from empirical data to support decision making in clinical practice? *Clinical Psychology & Psychotherapy, 13*, 223–32.

Meehl, P. E. (1954). *Clinical versus statistical prediction*. Minneapolis: University of Minnesota Press.

Miller, S. D., & Duncan, B. L. (2004). *The Outcome and Session Rating Scales: Administration and scoring manual*. Chicago: Institute for the Study of Therapeutic Change.

Miller, S. D., Duncan, B. L., Brown, J., Sparks, J. A., & Claud, D. A. (2003). The outcome rating scale: A preliminary study of the reliability, validity, and feasibility of a brief visual analog measure. *Journal of Brief Therapy, 2*, 91–100.

Miller, S. D., Duncan, B. L., Sorrell, R., & Brown, G. S. (2005). The Partners for Change Outcome System. *Journal of Clinical Psychology: In Session, 61*, 199–208.

National Advisory Mental Health Council. (2001). *Blueprint for change: Research on child and adolescent mental health. A report by the National Advisory Mental Health Council's Workgroup on Child and Adolescent Mental Health Intervention Development and Deployment*. Bethesda, MD: National Institutes of Health/National Institute of Mental Health.

Percevic, R., Lambert, M. J., & Kordy, H. (2006). What is the predictive value of responses to psychotherapy for its future course? Empirical explorations and consequences for outcome monitoring. *Psychotherapy Research, 16*, 364–73.

*Reese, R. J., Norsworthy, L., & Rowlands, S. (2009). Does a continuous feedback system improve psychotherapy outcome? *Psychotherapy: Theory, Research, Practice, & Training, 46*, 418–31.

Riemer, M., & Bickman, L. (2004) *The Contextualized Feedback Intervention Theory: A theory of guided behavior change.* Unpublished manuscript.

Riemer, M., Rosof-Williams, J., & Bickman, L. (2005). Theories related to changing clinician practice. *Child Adolescent Psychiatric Clinics of North America, 14,* 241–54.

Ringel, J. S., & Sturm, R. (2001). National estimates of mental health utilization and expenditures for children in 1998. *Journal of Behavioral Health Services & Research, 28,* 319–33.

Safran, J. D., Muran, J. C., Samstang, L. W., & Winston, A. (2005). Evaluating alliance-focussed intervention for potential treatment failures: A feasibility and descriptive analysis. *Psychotherapy: Theory, Research, Practice, & Training, 42,* 512–531.

Sapyta, J., Riemer, M., & Bickman, L. (2005). Feedback to clinicians: Theory, research, and practice. *Journal of Clinical Psychology, 62,* 145–53.

Shadish, W. R., Matt, G. E., Navarro, A. M., Siegle, G., Crits-Christoph, P., Hazelrigg, M. D., et al. (1997). Evidence that therapy works in clinically representative conditions. *Journal of Consulting and Clinical Psychology, 65,* 355–65.

Shimokawa, K., Lambert, M. J., & Smart, D. W. Enhancing treatment outcome of patients at risk of treatment failure: Meta-analytic and mega-analytic review of a psychotherapy quality assurance system. (2010). *Journal of Consulting & Clinical Psychology, 78,* 298–311.

*Slade, K., Lambert, M. J., Harmon, S. C., Smart, D. W., & Bailey, R. (2008). Improving psychotherapy outcome: The use of immediate electronic feedback and revised clinical support tools. *Clinical Psychology & Psychotherapy, 15,* 287–303.

Smith, M. L., Glass, G. V., & Miller, T. L. (1980). *The benefits of psychotherapy.* Baltimore: The Johns Hopkins University press.

Spielmans, G. I., Masters, K. S., & Lambert, M. J. (2006). A comparison of rational versus empirical methods in prediction of negative psychotherapy outcome. *Clinical Psychology & Psychotherapy, 13,* 202–214.

Vermeersch, D. A., Lambert, M. J., & Burlingame, G. M. (2000). Outcome Questionnaire: Item sensitivity to change. *Journal of Personality Assessment, 74,* 242–61.

Vermeersch, D. A., Whipple, J. L., Lambert, M. J., Hawkins, E. J., Burchfield, C. M., & Okiishi, J. C. (2004). Outcome Questionnaire: Is it sensitive to changes in counseling center clients? *Journal of Counseling Psychology, 51,* 38–49.

Walfish, S., McAlister, B., O'Donnell, P., & Lambert, M. J. (2010). *Are all therapists from Lake Wobegon?: An investigation of self-assessment bias in mental health providers.* Unpublished manuscript.

Wampold, B. (2008). *The great psychotherapy debate* (2nd.ed.). Mahwah, NJ: Erlbaum.

Warren, J. S., Nelson, P. L., Mondragon, S. A., Baldwin, S. A., & Burlingame, G. M. (2010). Youth psychotherapy change trajectories & outcome in usual care: Community mental health versus managed care. *Journal of Consulting & Clinical Psychology, 78,* 144–55.

Weiss, B., Catron, T., Harris, V., & Phung, T. M. (1999). The effectiveness of traditional child psychotherapy. *Journal of Consulting and Clinical Psychology, 67,* 82–94.

Weiss, B., Catron, T., Harris, V., & Phung, T. M. (1999). The effectiveness of traditional child psychotherapy. *Journal of Consulting and Clinical Psychology, 67,* 82–94.

Weisz, J. R. (2004). *Psychotherapy for children and adolescents: Evidence-based treatments and case examples.* New York: Cambridge University Press.

Weisz, J. R., Donenberg, G. R., Han, S. S., & Weiss, B. (1995). Bridging the gap between laboratory and clinic in child and adolescent psychotherapy. *Journal of Consulting and Clinical Psychology, 63,* 688–701.

Whipple, J. L., Lambert, M. J., Vermeersch, D. A., Smart, D. W., Nielsen, S. L., & Hawkins, E. J. (2003). Improving the effects of psychotherapy: The use of early identification of treatment failure and problem solving strategies in routine practice. *Journal of Counseling Psychology, 58,* 59–68.

Wolf, F. M. (1986). *Meta-analysis: Quantitative methods for research synthesis.* Sage University Paper series on quantitative applications in the social sciences. Beverly Hills, CA: Sage Publications.

11 Repairing Alliance Ruptures

Jeremy D. Safran, J. Christopher Muran, *and* Catherine Eubanks-Carter

One of the most consistent findings emerging from psychotherapy research is that the quality of the therapeutic alliance is a robust predictor of outcome across a range of different treatment modalities (e.g., Chapters 2, 3, and 4) and that, conversely, weakened alliances are correlated with unilateral termination by the patient (e.g., Horvath & Bedi, 2002; Martin, Garske, & Davis, 2000; Samstag, Batchelder, Muran, Safran, & Winston, 1998; Tryon & Kane, 1990, 1993, 1995). In the last two decades, there has emerged what we have characterized as a "second generation" of alliance research that attempts to clarify the factors leading to the development of the alliance, as well as those processes involved in repairing ruptures in the alliance when they occur (Safran & Muran, 2006; Safran et al., 2002). In this chapter, we provide a review of this research and meta-analyses of two different types of relevant studies. The first meta- analysis examines the association between the presence of rupture repair episodes and treatment outcome. The second examines the impact of rupture resolution training or supervision on patient outcome by assessing patient change from therapy intake to termination. We will also briefly review the task analytic studies investigating processes associated with alliance rupture repair.

Definitions and Measures

A rupture in the therapeutic alliance can be defined as a tension or breakdown in the collaborative relationship between patient and therapist (Safran & Muran, 2000, 2006). Although the term *rupture* may imply to some a dramatic breakdown in collaboration, ruptures vary in intensity from relatively minor tensions, which one or both of the participants may be only vaguely aware of, to major breakdowns in collaboration, understanding, or communication. Concepts that are similar or overlapping with the construct of the alliance rupture include empathic failure (Kohut, 1984), therapeutic impasse, and misunderstanding event (Rhodes et al., 1994). Alliance ruptures and repairs can be measured from patient, therapist, and observer perspectives. They can focus on rupture repair events that take place either within session or over the course of treatment.

Patient Self-Report of Within-Session Ruptures

One method of identifying alliance ruptures and repairs involves obtaining patient and therapist reports of shift in quality of the alliance, or perception of alliance rupture and degree of resolution within session, using session impact questionnaires.

For example, in a study comparing the efficacy of brief relational therapy, cognitive behavioral therapy, and short-term dynamic therapy with personality-disordered patients (Muran et al., 2005), patients completed postsession questionnaires (PSQ; Muran, Safran, Samstag, & Winston, 1992), which included self-report measures of the alliance (12-item Working Alliance Inventory, WAI; Horvath & Greenberg, 1989; Tracey & Kokotovic, 1989), as well as self-report indices measuring the occurrence of ruptures, rupture intensity, and the extent to which ruptures were resolved. Ruptures occurred frequently across the three treatments: in the first six sessions of treatment, ruptures were reported by 37% of patients and 56% of therapists (Muran et al., 2009). Ruptures were also found to be significantly related to outcome. Higher rupture intensity, as reported jointly by patients and therapists, was associated with poor outcome on measures of interpersonal functioning. Failure to resolve these ruptures was predictive of dropout. Another study (Eames & Roth, 2000) also administered the WAI items and the rupture indices from the PSQ to 30 patients receiving treatment as usual. Therapists reported ruptures more often, reporting them in 43% of sessions, while patients reported them in 19%.

Patient Fluctuations in Alliance Measures across Sessions

Another method of identifying alliance ruptures and their repairs has been to track fluctuations in patients' alliance scores across the course of therapy. For example, Strauss and colleagues (2006) sought to identify rupture repair episodes in a sample of 30 patients with avoidant and obsessive-compulsive personality disorders who received up to a year of cognitive therapy. They developed criteria for rupture and resolution sessions by looking for fluctuations in scores on the California Psychotherapy Alliance Scale

(CALPAS; Marmar, Weiss, & Gaston, 1989) that were at least as large as the mean standard deviation of alliance scores across the sample. Of the patients with at least three alliance assessments, rupture repair sequences occurred in 56% of the cases. For another example, Stevens and associates (2007) developed criteria for identifying rupture repair sequences from fluctuations in WAI scores in a sample of 44 patients drawn from the personality disorder cases. Ruptures were defined as decreases of at least one point on the WAI; ruptures were deemed to be resolved if the alliance score rose to within 0.25 points of the prerupture score in three to five sessions. Fully 50% of the cases included episodes that met these rupture repair criteria.

Observer-Based Methods

Differences between patient and therapist perspectives of the alliance ruptures raise the concern that patients may underreport ruptures due to a lack of awareness of them or discomfort with acknowledging them. One way to address this problem is to use observer-based measures to detect ruptures and resolution processes. An early example of this is the study of "weakenings" in the therapeutic alliance (Lansford, 1986). Using audiotapes of six sessions of time-limited dynamic therapy, raters identified ruptures and repairs and then examined the relationship between occurrence of ruptures and treatment outcome. The study found that the most successful outcomes were associated with patients and therapists who actively dealt with alliance ruptures (Lansford, 1986).

In a study of 151 sessions from five patients in psychodynamic therapy (Sommerfeld et al., 2008), the difference between patient self-report of ruptures and observer-based report was directly examined. Patients completed a brief version of PSQ after each session that included the alliance measure, self-reports of ruptures and resolution, and items tapping into the depth and smoothness of the session from the Session Evaluation Questionnaire (SEQ; Stiles, 1980). Patients reported ruptures in 42% of the sessions. Using transcripts of these same sessions, judges identified confrontation and withdrawal ruptures using Harper's unpublished coding system (1989a, 1989b); rupture markers were identified by observers in 77% of sessions. There was no significant association between the observer and client perspectives. But sessions where both patient and observer saw a rupture were rated as having greater depth by the patient. As ruptures that are identified by both self- and observer-report are likely ones that are explicitly discussed in the session, this finding suggests that patients find therapy more helpful when therapists are sensitive to subtle indications of ruptures and encourage patients to explore them.

The researchers also found a significant association between the occurrence of ruptures and the appearance of dysfunctional interpersonal schemas involving the therapist, identified using the core conflictual relationship theme method (CCRT; Luborsky & Crits-Christoph, 1998). This finding suggests that when ruptures occur, dysfunctional interpersonal schemas are likely to be active. Thus, ruptures provide critical opportunities to identify, explore, and change patients' self-defeating patterns of thought and behavior.

Colli and Lingiardi (2009) have developed an observer-based method that codes transcribed sessions for both alliance ruptures and resolutions: the Collaborative Interaction Scale (CIS). A strength of the CIS is that it assesses both patients' and therapists' positive and negative contributions to the therapeutic process. The CIS has also demonstrated good interrater

reliability with graduate student raters (Colli & Lingiardi, 2009). The patient rupture markers and therapist intervention items were largely derived from the Rupture Resolution Scale (Samstag, Safran, & Muran, 2004).

Given that most observer-based methods for coding ruptures and resolutions rely on the use of transcripts or the use of highly experienced clinicians as judges (e.g., Aspland et al., 2008; Bennett et al., 2006), our research team has sought to develop a coding system that is accessible to graduate student raters and does not require transcription of sessions. The Rupture Resolution Rating System (3RS; Eubanks-Carter, Muran, & Safran, 2009) draws on Harper's (1989a, 1989b) manual for coding confrontation and withdrawal ruptures, as well as the Rupture Resolution Scale (Samstag, Safran, & Muran, 2004). Preliminary findings from the 3RS are consistent with the evidence that alliance ruptures identified through observer-based coding systems are more frequent than those identified by patient self-report (Mitchell et al., 2010).

Prevalence of Ruptures
However measured, ruptures in individual psychotherapy are quite frequent. Table 11.1 summarizes the frequency of alliance ruptures and rupture repair sequences across eight studies employing either patient report, therapist report, or observer ratings. These studies demonstrate that (1) patients report ruptures in 19% to 42% of sessions, (2) therapists report them in 43% to 56% of sessions, and (3) third-party raters observe ruptures anywhere from 41% to 100% of sessions. In studies that examined postsession alliance ratings to identify the prevalence of rupture repair sequences, patients reported such sequences in 22% to 56% of cases.

Table 11.1   Prevalence of Alliance Ruptures and Rupture Repair Sequences

Study		Method	Frequency
Colli & Lingiardi (2009)	16 patients, 32 sessions	Observer-based	Indirect ruptures: 100% of sessions
			Direct ruptures: 43% of sessions
Eames & Roth (2000)	30 patients, sessions 2-5	In session self-report, patient	19% of sessions
		In session self-report, therapist	43% of sessions
Mitchell et al. (2010)	9 patients, 24 sessions	In-session self-report, patient	41% of sessions
		In-session self-report, therapist	59% of sessions
		Observer-based	Withdrawal ruptures: 74% of sessions
			Confrontation ruptures: 44% of sessions
Muran et al. (2009)	128 patients, Sessions 1–6	In-session self-report, patient	37% of cases
		In-session self-report, therapist	56% of cases
Sommerfeld et al. (2008)	5 patients, 151 sessions	In-session self-report, patient	42% of sessions
		Observer-based	77% of sessions
Stevens et al. (2007)	44 patients	In-session self-report	Rupture repair sequences: 50% of cases
Stiles et al. (2004)	79 patients	In-session self-report	Rupture repair sequences: 21.5% of cases
Strauss et al. (2006)	25 patients	In-session self-report	Rupture repair sequences: 56% of cases

Clinical Examples

Following Bordin's (1979) understanding of the alliance, we find it useful to conceptualize ruptures in the alliance as consisting of (1) disagreements about the tasks of therapy, (2) disagreement about the treatment goals, or (3) strains in the patient–therapist bond. An example of a disagreement about the goal dimension would be a situation in which the patient begins treatment seeking immediate relief from his or her panic symptoms, but the therapist believes the goal should be one of obtaining insight rather than immediate symptom relief. An example of a disagreement about the task dimension would be a situation in which the patient believes that it is important to spend time reviewing and making sense of his or her history, but the therapist has a present-focused, pragmatic orientation. An example of a strain in the bond dimension would be a situation in which the patient feels patronized or misunderstood by the therapist.

These three types of ruptures are, of course, not mutually exclusive. For example, the patient whose therapist is unwilling to negotiate the tasks or goals of treatment may feel misunderstood or disrespected. Conversely, a patient who feels mistrusting of his or her therapist will be more likely to disagree with the therapist about a therapeutic task or goal.

Understanding the typical clinical manifestations of alliance ruptures leads naturally to common rupture repair interventions on the part of the psychotherapist:

1. *Repeating the Therapeutic Rationale.* Outlining the therapeutic rationale at the beginning of treatment can play an important role in developing the alliance at the outset. Reiterating the rationale throughout treatment can help to repair a strained alliance. For example, the therapist can help to repair an alliance rupture resulting from his or her attempt to make a transference interpretation by reiterating that exploring parallels between the therapeutic relationship and other relationships can help the patient to become aware of self-defeating patterns.

2. *Changing Task or Goals.* In this intervention, the therapist responds to ruptures resulting from disagreements about tasks or goals by modifying his behaviors in a fashion that feels meaningful to the patient. For example,

a rupture ensues when a therapist attempts to challenge a patient's dysfunctional thinking style. In response the therapist shifts to validating his experience rather than challenging his perception. A patient is frustrated by the therapist's attempt to explore his feelings and asks for more direct guidance. In response the therapist shifts to providing direct advice or engaging in collaborative problem solving with the patient.

3. *Clarifying Misunderstandings at a Surface Level.* For example, a therapist notices that her patient seems withdrawn and initiates an exploration of what is going on in the here and now of their relationship. The patient admits to feeling criticized by the therapist. The therapist responds in a nondefensive fashion and acknowledges that she can see how the patient might have felt criticized by what she said.

4. *Exploring Relational Themes Associated with the Rupture.* In some situations, the process of clarifying factors leading to a rupture can lead to an exploration of underlying relational themes. For example, a patient may experience the therapist's questions about her inner experience as intrusive. Exploring the meaning and nature of this experience for the patient may reveal that it is related to a more general experience on her part of feeling intruded upon by others. A patient who fails to do his homework assignments in cognitive therapy may have a particular sensitivity to feeling dominated and controlled by others. A patient's feeling of being misattuned to by the therapist may reflect a narcissistic sensitivity that becomes a major focus of the treatment.

5. *Linking the Alliance Rupture to Common Patterns in a Patient's Life.* In some situations resolving a rupture can involve explicitly exploring the link between the rupture that occurs

in the session. For example, a therapist explores similarities between the control struggles occurring the therapeutic relationship and the patient's parallel tendency to become involved in controls struggles with others in his or her life.

6. *New Relational Experience.* The therapist acts in a way that he or she hypothesizes will provide the patient with an important new relational experience without explicitly exploring the underlying meaning of the interaction. This intervention is particularly important when the patient has difficulty exploring the therapeutic relationship in the here and now. For example, a therapist decides to answer a patient's request for advice because she formulates the situation as one in which the decision to do so will provide a corrective contrast to the patient's abandoning mother.

Meta-Analytic Review

Two sets of meta-analyses were conducted. The first set of analyses examined the association between the presence of rupture repair episodes and treatment outcome. The second set of analyses examined the impact of rupture resolution training or supervision on patient outcome.

Search Strategy and Inclusion Criteria

To identify potential studies, we searched the reference sections of several recent reviews of the alliance rupture literature (i.e., Eubanks-Carter, Muran, & Safran, 2010; Eubanks-Carter, Muran, Safran, & Hayes, 2011; Safran, Muran, Samstag, & Stevens, 2002). In addition, we conducted a computerized search of the PsycINFO database. Using the search terms *alliance* and *outcome*, and the terms *alliance* and *rupture*, a list of 578 journal articles was generated on April 15, 2010. These articles were inspected for studies meeting the following inclusion criteria: (a) the study

was published in English in a peer-reviewed journal, and (b) it included a quantifiable measure of outcome at the beginning and termination of treatment. To be included in the meta-analysis of rupture repair episodes, a study also had to use quantitative criteria to identify patients who experienced discrete ruptures and rupture repairs or resolutions over the course of treatment.

In order to be included in the meta-analysis of rupture resolution training and supervision, a study also had to constitute an investigation of therapist training or supervision focused on improving therapists' abilities to build and/or maintain good alliances with their adult patients in individual, in-person psychotherapy. Many psychotherapy treatments include attention to the alliance; in order to be included in this analysis, the alliance-focused training or supervision had to include a *specific* focus on helping therapists to manage alliance ruptures or problems in the therapeutic relationship.

The literature search identified four studies that met the inclusion criteria for the rupture repair analysis. Three of these studies (Stiles et al., 2004; Stevens et al., 2007; Strauss et al., 2006) defined rupture repair episodes based on session-to-session fluctuations in alliance scores, and they examined the relation between the presence of these episodes and outcome. A fourth study (Muran et al., 2009) examined ruptures and repairs that occurred within the first six sessions of treatment for patients with Cluster C and Personality Disorder NOS diagnoses, based on patient and therapist self-reports. This study reported findings regarding the relation between rupture repair episodes and outcome, namely that higher rupture intensity was associated with poor outcome on measures of interpersonal functioning ($r = -0.35$, $p < 0.01$), and rupture repair was predictive of retention in treatment ($r = 0.29$, $p < 0.05$).

However, due to the significant methodological difference of examining rupture repairs within sessions, rather than between sessions, this study was excluded from the meta-analysis.

The literature search identified nine studies that met the inclusion criteria for the rupture resolution training analysis. However, one study (Safran et al., 2005) was excluded from the meta-analysis due to its markedly different design, which included unique selection criteria and a change in treatment conditions during the course of the study. Specifically, a subset of patients in the CBT and dynamic supervision conditions of the Muran et al. (2005) study were identified as potential treatment failures based on patient and therapist postsession questionnaire ratings, and these patients were given the opportunity to switch midtreatment to one of the other treatment conditions. Those who agreed to switch were randomly assigned to either rupture resolution supervision condition or the other standard treatment condition (CBT or dynamic therapy). This study found that patients who switched into the rupture resolution condition were significantly more likely to remain in treatment than those who switched into another treatment condition.

The remaining eight studies in the rupture resolution training analysis all presented intake and termination data for therapists who received some form of rupture resolution training and/or supervision. Seven of the eight studies also included a control condition; however, these control groups varied considerably. They included a wait list control (Castonguay et al., 2004), an unsupervised active treatment (Bambling et al., 2006), supervised active treatments (Constantino et al., 2008; Muran et al., 2005; Newman et al., 2008), and therapists serving as their own controls in studies that compared outcomes obtained with different patients before and after therapists received rupture resolution training or supervision. The first of these was the Vanderbilt II study conducted by Hans Strupp and colleagues (Bein et al., 2000). The second was conducted by Crits-Christoph et al. (2006). One study (Hilsenroth et al., 2007) did not include a control group. In order to include all of the eligible studies, we chose to first conduct a meta-analysis of all eight studies using standardized mean gain effect sizes comparing pretreatment to posttreatment scores. However, given that pre-post comparisons typically yield very large effect sizes due to their failure to control for confounds such as the passage of time, we also conducted a meta-analysis of the standardized mean difference scores of the seven studies that included control conditions.

Methodological Considerations

Not all studies reported effect sizes, and those that did varied as to the effect size statistic used as well as the data on which it was based (e.g., termination vs. follow-up data, all outcome measures or a subset of outcome measures). In order to achieve greater methodological consistency, effect sizes were recalculated for all studies. First, standardized mean differences (or, in the case of pre-post effect sizes, standardized mean gains) were calculated based on means and standard deviations or F ratios provided in the articles or directly from the authors. The standardized mean scores were then converted into r effect sizes. When studies reported more than one outcome measure or finding for more than one subgroup, effect sizes were calculated for each outcome measure or each subgroup, and then averaged to form one effect size per study. The meta-analyses were conducted using random-effects models, with each effect size weighted by the inverse of its variance. Comprehensive Meta-Analysis,

Version 2.0, was used for all analyses (Borenstein, Hedges, Higgins, & Rothstein, 2005).

Results

Table 11.2 presents the correlations between the presence of rupture repair episodes and treatment outcome in three studies. The aggregated correlation was 0.24, $z = 3.06$, 95% CI (0.09–0.39), $p = 0.002$, a medium size effect that indicates that the presence of rupture repair episodes was positively related to good outcome.

Our second set of meta-analyses examined the impact of rupture resolution training or supervision on patient outcome in eight published studies. Both pre-post and group contrast effect sizes were calculated; the results are presented in Table 11.3. The mean weighted pre-post r for the rupture resolution training studies was 0.65, $z = 5.56$, 95% CI (0.46–0.78.), $p < 0.001$. Given the particularly large effect sizes produced by two studies (Bambling et al., 2006; Castonguay et al., 2004), the results were recalculated excluding these studies, yielding an effect size of 0.52, $z = 6.94$, 95% CI (0.40–0.63), $p < 0.001$. These results provide evidence that rupture resolution training/supervision led to significant patient improvement; however, with a pre-post design, we cannot determine whether this improvement was greater than what patients would experience with treatment from therapists who were not trained in rupture resolution.

A meta-analysis of the between-group effect sizes for the seven studies with control conditions yielded a mean weighted effect size of 0.15, $z = 2.66$, 95% CI (0.04–0.26), $p = 0.01$. When one outlier study was removed (Castonguay et al., 2004), the mean weighted effect size was reduced to 0.11, $z = 2.24$, 95% CI (0.01–0.21), $p = 0.03$. These results indicate that rupture resolution training/supervision leads to small but statistically significant patient improvements relative to treatment by therapists who did not undergo such training.

Moderators and Mediators

The meta-analysis examining the relation between rupture repair and outcome included only three studies, which precludes most moderator analyses. Furthermore, across these three studies, mean weighted effect sizes were not significantly heterogeneous, $Q(2) = 0.99$, $p = 0.61$.

For the analysis of pre-post effect sizes of rupture resolution training, mean weighted effect sizes across the studies were significantly heterogeneous, $Q(7) = 203.85$, $p < 0.001$. Potential moderators that might explain this variability were examined. To examine whether effect sizes varied as a function of patient diagnosis, studies were divided into two groups: a group of studies

Table 11.2 Correlation between Rupture Repair and Outcome

Study	Treatment	Patient diagnostic criteria	N	Outcome measure	r	Lower limit (r)	Upper limit (r)	Z-value (r)	p-value (r)
Stiles et al. (2004)	CBT and PI	Depression	79	BDI, GSI, IIP, SAS, Self-esteem	0.19	−0.04	0.39	1.64	0.10
Stevens et al. (2007)	BRT, CBT, and STDP	Cluster C or PDNOS	44	GAS, GSI, IIP, TC, WISPI	0.26	−0.03	0.50	1.77	0.08
Strauss et al. (2006)	CT for PDs	AVPD and OCPD	25	BDI, SCID II, WISPI	0.39	0.03	0.66	2.12	0.03

Table 11.3 Rupture Resolution Training/Supervision Effect Sizes

Study	Treatment	Patient diagnostic criteria	Outcome measure	Pre-post r	95% CI	Z-value	Control group	Between-groups r	95% CI	Z-value
Bambling et al. (2006)	PST with process-focused supervision (N = 34)	Major depression	BDI	0.89	0.84–0.92	15.62**	PST with no supervision (N = 38)	0.18	0.02–0.33	2.13*
Bambling et al. (2006)	PST with skills-focused supervision (N = 31)	Major depression	BDI	0.85	0.79–0.89	13.56**				
Bein et al. (2000)	TLDP (N = 32)	Interpersonal problems	GAS, GSI, IDI, MCMI	0.30	0.20–0.39	5.82**	Pretraining (n = 32)	0.09	-0.16–0.32	0.70
Castonguay et al. (2004)	ICT (N =11)	Major depression	BDI, GAF, HAM-D	0.86	0.77–0.91	9.94**	Wait list (n = 10)	0.54	0.21–0.76	3.02**
Constantino et al. (2008)	ICT (N = 11)	Major depression	BDI, BSI	0.66	0.51–0.78	6.64**	CT (n = 11)	0.19	-0.22–0.54	0.92
Crits-Christoph et al. (2006)	Alliance-fostering therapy (N = 14)	Major depression	BDI, HAM-D, QOLI	0.57	0.43–0.69	6.72**	Pretraining (n = 14)	0.15	-0.23–0.49	0.76
Hilsenroth et al. (2007)	STPP (N = 33)	Major depression and BPD	MDE criteria, BSI, GARF	0.51	0.44–0.58	11.51**	N/A			
Muran et al. (2005)	BRT (N = 33)	Cluster C PD or PD NOS	GAS, GSI, IIP, TC, WISPI	0.38	0.27–0.48	6.41**	CBT (n = 29) and STDP (n = 22)	0.02	-0.16–0.20	0.19
Newman et al. (2008)	CBT with I/EP (N = 18)	GAD	Assessor severity, daily diary, HAM-A, PSWQ, RRAQ, STAI-T	0.69	0.59–0.77	9.86**	CBT with SL (n = 3)	0.14	-0.27–0.51	0.65

Note. Although the two conditions of the Bambling et al. (2006) study are listed separately in the table, the conditions were combined to create one effect size for use in the meta-analyses.

focused on patients with Axis I disorders (depression and anxiety), and a group of studies that targeted patients with Axis II disorders or interpersonal problems. We observed that these groupings also reflected treatment length: studies targeting Axis I disorders provided between 8 and 20 sessions of treatment, while studies targeting Axis II disorders or interpersonal problems provided 25 or more sessions. With the exception of one 16-session dynamic treatment targeting major depression (Crits-Christoph et al., 2006), these groupings also reflected the theoretical orientation of the treatments administered by the therapists receiving rupture resolution training: the briefer, Axis I treatments were cognitive behavioral, while the longer treatments targeting personality and interpersonal problems were dynamic and/or relational. Mean weighted effect sizes were computed for each of these groups, and they differed significantly, $Q(1) = 10.96$, $p = 0.001$, with briefer, predominantly cognitive-behavioral treatments that targeted Axis I disorders showing more patient improvement from intake to termination ($r = 0.76$, $z = 6.62$, $p < 0.001$) than longer dynamic and relational treatments that targeted Axis II disorders or interpersonal problems ($r = 0.40$, $z = 5.34$, $p < 0.001$). The smallest pre-post effect size found was for the Vanderbilt II study. In some respects, this is not surprising given the fact that the study found that therapists' skills in some respects actually deteriorated after training, and that a majority of the therapists had not achieved basic competence in TLDP (Bein, 2000).

In contrast to the pre-post effect sizes, the between-groups effect sizes comparing rupture resolution supervision/training to a control condition were not significantly heterogeneous, $Q(6) = 7.65$, $p = 0.27$. However, to facilitate comparison with the pre-post meta-analysis, we examined potential moderators by dividing the studies into the two groups compared in the moderator analysis above. The briefer, predominantly CBT treatments targeting Axis I disorders again yielded a higher mean weighted effect size ($r = 0.22$, $z = 3.18$, $p = 0.001$) than the longer, dynamic and relational treatments targeting Axis II disorders ($r = 0.04$, $z = 0.57$, $p = 0.57$); however, the difference between the two groups failed to reach statistical significance, $Q(1) = 3.14$, $p = 0.08$.

Task-Analytic Studies

Task analysis is a programmatic research paradigm that employs a combination of qualitative and quantitative research methodologies. Since most of the task analysis research on the rupture resolution process is still at the qualitative stage, it cannot be reviewed through meta-analytic procedures. Nevertheless, the review of this emerging literature is valuable for the purpose of providing a preliminary view of ways in which the process of rupture resolution may vary in different treatments.

From a series of task-analytic studies in the 1990s (Safran & Muran, 1996; Safran et al., 1990, 1994), we developed a four-part stage model: (1) attending to the rupture marker, (2) exploring the rupture experience, (3) exploring the avoidance, and (4) emergence of wish/need. We distinguished between two types of patient communications or behaviors marking a rupture—withdrawal and confrontation markers. In withdrawal markers, the patient withdraws or partially disengages from the therapist, his or her own emotions, or some aspect of the therapeutic process. In confrontation ruptures, the patient directly expresses anger, resentment, or dissatisfaction with the therapist or some aspect of the therapy in an attempt to control the therapist.

We observed that the type of rupture marker dictated differences in the resolution process. The common progression in the resolution of withdrawal ruptures consists of moving through increasingly clearer articulations of discontent to self-assertion, in which the need for agency is realized and validated by the therapist. The progression in the resolution of confrontation ruptures consists of moving through feelings of anger, to feelings of disappointment and hurt over having been failed by the therapist, to contacting vulnerability and the wish to be nurtured and taken care of. Typical avoidant operations that emerge, regardless of rupture type, concern anxieties and self-doubts resulting from the fear of being too aggressive or too vulnerable associated with the expectation of retaliation or rejection by the therapist.

Building on this research, three studies, using the task-analytic paradigm have found preliminary evidence of somewhat similar rupture resolution procedures in other treatment modalities. Agnew, Harper, Shapiro, and Barkham (1994) tested a psychodynamic-interpersonal model of resolution of confrontation ruptures using one good-outcome case of eight-session psychodynamic-interpersonal therapy from the Sheffield study of treatment for depression. One rupture and one resolution session were selected based on changes in alliance scores measured using the Agnew Relationship Measure (ARM; Agnew-Davies, Stiles, Hardy, Barkham, & Shapiro, 1998), which was completed by the patient after each session. Consistent with Safran and Muran's resolution model, Agnew and colleagues observed that the resolution process involves the therapist acknowledging the rupture and then exploring the rupture collaboratively with the patient in order to reach a shared understanding. However, whereas Safran and Muran's model depicts resolution as a progression toward clarification of the patient's underlying wish or need, therapists in Agnew et al.'s study tended to place greater focus on linking the

alliance rupture to situations outside of therapy and discussing new ways to handle those situations.

Bennett et al. (2006) used task analysis to examine rupture resolution in cognitive-analytic therapy (CAT: Ryle, 1997) for borderline personality disorder. The task analysis was performed using 6 cases - 4 with good outcome and 2 with poor. Rupture sessions were selected based on deviations in scores on the Therapy Experience Questionnaire (TEQ: Ryle, 1995), which was completed by the patient after every session. Bennett et al. found that in good-outcome cases, therapists recognized and focused attention on the majority of ruptures, while in poor-outcome cases they usually failed to notice or draw attention to the alliance threat. They also found that therapists in good-outcome cases tended to have a nondefensive stance. However, in contrast to Safran and Muran's findngs that therapists in resolved ruptures tend to focus on the immediate process and progressive clarification of the patient's underlying needs, Bennett et al.'s therapists in good-outcome cases placed greater emphasis on linking the rupture to a preestablished case formulation and to the patient's other relationships.

Aspland, Llewelyn, Hardy, Barkham, and Stiles (2008) used task analysis procedures to begin the process of clarifying the way ruptures are successfully resolved in CBT. They examined ruptures and resolution in two good-outcome cases of CBT for depression from the Second Sheffield Psychotherapy Project (Shapiro et al., 1994). Cases were identified based on changes in alliance scores, measured using the ARM, following a naturalistic observation (Stiles et al., 2004). Two experienced clinicians examined transcripts of the sessions and identified confrontation and withdrawal markers. After close examination of rupture and resolution markers, Aspland and colleagues (2008) observed that most ruptures appeared to arise from unvoiced disagreements about the tasks and goals of therapy, which led to negative complementary interactions in which the therapist focused on the task and the patient withdrew. Resolution occurred when therapists shifted their focus from the therapy task to issues that were salient for the patient. Consistent with the other rupture resolution models described above, Aspland et al.'s (2008) preliminary model emphasized the therapist's collaborative stance, but in contrast to the other resolution models, Aspland et al.'s (2008) model did not include any overt recognition or discussion of the rupture itself. The authors noted that the lack of explicit discussion of the rupture may have been due to the predominance of withdrawal ruptures over confrontation ruptures in their sample.

Limitations of the Research

There are a number of limitations to the studies included in our meta-analyses. At this point in time, there are a limited number of relevant studies. A number of the studies are correlational in nature. The studies included were heterogeneous with respect to design, treatment modality tested, treatment length, and client population. Some of the outcome studies included were not randomized clinical trials. The majority of the outcome studies included evaluated the efficacy of alliance-focused treatments (or treatments enhanced with alliance-focused interventions) but did not directly test the hypothesis that training in the implementation of an alliance-focused treatment improved therapists' ability to work with challenging patients. Finally, none of the studies included in the meta-analyses investigated the processes through which alliance ruptures are resolved. The task-analytic research programs investigating these processes are at this point limited

in number and at an early stage of development. The most well-established research program in this area (Safran and colleagues) has some verification or hypothesis-testing data in support of its model, but even these findings are based on small samples and have not been replicated in multiple samples or by independent investigators.

Therapeutic Practices

In the first edition of *Psychotherapy Relationships That Work* (Norcross, 2002), we reviewed the existing evidence suggesting that the process of repairing alliance ruptures may be related to good positive outcome. In this chapter, we have reviewed the growing body of evidence indicating that repairing ruptures in the alliance is related to positive outcome. We have also reviewed some of the similarities and differences in principles relevant to alliance rupture resolution in different treatment approaches. On the basis of these reviews, we describe below research-supported therapeutic practices:

• Practitioners should be aware that patients often have negative feelings about the psychotherapy or the therapeutic relationship that they are reluctant to broach for fear of the therapist's reactions. It is thus important for therapists to be attuned to subtle indications of ruptures in the relationship and to take the initiative in exploring what is transpiring in the relationship when they suspect that a rupture has occurred.

• It is probably helpful for patients to express negative feelings about the therapy to the therapist should they emerge or to assert their perspective on what is going on when it differs from the therapist's.

• When this takes place, it is important for therapists to attempt to respond in an open or nondefensive fashion, and to accept responsibility for their contribution to the interaction, as opposed to blaming the patient for misunderstanding or distorting.

• It is also important for therapists to empathize with their patients' experience and to validate them for broaching a potentially divisive topic in session.

• In some forms of treatment, the primary intervention may consist of the therapist changing the tasks or goals of treatment without necessarily explicitly addressing the rupture with the patient.

• In other forms of treatment, resolving alliance ruptures may involve more in-depth exploration of what is transpiring between the therapist and patient as well as in-depth exploration of the patient's experience.

• There is also preliminary evidence to suggest that in some approaches it may be useful for the therapist to explicitly establish a link between the rupture event and characteristic interpersonal patterns in the patient's life. This evidence should, however, be interpreted cautiously in light of the growing body of evidence indicating that frequent transference interpretations linking what is taking place in the therapeutic relationship to other relationships in the patient's life can exert negative effects (e.g., Crits-Christoph & Gibbons, 2002; Henry, Strupp, Schacht, & Gaston, 1994). The quality of the interpretation (as opposed to the quantity) and the collaborative style in which it is tendered appear to make the difference between a positive and negative effect on the patient.

References

An asterisk (*) indicates studies included in the meta-analysis.

Agnew, R. M., Harper, H., Shapiro, D. A., & Barkham, M. (1994). Resolving a challenge to the therapeutic relationship: A single case study. *British Journal of Medical Psychology, 67,* 155–170.

Agnew-Davies, R., Stiles, W. B., Hardy, G. E., Barkham, M. & Shapiro, D. A. (1998). Alliance structure assessed by the Agnew Relationship Measure (ARM). *British Journal of Clinical Psychology, 37,* 155–172.

Aspland, H., Llewelyn, S., Hardy, G. E., Barkham, M., & Stiles, W. (2008). Alliance ruptures and rupture resolution in cognitive-behavior therapy: A preliminary task analysis. *Psychotherapy Research, 18,* 699–710.

*Bambling, M., King, R., Raue, P., Schweittzer, R., & Lambert, W. (2006). Clinical supervision: Its influence on client-rated working alliance and client symptom reduction in the brief treatment of major depression. *Psychotherapy Research, 16,* 317–331.

*Bein, E., Anderson, T., Strupp, H., Henry, W. P., Schacht, T. E., Binder, J., et al. (2000). The effects of training in time-limited dynamic psychotherapy: Changes in therapeutic outcome. *Psychotherapy Research, 10,* 119–132.

Bennett, D., Parry, G., & Ryle, A. (2006). Resolving threats to the therapeutic alliance in cognitive analytic therapy of borderline personality disorder: A task analysis. *Psychology and Psychotherapy: Theory, Research, and Practice, 79,* 395–418.

Bordin, E. (1979). The generalizability of the psychoanalytic concept of the working alliance. *Psychotherapy: Theory, Research, and Practice, 16,* 252–260.

Borenstein, M., Hedges, L., Higgins J., & Rothstein, H. (2005). *Comprehensive meta-analysis: Version 2,* Biostat, Englewood NJ (2005).

*Castonguay, L. G., Schut, A. J., Aikins, D., Constantino, M. J., Lawrenceau, J.P., Bologh, L., & Burns, D. (2004). Integrative cognitive therapy for depression: A preliminary investigation. *Journal of Psychotherapy Integration, 14,* 4–20.

Colli, A., Lingiardi, V. (2009). The Collaborative Interactions Scale: A new transcript-based method for the assessment of the therapeutic alliance ruptures and resolutions in psychotherapy. *Psychotherapy Research, 19,* 718–734.

*Constantino, M. J., Marnell, M. E., Haile, A. J., Kanther-Sista, S. N., Wolman, K., Zappert, L., & Arnow, B. A. (2008). Integrative cognitive therapy for depression: A randomized pilot comparison. *Psychotherapy: Theory, Research, Practice, Training, 45,* 122–134.

*Crits-Christoph, P., Gibbons, M. B., Crits-Christoph, K., Narducci, J., Schramberger, M.,

& Gallop, R. (2006). Can therapists be trained to improve their alliances? A preliminary study of alliance-fostering psychotherapy. *Psychotherapy Research, 16,* 268–281.

Eames, V., Roth, A. (2000). Patient attachment orientation and the early working alliance: A study of patient and therapist reports of alliance quality and ruptures. *Psychotherapy Research, 10,* 421–434.

Eubanks-Carter, C., Muran, J. C., & Safran, J. D. (2009). Rupture Resolution Rating System (3RS): Manual. Beth Israel Medical Center. New York: New York.

Eubanks-Carter, C. Muran, J.C., Safran, J.D., & Hayes, J. A. (2011). Interpersonal interventions for maintaining an alliance. In L.M. Horowitz & S. Strack (Eds.), *Handbook of interpersonal psychology: Theory, research, assessment, and therapeutic interventions* (pp. 519–531). Hoboken, NJ: John Wiley & Sons.

Harper, H. (1989a). *Coding guide I: Identification of confrontation challenges in exploratory therapy.* Sheffield, England: University of Sheffield.

Harper, H. (1989b). *Coding guide II: Identification of withdrawal challenges in exploratory therapy.* Sheffield, England: University of Sheffield.

Henry, W. P., Schacht, T. E., Strupp, H. H., Butler, S. F., & Binder, J. L. (1993). Effects of training in time-limited dynamic psychotherapy: Mediators of therapists' responses to training. *Journal of Consulting and Clinical Psychology, 61,* 441–447.

*Hilsenroth, M., Defife, J., Blake, M., & Cromer, T. (2007). The Effects of Borderline Pathology on Short-Term Psychodynamic Psychotherapy for Depression. *Psychotherapy Research, 17,* 175–188.

Horvath, A. O., & Bedi, R. P. (2002). The alliance. In J. C. Norcross (Ed.), *Psychotherapy relationships that work.* New York: Oxford University Press.

Horvath, A. O., & Greenberg, L. S. (1989). Development and validation of the Working Alliance Inventory. *Journal of Consulting and Clinical Psychology, 36,* 223–233.

Kohut, H. (1984). *How does analysis cure?* Chicago: University of Chicago Press.

Lansford, E. (1986). Weakenings and repairs of the working alliance in short-term psychotherapy. *Professional Psychology: Research and Practice, 17,* 364–366.

Luborsky, L., Crits-Christoph, P. (1998). *Understanding transference: The core conflictual relationship theme method* (2nd ed.). Washington DC: American Psychological Association.

Marmar, C. R., Weiss, D. S., & Gaston, L. (1989). Toward the validation of the California Therapeutic Alliance Rating System. *Psychological Assessment, 1,* 46–52.

Martin, D. J., Garske, J. P., & Davis, M. K. (2000). Relation of the therapeutic alliance with outcome and other variables: A meta-analytic review. *Journal of Counseling and Clinical Psychology, 68,* 438–450.

Mitchell, A., Eubanks-Carter, C., Safran, J. D., & Muran, J.C. (2010). Rupture resolution rating system, version 2: An observer-based measure. *Society for Psychotherapy Research Annual Conference.* June, Asilomar, California.

*Muran, J. C., Safran, J. D., Gorman, B. S., Samstag, L. W., Eubanks-Carter, C., & Winston, A. (2009). The relationship of early alliance ruptures and their resolution to process and outcome in three time-limited psychotherapies for personality disorders. *Psychotherapy: Theory, Research, Practice, Training, 46,* 233–248.

Muran, J. C., Safran, J. D., Samstag, L. W., & Winston, A. (2005). Evaluating an alliance-focused treatment for personality disorders. *Psychotherapy: Theory, Research, Practice, Training, 42,* 532–545.

*Newman, M. G., Castonguay, L. G., Borkovec, T. D., Fisher, A. J., & Nordberg, S. S. (2008). An open trial of integrative therapy for generalized anxiety disorder. *Psychotherapy: Theory, Research, Practice, Training, 45,* 135–147.

Norcross, J. C. (2002). Empirically supported therapy relationships. In J. C. Norcross (Ed.), *Psychotherapy relationships that work* (pp. 3–16). New York: Oxford University Press.

Rhodes, R., Hill, C., Thompson, B., & Elliot, R. (1994). Client retrospective recall of resolved and unresolved misunderstanding events. *Counseling Psychology, 41,* 473–483.

Ryle, A. (1995). Transference and countertransference variations in the course of cognitive-analytic therapy of two borderline patients: The relation to the diagrammatic reformulation of self-states. *British Journal of Medical Psychology, 68,* 109–124.

Ryle, A. (1997). *Cognitive analytic therapy and borderline personality disorder: The model and the method.* Chichester, UK: Wiley.

Safran, J. D., Crocker, P., McMain, S., & Murray, P. (1990). The therapeutic alliance rupture as a therapy event for empirical investigation. *Psychotherapy: Theory, Research, and Practice, 27,* 154–165.

Safran, J. D., & Muran, J. C. (1996). The resolution of ruptures in the therapeutic alliance. *Journal of Counseling and Clinical Psychology, 64,* 447–458.

Safran, J. D., & Muran, J. C. (2000). *Negotiating the therapeutic alliance: A relational treatment guide.* New York: Guilford Press.

Safran, J. D., & Muran, J. C. (2006). Has the concept of the alliance outlived its usefulness? *Psychotherapy, 43,* 286–291.

Safran, J. D., Muran, J. C., & Samstag, L. W. (1994). Resolving therapeutic alliance ruptures: A task analytic investigation. In A. O. Horvath & L. S. Greenberg (Eds.), *The working alliance: Theory, research, and practice.* (pp. 225–255). New York: Wiley.

Safran, J. D., Muran, J. C., Samstag, L. W., & Stevens, C. (2002). Repairing alliance ruptures. In J. C. Norcross (Ed.), *Psychotherapy relationships that work.* New York: Oxford University.

Samstag, L. W., Batchelder, S., Muran, J. C., Safran, J. D., & Winston, A. (1998). Predicting treatment failure from in-session interpersonal variables. *Journal of Psychotherapy Practice and Research, 5,* 126–143.

Shapiro, D., Barkham, M., Rees, A., Hardy, G. E., Reynolds, S., & Startup, M. (1994). Effects of treatment duration and severity of depression on the effectiveness of cognitive-behavioral and psychodynamic interpersonal psychotherapy. *Journal of Consulting and Clinical Psychology, 62,* 522–534.

Sommerfeld, E., Orbach, I., Zim, S., & Mikulincer, M. (2008). An in-session exploration of ruptures in working alliance and their associations with clients' core conflictual relationship themes, alliance-related discourse, and clients'

postsession evaluation. *Psychotherapy Research, 18,* 377–388.

*Stevens, C. L., Muran, J. C., Safran, J. D., Gorman, B. S., & Winston, A. (2007). Levels and patterns of the therapeutic alliance in brief psychotherapy. *American Journal of Psychotherapy, 61,* 109–129.

Stiles, W. B. (1980). Measurement of the impact of psychotherapy sessions. *Journal of Consulting and Clinical Psychology, 48,* 176–185.

*Stiles, W. B., Glick, M. J., Osatuke, K., Hardy, G. E., Shapiro, D. A., & Agnew-Davies, R. (2004). Patterns of alliance development and the rupture-repair hypothesis: Are productive relationships U-shaped or V-shaped? *Journal of Counseling Psychology, 51,* 81–92.

*Strauss, J. L., Hayes, A. M., Johnson, S.L., Newman, C. F., Brown, G. K., Barber, J. P., et al. (2006). Early alliance, alliance ruptures, and symptom change in a nonrandomized trial of cognitive therapy for avoidant and obsessive-compulsive personality disorders. *Journal of Consulting and Clinical Psychology, 74,* 337–345.

Tracey, T. J., & Kokotovic, A. M. (1989). Factor structure of the Working Alliance Inventory. *Psychological Assessment, 1,* 207–210.

Tryon, G. S., & Kane, A. S. (1990). The helping alliance and premature termination. *Counseling Psychology Quarterly, 3,* 233–238.

Tryon, G. S., & Kane, A. S. (1993). Relationship of working alliance to mutual and unilateral termination. *Journal of Counseling Psychology, 40,* 33–36.

Tryon, G. S., & Kane, A. S. (1995). Client involvement, working alliance, and type of therapy termination. *Psychotherapy Research, 5,* 189–198.

CHAPTER

12   Managing Countertransference

Jeffrey A. Hayes, Charles J. Gelso, *and* Ann M. Hummel

Authors' Note. We are grateful to Mark Hilsenroth and Marc Diener for providing consultation on the meta-analyses.

The concept of countertransference is about as old as psychotherapy itself. Like so many fundamental constructs in psychotherapy, the term was created by Freud (1910), shortly after the turn of the twentieth century. Although Freud did not write extensively about countertransference (CT), it was clear that he viewed it as problematic and needing to be managed. For example, Freud (1910, pp. 144–145) commented that: "We have begun to consider the 'counter-transference' which arises in the physician as a result of the patient's influence on his unconscious feelings, and have nearly come to the point of requiring the physician to recognize and overcome this countertransference in himself." Freud noted that anyone who fails to overcome CT may at once "give up any idea of being able to treat patients by analysis."

Freud's negative view of CT likely led to the field's neglect of the topic for many decades. It became simply something to be done away with, not something to be examined or even used beneficially. The good analyst was, in fact, thought to be capable of maintaining objectivity and keeping personal conflicts out of the therapeutic

relationship. During those early days, CT attained the status of a taboo topic.

Newer conceptions of CT, to be discussed subsequently, began emerging in the 1950s. During this decade, the first empirical studies on the topic also emerged (e.g., Cutler, 1958; Fiedler, 1951). From that point on, there has been a steady increase in both clinical and theoretical writing on CT. As is so often the case, however, empirical efforts lagged markedly behind theoretical work. Research on CT has gained momentum during the past quarter century, however, to the point where substantive reviews of the empirical literature have become possible (e.g., Fauth, 2006; Hayes, 2004; Hayes & Gelso, 2001; Rosenberger & Hayes, 2002a).

In the present chapter, we present the results of an original meta-analysis on the relation of CT to psychotherapy outcome. Particular emphasis is placed on the management of CT and its role in enhancing the success of psychotherapy. The chapter incorporates studies conducted within all research traditions: field, laboratory, survey, experimental, correlational, and qualitative. We begin by describing varying definitions of CT, identifying its common measures, and then examining research as it bears upon the question of the effects of

CT and CT management on treatment outcome.

Definitions and Measures

Four conceptions of CT have emerged as the most prominent over the years: the *classical*, the *totalistic*, the *complementary*, and the *relational* (Gelso & Hayes, 2007). In the classical definition, originated by Freud (1910), CT is seen as the therapist's unconscious, conflict-based reaction to the patient's transference. Unresolved conflicts originating in the therapist's childhood are triggered by the patient's transference and are acted out by the therapist in one way or another. Advocates of this view of CT see little or no benefit to CT. They do not generally believe CT can be used to enhance understanding, nor to promote therapeutic gain.

The totalistic conception of CT originated in the 1950s (Heimann, 1950; Little, 1951). According to this conception, CT represents *all* of the therapist's reactions to the patient. All reactions are important, all should be studied and understood, and all are usefully placed under the broad umbrella of CT. This definition served to legitimize CT and make it an object of the therapist's self-investigation and use. Accordingly, as the totalistic view gained ascendancy, CT became seen more and more as potentially beneficial to the work, if therapists studied their reactions and used them to further their understanding of patients.

In the third, or complementary, conception of CT, the therapist's reactions are viewed as a complement to the patient's style of relating (Levenson, 1995; Racker, 1957; Teyber, 1997). That is, the patient exhibits certain "pulls" on the therapist. The well-functioning therapist, however, does not act out *lex talionis* (an eye for an eye, a tooth for a tooth), even though it is the typical, and expected, reaction elicited by the patient in others. Ideally, therapists restrain their "eye-for-an-eye" impulse and seek to understand what the patient is doing to stir up these reactions. This allows for an understanding of the patient's interpersonal style of relating and for the effective framing of therapeutic interventions.

Finally, the relational perspective views CT as mutually constructed by the patient and the therapist (Mitchell, 1993). The needs, unresolved conflicts, and behaviors of both contribute to the manifestation of CT in session.

In the literature and in everyday dialogue, these four conceptions of CT are all used, confusingly and sometime in contradiction. The problem is that it is often unclear which of the four, or which combination, is intended at any given time. Many literature reviews and clinical exchanges are marred by the disparate definitions of the phenomenon.

Beyond ambiguity of usage, each of the four views of CT possesses fundamental limitations. The classical view is overly restrictive in that its focus is solely on the therapist's reactions to transference. In addition, it construes CT in almost exclusively negative terms, and it ignores the natural, inevitable reactions of the therapist that are tied to powerful "pulls" by the patient. Similarly, the totalistic position, in its attempt to encompass all of the therapist's reactions, may render the concept of CT meaningless. If all reactions are construed as CT, then no reactions are not CT, and there is no need for the term; *CT* is simply redundant with the phrase "therapist reactions." However, there are varying kinds and causes of therapist reactions and it is helpful to distinguish them. For example, adverse reactions that are due to therapists' unresolved personal conflicts may be usefully addressed in the therapist's supervision or personal treatment, whereas reactions due to inexperience or fatigue at the end of a long day require different interventions. The complementary conception is limited in the sense that, in its focus on CT as "pulls" emanating from the patient, it does not take into enough account the therapist's personality, including his or her own interpersonal style and unresolved conflicts. This same limitation applies to the relational view.

Although each of the common conceptions is seriously limited, all four point to important elements of CT. We favor an integrative definition that includes lessons from all four (Gelso & Hayes, 2007). We believe it is important to limit the definition of CT to reactions in which unresolved conflicts of the therapist are implicated. All of the therapist's reactions are significant and worthy of investigation, clinically and empirically, but the definition of CT must be narrower than the totalistic one if it is to be scientifically useful and clinically meaningful. Whereas our conception of CT is similar to the classical view in its focus on the therapist's unresolved conflicts as the source of CT, it is different in that CT is seen as a potentially useful phenomenon if therapists successfully understand their reactions and use them to help understand the patient. Thus, in seeing CT as both a hindrance and a potential benefit to treatment, an integrative definition picks up on the two thematic constructs that have been intertwined, like a double helix, throughout the history of thought about CT (Epstein & Feiner, 1988). In addition, like the totalistic position, we consider CT to be inevitable. This is so because all therapists, by virtue of their humanity, have unresolved conflicts, personal vulnerabilities, and unconscious "soft spots" that are touched upon in one's work. Finally, like the complementary and relational views, our integrative definition of CT does not simply focus on the therapist's reaction to the patient's transference.

Rather, it incorporates the therapist's reaction to all clinically relevant material, including the patient's personality style, the actual content that the patient is presenting, and even the patient's appearance.

Measuring CT

Despite the history of definitional inconsistency, most empirical studies on CT have employed a definition that implicates the therapist's unresolved conflicts as the source, often with one or more characteristics of the patient as the trigger. Furthermore, most research on CT has examined either internal or external manifestations of CT. As an internal emotional state, CT may be reflected in therapist anxiety, anger, boredom, despair, arousal, disgust, and so on. These feelings not only range in valence from highly pleasant to highly unpleasant, but they also vary in intensity, from too intense to not strong enough. To measure CT emotions, researchers have used instruments such as the State Anxiety Inventory (cf. Hayes & Gelso, 1991, 1993) and the Therapist Appraisal Questionnaire (cf. Fauth & Hayes, 2006), as well as qualitative methods (Hayes et al., 1998).

As an internal cognitive phenomenon, CT may manifest itself in therapists' failure to accurately recall therapy-specific events and to misperceive clients as overly similar to or dissimilar from themselves (Cutler, 1958; Gelso, Fassinger, Gomez, & Latts, 1995). To measure these cognitive aspects of CT, researchers have compared the therapist's perception of the session or client with objective or factual data (e.g., from transcripts of sessions or personality assessments).

In terms of overt behavior, CT typically has been studied as the therapist's withdrawal, underinvolvement, or avoidance of the patient's material or, at times, as therapists' overinvolvement with patients. These assessments typically are made by trained raters who assess transcripts and/or tapes of therapy sessions (e.g., Rosenberger & Hayes, 2002b). CT behavior also has been measured via raters' or clinical supervisors' assessments of therapists' behavior on a one-item measure (the CT Index; Hayes, Riker, & Ingram, 1997), the 21-item Index of Countertransference Behavior (ICB; Friedman & Gelso, 2000), or the 10-item Countertransference Behavior Measure (CBM; Mohr, Gelso, & Hill, 2005). The ICB contains two subscales reflecting CT behaviors that have a positive (e.g., befriending the client) or negative (e.g., punishing the client) valence. The CBM contains items that reflect therapist behaviors that are dominant, hostile, or distant. More recently, a Countertransference Measure was developed via experts' ratings of prototypical CT reactions (Hofsess & Tracey, 2010).

Generally, CT behavior is seen as hindering because it is based more on the therapist's needs than the patient's. Internal CT, on the other hand, is seen as potentially helpful. If therapists can understand these reactions and how they may relate to the patient's inner life and behavior, then this understanding can facilitate work with the patient. Such management of CT has been measured almost exclusively with the 50-item Countertransference Factors Inventory (CFI; Van Wagoner, Gelso, Hayes, & Diemer, 1991) or one of two abbreviated, revised versions (CFI-D; Gelso, Latts, Gomez, & Fassinger, 2002; CFI-R, Hayes et al., 1997). The CFI contains items tapping therapists' CT-relevant tendencies in general, whereas the CFI-R contains 27 items from the CFI that were rated highly by experts in a content validity study (Hayes, Gelso, Van Wagoner, & Diemer, 1991). The CFI-D contains 21 items only about the therapist's functioning during psychotherapy.

All three versions of the CFI contain five subscales reflecting therapist attributes thought to be important to successful CT management: self-insight, self-integration, anxiety management, empathy, and conceptualizing ability. *Self-insight* refers to the extent to which the therapists are aware of and understand their own feelings, attitudes, personalities, motives, and histories. *Self-integration* taps the therapist's possession of an intact, basically healthy character structure. In the therapy interaction, self-integration manifests itself as an ability to differentiate self from other. *Anxiety management* refers to therapists allowing themselves to experience anxiety and possessing the internal skill to control and understand anxiety so that it does not bleed over into their responses to patients. *Empathy*, or the ability to partially identify with and put one's self in the other's shoes, permits the therapist to focus on the patient's needs despite difficulties he or she may be experiencing in the moment. Finally, *conceptualizing ability* reflects the therapist's ability to draw on theory and understand the patient's role in the therapeutic relationship.

Although the CFI, CFI-R, and CFI-D can be completed via self-report (e.g., Rosenberger & Hayes, 2002b), in most research supervisors have assessed trainee CT management. In fact, trainees seem to have difficulty accurately assessing their own CT management abilities (Hayes et al., 1997; Hofsess & Tracey, 2010). In some studies, typically those conducted prior to the development of the CFI, several of the constructs measured by the CFI were assessed via other instruments, such as the Empathy Scale of the Barrett-Lennard Relationship Inventory (Peabody & Gelso, 1982), a measure of the ability to conceptually understand CT reactions (Robbins & Jolkovski, 1987), and a self-awareness index (Williams, Hurley, O'Brien, & Degregorio, 2003).

Clinical Example

Examples of countertransference are ubiquitous. They range from the obvious, aggressive acting out to more subtle, seductive comments. We suspect that in many or even most cases in which the therapist's intense reaction is a "natural" response to the patient, therapist unresolved conflicts are implicated. An example helps illustrate this point.

The trainee was in her fourth practicum of a doctoral training program and by every indication appeared to have extraordinary potential as a psychotherapist. In the early part of her treatment with a 20-year-old male patient, she experienced continued strong irritation, and she reacted to the patient in a controlled, muted, and metallic manner. For his part, the patient was an angry, obsessional young man suffering from many borderline features. He negated the therapist's attempts to help him understand how his conflicts might be contributing to his ongoing problems with women, and he denied that the treatment could have any impact. Also, he usually negated the therapist's observations about what he might be feeling. Clearly the therapist's emotional reactions were "natural," given the patient's negativity and hostility. Yet, the therapist's unresolved anxieties about not being good enough, about fearing that she could not take care of others sufficiently, and about some transference-based fears of her supervisor's evaluation of her were clearly implicated in her irritation and her muted reaction to the patient. As she came to understand these dynamics, her irritation with the patient lessened, and she empathically grasped the terrifying emotions that were underlying much of his negativity.

Had the supervisor rated this trainee's in-session behavior on the CFI early in her work with the client, CFI items that might have captured her difficulties managing CT include "does not become overly anxious in the presence of most client problems" and "is able to manage her need for approval."

The therapist's eventual success managing her CT may have been captured in items on the CFI that reflected her ability "to distinguish between the client's needs and her own needs," her capacity to "restrain herself from excessively identifying with clients' conflicts," and her ability to "conceptualize her role in what transpires in the counseling relationship."

Meta-Analytic Review

In the following sections, we present meta-analytic findings pertaining to CT and its management, particularly in relation to psychotherapy outcome. First, we establish that CT reactions themselves plausibly influence outcome by reviewing research evidence on the association of CT to outcome t. Second, we examine studies that address whether CT management reduces actual CT reactions. Third, we review the research that bears directly on the relationship between CT management and outcome. For each of these questions, both quantitative and qualitative research is reviewed, and the findings from quantitative research are summarized in meta-analytic form.

Search Strategy

The literature search for identifying possible articles for the meta-analyses involved three strategies. First, the reference lists of two comprehensive reviews of the literature were consulted (Gelso & Hayes, 2007; Rosenberger & Hayes, 2002a). Second, a search of PsycINFO and the Psychology and Behavioral Sciences Collection was conducted by title, keyword, and subject for the term "countertransference." Finally, EBSCO databases offers a feature called "related articles," which suggests articles similar to an article being viewed; suggested articles that had not already been found through the first two search methods were considered for the meta-analyses.

A total of 126 articles and dissertations were identified in these ways. We subsequently analyzed whether they were quantitative studies. Fifty-five published articles and 21 dissertations were categorized as quantitative studies.

These studies were then analyzed by three coders coming to consensus to determine suitability for the meta-analyses. For inclusion, each study needed to include at least two of three variables: CT, CT management, and psychotherapy outcome. Thus, studies that focused simply on predictors of CT that did not include outcome or CT management were not considered suitable for the meta-analyses. Some studies included variables that could be considered proxies for the three variables of interest (see the distinction between big O and little o outcome in Greenberg & Pinsof, 1986). For example, working alliance and session evaluation could be considered proximal outcomes; self-awareness could be considered a type of CT management. Studies that used proxies of criterion variables were included and coded. The studies were coded by one male doctoral-level psychologist (second author), one female counseling psychology doctoral student (third author), and one female postbaccalaureate research assistant. All published articles were coded simultaneously by the three coders, although each coder also previewed articles independently and then coded the articles together with the other two coders. Dissertations were coded independently by the postbaccalaureate coder and then reviewed by all three coders, who reached consensus on the coding for each dissertation. Disagreements on coding were resolved through discussion until consensus was achieved. Of the 55 published articles, 22 were found to be suitable for the meta-analysis; of the 21 dissertations, 5 were suitable. Two dissertations had been subsequently published as articles, so the

published articles were included in the meta-analyses in place of the dissertations.

Study Coding

Characteristics that were coded for each study included research design (correlational or experimental), research setting (field or lab), outcome type (proximal or distal), therapist type, client type, participant demographics, and the inferential statistics reported. Using an established method (Chatzisarantis & Stoica, 2009), moderators were tested in each meta-analysis when there were a sufficient number of studies in each category. Mediators were considered for coding, but there were no reported instances of mediation in the studies.

Statistical Methods

Because the goal of the meta-analysis was to obtain overall weighted rs for the relationships between each set of variables, results that that did not report correlation coefficients were converted to rs (see Diener et al., 2008; Rosenthal & DiMatteo, 2001). In some cases, authors were contacted to provide additional data, such as secondary tests or additional statistics when nonsignificant findings were reported. These instances are noted in Tables 12.1, 12.2, and 12.3, which present the coded studies. Average rs were calculated for studies that reported multiple results, so that each study had one r to contribute to the overall meta-analyses (Diener et al., 2008). The Hunter-Schmidt random-effects model was used to calculate an average weighted r and 95% confidence intervals. A χ^2 was calculated to test for homogeneity of effect sizes in each meta-analysis. We also report the standard deviation of the weighted rs. Note that when confidence intervals do not overlap, $p < 0.05$.

Although unpublished dissertations were included in the meta-analyses, it is possible that other studies exist that were not

Table 12.1 Summary of Studies Relating Countertransference to Outcome

Authors	Year	Design	Setting	Predictor	Criterion	Outcome	Moderator	N	Therapists	Clients	% Male	Ethnicity (% white)	Age mean (SD)	CT rater type	r	p value 1-tailed
Bandura, Lipsher, & Miller	1960	Corr	Field	Approach-avoidance	Hostility	Proximal		12 TH 17 CL	Prof	Parents	83 TH	Not reported	Not reported	Observer	-0.53	0.04
Yeh & Hayes	2010	Exp	Lab	TH disclosure	CL rated TH quality & session quality	Proximal		116	Video	Video	22	88	21 (18–44)	Student-participant	-0.38	0.00
Williams & Fauth *	2005	Corr	Lab	Negative stress	Session eval.	Proximal		18 TH 18 CL	Mix	Students	28 TH 11 CL	94 TH 75 CL	TH ´36(10.3) CL ´ 22 (8.2)	TH	-0.37	0.07
Hayes, Yeh, & Eisenberg*	2007	Corr	Field	Missing (subscale of TRIG)	TH empathy, CERS, WAI-S, SEQ-D	Proximal		69 TH 69 CL	Bereavement TH	Clients	19 TH 10 CL	89 TH 93 CL	53.5 (8.6) TH 46.5 (12.8) CL	TH	-0.03	0.40
Hayes, Riker, & Ingram	1997	Corr	Field	CT behavior	Composite CSAB	Distal	Case success	20 TH; 20 CL	Trainees	Students	25 TH 50 CL	80 TH 85 CL	30.8 (7.4) TH 25.4 (7.0) CL	TH Supervisor observer	-0.33	0.08
Ligiéro & Gelso	2002	Corr	Field	Negative CT	Working alliance	Proximal		50	Trainees	Students	26	70	Not reported	TH	-0.32	0.01
Rosenberger & Hayes	2002b	Corr	Field	CT avoidance behavior	WAI, EAT, SEQ	Proximal	None	1 TH 1 CL	Prof	Student	0 TH 0 CL	100 TH 100 CL	TH = 34 CL = 21	TH	-0.06	0.42
Cutler	1958	Corr	Field	CT (conflicted/nonconflicted area)	Task vs. ego-oriented responses	Proximal		2 TH 5 CL	Trainees	Students, Veterans	100 TH	Not reported	Not reported	Observer	-0.24	0.30
Myers & Hayes	2006	Exp	Lab	CT	EAT; session quality	Proximal	Working alliance	224	Video	Students	33	89	20.4	Exp. Manipulation	-0.04	0.28
Mohr, Gelso, & Hill*	2005	Corr	Lab	CT behavior	Session eval– depth, smoothness	Proximal		88 CL 27 TH 12 Sup	Trainees	Students	13 TH 7 Super 93 CL	Not reported	Not reported	Supervisor	-0.04	0.37

Note: diss = dissertation; corr = correlational, exp = experimental; TH = therapist, CL = client, prof = professional; sup = supervisor.
* Additional data were provided by the authors.

Table 12.2 Summary of Studies Relating Countertransference Management to Countertransference

Authors	Year	Design	Setting	Predictor	Criterion	Outcome	Moderator	N	Therapists	Clients	% Male	Ethnicity (% white)	Age mean (SD)	CT rater type	r	p value 1-tailed
Friedman & Gelso	2000	Corr	Field	CFI-R	Inventory of CT Behavior	Distal		149	Prof	Clients	58	91	49 (8.7)	Supervisor	−0.59	0.00
Hofsess & Tracey	2010	Corr	Field	CFI	Experiences with CT	Distal		35 TH 12 Sup	Trainees	In general	20 TH 42 Sup	54 TH 67 Sup	28 TH 38 Sup (SD not reported)	TH	−0.57	0.00
Latts & Gelso	1995	Corr	Lab	Awareness of feelings; use of theory	Avoidance	Distal	Awareness of feelings and use of theory	47.00	Trainees	Video	65.00	25	29 (SD not reported)	Observer	−0.45	0.00
Williams & Fauth [*]	2005	Corr	Lab	Self-awareness	Negative stress	Proximal		18 TH 18 CL	Mix	Students	28 TH 11 CL	94 TH 75 CL	36 (10.3) TH 22 (8.22) CL	TH	−0.43	0.00
Williams, Hurley, O'Brien, & Degregorio	2003	Corr	Field	Management strategies	Hindering self-awareness	Proximal		301	Prof	In general	44.00	92	51.2 (9.3)	TH	0.29	0.04
Peabody & Gelso	1982	Corr	Field	Therapist empathy	CT behavior	Proximal		20 TH-CL pairs	Trainees	Students and video	100 TH 0 CL	Not reported	Not reported	Observer	−0.24	0.15

Hayes, Riker, & Ingram	1997	Corr	Field	CFI-R	CT Index; avoidance	Distal	CT rater	20 TH 20 CL	Trainees	Students	25 TH 50 CL	80 TH 85 CL	31 (7.4) TH 25 (7) CL (*SD* not reported)	TH sup observer	−0.18 0.22
Kholooci	2007	Corr	Field	Mindfulness	CT Questionnaire	Distal		203	Mix	Client	30 TH 36 CL	90 TH 80 CL	42 TH 40 CL (*SD* not reported)	TH	−0.15 0.19
Forester	2001	Corr	Field	Body awareness	Vicarious traumatization	Proximal		96	Prof	In general	33	60	39.4 (*SD* not reported)	TH	−0.10 0.17
Robbins & Jolkovski	1987	Corr	Lab	Awareness of feelings; use of theory	Withdrawal of involvement	Distal	Awareness of feelings and use of theory	58	Trainees	Video	53	91	29 (5.3)	Observer	−0.04 0.38
Gelso, Fassinger, Gomez, & Latts	1995	Exp	Lab	CFI	Cognitive, affective, behavioral CT	Distal	Sexual orientation of client	68	Trainees	Video	29	56	Not reported	TH, observer	−0.04 0.40

Note. diss = dissertation; corr = correlational; exp = experimental; TH = therapist; CL = client; prof = professional; sup = supervisor; CFI = the Countertransference Factors Inventory.
* Additional data were provided by the authors.

Table 12.3 Summary of Studies Relating Countertransference Management to Outcome

Authors	Year	Design	Setting	Predictor	Criterion	Outcome	Moderator	N	Therapists	Clients	% Male	Ethnicity (% white)	Age mean (SD)	CTMGMT rater type	r	p value 1-tailed
Latts	1996	Corr	Field	CFI	TH effectiveness	Proximal	None	77 TH 77 Sup	Trainees	Not reported	29 TH 42 sup	69 TH 74 Sup	29 TH 41 Sup (SD not reported)	Sup	0.89	0.00
Van Wagoner, Gelso, Hayes, & Diemer	1991	Exp	Lab	CFI	TH excellence	Proximal	None	122	Prof	None	36 TH	Not reported	47.90 (SD not reported)	Study participants	0.55	0.00
Peabody & Gelso	1982	Corr	Field	Openness to CT feelings	TH empathy	Proximal	None	20 TH–CL pairs	Trainees	Students	100 TH 0 CL	Not reported	Not reported	Observer	0.42	0.03
Gelso, Latts, Gomez, & Fassinger	2002	Corr	Field	CFI	TH-rated CL outcome; Sup rated CL outcome	Distal	None	32 TH 15 Sup 63 CL	Trainees	Students	34 TH 40 Sup CL not reported	Not reported	29 (5.5) TH Sup not reported CL not reported	TH Sup	0.39	0.01
Williams & Fauth*	2005	Corr	Lab	Self-awareness	Session eval	Proximal	None	18 TH 18 CL	Mix	Students	28 TH 11 CL	94 TH 75 CL	36 (10.3) TH 22 (8.22) CL	TH	0.18	0.25
Fauth & Williams	2005	Corr	Lab	Self-awareness	CL rated TH helpfulness	Proximal	None	17 TH 17 CL	Trainees; undergrads with counseling experience	Students	35 TH 24 CL	65 TH 82 CL	24.3 (6.26) TH 21.9 (3.76) CL	TH	0.17	0.00
Rosenberger & Hayes	2002b	Corr	Field	CFI-R	WAI, EAT, SEQ	Proximal	None	1 TH 1 CL	Prof	Student	0 TH 0 CL	100 TH 100 CL	TH = 34 CL = 21	TH	0.38	0.00

Note: dis = dissertation, corr = correlational; exp = experimental; TH = therapist, CL = client, prof = professional; sup = supervisor; CFI = the Countertransference Factors Inventory; MGMT = management; WAI = Working Alliance Inventory, SEQ = Session Evaluation Questionnaire, and EAT = Expertness, Attractiveness, Trustworthiness.
* Additional data were provided by the authors.

included, such as masters theses or studies that were not published. Thus, a file drawer analysis (Diener et al., 2008) was used to calculate how many studies with null results would be necessary to bring the weighted average r to equal 0.10 and 0.20. The statistical program used for the meta-analysis can be accessed at www.informaworld.com/mpp/uploads/metaanalysisprogramv.3.4.xls (Diener et al., 2008).

Do CT Reactions Affect Psychotherapy Outcomes?

Treatment outcomes exist on a continuum from immediate to distal. Immediate outcomes pertain to the effects of or on a given phenomenon within the session, whereas distal outcomes address the effects of treatment on client functioning at the end of treatment or after termination. In between immediate and distal outcomes reside a wide range of what might be called proximate outcomes: those pertaining to a given session or series of sessions, as well those presumed to be the way station for more distal outcomes. For example, increased patient experiencing may be seen as proximal to improvement in patient interpersonal functioning, itself a more distal outcome.

A striking feature of the empirical CT literature is the limited amount of research seeking to connect CT to more distal outcomes. We shall have more to say about this later, but for now we simply note that nearly all research on CT effects focuses on immediate or proximate outcomes.

The 10 quantitative studies permitted a numerical estimate of the relationship between CT and outcome. A summary of the studies is presented in Table 12.1. The average weighted r of CT with outcome in these studies was significant and small ($r = -.16$; 95% confidence interval = $-.26$ to $-.06$). File drawer analysis indicates that 6 studies with null findings with an average sample size of 60 would have to exist for the average weighted r to be increased to $-.10$. The test for heterogeneity was not significant ($\chi^2 = 16.31, p = 0.06$), with 46% of the observed variance due to true differences between studies ($I^2 = 46.15\%$). The standard deviation of the rs from the 10 studies was 0.16, and the range of rs was $-.53 \leq r \leq -.03$. The hypothesis that CT is inversely related to outcome was supported by the meta-analysis, though the relationship appears modest.

Type of outcome (proximal vs. distal) was found to moderate the overall weighted r. Studies with distal outcomes had a higher ($p < 0.05$) average r ($k = 3$; $r = -.36$; 95% confidence interval: $-.40$ to $-.32$; $I^2 = 0\%$) than studies with proximal outcomes ($k = 7$; $r = -.09$; 95% confidence interval: $-.18$ to 0.01; $I^2 = 4.11\%$).

In what follows, we illustrate these meta-analytic results with select studies. One of the first studies of CT demonstrated that CT can have detrimental effects (Cutler, 1958). The work of two therapist-trainees was examined in depth, and it was found that when patient material was related to areas of unresolved conflict in the therapist, the therapist's interventions were judged by supervisors to be less effective. These findings are comparable with those from a more recent study that detected that therapist experience of stress in session was associated with poorer evaluations of the sessions (Williams & Fauth, 2005). Similar results were found in a case study of 13 therapy sessions conducted by an experienced female therapist (Rosenberger & Hayes, 2002b). In particular, the more the patient talked about topics that were related to unresolved conflict in the therapist, the less the therapist perceived herself as expert, attractive, and trustworthy, and the more she viewed sessions as shallow.

The aforementioned case study also reported an inverse relation between CT behavior and the working alliance

(Rosenberger & Hayes, 2002b). Specifically, the more avoidance behavior the therapist exhibited in the work, the lower were her ratings of the overall alliance. Also, trained judges' ratings of avoidant behavior in sessions were related to the bond aspect of the working alliance, as assessed by both the therapist and the client. The greater the amount of avoidance behavior, the weaker was both participants' experience of their working alliance bond. One possible explanation for these findings is that avoidance behavior on the therapist's behalf can suppress expression of affect by patients (Bandura, Lipsher, & Miller, 1960), thus limiting the emotional bond between therapists and patients.

CT also was found to be negatively related to the alliance in a field study of 51 doctoral students and their clinical supervisors (Ligiéro & Gelso, 2001). Supervisors rated therapists' CT behavior during the middle phase of treatment. Both supervisors and therapists rated the working alliance between therapists and their clients. Results indicated that negative CT behavior was inversely related to both supervisor ($r = -0.58$) and therapist ($r = -0.34$) ratings of the working alliance. Also, positive CT (e.g., too much support, colluding with the client) related negatively to supervisors' ratings of the bond aspect of the alliance ($r = -0.36$). Thus, negative CT behavior, and perhaps positive CT as well, seems to be associated with the development of weaker alliances.

In a rare study that examined the relation of CT to distal outcome, 20 cases of brief therapy conducted by therapist-trainees were examined (Hayes et al., 1997). Supervisors observed each session and rated CT. For the less successful cases, a strong negative relationship was found between CT behavior as rated by both supervisor ($r = -0.87$) and counselor ($r = -0.69$) and a composite measure of outcome rated by therapists,

supervisors, and clients. For the more successful cases, however, no relationship was found. The authors speculated that in the more successful cases, a strong working alliance mitigated the negative effects of CT.

Several qualitative studies, not included in our meta-analyses, also have examined the effects of CT. In one of these, (Hill, Nutt-Williams, Heaton, Thompson, & Rhodes, 1996), factors that cause impasses, or disagreements between clients and therapists, that end in termination were examined. The researchers studied 12 experienced therapists of varying theoretical persuasions, and each reported on one case with such an impasse. As expected, many factors were found to be implicated in the impasses, and CT was among the most prominent. Most therapists indicated that their own personal conflicts were involved in the impasses. For example, two therapists had a parent who had committed suicide, which led the therapists to feel especially vulnerable when their clients threatened suicide.

In another qualitative study, 11 experienced therapists were interviewed to examine their reactions to transference in cases of successful, long-term dynamic therapy (Gelso, Hill, Mohr, Rochlen, & Zack, 1999). Even within these successful cases, therapists reported many instances of CT. An example of CT was a case in which the "therapist reported that he admired the client for doing things in his life that the therapist could not do, and at the same time enjoyed being idealized by the client. Tied to these reactions, the therapist felt he did not give the client enough permission to express negative transference feelings" (p. 264).

In another qualitative study, the focus was entirely on CT (Hayes et al., 1998). Eight experienced therapists identified as experts by peers each treated one patient for between 12 and 20 sessions. Therapists identified CT as operative in fully 80% of their 127 sessions, and it appeared that CT was prominent in each case. Such findings support the proposition that CT is a universal phenomenon in therapy, even when defined from an integrative rather than totalistic perspective (Gelso & Hayes, 1998, 2007). The findings, of course, run counter to what may be seen as the Freudian myth that good therapists do not experience CT. As regards the effects of CT on treatment outcome, the data contained evidence of both hindering and facilitative effects. For example, one therapist was too immersed in her CT issues of strength and independence to connect with her dependent client and help her work through her problems. On the other hand, another therapist was able to make use of her CT-based needs to nurture and be a good parent by appropriately supporting and being patient with her client. The researchers offered the working hypothesis that "the more resolved an intrapsychic conflict is for a therapist, the greater the likelihood that the therapist will be able to use his or her countertransference therapeutically (e.g., to deepen one's understanding of the client)" (p. 478). Conversely, the less resolved the conflict, the greater the likelihood that CT will have antitherapeutic effects.

In sum, then, the results of both quantitative and qualitative studies support the idea that CT does adversely affect outcomes.

Does CT Management Reduce CT Manifestations?

Since the 1950s, the clinical literature on CT has been replete with writing about its potential to aid therapy. A fundamental concept in this literature is that if CT is to be a help rather than a hindrance, the therapist must do something to, with, or about CT, other than acting it out in therapy. A significant aspect of all of this may be termed CT management.

We conducted a meta-analysis to summarize findings from 11 quantitative studies pertaining to the relationship between CT management and CT. Here, studies were selected that explicitly employed the term CT management, or incorporated processes that were clearly indicative of therapists' control of and effort to manage their countertransference reactions (e.g., therapist self-awareness, therapist use of mindfulness). The average weighted r for the relation between CT management and CT was significant and small, $r = -.14$, 95% confidence interval: -0.30 to -0.03. Four studies with null findings with an average sample size of 89 would have to exist for the average weighted r to be increased to -0.10. The test for heterogeneity was significant ($\chi^2 = 76.89$, $p < 0.01$), with about 89% of the observed variance due to true between-study differences ($I^2 = 88.79\%$). The standard deviation of the rs was 0.28, and the range was $-0.59 \leq r \leq 0.18$, indicating variability in effect sizes among the studies. Overall, the expectation that CT management is negatively related to CT was supported by the results of the meta-analysis.

Operationalization of CT management was found to moderate the overall weighted r. Studies using the CFI had a larger ($p < 0.05$) average r ($k = 4$; $r = -0.46$; 95% confidence interval: -0.68 to -0.24; $I^2 = 80.15\%$) than studies using other CT management measures ($k = 7$; $r = -0.03$; 95% confidence interval of -0.17 to 0.12; $I^2 = 79.32\%$). CT rater also was found to moderate the overall weighted r. When therapists rated their own CT, the average r ($k = 5$; $r = -0.02$; 95% confidence interval of -0.21 to 0.17; $I^2 = 31.58\%$) was smaller (p < 0.05) than when supervisors or other observers rated CT ($k = 3$; $r = -0.53$; 95% confidence interval: -0.65 to -0.41; $I^2 = 44.79\%$). A summary of the studies is presented in Table 12.2. Taken together, these studies suggest that CT management ability aids therapists in containing their CT responses in sessions.

Here we present the findings of several studies to amplify and illustrate these meta-analytic results. Reich (1960) observed many years ago that therapy involves a partial identification with the patient. In this identification, the therapist seeks to understand and feel, perhaps even viscerally, the patient's experience. In this way, then, the therapist's internal experience is an important clue to what is going on with the patient beyond the surface. If the process is to work effectively, however, the therapist has to swing to an "outside" position and inspect what is being experienced. In Reich's words, therapists "should be alert to our own feelings, stop to investigate them, and analyze what is going on" (p. 392). In this statement, three factors are highlighted that may be fundamental to CT management: therapist empathy (partial identification), awareness of CT feelings, and the ability to make sense of these feelings.

An initial study on CT management addressed these three factors (Peabody & Gelso, 1982). In a sample of 20 trainees, therapists' general empathic ability related negatively to CT behavior under conditions the researchers speculated to be the most threatening to therapists. Further, the greater their empathic ability, the more openness these therapists had to their CT feelings. Empathic ability and openness to CT feelings (two of Reich's factors) appear to be interrelated as expected, and empathy may prevent CT behavior when the therapist deals with threatening material.

In support of these laboratory findings with trainees, the central role that empathy plays in managing CT also was identified in a qualitative study of 12 highly experienced therapists (Baehr, 2004). This same study suggested that therapists' self-care behaviors between sessions, such as meditating, resting, reading for pleasure, exercising, and not overscheduling patients, were helpful in reducing the incidence and intensity of CT behaviors during sessions.

Robbins and Jolkovski (1987) similarly reasoned that CT management would be aided by therapists' openness to CT feelings (referred to as CT awareness). However, they also theorized that another of Reich's factors, ability to analyze and make sense of these feelings, was implicated. They operationalized the latter as what they called the "theoretical framework" or the extent to which the therapist uses formal or informal theory to explain the events of the hour, or make them intelligible. Fifty-eight trainees listened and responded verbally at certain stopping points to an audiotaped client as if they were working with the client. It was found that awareness of CT feelings, as expected, was associated with fewer CT behaviors. Also, CT awareness and theoretical framework interacted, such that high awareness and high theoretical framework resulted in the least CT behavior, whereas use of theory in conjunction with low awareness resulted in the most CT behavior. These findings were replicated in a subsequent study despite the fact that different stimulus materials were used (Latts & Gelso, 1995). Similarly, a recent study (Hofsess & Tracey, 2010) found that trainees' conceptual abilities, in and of themselves, were not predictive of actual CT behavior. Thus, a merely intellectual approach to managing CT appears ineffective, at best. However, when one is aware of CT feelings and utilizes theory to understand them, CT management seems most effective.

Does CT Management Improve Psychotherapy Outcomes?

The previous two sections of the chapter have established that CT is associated, though modestly, with less desirable psychotherapy outcomes and that effective CT management is associated with decreased CT reactions. By extension, then, it could be inferred that effective CT management enhances psychotherapy outcomes.

We conducted a meta-analysis on the seven identified studies that addressed the relation between CT management and treatment outcome. A summary of the studies is presented in Table 12.3. The average weighted r of CT management to outcome was significant and large, $r = 0.56$ (95% confidence interval: 0.40 to 0.73). Thirty-two studies with null findings with an average sample size of 41 would have to exist for the average weighted r to be reduced to 0.10. The test for heterogeneity was significant ($\chi^2 = 31.8$, $p < 0.01$), with 88% of the variance reflecting real differences in effect size ($I^2 = 88.03\%$). The standard deviation of the rs was 0.23, and the range was $0.17 \leq r \leq 0.89.$, indicating that there is variability in effect sizes among the studies. An analysis of the distribution suggested that the $r = 0.89$ could be an outlier. When that finding was excluded from the meta-analysis, the average weighted r still was significant and large ($r = 0.45$; 95% confidence interval: 0.34 to 0.56; $I^2 = 0\%$). Even with this reduction in data, the hypothesis that CT management is positively related to outcome is supported.

Operationalization of CT management was found to moderate the relationship between CT management and outcome. The average r for studies using the CFI ($k = 4$, $r = 0.64$; 95% confidence interval: 0.45 to 0.82; $I^2 = 36.69\%$) was higher ($p < 0.05$) than for studies using other measures of CT management ($k = 3$, $r = 0.26$; 95% confidence interval of 0.13 to 0.40; $I^2 = 0\%$). Sample size also was a moderator. For testing the effects of sample size, the distribution of sample size appeared bimodal, so the studies were split at the median ($n = 32$). The average r of studies with larger samples ($k = 3$; $r = 0.64$, 95% confidence interval: 0.43 to 0.85; $I^2 = 94.53\%$) was higher ($p < 0.05$) than that of studies with smaller samples ($k = 4$; $r = 0.27$, 95% confidence interval: 0.15 to 0.38; $I^2 = 0\%$). Finally, CT management rater was found to moderate the overall weighted r as well. When therapists rated their own CT management, the average r ($k = 3$; $r = 0.18$; 95% confidence interval: 0.13 to 0.24, $I^2 = $ indeterminate) was lower ($p < 0.05$) than when others rated the therapists' CT management ($k = 4$; $r = 0.62$; 95% confidence interval: 0.44 to 0.81; $I^2 = 39\%$).

Below we review a couple of studies in the meta-analysis to flush out the numerical results. In a mail survey, 122 therapists rated either a particular therapist whom they considered to be excellent or therapists in general on the CFI (Van Wagoner et al., 1991). Excellent therapists were rated more favorably on all five CFI factors than therapists in general. These results are consistent with a study that found that overall CT management ability was directly associated with 77 supervisors' ratings of their trainees' therapeutic excellence (Latts, 1996).

Although such studies present results relevant to outcome, each captures only proximal aspects of outcome. Only one study to date has directly assessed the relation of CT management to distal therapy outcome (Gelso et al., 2001). In this study, 32 therapist-trainees and their supervisors rated treatment outcomes of one case, while the supervisors also evaluated the supervisees' CT management ability on the CFI. Outcome ratings by both therapists and supervisors (controlling for initial level of client disturbance) were positively related to supervisor-rated CFI scores overall and on three of the five subscales.

Taken together, the quantitative findings on CT management are promising. It appears that such management is a characteristic of therapists seen as excellent by their peers, aids in controlling the manifestation of CT, and is probably related to treatment outcome. In addition to these quantitative studies, five qualitative investigations (Baehr, 2004; Gelso et al., 1999; Hayes et al., 1998; Hill et al., 1996; Williams et al., 1997) all point to the importance of CT management in the judgment of therapists whose views about particular clients were studied. These qualitative studies are especially significant in that four of them sampled highly experienced therapists.

Patient Contribution

Perhaps as much as any relationship element addressed in this book, CT management is largely up to psychotherapists. If therapists evidence specific attributes (e.g., self-awareness) or engage in particular activities (e.g., meditation), they may be better positioned to manage CT. At the same time, there are certain patients who are simply more difficult for most therapists to work with, and these patients are likely to evoke CT reactions that are challenging to manage. The patient influences the therapist to a marked degree and in predictable ways (Singer & Luborsky, 1977). Two studies found surprisingly similar results in their surveys of psychotherapists' perceptions of stressful client behavior (Deutsch, 1984; Farber, 1983). In both studies, suicidal statements were the most stressful type of client behavior. Others were aggression and hostility, severe depression, apathy or lack of motivation, and agitated anxiety. From a different perspective, the APA Insurance Trust has identified types of patients who are more likely to result in unfavorable outcomes and increased probability of malpractice suits. These include borderline and narcissistic personality disorders, dissociative disorder, PTSD, suicidal and violent patients, and abuse victims. These patients, who typically have poor prognoses, are likely to prompt CT. Therefore, the inverse association between CT and outcome may be understood as due, in part, to patient variables.

Although the three meta-analyses presented in this chapter did not identify consistent patient characteristics that contributed to CT reactions or interfered with their management, this is somewhat understandable given the relatively small number of studies reviewed. We will expand on this point in the next section.

Limitations of the Research

CT does seem to adversely affect important outcomes of psychotherapy, but the link between CT behavior and outcome is a tenuous one. Effects of CT on outcome may be inferred from the data. However, there is precious little direct empirical support for such conclusions. In other words, it seems obvious that if CT behavior is negatively related to sound working alliances and to supervisors' evaluations of trainees, then it also seems safe to suggest that uncontrolled CT is harmful to treatment. At the same time, we could locate only one study (Hayes et al., 1997) that connected CT behavior to treatment outcomes beyond proximate outcomes, and the results of that study only partially supported the link of CT to outcome.

Furthermore, there are a few ways in which our three meta-analyses fall short of the ideal. First, the number studies for each was small, especially for the CT-management-to-outcome analysis, which limits the extent to which one can address heterogeneity of effect sizes and potential moderators. Second, there might be researcher bias within the findings because many of the studies were conducted by the same set of scholars, or by researchers who were trained at the same university, or trained by faculty from the same university. These connections among researchers may have been responsible for the similarity in measures in most studies. Such similarity is helpful in creating consistency between studies but could also affect external validity and inflate the relations found.

As far as limitations of research methods, the enormous complexity of CT led early studies not "to work very well with the more subtle, yet substantial, aspects of countertransference. Rather . . . studies have been limited to more simplified and superficial problems, and restricted in terms of what could be measured" (Singer and Luborsky, 1977, p. 448). Have we progressed beyond this point? Our evaluation leads to a "yes" and "no" answer. On the affirmative side, although many of the studies reviewed in this chapter were laboratory experiments, these investigations have moved forward in terms of both realism and complexity. For example, videotapes have replaced audiotapes as client stimuli, and rather than choose from predetermined written responses, therapist participants usually generate their own verbal responses to the client stimulus. Also, in recent laboratory studies, CT tends to be operationalized multidimensionally along affective, cognitive, and behavioral lines. A further advance has been the development of a line of research on CT management. Such work moves the field toward studying the ways in which CT may be beneficially used (Jacobs, 1991).

On the negative side, laboratory studies possess inherent limitations. Experimental manipulations are inevitably highly simplified. Clinical meaning and external validity are sacrificed for experimental control. However, we would offer that such simplifications are a reasonable and helpful way to proceed, so long as a sufficient number of field studies are done to complement the analogues and to allow for methodological triangulation. Field studies have begun to accumulate, as have qualitative studies, both of which have served to advance knowledge valuably. Still, there is a great need for more controlled, quantitative field research in the CT area.

Therapeutic Practices

The meta-analytic evidence points to the likely conclusion that the acting out of CT is harmful and that CT management is helpful. Several therapeutic practices follow directly from these research-driven conclusions.

• The effective psychotherapist can work at preventing such acting out and must manage internal CT reactions in a way that benefits the work.

• Several therapist behaviors appear to be a useful part of this process. Using self-insight and self-integration as examples, the therapist's struggle to gain self-understanding and work on his or her own psychological health, including boundary issues with patients, are fundamental to managing and effectively using one's internal reactions. These two factors allow the therapist to pay attention to client behaviors that are affecting the therapist in particular ways, and why. As the therapist seeks to understand what internal conflicts are being stirred by the patient's material, the therapist also considers how this process may relate to the patient's life outside the consulting room. Then the therapist may be in a good position to devise responses that will be helpful to the patient.

• One aspect of CT management, self-integration, underscores the importance of the therapist resolving his or her major conflicts, which in turn points to the potential value of personal therapy for the psychotherapist. Personal therapy for the therapist seems especially important when dealing with chronic CT problems. Although we believe the evidence supports the pervasive nature of CT, it seems obvious that chronic CT problems need to be dealt with by the therapist, and that personal treatment is a likely vehicle for such resolutions. Clinical supervision, for experienced therapists as well as trainees, is another key factor in understanding and managing CT and in using it to benefit the work of therapy.

• The psychotherapist can deal with CT that has already been acted out in the session. In addition to the need for the therapist to understand that indeed he or she was acting out personal conflicts, some research (Hill et al., 1996) points to the value to therapists' admission that a mistake was made and that it was the therapists' conflicts that were the source. Therapists need not go into detail about the specific nature of those problems, for we suggest that doing so often serves the therapist's needs more than the patient's (Myers & Hayes, 2006; Yeh & Hayes, 2010).

• If CT is to be managed and used for therapeutic gain, having and using a theory are not enough. Theory alone may be used defensively, but the evidence suggests that theory in conjunction with personal awareness is a key to the therapeutic use of CT.

References

An asterisk (*) indicates studies included in the meta-analysis.

Baehr, A. (2005). *Wounded healers and relational experts: A grounded theory of experienced psychotherapists' management and use of countertransference.* Dissertation completed at Penn State University.

*Bandura, A., Lipsher, D. H., & Miller, P. E. (1960). Psychotherapists' approach-avoidance reactions to patients' expressions of hostility. *Journal of Consulting Psychology, 24*, 1–8.

Chatzisarantis, N. L. D., & Stoica, A. (2009). A primer on the understanding of meta-analysis. *Psychology of Sport and Exercise, 10*, 498–501.

*Cutler, R. L. (1958). Countertransference effects in psychotherapy. *Journal of Consulting Psychology, 22*, 349–356.

Deutsch, C. J. (1984). Self-reported sources of stress among psychotherapists. *Professional Psychology: Research and Practice, 15*, 833–845.

Diener, M., Hilsenroth, M., & Weinberger, J. (2008). A primer on meta-analysis of correlation coefficients: The relationship between patient-reported therapeutic alliance and adult attachment style as an illustration. *Psychotherapy Research, 18*, 1–9.

Epstein, L., & Feiner, A. H. (1988). Countertransference: The therapist's contribution to treatment. In B. Wolstein (Ed.), *Essential papers on countertransference* (pp. 282–303). New York: New York University Press.

Fauth, J. (2006). Toward more (and better) countertransference research. *Psychotherapy, 43*, 16–31.

Fauth, J, & Hayes, J. A. (2006). Counselors' stress appraisals as predictors of countertransference behavior with male clients. *Journal of Counseling and Development, 84*, 430–439.

*Fauth, J., & Williams, E. N. (2005). The in-session self-awareness of therapist- trainees: Hindering or helpful? *Journal of Counseling Psychology, 52*, 443–447.

Fiedler, F. E. (1951). A method of objective quantification of certain countertransference attitudes. *Journal of Clinical Psychology, 7*, 101–107.

*Forester, C. (2001). Body awareness: An aspect of countertransference management that moderates vicarious traumatization. *Dissertation Abstracts International, 61* (5561).

Freud, S. (1910/1957). Future prospects of psychoanalytic therapy. In J. Strachey (Ed.), *The standard edition of the complete works of Sigmund Freud* (Vol. 11, pp. 139–151). London: Hogarth Press.

*Friedman, S. C., & Gelso, C. J. (2000). The development of the Inventory of Countertransference Behavior. *Journal of Clinical Psychology, 56*, 1221–1235.

*Gelso, C. J., Fassinger, R. E., Gomez, M. J., & Latts, M. G. (1995). Countertransference reactions to lesbian clients: The role of homophobia, counselor gender, and countertransference management. *Journal of Counseling Psychology, 42*, 356–364.

Gelso, C. J., & Hayes, J. A. (1998). *The psychotherapy relationship: Theory, research, and practice.* New York: Wiley.

Gelso, C. J., & Hayes, J. A. (2007). *Countertransference and the inner world of the psychotherapist: Perils and possibilities.* Mahwah, NJ: Erlbaum.

Gelso, C. J., Hill, C. E., Mohr, J. J., Rochlen, A. B., & Zack, J. (1999). Describing the face of transference: Psychodynamic therapists' recollections about transference in cases of successful long-term therapy. *Journal of Counseling Psychology, 46*, 257–267.

*Gelso, C. J., Latts, M., Gomez, M., & Fassinger, R. E. (2002). Countertransference management and therapy outcome: An initial evaluation. *Journal of Clinical Psychology, 58*, 861–867.

Greenberg, L. S., & Pinsof, W. M. (1986). Process research: current trends and future perspectives. In L. S. Greenberg & W. M. Pinsof (Eds.), *The psychotherapeutic process: A research handbook* (pp. 3–20). New York: Guilford.

Hayes, J. A. (2004). The inner world of the psychotherapist: A program of research on countertransference. *Psychotherapy Research, 14*, 21–36.

Hayes, J. A. & Gelso, C. J. (1991). Effects of therapist-trainees' anxiety and empathy on countertransference behavior. *Journal of Clinical Psychology, 47*, 284–290.

Hayes, J. A. & Gelso, C. J. (1993). Male counselors' discomfort with gay and HIV-infected clients. *Journal of Counseling Psychology, 40*, 86–93.

Hayes, J. A. & Gelso, C. J. (2001). Clinical implications of research on countertransference: Science informing practice. *Journal of Clinical Psychology, 57*, 1041–1051.

Hayes, J. A., Gelso, C. J., VanWagoner, S. L., & Diemer, R. (1991). Managing countertransference: What the experts think. *Psychological Reports, 69*, 139–148.

Hayes, J. A., McCracken, J. E., McClanahan, M. K., Hill, C. E., Harp, J. S., & Carozzoni, P. (1998). Therapist perspectives on countertransference: Qualitative date in search of a theory. *Journal of Counseling Psychology, 45*, 468–482.

*Hayes, J. A., Riker, J. B. & Ingram, K. M. (1997). Countertransference behavior and management in brief counseling: A field study. *Psychotherapy Research, 7*, 145–154.

*Hayes, J. A, Yeh, Y., & Eisenberg, A. (2007). Good grief and not-so-good grief: Countertransference in bereavement therapy. *Journal of Clinical Psychology, 63*, 345–356.

Heimann, P. (1950). Countertransference. *British Journal of Medical Psychology, 33*, 9–15.

Hill, C. E., Nutt-Williams, E., Heaton, K. J., Thompson, G. B. J., & Rhodes, R. H. (1996). Therapist retrospective recall of impasses in long-term psychotherapy: A qualitative analysis. *Journal of Counseling Psychology, 43*, 201–217.

*Hofsess, C. D., & Tracey, T. J. G. (2010). Countertransference as a prototype: The development of a measure. *Journal of Counseling Psychology, 57*, 52–67.

Jacobs, T. J. (1991). *The use of the self: Countertransference and communication in the analytic situation.* Madison, CT: International Universities Press.

*Kholooci, H. (2007). An examination of the relationship between countertransference and mindfulness and its potential role in limiting therapist abuse. *Dissertation Abstracts International, 68* (9-B), 6312.

*Latts, M. G. (1996). *A revision and validation of the Countertransference Factors Inventory.* Unpublished doctoral dissertation, University of Maryland, College Park.

*Latts, M. G., & Gelso, C. J. (1995). Countertransference behavior and management with survivors of sexual assault. *Psychotherapy, 32*, 405–415.

Levenson, H. (1995). *Time-limited dynamic psychotherapy.* New York: Basic Books.

*Ligiéro, D., & Gelso, C. (2002). Countertransference, attachment, and the working alliance: The therapist's contribution. *Psychotherapy, 39*, 3–11.

*Little, M. (1951). Countertransference and the patient's response to it. *International Journal of Psychoanalysis, 32*, 32–40.

Mitchell, S. A. (1993). *Hope and dread in psychoanalysis.* New York: Basic Books.

*Mohr, J. J., Gelso, C. J., & Hill, C. E. (2005). Client and counselor trainee attachment as predictors of session evaluation and countertransference behavior in first counseling sessions. *Journal of Counseling Psychology, 53*, 298–309.

*Myers, D., & Hayes, J. A. (2006). Effects of therapist general self-disclosure and countertransference disclosure on ratings of the therapist and session. *Psychotherapy, 43*, 173–185.

*Peabody, S. A., & Gelso, C. J. (1982). Countertransference and empathy: The complex relationship between two divergent concepts in counseling. *Journal of Counseling Psychology, 29*, 240–245.

Racker, H. (1957). The meanings and uses of countertransference. *Psychoanalytic Quarterly, 26*, 303–357.

Reich, A. (1960). Further remarks on countertransference. *International Journal of Psychoanalysis. 41*, 389–395.

*Robbins, S. B. & Jolkovski, M. P. (1987). Managing countertransference feelings: An interactional model using awareness of feeling and theoretical framework. *Journal of Counseling Psychology, 34,* 276–282.

Rosenberger, E. W., & Hayes, J. A. (2002a). Therapist as subject: A review of the empirical countertransference literature. *Journal of Counseling and Development, 80,* 264–270.

*Rosenberger, E. W., & Hayes, J. A. (2002b). Origins, consequences, and management of countertransference: A case study. *Journal of Counseling Psychology, 49,* 221–232.

Rosenthal, R., & DiMatteo, M. R. (2001). Meta-analysis: Recent developments in quantitative methods for literature reviews. *Annual Review of Psychology, 52,* 59–82.

Singer, B. A., & Luborsky, L. (1977). Counter-transference: The status of clinical versus quanti-tative research. In A. S. Gurman & A. M. Razin (Eds.), *Effective psychotherapy: Handbook of research* (pp. 433–451). New York: Pergamon.

Teyber, E. (1997). *Interpersonal process in psychotherapy: A relational approach.* Pacific Grove, CA: Brooks/Cole.

*VanWagoner, S. L., Gelso, C. J., Hayes, J. A., & Diemer, R. (1991). Countertransference and the reputedly excellent psychotherapist. *Psychotherapy, 28,* 411–421.

*Williams, E. N., & Fauth, J. (2005). A psycho-therapy process study of therapist in session self-awareness. *Psychotherapy Research, 15,* 374–381.

*Williams, E. N., Hurley, K., O'Brien, K., & Degregorio, A. (2003). Development and vali-dation of the Self-Awareness and Management Strategies (SAMS) scale for therapists. *Psycho-therapy, 40,* 278–288.

Williams, E. N., Judge, A. B., Hill, C. E., & Hoffman, M. A. (1997). Experiences of novice therapists in prepracticum: Trainees,' clients,' and supervisors' perceptions of therapists' personal reactions and management strateg-ies. *Journal of Counseling Psychology, 44,* 390–399.

*Yeh, Y., & Hayes, J. A. (in press). How does disclosing countertransference affect perceptions of the therapist and the session? *Psychotherapy.*

PART 3

Tailoring the Therapy Relationship to the Individual Patient: What Works in Particular

13 Reactance/Resistance Level

Larry E. Beutler, T. Mark Harwood, Aaron Michelson, Xiaoxia Song, *and* John Holman

While it may be conceptualized differently, psychotherapists from all professions and perspectives struggle to overcome patients' apparent resistance to change. This resistance is seen in more than simply a failure to improve; it is often seen in the patient's behaving in ways that are directly contrary to the recommendations of the therapist and/or to the health of the patient. This great paradox of psychotherapy suggests that even the most well-intentioned patients may possess ambivalence about making changes that will help them and thus may fail to act in their own self-interest.

Patients who fail to comply with therapy procedures, even when they believe that doing so will be helpful, are usually described as *resistant*. But such a label implies that the problem is simply and solely that of the patient and would disappear if the patient were more committed. Such an unwarranted assumption offers little to help the therapist improve the outcomes of work with such patients. It is more accurate, we believe, to talk about the failure of one to respond in his or her own best interest as a problem of *reactance* rather than a problem of resistance.

Reactance implies that the psychotherapy environment itself is a partner in inducing noncompliance, and by extension, that the therapist has some control over the failure of therapy. The failure to change is not merely a product of the patient's poor motivation—it is also a failure of the therapist to fit the treatment to the patient. It is in consideration of this viewpoint that we have included a discussion of *reactance* in this chapter and tend to use this term interchangeably with the more usual term, *resistance*. By either term, our explicit objective in this chapter is to consider how a patient's failure to thrive may be a reflection of the therapy rather than of the patient alone. We will address the notion that, by looking beyond the patient to the demands of the therapeutic environment, we can identify and target those processes that can facilitate patient cooperation and improve outcomes.

The literature on patient resistance and reactance has arisen from two simple observations: First, in every form of psychotherapy, some individuals don't change, no matter how skilled or knowledgeable the therapist (Howard, Krause, & Lyons, 1993), and second, in the end, most psychotherapies seem to achieve similar amounts of change to one another, a phenomenon characterized as the *dodo bird verdict* (e.g., Beutler, 2009; Budd & Hughes, 2009; Wampold, 2001; Wampold et al., 1997).

Since the mid-1970s, the preferred methodology of comparative psychotherapy research has been the randomized clinical trial (RCT). This methodology has been considered, in most circles, to be the "gold standard" for identifying research-supported treatments (variously called research-informed, evidence-based, and empirically-supported; c.f. Norcross, Beutler, & Levant, 2007). This methodology compares a manualized treatment with another manualized treatment or with a delayed or no-treatment control group. In actuality, these "treatments" are not homogeneous but are represented by one or more clusters of interventions that may differ widely in what they are intended to do. Typically, the discrete interventions within any "treatment" are aimed at multiple goals, reflecting efforts both to create a therapeutic environment or process and to affect the end point of treatment itself. These multiple objectives represent the goals that are valued by the theoretical model and underlie the particular treatment approach. These treatments (or more accurately, clusters of interventions bound to a given theory) are applied by specially trained therapists to selected groups of patients, all of whom share a common diagnosis and who are randomly assigned to treatments. The specific training provided ensures that the therapists deliver the treatment in a manner that is as similar as possible. Those who depart too far from the ideal treatment behavior are subject to being dropped or retrained to ensure that similarity among therapists is maintained in how treatment is delivered.

The effects of the therapist variability, the influence of the treatment relationship, and all other factors that are thought to be extraneous to the specific "treatment" studied are ostensibly controlled through training, randomization, or the application of statistical controls. Unfortunately, this effort to eliminate variance associated with therapists, relationships, and contexts by RCT methodologies inadvertently eliminates from study the very aspects of psychotherapy that would allow us to understand and overcome patient resistance. Cognitive therapy (or any other treatment studied), the training of cognitive therapists, and the diagnosis of patients (and any other homogenizing condition) are implicitly assumed to accurately and sufficiently describe patients, therapists, treatments, and contexts. Limiting study to what the similarly trained therapists do in common, to similarly diagnosed patients, rather than including either the variations that exist among commonly trained therapists, the variability among patients within diagnostic groups, or the nature of the therapy's context may obscure important relational, patient, and therapist contributions to psychotherapy outcome (Beutler, 2009).

In response to the foregoing concerns, contemporary research has begun to look for aptitude by treatment interactions (ATIs). This research largely has investigated how different classes of treatment methods and the pattern of their use (rather than the clusters of interventions valued by broad theories of psychotherapy) interact with specifically defined (and often extradiagnostic) characteristics of patients (e.g., Beutler, Clarkin, & Bongar, 2000; Castonguay & Beutler, 2007). That is, it is increasingly thought that the fit or match between specific interventions that share common characteristics (rather than either the broader treatment or a specific technique) and the personal (usually non-diagnostic) attributes of particular subgroups of patients is what primarily instigates and maintains change.

This chapter examines the value of this matching approach as applied to patient resistance or reactance. Specifically, we will report the results from an original meta-analysis on matching a nondiagnostic patient variable (resistance) to a group of therapy interventions that share a common level of therapist directiveness. Our review will assess the prevailing hypothesis that treatment outcomes are enhanced by a good (in this case, an inverse) fit between the patient's level of trait-like resistance and the level of therapist directiveness.

Definitions and Measures
Patient Resistance/Reactance

The concept of resistance began to take shape in psychology with the development of psychoanalytic theory. Classical psychoanalytic theory characterized resistance as the patient's unconscious avoidance of or distraction from the analytic work. Resistance was an inherent, unconscious striving to avoid, repress, or control conflicted thoughts and feelings that threatened to become expressed toward a therapist or family member. For example, a patient with significant past trauma may feel threatened by an inquisitive therapist and protectively divert attention away from the threatening material through unconscious processes, or consciously attempt to withhold, falsify, or even refuse disclosure of relevant information.

This concept of resistance has been incorporated into much of contemporary literature, movies, and even common parlance. Take, for example, the frequently confrontational phrase, "you are in denial" to alert a person to his or her resistance to admitting an addiction or other problem.

Outside of psychotherapy and particularly outside of psychoanalytic thought, the concept of resistance has achieved its greatest recognition within the field of social psychology, under the label, *reactance*. In 1966, J. W. Brehm proposed a theory of psychological reactance, defining this term as a ". . . state of mind aroused by a threat to one's perceived legitimate freedom, motivating the individual to restore the thwarted freedom" (Brehm & Brehm, 1981, p. 4).

In spite of the similarity in the definitions of resistance and reactance, there are several distinguishing features. We have already mentioned that reactance invokes a consideration of the evoking environment whereas resistance implies a problem contained within the skin of the person. Beyond this important difference, resistance implies both a state and a traitlike quality associated with psychopathology, while reactance is confined to statelike behavior that occurs in normal personality expression. Finally, reactance, by definition, is expressed as directly oppositional behavior while resistance can be identified by failure to act—stubbornness—as well as obstructionism and rebellion.

In other words, reactance seems to be a special expression of resistance that occurs in the form of rebellion and that is situationally induced (Brehm, 1976). As such, reactance may be affected by one's tolerance for events that limit freedom—it is responsive to traitlike sensitivities as well as statelike properties of the environment. Whether these oppositional behaviors are manifest in any particular situation depends both on the level of traitlike sensitivity (i.e., "resistance") present to stimulate "reactance" and the forcefulness of the external demand to comply. An adequate external demand is one that limits a person's options; this stimulates oppositional behavior (J. W. Brehm, 1976). Clients rarely attribute active opposition as a characteristic of their own behavior in psychotherapy (Kirmayer, 1990). Most ascribe their oppositional response to the effect of being a victim of circumstance, of disease, of others' malevolence or of the therapy itself.

Once activated by the environment, resistance propensities can escalate to become reactant—oppositional, noncompliant, and rigid (Tennen et al., 1981). An adolescent may be quick to perceive his or her freedom as being threatened by a parent and may resist in reactant ways—rebellious and oppositional behaviors. An adolescent with high traitlike resistance may be particularly sensitive to threats to freedom (e.g., being disciplined by a parent) and consequently may exhibit a reactant oppositional behavior.

Resistance, as applied to a client's behavior, implies that both the static refusal to cooperate or change and manifest rebellion are active processes driven by a common need to escape the therapist's effort to limit his or her behavior, whether through direct suggestion or via the inherent demands for change within the therapy process. It follows that a therapist may elicit resistant behavior from a client by assuming more control of the patient's behavior within and outside of the therapy sessions than the recipient of these efforts can tolerate, by using confrontational techniques, or by creating or failing to mend alliance ruptures, among other things. Thus, as we look for aspects of the therapeutic environment that may evoke resistance, therapist directiveness has become the major contender (e.g., Beutler, 1983; Rohrbaugh, Tennen, Press, & White, 1981; Shoham-Solomon & Hannah, 1991).

Therapist Directiveness

Therapist directiveness refers to the extent to which a therapist dictates the pace and direction of therapy and implicates a direction of needed change, as well as the overall predominance of interventions chosen by the therapist to elicit change, insight, or well-being. In other words, directiveness refers to the degree to which the therapist becomes the primary agent of therapeutic process or change, whether through the selection of specific techniques or the adoption of a specific interpersonal demeanor. High therapist directiveness is illustrated by use of instruction, guidance, interpretations, experiential procedures, and in some cases, more confrontational therapeutic styles; however, directiveness should not be equated with a particular kind of treatment. Any therapist decision to vary usage of self-help resources, to use suggestions rather than directions, to use reflections versus interpretations, to use the application of self-guided as opposed to therapist-guided homework assignments, and to use paradoxical interventions (Beutler & Harwood, 2000; Malik et al., 2003) are all indicative of low levels of therapist directiveness. Early research indicated that effective therapeutic change is greatest when the level of a given therapist's directiveness corresponds inversely to a given patient's level of resistance (e.g., Beutler & Harwood, 2000).

Measuring Resistance and Therapist Directiveness

For it to be useful in psychotherapy planning, resistance/reactance must occur with some degree of consistency. We must start with the awareness that resistance, as a trait, is something that all individuals have. Variability among people is a matter both of degree (extremeness of reaction) and sensitivity (the likelihood of activating reactance). Thus, measures that identify a patient's traitlike qualities of resistance are preferred for treatment planning. Unfortunately, there are no current measures that reliably predict when one's predisposition to resistance will become oppositional/reactant; however, we can measure the strength of resistance by assessing the likelihood of its being observed in different situations.

That is, resistant traits in psychotherapy are identified by assessing the sensitivity of a patient to external demands that reduce his or her choices. A highly trait-resistant individual is easily stimulated to behave with opposition to a situation in which external restraints to freedom are placed on him or her. High traitlike resistance may or may not lead to broader psychopathology; however, easy arousal of resistance behaviors is likely to be disruptive to relationships and social activities of many varieties. At this point, it is important to remember that resistance is not isomorphic with any particular kind of psychopathology or set of diagnoses. In other words, resistance is a normal process evoked within most people under the right circumstances; however, some individuals are more easily aroused to resistant behaviors than others. Resistance is not the prerogative of any diagnostic group or groups; it is best considered a nonpathological process rather than a pathology characteristic of one's unconscious urges and impulses. Thus, resistance will be a potentially observable event when any person has been subject to persuasion and social influence to change his or her behavior, thoughts, and feelings. Resistance occurs when a patient perceives his or her options as being arbitrarily limited by this influence (e.g., Beutler, 1983; J.W. Brehm, 1966; S. S. Brehm, 1976).

Given the variability of individual sensitivity and thresholds that comprise resistance, it is not likely to be reliably measured as a grouping variable embedded within diagnoses. Neither are the efforts to circumvent resistance best measured at the level of treatment brand. Resistance is most sensitively measured by individual observations of a patient's tendency to act against or in opposition to those persuasive acts of others that are designed to induce change. Relatedly, intervention is best measured at the level of individual therapists and interventions, with judgments based on the degree to which the interventions limit choice.

Direct observer ratings of patient behavior and of therapists evoking behavior, within the therapy session, have been used in several research studies (e.g., Karno & Longabaugh, 2005a, 2005b; Shoham-Salomon, Avner, & Neeman, 1989). In observational methods, a rater typically codes such patient behaviors as failure to keep appointments, failure to complete homework assignments or other contractual agreements, anger at the therapist, criticism of the therapy, anger at the therapist's interventions, and the like as instances of resistance. Therapist behaviors that include directions, homework assignments, teaching activities, and guidance are coded as examples of directiveness.

Alternatively, some studies have employed paper and pencil tests to tap patient trait-like, resistant qualities (e.g., Beutler et al., 2003; Karno, Beutler, & Harwood, 2002; Piper, Joyce, McCallum, & Azim, 1998); these tests ask the patient to rate their own tendencies to get in arguments, the frequency of past conflicts with authorities, attitudes toward psychotherapy, and rated ease of changing behaviors that are offensive to others.

For example, The Systematic Treatment Selection-Clinician Rating Form (STS-CRF; Beutler, Clarkin, & Bongar, 2000) illustrates an observer-based rating of patient traitlike behavior while the use of the MMPI Dominance or Treatment Readiness (TRT) Scales to measure resistant tendencies represents examples of a self-report rating system.

Not all patient measures of resistance are aimed at general traitlike qualities. Both observer-based ratings and self-report methods are also available as measures that are specific to identifying resistance in psychotherapy. For example, the STS-CRF requires the clinician to rate the patient's previous responses to mental health treatment as a means of predicting a particular patient's resistance to treatment. From a self-report perspective, the TRT (Negative Treatment Indicators) is a content scale included in and extrapolated from the MMPI-2 (Butcher, Dahlstrom, Graham, Tellegen, & Kaemmer, 1989) to assess resistance to the specific case of mental health treatment. Another example of a state-based self-report measure is the Patient Resistance Inventory (PRI) developed by Dowd and colleagues (Dowd, Milne, &

Wise, 1991; Dowd, Wallbrown, Sanders, & Yesenosky, 1994) as a specific measure of resistance in psychotherapy. All of these measures are examples of direct and individualized methods of assessing each individual patient's level of resistance.

Corresponding measures of the therapist's actions are even less frequently used than measures of individual patient behavior. Treatment type, embodied in a manual, is usually considered a proxy for all therapist behaviors; however, it is not very likely that one can accurately infer the therapist's proclivities for directiveness from a treatment manual. Certainly, directiveness cuts across therapeutic schools broadly (e.g., Malik et al., 2003) and dilutes estimates of directiveness on the basis of school or manual adherence. Thus, most comparisons of different treatments do not include an individualized, direct assessment of either resistance or therapy directiveness. In the current review, for example, we found that relatively few of the many studies on psychotherapy had utilized a direct measure of patient resistance and that even fewer used a direct measure of therapist directiveness. The absence of appropriate measures was so pervasive that we had to resort to including a few studies that used group-based measures of both patient and therapy qualities. While it is possible, under ideal conditions, to estimate patient resistance by identifying certain group-level characteristics of the patients in the sample and, perhaps, certain levels of directiveness based on the comparative treatments studied, we reserved the use of this procedure to fewer than 50% of the studies reported and to exceptional circumstances where the homogeneity of the group or the disparity of the comparative treatments was sufficiently documented to warrant equating a group-level quality with an individual assessment. It should be noted that such a group classification procedure introduces insensitivity into the measurement of what are individual patient and treatment qualities.

In the rare instances in which the shared characteristics of groups of individuals could be used to infer the presence of individual trait-like levels of resistance traits, these shared characteristics (primarily diagnoses) were used to indirectly reflect in session levels of resistance levels. Such a leap from a grouping variable to an estimate of an individual trait of resistance was easiest for patients who were diagnosed with borderline personality disorder (BPD), and then only when the samples were sufficiently described and documented as having behavioral characteristics of resistance. Likewise, when a treatment that dictated directive interventions was compared with one that clearly represented a less directive approach (e.g., behavior therapy vs. nondirective therapy, as per Beutler, Mohr, et al., 1991; Karno & Longabaugh, 2005b; or interpretive vs. insight-supportive therapy as per Piper et al,. 1999), one might infer a difference in directiveness sufficient to permit analyses. In the current review, such decisions were based on a nomination and review process described further in the following sections.

Clinical Examples

There are many examples of resistance in psychotherapy: The patient who consistently fails to complete homework assignments, the chronically late patient, the patient who agrees and then disagrees ("yes, but . . ."), and the patient who becomes angry and verbally attacks the therapist's skill or interventions. While any patient may show some of these signs when the therapist moves too fast or makes a tactical error, patients who show consistent, cross-situational resistant behaviors may be spoken validly of as a "resistant patient."

Lisa was a 37-year-old European-American female in her third marriage.

She sought psychotherapy because of mild depressive symptoms. She presented with a matter-of-fact and assertive style. She revealed that she had marital problems and described escalating arguments that lasted several hours. She indicated that her primary goal was learning how to communicate in a more effective way with her husband. The client admitted that her husband was the one who told her to come to therapy, although he was unwilling to engage in couples therapy himself.

Lisa defended her decision to undertake psychotherapy by describing the history of her symptoms in detail and reporting her background. She opened the third treatment session by asking, "So, what do we do now?" This was the client's first therapy experience, and she declared she wanted to move through the process and find a solution as quickly as possible. She expected to be through with therapy in 6 months. This form of resistance may simply result from misunderstanding the nature of psychotherapy and the demands and time requirements associated with change. Such resistance can often be countered by providing education about the treatment process.

By contrast, Ray was a 34-year-old cocaine abuser who was sent to treatment by his lawyer. He openly expressed a lack of interest in participating and spent the first two sessions sitting quietly but sullenly. He failed to complete homework assignments or performed them in an obviously incorrect and antagonistic way. This "reactant" behavior exemplifies the conditions in which fear of losing face, control, or freedom, and a resulting open distrust of the process, can drive oppositionalism and avoidance. Working with this magnitude and type of resistance requires either a very slow and nondirective treatment in which trust is developed gradually and painfully, or the use of paradoxical strategies in which resistance is not only tolerated but prescribed.

In this latter tactic, the therapist attempts to gain the patient's trust by acknowledging, agreeing with, or even encouraging the avoidance, with such assertions as, "Make sure you don't reveal more than you want to" and "it is not wise to rush into change." At other times, the therapist provides an interpretation to accompany the paradoxical assertion. This interpretation is framed with a twist in which the encouragement of the patient's defensiveness is given a negative valence. For example, it may be interpreted as a natural process that will pass when sufficient maturity or strength is achieved. The implication is that the patient is not yet strong, and until he is, he should resist and avoid anything that might frighten him. This interpretation is designed to mobilize the patient's oppositional tendencies against his or her own resistance.

For example, the therapist suggested to Ray that he had failed to yet develop the strength to face aspects of his relationships and that until he developed this level of experience and maturity, the therapist would continue to encourage him to avoid discussing anything personal about himself. His resistance to being classified as weak helped move him toward greater self-disclosure.

Another variety of resistance comes in the form of periodic cooperation interspersed with periods of anger at, rebellion against, or distrust of the therapist. Barbara, for example, seemed very interested in finding ways to better develop relationships with others. She had a long history of beginning relationships, becoming intensely involved, and then being abandoned and rejected. She could not keep a relationship going for longer than a few months, and the end of the relationship was always difficult, filled with ambivalence and hostility. She vacillated between being angry with and being dependent on others. Her relationship with the therapist was similar. She quickly came to depend on her therapist's suggestions, even to the point of calling in several times a week to make sure that her decisions were appropriate. But on those occasions when her decisions did not meet her therapist's ready approval or did not produce the desirable results, Barbara became angry. Initially she expressed the anger in a heated fashion and then immediately apologized and pleaded for understanding; however, as time passed, she became more overt with the expression of her anger and began to distrust the therapist's motives. She accused her therapist of lying to her, asserted that therapy was just a way of manipulating her, and frequently became distraught if the therapist did not give direct answers to her many questions.

Barbara represents a particularly difficult pattern in which her early behavior tended to seduce the therapist into a pattern of answering questions and giving direction. But, as soon as this pattern became established, the patient then reversed her behavior and became angry at the therapist's control—the very behaviors that she initially desired and solicited from the therapist. The situation calls for the therapist to back away from providing direction, to rethink the processes by which help is being offered, and to give space to the patient to make her own choices. In these instances, the therapist has a difficult task of letting the patient struggle to regain control. As the therapist adopts a less directive approach, dropping her agenda of trying to change the patient, and becomes reflective and more able to listen, the patient is likely to open up and express more feelings about her fears.

Previous Reviews

In the first edition of this volume, Beutler, Harwood, Alimohamed, and Malik (2002) identified nearly 30 studies that either addressed the independent role of patient resistance on psychotherapy outcome or the impact of "fit" and "misfit" between patient resistance and therapist directiveness on outcome. They concluded that, in both cases, more than 80% of studies cited confirmed one of two relationships. The first relation found was that patient resistance was consistently and negatively related to the achievement of therapeutic gains. The second relation that predicted treatment benefit was a consistent but inverse correlation between patient resistance and the level of therapist directiveness. That is, when this inverse relationship was present, the likelihood and magnitude of positive change increased.

Based on these two findings, the authors concluded that measures of resistance/reactance could be used to tailor therapeutic interventions and optimize gains. Advantageous outcomes would most likely occur if therapists could selectively fit treatments that vary in the level of applied control, structure, and directiveness in order to optimally fit both the high- and the low-resistance patient.

Meta-Analytic Review
Inclusion Criteria and Search Strategy

The overriding objective of the current review was to investigate the hypothesis that an inverse fit between patient level of resistance and therapist directiveness is conducive to enhanced treatment benefit. In order to ensure an optimal and reliable test of this hypothesis, we began with the description of an ideal prototypic study that could best address the research question of fit. The qualities of this prototypic study included the following:

1. A wide breadth of reliably applied therapeutic approaches and trained therapists to ensure variance on the dimension of directiveness

2. A similarly wide range of moderately impaired patients in order to ensure

variability on the dimension of traitlike resistance

3. Individualized, direct measures of both patient resistance and therapy/therapist directiveness in order to avoid equating directiveness with a particular brand of treatment and resistance with a particular diagnosis

4. Random assignment of patients to therapists within treatments in order to ensure equivalent dispersal of patients to directive and nondirective interventions

5. Systematic monitoring both of treatment variability/consistency on the dimension of directiveness and of patient resistance.

6. Objective and uniform outcome measurement that included analysis of fit between patient resistance and therapy/therapist directiveness.

We eliminated from consideration studies that looked only at statelike qualities of resistance since such measures would have little implication for pretreatment selection and confounded resistance with intervention.

To aid our selection further, we identified a study that represented this model most closely, which then served as a template for evaluating other studies that we identified. The study we used as a template (Beutler et al., 2003) had the following methodological features:

1. Three manualized treatments to ensure treatment breadth. cognitive, narrative, and prescriptive therapies were designed to ensure variability of therapy actions across therapies.

2. Patients were those with comorbid conditions of mild-to-moderate depression and substance abuse disorder.

3. Patient *resistance* was measured before therapy using a self-report measure (the MMPI-2 TRT scale). This avoided the tendency to equate level of resistance with patient diagnosis. Likewise, *directiveness* was assessed through patient-level ratings of therapist actions using external raters applying a pretested scale (the Therapy Process Rating Scale).

4. Patients were randomly assigned to treatment type and then randomly assigned to therapist within treatment type.

5. Directiveness of treatment was monitored in early and late sessions, and resistance was monitored after every five sessions to ensure constancy of both treatment and fit.

6. Outcome was assessed using standard scales for depression and drug abuse, including biological tests of use. Fit of treatment and patient was systematically measured and assessed against patient, treatment, and relationship contributors to outcome at the end of treatment and 6 months later.

The foregoing study represents a good fit with our ideal prototype but was not used as one of the studies that were subjected to meta-analysis because the measure of fit was a composite measure that included the fit of resistance and directiveness along with two other measures of fit. While a significant finding was obtained, the fit of resistance and directives could not be teased out of the composite score from the published data.

The next step in our procedure was to identify studies that most closely approximated our ideal and to retain these for the meta-analysis. Our scope included studies published within a 20-year span from 1988 to 2008. We began by collecting studies that had addressed patient resistance as a mediator between treatment directiveness and outcome from among the studies of resistance × directiveness that were reviewed in the first edition. This resulted in a list of 20 studies, and we added to this list by searching the PSYCInfo database using search words associated with resistance/reactance, therapy directiveness, and the like. The final step was to hand-search the past year's volumes of the most widely cited journals that emerged from our search. These included the *Journal of Consulting and Clinical Psychology*, the *Journal of Counseling Psychology*, *Clinical Psychology: Science and Practice*, and the *Journal of Clinical Psychology*.

Few studies were found that met all six criteria in our methodological ideal. The search yielded a total of 27 studies that complied with three or more of our six inclusion criteria and only five that complied with all six of the criteria sufficiently that we could extract effect size estimates. The penultimate sample was comprised of 10 studies that met five or more of the six prototypic criteria. The most usual departure from our ideal was the failure to use individual/direct measures of either resistance or directiveness or the failure to adequately describe the treatment(s) or patients in sufficient detail as to ensure compliance with the first two criteria. Failure to report necessary statistics to ensure that level of fit was assessed against a reliable outcome measure was a close second reason for rejecting studies.

At this point, we elected to expand the data set to include two more studies in order to reach a sample of 12 studies for our analysis. We invited each of the coauthors to nominate studies that they thought came closest to the ideal prototype, though not in compliance with all six selection criteria. We accepted nominations of studies that departed from the criteria but included only as many as would ensure that the preponderance of the final data set were in substantial compliance with the quality criteria that we identified. The two senior authors made final decisions by a review of the methodology of each nominated study

without reference to the findings. This decision provided some confidence that the body of studies we included were of a high enough quality to estimate the effects of treatment by patient fit.

Our meta-analysis was based on this carefully selected sample of studies, all of which maintained a relatively uniform methodology and adequate description to ensure consistency in the calculation of effect sizes. All but one of the selected studies employed a manual-driven and randomized assignment (RCT) of therapy. The one partial exception (Calvert, Beutler, & Crago, 1988) did not employ a manualized psychotherapy but otherwise met criteria for an RCT design. It also had the advantages of a large sample and was the only study that applied the concepts to psychiatric inpatients. Two studies reported initial and follow-up data on the same sample (Piper et al., 1998 and Piper et al., 1999), but only one provided a sufficiently convincing measure of the patient resistance variable to include.

The 12 studies, involving 1,103 psychotherapy patients, are summarized in Table 13.1. We discuss the result of the meta-analysis in the following paragraphs, both in terms of main effects of resistance and directiveness as well as the mediational effects of matching patient resistance levels with therapist directiveness.

Calculation of Effect Sizes

Effect sizes (ESs) associated with the fit of treatment directiveness and patient resistance levels were calculated by the use of several different formulas, each being selected to best fit the characteristics of the data presented in an individual study. Cohen's *d* was calculated in all cases and, when ESs were presented as correlations or regressions, transformations were conducted (using Borenstein, Hedges, Higgins, and Rothstein, 2009, as our general guide; Lipsey & Wilson, 2001, and Hunter &

Table 13.1   Resistance and Psychotherapy Directiveness

Study name	N	Design	Measure resistance	Measure directiveness	N ES/study	M ES (direct)	M ES (resist)	M ES (fit)	95% CI
Calvert et al. (1988)	108	RCT	D (FIRO-B)	D (TOQ)	1			0.52	0.42–0.61
Beutler, Engle,, et al. (1991)	62	RCT	D (MMPI)	I (CBT v FEP v S/Sd)	3	0.34		0.88	0.79–0.96
Beutler, Mohr, et al. (1991)	63	RCT	D (9 scales)	I (BEH Vs ND)	9			0.62	0.50–0.73
Beutler et al. (1993)	46	RCT	D (MMPI)	D (TPRS)	1	0.33		1.40	1.18–1.61
Piper et al. (1999)	98	RCT	D (QOR)	I (Interp v insight)	4	0.31	0.43	0.64	0.54–0.58
Karno et al. (2002)	47	RCT	D (MMPI)	I (FST v CBT)	1	0.46	0.42	0.65	0.51–0.78
Karno & Longabaugh									
(2004)	140	RCT	D (anger)	D (TPRS)	3			1.16	1.04–1.33
	138	RCT	D (anger)	I (MET v CBT)	2			0.43	0.33–0.50
(2005a)	169	RCT	D (obs)	D (obs)	4			1.21	1.12–1.29
(2005b)	139	RCT	D (self-re)	I (TPRS)	6			1.12	1.05–1.18
Clarkin et al. (2007)	62	RCT	I (BPD)	I (DBT v Pdyn v Support)	3			0.14	0.10–0.17
Gregory et al. (2008)	30	RCT	I (BPD)	I (Pdyn v TAU)	4			0.52	0.34–0.69
Total N	1102								
Summary weighted ESs						0.38		0.82	
95%CIs for summary weighted ESs =						0.32–0.43		0.81–0.86	

Note: For ease of interpretation, all effect sizes have been reported as positive values if they support the specified hypotheses. Negative values indicate a failure to support the hypothesized relationships.

Key: Design = RCT (randomized clinical trial)

Measures of resistance and directiveness = Measure of resistance and directiveness are either directly measured (D) or indirectly measured (I). Specifically, *D* indicates the use of direct observational ratings of directiveness (obs) or a standardized trait measure (e.g., the MMPI, QOR-Quality of Object Relationships, FIRO-B, or STS-Clinician Rating Form) applied to each individual. *I* indicates that an indirect measure of resistance was used based upon a grouping variable such as patient diagnosis—e.g., borderline personality disorder (BPD) or substance abuse disorder (SAD) to indicate resistant groups.

Among measures of Directiveness, *D* indicates the use of a direct rating of therapist acts in treatment—e.g., using an observational rating like the Therapy Process Rating Form (TPRS), or a simple observational rating (obs). *I* indicates the use of an indirect measure of directiveness, based on the general directiveness of the treatment model used. Below are identifiers of the direct and indirect measures of the directive and nondirective treatments employed.

TOQ = Therapist Orientation Questionnaire—a measure of therapist directiveness

Pdyn = psychodynamic treatment—moderately directive; TAU = treatment as usual, nondirective; BEH = Behavioral Tx, directive; ND = nondirective or reflective, nondirective; CBT = cognitive therapy, directive; FEP = focused expressive therapy, low directive; Interp = interpretive, highly directive; FST = family systems; NT = narrative therapy; MET = motivational interviewing, nondirective; DBT = dialectic behavior therapy, directive

Support = supportive therapy, nondirective

N ES/Study = Number of effect sizes calculated for this study

M ES (Direct) = the mean effect size attributable to the directiveness of the treatment—combining all treatments

M ES (Resist) = the mean effect size attributable to the resistance variable—combining all varieties

M ES (Fit) = the mean difference between Effect sizes for "good" and "poor" fit, estimated in MR/Nat studies from correlational data. All ESs are expressed as *d*.

Total effect size is weighted by the sample sizes of all studies.

Schmidt, 2004, were used as supplemental sources). In all cases, the signs of the effect sizes were changed where necessary in Table 13.1 to ensure that positive signs indicated support for one of three hypotheses: (1) positive outcomes are associated with low levels of resistance, (2) positive outcomes are associated with high levels of directiveness, and (3) good outcomes are associated with an inverse fit between patient resistance and therapist directiveness.

In calculating the mean effect sizes, we weighted each mean ES estimate by the N of the study in which it occurred. This ensured that the vagaries of small samples would not overly influence the conclusions. Finally, we calculated 95% confidence intervals for all d values, utilizing the procedures outlined by Smithson (2003).

Meta-Analytic Results

Resistant patients are assumed to experience less benefit and are more prone to prematurely terminate from treatment than those who are cooperative. Unfortunately, while the preponderance of studies available in the literature is supportive of this claim, the reliability of the findings is less than optimal. In our sample of 12 controlled studies, for example, only two provided reliable data on which to calculate an effect size attributable to patient resistance (Karno, Beutler, & Harwood, 2002; Piper et al, 1999). These effect sizes were −.43 and −.42 (note: the signs are changed in Table 13.1 to preserve consistency), suggesting that high resistance was related to low outcomes. Though meager, this finding is consistent with the evidence reported in our earlier review published in the first edition of this book based on a box score count of the preponderance of findings. Thus, we tentatively reaffirm that our earlier recommendation that psychotherapists avoid inciting patient resistance may be valid.

All of the studies in our meta-analysis addressed the role of therapist directiveness and the differential or mediating effects of resistance on different treatments. Four analyses in this series were conducted on a single sample from Project Match and three associated publications of these data (Karno & Longabaugh, 2004, 2005a, 2005b). These analyses were included separately because they entailed different measures of both resistance and directiveness and varied in the samples used; however, the presence of some redundancy among these studies led us to later summarize the data with and without this replication.

All studies in this series involved random assignment of patients to therapists, and all but one included randomization to a manualized treatment as well. In 10 of the 12 studies in our analyses, we evaluated the fit of directiveness to patient resistance through individual, direct measure of the patient's resistance, the therapist's directiveness, or both. This assessment at the level of the person and session avoided equating treatment type with directiveness or diagnosis with patient resistance, and it assures independence of measurement. Addressed in this way, we were able to disentangle therapist intervention from treatment. Thus, it was possible to extract an effect size estimate for the use of directive procedures, independently of patient resistance levels, based on four of the studies. The weighted effect size of this analysis was 0.38. This ES is considered a significant, moderate effect and provides support that directive treatments tend to be relatively powerful compared with nondirective ones.

As noted in Table 13.1, the mean ESs (d) associated with matching effects, summing across different measures across these studies, earned a large mean, weighted d of 0.82. The effect size of 0.82 suggests that approximately 15% of the variance in outcome may be reflective of the fit of directiveness and patient resistance; however, the range was relatively wide with 0.14 (Clarkin et al., 2007) being the low value and 1.40 (Beutler et al., 1993) marking the high value. Such variation suggests that the fit of treatment and patient is important, but that additional mediators also are at work and are not accounted for in the data.

One yet unpublished (and hence, not included) study (Johannsen, reported in Beutler, 2009), comparing U.S. and Argentine samples, suggested that one of these additional moderating variables might include variations among cultures. However, the one non–North American sample included in the current meta-analysis (Beutler, Mohr, et al., 1991) was based on a Swiss sample and reported results that were comparable to others in the set (see Table 13.1). Moreover, when only the first of the four analyses of Project Match data by Karno and Longabaugh (2004) was included in deriving the effect size, the result (d = 0.76) continued to be high and supportive of the mediational hypothesis.

It bears noting that Karno and Longabaugh (2004) conducted two analyses of the same patients, one in which individualized measures were taken of both patient resistance (anger levels) and of therapist directiveness (rater observations) and the other that substituted a group measure of treatment directiveness based on the global treatments compared. While the individualized measurement yielded an effect size (d) of 1.16, a high value, the grouping method earned only an effect size of (d) 0.43. The magnitude of this difference suggests the degree of dilution that can be obtained by the use of group methods of clustering treatments (and patients) as opposed to the more sensitive, individualized ones.

Representative Studies

To give further flavor of the ways in which these indications of treatment–patient fit were studied, a review of several studies and their findings may prove helpful. Piper and colleagues (1999), for example, compared interpretative (directive) and supportive (nondirective) therapies among patients who varied on their interpersonal receptivity and attachment patterns (Quality of Object Relations). In our analysis, we used the latter measure as a proxy measure of patient resistant tendencies. Piper et al. found that directive interventions evoked higher rates of dropout than supportive ones, and that among patients with high receptivity, the application of directive interventions resulted in positive effects, while patient with poor receptivity/object relations responded poorly to directive interventions.

For another example, Beutler, Engle, and colleagues (1991) demonstrated that directive therapies (cognitive therapy) and nondirective interventions (self-directed therapy) were differentially effective for reducing depressive symptoms, depending on the patient's level of resistance. Among very resistant patients, a self-directed therapy regimen surpassed a directive one in affecting therapeutic gain. Conversely, patients who were low on resistance did best with directive, cognitive therapy procedures. These results were cross-validated at 1-year follow-up (Beutler, Machado, Engle, & Mohr, 1993) and independently replicated in a cross-cultural sample of depressed patients treated with behavioral and nondirective therapies (Beutler, Mohr, Grawe, Engle, & McDonald, 1991).

Reactance theorists have suggested that paradoxical interventions may be differentially effective among highly reactant patients since they capitalize on the patient's tendency to respond in oppositional ways. These studies were not included in the current analysis because they usually involved subject analog designs. For example, Shoham-Saloman, Avner, and Neemen (1989) examined the mechanisms of change under paradoxical interventions (defined as therapeutic directives whose common denominator is to attempt to induce change by discouraging it). Although conducted with a nonclinical population, their study revealed that, under paradoxical interventions, subjects who were high on resistance benefitted more than those low on resistance.

Patient Contribution

The negative relationship between patient resistance and therapy outcome may evoke some criticism among those who believe that patient resistance represents a core conflict that must be exposed and excised in order for benefit to be achieved. One of the implications of the current findings is that it may be advisable to reframe our conventional wisdom about the role of interpreting and inciting resistance in psychotherapy. Rather than being a patient process that must be expunged in order to promote change, resistance may best be viewed as a signal to the therapist that ineffective methods are being used. Namely, the therapist may better view some forms of resistance as a problem of inadequately or inappropriately selecting interventions that evoke resistance. Although some patients may enter treatment with a certain level of resistance, reactance, or suspicion of the motives of the therapist, in general, resistance is typically evoked through poor selection of interventions; therefore, resistance is best viewed as a problem of therapy, not of the patient, and as such, it becomes a problem for the therapist to solve. The therapist can then find the appropriate therapeutic means that both stimulate movement and reduce fear of losing control or freedom.

Limitations of the Research

Because resistance cannot be randomly assigned to patients, they are not subject to experimental designs that require direct random assignment. Randomized controlled trials are possible by randomly assigning patients (who vary in resistance) to treatments (which vary in the amount of directiveness), and to therapists within treatments (whose differential proclivities to adopt directive interventions can be measured). Our meta-analysis relied heavily on such evidence and excluded studies that did not utilize randomized procedures for assigning patients to treatments and therapists. Many naturalistic and quasi-experimental studies failed to include sufficient controls to meet our standards for calculating meaningful effect size estimates.

Based on 12 studies that we believe are representative of the best available, we found that the evidence supports the hypotheses posed; however, we recognize that there is a particular weakness within this body of studies. More specifically, they are not equally inclusive of other potential mediators. For example, the study that we used to exemplify a prototypic methodology model (Beutler et al., 2003) investigated the joint relationship of three pairs of mediating variables. They observed effect sizes that accounted for over 40% of the outcome variance. Such effects are higher than any of those reported here for the single resistance–directiveness dimension and suggest that there are multiple dimensions on which matching can be beneficial, each of which may add independent variance to the predictive equation. The role of patient coping style, stage of change, cultural beliefs, and symptom severity are all cases in point where patient and treatment factors probably interact.

Another limitation in studying patient resistance is the absence of consensually accepted measures of traitlike resistance.

There is a certain circularity to the definition of resistance that almost, by definition, determines that those patients who have it will not do as well in psychotherapy as those who do not. At least this is true if we retain the view that resistance is a characteristic of the patient rather than a signal to or a characteristic of the therapist's interventions. Escaping the circularity would be assisted if there were generally accepted measures of resistance traits. Numerous measures have been developed, but they suffer from low or inconsistent intercorrelations. The presence of stable predictive measures would greatly add to the draw that this area has on contemporary researchers.

Another concern is the role played by different theories of psychotherapy in setting the level of therapist directiveness. Much of the research initially reviewed (but rejected in this analysis) assumed that different treatment types are distinguished by definably different levels of directiveness. To the degree that this assumption is accurate (and that has not been adequately demonstrated), it follows that different treatments may be more or less appropriate for patients, depending on the level of resistance that these patients evince. Therapies that are thought to be directive (behavioral and cognitive-behavioral) or nondirective (self-directed or evocative) are presumed to be advantageous for different patients, though directiveness alone seems to offer a better prospect of treatment outcome than if it is nondirective. Indeed, cognitive and behavioral therapies have been found to be most useful for patients who are relatively low in resistance, whereas self-directed and client-centered therapies have been found to be of most value for those who are highly resistant. Of course, such demonstrations are only interpretable if it can be assured that different psychotherapies actually differ in level of therapist direction.

Therapeutic Practices

Collectively, the foregoing results provide strong evidence that, other things being equal, low traitlike resistance serve as an indicator for patients who respond to directive interventions. Conversely, high resistance-like traits are markers for identifying patients who may respond poorly to interventions that are authoritative and directive, evoking states of resistance that interfere with progress, increase the likelihood of dropout, and reduce effectiveness of treatment.

In practice, we recommend the following on the basis of these results:

• Psychotherapists can learn to recognize the manifestations of resistance both as a state and as a trait. Cues for statelike manifestations of resistance include expressed anger at the treatment or therapist, ranging from simple dissatisfaction with therapeutic progress to overt expressions of resentment and anger. Three responses to these expressions of resistant states entail: (1) acknowledgment and reflection of the patient's concerns and anger, (2) discussion of the therapeutic relationship, and (3) renegotiation of the therapeutic contract regarding goals and therapeutic roles. These responses are designed to defuse the immediate consequences of resistance and to infuse the patient with some sense of control, as suggested in formulations of reactance theory (Beutler & Harwood, 2000; also see Chapter 11 by Safran, Muran, and Eubanks-Carter, this volume).

• Anticipate these reactions by initially assessing the level of patient reactance. Patterns are assessed either by standardized psychological tests that tap interpersonal suspiciousness and distrust or by attending to the historical patterns that have characterized the patient's responses to authority. Patients with high resistance traits typically manifest a history of difficulty taking direction, a tendency toward stubbornness and obstructiveness, and difficulty working cooperatively in groups.

• Match therapist directiveness to patient reactance. High reactance indicates a treatment that will deemphasize therapist authority and guidance, employ tasks that are designed to bolster patient control and self-direction, and deemphasize the use of rigid homework assignments. Among high-reactance patients, homework assignments can be constructed as experiments that require minimal overt action on the part of the patient, in order to avoid failure and to reduce the opportunities for oppositional behavior. The relative amount of listening versus talking should shift more toward the patient, and fewer instructions should be used. Self-directed assignments and reading might replace the usual instructional activities of the therapist.

• Beware to avoid matching the level of therapist directiveness to the *therapist's* reactance level. This surfaces as a common occurrence among neophyte therapists who unwittingly project their own personality structure onto their clients. It is the patient's, not the therapist's, level of reactance that provides the optimal fit.

• Avoid stimulating the patient's level of resistance. Based on the current review, we conclude that there is strong and consistent support for a negative relationship between raising patient resistance and therapeutic outcome. While a causal chain cannot be certain, the consistency of the correlational evidence is persuasive.

• Consider directive interventions as a class to be modestly more effective than nondirective ones. This conclusion supports a recent meta-analyis of three

decades of study on psychotherapy outcomes among depressed adults, which found a modest effect favoring directive models and dis-favoring nondirective ones (Cuijpers, van Straten, Andersson, & van Oppen, 2008). To the degree that specific treatments are found to differ in efficacy, it may well be by virtue of how they differ in the use of such common treatment characteristics as level of directiveness rather than in how accurately they conceptualize psychopathology or psychotherapy processes.

• View some manifestations of client resistance as a signal that ineffective methods are being used. That is, resistance is best characterized as a problem of therapy delivery (not of the patient) and as such becomes a problem for the therapist to solve. The therapist can find a means that both stimulates movement and reduces fear of losing control or freedom.

References

* = Studies included in the meta-analysis.

Arlow, J. A. (2000). Psychoanalysis. In R. J. Corsini & D. Wedding (Eds.), *Current Psychotherapies* (6th ed.),. Itasca, IL: Peacock Press.

Beutler, L. E. (1981). Convergence in counseling and psychotherapy: A current look. *Clinical Psychology Review, 1*, 79–101.

Beutler, L. E. (1983). *Eclectic psychotherapy: A systematic approach.* New York: Pergamon Press.

Beutler, L. E. (2009). Making science matter in clinical practice: Redefining psychotherapy. *Clinical Psychology: Science and Practice, 16*, 301–317.

Beutler, L. E., & Clarkin, J. (1990). *Systematic treatment selection: Toward targeted therapeutic interventions.* New York: Brunner/Mazel.

Beutler, L. E., Clarkin, J. F., & Bongar, B. (2000). *Guidelines for the systematic treatment of the depressed patient.* New York: Oxford University Press.

*Beutler, L. E., Engle, D., Mohr, D., Daldrup, R. J., Bergan, J., Meredith, K., et al. (1991). Predictors of differential and self-directed psychotherapeutic procedures. *Journal of Consulting and Clinical Psychology, 59*, 333–340.

Beutler, L. E., Goodrich, G., Fisher, D., & Williams, O. B. (1999). Use of psychological tests/instruments for treatment planning. In M. E. Maruish (Ed.), *The use of psychological tests for treatment planning and outcome assessment* (2nd ed., pp. 81–113). Hillsdale, NJ: Lawrence Erlbaum.

Beutler, L. E., & Harwood, M. T. (2000). *Prescriptive therapy: A practical guide to systematic treatment selection.* New York: Oxford University Press.

Beutler, L. E., Harwood, T. M., Alimohamed, S., & Malik, M. (2002). Functional impairment and coping style. In J. Norcross (Ed), *Psychotherapy relationships that work* (pp. 145–70). New York: Oxford University Press.

*Beutler, L. E., Machado, P. P., Engle, D., & Mohr, D. (1993). Differential patient X treatment maintenance of treatment effects among cognitive, experiential, and self-directed psychotherapies. *Journal of Psychotherapy Integration, 3,*15–32.

*Beutler, L. E., Mohr, D. C., Grawe, K., Engle, D., & McDonald, R. (1991). Looking for differential effects: Cross-cultural predictors of differential psychotherapy efficacy. *Journal of Psychotherapy Integration, 1,* 121–42.

Beutler, L. E., Moleiro, C., Malik, M., Harwood, T. M., Romanelli, R., Gallagher-Thompson, D., et al. (2003). A comparison of the Dodo, EST, and ATI indicators among co-morbid stimulant dependent, depressed patients. *Clinical Psychology & Psychotherapy, 10,* 69–85.

Borenstein, M., Hedges, L., Higgins, J., & Rothstein, H. (2009). *Introduction to meta-analysis.* Chichester, UK: Wiley.

Brehm, J. W. (1966). *A theory of psychological reactance.* New York: Academic Press.

Brehm, S. S. (1976). *The application of social psychology to clinical practice.* Washington, DC: Hemisphere.

Brehm, S. S. & Brehm, J.W. (1981). *Psychological reactance: A theory of freedom and control.* New York: Wiley Press.

Budd, R., & Hughes, I. (2009). The dodo bird verdict—controversial, inevitable and important: A commentary on 30 years of meta-analyses. *Clinical Psychology and Psychotherapy, 16,* 510–22.

Butcher J. N., Dahlstrom W. G., Graham J. R., Tellegen, A., & Kaemmer, B. (1989). *Minnesota Multiphasic Personality Inventory-2: Manual for administration and scoring.* Minneapolis, MN: National Computer Systems.

*Calvert, S. J., Beutler, L. E., & Crago, M. (1988). Psychotherapy outcome as a function of therapist-patient matching on selected variables. *Journal of Social and Clinical Psychology, 6,* 104–117.

Castonguay, L. G., & Beutler, L. E. (Eds.) (2006). *Principles of therapeutic change that work: Integrating relationship, treatment, client, and therapist factors.* New York: Oxford University Press.

*Clarkin, J. F., Levy, K. N., Lezenweger, M. F., & Kernberg, O. F. (2007). Evaluating three treatments of borderline personality disorder: A multiwave study. *American Journal of Psychiatry, 164,* 922–28.

Cortina, J. M., & Nouri, H. (2000). *Effect size for ANOVA designs.* Thousand Oaks, CA: Sage Publications.

Cuijpers, P., van Straten, A., Andersson, G., & van Oppen, P. (2008). Psychotherapy for depression in adults: A meta-analysis of comparative outcome studies. *Journal of Consulting and Clinical Psychology, 76,* 909–22.

Dowd, E. T., Milne, C. R., & Wise, S. L. (1991). The therapeutic reactance scale: A measure of psychological reactance. *Journal of Counseling and Development, 69,* 541–45.

Dowd, E. T., Wallbrown, F., Sanders, D., & Yesenosky, Y. (1994). Psychological reactance and its relationship to normal personality variables. *Cognitive Therapy and Research, 18,* 601–613.

*Gregory, R. J., Chlebowski, S., Kang, D., Remen, A. L., Soderberg, M. G., Stepkovitch, J., et al. (2008). A controlled trial of psychodynamic psychotherapy for co-occurring borderline personality disorder and alcohol use disorder. *Psychotherapy, 45*(1), 28–41.

Howard, K. I., Krause, M. S., & Lyons, J. (1993). When clinical trials fail: A guide for disaggregation. In L. S. Onken & J. D. Blaine (Eds.), *Behavioral treatments for drug abuse and dependence* (pp. 291–302) (NIDA Research Monograph No. 137). Washington, DC: National Institute of Drug Abuse.

Hunter, J. E., & Schmidt, F. L. (2004). *Methods of meta-analysis: Correcting error and bias in research findings, 2nd edition.* Thousand Oaks, CA: Sage Publications.

*Karno, M. P, Beutler, L. E., & Harwood, M. (2002). Interactions between psychotherapy process and patient attributes that predict alcohol treatment effectiveness: A preliminary report. *Journal of Alcohol Studies, 27,* 779–97.

*Karno, P. M., & Longabaugh, R. (2004). What do we know? Process analysis and the search for a better understanding of Project Match's anger-by-treatment matching effect. *Journal of Studies in Alcohol*, 65, 501–512.

*Karno, P. M., & Longabaugh, R. (2005a). Less directiveness by therapists improves drinking outcomes of reactance client in alcoholism treatment. *Journal of Consulting and Clinical Psychology*, 73, 262–67.

*Karno, P. M., Longabaugh, R. (2005b). An examination of how therapist directiveness interacts with patient anger to predict alcohol use. *Journal of Studies on Alcohol*, 66, 825–32.

Kirmayer, L. J. (1990). Resistance, reactance, and reluctance to change: A cognitive attributional approach to strategic interventions. *Journal of Cognitive Psychotherapy: An International Quarterly*, 4, 83–103.

Kirsch, I., & Sapirstein, G. (1998). Listening to Prozac by hearing placebo: A meta-analysis of antidepressant medications. *Treatment and Prevention*, 1(1), Article 0001c, at *http://journals.apa.org/prevention/volume 1/pre 0010001c.html*. November, 1998.

Lipsey, M. W., & Wilson, D. B. (2001) *Practical meta-analysis. Applied social research methods series, Volume 49.* Thousand Oaks, CA: Sage Publications.

Malik, M. L., Beutler, L. E., Gallagher-Thompson, D., Thompson, L., & Alimohamed, S. (2003). Are all cognitive therapies alike? A comparison of cognitive and non-cognitive therapy process and implications for the application of empirically supported treatments (ESTs). *Journal of Consulting and Clinical Psychology*, 71, 150–58.

Norcross, J., Beutler, L. E., & Levant, R. (Eds.) (2006). *Evidence based practices in mental health: Debate and dialogue on the fundamental questions.* Washington, DC: American Psychological Association.

Piper, W. E., Joyce, A. S., McCallum, M., & Azim, H. F. (1998). Interpretative and supporive forms of psychotherapy and patient personality variables. *Journal of Consulting and Clinical Psychology*, 66(3), 558–67.

*Piper, W. E., McCallum, M., Joyce, A. S., Azim, H. F., & Ogrodniczuk, J. S. (1999). Follow-up findings for interpretive and supportive forms of psychotherapy and patient personality variables. *Journal of Consulting and Clinical Psychology*, 67, 267–273.

Rohrbaugh, M., Tennen, H., Press, S., & White, L. (1981). Compliance, defiance, and therapeutic paradox: Guidelines for strategic use of paradoxical interventions. *American Journal of Orthopsychiatry*, 51, 454–67.

Shoham-Salomon, V., Avner, R., & Neemen, R. (1989). You're changed if you do and changed if you don't: Mechanisms underlying paradoxical interventions. *Journal of Consulting and Clinical Psychology*, 57(5), 590–98.

Shoham-Salomon, V., & Hannah, M. T. (1991). Client-treatment interaction in the study of differential change processes. *Journal of Consulting and Clinical Psychology*, 59, 217–25.

Smithson, M. (2003). *Confidence intervals. Series: Quantitative applications in the social sciences, No. 140.* Thousand Oaks, CA: Sage Publications.

Tennen, H., Rohrbaugh, M., Press, S., & White, L. (1981). Reactance theory and therapeutic paradox: A compliance defiance model. *Psychotherapy*, 18(1), 14–22.

Thalheimer, W., & Cook, S. (2002). How to calculate effect sizes from published research articles: A simplified methodology. Retrieved March 15, 2009 from http://work-learning.com/effect_sizes.htm.

Wampold, B. E. (2001). *The great psychotherapy debate: Models, methods, and findings.* Hillsdale, NJ: L. Erlbaum Associates.

Wampold, B. E., Mondin, G. W., Moody, M., Stich, F., Benson, K., & Ahn, H. (1997). A meta-analysis of outcome studies comparing bona fide psychotherapies: Empirically, "All must have prizes." *Psychological Bulletin*, 122, 203–215.

14   Stages of Change

John C. Norcross, Paul M. Krebs, *and* James O. Prochaska

In the transtheoretical model, behavior change is conceptualized as a process that unfolds over time and involves progression through a series of five stages: precontemplation, contemplation, preparation, action, and maintenance. At each stage of change, we propose that different change processes and relational stances produce optimal progress. Matching psychotherapy to the individual patient thus requires matching the processes of change and the therapeutic relationship to his/her stage of change. Furthermore, as clients progress from one stage to the next, the therapeutic relationship also progresses.

In this chapter, we review the voluminous research evidence on the stages of change as it applies to psychotherapy. Our meta-analysis is intended to address two specific aims: First, to assess the ability of stages of change and related readiness measures to predict psychotherapy outcomes; and second, to assess the outcomes from psychotherapy studies that matched treatment to specific stages or readiness levels of change. We illustrate the meta-analytic results with examples from select studies using the stages of change.

Definitions and Measures
Stages of Change

Following are brief descriptions of each of the five stages of change. Each stage

represents a period of time as well as a set of tasks needed for movement to the next stage. Although the time an individual spends in each stage may vary, the tasks to be accomplished are assumed to be invariant.

Precontemplation is the stage at which there is no intention to change behavior in the foreseeable future. Most patients in this stage are unaware or under-aware of their problems. Families, friends, neighbors, or employees, however, are often well aware that the precontemplators have problems. When precontemplators present for psychotherapy, they often do so because of pressure from others. Usually they feel coerced into changing by a spouse who threatens to leave, an employer who threatens to dismiss them, parents who threaten to disown them, or courts that threaten to punish them. Resistance to recognizing or modifying a problem is the hallmark of precontemplation.

Contemplation is the stage in which patients are aware that a problem exists and are seriously thinking about overcoming it but have not yet made a commitment to take action. Contemplators struggle with their positive evaluations of their dysfunctional behavior and the amount of effort, energy, and loss it will cost to overcome it. People can remain stuck in the contemplation stage for long periods. In one study, we followed a group of 200 smokers in the contemplation stage for 2 years. The modal response of this group was to remain in the contemplation stage for the entire 2 years of the study without ever moving to significant action (Prochaska & DiClemente, 1983). Serious consideration of problem resolution is the central element of contemplation.

Preparation is a stage that combines intention and behavioral criteria. Individuals in this stage are intending to take action in the next month and have unsuccessfully taken action in the past year. As a group, patients prepared for action report some small behavioral changes—"baby steps," so to speak. While they have made some reductions in their problem behaviors, patients in the preparation stage have not yet reached a criterion for effective action, such as abstinence from smoking, alcohol abuse, or heroin use. They are intending, however, to take such action in the immediate future.

Action is the stage in which individuals modify their behavior, experiences, and/or environment in order to overcome their problems. Action involves the most overt behavioral changes and requires considerable commitment of time and energy. Modifications of the problem made in the action stage tend to be most visible and receive the greatest external recognition. Individuals are classified in the action stage if they have successfully altered the dysfunctional behavior for a period from 1 day to 6 months. Modification of the target behavior to an acceptable criterion and significant overt efforts to change are the hallmarks of action.

Maintenance is the stage in which people work to prevent relapse and consolidate the gains attained during action. For addictive behaviors this stage extends from 6 months to an indeterminate period past the initial action. For some behaviors, maintenance can be considered to last a lifetime. Remaining free of the problem behavior and/or consistently engaging in a new incompatible behavior for more than 6 months are the criteria for considering someone to be in the maintenance stage. Stabilizing behavior change and avoiding relapse are the hallmarks of maintenance.

Measures of Stages and Readiness

Multiple assessment devices have been developed over the years to assess a person's stage of change or "readiness to change." The measures vary in format—questionnaires, algorithms, ladders, and interviews—as well as in specificity—generic measures for various problems and disorder-specific measures (see the Measures link at www.uri.edu/research/cprc/).

The most frequent measure in psychotherapy research studies is the University of Rhode Island Change Assessment (URICA; McConnaughy et al., 1983, 1989). This 32-item questionnaire yields separate scores on four continuous scales: Precontemplation, Contemplation, Action, and Maintenance (people in preparation score high on both the contemplation and action scales). Items that are used to identify precontemplation include "As far as I'm concerned, I don't have any problems that need changing" and "I guess I have faults but there's nothing that I really need to change." Contemplators endorse such items as "I have a problem and I really think I should work on it" and "I've been thinking that I might want to change something about myself." Patients in the action stage endorse statements like, "I am really working hard to change" and "Anyone can talk about changing; I am actually doing something about it." Representative maintenance items are, "I may need a boost right now to help me maintain the changes I've already made" and "I'm here to prevent myself from having a relapse of my problem."

Other researchers have constructed additional measures of readiness to change.

The Stages of Change Readiness and Treatment Eagerness Scale (SOCRATES) was developed for measuring readiness for change with regard to problem drinking as an alternate measure to the URICA (Miller & Tonigan, 1996). This 19-item measure produces three continuous scales: Ambivalence, Recognition, and Taking Steps, which are considered to represent continuously distributed motivational processes. The SOCRATES has been found to be related to quit attempts for smoking cessation (DiClemente et al., 1991), alcohol use (Isenhart, 1997; Zhang, Harmon, Werkner, & McCormick, 2004), and drug use (Henderson, Saules, & Galen, 2004).

In fewer research studies but more frequently in clinical practice, the stages are measured using a series of questions that result in a discrete categorization. We ask if the individual is seriously intending to change the problem in the near future, typically within the next 6 months. If not, they are classified as precontemplators. Clients who state that they are seriously considering changing the problem behavior in the next 6 months are classified as contemplators. Those intending to take action in the next month are in the preparation stage. Clients who state that they are currently changing their problem are in the action stage.

Processes of Change

The stages of change represent when people change; the processes of change entail how people change. The processes of change represent an intermediate level of abstraction between metatheoretical assumptions and specific techniques spawned by those theories. While there are 400-plus ostensibly different psychotherapies, we have been able to identify only 8 to 10 different processes of change based on principal components analysis. We prefer to conceptualize change in terms of processes or principles, not in terms of specific techniques.

Change processes are overt and covert activities that individuals engage in when they attempt to modify problem behaviors. Each process is a broad category encompassing multiple techniques, methods, and relationship stances traditionally associated with disparate theoretical orientations.

Table 14.1 presents the processes receiving the most theoretical and empirical

Table 14.1 Definitions and Representative Interventions of the Processes of Change

Process	Definition: Interventions
Consciousness raising	Increasing information about self and problem: observations; confrontations; interpretations; awareness exercises; bibliotherapy
Self-reevaluation	Assessing how one feels and thinks about oneself with respect to a problem: value clarification; imagery; corrective emotional experience
Dramatic relief (emotional arousal)	Experiencing and expressing feelings about one's problems and solutions: psychodrama; cathartic work; grieving losses; role-playing
Self-liberation	Choosing and commitment to act or believe in ability to change: decision-making methods; motivational interviewing; commitment-enhancing techniques
Counterconditioning	Substituting alternative or incompatible behaviors for problem: relaxation; desensitization; assertion; cognitive restructuring; behavioral activation.
Stimulus control	Avoiding or controlling stimuli that elicit problem behaviors: restructuring one's environment; avoiding high-risk cues; fading techniques; altering relationships
Reinforcement	Rewarding one's self or being rewarded by others for making changes: contingency contracts; overt and covert reinforcement; self-reward

support in our work along with their definitions and representative interventions. A common and finite set of change processes has been repeatedly identified across diverse disorders (Prochaska & DiClemente, 1985).

Stages × Processes

The transtheoretical model posits that different processes of change are differentially effective in certain stages of change. In general terms, change processes traditionally associated with the experiential, cognitive, and psychoanalytic persuasions are most useful during the earlier precontemplation and contemplation stages. Change processes traditionally associated with the existential and behavioral traditions, by contrast, are most useful during action and maintenance.

Consciousness raising will help clients progress from precontemplation to contemplation. In particular, patients need to increase their awareness of the advantages of changing and the multiple benefits of psychotherapy. They also typically benefit from enhanced awareness of themselves, their disorders, and their defenses.

Contemplation can be a safe haven for clients and therapists alike. Clients are intending to make major changes, but not right now. First they need to increase consciousness more and more and more. Reflecting, feeling and reevaluating how they have been and how they might become can be hard work at times. But it can also be very meaningful and even fun. And such sharing builds a therapeutic bond that can be hard to let go. Who wants to give up such a close relationship? How can you fail as a therapist by having such a good therapeutic relationship? By allowing your client to stay stuck in contemplation.

The process of *dramatic relief* (emotional arousal) can include anticipatory grieving, the sadness and loss of letting go of a best friend in a bottle, of a childlike way of

relating that encourages others to take care of us, or a sense of self-worth based on suffering and self-sacrifice. Dramatic relief can also include facing the fear, guilt or regret that would come from not changing. If a patient clings tenaciously on to safe and secure patterns that are also self-defeating and self-destructive, how will he/she feel in the future?

As people progress from precontemplation to contemplation, they rely more on the process of *self-reevaluation*. "How do I think and feel about myself as a couch potato or a passive person? How will I think and feel about myself as a more active or proactive person?" Many couch potatoes perceive joggers as road hazards, public nuisances. Why would they want to become one of them? The lesson learned here is that psychotherapy can help people find positive images that can draw them into a healthier future, just as the tobacco industry provides attractive images that draw young people into an unhealthy future.

As patients progress into the preparation stage, they rely more on the process of *self-liberation*. This is the belief that they have the ability to change their behavior and the commitment and recommitment to act on that belief. This process is what the public calls willpower. People often overrely on this process. And when they relapse because of overreliance on one change process, they attribute their failure to lack of willpower.

Self-liberation can be enhanced via many routes. As with each change process, we try to provide expert guidance as to whether clients are overutilizing, underutilizing, or appropriately utilizing willpower compared with their peers who have been most successful in progressing from preparation to action. Such feedback requires scientific assessments with adequate reliability and validity. Another way to enhance self-liberation is to give clients choices. If we only give them one choice (go to AA), they won't be as committed as they would be if we gave them two choices (AA or motivational interviewing). Two choices won't enhance willpower as much as three choices (AA or motivational interviewing or cognitive-behavioral therapy).

During action, clients receiving adequate *reinforcement* for their efforts secure better treatment outcomes. One problem is they expect to be reinforced by others much more than others will reinforce them. Average acquaintances are good for one or two reinforcements before they start to take the change for granted. Thus, clients need to be prepared to rely more on self rather than social reinforcements, including from the therapist.

Clients will learn and practice *counterconditioning* (response substitution) as they replace healthier and happier behaviors for their problem behaviors. This process includes the classic reciprocal inhibition methods: assertion to counter passivity; relaxation to replace anxiety; cognitive substitutions instead of negative thinking; exposure to counter avoidance.

As clients progress into the maintenance stage, they do not have to work as hard, but they have to apply change processes to prevent relapse. They particularly have to be prepared for the situations that are most likely to induce relapse.

But for all, psychotherapy will probably terminate before the problem is terminated. This is one reason why therapists and clients alike can feel anxious about termination. They both know that under certain conditions the risk of relapse is real. Of course, clients can return for brief therapy if they lapse or relapse. They can analyze what they did right, what mistakes they made, and what they need to do differently to keep moving ahead.

Clinical Examples

The following exchange from a psychotherapy session demonstrates the relational stance a transtheoretical therapist (Prochaska) would adopt with a patient in the precontemplation stage. The client is a 32-year-old stockbroker in precontemplation for chronic cocaine abuse. The stage of change was briefly outlined, and then the client, Donald, was given feedback that his assessment indicated he was in the precontemplation stage. Did he concur? "Yeh, probably."

> *Therapist*: We know that individuals in the precontemplation stage often feel coerced into entering therapy rather than being there by choice. What pressures were there on you to seek psychotherapy?
>
> *Client*: Lots of people have been on my back. My girlfriend, my mother. My job may be in jeopardy. They all think it's caused by cocaine. But I've been using it for years, and it's never been a problem.
>
> *Therapist*: How do you react when people pressure you to quit cocaine when you're not ready?
>
> *Client*: I get angry. I tell them to mind their own business.
>
> *Therapist*: You get defensive.
>
> *Client*: Sure, wouldn't you? Nobody likes to be told what to do, to be treated like a kid.
>
> *Therapist*: How would you react if I told you to quit cocaine?
>
> *Client*: I would get angry. I would tell myself you're just like all the others— think you know better than me how to run my life.
>
> *Therapist*: Would you want to drop out of therapy?
>
> *Client*: Probably. I don't react well to being controlled.
>
> *Therapist*: I appreciate you sharing your reactions with me. Let me share my main concern. I am concerned that you might drop out of therapy before

I have a chance to make a significant difference in your life. I don't want to coerce or control you. I do want to help you to be freer to do what is best for your life. So will you let me know if I am pressuring you or parenting you?

Client: You'll know.

Historically, confrontation was one of the recommended ways of relating to defensive and resistant clients. By consistently confronting patients' defenses and resistance, therapists expected to be able to break through their denial and other defenses. Research has shown, however, that a confrontational style of relating drives many patients away and increases premature termination (Miller & Rollnick, 2002; Miller, Wilbourne, & Hettema, 2003).

Later, in the same session, the therapist adopts an affirming, Socratic style and relies primarily on consciousness-raising strategies that the research evidence suggests will assist a patient to progress from precontemplation to contemplation. This entails increasing awareness of the pros of changing and the multiple benefits of sticking with treatment.

Therapist: We know people are likely to complete therapy if they appreciate its many benefits. Donald, how do you think people benefit from therapy?
Client: It makes the therapist better off.
Therapist: That's good! And how about the client?
Client: I expect it helps them solve their problems.
Therapist: That's true. And would that help them to feel better about themselves?
Client: Yeah, it should.
Therapist: And would that improve their moods?

Client: Sure.
Therapist: Would that improve their relationships?
Client: It should.
Therapist: And be more open and less defensive.
Client: I can see that.
Therapist: And do better in their job and make more money.
Client: I don't know about that.
Therapist: It's true. How about we make a deal. If your income goes up 10%, my fee goes up 10%?
Client: That would be worth it.
Therapist: You might not believe this, but there's only one other thing you could do for an hour a week that would give you more benefits than therapy.
Client: What's that?
Therapist: I'm not going to tell you because you might invest in that instead.
(Donald laughs!)

The psychotherapist's relational stance at different stages can be characterized as follows. With patients in precontemplation, often the role is like that of a *nurturing parent* joining with a resistant youngster who is both drawn to and repelled by the prospects of becoming more independent. With clients in contemplation, the role is akin to a *Socratic teacher* who encourages clients to achieve their own insights into their condition. With clients who are in the preparation stage, the stance is more like that of an *experienced coach* who has been through many crucial matches and can provide a fine game plan or can review the participant's own plan. With clients who are progressing into action and maintenance, the psychotherapist becomes more of a *consultant* who is available to provide expert advice and support when action is not progressing as smoothly as expected. As termination approaches in lengthier treatment, the therapist is consulted less and less often as the client experiences greater autonomy and ability to live a life freer from previously disabling problems.

Previous Meta-Analyses

Empirical research on the stages of change has taken a number of tacks over the past 30 years (for reviews, see Prochaska et al., 2001; Prochaska & Norcross, 2010), resulting in a vast literature. In this section, we review the results of earlier meta-analyses on the integration of the stages and processes of change and on the ability of the stages of change to predict the outcomes of behavior change.

Stages × Processes

Years of research in behavioral medicine and psychotherapy converge in showing that different processes of change are differentially effective in certain stages of change. Rosen (2000) performed a meta-analysis of 47 cross-sectional studies examining the relations of the stages and the processes of change. The studies involved smoking, substance abuse, exercise, diet, and psychotherapy. The mean effect sizes (d) were approximately 0.70 for variation in cognitive-affective processes by stage and 0.80 for variation in behavioral processes by stage, both moderate-to-large effects. Effect sizes for stages by processes did not vary significantly by the problem treated. For the five studies that examined the change processes in psychotherapy, behavioral processes peaked in action while cognitive-affective processes peaked in contemplation or preparation. Of particular interest was the finding that "use of helping relationships was strongly related to stages in studies of psychotherapy" (Rosen, 2000, p. 601).

Tailoring Treatments to Stages

A large number of psychosocial treatments have been tailored to stage of change or readiness for change. These have primarily been population-based studies delivered via computer, mail, or phone, with a focus on health behavior change. Such interventions have assessed and provided specific feedback by stage of change and other constructs, such as self-efficacy. Results of these studies clearly show the effectiveness of tailoring or matching to the patient's stage of change.

We conducted a meta-analysis on 87 prospective, tailored interventions delivered via computer or mail across smoking cessation, physical activity, healthy diet, and mammography screening (Krebs, Prochaska, & Rossi, in press). The mean effect size of $d = 0.18$ (95% CI = 0.16–0.20) represents a 39% increase ($OR = 1.39$) over the assessment or minimal care conditions with which the interventions were compared and indicates a medium-size effect for population-based interventions (Rossi, 2002). The subset of studies that intervened on smoking cessation, for instance, resulted in an absolute increase of 6% in quit rates, a rate comparable to that observed with 4 to 8 individual in-person counseling sessions (Fiore et al., 2008).

Although supportive of matching or tailoring to the patient's stages of change, these studies did not include face-to-face psychotherapy, nor did they address the disorders most commonly treated by mental health professionals. Thus, we undertook a new meta-analysis specifically focusing on the stages of change in psychotherapy.

Meta-Analytic Review: Stages Predicting Outcome

Here, we present the results of an original meta-analysis conducted with aim of gauging the ability of the stages of change to predict psychotherapy outcomes.

Search Strategy and Criteria

A combination of search methods was used to locate all published and in-press studies that matched psychotherapy to stage of change or that employed a measure of readiness for change to predict outcomes after a course of treatment. The electronic databases PsycINFO and PubMed were searched for studies indicating reference to psychotherapy and stages of change, readiness, and motivation as well as for instruments used to measure these constructs (e.g., URICA, SOCRATES, Contemplation Ladder). To locate studies that may have employed similar techniques, we also conducted a forward search for articles that cited identified studies, examined reference lists from published studies, and searched for articles published by authors of studies deemed suitable for inclusion.

Studies selected for analysis met the following criteria, which were consistent with inclusion criteria for other meta-analytic reviews in this volume: (a) studies reported results of behavioral/psychological face-to-face treatment; (b) treatment was provided by mental health professionals; (c) patients had a DSM-III or IV diagnosis; (d) treatments consisted of at least three group or individual sessions; (e) readiness to change measured prior to treatment was used to predict treatment outcome; and (f) sufficient statistical information was available to calculate an effect size.

The search yielded 1,686 references, the abstracts of which were reviewed for possible inclusion. Of these, 113 papers were chosen for full text review, and 39 studies met inclusion criteria and were included in the present analysis.

Methodological Decisions

The primary database was created, and the results were analyzed using the Comprehensive Meta-Analysis software package (Biostat, 2006). Effect sizes were calculated using the standardized mean difference (Cohen's d). Results reported as correlations (r), mean differences (F or t), or tests of variance (X^2) were transformed to d (per Lipsey & Wilson, 2001). Each obtained effect size estimate was weighted by the inverse of the variance of the estimate, which gives greater weight to studies with better estimates (for the most part, studies with larger sample sizes). If insufficient information was reported for effect size calculation, the study was excluded, but if the study indicated that the effect was simply "nonsignificant," it was included with the effect size entered as zero, a conservative strategy that nevertheless preserves some data.

We employed a random-effects variance estimation model. This model assumes both study-level error and, as well, variability among studies due to sampling of studies from a population of studies. This enables generalization to a population of studies. Variability of the random-effects variance component was tested with the Q test, the significance of which indicates that there is variability among the effect size of the sampled studies and suggests that there are factors (i.e., moderators) that could explain this variability.

Publication bias, the tendency for significant study results to get reported more often than nonsignificant results, can upwardly skew effect size estimates in meta-analysis. Mean effects were assessed for degree of publication bias using two techniques: fail-safe N, and trim and fill. Fail-safe N calculates the number of unpublished studies with a null effect size needed to reduce the overall effect to nonsignificance. Trim and fill (Duval & Tweedie, 2000) assesses the symmetry of a plot of effect size by sample size (funnel plot) under the assumption that when publication bias exists, a disproportionate number of studies will fall to the bottom right of the plot. This technique thus determines the number of asymmetrical outcomes, imputes their counterparts to the left, and estimates a corrected mean effect size.

The 39 analyzed studies represented a variety of diagnoses and outcome measures with some studies reporting more than one outcome (e.g., substance use and treatment dropout). To ensure statistical independence of outcomes, where studies reported more than one outcome, an overall mean effect size per study was included for calculating the overall mean effect.

The Studies

Table 14.2 summarizes the attributes of the 39 studies, encompassing 8,238 psychotherapy patients. All studies reported data

Table 14.2 Summary of Studies and Samples (k = 39) included in the Meta-Analysis

Characteristic	k	%
Country		
United States	25	64%
Canada	7	18%
Australia	2	5%
United Kingdom	2	5%
Spain	2	5%
Germany	1	3%
Study design		
Single group pre-post	24	62%
Randomized controlled trial	15	38%
Patient age		
Adult (18+)	33	85%
Adolescent (13–17)	6	15%
Patient race/ethnicity		
White (>60% of sample)	26	67%
Mix (none greater than 60% of sample)	6	15%
African American (>60% of sample)	4	10%
Data not reported	3	8%
Treatment setting		
Outpatient	25	64%
Inpatient	14	36%
Treatment manual used	12	31%
Number of treatment sessions		
<10	4	10%
10–19	13	33%
20+	4	10%
Data not reported	17	44%
Treatment orientation		
Cognitive-behavioral	19	49%
12-step	4	10%
Other	5	13%
Data not reported	17	44%
Readiness Measure		
University of Rhode Island Change Assessment	27	69%
Stages of Change Readiness and Treatment Eagerness Scale (SOCRATES)	5	13%
Anorexia Stages of Change Questionnaire	2	5%
Other	5	13%

only from final follow-ups, which were mostly conducted immediately upon treatment completion. Thirteen studies were randomized controlled trials while the remainder used a one-group pre-post design. Six studies concerned treatments for adolescents (ages 13–17), while the others focused on adults (18+). Sample sizes ranged from $N = 42$ to $N = 1,075$, with an average of 211 participants at recruitment and a 77% retention rate at follow-up. Most samples ($k = 26$) were comprised of primarily white participants (>60%), four with primarily African-American participants (>60%), and six studies recruited a racially mixed sample. (Note that k denotes the number of studies, in contrast to N, which refers to the number of participants in a study.) Samples on average were 38% female (and ranged 0%–100%). Fourteen studies conducted interventions in an inpatient setting, and the number of treatment sessions ranged from 4 to 28 with 12 being the modal number. Twelve studies reported using a treatment manual, with cognitive-behavioral treatment the most common theoretical orientation guiding treatment ($k = 19$). The most common readiness measures were the University of Rhode Island Change Assessment (URICA; $k = 27$) and the Stages of Change Readiness and Treatment Eagerness Scale (SOCRATES; $k = 5$).

Effect Size

The 39 studies reported 71 separate outcomes. Results of the individual studies are summarized in Table 14.3. The mean effect size was $d = .46$ with a 95% confidence interval of .35 to .58 (range −.20 to 2.7), $Q(38) = 186.05$, $p < 0.001$. Analysis of publication bias suggested a fail-safe N of 2,554.

By convention, a d of .46 indicates a medium effect, demonstrating that the

stages of change reliably predict outcomes in psychotherapy. That is, the amount of progress clients make during treatment tends to be a function of their pretreatment stage of change. For example, an intensive action- and maintenance-oriented smoking cessation program for cardiac patients achieved success for 22% of precontemplators, 43% of the contemplators, and 76% of those in action or prepared for action 6 months later (Ockene et al., 1992).

If patients progress from one stage to the next during the first month of treatment, they can double their chances of taking action in the next 6 months. Of the precontemplators who were still in precontemplation at 1-month follow-up, only 3% took action by 6 months. For the precontemplators who progressed to contemplation at 1 month, 7% took action by 6 months. Similarly, of the contemplators who remained in contemplation at 1 month, only 20% took action by 6 months. At 1 month, 41% of the contemplators who progressed to the preparation stage attempted to quit by 6 months (Prochaska, DiClemente, Velicer, et al. 1985). Such data indicate that treatments designed to help patients progress just one stage in a month can double the chances of participants taking action in the near future.

Effect Size by Outcome

We analyzed the effect size for the stages of change for two particular outcomes of interest: enhancement of the working alliance ($k = 4$) and adherence to treatment/premature dropout ($k = 24$). Three studies included working alliance as an outcome with one reporting outcomes from two samples (Connors et al., 2000). The mean effect size for these four outcomes was $d = .61$ (95% CI = .36–.86, $p < 0.001$).

Table 14.3 Effect Sizes by Study

Study	Primary diagnosis	Readiness measure	N	d	SE	95% CI Lower	Upper
Alexander & Morris, 2008	Domestic abuse	URICA	210	0.44	0.19	0.08	0.81
Ametller et al., 2005	Eating disorder	Anorexia Stage of Change	70	0.34	0.12	0.10	0.58
Blanchard et al., 2003	Substance abuse	URICA	252	0.16	0.13	−0.10	0.42
Brodeur et al., 2008	Domestic abuse	URICA-DV	302	0.11	0.12	−0.12	0.34
Callaghan et al., 2005	Substance abuse	URICA	130	0.74	0.19	0.37	1.11
Callaghan et al., 2008 (Budney, 2000)	Substance abuse	URICA	60	0.37	0.41	−0.44	1.18
Callaghan et al., 2008 (Budney, 2006)	Substance abuse	URICA	90	0.62	0.29	0.05	1.20
Carpenter et al., 2002	Substance abuse	URICA	174	0.49	0.22	0.05	0.92
Chung & Maisto, 2009	Substance abuse	Contemplation Ladder	142	0.03	0.23	−0.43	0.49
Connors et al., 1998a	Alcohol abuse	URICA	682	0.49	0.08	0.34	0.65
Connors et al., 1998b	Alcohol abuse	URICA	465	0.52	0.10	0.33	0.70
Demmel et al., 2004	Alcohol abuse	SOCRATES	350	0.58	0.13	0.33	0.83
Derisley et al., 2000	General therapy	URICA	60	1.30	0.32	0.68	1.92
Dozois et al., 2004	Anxiety	URICA	81	0.34	0.24	−0.12	0.80
Eckhardt et al., 2008	Domestic abuse	URICA-DV	199	0.52	0.16	0.21	0.84
Geller et al., 2004	Eating disorder	RMI	60	0.78	0.35	0.10	1.47
Gossop et al., 2006	Substance abuse	SOCRATES	1,075	0.23	0.08	0.08	0.38
Haller et al., 2004	Substance abuse	URICA	75	0.87	0.26	0.36	1.38
Henderson et al., 2004	Substance abuse	URICA	96	0.63	0.22	0.20	1.06
Hewes & Janikowski, 1998	Alcohol abuse	SOCRATES	58	2.49	0.60	1.31	3.68
Hunt et al., 2006	PTSD	URICA	42	0.68	0.35	0.00	1.36
Isenhart 1997	Alcohol abuse	SOCRATES	125	0.69	0.19	0.32	1.07
Kerns et al., 2000	Pain management	Pain Stages of Change	68	0.24	0.10	0.05	0.44
Kinnaman et al., 2007	Alcohol abuse	URICA	120	−0.02	0.19	−0.39	0.34
Lewis et al., 2009	Depression	Stage of Change Q	332	0.30	0.12	0.08	0.53
Mitchell, 2006	Substance abuse	SOCRATES	357	0.71	0.11	0.49	0.93
Pantalon et al., 2002	Substance abuse	URICA	117	0.14	0.20	−0.25	0.52
Pantalon et al., 2003	Psychiatric inpatients	URICA	120	−0.20	0.09	−0.38	−0.02
Petry et al., 2005	Gambling disorder	URICA	234	0.70	0.16	0.38	1.01
Project Match Group, 1999	Alcohol abuse	URICA	806	0.28	0.07	0.14	0.42

(Continued)

Table 14.3 Continued

Study	Primary diagnosis	Readiness measure	N	d	SE	95% CI Lower	Upper
Rooney et al., 2007	PTSD	URICA	50	0.63	0.31	0.03	1.23
Scott & Wolfe, 2003	Domestic abuse	URICA	194	0.63	0.21	0.23	1.04
Smith et al., 1995	General therapy	URICA	74	1.84	0.33	1.20	2.48
Soler et al., 2008	Borderline PD	URICA	60	0.54	0.61	−0.67	1.74
Stotts et al., 2003	Alcohol abuse	URICA	115	0.49	0.24	0.03	0.96
Tambling & Johnson, 2008	Relational problem	URICA	469	−0.09	0.13	−0.34	0.15
Treasure et al., 1999	Eating disorder	URICA	125	0.70	0.47	−0.22	1.61
Wade et al., 2009	Eating disorder	Anorexia Stage of Change	47	2.67	0.50	1.68	3.65
Willoughby et al., 1996	Alcohol abuse	URICA	152	−0.15	0.17	−0.49	0.18
Overall Effect Size				**0.46**	**0.06**	**0.35**	**0.58**

URICA = University of Rhode Island Change Assessment; SOCRATES = Stages of Change Readiness and Treatment Eagerness Scale; RMI = Readiness and Motivation Interview.

For the 24 studies that reported client adherence to suggested treatment or premature dropout from treatment, the mean effect size was $d = .42$ (95% CI = .24–.60).

The stage of change reliably predicts psychotherapy dropout, which is an important finding given that a review of 126 studies found that about 50% of patients will leave treatment prematurely (Pekarik & Wierzbicki, 1986). While stage of change alone is an important indicator of treatment dropout, we found in a separate study that assessing both stage and processes of change predicted psychotherapy dropout with 90% accuracy among clients with a variety of mental health problems (Brogan, Prochaska, & Prochaska, 1999). The 40% of the patients who terminated quickly (less than three sessions) and prematurely, as judged by their therapists, had a group profile representing the precontemplation stage. The 20% of patients who terminated quickly but appropriately had a group profile representing action, while the 40% who remained in psychotherapy had a stage profile similar to contemplation.

Potential Moderators

Categorical moderators were examined using a statistical test for meta-analysis that employs weighted data and compares within- and between-group heterogeneity using the Q statistic as employed by the Comprehensive Meta-analysis software package (Biostat, 2006). A sample size of 10 or more studies is necessary to provide sufficient statistical power for detecting differences between groups (Lipsey & Wilson, 2001). Continuous moderators were examined using meta-regression techniques, which correct variance estimates for sample size.

The significant Q test for our meta-analysis indicated that there was sufficient variability among the effect sizes of the studies to look for moderators that could explain this variability. We conducted moderator analyses for patient characteristics, treatment features, and diagnostic categories. We could not search for potential moderators of assessment time or rater perspective as all stage measures were completed by patients at the beginning of intake or treatment.

Nor was there sufficient variability in these 39 studies in the measures used to assess stages to explore moderators; more than 30 studies employed the University of Rhode Island Change Assessment (URICA).

For patient characteristics, we found no statistically significant difference between adolescent and adult populations, nor by race/ethnicity (all $ps > .10$). However, effect size was positively correlated with having a larger number of female participants ($p = .02$). For treatment features, we found no differences in effect size between inpatient and outpatient treatment settings, between treatments that used a manual or those that did not, nor by number of treatment sessions. However, for studies reporting primary theoretical orientation, 12-step programs had the highest effect size ($k = 4$, $d = .73$) as compared to cognitive-behavioral treatment ($k = 19$, $d = .39$) or other orientations ($k = 5$, $d = .24$; $p = .001$).

We also analyzed the effect size of the stages of change for particular diagnostic categories: addictions, eating disorders, and mood disorders. Fourteen studies predicted addiction outcomes using baseline readiness to change. The most frequently used outcome measures were the Addiction Severity Index, Severity of Dependence Scale, Timeline Followback, and the Alcohol Use Questionnaire. The mean effect for the 14 studies was $d = .37$ (95% CI = .23–.52, $p < .001$). Four studies assessed the relationship between baseline readiness to change and prediction of eating disorder outcomes. Two studies employed the Eating Disorders Inventory, one a measure from the European COST Action B6 Project, and one a count of relapse to assess outcomes. The mean effect size was $d = .99$ (95% CI = 0.24–1.74, $p < .001$). Seven studies assessed the relationship between baseline readiness to change and prediction of mood disorder symptoms or relational

distress, which were deemed sufficiently similar to group together to increase reliability of the estimate. Outcome measures included the State-Trait Anxiety Inventory, Beck Depression Inventory, Children's Depression Rating Scale, and the Outcome Questionnaire 45. The mean effect size was $d = .45$ (95% CI = .19–.71, $p < .001$).

Across studies, readiness to change was moderately to strongly related to progress in psychotherapy for various DSM-IV disorders. For instance, low motivation as indicated on the Anorexia Nervosa Stages of Change Questionnaire predicted hospitalization in adolescent patients (Ametller et al., 2005) as well as improvement in problem eating (Wade et al., 2009). Changes in stages predicted PTSD symptom severity in a population of veterans at treatment follow-up 3 months later (Rooney et al., 2007). Improvement in Action scores during psychotherapy was positively related to decreases on the Children's Depression Rating Scale after 12 weeks of treatment (Lewis et al., 2009).

Meta-Analytic Review: Stage-Matched Treatments

Our second aim was to conduct a meta-analysis that assessed the outcomes from psychotherapy studies that matched treatment to specific stages or readiness levels of change. We were interested in learning whether stage-matching clients in psychotherapy produced the superior results found in behavioral medicine and population-based studies reviewed earlier. Unfortunately, we located no controlled group studies meeting our inclusion criteria that matched psychotherapy to client stage or readiness. As a result, we could not perform a meta-analysis.

A number of studies did use in-person sessions and delivered treatment based on stage or readiness to change but otherwise did not meet inclusion criteria in that treatment either was a single session, provided by medical staff, or focused on health behaviors such as smoking, physical activity, or diabetes management (Champion et al., 2003; Chouinard & Robichaud-Ekstrand, 2007; Clark, Hampson, Avery, & Simpson, 2004; Patten, et al., 2008; Van Sluijs, Van Poppel, Twisk, Brug, & Van Mechelen, 2005; Wiggers et al., 2005). The one study that intervened on psychiatric and substance use diagnoses was not individually stage tailored (James et al., 2004). All of the studies we did locate reported findings in support of stage-matching treatments.

The failure to locate stage-matching studies in psychotherapy reflects, first, the obvious dearth of such studies, and second, the limited reach of conventional psychotherapy. Psychotherapy has traditionally taken a passive and narrow approach to health care—passively waiting for individuals suffering from mental disorders in the contemplation or preparation stages to contact their offices. When psychotherapy proactively reaches out to individuals and populations alike, suffering from all behavioral health conditions, in all stages of change, then we will achieve a transformation in psychotherapy.

To illustrate, several of our studies investigated the results of reaching out to patient populations. A series of clinical trials applying stage-matched interventions for health behavior change have been conducted. In our first large-scale clinical trial, we compared four treatments: a home-based action-oriented tobacco cessation program (standardized); stage-matched manuals (individualized); expert system computer reports plus manuals (interactive); and counselors plus computers and manuals (personalized). We randomly assigned by stage 739 smokers to one of the four treatments (Prochaska, DiClemente, Velicer, & Rossi, 1993).

In the computer condition, participants completed by mail or telephone 40 questions that were entered into computers that generated feedback reports. These reports informed participants about their stage of change, their pros and cons of changing, and their use of change processes appropriate to their stages. At baseline, participants were given positive feedback on what they were doing correctly and guidance on which principles and processes they needed to apply more in order to progress. In two progress reports delivered over the next 6 months, participants also received positive feedback on any improvement they made on any of the variables relevant to progressing.

In the personalized condition, smokers received four proactive counselor calls over the 6-month intervention period. Three of the calls were based on the computer reports. Counselors reported much more difficulty in interacting with participants without any progress data. Without scientific assessments, it was harder for both clients and counselors to tell whether any significant progress had occurred since their last interaction.

Abstinence rates were compared for each of the four treatment groups over 18 months with treatment ending at 6 months. The two self-help manual conditions paralleled each other for 12 months. At 18 months, the stage-matched manuals moved ahead (18% vs. 11% abstinent). This is an example of a delayed action effect, which we often observe with stage-matched programs specifically and which others have observed with self-help programs generally. It takes time for participants in early stages to progress all the way to action. Therefore, some treatment effects as measured by action will be observed only after considerable delay.

The results of the computer alone and computer plus counselor conditions paralleled each other for 12 months. Then, the effects of the counselor condition flattened out (18%) while the computer condition effects continued to increase (25% abstinent). We can only speculate as to the delayed differences between these two conditions. Participants in the personalized condition may have become somewhat dependent on the social support and social control of the counselor calling. The last call was after the 6 months assessment and benefits would be observed at 12 months. Termination of the counselors could result in no further progress because of the loss of social support. The classic pattern for therapies for all addictions is rapid relapse beginning as soon as the treatment is terminated. Some of this rapid relapse could well be due to the sudden loss of social support or social control provided by the counselors and other participants in therapy programs.

The next test was to demonstrate the efficacy of the expert system when applied to an entire population recruited proactively. With over 80% of 5,170 smokers participating and fewer than 20% in the preparation stage, we demonstrated significant benefit of the expert system at each 6-month follow-up (Prochaska et al., 2005). The point prevalence abstinence rates for expert stage-matched systems versus assessment alone were: 9.7% vs. 7.4%; 18.0% vs. 14.5%; 21.7% vs. 16.6%; and 25.6% vs. 19.7% at 6, 12, 18, and 24 months, respectively. The advantages over proactive assessment alone increased at each follow-up for the full 2 years assessed. The implications here are that stage-matched interventions in a population can continue to demonstrate benefits long after the intervention has ended.

The system's efficacy was replicated in an HMO population of 4,000 smokers with 85% participation (Prochaska et al., 2001). In the first population-based study,

the expert system proved 34% more effective than assessment alone; in the second population study, it was 31% more effective (23.2% abstinent vs. 17.5%). Working with populations, we were able to produce the outcomes normally found in intense clinic-based programs with low participation rates of much more selected samples of smokers, namely, about 25% abstinence at long-term follow-up. The research to date indicates that proactive, stage-matched treatments emerge as a powerful and inclusive approach to behavior change.

Limitations of the Research

Although more than 1,500 research studies have been conducted on the stages of change, none have directly and prospectively matched and mismatched psychotherapy to the patient's stage of change. Rather, the available research concerns the predictive utility of the stages of change in terms of outcomes and dropouts, the differential use of the processes of change at various stages of change, and the relative efficacy of diverse forms of service delivery. Further, the majority of published research concerns health behaviors and addictive disorders, as contrasted to the wide range of neurotic disorders.

Therapeutic Practices

Three decades of clinical research on the stages of change, including the meta-analyses reviewed in this chapter, have identified a number of therapist behaviors that will improve psychotherapy outcomes.

• *Assess the client's stage of change.* Probably the most obvious and direct implication is to assess the stage of a client's readiness for change and to tailor treatment accordingly. In clinical practice, assessing stage of change typically entails a straightforward question: "Would you say you are not ready to change in the next

6 months (precontemplation), are thinking about changing in the next 6 months (contemplation), are thinking about changing in the next month (preparation), or have already made some progress (action)?" The stages are problem specific, so the question will probably be asked several times for multidisordered patients.

• *Beware treating all patients as though they are in action.* Professionals frequently design excellent action-oriented treatments but then are disappointed when only a small percentage of clients seek that therapy or remain in therapy. The vast majority of patients are *not* in the action stage. Aggregating across studies and populations (Velicer et al., 1995), we estimate that 40% are in precontemplation, 40% in contemplation, and only 20% prepared for action. Thus, professionals offering only action-oriented programs are likely to underserve or misserve the majority of their target population. The therapeutic recommendation is to move from an action paradigm to a stage paradigm.

• *Set realistic goals by moving one stage at a time.* A goal for many patients, particularly in a time-limited managed care environment, is to set realistic goals, such as helping patients progress from precontemplation to contemplation. Such progress means that patients are changing if we view change as a process that unfolds over time, through a series of stages. Helping patients break out of the chronic, stuck phase of precontemplation is a therapeutic success, since it almost doubles the chances that patients will take effective action in the next 6 months. If we can help them progress two stages with brief therapy, we triple the chances they will take effective action.

• *Treat precontemplators gingerly.* We know that, across every disorder that has been studied, people in precontemplation underestimate the pros of changing, overestimate the cons, and are not particularly conscious that they are making such mistakes (Prochaska, 1994). Compared with their peers in other stages, precontemplators rate the cons of changing—and of psychotherapy—as higher than the pros (Hall & Rossi, 2008). No wonder they are at a high risk for dropping out. If psychotherapists try to impose action on these patients, they are likely to drive them away, consequently blaming the clients for being resistant, unmotivated, noncompliant, or not ready for therapy. Historically, it has been therapists who were not ready or motivated to match their relationship and interactions to the clients' needs, and who were resistant to trying new approaches to retaining more clients. Motivational Interviewing (Miller & Rollnick, 2002) has brilliantly incorporated these lessons into its philosophical spirit and its treatment methods.

• *Tailor the processes to the stages.* The research reliably demonstrates that patients optimally progress from precontemplation and contemplation into preparation by use of consciousness raising, self-liberation, and dramatic relief/emotional arousal. Patients progress best from preparation to action and maintenance by use of counterconditioning, stimulus control, and reinforcement management. To simplify: change processes traditionally associated with the insight or awareness therapies for the early stages, and change processes associated with the action therapies for the later stages.

• *Avoid mismatching stages and processes.* A person's stage of change provides proscriptive as well as prescriptive information on treatments of choice. Action-oriented therapies may be quite effective with individuals who are in the preparation or action stages. These same programs tend to be ineffective or detrimental, however, with individuals in precontemplation or contemplation.

We have observed two frequent mismatches (Prochaska, Norcross, & DiClemente, 1995). First, some therapists rely primarily on change processes most indicated for the contemplation stage— consciousness raising, self-reevaluation— while they are moving into the action stage. They try to modify behaviors by becoming more aware, a common criticism of classical psychoanalysis: insight alone does not necessarily bring about behavior change. Second, other therapists rely primarily on change processes most indicated for the action stage—reinforcement management, stimulus control, counterconditioning— without the requisite awareness, decision making, and readiness provided in the contemplation and preparation stages. They try to modify behavior without awareness, a common criticism of radical behaviorism: overt action without insight is likely to lead to temporary change.

• *Prescribe stage-matched "relationships of choice" as well as "treatments of choice."* We conceptualize this practice, paralleling the notion of "treatments of choice" in terms of treatment methods, as offering "therapeutic relationships of choice" in terms of interpersonal stances (Norcross & Beutler, 1997). Once you know a patient's stage of change, then you will know which relationship stances to apply in order to help him/her progress to the next stage and eventually maintenance. Rather than apply therapy relationships in a haphazard or trial-and-error manner, practitioners can use them in a more systematic style across the course of psychotherapy.

These relational matches, as reviewed earlier, entail a nurturing parent stance with a precontemplator, a Socratic teacher role with contemplator, an experienced coach with a patient in action, and then a consultant once into maintenance.

• *Practice integratively.* Psychotherapists moving with their patients through the stages of change over the course of treatment will probably employ relational stances and change processes traditionally emphasized by disparate systems of psychotherapy. That is, they will practice integratively (Norcross & Goldfried, 2005). Competing systems of psychotherapy have promulgated purportedly rival processes of change. However, ostensibly contradictory processes become complementary when embedded in the stages of change. While some psychotherapists insist that such theoretical integration is philosophically impossible, our research has consistently documented that psychotherapists in their consultation rooms can be remarkably effective in synthesizing powerful change processes across the stages (Valasquez, Maurer, Crouch, & DiClemente, 2001).

• *Anticipate recycling.* Most psychotherapy patients will recycle several times through the stages before achieving long-term maintenance. Accordingly, professionals and programs expecting people to progress linearly through the stages of change are likely to gather disappointing results. Be prepared to include relapse prevention in treatment, anticipate the probability of recycling patients, and try to minimize therapist guilt and patient shame over recycling (Prochaska, Norcross, & DiClemente, 2005).

• *Shift to an expanded view of psychotherapy as proactive, population-based health care.* Psychotherapists need not discard effective means of assisting individuals suffering from mental disorders. Instead, we can add to these invaluable services by providing proactive recruitment and treatment of entire populations suffering from chronic biobehavioral conditions. Such an expansion could produce unprecedented impacts on the health and happiness of the populace.

References

Biostat. (2006). *Comprehensive meta-analysis.* Englewood, NJ: Author.

Brogan, M. M., Prochaska, J. O., & Prochaska, J. M. (1999). Predicting termination and continuation status in psychotherapy using the transtheoretical model. *Psychotherapy, 36,* 105–113.

Budney, A. J., Moore, B. A., Rocha, H. L., & Higgins, S. T. (2006). Clinical trial of abstinence-based vouchers and cognitive-behavioral therapy for cannabis dependence. *Journal of Consulting and Clinical Psychology, 74,* 307–316.

Budney, A. J., Higgins, S. T., Radonovich, K. J., & Novy, P. L. (2000). Adding voucher-based incentives to coping skills and motivational enhancement improves outcomes during treatment for marijuana dependence. *Journal of Consulting and Clinical Psychology, 68,* 1051–1061.

Champion, V., Maraj, M., Hui, S., Perkins, A. J., Tierney, W., Menon, U., et al. (2003). Comparison of tailored interventions to increase mammography screening in nonadherent older women. *Preventive Medicine, 36*(2), 150–58.

Chouinard, M. C., & Robichaud-Ekstrand, S. (2007). Predictive value of the transtheoretical model to smoking cessation in hospitalized patients with cardiovascular disease. *European Journal of Cardiovascular Prevention and Rehabilitation, 14*(1), 51–58.

Clark, M., Hampson, S. E., Avery, L., & Simpson, R. (2004). Effects of a tailored lifestyle self-management intervention in patients with Type 2 diabetes. *British Journal of Health Psychology, 9*(3), 365–79.

Connors, G. J., DiClemente, C. C., Dermen, K. H., Kadden, R., Carroll, K. M., & Frone, M. R. (2000). Predicting the therapeutic alliance in alcoholism treatment. *Journal of Studies on Alcohol, 61*(1), 139–49.

DiClemente, C. C. (1991). Motivational interviewing and the stages of change. In W. R. Miller &

S. Rollnick (Eds.), *Motivational interviewing: Preparing people for change.* New York: Guilford.

DiClemente, C. C., Prochaska, J. O., Fairhurst, S. K., Velicer, W. F., Velasquez, M. M., & Rossi, J. S. (1991). The process of smoking cessation: An analysis of precontemplation, contemplation and preparation stages of change. *Journal of Consulting and Clinical Psychology, 59,* 295–304.

Duval, S., & Tweedie, R. (2000). Trim and fill: A simple funnel-plot-based method of testing and adjusting for publication bias in meta-analysis. *Biometrics, 56*(2), 455–63.

Fiore, M., Jaen, C. R., Baker, T. B., et al. (2008). *Treating tobacco use and dependence: 2008 Update.* Rockville, MD: U.S. Department of Health & Human Services. Public Health Service.

Hall, K. L., & Rossi, J. S. (2008). Meta-analytic examination of the strong and weak principles across 48 health behaviors. *Preventive Medicine, 46*(3), 266–74.

Henderson, M. J., Saules, K. K., & Galen, L. W. (2004). The predictive validity of the University of Rhode Island Change Assessment questionnaire in a heroin-addicted polysubstance abuse sample. *Psychology of Addictive Behaviors, 18*(2), 106–112.

Isenhart, C. E. (1997). Pretreatment readiness for change in male alcohol dependent subjects: Predictors of one-year follow-up status. *Journal of Studies on Alcohol, 58*(4), 351–57.

James, W., Preston, N. J., Koh, G., Spencer, C., Kisely, S. R., & Castle, D. J. (2004). A group intervention which assists patients with dual diagnosis reduce their drug use: A randomized controlled trial. *Psychological Medicine, 34*(6), 983–90.

Krebs, P., Prochaska, J. O., & Rossi, J. S. (in press). Defining what works in tailoring: A meta-analysis of computer-tailored interventions for cancer-preventive behavior change. *Preventive Medicine.*

Lipsey, M., & Wilson, D. B. (2001). *Practical meta-analysis.* Thousand Oaks, CA: Sage.

McConnaughy, E. A., DiClemente, C. C., Prochaska, J. O., & Velicer, W. F. (1989). Stages of change in psychotherapy: A follow-up report. *Psychotherapy, 26,* 494–503.

McConnaughy, E. A., Prochaska, J. O., & Velicer, W. F. (1983). Stages of change in psychotherapy: Measurement and sample profiles. *Psychotherapy, 20,* 368–75.

Miller, W. R., & Rollnick, S. (2002). (Eds.), *Motivational interviewing: Preparing people for change* (2nd ed.). New York: Guilford.

Miller, W. R., & Tonigan, J. S. (1996). Assessing drinkers' motivation for change: The Stages of Change Readiness and Treatment Eagerness Scale (SOCRATES). *Psychology of Addictive Behaviors, 10*(2), 81–89.

Miller, W. R., Wilbourne, P. L., & Hettema, J. E. (2003). What works? A summary of alcohol treatment outcome research. In R. K. Hester & W. R. Miller (Eds.), *Handbook of alcoholism treatment approaches: Effective alternatives* (3rd ed., pp. 13–63). Boston: Allyn & Bacon.

Norcross, J. C., & Beutler, L. E. (1997). Determining the therapeutic relationship of choice in brief therapy. In J. N. Butcher (Ed.), *Objective psychological assessment in managed health care: A practitioner's guide.* New York: Oxford University Press.

Norcross, J. C., & Goldfried, M. R. (Eds.). (2005). *Handbook of psychotherapy integration* (2nd ed.). New York: Oxford University Press.

Ockene, J., Kristellar, J., Ockene, I., & Goldberg, R. (1992). Smoking cessation and severity of illness. *Health Psychology, 11,* 119–26.

Patten, C. A., Decker, P. A., Dornelas, E. A., Barbagallo, J., et al. (2008). Changes in readiness to quit and self-efficacy among adolescents receiving a brief office intervention for smoking cessation. *Psychology, Health and Medicine, 13*(3), 326–36.

Pekarik, G., & Wierzbicki, M. (1986). The relationship between clients' expected and actual treatment duration. *Psychotherapy, 23*(4), 532–34.

Prochaska, J. O. (1994). Strong and weak principles for progressing from precontemplation to action on the basis of twelve problem behaviors. *Health Psychology, 13*(1), 47–51.

Prochaska, J. O., & DiClemente, C. C. (1983). Stages and processes of self-change in smoking: Toward an integrative model of change. *Journal of Consulting and Clinical Psychology, 5,* 390–95.

Prochaska, J. O., & DiClemente, C. C. (1985). Common processes of self-change in smoking, weight control, and psychological distress. In S. Shiffman & T. Wills (Eds.), *Coping and substance abuse: A conceptual framework.* New York: Academic Press (pp. 345–63).

Prochaska, J. O., DiClemente, C. C., & Norcross, J. C. (1992). In search of how people change: Applications to addictive behaviors. *American Psychologist, 47,* 1102–1114.

Prochaska, J. O., DiClemente, C. C., Velicer, W. F., Ginpil, S., & Norcross, J. C. (1985). Predicting change in smoking status for self-changers. *Addictive Behaviors, 10,* 395–406.

Prochaska, J. O., DiClemente, C. C., Velicer, W. F., & Rossi, J. S. (1993). Standardized, individualized, interactive, and personalized self-help programs for smoking cessation. *Health Psychology, 12*(5), 399–405.

Prochaska, J. O., & Norcross, J. C. (2010). *Systems of psychotherapy: A transtheoretical analysis* (7th edition). Pacific Grove, CA: Brooks/Cole.

Prochaska, J. O., Norcross, J. C., & DiClemente, C. C. (1995). *Changing for good.* New York: Avon.

Prochaska, J. O., Norcross, J. C., & DiClemente, C. C. (2005). Stages of change: Prescriptive guidelines. In G. P. Koocher, J. C. Norcross, & S. S. Hill. (Eds.), *Psychologists' desk reference* (2nd edition). New York: Oxford University Press.

Prochaska, J. O., Norcross, J. C., Fowler, J, Follick, M., & Abrams, D. B. (1992). Attendance and outcome in a work-site weight control program: Processes and stages of change as process and predictor variables. *Addictive Behaviors, 17,* 35–45.

Prochaska, J. O., Redding, C. A., & Evers, K. (2001). The transtheoretical model and stages of change. In K. Glanz, F. M. Lewis, & B. K. Rimer (Eds.), *Health behavior and health education* (3rd Edition). San Francisco: Jossey-Bass.

Prochaska, J. O., Velicer, W. F., Fava, J. L., Ruggiero, L., Laforge, R. G., Rossi, J. S., et al. (2001). Counselor and stimulus control enhancements of a stage-matched expert system intervention for smokers in a managed care setting. *Preventive Medicine, 32*(1), 23–32.

Prochaska, J. O., Velicer, W. F., Fava, J. L., Rossi, J. S., & Tsoh, J. Y. (2001). Evaluating a population-based recruitment approach and a stage-based expert system intervention for smoking cessation. *Addictive Behaviors, 26,* 583–602.

Prochaska, J. O., Velicer W. F., Redding, C. A., Rossi, J. S., Goldstein, M., DePue, J., et al. (2005). Stage-based expert systems to guide a population of primary care patients to quit smoking, eat healthier, prevent skin cancer and receive regular mammograms. *Preventive Medicine, 41,* 406–416.

Project MATCH Research Group. (1999). Matching alcoholism treatments to client heterogeneity: Project MATCH posttreatment drinking outcomes. *Journal of Studies on Alcohol, 58,* 7–29.

Rosen, C. S. (2000). Is the sequencing of change processes by stage consistent across health problems? A meta-analysis. *Health Psychology, 19*(6), 593–604.

Rossi, J. S. (2002). *Comparison of the use of significance testing and effect sizes in theory-based health promotion research*. Paper presented at the 43rd Annual Meeting of the Society for Multivariate Experimental Psychology.

Valasquez, M. M., Maurer, G., Crouch, C., & DiClemente, C. C. (2001). *Group treatment for substance abuse: A stages-of-change therapy manual*. New York: Guilford.

Van Sluijs, E. M. F., Van Poppel, M. N. M., Twisk, J. W. R., Brug, J., & Van Mechelen, W. (2005). The positive effect on determinants of physical activity of a tailored, general practice-based physical activity intervention. *Health Education Research, 20*(3), 345–56.

Velicer, W. F., Fava, J. L., Prochaska, J. O., Abrams, D. B., Emmons, K. M., & Pierce, J. P. (1995). Distribution of smokers by stage in three representative samples. *Preventive Medicine, 24*(4), 401–411.

Wiggers, L. C. W., Oort, F. J., Dijkstra, A., De Haes, J. C. J. M., Legemate, D. A., & Smets, E. M. A. (2005). Cognitive changes in cardiovascular patients following a tailored behavioral smoking cessation intervention. *Preventive Medicine, 40*(6), 812–21.

Zhang, A. Y., Harmon, J. A., Werkner, J., & McCormick, R. A. (2004). Impacts of motivation for change on the severity of alcohol use by patients with severe and persistent mental illness. *Journal of Studies on Alcohol, 65*(3), 392–97.

Studies Included in the Meta-Analysis

Alexander, P. C., & Morris, E. (2008). Stages of change in batterers and their response to treatment. Violence and Victims, 23(4), 476–92.

Allen, J., Anton, R. F., Babor, T. F., Carbonari, J., Carroll, K. M., Connors, G. J., et al. (1998). Matching alcoholism treatments to client heterogeneity: Project MATCH three-year drinking outcomes. *Alcoholism: Clinical and Experimental Research, 22*(6), 1300–1311.

Ametller, L., Castro, J., Serrano, E., Martínez, E., & Toro, J. (2005). Readiness to recover in adolescent anorexia nervosa: Prediction of hospital admission. *Journal of Child Psychology and Psychiatry and Allied Disciplines, 46*(4), 394–400.

Blanchard, K. A., Morgenstern, J., Morgan, T. J., Labouvie, E., & Bux, D. A. (2003). Motivational subtypes and continuous measures of readiness for change: Concurrent and predictive validity. *Psychology of Addictive Behaviors, 17*(1), 56–65.

Brodeur, N., Rondeau, G., Brochu, S., Lindsay, J., & Phelps, J. (2008). Does the transtheoretical model predict attrition in domestic violence treatment programs? *Violence and Victims, 23*(4), 493–507.

Callaghan, R. C., Hathaway, A., Cunningham, J. A., Vettese, L. C., Wyatt, S., & Taylor, L. (2005). Does stage-of-change predict dropout in a culturally diverse sample of adolescents admitted to inpatient substance-abuse treatment? A test of the transtheoretical model. *Addictive Behaviors, 30*(9), 1834–47.

Callaghan, R. C., Taylor, L., Moore, B. A., Jungerman, F. S., Vilela, F. A. D. B., & Budney, A. J. (2008). Recovery and URICA stage-of-change scores in three marijuana treatment studies. *Journal of Substance Abuse Treatment, 35*(4), 419–26.

Carpenter, K. M., Miele, G. M., & Hasin, D. S. (2002). Does motivation to change mediate the effect of DSM-IV substance use disorders on treatment utilization and substance use? *Addictive Behaviors, 27*(2), 207–25.

Chung, T., & Maisto, S. A. (2009). "What I got from treatment": Predictors of treatment content received and association of treatment content with 6-month outcomes in adolescents. *Journal of Substance Abuse Treatment, 37*(2), 171–81.

Demmel, R., Beck, B., Richter, D., & Reker, T. (2004). Readiness to change in a clinical sample of problem drinkers: Relation to alcohol use, self-efficacy, and treatment outcome. *European Addiction Research, 10*(3), 133–38.

Derisley, J., & Reynolds, S. (2000). The transtheoretical stages of change as a predictor of premature termination, attendance and alliance in psychotherapy. *British Journal of Clinical Psychology, 39*(4), 371–82.

Dozois, D. J. A., Westra, H. A., Collins, K. A., Fung, T. S., & Garry, J. K. F. (2004). Stages of change in anxiety: Psychometric properties of the University of Rhode Island Change Assessment (URICA) scale. *Behaviour Research and Therapy, 42*(6), 711–29.

Eckhardt, C., Holtzworth-Munroe, A., Norlander, B., Sibley, A., & Cahill, M. (2008). Readiness to change, partner violence subtypes, and treatment outcomes among men in treatment for partner assault. *Violence and Victims*, *23*(4), 446–75.

Geller, J., Drab-Hudson, D. L., Whisenhunt, B. L., & Srikameswaran, S. (2004). Readiness to change dietary restriction predicts outcomes in the eating disorders. *Eating Disorders: The Journal of Treatment & Prevention*, *12*(3), 209–24.

Gossop, M., Stewart, D., & Marsden, J. (2007). Readiness for change and drug use outcomes after treatment. *Addiction*, *102*(2), 301–308.

Haller, D. L., Miles, D. R., & Cropsey, K. L. (2004). Smoking stage of change is associated with retention in a smoke-free residential drug treatment program for women. *Addictive Behaviors*, *29*(6), 1265–70.

Henderson, M. J., Saules, K. K., & Galen, L. W. (2004). The predictive validity of the University of Rhode Island Change Assessment questionnaire in a heroin-addicted polysubstance abuse sample. *Psychology of Addictive Behaviors*, *18*(2), 106–112.

Hewes, R. L., & Janikowski, T. P. (1998). Readiness for change and treatment outcome among individuals with alcohol dependency. *Rehabilitation Counseling Bulletin*, *42*(1), 76–93.

Hunt, Y. M., Kyle, T. L., Coffey, S. F., Stasiewicz, P. R., & Schumacher, J. A. (2006). University of Rhode Island Change Assessment - Trauma: Preliminary psychometric properties in an alcohol-dependent PTSD sample. *Journal of Traumatic Stress*, *19*(6), 915–21.

Isenhart, C. E. (1997). Pretreatment readiness for change in male alcohol dependent subjects: Predictors of one-year follow-up status. *Journal of Studies on Alcohol*, *58*(4), 351–57.

Kerns, R. D., Wagner, J., Rosenberg, R., Haythornthwaite, J., & Caudill-Slosberg, M. (2005). Identification of subgroups of persons with chronic pain based on profiles on the pain stages of change questionnaire. *Pain*, *116*(3), 302–310.

Kinnaman, J. E. S., Bellack, A. S., Brown, C. H., & Yang, Y. (2007). Assessment of motivation to change substance use in dually-diagnosed schizophrenia patients. *Addictive Behaviors*, *32*(9), 1798–1813.

Lewis, C. C., Simons, A. D., Silva, S. G., Rohde, P., Small, D. M., Murakami, J. L., et al. (2009). The role of readiness to change in response to treatment of adolescent depression. *Journal of Consulting and Clinical Psychology*, *77*(3), 422–28.

Mitchell, D., & Angelone, D. J. (2006). Assessing the validity of the Stages of Change Readiness and Treatment Eagerness Scale with treatment-seeking military service members. *Military Medicine*, *171*(9), 900–904.

Pantalon, M. V., Nich, C., Frankforter, T., & Carroll, K. M. (2002). The URICA as a measure of motivation to change among treatment-seeking individuals with concurrent alcohol and cocaine problems. *Psychology of Addictive Behaviors*, *16*(4), 299–307.

Pantalon, M. V., & Swanson, A. J. (2003). Use of the University of Rhode Island change assessment to measure motivational readiness to change in psychiatric and dually diagnosed individuals. *Psychology of Addictive Behaviors*, *17*(2), 91–97.

Petry, N. M. (2005). Stages of change in treatment-seeking pathological gamblers. *Journal of Consulting and Clinical Psychology*, *73*(2), 312–22.

Rooney, K., Hunt, C., Humphreys, L., Harding, D., Mullen, M., & Kearney, J. (2005). A test of the assumptions of the transtheoretical model in a post-traumatic stress disorder population. *Clinical Psychology and Psychotherapy*, *12*(2), 97–111.

Scott, K. L., & Wolfe, D. A. (2003). Readiness to change as a predictor of outcome in batterer treatment. *Journal of Consulting and Clinical Psychology*, *71*(5), 879–89.

Smith, K. J., Subich, L. M., & Kalodner, C. (1995). The transtheoretical model's stages and processes of change and their relation to premature termination. *Journal of Counseling Psychology*, *42*(1), 34–39.

Soler, J., Trujols, J., Pascual, J. C., Portella, M. J., Barrachina, J., Campins, J., et al. (2008). Stages of change in dialectical behaviour therapy for borderline personality disorder. *British Journal of Clinical Psychology*, *47*(4), 417–26.

Stotts, A. L., Schmitz, J. M., & Grabowski, J. (2003). Concurrent treatment for alcohol and tobacco dependence: Are patients ready to quit both? *Drug and Alcohol Dependence*, *69*(1), 1–7.

Tambling, R. B., & Johnson, L. N. (2008). The relationship between stages of change and outcome in couple therapy. *American Journal of Family Therapy*, *36*(3), 229–41.

Treasure, J. L., Katzman, M., Schmidt, U., Troop, N., Todd, G., & De Silva, P. (1999). Engagement and outcome in the treatment of bulimia nervosa: First phase of a sequential design comparing motivation enhancement therapy and cognitive behavioural therapy. *Behaviour Research and Therapy, 37*(5), 405–418.

Wade, T. D., Frayne, A., Edwards, S. A., Robertson, T., & Gilchrist, P. (2009). Motivational change in an inpatient anorexia nervosa population and implications for treatment. *Australian and New Zealand Journal of Psychiatry, 43*(3), 235–43.

Willoughby, F. W., & Edens, J. F. (1996). Construct validity and predictive utility of the stages of change scale for alcoholics. *Journal of Substance Abuse, 8*(3), 275–91.

15 Preferences

Joshua K. Swift, Jennifer L. Callahan, *and* Barbara M. Vollmer

In recent years, health care professions have emphasized the inclusion of patient preferences as an essential part of best practice standards (e.g., American Psychological Association, 2006; Institute of Medicine, 2001). In psychology, client preferences have been identified as one of the three key components of evidence-based practice, along with the best available research and clinical expertise. In particular, APA's (2006) evidence-based practice policy states that treatment decisions should be made in collaboration with the patient, with the central goal to maximize patient choice. Involving clients in the decision-making process when providing psychological treatments is important not only because it allows them the freedom to direct their own lives and determine their care, but also because it might provide them with preferred services thought to lead to improved therapy outcomes.

The impact of client preferences on therapy outcomes has been studied empirically for at least 40 years. In perhaps the earliest review of the topic, Rosen (1967) surveyed a number of studies that examined preferences, but discussed only one study that actually looked at the influence preferences exert on treatment outcomes. Based on this early review, Rosen concluded that preferences "might" have an effect on a number of outcome-related variables. In the previous edition of this chapter, Arnkoff, Glass, and Shapiro (2002) reviewed 10 studies examining the relation between therapy outcomes and matching clients to a preferred treatment. Results from their review were inconclusive, with only 2 of the 10 studies finding a significant positive relationship between treatment preference matching and outcome.

Since the 2002 review, there has been increased interest in studying the preference effect; compared with the 10 studies found in 2002, Swift and Callahan (2009) identified 28 studies that tested this effect. Their meta-analysis found that clients who received their preferred treatments were significantly less likely to drop out from therapy prematurely and were significantly more likely to show improved outcomes compared with clients whose preferences were either not considered or not matched. Unfortunately, Swift and Callahan's review only examined preferences for treatment type. Thus, in order to further our understanding of the influence of client preferences on therapy, an updated meta-analysis of the preference effect for all types of client preferences is needed.

In this chapter, we review the empirical evidence supporting the accommodation of patient preferences when providing psychological treatments. Specifically, we examine whether providing patients with their preferred therapy conditions influences rates of premature termination and overall therapy outcomes. We begin by defining and providing clinical examples of preference matching, then provide a summary of our meta-analysis of the research looking at outcome and dropout effects, and conclude with recommendations for therapeutic practices.

Definitions and Measures

In the previous edition of this chapter, client preferences were defined as the behaviors or attributes of the therapist or therapy that clients value or desire (Arnkoff et al., 2002). In other words, client preferences represent what clients would want the therapy encounter to be like if the choice were left to them. This definition of preferences based on *desires* and *values* should be contrasted to definitions of the similar concept of client expectations, which focus more on what the client actually *believes* should or will happen in therapy (see Chapter 18 for a review of expectations). Studies have indicated that although these two constructs are correlated, client preferences and expectations are distinct phenomena that can influence therapy in different ways (Proctor & Rosen, 1981; Tracey & Dundon, 1988).

Three main types of client preferences have been identified in the literature: role preferences, therapist preferences, and treatment type preferences. *Role preferences* involve the behaviors and activities that clients desire themselves and their therapists to engage in while in therapy (e.g., preferring the therapist to take an active advice-giving role versus a listening role, preferring that cognitive-behavioral treatment be administered in a group format rather than an individual format). *Therapist preferences* entail characteristics that clients hope their therapists will possess (e.g., preferring the therapist to have had many years of clinical experience, preferring the therapist to have a similar ethnic background,

preferring to have a therapist that has a empathetic personality style). Finally, *treatment preferences* involve specific desires for the type of intervention that will be used (e.g., preferring a psychodynamic approach versus a behavioral approach, preferring psychotherapy compared to pharmacotherapy).

Various ways of measuring patient preferences can be found in the literature. Perhaps the most popular measure has been to directly ask patients what condition they would prefer to receive: for example, asking patients if they would prefer medication, psychotherapy, or a combination treatment (Kocsis et al., 2009), or asking patients if they would prefer a male or a female therapist (Zlotnick, Elkin, & Shea, 1998). In a variation of this type of measure, a few studies have provided patients with descriptions and/or demonstrations of their options prior to asking them to state a preference. For example, some researchers have played audiotapes of therapists providing descriptions of themselves and their approaches to therapy and then asked patients to indicate which therapist they would prefer to work with (Manthei, Vitalo, & Ivey, 1982). Other researchers have had clients briefly discuss therapy options with a psychotherapist or physician prior to being asked to state a preference for one treatment or another (Adamson, Sellman, & Dore, 2005; Calsyn, Winter, & Morse, 2000). The Treatment Preference Interview (Vollmer, Grote, Lange, & Walker, 2009) is one example of a discussion-based measure that allows clients to express preferences for each of the three main preference domains: roles, therapists, and treatments.

In contrast to directly asking patients for their preferences, some researchers have employed questionnaires or rating scales that assess preferences as well as their degree or strength. Assessing preference strength is of value because one might expect that stronger preferences, compared with slighter preferences, would have a greater influence on treatment outcomes. For example, researchers have not only invited depressed patients to indicate if they preferred interpersonal psychotherapy or pharmacotherapy, but they also asked them to rate on a five-point, Likert-type scale how strongly they wanted their preferred treatment (Raue, Schulberg, Heo, Klimstra, & Bruce, 2009). Similarly, the Treatment Preferences and Experiences Questionnaire (Berg, Sandahl, & Clinton, 2008) was developed to allow patients to rate their preferences according to four intervention and behavior domains: outward orientation (concrete and directive problem-solving interventions), inward orientation (interventions focusing on reflection and inner mental processes), support (wanting advice, encouragement, and sympathy from the therapist), and catharsis (focusing on expressive interventions).

Clinical Examples

The following case examples demonstrate how client preferences can be incorporated into initial treatment planning as well as ongoing therapy decision making. In both cases, the client's preferences were assessed during an intake appointment using the Treatment Preference Interview (Vollmer et al., 2009; Table 15.1). This interview was again administered at every third session, allowing these clients to indicate whether their preferences had changed and whether therapy was accommodating their preferences.

Case Example 1

"Linda," a 55-year-old divorced, Caucasian woman, contacted the clinic because she felt that her gambling was out of control. While she thought that her work performance had not suffered, other aspects of her life had. Linda's financial problems had worsened: she had to sell her home, was thousands of dollars in debt, and was constantly being called by collection agencies. Her family members, who were her only support system since she no longer had friends, had lost respect for her. She reported feeling depressed about the impact gambling had on her life. At the beginning of

Table 15.1   Treatment Preference Interview

Preference factor	Question content and examples
Therapist's characteristics	Strong preferences for counselor's: gender, age, ethnicity or race, language, sexual orientation, religion, or other?
Role preferences	Prior therapy or experience being helped: What was most helpful? What was the worst a therapist could do?
	Preferences for the counselor's approach: Preference for a therapist who takes charge, is active/talkative and expressive/warm, or client taking charge, and the therapist is more quiet and reserved?
	Preferences for treatment modality: Individual, couple, group, or family sessions?
	Preferences for therapy tasks: Try new things between sessions, reading self-help books, watching self-help movies, going online for information
Type of therapy	Beliefs about the causes of the problem: Will of God, unlucky experiences, biological makeup, unmet emotional needs, unrealistic expectations, relationship conflicts, lack of self-knowledge, lifestyle, or lack of will power?
	Preferences for type of therapy: solution-focused, cognitive-behavioral, or psychodynamic therapy? (Therapy descriptions were also provided, including typical goals, therapist–client relationship, and tasks.)
	Preferences for who decides about the type of therapy: Client makes the decision, client and therapist collaborate, or therapist makes the decision?

her therapy, Linda scored 68 on the Outcome Questionnaire 45.2 (OQ-45.2; Lambert et al., 1996), in the clinical range of disturbance, and she met diagnostic criteria for pathological gambling.

Linda responded positively to the possibility of being asked about her preferences. She stated that preferences were important to her "in order to individualize her treatment, since no one treatment is best for every person." During the Treatment Preference Interview, Linda was first asked about her preferences for therapist characteristics. Linda expressed a strong preference for a female therapist, partially due to a positive past experience with a female counselor and partially due to the difficulty she had in trusting men after an abusive marriage. In addition, she indicated that she preferred a therapist "who is warm, caring, and shows emotions" as well as empathy. In terms of role preferences, Linda strongly preferred individual therapy sessions compared with family or group therapy. Additionally, Linda did not want her therapist to "take a more directive and active approach . . . by giving opinions and making suggestions." She indicated that she desired to have a "collaborative" relationship with her therapist, "having specific goals to guide our work together."

In terms of treatment preferences, Linda responded positively to two therapy descriptions. Her first choice was psychodynamic, particularly because she was interested in identifying repetitive patterns in her life and relationships. Her second choice was motivational enhancement. This option appealed to Linda because of the collaborative nature of the relationship and elements that drew upon her strengths while still acknowledging her weaknesses. Linda strongly disliked twelve-step facilitation as a result of her experience at Gamblers Anonymous meetings. She did not identify with the spiritual principles prevalent in the twelve-step approach nor the individuals who attended meetings, as they did not seem to have problems with Internet gambling. Linda stated that her treatment goals were to regain her "sense of empowerment," to earn the perception of being a "strong woman" from her family members, to learn how to take better care of her health, and to change her gambling habit.

For the most part, the therapist adhered to Linda's preferences. Throughout their sessions, the therapist focused on Linda's feelings and the meanings attached to them. The therapist noted that Linda found it much easier to express her thoughts rather than her emotions. By the fourth session, Linda provided written feedback that she wanted therapy to continue to focus on building awareness of her feelings, and that she found the realization of a connection between her emotions and actions to be enlightening.

Although the therapist largely adhered to Linda's preferences for roles and type of therapy, the therapist noted that she breached them during the 12th session when she introduced the principles of cognitive-behavioral therapy (CBT) and the idea of a thought log as a homework exercise. The therapist quickly noticed that Linda became disengaged when discussing CBT and concluded that the introduction of CBT and homework was a mistake because it had not accommodated Linda's preferences. The therapist's observation was corroborated in Linda's ratings of the working alliance for that session; the item asking about whether "my therapist and I agree on ways to achieve my goals" was rated lower.

The therapist and client mutually terminated after 16 sessions. By this time Linda's OQ-45.2 score had dropped into the normal range, 47, indicating a clinically significant improvement. Her rating of the working alliance had also improved; going from an initial score of 9 to a score of 14.5

on the revised short version of the Working Alliance Inventory (WAI-S; Hatcher & Gillaspy, 2006). Overall, the client reported that working on family issues had been helpful, that her urge to gamble had dissipated, and that she was taking better care of herself. At her termination session, Linda's written response to the question "Do you feel that your therapist had a good understanding of your goal(s) for therapy?" was as follows: "Yes—She took my lead and went with it . . . I believe it was a good match. I respect and admire her."

Case Example 2

"Ruth," a 39-year-old pregnant Caucasian woman, contacted the clinic for assistance with relationship problems with her boyfriend, indicating that she had become increasingly concerned about his problems with alcohol. Ruth reported that he became emotionally abusive when he was drinking, and this was not the type of relationship she was hoping for when starting a family. Ruth wanted to be able to enjoy her pregnancy and look forward to becoming a parent. Her friends urged her to leave her boyfriend; however, she hoped that he would change and become a good father for his child. At the beginning of her therapy, Ruth scored 82 on the OQ-45.2, falling in the clinical range.

During the Treatment Preference Interview, Ruth indicated that she had no strong preferences for her therapist's age, gender, or sexual orientation. However, she did state that she wanted a therapist whom she could "connect" to, who would actively work with her on an equal basis, who would not be too confronting or challenging, and who would not "judge her too harshly" for being pregnant and unmarried. When asked about role preferences, Ruth expressed a desire for self-help books and self-help movies to be incorporated into her counseling, and openness to completing homework assignments between sessions. In terms of treatment preferences, Ruth strongly desired a CBT approach to her therapy. Ruth's treatment goals were to improve communication with her boyfriend, friends, and coworkers; to adjust better to her partner's reemergence of alcohol abuse; and to learn better problem-solving and decision-making skills.

Ruth started therapy by "no-showing" for the second session. When her therapist called to encourage her to continue treatment, she responded by returning and regularly attending after that point. Her therapist attributed Ruth's "no-show" as a test of whether the therapist would be non-judgmental and willing to work with her. Therapy primarily focused on Ruth's automatic thoughts of not feeling worthy to have a good life and her need to look to others for validation. Ruth indicated that therapy helped her learn to recognize and challenge her maladaptive thinking patterns and develop more assertive behaviors in her social and work relationships. When assessed at different time points during therapy, Ruth continued to express a preference for CBT. For example, when her therapist introduced thought logs, she wrote on her Session Feedback Survey that she "liked CBT."

Throughout therapy, Ruth continued to express hope that her boyfriend would change his behaviors. As might have been expected from her original goals, Ruth responded more positively to discussions concerning ways to manage her conflicts with her boyfriend, rather than to questions about the evidence that he would change. However, by the end of therapy she was able to look at her relationship in terms of her assumptions and beliefs and was able to state "If my partner behaves poorly, it is not a reflection on me," and "People are responsible for their own behavior." Interestingly, on the occasions when her therapist was challenging, such as suggesting her need to set better boundaries, Ruth rated the working alliance as lower for those sessions.

Ruth attended a total of 20 sessions. After the 11th session, she took a break from therapy when she was about to give birth. She later returned to therapy for an additional nine sessions. This return to therapy included a switch to a new male therapist as compared with the previous female one. Perhaps due to the lack of preference concerning therapist demographic characteristics, which was expressed prior to therapy, Ruth transitioned easily to her second therapist. Ruth, in her written comments about both therapists, noted several times that they were nonjudgmental and that she found it helpful to feel that she could talk about personal concerns in confidence. By the end of treatment, Ruth's OQ-45.2 score had dropped to the low 60s, indicating clinically significant improvement. Her WAI-S score had improved to 12.25 out of 15 points.

Meta-Analytic Review

The preceding case examples illustrate the probable influence of patient preferences on treatment progress, but here we examine more systematically the relation of patient preferences to psychotherapy outcomes. We summarize the results of our meta-analysis of studies comparing dropout rates and/or outcomes between preference-matched and preference non-matched patients.

Search Strategy

We began with an initial search of PsycINFO for articles published between 1967 (Rosen's review of client preferences) and September 2009. The electronic search was conducted using the following terms: *preference* or *choice,* in combination with *therapy* or *psychotherapy* or *treatment* or *therapist* or *counselor* or *therapeutic alliance* or *role,* and *matching*

or *outcome.* Using these terms, 3,895 citations were identified. Several journals were also hand searched for relevant studies. Further search strategies included pulling citations from the reference lists of relevant articles and exploring all studies in PsycINFO that cited a relevant study. All abstracts from the resulting citations were reviewed. Based on the abstracts, 134 potentially relevant articles were further evaluated to determine if they met inclusion criteria.

Inclusion Criteria

All published studies in the English language that assessed client preferences prior to treatment and examined the effect (on therapy dropout or outcome) of matching clients to their preferred therapy conditions were included in this meta-analysis. Studies were excluded if they used a nonclinical sample (e.g., students participating for course credit), studied a variable not related to a clinical problem (e.g., speed reading), did not involve matching of at least part of the sample to their preferred therapy condition, did not involve the administration of a psychological treatment (e.g., use of only medication groups, use of interview-only interventions), or did not include a measure of therapy dropout or outcome (e.g., examined the preference effect for treatment satisfaction). Where multiple studies analyzed the data from the same group of clients, the study with the most recent follow-up period or with the largest sample was used in the analysis. After further review, a total of 38 studies were deemed eligible for inclusion in the meta-analysis.

Study Coding

These 38 studies were coded by two independent evaluators to assess a number of variables: the type of preference (role, therapist, or treatment), problem treated, treatments that were provided (e.g., CBT, IPT, pharmacotherapy, psychodynamic), method of allocation to preference conditions (partially randomized preference trial, randomized/assigned to treatment conditions, or randomized/assigned to preference match conditions), and primary outcome (identified through statements/hypotheses made by the original authors). The two independent coders showed a high level of agreement (97.78%) across all variables. Where a discrepancy was found, a third coder was asked to code the relevant variable.

Methodological Decisions

We were interested in measuring outcome and dropout differences between those clients who were matched and those clients who were not matched to preferred therapy conditions. The results from each of the studies were summarized using odds ratios when examining therapy dropout and Cohen's d when examining therapy outcome. Of the 38 studies deemed eligible for inclusion, 3 did not contain sufficient outcome or dropout data to include their results in either analysis; thus, 35 studies were included in the remaining analyses. Where outcome results were reported for multiple measures within a single study, only one primary outcome measure (see study coding above) from each study was used in our analyses.

Effect sizes and confidence intervals for each of the studies were calculated, following which an aggregate effect size was then calculated across studies using a random-effects model. A fail-safe N was calculated, representing the number of nonsignificant, nonpublished studies that would be needed to dilute the results of the meta-analysis. Moderators were next tested using the Q-statistic and a random-effects model. A significant Q-statistic between groups indicates a difference that is greater than expected by chance. In addition, the I^2 statistic was calculated for each group of

moderators, estimating the percentage of variability due to true differences among the studies. Calculations were completed using Comprehensive Meta-Analysis, Version 2 (Borenstein, Hedges, Higgins, & Rothstein, 2005).

Effect on Dropout

Eighteen of the 35 studies compared dropout rates between clients who received their preferred therapy conditions and those who did not. An odds ratio effect size was calculated for each of the studies, which represents the ratio of dropouts versus completers between the compared groups. While an odds ratio of 1 indicates that an equal number of clients dropped out of each group, in our analyses an odds ratio less than 1 indicates fewer clients dropped out of the preference-matched groups, and an odds ratio greater than 1 indicates fewer clients dropped out of the preference non-matched groups. A forest plot of the odds ratio effect sizes for each study and the aggregate effect can be viewed in Figure 15.1. The overall effect on dropout was significant ($OR = 0.59$, $CI_{.95}$: 0.44 to 0.78, $p < 0.001$), indicating that clients who received their preferred conditions were between a half and a third less likely to drop out of therapy prematurely compared with clients who did not receive their preferred therapy conditions, or for every 5 non-matched clients who dropped out prematurely, only 3 matched clients dropped out. Heterogeneity between studies was not found [$Q(17) = 22.46$, $p = 0.17$, $I^2 = 24.31$]. Calculation of the fail-safe N indicated that 89 unpublished studies with nonsignificant results would be required to reduce the results of the preference effect on therapy dropout to a nonsignificant level.

Effect on Outcome

Thirty-three of the 35 studies included an outcome comparison between clients who

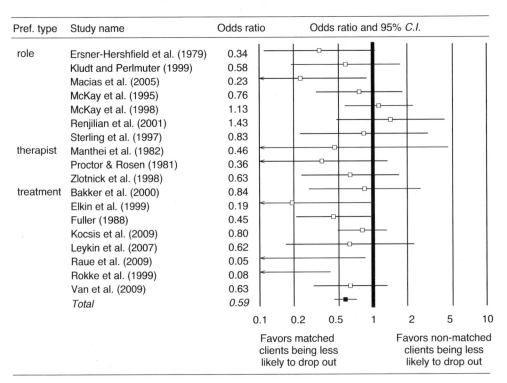

Pref. type	Study name	Odds ratio	Odds ratio and 95% C.I.
role	Ersner-Hershfield et al. (1979)	0.34	
	Kludt and Perlmuter (1999)	0.58	
	Macias et al. (2005)	0.23	
	McKay et al. (1995)	0.76	
	McKay et al. (1998)	1.13	
	Renjilian et al. (2001)	1.43	
	Sterling et al. (1997)	0.83	
therapist	Manthei et al. (1982)	0.46	
	Proctor & Rosen (1981)	0.36	
	Zlotnick et al. (1998)	0.63	
treatment	Bakker et al. (2000)	0.84	
	Elkin et al. (1999)	0.19	
	Fuller (1988)	0.45	
	Kocsis et al. (2009)	0.80	
	Leykin et al. (2007)	0.62	
	Raue et al. (2009)	0.05	
	Rokke et al. (1999)	0.08	
	Van et al. (2009)	0.63	
	Total	*0.59*	

0.1 0.2 0.5 1 2 5 10

Favors matched clients being less likely to drop out — Favors non-matched clients being less likely to drop out

Fig. 15.1 Dropout effect sizes (odd ratios) for preference match vs. nonmatch groups.

did and did not receive a preferred therapy condition. Cohen's *d* was calculated for each of these studies, and a forest plot of the effect sizes can be viewed in Figure 15.2. The overall effect size was $d = 0.31$ ($CI_{.95}$: 0.20 to 0.43), indicating a small but significant ($z = 5.39$, $p < 0.001$) outcome effect in favor of those clients who received their preferred therapy conditions. Heterogeneity between the 33 studies was found [$Q(32) = 57.78$, $p < 0.01$, $I^2 = 44.63$], indicating that the studies did differ significantly in their outcome effect size estimates. Calculation of the fail-safe *N* indicated that 427 unpublished studies with nonsignificant results would be required to reduce the results of the preference effect on treatment outcome to a nonsignificant level.

Moderators
Preference Characteristics
Preference Type. The effect of receiving or not receiving a preferred therapy condition may be moderated by what type of preference is

considered—role, therapist, or treatment. Preference type was tested as a moderating variable for the preference effect on therapy dropout and therapy outcome. A total of 11 studies examined role preferences, 3 examined therapist preference, and 21 examined treatment preferences. Of the 18 studies that reported dropout rates, the difference in effect size estimates between these groups was not significant [$Q(2) = 1.59$, $p = 0.45$], indicating that therapy dropout was similarly influenced by matching clients to any of the three preferred therapy conditions. In terms of treatment outcome, the difference between preference type groups was also not significant [$Q(2) = 0.10$, $p = 0.88$], indicating that treatment outcome was also similarly influenced by matching clients to their preferred therapy roles, therapists, or types of treatment.

Preference for or against Pharmacotherapy. Several studies specifically examined the preference effect when psychotherapy was compared with pharmacotherapy. Of the

Pref. type	Study name	Effect size d	Effect size and 95% C.I.
role	Al-Otaiba et al. (2008)	0.52	
	Cooper (1980a)	0.69	
	Cooper (1980b)	0.54	
	Gossop et al. (1986)	0.51	
	Kludt and Perlmuter (1999)	0.14	
	Macias et al. (2005)	0.08	
	McKay et al. (1995)	0.09	
	McKay et al. (1998)	0.25	
	Renjilian et al. (2001)	−0.14	
	Sterling et al. (1997)	0.47	
therapist	Manthei et al. (1982)	0.23	
	Zlotnick et al. (1998)	0.37	
treatment	Adamson et al. (2005)	0.52	
	Bakker et al. (2000)	0.31	
	Berg et al. (2008)	0.65	
	Brown et al. (2002)	0.37	
	Calsyn et al. (2000)	0.10	
	Chilvers et al. (2001)	0.33	
	Devine & Fernald (1973)	1.19	
	Dyck & Spinhoven (1997)	0.10	
	Elkin et al. (1999)	1.15	
	Fuller (1988)	−0.27	
	Gum et al. (2006)	0.07	
	Iacoviello et al. (2007)	1.15	
	Kadish (1999)	0.22	
	Kocsis et al. (2009)	1.01	
	Leykin et al. (2007)	0.31	
	Lin et al. (2005)	0.23	
	Raue et al. (2009)	−0.18	
	Rokke et al. (1999)	0.37	
	Van et al. (2009)	0.10	
	Wallach (1988)	0.44	
	Ward et al. (2000)	−0.08	
	Total	*0.31*	

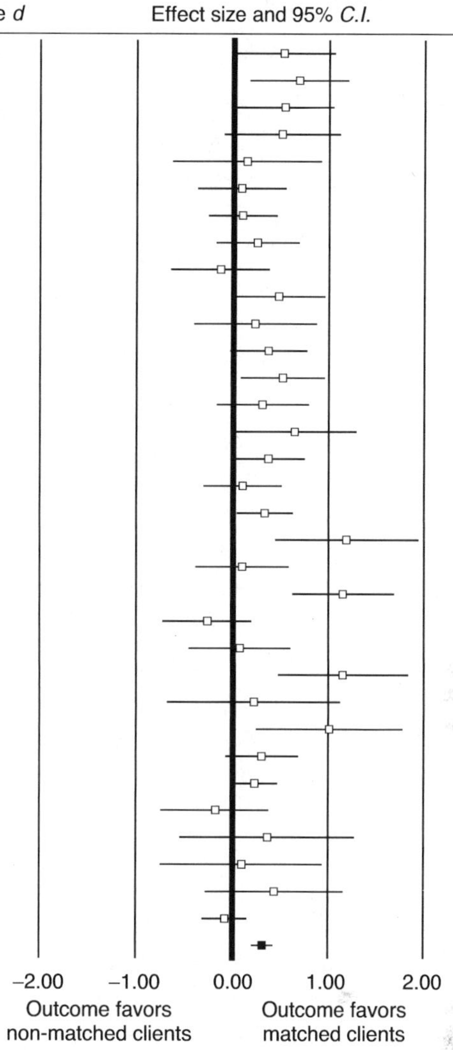

−2.00   −1.00   0.00   1.00   2.00

Outcome favors non-matched clients   Outcome favors matched clients

Fig. 15.2 Outcome effect sizes (d) for preference match vs. nonmatch groups.

studies that reported dropout rates, 7 examined the preference effect for psychotherapy versus pharmacotherapy and 11 examined the preference effect for one form of psychotherapy versus another. The difference between these groups was not significant [$Q(1) = 0.37$, $p = 0.55$]. In terms of treatment outcome, the average effect size for studies comparing preferences for psychotherapy versus pharmacotherapy ($k = 12$) was $d = 0.36$ ($CI_{.95}$: 0.24 to 0.49), while the average effect size for studies comparing preference for one form of psychotherapy versus another form of psychotherapy ($k = 21$) was $d = 0.21$ ($CI_{.95}$: 0.10 to 0.31). This difference showed a trend toward significance [$Q(1) = 3.49$, $p = 0.06$], indicating that preferences for psychotherapy versus pharmacotherapy may have a greater influence on treatment outcome than preferences between two forms of psychotherapy.

Client Characteristics

The only client characteristic that was reliably reported across studies and that could be compared between studies was client diagnosis/problem (e.g., anxiety, depression, substance abuse). In terms of therapy dropout, average odds ratios between the three compared groups (depression, substance abuse, and obesity) were not significantly different [$Q(2) = 3.04$, $p = 0.22$], indicating that matching clients to their preferred therapy conditions had a similar effect on therapy dropout rates regardless of the problem being treated. In terms of therapy outcome, studies of anxiety ($k = 6$) found an average preference effect of $d = 0.49$ ($CI_{.95}$: 0.19 to 0.79), studies of depression ($k = 12$) found an average preference effect of $d = 0.35$ ($CI_{.95}$: 0.13 to 0.57), studies of a health concern ($k = 3$) found an average preference effect of $d = -.07$ ($CI_{.95}$: $-.43$ to 0.29), studies of serious mental illness ($k = 2$) found an average preference effect of $d = 0.09$ ($CI_{.95}$: $-.22$ to 0.40), and studies of substance abuse ($k = 8$) found an average preference effect of $d = 0.34$ ($CI_{.95}$: 0.18 to 0.51). Preference effect differences between these groups showed a trend toward significance [$Q(4) = 7.71$, $p = 0.10$]. While matching client preferences did positively influence treatment outcomes for anxiety, depression, and substance abuse, preference matching showed little benefit in the treatment of health concerns and serious mental illness.

Design Characteristics

Study Design. The studies included in this meta-analysis varied in the designs used to examine the preference effect. These designs included partially randomized preference trials (PRPTs), studies that randomized or assigned clients to a treatment condition, and studies that randomized or assigned clients to a preference condition. The differences between studies in terms of design may have influenced the magnitude of the preference effect. Because PRPTs actually only compare clients who express preferences with clients who do not express strong preferences, these studies may underestimate the influence preferences have on

treatment dropout and outcome. In contrast, the other two types of designs make comparisons between clients who are given a therapy that matches their preferences and clients who are given a therapy that directly opposes their preferences, thus maximizing the differences between groups.

Type of study design was tested as a moderator for the preference effect for both therapy dropout and outcome. In terms of therapy dropout, the difference between the three design groups was not significant [$Q(2) = 3.33$, $p = 0.19$], indicating that study design did not moderate the effect preferences had on therapy dropout. In terms of therapy outcome, the three types of study design [PRPTs ($d = 0.16$, $CI_{.95}$: 0.00 to 0.32), studies allocating to preference conditions ($d = 0.24$, $CI_{.95}$: 0.01 to 0.46), and studies allocating to treatment conditions ($d = 0.45$, $CI_{.95}$: 0.28 to 0.62)] were found to be significantly different in their estimates [$Q(2) = 6.17$, $p = 0.02$]. While the largest outcome difference between matched and nonmatched clients was found in studies that randomized or assigned clients to a treatment condition, the smallest outcome difference between preference-matched and nonmatched clients was found in the group of PRPTs, as predicted.

Dropout/Outcome Measurement Type. The studies included in this meta-analysis differed both in how therapy dropout was defined (for those that included an assessment of dropout) and in how treatment outcome was measured. Thus, measurement type was also tested as a design moderator for the overall preference effects. Regarding outcomes, 7 studies measured outcome by ratings from an independent rater (e.g., HRSD, SCID), 6 studies used an objective measurement (e.g., BMI, urine analysis), and 19 studies measured outcome by patient self-report. A significant difference in effect size estimates between these groups was not found [$Q(3) = 0.10$, $p = 0.99$].

In terms of the preference dropout effect by assessment type, the studies ($k = 11$) that defined dropout as not completing a full treatment protocol found an average preference effect size of $OR = 0.73$ ($CI_{.95}$: 0.56 to 0.94), while the studies ($k = 2$) that assessed dropout by therapist rating found an average preference effect size of $OR = 0.38$ ($CI_{.95}$: 0.12 to 1.20) and the studies ($k = 5$) that defined dropout as having attended less than a set number of sessions found an average preference effect size of $OR = 0.34$ ($CI_{.95}$: 0.19 to 0.60). The effect size estimates from these three groups showed a trend toward significance [$Q(2) = 5.63$, $p = 0.06$]. When dropout was defined by completion of a treatment protocol, smaller differences (compared with differences found by the other two definitions of dropout) between those who received a preferred therapy condition and those who received a nonpreferred therapy condition were observed. Perhaps clients who received a nonpreferred therapy were willing to "stick it out" through a treatment that had a defined number of sessions in its protocol, but these nonmatched clients prematurely terminated when a predetermined number of treatment sessions had not been set.

Time of Outcome Measurement. Time of outcome measurement was also assessed as a design characteristic that may have had an influence on the overall preference effect. In testing this variable, we were examining whether receiving a preferred therapy condition resulted in improved outcomes (over clients who did not receive a preferred condition) equally early on in therapy, immediately after the completion of therapy, and at follow-up time points. There was not a significant difference in the effect size estimates between these groups [$Q(2) = 0.41$, $p = 0.82$], indicating that

time of outcome measurement was not a moderating variable.

Patient Contributions

In our meta-analysis we saw that client preferences influenced both who dropped out of therapy prematurely and who showed greater improvements while in therapy, thus illustrating the importance of accommodating client preferences in the therapy encounter. Patient preferences can be viewed as a variable that patients contribute to the therapy relationship because most patients enter therapy with specific desires or hopes concerning what treatment will be like. Patient preferences have been found to be influenced by a number of other variables, such as demographic characteristics, beliefs about the nature of their problems, level of symptom severity, previous experience with therapy, expectations for therapy, and other life experiences (e.g., Bedi et al., 2000; Churchill et al., 2000; Ertl & McNamara, 2000; Gum et al., 2006; Riedel-Heller, Matschinger, & Angermeyer, 2005; Vincent & LeBow, 1995; Wanigaratne & Barker, 1995; Wong, Kim, Zane, Kim, & Huang, 2003). Given the number of variables that could possibly influence preferences for therapy, each client should be viewed as a unique individual with different hopes or desires for what therapy will be like. It may well be labeled as the therapist's responsibility to elicit these individual preferences and then make treatment decisions in conjunction with their clients.

In turn, it could be considered a patient responsibility to be forthcoming with therapists concerning treatment preferences. If therapists are unaware of their patients' preferences, they will not likely accommodate them. However, some clients may be hesitant about expressing their preferences due to a number of factors. For example, clients who specifically enter treatment to work on an addictive behavior may indicate a preference to work on another problem or to use a treatment that is not as directed at their addiction because they are not yet ready to change. Some clients may also be hesitant about expressing preferences because they do not know that it is appropriate to do so or because they are unaware that different treatment options even exist. Additionally, patients who see their therapists as authority figures or who have yet to develop trust in their therapists may be hesitant because they think the therapists know best, or they worry that their preferences will be ignored or not taken seriously. In each of these situations, therapists should seek to overcome the barriers that prevent clients from expressing their preferences.

At the same time, some patients may be hesitant about airing their preferences because they do not want their preferences to be taken into account when treatment decisions are made. In one psychology department clinic, 42% of the clients preferred therapists to make treatment decisions, compared with clients making the decision, or clients and therapists collaborating to make treatment decisions together (Grote, Lange, Walker, & Vollmer, 2009). Yet, a client's desire to not be involved in the treatment decision-making process remains a preference that therapists can elicit and address.

Limitations of the Research

A number of limitations exist with the current body of research. Although this area of research has a history dating back over 40 years, the number of published studies is still relatively small. This limitation is particularly evident for studies examining clients' preferences for their therapists, with only three studies being found. In addition, research has primarily examined the preference effect post hoc in studies that were designed to study treatment effects. Although randomized controlled trials (RCTs) have

been identified as the gold standard for measuring treatment effects, patients in these trials are not randomized into preference (matched versus not-matched) conditions; thus, there is no guarantee that patients in the preference conditions are similar or even comparable. RCTs may also fail to properly account for client preferences because many clients who hold strong preferences (the group where one might expect to see the largest preference effect) refuse randomization into treatment groups. In response to this limitation, the PRPT has been developed. Although clients with strong preferences are more likely to be included in studies using this design, in PRPTs the preference effect is likely to be attenuated because no clients actually receive a nonpreferred treatment. PRPTs only compare clients who have stronger preferences with clients who hold weaker or no preferences. We believe the most clinically appropriate and methodologically sound design to measure the preference effect is to randomize clients into preference conditions. Regrettably, only about a third of the preference effect studies that have been conducted have used this design.

An additional limitation of the research reviewed is that most studies have failed to examine how other client variables influence the preference effect. None of the studies included in this review examined whether patient gender, age, or race/ethnicity affected whether preferences impacted therapy dropout or treatment outcomes. One might hypothesize that just as client diagnosis moderates the preference effect, other demographic variables could also moderate the magnitude of the overall effect.

A final concern is that very few of the studies identified employed a measure of preference strength; only one study in this meta-analysis assessed whether preference strength influenced the preference effect.

One might expect that receiving or not receiving a preferred therapy condition would exert large dropout and outcome effects for clients who strongly desire a given condition. On the other hand, receiving a preferred therapy condition may make little difference to patients who only slightly prefer one condition over another. However, given the lack of assessment of preference strength in the current research, this hypothesis could not be tested.

Therapeutic Practices

Based on the existing research, we can conclude that client preferences exert an influence on therapy dropout and treatment outcomes. Specifically, clients who receive a treatment that matches or considers their preferences, compared with clients who receive non-preferred conditions or clients whose preferences are ignored, are about one-half to one-third less likely to drop out of treatment prematurely and are more likely to show improved therapy outcomes. Given this significant preference effect, we offer the following clinical recommendations:

• Assess clients' preferences prior to the start of treatment. This assessment can address preferences for therapy roles, therapist characteristics, and treatment types.

• Seek to overcome barriers that might prevent clients from expressing their preferences, such as paucity of information about therapy options, lack of trust in the therapist, or low readiness to change.

• Address client preferences throughout the therapy process. Clients may change their preferences after starting treatment, or clients may feel as if their preferences are not being addressed despite therapists' attempts to do so.

• Accommodate client preferences whenever possible. The findings from this meta-analysis illustrate that when client preferences are addressed, fewer clients drop out of therapy prematurely, and clients show greater improvements in therapy outcomes.

• When a therapist believes that a client's preferences for therapy are not in the client's best interest, share these concerns with the client so that treatment decisions can still be made collaboratively.

References

An asterisk (*) indicates studies included in the meta-analysis.

*Adamson, S. J., Sellman, J. D., & Dore, G. M. (2005). Therapy preference and treatment outcome in clients with mild to moderate alcohol dependence. *Drug and Alcohol Review, 24,* 209–216.

*Al-Otaiba, Z., Worden, B. L., McCrady, B. S., & Epstein, E. E. (2008). Accounting for self-selected drinking goals in the assessment of treatment outcome. *Psychology of Addictive Behaviors, 22,* 439–43.

American Psychological Association Presidential Task Force on Evidence-Based Practice (2006). Evidence-based practice in psychology. *American Psychologist, 61,* 271–85.

Arnkoff, D. B., Glass, C. R., & Shapiro, S. J. (2002). Expectations and preferences. In J. C. Norcross (Ed.), *Psychotherapy relationships that work: Therapist contributions and responsiveness to patients.* (pp. 335–56). New York: Oxford University Press.

*Bakker, A., Spinhove, P., Van Balkom, A. J. L. M., Vleugel, L., & Van Dyck, R. (2000). Cognitive therapy by allocation versus cognitive therapy by preference in the treatment of panic disorder. *Psychotherapy and Psychosomatics, 69,* 240–43.

Bedi, N., Chilvers, C., Churchill, R., Dewey, M., Duggan, C., Fielding, K., et al. (2000). Assessing effectiveness of treatment of depression in primary care: Partially randomized preference trial. *British Journal of Psychiatry, 177,* 312–318.

*Berg, A. L., Sandahl, C., & Clinton, D. (2008). The relationship of treatment preferences and experiences to outcome in generalized anxiety disorder. *Psychology and Psychotherapy: Theory, Research, and Practice, 81,* 247–259.

Borenstein, M., Hedges, L. V., Higgins, J. P. T., & Rothstein, H. R. (2005). Comprehensive meta-analysis, Version 2. Englewood, NY: Biostat.

*Brown, T. G., Seraganian, P., Tremblay, J., & Annis, H. (2002). Matching substance abuse aftercare treatments to client characteristics. *Addictive Behaviors, 27*, 585–604.

*Calsyn, R. J., Winter, J. P., & Morse, G. A. (2000). Do consumers who have a choice of treatment have better outcomes? *Community Mental Health Journal, 36*, 149–60.

*Chilvers, C., Dewey, M., Fielding, K., Gretton, V., Millwer, P., Palmer, B., et al. (2001). Antidepressant drugs and generic counseling for treatment of major depression in primary care: Randomized trial with patient preference arms. *British Medical Journal, 322*, 1–5.

Churchill, R., Khaira, M., Gretton, V., Chilvers, C., Dewey, M., Duggan, C., et al. (2000). Treating depression in general practice: Factors affecting patients' treatment preferences. *British Journal of General Practice, 50*, 905–906.

*Cooper, J. (1980). Reducing fears and increasing assertiveness: The role of dissonance reduction. *Journal of Experimental Social Psychology, 16*, 199–213.

*Devine, D. A., & Fernald, P. S. (1973). Outcome effects of receiving a preferred, randomly assigned, or nonpreferred therapy. *Journal of Consulting and Clinical Psychology, 41*, 104–107.

*Dyck, V. R., & Spinhoven, P. (1997). Does preference for type of treatment matter?: A study of exposure in vivo with or without hypnosis in the treatment of panic disorder with agoraphobia. *Behavior Modification, 21*, 172–86.

*Elkin, I., Yamaguchi, J. L., Arnkoff, D. B., Glass, C. R., Sotsky, S. M., & Krupnick, J. L. (1999). "Patient-treatment fit" and early engagement in therapy. *Psychotherapy Research, 9*, 437–51.

*Ersner-Hershfield, S., Abramowitz, S. I., & Baren, J. (1979). Incentive effects of choosing a therapist. *Journal of Clinical Psychology, 35*, 404–406.

Ertl, M. A., & McNamara, J. R. (2000). Predicting potential client treatment preferences. *Psychotherapy, 37*, 219–27.

*Fuller, T. C. (1988). The role of patient preference for treatment type in the modification of weight loss behavior. *Dissertation Abstracts International, 49*, 2932.

*Gossop, M., Johns, A., & Green, L. (1986). Opiate withdrawal: Inpatient versus outpatient programmes and preferred versus random assignment to treatment. *British Medical Journal, 293*, 103–104.

Grote, J., Lange, R., Walker, C., & Vollmer, B. (2009). The effect of client choice on treatment outcomes. Presentation at the American Psychological Convention, Toronto, Canada.

*Gum, A. M., Arean, P. A., Hunkeler, E., Tang, L., Katon, M., Hitchcock, P., et al. (2006). Depression treatment preferences in older primary care patients. *The Gerontologist, 46*, 14–22.

Hatcher, R. L., & Gillaspy, J. A. (2006). Development and validation of a revised short version of the Working Alliance Inventory. *Psychotherapy Research, 16*, 12–25.

*Iacoviello, B. M., McCarthy, K. S., Barrett, M. S., Rynn, M., Gallop, R., & Barber, J. P. (2007). Treatment preferences affect the therapeutic alliance: Implications for randomized controlled trials. *Journal of Consulting and Clinical Psychology, 75*, 194–98.

Institute of Medicine (2001). *Crossing the quality chasm: A new health system for the 21st century.* Washington, DC: Institute of Medicine.

*Kadish, D. A. (1999). Psychological mindedness and psychotherapy orientation preference as predictors of treatment outcome for social phobia. *Dissertation Abstracts International, 60*, 832.

*Kludt, C. J., & Perlmuter, L. (1999). Effects of control and motivation on treatment outcome. *Journal of Psychoactive Drugs, 31*, 405–414.

*Kocsis, J. H., Leon, A. C., Markowitz, J. C., Manber, R., Arnow, B., Klein, D. N., & et al. (2009). Patient preference as a moderator of outcome for chronic forms of major depressive disorder treated with Nefazodone, Cognitive Behavioral Analysis System of Psychotherapy, or their combination. *Journal of Clinical Psychiatry, 70*, 354–61.

Lambert, M. J., Hansen, N. B., Umpress, V., Lunnen, K., Okiishi, J., & Burlingame, G. M. (1996). *Administration and scoring manual for the OQ-45.2.* Stevenson, MD: American Professional Credentialing Services LLC.

*Leykin, Y., DeRubeis, J., Gallop, R., Amsterdam, J. D., Shelton, R. C., & Hollon, S. D. (2007). The relation of patients' treatment preferences to outcome in a randomized clinical trial. *Behavior Therapy, 38*, 209–217.

*Lin, P., Campbell, D. G., Chaney, E. F., Liu, C., Heagerty, P., Felker, B. L., et al. (2005). The influence of patient preference on depression treatment in primary care. *Annals of Behavioral Medicine, 30*, 164–73.

*Macias, C., Barreira, P., Hargreaves, W., Bickman, L., Fisher, W., & Aronson, E. (2005). Impact of referral source and study applicants' preference for randomly assigned service on research enrollment, service engagement, and evaluative outcomes. *American Journal of Psychiatry, 162*, 781–87.

*Manthei, R. J., Vitalo, R. L., & Ivey, A. E. (1982). The effect of client choice of therapist on therapy outcome. *Community Mental Health Journal, 18*, 220–29.

*McKay, J. R., Alterman, A. I., McLellan, A. T., Boardman, C. R., Mulvaney, F. D., & O'Brien, C. P. (1998). Random versus nonrandom assignment in the evaluation of treatment for cocaine abusers. *Journal of Consulting and Clinical Psychology, 66*, 697–701.

*McKay, J. R., Alterman, A. I., McLellan, A. T., Snider, E. C., & O'Brien, C. P. (1995). Effect of random versus nonrandom assignment in a comparison of inpatient and day hospital rehabilitation for male alcoholics. *Journal of Consulting and Clinical Psychology, 63*, 70–78.

*Proctor, E. K., & Rosen, A. (1981). Expectations and preferences for counselor race and their relation to intermediate treatment outcomes. *Journal of Counseling Psychology, 28*, 40–46.

*Raue, P. J., Schulberg, H. C., Heo, M., Klimstra, S., & Bruce, M. L. (2009). Patients' depression treatment preferences and initiation, adherence, and outcome: A randomized primary care study. *Psychiatric Services, 60*, 337–43.

*Renjilian, D. A., Nezu, A. M., Shermer, R. L., Perri, M. G., McKelvey, W. G., & Anton, S. D. (2001). Individual versus group therapy for obesity: Effects of matching participants to their treatment preferences. *Journal of Consulting and Clinical Psychology, 69*, 717–21.

Riedel-Heller, S. G., Matschinger, H., & Angermeyer, M. C. (2005). Mental disorders—Who and what might help? Help-seeking and treatment preferences of the lay public. *Social Psychiatry and Psychiatric Epidemiology, 40*, 167–74.

*Rokke, P. D., Tomhave, J. A., & Jocic, Z. (1999). The role of client choice and target selection in self-management therapy for depression in older adults. *Psychology and Aging, 14*, 155–69.

Rosen, A. (1967). Client preferences: An overview of the literature. *The Personnel and Guidance Journal, 45*, 785–89.

*Sterling, R. C., Gottheil, E., Glassman, S. D., Weinstein, S. P., & Serota, R. D. (1997). Patient treatment choice and compliance: Data from a substance abuse treatment program. *The American Journal on Addictions, 6*, 168–76.

Swift, J. K., & Callahan, J. L. (2009). The impact of client treatment preferences on outcome: A meta-analysis. *Journal of Clinical Psychology, 65*, 368–81.

Tracey, T. J., & Dundon, M. (1988). Role anticipations and preferences over the course of counseling. *Journal of Counseling Psychology, 35*, 3–14.

*Van, H. L., Dekker, J., Koelen, J., Kool, S., Aalst, G. V., Hendriksen, M., et al. (2009). Patient preference compared with random allocation in short-term psychodynamic supportive psychotherapy with indicated addition of pharmacotherapy for depression. *Psychotherapy Research, 19*, 205–212.

Vincent, N., & LeBow, M. (1995). Treatment preference and acceptability: Epistemology and locus of control. *Journal of Constructivist Psychology, 8*, 81–96.

Vollmer, B., Grote, J., Lange, R., & Walker, C. (2009). A Therapy Preferences Interview: Empowering clients by offering choices. *Psychotherapy Bulletin, 44*, 33–37.

*Wallach, H. S. (1988). Clients' expectations and results of psychological therapy for dysmenorrheal. *Dissertation Abstracts International, 49*, 1961.

Wanigaratne, S., & Barker, C. (1995). Clients' preferences for styles of therapy. *British Journal of Clinical Psychology, 34*, 215–22.

*Ward, E., King, M., Lloyd, M., Bower, P., Sibbald, B., Farrelly, S., et al. (2000). Randomized controlled trial of non-directive counseling, cognitive-behavior therapy, and usual general practitioner care for patients with depression I: Clinical effectiveness. *British Medical Journal, 321*, 1383–88.

Wong, E. C., Kim, B. S. K., Zane, N. W. S., Kim, I. J., & Huang, J. S. (2003). Examining culturally based variables associated with ethnicity: Influences on credibility perceptions of empirically supported interventions. *Cultural Diversity & Ethnic Minority Psychology, 9*, 88–96.

*Zlotnick, C., Elkin, I., & Shea, M. T. (1998). Does the gender of a patient or the gender of a therapist affect the treatment of patients with major depression? *Journal of Consulting and Clinical Psychology, 66*, 655–59.

16 Culture

Timothy B. Smith, Melanie M. Domenech Rodríguez, *and* Guillermo Bernal

The therapist–client relationship is highly dependent on context. Factors such as the therapy format (e.g., family, individual therapy), clinical setting (e.g., group home, wilderness retreat), and personal characteristics of the participants (e.g., age, gender, culture) influence the content and process of therapy. Psychotherapy can be adapted across nearly infinite therapist–client combinations to achieve positive client outcomes, as evidenced across the other chapters in this volume.

In this chapter, we focus on the context of client culture. We situate this discussion in the context of evidence-based practice (EBP), defined by the American Psychological Association Presidential Task Force on Evidence-Based Practice (APA, 2006) as "the integration of the best available research with clinical expertise in the context of patient characteristics, *culture* [emphasis added] and preferences." (p. 273). Client culture is an essential context with which therapy should align.

Professional standards and guidelines across the mental health professions recognize the centrality of cultural contexts. The Guidelines for Providers of Psychological Services to Ethnic, Linguistic, and Culturally Diverse Populations (APA, 1993), for one prominent example, unequivocally state that culture and language impact psychological services. Psychotherapists are tasked

with considering culture in a "systematic fashion" in broad areas of practice. The more recent Guidelines on Multicultural Education, Training, Research, Practice, and Organizational Change for Psychologists (APA, 2003) specify that psychologists apply culturally appropriate skills in psychological practice, taking cultural context into account at all times. In short, recognizing and aligning with client culture is not only best practice, it is ethical practice (APA, 2002; Bernal, Jiménez-Chafey, & Domenech Rodríguez, 2009; Smith, 2010).

Despite the clear professional mandates to account for client culture, the implementation of these standards appears limited. Engagement into mental health services for ethnic minorities has been low (U.S. Surgeon General, 2001) and continues to be so (Gonzalez et al., 2010). Some scholars have argued that this low engagement is a result of incongruous therapy–client match (Dumas, Moreland, Gitter, Pearl, & Nordstrom, 2008) and low relevance of available treatments to ethnic minorities (Miranda, Azocar, Organista, Muñoz, & Lieberman, 1996). Other evidence points to language, economic, and structural barriers, such as a lack of mental health clinics in ethnic neighborhoods (Alegría et al., 2002).

Disproportionately low rates of utilization and retention among ethnic minorities may also be related to practitioner demographics. In the United States, the vast majority of treatment professionals are white/European American, primarily English-speaking (APA, 2009; NSF, 2009). In a survey of psychologists, only 12% of respondents reported speaking a language other than English well enough to provide services in that language, and 9% reported actually providing services in another language (APA, 2010). Meanwhile nearly 20% of the U.S. population speaks a language other than English in the home (Shin & Kominski, 2010). Ethnic minorities represent roughly 25% of the population in the United States and are expected to surpass 50% between 2040 and 2050 (Ortman & Guarnieri, 2009). While neither therapist ethnicity nor non–English language fluency imply cultural competence or lack thereof (Schwartz et al., 2010), the demographic mismatch between therapists and clients may present challenges to client engagement in therapy (e.g., Ridley, 1984).

In this chapter, we consider adaptations to psychotherapy based on client culture and present relevant clinical examples. We then present an original meta-analysis of culturally adapted treatment in mental health. We conclude with probable moderators, limitations of the research reviewed, and recommended therapeutic practices based on the research evidence.

Definitions and Measures

Although sometimes broadly considered *culture relevant* or *culture sensitive* (Atkinson, Bui, & Mori, 2001; Hall, 2001; LaRoche & Christopher, 2009; Tanaka-Matsumi, 2008), the term *culturally adapted* treatments has been used frequently in the literature. A precise definition of cultural adaptation is "the systematic modification of an evidence-based treatment (EBT) or intervention protocol to consider language, culture, and context in such a way that it is compatible with the client's cultural patterns, meanings, and values" (Bernal et al., 2009, p. 362).

A less structured conceptualization of cultural adaptation considers mental health treatments tailored to clients' cultural beliefs and values, provided in a setting considered "safe" by the client and conducted in the clients' preferred language (Miranda, Nakamura, & Bernal, 2003; Whaley & Davis, 2007). For instance, mental health clinics provide culturally adapted services when they regularly consult with cultural group representatives, provide language-appropriate resources, or modify their intake procedures to help orient clients unfamiliar with psychotherapy (Muñoz, 1982).

Guidelines for adapting therapy to clients' cultures have emerged (Barrera & González Castro, 2006; Bernal, Bonilla, & Bellido, 1995; Castro, Barrera, & Martínez, 2004; Hwang, 2006, 2009; Lau, 2006; Leong, 1996; Leong & Lee, 2006; Whitbeck, 2006), built on several decades of scholarship (Pedersen, 1999). A synthesis of the work of several international scholars with expertise in cross-cultural psychotherapy identified common themes regarding cultural adaptation:

- Therapists must practice flexibly.
- Therapists must remain open to what clients bring to therapy.
- Services must be meaningful within the cultural context that they are delivered.
- Assessments should be conducted prior to implementing treatment.
- Traditional treatments should not be summarily dismissed but rather used as an existing resource.
- Therapists must experience and communicate empathy with the client in a culturally appropriate manner.
- Observations of therapy across cultures provide an opportunity to

learn more about important cultural features.

- Therapists must proceed with caution in interpreting cultural differences as deficits (Draguns, 2008).

These common themes can be clinically actualized by eight elements of culturally adapted treatments: language, persons, metaphors, content, concepts, goals, methods, and context (Bernal & Sáez-Santiago, 2006). A *language*-appropriate service refers to not only the use of clients' preferred language but also to understanding the meaning of particular uses of language by different groups such as adolescents. *Person* factors include characteristics such as race and ethnicity. Studies of racial, ethnic, and language match generally show that clients both prefer therapists matched to themselves and typically remain in treatment longer compared with those who are not matched (e.g., Coleman, Wampold, & Casali, 1995). Infusion of cultural *metaphors*, symbols, and overarching cultural concepts can align therapy with existing client heuristics. For instance, cultural sayings can be used in therapy to more clearly convey meaning or insight. Attending to the cultural *content* of a mental health treatment can enhance alignment with client worldviews. For example, some groups are more collectivistic than others, so notions such as individuation, differentiation, and dependence may need to be contextualized so as to not pathologize clients with a collectivistic worldview. The categories of *goals* and *methods* imply the consideration of customs and cultural values in setting treatment goals and establishing suitable procedures to reach those goals. And finally, by the consideration of *context*, broader issues come into focus such as the social and economic realities that may include acculturative stress, migration, availability of social supports, and so on. In brief, explicit consideration of these eight elements

can help the psychotherapist align treatment with the client rather than presume that the client will accommodate to the psychotherapy.

In addition to considering when and how to culturally adapt a treatment, psychotherapists may want to consider the tension between population fit and treatment fidelity. If a traditional intervention such as cognitive therapy is adapted in content and format with an Asian American client by infusing the Buddhist principle of mindfulness, for example, there comes a point at which the causal explanations of cognitive therapy may no longer predominate in the adapted treatment (e.g., therapy may facilitate meditative relaxation/awareness over the explicit refutation of irrational thoughts).

Research contains a broad spectrum of opinions about maintaining traditional treatment fidelity when working with ethnic minority clients. Some scholars call for the creation of new therapies specific to each cultural group that are explicitly aligned with their beliefs, values, and practices (Comas-Diaz, 2006; Gone, 2009), yet others propose implementing traditional EBTs with minimal or no alterations (Chambless & Ollendick, 2000). Many scholars, however, seem to opt for an integrated or hybrid model of cultural adaptation that takes into account both fidelity and fit (Castro et al., 2004; Domenech Rodríguez & Wieling, 2004; Hwang, 2006, 2009; Lau, 2006; Whitbeck, 2006).

These scholars recommend adaptation of existing evidence-based therapies for cultural fit while retaining the original mechanisms of behavioral change or symptom reduction. For example, a Parent Management Training–Oregon (PMTO) intervention (Domenech Rodríguez, Baumann, & Schwartz, 2011) with Spanish-speaking Latino families maintained behavioral therapy principles, such as applying immediate contingencies for desired behaviors, but the specific behaviors thought to be desirable, the specific contingencies used, the context in which they are presented and delivered, the frames or metaphors used to explain the concepts to caregivers, and the therapeutic process are all changeable or decentrable (for a description of the concept of decentering, see Domenech Rodríguez & Wieling, 2004). To facilitate precise descriptions and evaluations of these types of adaptations, an observational measure of cultural adaptation is being developed by the PMTO team.

Clinical Examples

In a broad sense, all mental health treatments are informed by cultural contexts. What have been termed "traditional" Western treatments are inextricably interwoven with European/European-American culture, so much so as to render the cultural influences nearly invisible (Smith, Richards, Granley, & Obiakor, 2004). Yet, in an increasingly multicultural society, culture cannot remain invisible.

There are a number of ways in which cultural centering of mental health interventions can be achieved (Barrera & González Castro, 2006; Bernal et al., 1995; Castro et al., 2004; Domenech Rodríguez & Wieling, 2004; Hwang, 2006, 2009; Lau, 2006; Leong, 1996; Leong & Lee, 2006; Whitbeck, 2006). Still other ways to adapt therapy to better serve ethnic minority clients include: providing additional or ancillary services (e.g., child care, home visits, referrals for legal or medical assistance), supporting consultation/collaboration with community/family (e.g., religious clergy and indigenous healers such as *curanderos* or *santeros*), and providing outreach services that move beyond the traditional patient–therapist office visit to facilitate access to services by disadvantaged populations (e.g., Alberta & Wood, 2009; Miranda, 2006; Pedersen, 2000; Sue & Sue, 2008).

For instance, in the course of psychotherapy focused on improving parenting practices, one clinician supported linkages to medical practitioners when a family's inability to communicate in English interfered with their ability to secure urgent medical care for a child (Domenech Rodríguez, McNeal, & Cauce, 2008). The therapist's actions went beyond traditional services by making contact with the clients at home in their preferred language (Spanish), conducting an evaluation that went beyond presenting symptoms (in this case, a child's sleep disturbance turned out to be caused by persistent stomach pain) to include cultural and contextual information, respecting the father's role in the family and working within the cultural worldview of the parents, alleviating parents' fears about seeking medical care that were based on their undocumented immigration status, arranging for payment of medical services through a public health program, accompanying the parents to the medical office visit, and linking the family with a Hispanic community liaison who could provide subsequent assistance.

Oppositely, in a recent and poignant negative example, Dr. Guerda Nicholas, a well-known Haitian psychotherapist, had sharp words for practitioners wishing to engage in relief work in Haiti following the January 12, 2010 earthquake in Haiti that claimed hundreds of thousands of lives. Dr. Nicolas was quoted as saying "Please stay away—unless you've really, really done the homework" (Marcus, 2010). Among her examples, Dr. Nicolas shared a situation in which a psychologist from the United States was speaking with a Haitian woman who had lost her child, her home, and a leg. The woman was most upset about losing her leg, but the psychologist, apparently believing that the woman was avoiding a sensitive topic, insisted on discussing the child's death. Dr. Nicolas lamented that this psychologist had added one more task to the work of local therapists in Haiti: that of ensuring that the woman and other Haitians understood that not all therapists would respond in the same unhelpful manner. In this example it is evident that the psychotherapist privileged his or her own understanding of trauma over the client's experience, failing to connect with the client. Rather than assume that clients will adapt their ways to fit Western psychological theories, psychotherapists need to make concerted efforts to align their practices with clients' lived experiences.

This principle is demonstrated in an innovative study conducted in Australia with Aboriginal people suffering from chronic mental illness (Nagel, Robinson, Condon, & Trauer, 2009). The study had several notable features. First, it employed a mixed-methods design that entailed a 12-month qualitative phase followed by a nested randomized controlled trial. The treatment development invited both Aboriginal mental health workers and recovered patients as key informants to understand indigenous views of mental illness. Group and individual in-depth interviews were conducted as well as field observations. The themes that emerged were the importance of the family, strength derived from cultural traditions, and the value of storytelling to share information. These themes were used to inform the process and content of the assessment, intervention, and ancillary materials. The resulting culturally adapted treatment was subsequently compared with treatment as usual. In all, 49 patients were randomly assigned, and outcomes were evaluated at baseline, 6-, 12-, and 18-month follow-ups. The culturally adapted intervention produced better outcomes in well-being, health, and substance dependence with changes maintained over time. Conducted in a remote indigenous area of Australia with a historically underserved population, this study is an excellent clinical (and

research) example of collaboratively accessing experiential phenomena and then directly applying that understanding to the treatment rendered.

Previous Meta-Analyses

Evidence has slowly accumulated regarding the efficacy and effectiveness of culturally adapted treatments. In a comprehensive analysis of a decade of the randomized clinical trials (RCT) conducted with NIH funds, less than 50% of the studies reported any data specific to client culture, and all groups except white/European Americans and African Americans were underrepresented (Mak, Law, Alvidrez, & Pérez-Stable, 2007). Previous reviews have indicated that psychotherapy with ethnic minority clients is equally effective as that with white/European Americans (Hall, 2001; Miranda et al., 2005; Sue, 1988; Zane et al., 2004), but these reviews cite a limited number of RCTs.

Two meta-analyses of culturally adapted interventions, one specific to children and youth (Huey & Polo, 2008) and another with clients of all ages (Griner & Smith, 2006), found average effect sizes of moderate magnitude ($d = 0.44$ and $d = 0.45$, respectively), although the results of both meta-analyses were moderated by several factors. The overall positive meta-analytic findings have been somewhat surprising, given the lack of direct measurement of cultural adaptation and sparse information available on how cultural adaptations were implemented.

Meta-Analytic Review
Methods
Inclusion and Exclusion Criteria. We included in our meta-analysis those studies that provided quantitative data regarding clients' experiences in mental health treatments that explicitly accounted for clients' culture, ethnicity, or race. We included treatments

for mental illness, emotional distress/well-being, family problems, and problem behaviors (such as physical aggression but not pregnancy or sexual behavior). Substance abuse prevention and treatment programs were excluded unless they also targeted psychological variables (e.g., depression, self-esteem). We excluded studies that accounted for generic contextual/ecological factors (such as poverty or family systems) or other client characteristics (such as gender) unless they explicitly accounted for culture, ethnicity, or race (e.g., Latina women). Selection of clients from a particular group or assignment of clients to therapists of the same ethnic group or native language (ethnic or language matching) were insufficient criteria for inclusion; some aspect of the content, format, or delivery of the intervention had to be purposefully changed to align with clients' culture, ethnicity, or race. We extracted effect size data from psychological and behavioral outcomes but not educational, substance use/abuse, or physical health outcomes if reported.

A previous meta-analysis (Griner & Smith, 2006) aggregated studies using disparate research designs. This procedure is problematic because correlational designs, single-group pre- to posttest designs, and experimental designs provide distinct data that also typically differ in terms of effect size magnitude. Moreover, potential threats to internal validity plague single-group designs (Campbell & Stanley, 1966). We therefore restricted the present meta-analytic review to quasi-experimental and experimental designs.

Search Strategies. We included studies identified in prior meta-analyses and reviews (Griner & Smith, 2006; Hall, 2001; Huey & Polo, 2008; Miranda et al., 2005; Smith, 2010; Zane et al., 2004). We subsequently searched for additional published and unpublished studies that had appeared from January 2004 to July 2009 using several electronic databases: Academic Search Premier, Dissertation Abstracts, Mental Health Abstracts, and PsycINFO. Search terms included a list of root words relevant to psychotherapy (*clinic, counsel, intervention, psychotherapy, service, therapy,* and *treatment*) that were crossed with combinations of the root terms *culture/cultural, ethnic, multicultural,* and *race/racial* that were crossed with root terms *adapt, appropriate, consonant, compatible, competent, congruent, focused, informed, relevant, responsive, sensitive, skill,* and *specific.* Three undergraduate research assistants sequentially reviewed retrieved titles, then abstracts and full texts of apparently relevant reports. One of these assistants manually examined the reference sections of past reviews and of studies meeting the inclusion criteria to locate articles not identified in the database searches. Finally, we sent personal e-mail requests to several colleagues and posted general solicitations on several professional listservs: APA Division 12 Section VI: Clinical Psychology of Ethnic Minorities; APA Division 45; Association of Black Psychologists; National Latino/a Psychological Association; and the Society of Indian Psychologists.

Coding Procedures. Coders were six undergraduate and four graduate students with prior experience and training in meta-analytic coding. To increase the accuracy of coding and data entry, two team members coded each article. Subsequently, two different team members coded the same article. Coders extracted several objectively verifiable characteristics of the studies, including participants' age, gender, and race; the outcome evaluated; and components of the research design and intervention. Discrepancies across coding pairs were resolved through further scrutiny of the manuscript to the point of consensus.

Statistical Methods. Data within studies were transformed to the metric of Cohen's *d*. Across all studies we assigned positive *d* values to indicate beneficial results and negative *d* values to comparatively worse results for the culturally adapted intervention.

When multiple effect sizes were reported within a study (e.g., across different measures of outcome), we averaged the several values (weighted by N) to avoid violating the assumption of independent samples. Aggregate effect sizes were calculated using random effects models following confirmation of heterogeneity. A random effects approach produces results that best generalize beyond the sample of studies reviewed. The assumptions made in this meta-analysis clearly warrant this method: The belief that different kinds of modifications to mental health treatments and client characteristics moderate the effectiveness of psychotherapy implies that the studies reviewed will estimate different population effect sizes. Random effects models take such between-studies variation into account.

Results

Statistically nonredundant effect sizes were extracted from 65 studies that evaluated culturally adapted interventions using quasi-experimental or experimental designs. These studies and their ESs are summarized in Table 16.1. Data were reported from 8,620 participants, with an average age of 24.4 years (range = 5 to 73; *SD* = 16); 55% of the participants within studies were female. Of the total, 39% were Asian American, 32% were Hispanic/Latino(a), 20% were African American, 4% were Native American, 1% were white/European American, and 4% indicated "other" affiliations including ethnic groups outside North America.

Across all 65 studies, the weighted average effect size was *d* = 0.46 (95% CI = 0.36–0.56). By conventional benchmarks, a *d* of 0.46 represents a medium effect size, indicating that patients receiving culturally adapted treatments typically experienced superior outcomes to those of patients in control groups. Substantial heterogeneity characterized the effect sizes (range = −.97 to 2.80), with 74% of the variability in effect sizes due to true between-study variability (I^2 = 74; $Q_{(64)}$ = 247, $p < 0.001$). No extreme outliers were observed.

We conducted several analyses to determine if the meta-analytic results may have been influenced by publication bias (the exclusion of studies with negative or nonsignificant results because they tend to be unpublished and difficult to locate). Calculation of Orwin's fail-safe *N* indicated that there would need to be at least 103 studies averaging *d* = 0 that were "missing" from our literature search for the overall results to be reduced to a trivial magnitude (*d* < 0.10). Although unlikely, it was possible that many studies with nonsignificant findings remained unaccounted for over a 30-year period, leaving open the possibility of publication bias. Egger's regression test reached statistical significance ($p < 0.001$), and our examination of the funnel plot of the effect sizes by their standard error indicated approximately 15 "missing" studies on the left side of the distribution, where statistically nonsignificant results would be located in the expected funnel-shaped distribution. When we reestimated the average weighted effect size using "trim and fill" methodology (Duval & Tweedie, 2000), the recalculated value was *d* = 0.27 (95% CI = 0.16 to 0.38).

Moderators and Mediators

Given the substantial heterogeneity in the omnibus effect size estimate, we evaluated what factors may have accounted for the variation across the 65 studies. Analyses of effect size moderation were conducted using random effects weighted correlations

Table 16.1 Studies Included in the Meta-Analysis

Study	N	Mean age	Effect size	Lower limit	Upper limit
Acosta, Yamamoto, Evans, & Skilbeck (1983)	151	31	0.42	0.08	0.76
Banks, Hogue, Timberlake, & Liddle (1998)	64	12	0.59	0.07	1.11
Belgrave (2002)	49		0.61	0.02	1.20
Botvin, Schinke, & Diaz (1994)	304	13	0.11	−0.09	0.30
Cardemil, Reivich, Beevers, Seligman, & James (2007)	168	11	0.15	−0.13	0.43
Costantino, Malgady, & Rogler (1994)	90	11	0.22	−0.17	0.61
Crespo (2006)	36	38	1.10	0.37	1.84
Dai et al. (1999)	30	73	0.96	0.08	1.83
Domenech Rodríguez & Crowley (2008)	195	23	0.29	0.01	0.56
Falconer (2002)	25	20	−0.20	−0.99	0.58
Gallagher-Thompson, Arean, Rivera, & Thompson (2001)	70	52	0.51	0.03	0.99
Garza (2004)	29	8	0.21	−0.53	0.94
Gilchrist, Schinke, Trimble, & Cvetkovich (1987)	97	11	0.04	−0.35	0.43
Ginsburg & Drake (2002)	9	16	0.87	−0.50	2.24
Gonzalez (2003)	57	10	0.27	−0.25	0.79
Grodnitzky (1993)	28	14	0.31	−0.45	1.07
Gutierrez & Ortega (1991)	73	19	0.60	0.09	1.12
Hammond & Yung (1991)	19	14	0.80	−0.16	1.76
Heppner, Neville, Smith, Kivlighan, & Gershuny (1999)	41	20	0.25	−0.37	0.87
Hinton et al. (2005)	40	52	2.80	1.92	3.68
Hinton, Hofmann, Pollack, & Otto (2009)	24	50	2.26	1.24	3.27
Hogue, Liddle, Becker, & Johnson-Leckrone (2002)	114	13	0.53	0.14	0.92
Huey & Rank (1984)	48		0.95	0.36	1.53
Huey & Pan (2006)	15	24	0.82	−0.25	1.90
Jackson (1997)	14	17	−0.05	−1.10	1.01
Johnson, & Breckenridge (1982)	128	5	0.20	−0.14	0.54
Jones (2008)	10	42	1.58	0.58	2.58
Kataoka et al. (2003)	198	11	0.46	0.12	0.80
Kim, Omizo, & D'Andrea (1998)	48	16	0.91	0.33	1.50

(Continued)

Table 16.1   Continued

Study	N	Mean age	Effect size	Lower limit	Upper limit
King (1999)	80	13	0.17	−0.27	0.60
Kohn, Oden, Muñoz, Robinson, & Leavitt (2002)	18	47	0.81	−0.15	1.77
Kopelowicz, Zárate, Smith, Mintz, & Liberman (2003)	162	38	0.85	0.51	1.19
LaFromboise, & Howard-Pitney (1995)	62	16	0.33	−0.19	0.85
Lau & Zane (2000)	317	37	0.14	0.07	0.21
Malgady, Rogler, & Constantino (1990a)	80	14	0.46	−0.02	0.94
Malgady, Rogler, & Constantino (1990b)	210	8	0.44	0.16	0.72
Malgady, Rogler, & Constantino (1990b)	90	14	0.27	−0.17	0.71
Martinez & Eddy (2005)	52	13	0.46	−0.10	1.01
Matos, Bauermeister, & Bernal (2009)	32	5	1.81	0.97	2.64
Mausbach, Bucardo, McKibbin, Cardenas, & Barrio (2008)	59	49	0.70	0.15	1.26
Mickens-English (1996)	60	35	−0.09	−0.61	0.43
Mokuau, Braun, Wong, Higuchi, & Gotay (2008)	10	57	1.21	−0.17	2.58
Moran (1999)	85	11	−0.23	−0.67	0.21
Myers et al. (1992)[1]	92	31	0.38	−0.06	0.82
Myers et al. (1992)[1]	81	33	0.78	0.34	1.22
Nagel, Robinson, Condon, & Trauer (2009)	49	33	0.67	0.08	1.26
Nyamathi, Leake, Flaskerud, Lewis, & Bennett (1993)	858	33	−0.11	−0.24	0.03
Ochoa (1981)	21	15	0.58	−0.32	1.48
Pantin et al. (2003)	167	12	0.35	0.07	0.62
Parker (1990)	23	17	0.22	−0.61	1.05
Rosselló & Bernal (1999)	59	15	0.81	0.23	1.40
Rosselló, Bernal, & Rivera-Medina (2008)	112	15	1.21	0.82	1.60
Rowland et al. (1995)	31	15	0.40	−0.31	1.11
Royce (1998)	55	14	0.04	−0.48	0.56
Santisteban et al. (2003)	85	16	0.46	0.03	0.90
Schwarz (1989)	72	38	0.18	−0.30	0.66
Shin (2004)	47	66	1.56	0.91	2.21
Shin & Lukens (2002)	47	37	1.07	0.45	1.69

(Continued)

Table 16.1 Continued

Study	N	Mean age	Effect size	Lower limit	Upper limit
Sobol (2000)	89		−0.16	−0.60	0.28
Szapocznik et al. (1986)	31	15	0.38	−0.32	1.09
Szapocznik et al. (1989)	76	9.4	0.30	−0.14	0.74
Telles et al. (1995)	40	30	−0.97	−1.62	−0.32
Timberlake (2000)	74		0.19	−0.29	0.67
Xiong et al. (1994)	62	31	0.51	−0.01	1.03
Zhang et al. (2002)	97	35	0.54	0.15	0.93

Note: Effect sizes and 95% confidence intervals are expressed in the metric of Cohen's *d*.
[1] The publication by Myers et al. (1992) contained two studies, both included in our analyses.

for continuous-level variables and random effects weighted analyses of variance for categorical variables.

Participant Characteristics

We evaluated the association between effect sizes and the following characteristics of study participants: gender composition (percentage of females), average age, mental health status (normal community members, at-risk group members, clients in clinical settings), and racial composition. Of these, participants' average age was significantly associated ($r = 0.39$ $p < 0.001$) with the magnitude of effect sizes within studies. Investigation of the associated scatter plot (funnel plot) revealed that studies with adult participants over age 35 tended to have effect sizes of larger magnitude than studies with children, adolescents, and young adults. Further investigation of the data revealed that there was substantial overlap between participant age and the clinical status of the population investigated: normal community samples had an average age of 20 years; at-risk groups had an average age of 21 years; and clinical populations had an average age of 32 years. Nevertheless, we confirmed through random effects weighted multiple regression that participant age ($p = 0.01$), not

clinical status ($p = 0.46$), moderated effect size magnitude.

Differences were observed between studies using participants of different races ($Q_{(3, 48)} = 12.8$, $p = 0.005$). Specifically, 7 studies with Asian American participants ($d = 1.18$, 95% CI = 0.79 to 1.60) had an average effect size of more than twice that of 14 studies of African American participants ($d = 0.47$, 95% CI = 0.19 to 0.76), 26 studies of Hispanic/Latino(a) participants ($d = 0.47$, 95% CI = 0.28 to 0.65), and 5 studies of Native American participants ($d = 0.22$, 95% CI = −.20 to 0.64). Differences were also found between studies using culturally homogeneous samples (i.e., all participants were of the same culture) and culturally heterogeneous samples ($Q_{(1, 63)} = 5.2$, $p = 0.02$). Interventions delivered to a specific cultural group were much more effective ($d = 0.51$, 95% CI = 0.40 to 0.63) than interventions delivered to mixed groups ($d = 0.18$, 95% CI = −.08 to 0.44).

Study Design Variables

We next evaluated the association between effect sizes and several characteristics of study design: random assignment, control group condition, type of outcome evaluated, and the time of outcome assessment administration (number of sessions completed at posttest). Of these, the only statistically significant difference observed was across the source of the outcome evaluation ($Q_{(2, 108)}$ = 6.7, p = 0.04); outcome evaluations provided by therapists tended to be associated with effect sizes of much lower magnitude (d = 0.09) than those provided by the clients (d = 0.45) or external observers (d = 0.45).

We next evaluated whether authors included descriptions of treatment components that aligned with the eight points of Bernal's model (Bernal et al., 1995; Bernal & Sáez-Santiago, 2006). Each of the eight components was assigned a binary value (yes = 1, no = 0), which we summed to obtain a total number of culturally adapted components described within each study. This total value was positively associated with effect sizes (r = 0.28, p = 0.007), indicating that studies describing treatments with relatively more cultural adaptations tended to be more effective than studies describing treatments with fewer cultural adaptations. To ascertain the amount of variance in effect sizes explained by the cultural adaptations described within studies, we simultaneously entered into a random effects weighted multiple regression of the eight binary variables of language matching, ethnic matching, metaphors, content, conceptualization, goals, methods, and context (described previously). The resulting model explained 20% of the variance in effect sizes (p = 0.03); the two variables that reached statistical significance were descriptions of therapeutic goals that explicitly matched clients' goals (b = 0.29, p = 0.02) and descriptions of using metaphors/symbols in therapy that matched client cultural worldviews (b = 0.37, p = 0.02).

Patient Contributions

There is a small but growing literature on client characteristics and their contribution to psychotherapy process and outcome (Zane et al., 2004). Yet, due in part to the limited outcome research with ethnic minorities, the available research on client characteristics relies on analog studies, and much of the work has focused on establishing efficacy (Miranda et al., 2005; Zane et al., 2004). Furthermore, the high degree of heterogeneity across the major ethnocultural groups—Native Americans, Asian Americans, African Americans, and Latinos—and diversity within those groups calls into question any generalization that can be made in linking client characteristics to the therapy relationship and even to outcome.

With this caveat in mind, we turn to the patient's contribution to the relationship in culturally adapted psychotherapies and the distinctive perspective he/she brings to the interaction. In a comprehensive review of the research on psychotherapy with diverse populations, Zane and colleagues (2004) examined several cultural groups and discussed the salient client variables that include: preference for a therapist of the same ethnicity and language, valuing interpersonal over instrumental orientation, the role of the experience of discrimination and prejudice, preference for therapists who evoke positive attitudes and trustworthiness, acculturation, causal attributions on the nature of illness and symptoms, and culturally specific symptoms in some populations. The authors found that the most salient commonality across the four groups examined was that a substantial number of ethnic minorities prefer therapists of their own ethnicity. Subsequent research has confirmed this finding of client preference but has failed to find evidence that treatment outcomes improve as a result of ethnic matching (Cabral & Smith, 2010).

Much work remains to be done to understand the impact of culture-specific patient characteristics on treatment impact. In much of treatment outcome research, cultural values are implied rather than measured (LaRoche & Christopher, 2009); for example, positive results may be the result of a cultural value such as *personalismo*, but *personalismo* is not directly measured. When clients are asked about these, some understanding of cultural values map onto clients' but others do not (Bermúdez, Kirkpatrick, Hecker, & Torres-Robles, 2010). A noteworthy example to the contrary measured Asian American and European American cultural values and found that both related to differential outcomes for Asian American clients (Kim, Ng, & Ahn, 2005).

Limitations of the Research

Psychotherapy outcome research has accumulated over several decades, with now thousands of research reports and hundreds of meta-analyses. By comparison, the research investigating culturally adapted treatments is miniscule. The amount and pace of clinical outcome research specific to clients' cultural backgrounds has remained consistently low. The studies included in this review appeared at a steady rate of about 2.3 per year since 1981. Because the long-term success of any initiative depends on the consistent replication of supportive findings, the single greatest limitation of the research specific to culturally adapted mental health interventions is that more evidence needs to accumulate.

Across the history of psychotherapy, there have been multiple cycles wherein a new theory or treatment attains popularity following initial research support, but then enthusiasm and implementation decline when subsequent research fails to replicate the initial positive results. This failure to replicate results can be partially attributable to increased empirical rigor and the identification of potential confounds omitted in previous studies. Researcher allegiance effects, in particular, have been identified as a confound in comparisons of specific therapies (Luborsky et al., 2006). Even though our analyses indicated that ratings of client outcomes provided by therapists were of lower magnitude than those provided by clients or external observers, researcher allegiance to culturally adapted interventions may nevertheless be associated with outcomes of the studies included in our review. Adjusting the results for apparently "missing" nonsignificant findings (due to possible publication bias) reduced the magnitude of the omnibus effect size. Until additional unpublished reports appear or until studies explicitly control for researcher allegiance, the adjusted value of $d = 0.27$ represents a lower estimate of the comparative benefit of culturally adapted interventions than the omnibus value of $d = 0.46$.

A third limitation of the research concerns the heterogeneity of the adapted treatments. Studies included in this review used a variety of means to align mental health interventions with clients' cultures, with an average of four of the eight components (Bernal et al., 1995; Bernal & Sáez-Santiago, 2006) being explicitly described by authors within studies. Specifically, 74% described providing therapy in the clients' preferred language, 53% matched clients with therapists of similar ethnic/racial backgrounds, 42% utilized metaphors/objects from client cultures, 77% included explicit mention of cultural content/values, 37% adhered to the client's conceptualization of the presenting problem, 14% solicited outcome goals from the client, 43% modified the methods of delivering therapy based on cultural considerations, and 55% addressed clients' contextual issues. A regression model including all of these variables explained 20% of effect size variation, and treatments that included greater numbers of these adaptations tended to be more effective than treatments with fewer cultural adaptations.

Another limitation of the research base was the lack of systematic measurement of cultural adaptation within studies. Few studies confirmed the fidelity of the treatments provided. All interventions in this review were developed by Western-trained professionals, with mention of consultation with indigenous healers or cultural experts in 30 of 65 studies (46%). Many authors adapted traditional (Western) mental health interventions, but evaluation of the fidelity to the causal mechanisms assumed by the traditional intervention was rare. In short, existing clinical outcome research of cultural adaptations has inconsistently achieved high levels of methodological rigor.

Finally, we observed that much of the research describes preventative interventions with at-risk populations. Although preventative interventions are essential in at-risk communities, the fact that only 20 of the 65 studies were conducted in clinical settings with mental health clients must be acknowledged as a gap in coverage. Although we have no reason to suspect that the benefit of culturally adapted interventions would differ between clinical populations and at-risk populations (and no differences were observed in the meta-analytic results), researchers have come to rely on greater aggregate numbers of clinical studies than present coverage allows.

Therapeutic Practices

Mental health treatments typically yield patient outcomes of similar magnitude, irrespective of differences in content (Lambert, 1999). Bona fide comparisons of client outcomes across different therapies usually average between a d of 0 and 0.20 (Wampold et al., 1997). By comparison, the omnibus effect size obtained in this meta-analysis ($d = 0.46$) exceeds those expected values. Even if we interpret the omnibus effect size adjusted for possible publication bias ($d = 0.27$), these results remain important. Culturally adapted mental health therapies are moderately

superior to those that do not explicitly incorporate cultural considerations.

Thus, we advance the following research-supported therapeutic practices:

• Clients will tend to benefit when psychotherapists make attempts to align treatment with clients' cultural backgrounds.

• Asian American clients and adult clients tended to benefit most from culturally adapted treatments relative to clients of other groups and younger ages. Nevertheless, because both age and Asian American culture are likely mediating factors of acculturation status (integration with mainstream Western society vs. maintaining ancestral cultural worldviews), therapists should particularly aware of how client age and acculturation interact with their treatments.

• Treatments explicitly aligned with clients' outcome goals will tend to be more effective than other treatments.

• Treatments involving cultural metaphors and modes of expression will tend to be more effective than other treatments. Whenever feasible, psychotherapy should be conducted in the client's preferred language.

• Different combinations of the eight components of culturally adapted interventions (Bernal et al., 1995) proved effective across studies. Rather than exert treatment-specific effects, it is possible that cultural adaptations to treatment influence common factors, such as the therapeutic alliance and patient preferences. The specific procedures taken to align therapy with client culture may matter less than the fact that therapists attempt to make the alignment by using several methods (Smith, 2010). Treatments that include multiple cultural adaptations will tend to be more effective than treatments with only a few cultural adaptations.

- Consistent components identified in culturally adapted therapies include the following:

  - Work to establish a strong therapeutic alliance. Desire to understand the client. Demonstrate that you hold the client in high regard.

  - Confirm client expression and reception, optimally in the client's preferred language.

  - Verify clients' expectations and conceptualizations of optimal mental health; align treatment goals accordingly.

  - Use therapeutic methods that are compatible with the clients' values and conceptualization of improvement.

  - Maintain a feedback loop whereby clients express progress and expectations. For clients preferring directive therapeutic approaches, completion of rating scales would be preferable to interpersonal dialogue about process issues.

  - Respond immediately to client feedback; verify the congruity of your response.

- Culturally adapted treatments were much more beneficial when they were specific to clients of a given ethnic group than when they were provided to a conglomerate of clients from many ethnocultural groups. The more culturally focused and specific the treatment, the more effective it will probably prove.

References

Citations marked with an asterisk were included in the meta-analysis.

*Acosta, F. X., Yamamoto, J., Evans, L. E., & Skilbeck, W. M. (1983). Preparing low-income Hispanic, Black, and White patients for psychotherapy: Evaluation of a new orientation program. *Journal of Clinical Psychology, 39*(6), 872–77.

Alberta, A. J., & Wood, A. H. (2009). A practical skills model for effectively engaging clients in multicultural settings. *The Counseling Psychologist, 37*(4), 564–79.

Alegría, M., Canino, G., Rios, R., Vera, M., Calderon, J., Rusch, D., et al. (2002). Inequalities in use of specialty mental health services among Latinos, African Americans, and non-Latino Whites. *Psychiatric Services, 53*(12), 1547–55.

American Psychological Association (1993). Guidelines for providers of psychological services to ethnic, linguistic, and culturally diverse populations. *American Psychologist, 48*(1), 45–48.

American Psychological Association (2002). Ethical principles of psychologists and code of conduct. *American Psychologist, 57*, 1060–73.

American Psychological Association (2003). Guidelines on multicultural education, training, research, practice, and organizational change for psychologists. *American Psychologist, 58*, 377–402.

American Psychological Association (2006). *Evidence-based practice in psychology: APA presidential task force on evidence-based practice. American Psychologist, 61*, 271–85.

American Psychological Association (2009). *2007 doctorate employment survey.* Retrieved online 5/17/2010 from http://www.apa.org/workforce/publications/07-doc-empl/index.aspx

American Psychological Association (2010). *2008 APA Survey of Psychology Health Service Providers. Special Analysis.* Washington, DC: American Psychological Association.

Atkinson, D. R., Bui, U., & Mori, S. (2001). Multiculturally sensitive empirically supported treatments—an oxymoron? In C. M. Alexander (Ed.), *Handbook of multicultural counseling (2nd ed.).* (pp. 542–74). Thousand Oaks, CA: Sage Publications, Inc.

*Banks, R., Hogue, A., Timerlake, T., & Liddle, H. (1998). An Afrocentric approach to group social skills training with inner-city African American adolescents. *Journal of Negro Education, 65*(4), 414–23.

Barrera, M., & González Castro, F. (2006). A heuristic framework for the cultural adaptation of interventions. *Clinical Psychology: Science & Practice, 13*(4), 311–316.

*Belgrave, F. Z. (2002). Relational theory and cultural enhancement interventions for African American adolescent girls. *Public Health Reports, 117*(1), 76–81.

Bernal, G., Bonilla, J., & Bellido, C. (1995). Ecological validity and cultural sensitivity for outcome research: Issues for cultural adaptation and development of psychosocial treatments with Hispanics. *Journal of Abnormal Child Psychology, 23*, 67–82.

Bernal, G., Jimenez-Chafey, M. I., & Domenech Rodriguez, M. M. (2009). Cultural adaptation of treatments: A resource for considering culture in evidence-based practice. *Professional Psychology: Research and Practice, 40*(4), 361–68.

Bernal, G., & Sáez-Santiago, E. (2006). Culturally centered psychosocial interventions. *Journal of Community Psychology, 34*, 121–32.

Bernal, G., & Scharrón-del-Río, M. (2001). Are empirically supported treatments valid for ethnic minorities? Toward an alternative approach for treatment research. *Cultural Diversity and Ethnic Minority Psychology, 7*, 328–42.

Bermúdez, J. M., Kirkpatrick, D. R., Hecker, L., Torres-Robles, C. (2010). Describing Latino families and their help-seeking attitudes: Challenging the family therapy literature. *Contemporary Family Therapy, 32*, 155–72.

*Botvin, G. J., Schinke, S. P., Epstein, J. A., & Diaz, T. (1994). Effectiveness of culturally focused and generic skills training approaches to alcohol and drug abuse prevention among minority youths. *Psychology of Addictive Behavior, 8*(2), 116–27.

Cabral, R. C., & Smith, T. B. (manuscript submitted). Racial/ethnic matching of clients and therapists in mental health services: A meta-analytic review of preferences, perceptions, and outcomes.

Campbell, D. T., & Stanley, J. C. (1966). *Experimental and quasi-experimental designs for research*. Chicago: Rand McNally.

*Cardemil, E. V., Reivich, K. J., Beevers, C. G., Seligman, M. E. P., & James, J. (2007). The prevention of depressive symptoms in low-income, minority children: Two-year follow-up. *Behaviour Research and Therapy, 45*(2), 313–27.

Castro, F. G., Barrera, M., & Martinez, C. R. (2004). The cultural adaptation of prevention interventions: Resolving tensions between fidelity and fit. *Prevention Science, 5*(1), 41–45.

Chambless, D., & Ollendick, T. (2001). Empirically supported psychological interventions: Controversies and evidence. *Annual Review of Psychology, 52*, 685–716.

Coleman, H. L. K., Wampold, B. E., & Casali, S. L. (1995). Ethnic minorities' ratings of ethnically similar and European American counselors: A meta-analysis. *Journal of Counseling Psychology, 42*(1), 55–64.

*Costantino, G., Malgady, R. G., & Rogler, L. H. (1994). Storytelling through pictures: Culturally sensitive psychotherapy for Hispanic children and adolescents. *Journal of Clinical Child Psychology, 23*(1), 13–20.

Comas-Diaz, L. (2006). Latino healing: The integration of ethnic psychology into psychotherapy. *Psychotherapy: Theory, Research, Practice, and Training, 4*, 436–453.

*Crespo, M. M. (2006). *Effects of culturally specific dynamically oriented group art therapy with immigrant Latinas*. Unpublished doctoral dissertation, California Institute of Integral Studies, San Francisco, CA.

*Dai, Y., Zhang, S., Yamamoto, J., Ao, M., Belin, T. R., Cheung, F., & Hifumi, S. S. (1999). Cognitive behavioral therapy of minor depressive symptoms in elderly Chinese Americans: A pilot study. *Community Mental Health Journal, 35*(6), 537–42.

Domenech Rodríguez, M. M., Baumann, A., & Schwartz, A. (2011). Cultural adaptation of an empirically supported intervention: From theory to practice in a Latino/a community context. *American Journal of Community Psychology 47*, 170–186.

*Domenech Rodríguez, M. M., & Crowley, S. L. (2008, August). *Criando con amor: Promoviendo armonia y superacion: Findings from a randomized trial of a culturally adapted PMTO intervention*. Paper presented at the annual meeting of the American Psychological Association, Boston.

Domenech Rodríguez, M., McNeal, C. T., & Cauce, A. M. (2008). Counseling the marginalized. In P. B. Pedersen, J. G. Daguns, W. J. Lonner, & J. E. Trimble (Eds.), *Counseling across cultures* (6th ed.) (pp. 223–38). Thousand Oaks, CA: Sage.

Domenech Rodríguez, M., & Wieling, E. (2004). Developing culturally appropriate, evidence-based treatments for interventions with ethnic minority populations. I. In M. Rastogin & E. Wieling (Eds.), *Voices of color: First person accounts of ethnic minority therapists* (pp. 313–33). Thousand Oaks, CA: Sage.

Draguns, J. G. (2008). What have we learned about the interplay of culture with counseling and psychotherapy? In U. P. Gielen, J. G. Draguns & J. M. Fish (Eds.), *Principles of multicultural counseling and therapy.* (pp. 393–417). New York: Routledge/Taylor & Francis Group.

Dumas, J. E., Moreland, A. D., Gitter, A. H., Pearl, A. M., & Nordstrom, A. H. (2008). Engaging parents in preventive parenting groups: Do ethnic, socioeconomic, and belief match between parents and group leaders matter? *Health Education & Behavior, 35*(5), 619–33.

Duval, S., & Tweedie, R. (2000). Trim and fill: A simple funnel-plot-based method of testing and adjusting for publication bias in meta-analysis. *Biometrics, 56*(2), 455–63.

*Falconer, J. (2002). *The effectiveness of a culturally relevant eating disorder prevention intervention with African American college women.* Unpublished doctoral dissertation, University of Missouri-Columbia.

*Gallagher-Thompson, D., Arean, P., Rivera, P., & Thompson, L. W. (2001). A psychoeducational intervention to reduce distress in Hispanic family caregivers: Results of a pilot study. *Clinical Gerontologist, 23*(1/2), 17–32.

*Garza, Y. (2004). *Effects of culturally responsive child-centered play therapy compared to curriculum-based small group counseling with elementary-age Hispanic children experiencing externalizing and internalizing behavior problems: A preliminary study.* Unpublished doctoral dissertation, University of North Texas, Denton.

*Gilchrist, L. D., Schinke, S. P., Trimble, J. E., & Cvetkovich, G. T. (1987). Skills enhancement to prevent substance abuse among American Indian adolescents. *The International Journal of the Addictions, 22*(9), 869–79.

*Ginsburg, G. S., & Drake, K. L. (2002). School-based treatment for anxious African-American adolescents: A controlled pilot study. *Journal of the American Academy of Child & Adolescent Psychiatry, 41*(7), 768–75.

Gone, J. P. (2009). A community-based treatment for Native American historical trauma: Prospects for evidence-based practice. *Journal of Consulting and Clinical Psychology, 77*(4), 751–62.

*Gonzalez, M. (2003). *The effectiveness of a culturally based social work activity group in the promotion of ethnic identity and adaptive behaviors: A study of Puerto Rican children.* Unpublished doctoral dissertation, Catholic University of America, Washington, DC.

Gonzalez, H. M., Vega, W. A., Williams, D. R., Wassim Tarraf, W., West, B. T., & Neighbors, H. W. (2010). Depression care in the United States: Too little for too few. *Archives of General Psychiatry, 67*, 37–46.

Griner, D., & Smith, T. B. (2006). Culturally adapted mental health intervention: A meta-analytic review. *Psychotherapy: Theory, Research, Practice, Training, 43*(4), 531–48.

*Grodnitzky, G. R. (1993). *Hero modeling versus non-hero modeling as interventions for Puerto-Rican and Anglo adolescents exhibiting behavior problems.* Unpublished doctoral dissertation, Hofstra University, Hempstead, NY.

*Gutierrez, L. M., & Ortega, R. (1991). Developing methods to empower Latinos: The importance of groups. *Social Work with Groups, 14*(2), 23–43.

Hall, G. C. N. (2001). Psychotherapy research and ethnic minorities: Empirical, ethical, and conceptual issues. *Journal of Counseling and Clinical Psychology, 69*, 502–510.

*Hammond, W. R., & Yung, B. R. (1991). Preventing violence in at-risk African-American youth. *Journal of Health Care for the Poor and Underserved, 2*(3), 359–73.

*Heppner, M. J., Neville, H. A., Smith, K., Kivlighan, D. M., & Gershuny, B. S. (1999). Examining immediate and long-term efficacy of race prevention programming with racially diverse college men. *Journal of Counseling Psychology, 46*(1), 16–26.

* Hinton, D., Chhean, D., Pich, V., Safren, S., Hofmann, S., & Pollack, M. (2005). A randomized controlled trial of cognitive-behavior therapy for cambodian refugees with treatment-resistant PTSD and panic attacks: A cross-over design. *Journal of Traumatic Stress, 18*(6), 617–29.

*Hinton, D. E., Hofmann, S. G., Pollack, M. H., & Otto, M. W. (2009). Mechanisms of efficacy of CBT for Cambodian refugees with PTSD: Improvement in emotion regulation and orthostatic blood pressure response. *CNS Neuroscience & Therapeutics, 15*(3), 255–63.

*Hogue, A., Liddle, H. A., Becker, D., & Johnson-Leckrone, J. (2002). Family-based prevention counseling for high-risk young adolescents: Immediate outcomes. *Journal of Community Psychology, 30*(1), 1–22.

*Huey, S. J., & Pan, D. (2006). Culture-responsive one-session treatment for phobic Asian Americans: A pilot study. *Psychotherapy: Theory, Research, Practice, Training, 43*(4), 549–54.

Huey, S., & Polo, A. (2008). Evidence-based psychosocial treatments for ethnic minority youth. *Journal of Clinical Child and Adolescent Psychology, 37*(1), 262–301.

*Huey, W. C., & Rank, R. C. (1984). Effects of counselor and peer-led group assertive training on Black adolescent aggression. *Journal of Counseling Psychology, 31*(1), 95–98.

Hwang, W. (2006). The psychotherapy adaptation and modification framework: Application to Asian Americans. *American Psychologist, 61*(7), 702–715.

Hwang, W. (2009). The formative method for adapting psychotherapy (FMAP): A community-based developmental approach to culturally adapting therapy. *Professional Psychology: Research and Practice, 40*(4), 369–77.

*Jackson, P. A. (1997). *The effect of exposure to culturally relevant/historically based material on level of frustration tolerance, level of depression, and mediation of anger in African-American young males.* Unpublished doctoral dissertation, The California School of Professional Psychology, Alameda.

*Johnson, D. L. & Breckenridge, J. N. (1982). The Houston Parent-Child Development Center and the primary prevention of behavior problems in young children. *American Journal of Community Psychology, 10*(3), 305–316.

*Jones, L. V. (2008). Preventing depression: Culturally relevant group work with black women. *Research on Social Work Practice, 18*(6), 626–34.

*Kataoka, S. H., Stein, B. D., Jaycox, L. H., Wong, M., Escudero, P., Tu, W., et al. (2003). A school-based mental health program for traumatized Latino immigrant children. *Journal of the American Academy of Child & Adolescent Psychiatry, 42*(3), 311–318.

Kim, B. S. K., Ng, G. F., & Ahn, A. J. (2005). Effects of client expectation for counseling success, client-counselor worldview match, and client adherence to Asian and European American cultural values on counseling process with Asian Americans. *Journal of Counseling Psychology, 52*(1), 67–76.

*Kim, B. S. K., Omizo, M. M., & D'Andrea, M. J. (1998) The effects of culturally consonant group counseling on the self-esteem and internal locus of control orientation among Native American adolescents. *Journal of Specialists in Group Work, 23*(2), 145–16.

*King, B. S. (1999). *The effect of a cultural-based life skills curriculum on American Indian adolescent self-esteem and locus of control.* Unpublished doctoral dissertation, University of Arkansas, Fayetteville.

*Kohn, L. P., Oden, T., Munoz, R. F., Robinson, A., & Leavitt, D. (2002). Adapted cognitive behavioral group therapy for depressed low-income African American women. *Community Mental Health Journal, 38*, 497–504.

*Kopelowicz, A., Zarate, R., Gonzalez Smith, V., Mintz, J., & Liberman, R. (2003). Disease management in Latinos with schizophrenia: a family-assisted, skills training approach. *Schizophrenia Bulletin, 29*(2), 211–27.

Lambert, M. J. (1999). Are differential treatment effects inflated by researcher therapy allegiance? could clever Hans count? *Clinical Psychology: Science and Practice, 6*(1), 127–30.

*LaFromboise, T., & Howard-Pitney, B. (1995). The Zuni life skills development curriculum: Description and evaluation of a suicide prevention program. *Journal of Counseling Psychology, 42*(4), 479–86.

La Roche, M., & Christopher, M. (2009). Changing paradigms from empirically supported treatment to evidence-based practice: A cultural perspective. *Professional Psychology: Research and Practice, 40*(4), 396–402.

Lau, A. S. (2006). Making the case for selective and directed cultural adaptations of evidence-based treatments: Examples from parent training. *Clinical Psychology: Science & Practice, 13*(4), 295–310.

*Lau, A., & Zane, N. (2000). Examining the effects of ethnic-specific services: An analysis of cost-utilization and treatment outcome for Asian American clients. *Journal of Community Psychology, 28*(1), 63–77.

Leong, F. T. L. (1996). Toward an integrative model for cross-cultural counseling and psychotherapy. *Applied & Preventive Psychology, 5*(4), 189–209.

Leong, F. T. L., & Lee, S. H. (2006). A cultural accommodation model for cross-cultural psychotherapy: Illustrated with the case of Asian Americans. *Psychotherapy: Theory, Research, Practice, Training, 43*, 410–423.

Luborsky, L. B., Barrett, M. S., Antonuccio, D. O., Shoenberger, D., & Stricker, G. (2006). What else materially influences what is represented and published as evidence? In R. F. Levant (Ed.), *Evidence-based practices in mental health: Debate and dialogue on the fundamental questions* (pp. 257–98). Washington, DC: American Psychological Association.

Mak, W., Law, R., Alvidrez, J., & Pérez-Stable, E. (2007). Gender and ethnic diversity in NIMH-funded clinical trials: Review of a decade of published research. *Administration and Policy in Mental Health and Mental Health Services Research, 34*(6), 497–503.

*Malgady, R. G., Rogler, L. H., & Costantino, G. (1990a). Hero/heroine modeling for Puerto

Rican adolescents: A preventive mental health intervention. *Journal of Counseling Psychology, 58*, 469–74.

*Malgady, R. G., Rogler, L. H., & Costantino, G. (1990b). Culturally sensitive psychotherapy For Puerto Rican children and adolescents: A program of treatment outcome research. *Journal of Consulting and Clinical Psychology, 58*(6), 704–712.

Marcus, E. (2010). PTSD manifests differently in Haitian patients, says researcher. Huffington Post. Retrieved online May 31, 2010 from http://www.huffingtonpost.com/erin-marcus/ptsd-manifests-differentl_b_580825.html

*Martinez C. R., Jr., & Eddy, J. M. (2005). Effects of culturally adapted parent management training on Latino youth behavioral health outcomes. *Journal of Consulting and Clinical Psychology, 73*(4), 841–51.

*Matos, M., Bauermeister, J. J., & Bernal, G. (2009). Parent-Child Interaction Therapy for Puerto Rican preschool children with ADHD and behavior problems: A pilot efficacy study. *Family Process, 48*, 232–52.

*Mausbach, B. T., Bucardo, J., McKibbin, C. L., Cardenas, V., & Barrio, C. (2008). Evaluation of a culturally tailored skills intervention for Latinos with persistent psychotic disorders. *American Journal of Psychiatric Rehabilitation, 11*(1), 61–75.

*Mickens-English, P. (1996). *The efficacy of an Afrocentric/holistic group psychotherapy approach for black women.* Unpublished doctoral dissertation, Kent State University, Ohio.

Miranda, J. (2006). Improving services and outreach for women with depression. In C. M. Mazure & G. P. Keita (Eds). *Understanding depression in women: Applying empirical research to practice and policy.* (pp. 113–35). Washington, DC: American Psychological Association.

Miranda, J., Azocar, F., Organista, K. C., Muñoz, R. F., & Lieberman, A. (1996). Recruiting and retaining low-income Latinos in psychotherapy research. *Journal of Consulting and Clinical Psychology, 64*(5), 868–74.

Miranda, J., Bernal, G., Lau, A., Kohn, L., Hwang, W., & La Framboise, T. (2005). State of the science on psychosocial interventions for ethnic minorities. *Annual Review of Clinical Psychology, 1*, 113–42.

Miranda, J., Nakamura, R., & Bernal, G. (2003). Including ethnic minorities in mental health intervention research: A practical approach to a long-standing problem. *Culture, Medicine and Psychiatry, 27*(4), 467–86.

*Mokuau, N., Braun, K. L., Wong, L. K., Higuchi, P., & Gotay, C. C. (2008). Development of a family intervention for native Hawaiian women with cancer: A pilot study. *National Association of Social Workers. 53*(1), 9–19.

*Moran, J. R. (1999). Preventing alcohol use among urban American Indian youth: The seventh generation program. *Journal of Human Behavior in the Social Environment, 2*, 51–67.

Muñoz, R. E (1982). The Spanish speaking consumer and the community mental health center. In E. E. Jones & S. Korchin (Eds.), *Minority mental health* (pp. 362–98). New York: Praeger.

*Myers, H. F., Alvy, K. T., Arrington, A., Richardson, M. A., Marigna, M., Huff, R., et al. (1992). The impact of a parent training program on inner-city African-American families. *Journal of Community Psychology, 20*, 132–47.

*Nagel, T., Robinson, G., Condon, J., & Trauer, T. (2009). Approach to treatment of mental illness and substance dependence in remote indigenous communities: Results of a mixed methods study. *The Australian Journal of Rural Health, 17*(4), 174–82.

National Science Foundation (2009). *Doctorate recipients from US universities: Summary report 2007–2008.* Retrieved online May 17, 2010 from http://www.nsf.gov/statistics/nsf10309/pdf/nsf10309.pdf

*Nyamathi, A. M., Leake, B., Flaskerud, J., Lewis, C., & Bennett, C. (1993). Outcomes of specialized and traditional AIDS counseling programs for impoverished women of color. *Research in Nursing & Health, 16*, 11–21.

*Ochoa, M. L., (1981). *Group counseling Chicana troubled youth: An exploratory group counseling project.* Unpublished doctoral dissertation, University of Massachusetts, Amherst.

Ortman, J. M., & Guarneri, C. E. (2009). United States population projections: 2000 to 2050. U.S. Census Bureau. Retrieved online June 1, 2010 from http://www.census.gov/population/www/projections/analytical-document09.pdf

*Pantin, H., Coatsworth, J. D., Feaster, D. J., Newman, F. L., Briones, E., Prado, G., et al. (2003). Familias Unidas: The efficacy of an intervention to promote parental investment in Hispanic immigrant families. *Prevention Science, 4*(3), 189–201.

*Parker, L. (1990). *The role of cultural traditions in alcohol and drug abuse prevention: A Native American study.* Unpublished doctoral dissertation, Brown University, Providence, RI.

Pedersen, P. B. (1999). *Multiculturalism as a fourth force*. Philadelphia: Brunner/Mazel.

Pedersen, P. B. (2000). *A handbook for developing multicultural awareness* (3rd ed.). Alexandria, VA: American Counseling Association.

Rey, G., & Sainz, M. (2007). Tailoring an intervention model to help indigenous families cope with excessive drinking in central Mexico. *Salud Mental, 30*(6), 32–42.

Ridley, C. R. (1984). Clinical treatment of the nondisclosing Black client: A therapeutic paradox. *American Psychologist, 39*, 1234–44.

*Rosselló, J. & Bernal, G. (1999). The efficacy of cognitive behavioral and interpersonal treatments for depressed Puerto Rican adolescents. *Journal of Consulting and Clinical Psychology, 67*, 734–45.

*Rosselló, J., Bernal, G., & Rivera-Medina, C. (2008). Individual and group CBT and IPT Puerto Rican adolescent with depressive symptoms. *Cultural Diversity and Ethnic Minority Psychology, 14*, 234–45.

*Rowland, M. D., Halliday-Boykins, C. A., Henggeler, S. W., Cunningham, P. B., Lee, T. G., Kruesi, M. J. P., et al. (2005). A randomized trial of multisystemic therapy with Hawaii's Felix Class youths. *Journal of Emotional and Behavioral Disorders, 13*(1), 13–23.

*Royce, D. (1998) Mentoring high-risk minority youth: Evaluation of the Brothers project. *Adolescence, 33*(129), 145–58.

*Santisteban, D. A., Coatsworth, J. D., Perez-Vidal, A., Kurtines, W. M., Schwartz, S. J., LaPerriere, A., et al. (2003). Efficacy of Brief Strategic Family Therapy in modifying Hispanic adolescent behavior problems and substance use. *Journal of Family Psychology, 17*(1), 121–33.

Schwartz, A. L., Domenech Rodríguez, M. M., Santiago-Rivera, A., Arredondo, P., & Field, L. D. (2010). Cultural and linguistic competence: Welcome challenges from successful diversification. *Professional Psychology: Research and Practice, 41*, 210–20.

*Schwarz, D. A. (1989). *The effect of a Spanish pre-therapy orientation videotape on Puerto Rican clients' knowledge about psychotherapy, improvement in therapy, attendance patterns and satisfaction with services*. Unpublished doctoral dissertation, Temple University, Philadelphia.

Shin, H. B., & Kominski, R. A. (2010). Language use in the United States: 2007. U.S. Census Bureau. Retrieved on line June 1, 2010 from http://www.census.gov/population/www/socdemo/language/ACS-12.pdf

*Shin, S. K., & Lukens, E. P. (2002). Effects of psychoeducation for Korean Americans with chronic mental illness. *Psychiatric Services, 53*(9), 1125–31.

*Shin, S. K. (2004). Effects of culturally relevant psychoeducation for Korean American families of persons with chronic mental illness. *Research on Social Work Practice, 14*(4), 231–39.

Smith, T. B. (2010). Culturally congruent practices in counseling and psychotherapy: A review of research. In J. G. Ponterotto, J. M. Casas, L. A. Suzuki, & C. M. Alexander (Eds.), *Handbook of multicultural counseling*. (3rd ed., pp. 439–50). Thousand Oaks, CA: Sage.

Smith, T. B., Richards, P. S., Granley, M., & Obiakor, F. (2004). Practicing multiculturalism: An introduction. In T. B. Smith (Ed.), *Practicing multiculturalism: Affirming diversity in counseling and psychology* (pp. 3–16). Boston: Allyn & Bacon.

*Sobol, D. A. (2000). *An adolescent-parent conflict resolution training program for ethnically diverse families*. Unpublished doctoral dissertation, University of Southern California, Los Angeles.

Sue, S. (1988). Psychotherapeutic services for ethnic minorities: Two decades of research findings. *American Psychologist, 43*(4), 301–308.

Sue, D. W., & Sue, D. (2008). *Counseling the culturally diverse: Theory and practice* (5th ed.). New York: John Wiley.

*Szapocznik, J., Rio, A., Perez-Vidal, A., Kurtines, W., Hervis, O., & Santisteban, D. (1986). Bicultural Effectiveness Training (BET): An experimental test of an intervention modality for families experiencing intergenerational/intercultural conflict. *Hispanic Journal of Behavioral Sciences, 8*(4), 303–30.

*Szapocznik, J., Santisteban, D., Rio, A., Perez-Vidal, A., Santisteban, D., & Kurtines, W. M. (1989). Family Effectiveness Training: An intervention to prevent drug abuse and problem behaviors in Hispanic adolescents. *Hispanic Journal of Behavioral Sciences, 11*(1), 4–27.

Tanaka-Matsumi, J. (2008). Functional approaches to evidence-based practice in multicultural counseling and therapy. In P. A. Hays & G. Y. Iwamasa (Eds.), *Principles of multicultural counseling and therapy.* (pp. 169–98). New York: Routledge/Taylor & Francis Group.

*Telles, C., Karno, M., Mintz, J., Paz, G., Arias, M., Tucker, D., et al. (1995). Immigrant families coping with schizophrenia: Behavioural

family intervention v. *case management with a low-income Spanish-speaking population. British Journal of Psychiatry, 167*(4), 473–79.

*Timberlake, T. L. (2000). *A comprehensive approach to social skills training with urban African American adolescents.* Unpublished doctoral dissertation, Temple University, Philadelphia.

U.S. Surgeon General (2001). *Mental health: Culture, race, and ethnicity. A supplement to mental health: A report of the surgeon general.* Rockville, MD: U.S. Department of Health and Human Services.

Wampold, B. E., Mondin, G. W., Moody, M., Stich, F., Benson, K., & Ahn, H. (1997). A meta-analysis of outcome studies comparing bona fide psychotherapies: Empirically, "all must have prizes." *Psychological Bulletin, 122*(3), 203–215.

Whaley, A. L., & Davis, K. E. (2007). Cultural competence and evidence-based practice in mental health services: A complementary perspective. *American Psychologist, 62*(6), 563–74.

Whitbeck, L. B. (2006). Some guiding assumptions and a theoretical model for developing culturally specific preventions with Native American people. *Journal of Community Psychology, 34*(2), 183–92.

*Xiong, W., Phillips, M. R., Hu, X., Wang, R., Dai, Q., Kleinman, J., et al. (1994). Family-based intervention for schizophrenic patients in China: A randomized controlled trial. *British Journal of Psychiatry, 165*(2), 239–47.

Zane, N., Hall, G. N., Sue, S., Young K., & Nuñez (2004). Research on psychotherapy with culturally diverse populations. In M. Lambert (Ed.), *Bergin and Garfield's Handbook of Psychotherapy and Behavior Change, 5th Edition* (767–804). New York: Wiley.

*Zhang, Y., Young, D., Lee, S., Li, L., Zhang, H., Xiao, Z., et al. (2002). Chinese Taoist cognitive psychotherapy in the treatment of generalized anxiety disorder in contemporary China. *Transcultural Psychology, 39*(1), 115–29.

17 Coping Style

Larry E. Beutler, T. Mark Harwood, Satoko Kimpara, David Verdirame, *and* Kathy Blau

It is important that children, early on, acquire the ability both to engage in self-reflection and to appraise the behavior of others. As children begin to look both internally and externally, they learn to integrate and compare the information obtained from each without becoming overwhelmed with either. The integration between internal sensitivity and external judgment, between the subjective and the objective, requires that humans maintain a complex but modulated response to both sources of information and rely on a flexible system of values by which to appraise both the impact of others on self and of self on others.

A perfect balance is unlikely and, not infrequently, an individual will develop a preference for, or sensitivity to, either internal experiences or external events. This preference results in governing temperaments of infants and, later in life, distinctive coping styles.

Kagan (1998) observed that some infants were, by nature, behaviorally highly reactive—very responsive—to internal events, resulting in a degree of emotionality that contributed to behavioral instability. He concluded that hyperreactive children were easily overwhelmed and distressed by sudden or novel stimuli in their environments. Their responses were characterized by high arousal, distress, and fear. They viewed both the occurrence and anticipation of external events as intrusions, as threats that upset their internal experiences and produced avoidance and seclusion. In later life, these children were observed frequently to develop substantial amounts of anxiety and to become overwhelmed by their fears and avoidant in their behaviors. They often became socially withdrawn, self-critical, phobic, and intolerant of emotional experience or environmental change. They turned to internal experience, fantasy, and obsessive reconstruction of events to achieve stability.

By contrast, Kagan observed that other infants were less reactive to these events and, instead, preferred attending to external happenings while ignoring internal experiences. Those with this temperament of low reactivity or low sensitivity were relatively more tolerant of novelty and change; they were observed to seek, rather than avoid, stimulation from their environment, to take action to engage and change their environments, and to be gregarious and outgoing in their relationships with others. When they did develop problems, the problems frequently expressed themselves as intrusive behaviors, insensitivity to other's feelings and needs, lack of empathy, and with overt signs of anger and rage.

Patterns like those observed by Kagan occur within all age groups. Introversion–extroversion (Eysenck, 1960), internalization–externalization (Welsh, 1952), and a bimodal array of similarly descriptive terms have characterized these distinctions among the experiences that people prefer and the way they adapt to change. These and related terms constitute psychometrically valid and clinically useful descriptors identifying a continuum of ways that people respond to novelty and change. At one end of this continuum are individuals who protect themselves from stimulation by being self-critical, avoiding change, and withdrawing in the face of anticipated change or discord. These individuals are sensitized and overreactive to change and are prone to be overwhelmed by fear. They seek stability and safety in a focus on internal experiences rather than on the instability and uncertainty of external events. At the other end of the continuum are individuals who prefer to embrace novelty and change with activity and assertion (e.g., Beutler, Moos, & Lane, 2003; Beutler, Clarkin, & Bongar, 2000). They seek contact with others, enjoy change, and are gregarious in their interactions with their world.

In virtually all cultures, individuals with a highly reactive temperament are described as internalizing, avoidant, restrained, or introverted. Those with a low reactive temperament, in contrast, have been described as externalizing, gregarious, and extroverted. Across cultures, there are preferences for one or another of these temperamental styles; Western cultures tend to foster the development of external, assertive, and individualistic styles of adjusting to change, while those living in Eastern cultures prefer more avoidant, self-inspection, and internalizing styles, even sharing attachments across the communal group (Kawai, 1993, 1996).

In their search for factors that mediate the effects of psychotherapy, researchers have been drawn to examine how patient attributes may determine one's response to different therapeutic interventions. One of these specific patient attributes is coping style, a patient dimension that is both reminiscent of the temperament described by Kagan (1998) and matched with the degree to which effective change is moderated by insight. Early research discovered a relation between patient coping style and the differential use of psychological treatments that either sought to change skills and behaviors directly or that focused on the indirect processes of achieving insight and internal awareness (Beutler & Clarkin, 1990). Specifically, among patients whose characteristic coping styles were identified as internalizing (or hyperreactive) outcomes were positively associated with the use of insight- or awareness-oriented therapies. The latter interventions include those focused on improved emotional awareness or interpersonal sensitivity. Conversely, among patients whose characteristic coping styles were identified as externalizing, positive outcomes were associated with therapies that rely largely on enhancing skill development and encouraging direct symptom change.

The chapter (Beutler et al., 2002) in the earlier edition of this volume provided a box score on the association of patient coping style with treatment type in predicting psychotherapy outcome. Fifteen of 19 studies confirmed the expected pattern between the goodness of patient–treatment fit and outcome; however, the inclusion criteria for those 19 studies were somewhat lenient, and the box score did not yield an index of the magnitude of the association.

In this chapter, we delve deeper into the rationale for patient coping style as an indicator for differential psychotherapy and will subject the hypotheses to a meta-analysis.

This will allow an assessment both of the statistical significance of the findings and the strength of this matching dimension as a contributor to outcome. Our meta-analysis will also permit us to analyze studies comprised mainly of patients with one type of coping style (external or internal), and a separate estimate can be derived for each of these styles and the differences can be compared.

Definitions and Measures

In order to determine the effectiveness of matching a patient's coping style to the focus of psychotherapeutic interventions, both the patient's coping style and the nature of treatments ranging from insight/awareness- to symptom-focused must be defined in operational terms. While numerous instruments have been developed to assess this distinction among treatments, few address the level of observed therapist behavior in these terms. One exception to this rule is an instrument developed by Beutler and colleagues to assess dimensions both of patients and treatments. This instrument conceptualizes both coping style and therapy focus as existing along a continuum, with the nature of the effective interaction assumed to vary as a function of the intersect between each continuum for a given patient and therapist. In measuring coping style, for example, ratings of externalization and internalization are ordered along a continuum based on the preponderance of actions that occur under conditions of environmental change (Beutler, Moos, & Lane, 2003). Likewise, measures of treatment focus consider it to be best described as a continuum that extends from being insight/awareness-oriented to symptom/skill-oriented. This latter designation is based both on a rating of the objectives of the treatment and the degree to which the efforts to induce change are aimed directly at symptomatic behaviors or indirectly

through increasing insight or personal awareness. These distinctions will become clear as we inspect some of the ways that these concepts have been defined and measured in the past.

Coping Style

Coping style has been described by different personality and psychopathology theorists via a collection of often unrelated-sounding but conceptually similar terms. Two conceptual aspects of coping have proven controversial. First, some theorists define coping style in terms of how one deals with environmental novelty and change under normal conditions (e.g., Lazarus & Folkman, 1984; McKay et al., 1998), whereas others emphasize the adaptability of one's of coping efforts when faced with stressful situations or unusual environmental changes (e.g., Eysenck, 1960; Latack & Havlovic, 1992). Second, some emphasize the role of traitlike aspects of coping (e.g., Endler, Parker, & Butcher, 1993), a position that is in contrast to those that concentrate on state or situational qualities of coping (e.g., Ouimette, Ahrens, Moos, & Finney, 1997).

We have incorporated these varying theoretical points within a broad, statistical definition (Beutler & Clarkin, 1990). We define coping style as the pattern of behavior that is predominantly employed when one faces a new or unusual situation. This definition combines both state- and trait aspects of one's response and removes the requirement that coping styles only be observed during and following *stressful* situations. Thereby, the definition effectively eliminates the need to judge the level of stress experienced or the generalizability of the situation in which it has occurred.

From this broader perspective, *coping styles* are recurrent patterns of behavior that characterize the individual when confronting new or problematic situations.

This style identifies one's vulnerability to change and one's predominant tendency to respond to novelty. Thus, coping styles are not discrete behaviors but are a cluster of related behaviors that are distinguished because they are repetitive, durable across similar events, and observable when problems or unexpected events are being addressed. Descriptively, the specific behaviors that form the clusters include both repetitive situational responses such as impulsivity, discrete acting-out behaviors, escape and direct avoidance, and general temperaments. Unlike more narrow definitions of coping style, definitions like ours are based upon correlated clusters of behaviors and are not explanatory concepts. Given the diversity of measurements used to study coping styles, we will adopt this broad definition in our meta-analysis.

Following the description of Eysenck (1957) and Kagan (1998), the quality that distinguishes internalizing traits and dispositions from other coping styles is that they are governed by the forces of inhibition and excitation. Internalizers/introverts are more easily overwhelmed by change and tend to become shy, withdrawn, and self-inspective, while externalizers/extroverts are more likely to act out, to seek stimulation and change, to directly escape or withdraw from conflict, and to be confrontational and gregarious in expressing problems. Animal behaviorists have extended these qualities to proactive versus reactive behaviors (Koolhaas et al., 1999), and others have incorporated similar concepts into the Big Five personality factors (Costa & McCrae, 1985).

For research purposes in psychotherapy, patient coping styles are typically measured objectively through individualized observations and ratings (e.g., Beutler, Clarkin, & Bongar, 2000) or through standardized, self-report, omnibus personality and psychopathology measures such as the Minnesota

Multiphasic Personality Inventory (MMPI-2; Butcher, 1990; Butcher & Beutler, 2003), supplemented by reviewing the patient's past and present reactions to problems. The internalization ratio (IR) formula, extracted from the MMPI-2, has been used frequently by our own research group to capture the interactive nature of coping style and treatment focus (e.g., Beutler, Engle, et al., 1991; Beutler, Moliero, et al., 2003). In our modification of a formula originally proposed by Welsh (1952), eight MMPI-2 subscale scores are entered as a standard T scores:

$$IR = \frac{Hy + Pd + Pa + Ma}{Hs + D + Pt + Si}$$

An IR that favors the numerator suggests that a patient is disposed to use externalizing coping behaviors. These individuals blame others for their feelings (Pa); they display active, dependent behaviors (Hy), high levels of unfocused energy (Ma), are impulsive, and frequently have social adjustment problems (Pd).

These individualized, patient-level methods of measurement serve the broad definition used in this literature somewhat better than more indirect measures that cluster groups of individuals under a categorical classification based on either coping (e.g., Lazarus & Folkman, 1984) or diagnosis. Using diagnosis as a proxy for coping style, for example, treats all patients within a diagnostic group as if they were identical on this dimension, occluding the many variations that exist within diagnostic groups; however, when using archival data, direct, individual-level measures of coping style are often not available. In such instances, a categorical definition of the patient's dominant coping style must be inferred through indirect observation of shared behaviors, using what information is available. Diagnostic problems that are characterized by intense distress, ruminations, and social withdrawal are usually indirectly identified as related to internalizing patterns of coping. Thus, Axis I diagnoses within the spectrum of anxiety disorders as well as Axis II avoidant personality disorders can usually be assumed to be internalizing conditions, while antisocial personality, substance abuse, and paranoid personality disorder can be seen as more highly dominated by externalizing patterns. Unfortunately, because they are diverse and do not reliably map onto individual coping style descriptions, reliance on diagnosis or other categorical definitions of personalities as a proxy for a patient's dominant coping style must be undertaken with considerable caution. This consideration led us to arbitrarily limit the proportion of studies in our meta-analysis that used such proxy measures to no more the 25% of the studies included in our analysis.

Treatment Focus

The therapist's treatment methods are also measured in two ways—through direct observations of each individual therapist's behaviors or by indirect measures based on the system of psychotherapy used. There is little doubt that the most sensitive measure of treatment focus is to observe and calibrate in-therapy actions and intentions of the therapist. Using individual, direct measuring methods, rating the use of various techniques such as interpretation, transference analysis, dream analysis, interpersonal analysis, and the like can identify procedures that are most frequently associated with the effort to evoke insight and awareness of previously cathected, unconscious, and symbolized material (e.g., Beutler, Moleiro, et al., 2003).

Direct observation such as the foregoing can yield numerical data on the frequency of any treatment methods. One can count the use of symptom reports, techniques based on reinforcement paradigms, therapist

instruction in the use of problem-solving strategies, or efforts to enhance patient self-monitoring in order to identify the predominant procedures used to evoke changes in symptoms and overt problems as well as to stimulate the resolution of inferred problems or causes. Where possible, the use of direct measures is advantageous in either case. The measures are reliable, easily tested for interrater validity, and can be used to rate a wide array of discrete techniques that share a common set of objectives.

Unfortunately, as with coping style, there are many instances when direct observations of therapy interactions are not possible. When using archival data or when working from published reports, the focus of the treatment often must be inferred from the theoretical rationale underlying the therapy used. Usually, it is most reliable simply to categorize the treatment model in terms of purity as a prototypic insight/awareness-oriented procedure or a symptom/skill-focused procedure. In this bifurcation, interpersonal, experiential, and psychodynamic therapies are usually classed as insight-focused procedures, and cognitive, cognitive-behavioral, and behavioral models are identified as symptom-focused interventions. However, it is an oversimplification to think of the distinction between direct, symptom change–focused and indirect change–focused interventions as discrete and finite. More accurately, psychological treatments are ordered along a continuum that ranges from the degree to which they address mediating variables to the degree to which they focus on the symptoms themselves (Beutler, Moleiro, et al., 2003). For example, in the purest form of symptom-focused interventions, behavior therapy directly addresses changes in symptoms and skills while eschewing the presence of "underlying" problems. These therapies take each symptom that is disruptive to the patient's adjustment or happiness at face value, working sequentially to eradicate it. At the other end of the treatment focus dimension, psychodynamic procedures make an indirect or mediated change on expressed problems and symptoms. These methods take little note of the symptom, itself, seeing it as merely a symbolized expression of some unseen and more important underlying conflict. That which is not directly seen, but which can be inferred from the theoretical model used, is then assumed as the point of focus for the change effort. Treatments that emphasize unconscious processes are examples of these indirect interventions.

The difficulty with this categorical classification can be seen when the therapies studied are those that attempt to achieve symptom change through indirect means. Interpersonal psychotherapy (IPT), for example, is explicitly *not* focused on improving historical insight in the same way that psychodynamic therapy is. Instead, it deals with improving one's awareness of interpersonal and emotional forces that affect one's behavior. Thus, it is focused on the enhancement of social and emotional awareness but not on insight, per se, and its status lies somewhere between the direct symptom focus of cognitive therapy and the indirect focus of psychodynamic therapy. While not as sensitive as therapist-level measures, a classification of treatment based on relative position along the continuum from insight/awareness to symptom/skill focus can be assessed for reliability. Descriptions of efforts to ensure treatment fidelity can be used in research practice to provide some cross-validation of one's classifications.

Clinical Examples

There are many examples of how patient coping styles manifest in psychotherapy. Even if the therapist does not have self-report measures, he/she may observe the patient's response to life crises by withdrawal and self-blame (internalizing) or by becoming angry, blaming, and avoidant (externalizing).

L.C. was a 42-year-old, married man who was referred for psychotherapy by his physician, who he also described as his best friend. The patient's presenting problems were many, including substance abuse, depression, impaired work performance, and deficits in interpersonal functioning. The patient recalled being "very depressed" since the age of 12 and described a family history of abuse, alcohol dependence, and finally, abandonment. He was on his own at age 16, and what had begun 3 years before as recreational marijuana use rapidly developed into extensive cocaine, methamphetamine, and heroin abuse. He held several jobs between the ages of 16 and 40, losing most because of behaviors related to chemical dependency. At age 29 he got married and was divorced by age 35. At age 40 he began his own Internet business in an effort to escape the rigid rules that had frequently led to his termination from other jobs. His progress had been uneven and slow; he maintained a marginal existence on the income that he could produce.

Direct and indirect measures of L.C.'s coping style indicated a mixed but predominantly internalizing style. Indirect measure, based on diagnosis, reveals a mix of internalizing depression and some substance acting out. A direct measure (the MMPI-2, IR) of L.C.'s coping pattern revealed that he had a mixture of both internalizing and externalizing coping patterns, with an overall balance favoring the use of internalizing strategies. Hypochondriasis, Depression, anxiety (Psychasthenia), and Social Introversion scales averaged 7 points higher than the corresponding externalizing scales. His internalizing style of coping was further illustrated and observed in how he conceptualized the cause and the consequences of his drug use. He expressed the belief that his drug abuse began because he was weak and defective—an introtensive injunction. He indicated that his problem had continued because he was not strong enough to follow his conscience—a self-critical injunction. While not a religious man, he expressed strong guilt for having "enticed" his wife into a marriage in which he was unable to take care of her.

In contrast, R.W. was a 43-year-old woman with a history of social avoidance and shyness. In her 20s and 30s, the problems had become so bad that she had to quit her job as a secondary school teacher because she could not face her class. At that time she was diagnosed with social phobia and with avoidant personality disorder. The MMPI-2 provided a direct confirmation for an internalizing coping style. The Internalization ratio showed dramatic elevations on Psychasthenia (Scale 7) and Social Introversion (Scale 10), with a secondary elevation on Depression (Scale 2), relative to the externalizing scales.

L.C. and R.W. would differ with respect to the symptoms that would be of primary focus during the early phase of treatment and in the theme that guided the insight-oriented work. For L.C. the initial symptom focus would probably be on behaviors that indicated risk for drug abuse and self-harm, with a secondary focus on social functioning. In contrast, the initial focus for R.W. would probably be on social withdrawal and depression with secondary attention given to any issues of self-harm that emerge.

R.W.'s theme is likely to be quite different than L.C.'s. R.W. may represent the hyperreactive temperament described by Kagan (1998) and, thus, be an early developmental phenomenon; therefore, hypervigilance, chronic fear, and a dread of appraisal from others would probably dominate the theme. Compared with L.C., the coping style is

likely to be much more consistently internalizing, with a lot of attention given to self-evaluation and criticism. This means that one would probably move quite quickly to a theme- or insight-focused intervention.

There are equivalent examples of the differential treatment of individuals who prefer externalizing coping styles. Patterns of consistent acting out and conflict with authorities are examples of individuals who cope in externalized ways. The identification of a preference for these externalized patterns may be inferred from diagnoses like antisocial personality disorder, borderline personality disorder, substance abuse or dependency, and varieties of impulse disorders. While these categorical, indirect measures of coping style are useful, they lack the sensitivity that a continuous measure might provide.

R.G., for example, was a 21-year-old woman referred for psychotherapy from her psychiatrist because of a long-standing pattern of explosive outbursts. In recent years, she had begun abusing alcohol and had been arrested for driving under the influence on two occasions. She had experienced problems in school because of her failure to control her temper and had been a chronic problem to her parents because of similar behavior. She had been in and out of treatment since age 8, but with little help. Except for her first experience with behavior therapy, her treatment had focused on allowing expression of her feelings, trying to uncover the source of her rage, and developing self-awareness and insight.

R.G.'s direct measure of coping style, using the Systematic Treatment Selection-Clinician Rating Form (STS-CRF, Fisher, Beutler, & Williams, 1999) and the MMPI-2, confirmed the dominance of impulsivity and confrontational coping behaviors over rational self-control. She evidenced poor insight, high levels of poorly directed energy, and a strong sense of persecution. Accordingly, treatment focused, not on self-expression and "unloading," but on control and tolerance for the discomfort associated with anger and environmental stimulation.

Psychotherapy began by identifying specific situations in which problematic behaviors and symptoms occurred. R.G. was taught to self-monitor her arousal and to identify risk-provoking situations. She then was engaged in learning stress tolerance, where negative emotions were selectively evoked by visual imagery and role playing. Instruction in prosocial behavior accompanied all of these interventions. For example, behavioral rehearsal was used to engage her in communication training and to develop useful skills in impulse control, self-appraisal, and tolerance for novelty and change.

Meta-Analytic Review
Literature Search and Inclusion Criteria

In undertaking our meta-analysis, our focus was to identify studies in which interaction of coping style and treatment focus could be assessed and effect sizes could be calculated. That is, they addressed the moderating role that patient coping style exerted on the effectiveness of a particular treatment focus (direct behavior change or indirect insight change). In addition, like the corresponding chapter in the earlier volume of this book, we also wanted to assess the independent effects of patient coping style, if any, on outcome. That is, we wanted to know the main effects of patient coping style. This latter, or main effect analysis, addresses a prognostic question while moderating studies address a treatment planning question: What treatment is best for what patient?

In identifying relevant literature, we followed the general outline that was used by Beutler, Harwood, Michelson, Song, and Holman (this volume, Chapter 13) in their meta-analytic review of matching treatment directiveness to patient resistance/reactance. This procedure began with identifying a set of six criteria that would characterize an ideal study:

1. A wide breadth of reliably applied therapeutic approaches and trained therapists to ensure variance on the dimension of treatment focus

2. A similarly wide range of moderately impaired patients in order to ensure variability on the dimension of coping style

3. Individualized (i.e., direct) measures of both patient coping style and treatment focus in order to avoid equating focus with a particular brand of treatment and coping style with a particular diagnosis

4. Random assignment of patients to therapists within treatments in order to ensure equivalent dispersal of patients to insight/awareness- and symptom/skill-focused interventions

5. Systematic monitoring both of treatment variability/consistency on the dimension of treatment focus and of patient coping style

6. Objective and uniform outcome measurement that included analysis of fit between patient coping style and treatment focus.

The second step was then to identify a model study, an investigation whose methods represented these criteria most closely. This model study then served as a template for evaluating other studies that we identified. The study (Beutler, Moleiro, et al., 2003) had all of the requisite methodological features for inclusion in our review except that it utilized a composite algorithm to fit treatment to patient. The composite included the fit of coping style to treatment focus but incorporated two other matching factors as well. Because it did not permit a pure test of the coping style by treatment focus "fit," it was not included in the current review as a primary study.

The next step in our procedure was to identify studies that most closely complied with the criteria established for inclusion in the meta-analysis. Our scope included studies published within a 19-year span from 1990 to 2009. We began by collecting studies that had addressed patient coping style explicitly as a mediator between treatment focus and outcome in the prior edition of this volume. This resulted in a list of 19 studies, and we added to this list by searching the PsychINFO database using search words associated with coping style, personality, introversion, extraversion, etc. The final step was to hand-search the 2009 volumes of the most widely cited journals that emerged from our search. These included the *Journal of Consulting and Clinical Psychology*, the *Journal of Counseling Psychology*, and the *Journal of Clinical Psychology*.

We excluded studies that had major methodological weaknesses and those whose results did not allow the calculation of an effect size (ES). Methodological weaknesses included the failure to use direct measures of coping style, absence of blind or masked outcome measures, indefinite forms of treatment in which the focus could not be defined with relative certainty, and inaccurate interpretations or calculations.

Applying both indirect measures of coping style and direct ones, we initially identified 26 studies that had addressed the roles of coping style (or a reasonable proxy measure) either as a main effect or as a mediator of treatment outcome. From the pool of 26 studies, 12 met at least four of the six criteria and permitted an analysis of ESs. The main reason studies were pared from the initial set of 26 studies was that they did not report data from which effect sizes could be computed. In many cases this was simply a failure on the part of the

investigator to conduct necessary analyses or report statistics. In other cases, the problem was that their statistical procedures provided data that were appropriate, but we were unable to reliably calculate effect sizes. Some examples of excluded studies may make the decision process more clear.

One excluded study (Beutler & Mitchell, 1981) reported the treatment outcomes of 40 patients. Patient coping style (internalizer or externalizer) was assessed using the MMPI. The results revealed systematic patient aptitude (coping style) × treatment interaction effects independent of diagnoses. Externalizing patients were found to achieve greater benefit from experiential treatment than from analytic-based therapy; however, among internalizing patients, insight-oriented (analytic) treatment achieved its greatest effects and, correspondingly, the behavioral therapies had the least beneficial impact. Unfortunately, these results were based on a box score tabulation of studies that were indicative of a relation between therapy–patient fit and outcome. The lack of more precise statistics rendered this study inappropriate for inclusion in the meta-analysis.

A study by Barber and Muenz (1996) was included as part of the meta-analysis in an early draft of this chapter but excluded in the final sample. The exclusion occurred because the two senior authors could not uniformly identify a difference in coping styles as being characteristic of the two subsamples studied. Obsessive and "avoidant" patients were both judged to be representative of predominantly internalizing coping styles.

Three widely regarded and large-sample studies also were excluded from our final analysis and deserve special attention here because of this. For example, Beutler, Clarkin, and Bongar (2000) compared several treatment fit dimensions in a large-scale study of 284 patients, nine treatments, and over 30 therapists. This study included specific and direct measures of both internal and external coping styles from the MMPI, as well as observational and direct measures of treatment focus. Unfortunately, the study also applied a complex Structural Equation Modeling (SEM) analysis to assess the findings, and we could find no reliable method to extract an effect size estimate for the interaction effects of the specific matching dimensions associated with coping style.

The second large-sample study, Project MATCH (Project Match Research Group, 1997), is the largest randomized clinical trial (RCT) of matching variables conducted to date. In this study, 952 outpatients and 774 inpatients diagnosed as alcohol dependent were assigned to one of three 12-week, manual-guided treatments (cognitive-behavioral coping skills therapy = CBT, motivational enhancement therapy = MET, or 12-step facilitation therapy = TSF). All three of the treatments were symptom focused. None of the treatments could reliably be judged by our raters as insight or awareness oriented. This precluded a reliable test of the fit between treatment focus and patient coping style.

The third large-sample study that was excluded was the United Kingdom Alcohol Treatment Trial (UKATT Research Team, 2007). Over 420 alcoholic patients were treated with one of two structured interventions. The treatments consisted of either motivational enhancement therapy (MET) or social behavior and network Therapy. Once again, our raters could not distinguish between the two treatments. Both were identified as being symptom and skill focused. This and the absence of specific outcome and follow-up data precluded a test of the treatment-fitting hypothesis regarding coping style and treatment focus.

Coding Studies and Calculating ESs

Effect sizes (ESs) associated with the fit of treatment focus and patient coping style were calculated as suggested by several sources.

We used the calculation procedure and formula that best fit the characteristics of the data presented in an individual study. We used Cohen's d in all cases, but ESs were often presented as correlation coefficients or even regression coefficients. In these cases, we transferred all estimates of ES to a d coefficient. Several sources were consulted in making this transformation. When there was a difference between formulas, and no single one was consensually accepted as the one of choice, which was often the case, we used the formula that was most consistent with other sources and that provided what appeared to be the most unbiased estimate of ES. We frequently calculated and recalculated formulas two or three times to ensure accuracy. If means, sample sizes, and SDs were available, we always employed the same formula across studies; however, when data were incomplete or reports did not contain some important information, we relied on accepted alternative procedures (e.g., Borenstein, Hedges, Higgins, & Rothstein, 2009; Lipsey & Wilson, 2001; Hunter & Schmidt, 2004). We also calculated an overall mean ES estimate across studies, weighting the individual study ds with the number of patients. Our source for the calculation of 95% confidence intervals was Smithson (2003).

Results: Main Effects of Coping Style and Treatment Focus

The 12 studies and their results are presented in Table 17.1. Only four of these studies provided information from which we could extract an ES estimate on the predictive value of coping style. Only one of these was on an internalizing group of patients (Knekt et al., 2008), and three (Beutler, Moliero, et al., 2003; Karno et al, 2002; Longabaugh et al, 1994) were on externalizing groups. Thus, the number of studies was insufficient to calculate a reliable

Table 17.1 Coping Style and Therapy Focus

Study	N	Design	Measure TX Focus	Sample coping style	N ESs/Study	M ES (focus)	M ES (CS)	M ES "fit"	95% CI
Beutler, Engle, et al. (1991)	63	RCT	I (FEP/ins vs. SSD/sym)	D (Int-Ext)	3	1.63		0.75	0.64–0.86
Litt, Babor, et al. (1992)	79	RCT	I (CST/Sym vs. Interact/Ins)	D (Ext)	2			0.63	0.52–0.74
Beutler, et al. (1993)	46	RCT	I (CT/Sym FEP/Ins & SSD/Ins)	D (Int-Ext)	4	1.16		1.64	1.34–1.94
Longabaugh, Rubin, et al. (1994)	140	RCT	I (CBT/Sym vs. ECBT/Ins)	I (Ext)	14	0.12		0.37	0.29–0.45
Calvert, Beutler, & Crago (1988)	108	MR/Q-E	D (TOQ) (Sym-Ins)	D (Int-Ext)	3		0.68	0.81	0.73–0.88
Kadden, et al., (1989)	96	Nat	I (CBT/sym vs. IPT/Ins)	D (Ext)	2			0.60	0.50–0.70
Karno et al. (2002)	47	RCT	I (CT/Sym vs. FST/Ins)	I (Ext)	4	0.02	0.30	0.50	0.36–0.64
Beutler, Moliero, et al. (2003)	40	RCT/MR	I (CT/Sym vs. NT/ins)	I/D (Ext)	4	1.01	0.99	0.71	0.57–0.85
Milrod, Leon, et al. (2007)	49	RCT	I (PFP/Ins vs. ART/Sym)	I (Int)	4	0.92		0.71	0.58–0.84
Knekt, Lindfors, et al. (2008)	326	RCT	I (SFT/Sym vs. STD/Ins & LTD/Ins)	D (Int)	1	0.94	0.94	0.17	0.13–0.21
Kimpara (in Beutler, 2009)	121	Nat	D (SFT/Ins vs. Sym)	D (Int)	1	1.17		0.76	0.68–0.84

	N	Design			
Johannsen (in Beutler, 2009)	92	Q-E/MR	D (TPRS/Ins vs. Sym)	D (Int-Ext)	1
Total N	1,291				
Summary weighted ESs			0.85*	0.55*	0.61
95% CIs for summary weighted ESs			0.82–0.88	0.52–0.58	0.51–0.71

N = Participants in study

Design = RCT (randomized clinical trial), MR (correlational), Nat (naturalistic), Q-E (quasi-experimental)

Measure Tx focus = either direct (designated as D) or indirect (designated as I). Indirect measures are based on the model of treatment used and identified as either either symptom- (Sym) or insight- (Ins) focused; direct measures are based on a individual measure of the use of insight or symptom change procedures.

Direct measures include: TOQ (Therapist Orientation Questionnaire), TPRS (Therapy Process Rating Scale).

Indirect measures of Tx Focus are based on the model of treatment studied:

CT = cognitive therapy; FEP = focused expressive therapy; SSD = supportive self-directed therapy;

CST = coping skills training; Interact = Interactive; CBT = cognitive behavioral therapy; ECBT = relationship enhanced CT;

IPT = interpersonal therapy; Interp = interpretive; Supp =supportive; FST = family systems; NT = narrative therapy;

PT = prescriptive therapy; PFP = panic-focused psychodynamic; ART = applied relaxation;

SFT = solution-focused therapy; STD = short-term dynamic therapy; LTD = long-term dynamic therapy

Sample/coping Style = coping style type. CS is measured either directly (designated as D) or indirectly (designated as I). Direct measures are an individual personality scale (unspecified here).

Indirect measures are based on the type or diagnosis of the patient group as either internalizing (Int) or externalizing (Ext) or both (In-Ext)

N ESs = Number of effect sizes calculated for this study

M ES (focus) = The mean effect size attributable to the treatment focus variable—combining all treatments

M ES (CS) = The mean effect size attributable to the CS variable—combining all varieties

M ES "fit" = The mean difference between effect sizes for "good" and "poor" fit, estimated in MR/Nat studies from correlational data

All ESs are expressed as d.

* designates a weighted mean effect size across studies.

difference among the effect sizes represented by the two coping styles. Thus, we are unable to conclude whether there was a substantial effect in favor of one or the other way of coping.

Estimating the effect of the therapist's treatment focus was an easier matter since all the treatments could be coded in the same direction relative to their insight or symptomatic focus. The results of these analyses indicated $d = 0.85$ ($p < 0.05$; CI = 0.82–0.88) favoring symptom-focused over insight-focused interventions. This is a large effect, and clearly, at least among treatments comprising the majority of this data set, a direct symptomatic focus is superior to an indirect, insight focus of treatment; however, this conclusion must be considered with caution because of several factors: (1) the included studies were selected because they allowed the assessment of a matching or selective treatment effect, and many studies that included variation in patient coping style without a corresponding measure of treatment focus may have been excluded; and (2) fully half of the studies included were conducted by members or former members of our own research group, leaving the conclusions subject to potential investigator bias.

Results: Moderated Effects of Patient Coping Style

The 12 studies in our final meta-analysis all allowed a test of the proposition that coping style could serve as a moderator of the effect of differential treatment focus. Nine of the 12 studies used a direct measure of patient coping style. Only three used a direct measure of therapy focus. The individual studies had from 1 to 14 effect sizes comparing the level of fit to outcome.

The statistic of interest in these analyses was the variance accounted for by "fitting" the patient's coping style to the treatment focus. A weighted composite mean effect

size (d) was computed for each study, based on all dependent variables. The size of the mean of means, then, indicated the role of treatment fit. A good fit was taken as being composed of either: (1) externalizing patients and symptom-focused therapy or (2) internalizing patients and insight-focused therapy. The overall mean of the estimated ES reflecting level of "fit" was $d = 0.55$ ($p < 0.05$; CI = 0.52–0.58). This value indicates a medium effect size (Cohen, 1988) associated with fitting patient coping style to treatment focus. The average well-matched treatment produced an 8% greater effect than a randomly matched treatment—the average patient with a good fit was better off than 58% of those with a poor match.

The findings were consistent across studies in demonstrating the selective efficacy of symptom/skill-building methods and insight-/interpersonally oriented methods as a function of patient coping style. All studies found results in the same direction; interpersonal and insight-oriented therapies are more effective among internalizing patients, whereas symptom and skill-building therapies are more effective among externalizing patients.

This meta-analytic result supports the conclusions of the earlier review and adds important information about the strength of the effect. Moreover, given the correspondence among the two reviews, one an inclusive review and this, a truncated review of only those studies that reported relevant statistics, the conclusion gains some veracity.

Patient Contributions

Coping style is a relatively stable and enduring patient quality; it is best conceptualized as a personality trait (Beutler, Moos, & Lane, 2003). Clearly, coping style is an aptitude that contributes to differential treatment outcome when it interacts with treatment focus. Its independent effect is uncertain, as noted previously. In the earlier edition of this volume, the review of coping style (Beutler et al., 2002) suggested that internalizing patients were better prognostic risks in psychotherapy than externalizing patients, but that finding does not achieve the level of consistency required for clinical application in the current analysis. In an effort to partially salvage a reliable test of this hypothesis, we looked at the relative effect sizes associated with treatment focus, separating and comparing the values for patients with each of the two coping styles. That is, we calculated the mean effect sizes associated with insight/awareness-focused and symptom/skill-building-focused therapies on samples of patients who were predominantly internalizing and compared them with samples of patients who were predominantly externalizing.

In our sample of 12 studies, there were three that were done on samples of patients whose diagnoses suggested that they may be dominantly internalizing coping types. These included patients diagnosed with chronic shyness and avoidant personality disorder (Kimpara—cited in Beutler 2009), those with chronic depression (Knekt et al., 2008), and those with anxiety disorders (Milrod et al., 2007). The effect sizes of these studies indicate, generally, that the impact of the focus of treatment was moderate. The weighted mean effect size (d) of these three studies was 0.37 ($p < 0.05$; CI = 0.27–0.47), indicating a medium effect size favoring insight/awareness treatments over symptom/skill-focused treatments.

By comparison, 5 of the 12 studies in our sample were conducted on patients whose diagnosis suggested a dominantly externalizing coping pattern (i.e., substance abusers; Litt et al., 1992; Longabaugh et al., 1994; Kadden et al., 1998; Karno et al., 2002; Beutler, Moliero et al., 2003). These studies earned a mean, weighted effect size of treatment focus (d) of 0.53 ($p < 0.05$; CI = 0.40–0.67), favoring the use of symptom/skill-focused interventions. Both values reflect medium effect sizes, but the difference between them ($d = 0.16$; $p < 0.10$) was nonsignificant. Thus, we are unable to conclude that those with one style of coping (e.g., internalizing) are more likely to benefit from psychotherapy than those with the other. Notably, this also means that we did not find evidence for Kagan's (1998) assumption either that the fearful, hypersensitive internalizer would be more of a prognostic risk than the under-responsive externalizer.

Judging from the current findings, patient's coping styles are distributed broadly within the population at large and all along the coping style continuum. Individuals with both internal and external styles of coping are capable of benefitting from psychotherapy, assuming that the nature of that treatment is appropriate to their own coping style.

Limitations of the Research

There are limitations to any research analysis, including meta-analyses. Three major threats need to be considered in our meta-analytic review. First, several studies are excluded because they do not include data that allows effect sizes to be constructed in a way that is comparable across studies. That was certainly a problem here where 12 studies found in our review of the literature were not included because of missing statistical information. Nonetheless, a tabulation of these studies confirmed that the direction of their findings were consistent with the direction of the effect sizes we computed.

Second, it is of some concern that 4 of the 12 studies in this meta-analysis utilized an indirect measure of patient coping style. While nine of the studies employed a categorical measure based on the treatment models/manuals employed, this is a much less serious breach of the criteria of adequacy than the use of a proxy measure for a patient trait. A diagnosis of alcohol dependence does not, logically, equate to a sensitive indication of one's dominant coping style of externalization. However, we limited the use of such proxy measures, and the limitation placed on the findings by this categorical proxy of coping style augurs well to ensure the results are conservative. In follow-up research, however, we urge those who seek to understand ATI relationships to employ direct, individual measures of both the treatment variable and, especially, the patient variable under investigation that reveals a masked relationship because the other studies do not have such a feature.

Third, the pool of 12 studies analyzed here may prove restrictive in another sense. This is a relatively small number of studies, the majority of which were conducted by one senior researcher (Beutler) and various colleagues. The possibility of the file drawer phenomenon was not also considered in the analyses. Although obviously not a concern in that the authors of this chapter would be aware of any unpublished studies of their own, we do not know if there exist other unpublished studies that were left in a file drawer because their results did not favor the predicted aptitude by treatment interaction.

Therapeutic Practices

Patient coping style emerges in the research as a moderator of the effects of treatment focus on outcomes. We offer, in closing, several practice recommendations based on the research reviews:

• Assess each patient's predominant coping style using a direct, individual measure in the interest of treatment planning. Assessment of these patient attributes need not be time consuming or tedious; cues for the identification of a variety of patient attributes are included in Beutler and Harwood (2000) to enable the clinician to make any necessary in-session treatment-matching adjustments. These procedures combine self-report and clinician ratings to define characteristic ways that the patient responds to change and novelty.

• Match the patient's coping style to the focus of treatment. Patients who manifest externalizing tendencies can be provided with treatments that are focused on skill building and on symptom change. In contrast, those who manifest patterns of self-criticism and emotional avoidance are more likely to benefit from an interpersonally focused and insight-oriented treatment.

• Even with internalizing patients, the research suggests that there is value in beginning treatment with direct, symptom-focused methods. As the coping style of the patient becomes clear, it may then be optimal to switch to a more indirect, insight approach if that patient's coping style is weighted toward internalizing patterns.

• More broadly, remember that the focus of treatment represents both an aspect of one's theoretical orientation and some personal proclivity or preference. Effective psychotherapists will recognize a patient's distinctive aptitude, such as coping style, reactance level, stage of change, ethnic/racial heritage, and other moderators, in order to modify treatment to fit the patient and his/her unique circumstances.

References

An asterisk (*) indicates studies included in the meta-analysis.

Badger, T. A., & Collins-Joyce, P. (2000). Depression, psychosocial resources, and functional ability in older adults. *Clinical Nursing Research*, 9(3), 238–55.

Barber, J. P., & Muenz, L. R. (1996). The role of avoidance and obsessiveness in matching patients to cognitive and interpersonal psychotherapy: Empirical findings for the treatment for depression collaborative research program. *Journal of Consulting and Clinical Psychology, 64,* 951–58.

Beutler, L. E., & Berren, M. R. (1995). *Integrative assessment of adult personality*. New York: EGuilford Press.

Beutler, L. E., & Clarkin, J. F. (1990). *Systematic treatment selection: Toward targeted therapeutic interventions*. New York: Brunner/Mazel.

Beutler, L. E., Clarkin, J. F., & Bongar, B. (2000). *Guidelines for the systematic treatment of the depressed patient*. New York: Oxford University Press.

*Beutler, L. E., Engle, D., Mohr, D., Daldrup, R. J., Bergan, J., Meredith, K., et al. (1991). Predictors of differential response to cognitive, experiential, and self-directed psychotherapeutic techniques. *Journal of Consulting and Clinical Psychology, 59,* 333–340.

Beutler, L. E., Goodrich, G., Fisher, D., & Williams, O. B. (1999). Use of psychological tests/instruments for treatment planning. In M. E. Maruish (Ed.), *The use of psychological tests for treatment planning and outcome assessment* (2nd ed., pp. 81–113). Hillsdale, NJ: Lawrence Erlbaum.

Beutler, L. E., & Harwood, T. M. (2000). *Prescriptive psychotherapy: A practical guide to systematic treatment selection*. New York: Oxford University Press.

Beutler, L. E., Kim, E. J., Davison, E., Karno, M., & Fisher, D. (1996). Research contributions to improving managed health care outcomes. *Psychotherapy, 33,* 197–206.

*Beutler, L. E., Machado, P. P. P., Engle, D., & Mohr, D. (1993). Differential patient X treatment maintenance aiming cognitive, experiential, and self-directed psychotherapies. *Journal of Psychotherapy Integration, 3,* 15–31.

Beutler, L. E., & Mitchell, R. (1981). Differential psychotherapy outcome among depressed and impulsive patients as a function of analytic and experiential treatment procedures. *Psychiatry, 44,* 297–306.

Beutler, L. E., Mohr, D. C., Grawe, K., Engle, D., & MacDonaled, R. (1991). Looking for differential treatment effects: Cross-cultural predictors of differential psychotherapy efficacy. *Journal of Psychotherapy Integration, 1*(121–41).

Beutler, L. E., Moleiro, C., Malik, M., & Harwood, T. M. (2000, June). *The UC Santa Barbara study of fitting therapy to patients: First results*. Paper presented at the International Society for Psychotherapy Research, Chicago.

*Beutler, L. E., Moleiro, C., Malik, M., Harwood, T. M., Romanelli, R., Gallagher-Thompson, D., et al. (2003). A comparison of the Dodo, EST, and ATI indicators among co-morbid stimulant dependent, depressed patients. *Clinical Psychology & Psychotherapy, 10,* 69–85.

Beutler, L. E., Moos, R. H., & Lane, G. (2003). Coping, treatment planning, and treatment outcome: discussion. *Journal of Clinical Psychology, 59,* 1151–67.

Billings, A. G., & Moos, R. H. (1985). Life stressors and social resources affect posttreatment outcomes among depressed patients. *Journal of Abnormal Psychology, 94,* 140–53.

Borenstein, M., Hedges, L., Higgins, J., & Rothstein, H. (2009). *Introduction to meta-analysis*. Chichester, UK: Wiley.

Bussing, R., Zima, B. T., & Perwien, A. R. (2000). Self-esteem in special education children with ADHD: Relationship to disorder characteristics and medication use. *Journal of the American Academy of Child & Adolescent Psychiatry, 39*(10), 1260–69.

Butcher, J. N. (1990). *The MMPI-2 in psychological treatment*. New York: Oxford University Press.

*Calvert, S. J., Beutler, L. E., & Crago, M. (1988). Psychotherapy outcomes as a function of therapist-patient matching on selected variables. *Journal of Social and Clinical Psychology, 6,* 104–117.

Cohen, J. (1988). *Statistical power analysis for the behavioral science* (*2nd ed.*). Hillsdale, NJ: Lawrence Erlbaum Associates.

Cortina, J. M., & Nouri, H. (2000). *Effect size for ANOVA designs*. Thousand Oaks, CA: Sage Publications.

Costa, P. T., Jr., & McCrae, R. R. (1985). *The NEO Personality Inventory manual*. Odessa, FL: Psychological Assessment Resources.

Ellicott, A., Hammen, C., Gitlin, M., Brown, G., & Jamison, K. (1990). Life events and the course of bipolar disorder. *American Journal of Psychiatry, 147,* 1194–1198.

Endler, N. S., Parker, J. D. A., & Butcher, J. M. (1993). A factor analytic study of coping styles and the MMPI-2 Content Scales. *Journal of Clinical Psychology, 49,* 523–527.

Eysenck, H. J. (1957). *The dynamics of anxiety and hysteria*. New York: Praeger.

Fahy, T. A., & Russell, G. F. M. (1993). Outcome and prognostic variables in bulimia-nervosa. *International Journal of Eating Disorders*, *14*, 135–45.

Fisher, D., Beutler, L. E., & Williams, O. B. (1999). STS Clinician Rating Form: Patient assessment and treatment planning. *Journal of Clinical Psychology*, *55*, 825–42.

Hoglend, P. (1993). Personality disorders and long-term outcome after brief dynamic psychotherapy. *Journal of Personality Disorders*, *7*(2), 168–81.

Hunter, J. E., & Schmidt, F. L. (2004). *Methods of meta-analysis: Correcting error and bias in research findings, 2nd edition*. Thousand Oaks, CA: Sage Publications.

Judd, L. L., Paulus, M. P., Wells, K. B., & Rapaport, M. H. (1996). Socioeconomic burden of subsyndromal depressive symptoms and major depression in a sample of the general population. *American Journal of Psychiatry*, *153*(11), 1411–1417.

*Kadden, R. M., Cooney, N. L., Getter, H., & Litt, M. D. (1989). Matching alcoholics to coping skills or interactional therapies: Posttreatment results. *Journal of Consulting and Clinical Psychology*, *57*, 698–704.

Kagan, J. (1998). *Galen's prophecy: temperament in human nature*. NY: Basic Books.

*Karno, M., Beutler, L. E., & Harwood, T. M. (2002). Interactions between psychotherapy procedures and patient attributes that predict alcohol treatment effectiveness: A preliminary report. *Addictive Behavior*, *27*, 779–797.

Kawai, H. (1993). *Monogatari to ningenno kagaku (Stories and human's science)*. Tokyo: Iwanami Books.

Kawai, H. (1996). *The Japanese psyche: Major motifs in the fairy tales of Japan*. Dallas, TX: Spring.

Keijsers, G. P. J., Hoogduin, C. A. L., & Schaap, C. P. D. R. (1994). Predictors of treatment outcome in the behavioral treatment of obsessive-compulsive disorder. *British Journal of Psychiatry*, *165*, 781–86.

*Knekt, P., Lindfors, O., Hrakanen, T., Valikoski, M., Virtala, E., & Laaksonen, M. A. (2008). Randomized trial of the effectiveness of long-term and short-term psychodynamic psychotherapy and solution-focused therapy on psychiatric symptoms during a 3-year follow up. *Psychological Medicine*, *38*, 689–703.

Koenig, H. (1998). Depression in hospitalized older patients with congestive heart failure. *General Hospital Psychiatry*, *20*(1), 29–43.

Koolhaas, J. M., Korte, S. M., De Boer, S. F., Van der Vegt, B. J., Van Reenan, C. G., Hopster, H., et al. (1999). Coping style in animals: Current status in behavior and stress-physiology. *Neuroscience and Biobehavioral Reviews*, *23*, 925–35.

Koran, L. M. (2000). Quality of life in obsessive-compulsive disorder. *The Psychiatric Clinics of North America*, *23*, 509–517.

Latack, J. C., & Havlovic, S. J. (1992). Coping with job stress: A conceptual evaluation framework for coping measures. *Journal of Organizational Behavior*, *13*, 479–508.

Lazarus, A. A. (1981). *The practice of multi-modal therapy*. New York: McGraw-Hill.

Lazarus, R. S., & Folkman, S. (1984). *Stress, appraisal and coping*. New York: Springer.

Lipsey, M. W., & Wilson, D. B (2001) *Practical meta-analysis. Applied social research methods series, Volume 49*. Thousand Oaks, CA: Sage Publications.

*Litt, M. D., Babor, T. F., DelBoca, F. K., Kadden, R. M., & Cooney, N. L. (1992). Type of alcoholics: II. Application of an empirically derived typology to treatment matching. *Archives of General Psychiatry*, *49*, 609–614.

Littlefield, C. H., Rodin, G. M., Murray, M. A., & Craven, J. L. (1990). Influence of functional impairment and social support on depressive symptoms in persons with diabetes. *Health Psychology*, *9*(6), 737–49.

*Longabaugh, R., Rubin, G. M., Malloy, P., Beattie, M., Clifford, P. R., & Noel, N. (1994). Drinking outcomes of alcohol abusers diagnosed as antisocial personality disorder. *Alcoholism: Clinical and Experimental Research*, *18*, 778–85.

Miller, W. R., & Joyce, M. A. (1979). Prediction of abstinence, controlled drinking, and heavy drinking outcomes following behavioral self-control training. *Journal of Consulting and Clinical Psychology*, *47*, 773–75.

*Milrod, B., Leon, A. C., Busch, F., Rudden, M., Schwalberg, M., Clarkin, J., et al. (2007). A randomized controlled clinical trial of psycho-analytic psychotherapy for panic disorder. *American Journal of Psychiatry*, *164*, 265–72.

Ouimette, P., Finney, J., & Moos, R. (1999). Two year posttreatment functioning and coping of patients with substance abuse and posttraumatic stress disorder. *Psychology of Addictive Behaviors*, *13*, 105–114.

Prochaska, J. O., & DiClemente, C. C. (1992). The transtheoretical approach. In J. C. Norcross

& M. R. Goldried (Eds.) *Handbook of psychotherapy integration.* (pp. 300–34). New York: Basic Books.

Project Match Research Group. (1997). Matching alcoholism treatments to client heterogeneity: Project Match posttreatment drinking outcomes. *Journal of Studies in Alcoholism, 58,* 7–29.

Shea, M. T., Elkin, I., Imber, S. D., Sotsky, S. M., Watkins, J. T., Collins, J. F., et al. (1992). Course of depressive symptoms over followup: findings form the National Institute of Mental Health Treatment of Depression Collaborative Research Program. *Archives of General Psychiatry, 49,* 782–87.

Thase, M. E., Simons, A. D., Cahalane, J., McGeary, J., & Harden, T. (1991). Severity of depression and response to cognitive behavior therapy. *American Journal of Psychiatry, 148,* 784–89.

UKATT Research Team. (2007). UK Alcohol Treatment Trial: Client-treatment matching effects. *Addiction, 103,* 228–38.

Veiel, H. O., Kuhner, C., Brill, G., & Ihle, W. (1992). Psychosocial correlates of clinical depression after psychiatric in-patient treatment: Methodological issue and baseline differences between recovered and non-recovered patients. *Psychological Medicine, 22,* 425–27.

Welsh, G. S. (1952). An anxiety index and an internalization ratio for the MMPI. *Journal of Consulting Psychology, 16,* 65–72.

18 Expectations

Michael J. Constantino, Carol R. Glass, Diane B. Arnkoff,
Rebecca M. Ametrano, *and* JuliAnna Z. Smith

Patients' expectations have long been considered a key ingredient and common factor of successful psychotherapy (e.g., Frank, 1961; Goldfried, 1980; Goldstein, 1960; Rosensweig, 1936; Weinberger & Eig, 1999). Influenced by classic social psychological findings that substantiated the influence of expectations on people's perceptions, motivations, and actions (e.g., Asch, 1946; Kelley, 1950; Secord, 1958), researchers and clinicians became interested in how expectations specifically affect psychotherapy. In his classic book, *Persuasion and Healing*, Frank (1961) argued that for any therapy to be effective there must be within the patient a mobilization of hope for improvement. According to Frank, patients enter therapy because they are demoralized, and restoring their hope and positive expectation is a powerful change ingredient. Others have since concurred with this perspective (e.g., Kirsch, 1985; Shapiro, 1981), some going so far as to suggest that most psychotherapies are inextricably linked with the manipulation and revision of patients' expectations (Greenberg, Constantino, & Bruce, 2006; Kirsch, 1990).

This chapter will review the research evidence linking patient expectations with treatment outcome across a variety of psychotherapies and clinical contexts. We consider both expectations about the consequences of participating in treatment (*outcome expectations*) and expectations about the nature and process of treatment (*treatment expectations*). For outcome expectations, we include a comprehensive meta-analysis of the association between pre- or early-therapy expectations and posttreatment outcome. Given the many types of treatment expectations and the heterogeneity of research methods used to study them, we did *not* conduct a meta-analysis of their association with outcome. Instead, we include a substantive, though not exhaustive, narrative review of that research. We also review (a) definitions of expectations and similar constructs, (b) expectancy measurement, (c) mediators and moderators of the expectation–outcome link, (d) patient factors related to expectations, and (e) limitations of the extant research base. In concluding, we offer therapeutic practices based on the research results.

Definitions and Measures
Outcome Expectations
Definitions. Outcome expectations reflect patients' prognostic beliefs about the consequences of engaging in treatment (Arnkoff, Glass, & Shapiro, 2002). In psychotherapy, outcome expectations are typically assessed on a continuum of the potential *benefits*

of treatment, with rare consideration of plausible expected *negative* effects (Schulte, 2008). Outcome expectations come in different guises. For example, patients have beliefs about a treatment's utility even before they have contact with a therapist or the treatment. Patients also have malleable during-treatment expectations that are influenced by their own history, their interactions with the therapist, and their ongoing appraisal of the treatment's course and efficacy (Schulte, 2008).

Outcome expectations are differentiated from constructs such as treatment motivation and therapy preferences. Motivation, which encompasses patients' desire and readiness for change, does not necessarily correspond to positive prognostic expectations (see Norcross, Krebs, & Prochaska, this volume, Chapter 14). Patients in distress might be highly motivated to engage in treatment yet have low expectation or faith that therapy can actually help them (Rosenthal & Frank, 1956). Preferences (see Swift, Callahan, & Vollmer, this volume, Chapter 15) are distinguishable from expectations in that they reflect something valued or desired, which might be distinct from what is expected (Arnkoff et al., 2002). For example, a patient might have a preference for working with a same-sex psychotherapist yet expect that it would be more helpful to work with an other-sex therapist.

Another related construct involves treatment credibility, or how plausible, suitable, and logical a treatment seems to the patient (Arnkoff et al., 2002). There is some debate over whether credibility and expectancy are distinct constructs. On the one hand, outcome expectations might develop, at least in part, from how credible a treatment seems (Hardy et al., 1995). Moderately significant correlations between expectancy and credibility/suitability scales support this perspective (e.g., Constantino,

Arnow, Blasey, & Agras, 2005; Safren, Heimberg, & Juster, 1997). On the other hand, pretreatment outcome expectations often exist *prior* to having any substantial information about the forthcoming treatment. Credibility, though, is a perception based on knowledge gained *through* direct experience or observation (Schulte, 2008; Tinsely, Bowman, & Ray, 1988). From another perspective, credibility reflects what a patient *thinks* will happen (a *cognitive* process), while expectations assess what a patient *feels* will happen (an *affective* process; Devilly & Borkovec, 2000). Thus, although conceptually related, expectancy and credibly are likely distinct.

Measures. Historically, patient expectations have been viewed as potential artifacts requiring control in experimental treatment trials. Thus, as predictive factors and potential change ingredients, expectations have tended to be undervalued, with few studies providing a primary assessment of expectations (Weinberger & Eig, 1999). Rather, expectations have often been assessed secondarily as a manipulation check, so that researchers can point to the comparability of expectancies engendered by different treatments, thus eliminating expectancy effects as a rival hypothesis to any between-group effects observed (Borkovec & Nau, 1972; Holt & Heimberg, 1990). Most expectation measures have been brief (in many cases one item only; e.g., Heine & Trosman, 1960) and often study specific (and thus lacking in psychometric validation; e.g., Barrios & Karoly, 1983). In some cases, the measures have been confounded with another belief construct (such as credibility; e.g., Hardy et al., 1995) or even an outcome measure (e.g., Evans, Smith, Halar, & Kiolet, 1985).

Borkovec and Nau (1972) pioneered the use of a brief (4-item) questionnaire to assess whether the rationale of placebo therapies generated equivalent ratings of credibility and treatment outcome expectancy as did behavioral treatments for public-speaking anxiety. Easily adaptable for different conditions, this measure became the most frequently used credibility/expectancy measure in psychotherapy research. Using trauma as an example, the measure includes three credibility items rated on a 9-point, Likert-type scale ("At this point, how logical does the therapy offered seem to you?" "At this point, how successful do you think this treatment will be in reducing your trauma symptoms?" "How confident would you be in recommending this treatment to a friend who experiences similar problems?"), and one outcome expectancy item rated from 0% to 100% ("By the end of the therapy period, how much improvement in your trauma symptoms do you think will occur?"). In subsequent psychometric analyses (Devilly & Borkovec, 2000), the three credibility items hung together, while the expectancy item hung together with two additional affectively anchored items ("At this point, how much do you really *feel* that therapy will help you to reduce your trauma symptoms?" "By the end of the therapy period, how much improvement in your trauma symptoms do you *feel* will occur?"). Devilly and Borkovec named their update to Borkovec and Nau's measure the Credibility/Expectancy Questionnaire (CEQ).

The Reaction to Treatment Questionnaire (RTQ; Holt & Heimberg, 1990) has also been used in several studies. This measure is comprised of the four Borkovec and Nau (1972) items (yielding a treatment "credibility score") and nine items assessing patients' confidence that the treatment would eliminate anxiety in specific social situations (a situationally based "confidence" or outcome expectancy scale). Scored in this manner, though, the credibility scale lacks differentiation between credibility and expectancy.

Perhaps one of the purest measures of outcome expectancy (aside from 1-item measures) is the Patient Prognostic Expectancy Inventory (PPEI; Martin & Sterne, 1975), although it has been used fairly infrequently. The PPEI assesses, on a 4-point response scale, patients' expected improvement as a result of hospital treatment across 15 domains (e.g., depression-sadness, feeling afraid, keeping a job).

The Expectations About Counseling measure (EAC; Tinsely, Workman & Kass, 1980) and its short form (Tinsely & Westcot, 1990) predominantly assess treatment expectations but also contain a 3-item scale assessing treatment outcome expectancies. This scale has strong psychometric properties.

Finally, a promising scale for independently assessing patients' outcome expectations and perceived treatment suitability is the Patients' Therapy Expectation and Evaluation (PATHEV; Schulte, 2008). This measure consists of three, factor analytically derived subscales: hope of improvement (confidence in treatment efficacy), fear of change, and suitability. Perhaps what is most promising about this measure is that it differentiates hope (e.g., "I believe my problems can finally be solved") and fear (e.g., "Sometimes I am afraid that my therapy will change me more than I want"), both of which are components of expectations (Heckhausen & Leppmann, 1991). The PATHEV also includes the assessment of pessimistic expectations (e.g., "Actually, I am rather skeptical about whether treatment can help me").

Treatment Expectations

Definitions. Treatment expectations reflect beliefs about what will transpire during treatment. One form of treatment expectation reflects *role* expectations, or beliefs about how a person occupying a given position should behave (Arnkoff et al., 2002).

Patients may have role expectations of both themselves (e.g., crying in session) and their psychotherapist (e.g., providing support). Patients also have *process* expectations about the type of work that will transpire and the duration of treatment (Greenberg et al., 2006). In this chapter we focus predominantly on role expectations but caution that in some cases researchers did not distinguish between role and process expectations, tending to use "role" as a blanket term.

Measures. Although many studies have employed idiosyncratic measures of treatment expectations, there are two widely used and well-validated measures. The aforementioned EAC (Tinsely et al., 1980) and its brief version (EAC-B; Tinsely & Westcot, 1990) assess four empirically derived expectancy domains: patient attitudes and behaviors (e.g., motivation, openness), counselor attitudes and behaviors (e.g., acceptance, confrontation), counselor characteristics (e.g., expertness, trustworthiness), and counseling process and outcome (e.g., immediacy, concreteness, and the aforementioned outcome scale) (see also Ægisdóttir, Gerstein, & Gridley, 2000 for a proposed three-factor solution).

The Psychotherapy Expectancy Inventory's (PEI; Rickers-Ovsiankina, Geller, Berzins, & Rogers, 1971) factor analytically derived scales correspond to Apfelbaum's (1958) three clusters of expected therapist roles: nurturant (to be guided by an affiliative other), model (to be guided to help oneself), and critical (to receive guidance and correction). The authors added a fourth dimension, cooperative (to become autonomous and equal to the counselor), which they purported comes about only toward treatment's end. Subsequent reanalysis led to the Psychotherapy Expectancy Inventory-Revised (PEI-R; Berzins, 1971), with renamed but conceptually consistent scales of approval seeking (e.g., "How strongly do you expect to be concerned with how you appear to your therapist?"), advice seeking (e.g., "How strongly do you expect to get definite advice from your therapist?"), audience seeking (e.g., "How strongly do you expect to feel like opening up without any help from your therapist?"), and relationship seeking (e.g., "How strongly do you expect to behave in a spontaneous manner?"). Subsequent analyses (Bleyen, Vertommen, Vander Steene, & Van Audenhove, 2001) found adequate support for this four-factor structure, but a better fit for a five-factor model that split the first factor into approval seeking and impression (e.g., "How strongly do you expect to be concerned with the impression you make on your therapist?").

Clinical Examples
Outcome Expectations
By definition, therapy outcome expectations are cognitions regarding a probable future resulting from treatment. Such expectations can be positive (e.g., "I have faith that I can do the work and feel better"), negative (e.g., "I can't imagine ever feeling better, even after this therapy"), or ambivalent (e.g., "Well, I am willing to give it a shot, but I'm just not sure this will work . . . I have been depressed for a long time"). Of course, patients' hopes and expectations may conflict. For example, a patient might have a desperate wish to feel emotional relief (e.g., "I hope to feel like my old self"), yet have what he or she deems a more reality-based expectation or prediction (e.g., "I expect that therapy might not help me completely and that I will never fully be what I used to be").

Prognostic expectations are also affected by context, including perhaps most powerfully one's own learning experiences. For example, a male patient might have had a positive therapy experience with an older female therapist in the past, which has led him to have greater faith in either recommencing therapy with this same therapist or seeing a new therapist with perceived salient similarities (e.g., gender, age, theoretical orientation).

Outcome expectations and treatment expectations probably interact. For example, a patient might generally have high outcome expectations prior to therapy and also expect therapy to focus exclusively on early childhood (treatment expectation). Upon meeting with a well-regarded therapist who tends to work from a here-and-now, problem-oriented perspective, this patient's outcome expectations might take a hit. However, psychotherapists can often frame their approach in accord with the patient's treatment expectations, thereby enhancing the patient's outcome expectations. For example, the therapist might say, "Actually, in discussing your current problems and relationships, we will likely see traces of these same problems and patterns from your earlier life. People learn many things early on that have a lasting influence on their present thoughts and feelings. Thus, although we might lean toward discussing the here-and-now, your childhood will not be off limits, and I suspect that we will learn something quite useful from connecting past to present. How does this sound to you?"

Treatment Expectations
In one study (Garfield & Wolpin, 1963), 27% of surveyed clinic patients expected that therapy would predominantly center on their early life, and 47% thought that the central focus would be on their life just before therapy. Half of the patients indicated that the most important thing a therapist does is to help patients understand themselves better, while 33% pointed to advice. Forty percent thought that the therapist could read their mind at least moderately. The authors concluded: "Patients appear to be seeking a sincere, understanding, sympathetic, interested and competent person who would be unlikely to engage in criticism, anger or ridicule. They also want someone who will not be pessimistic about them, nor turn them away, but who will at the same time not deny that the patient has difficulties" (p. 360).

But many patients have not formed pretreatment expectations for psychotherapy. In a study of former Veterans Administration clinic patients (Kamin & Caughlan, 1963), the authors concluded that ". . . almost 75% entered therapy with no clear concepts of its modus operandi. They understood neither their own role, nor that of the therapist . . . repeatedly commented that therapists were too passive, disinterested, cold, incomprehensible, enigmatic, even though polite, patient, and probably well meaning . . . therapists are analytically oriented, but the patients are not" (p. 666).

Other surveys indicated that many patients hold incongruent or unrealistic expectations, almost having a ". . . naive, wishful, or magical view of counseling" (Tinsley, Bowman, & Barich, 1993, p. 50). Some patients expect the psychotherapist, like their physician, will tell them what is wrong and fix them. Others seeing a cognitive-behavioral psychotherapist may expect to lay on a couch and talk about their childhood, while patients with psychodynamic or experiential psychotherapists may be frustrated by their clinician's limited input (Walborn, 1996).

Research Review
In this section, we provide research reviews for both outcome and treatment expectations. For the former, we summarize a previous box count review as well as present a comprehensive and original meta-analytic review of the association between pre- or early-therapy outcome expectations and treatment outcomes. For the latter, we

summarize a previous box count and offer a selective review of relevant studies published since the previous version of this chapter (Arnkoff et al., 2002). Our reviews are limited to clinical samples receiving psychotherapy, with more specific inclusion/exclusion criteria for the meta-analysis discussed below.

Outcome Expectations

Arnkoff and colleagues (2002) presented a box count review of studies through the year 2000 that examined the association between patient outcome expectations and psychotherapy outcomes (e.g., treatment continuation, patient self-report, behavior). They found that 12 studies revealed a significant positive association, 7 revealed mixed findings, and 7 others demonstrated no effect.

Since 2000, several other researchers have summarized research on patient expectations. A review of the psychiatric literature (Noble, Douglas, & Newman, 2001) found that research prior to 1980 generally suggested a curvilinear relationship between outcome expectations and outcome. That is, patients with moderate outcome expectations demonstrated better outcomes than those with extremely high or extremely low expectations (e.g., Goldstein, 1962). For the period from 1980 to 1999, several studies demonstrated a positive association (Hansson & Berglund, 1987; Sotsky et al., 1991), while one study revealed no significant effects (Basoglu et al., 1994) and another showed a negative association (Lax, Basoglu, & Marks, 1992). A review of additional studies from 2000 to 2005 (Greenberg et al., 2006) found several studies demonstrating a positive association between outcome expectations and either alliance quality (e.g., Constantino et al., 2005) or posttreatment outcomes (e.g., Joyce, Ogrodniczuk, Piper, & McCallum, 2003).

Given these mostly positive but still mixed findings, it remains difficult to determine the consistency of the outcome expectancy effect across various treatment contexts, as well as its magnitude. The current meta-analysis attempts to shed additional light on these questions by focusing on the aggregated effect of outcome expectations on posttreatment status. In addition to examining the overall effect of outcome expectations on treatment outcome, we examined the potential moderating influence of several clinical variables: presenting diagnosis, treatment orientation, treatment modality, treatment setting, design type, and date of publication.

Search and Inclusion Procedures. We first conducted an extensive PsycINFO database search for all references through December 2009. We included the following 14 searches (limited to published sources written in English): *expecta** (any derivation of *expectation*) in combination with *psychotherapy, treatment, therapy, counseling, counselling, outcome, improvement, change, dropout, dropping out, premature termination, duration, patient,* and *client*. This database search yielded 39,250 citations. We then searched PubMed using the terms *expecta** and *psychotherapy* and *expecta** and *counseling*, which yielded an additional 15 citations. Finally, we hand-searched the reference lists of prior review articles, as well as the last four issues of 10 clinical journals (to ensure that we did not miss any citations because of a lag before appearing in PsycINFO or PubMed). These hand searches revealed 13 additional citations for a total initial yield of 39,278 citations. We reviewed the titles and abstracts of all citations and applied the inclusion/exclusion criteria in the next paragraph to create a candidate list.

To be included in the meta-analysis, studies had to (a) be correlational (this is reflective of the field in that virtually no studies exist that experimentally manipulate *outcome expectations* in a way not confounded by treatment expectations), (b) include a measure of patients' *own* outcome expectations at pretreatment or following Session 1, and (c) include a posttreatment symptom outcome measure not explicitly referenced as a *follow-up* occasion. Studies were excluded if they (a) examined a nonclinical sample (e.g., students participating for course credit), (b) involved non-clinically-oriented outcomes (e.g., well-being behaviors such as exercise promotion programs), (c) focused solely on expectations other than for *treatment outcomes/consequences*, (d) did not involve a psychotherapist (e.g., self-help), (e) only *inferred* outcome expectation through tests of placebo treatment effects, (f) assessed outcome expectations with a measure that was capturing a related, but distinct construct (e.g., treatment credibility, motivation), (g) assessed outcome expectations retrospectively only, (h) employed an experimental manipulation of outcome expectancies, or (i) involved a treatment of fewer than three sessions.

Based on these criteria, 186 candidates were selected from the titles and abstracts review. We fully read these candidates and ruled out another 108 studies at this stage. Thus, 78 studies were fully coded (by the first four authors) for study characteristics relevant to this review. In the case of articles that included multiple studies on separate samples, we coded these samples separately. For studies from separate articles that analyzed data from the same sample, we coded them as one sample. We excluded studies that reported *only* multivariate effects because of the difficulty obtaining accurate estimates of comparable effects across studies (Lipsey & Wilson, 2001): the inclusion of other variables in the model equations means that even when standardized effects (such as standardized regression coefficients)

are reported, the actual parameters being estimated differ depending on which variables are included. In addition, there was generally insufficient information available to calculate standard errors of these estimates and, consequently, to determine accurate inverse variance weights for the meta-analysis. Thus, the total number of independent samples on which we conducted our meta-analysis was 46.

In some studies, researchers assessed outcome expectancies with more than one measure and/or at both baseline and postsession. Furthermore, in many studies, researchers assessed multiple treatment outcomes. For studies that included multiple outcomes, our goal was to identify and to code up to the three most psychometrically sound *symptom* measures. However, for the few studies that included more than three sound symptom measures, we coded more than three. In order to create a single effect size for each independent sample, we averaged across the multiple expectancy and/or outcome measures and time points by creating a weighted average based on the sample size for each effect reported.

Data Analyses. To estimate the direct effect of outcome expectations on outcome, we examined mean difference scores and bivariate associations. We also included effects between outcome expectations and treatment outcome that accounted for pretreatment levels of symptomatology (either with partial correlations, the use of researcher-derived change scores for an outcome variable, or patient-reported change on an outcome variable). We summarized the averaged results from each independent sample using the *r* statistic following the procedures outlined in Lipsey and Wilson (2001). In situations where the coefficient was unknown and reported only as nonsignificant, we used a conservative approach of setting *r* to zero.

We next calculated an overall r across samples. As sample sizes and, consequently, the precision of the effect size estimates varied from study to study, the effect sizes from the independent samples were weighted by the inverse of their variance. As we desired to generalize to a population of studies, we used a random-effects model.

Finally, we grouped samples on the various moderator characteristics and compared average weighted effect sizes using a mixed-effects model analogous to an ANOVA, which tests whether the systematic variance in r is a function of the categorical variable included (Lipsey & Wilson, 2001).

Results. The meta-analysis included 8,016 patients across the 46 samples. In all but one study, the patients were identified as predominantly (>80%) adult (age 18 to 65). In all studies that reported race (13 of 46), the patients were predominantly white (>60%). In the studies reporting gender (41 of 46), 53.7% included predominantly (>60%) women, 9.8% predominantly men, and 36.6% mixed (no predominant sex).

Table 18.1 includes averaged effect sizes on outcome across all relevant analyses for each independent sample. We coded the direction of the effect such that positive rs reflect positive associations between outcome expectations and favorable treatment outcome, whereas negative rs reflect a negative association. The overall weighted effect size across samples was $r = 0.12$, $p < 0.001$ ($CI._{95}$ 0.10 to 0.15), indicating a small, but significant positive effect. Expressed as Cohen's (1988) d, the effect size was 0.24.

A test of homogeneity revealed significant heterogeneity between studies, $Q(45) = 92.00$, $p < 0.001$, which is not surprising given the different study designs, instruments, and eras. To address potential publication

bias, we also calculated a fail-safe N to determine the number of nonsignificant file drawer studies that would be required to attenuate the current results to an effect less than $r = 0.10$ (i.e., less than a small effect in behavioral science research). The fail-safe N was 9 studies—that is, about 9 studies would need to have an average r of 0.00 to bring the weighted mean r below 0.10. Thus, it seems reasonable to suggest some caution in interpreting our meta-analytic findings.

We also examined the overall weighted effect without an outlier based on sample size (one study that contributed more than half of the total n to the meta-analysis). Without this study, the effect size and confidence intervals were essentially equivalent. The same was the case when we examined the overall effect removing a different outlier (i.e., a study that reported a moderate averaged *negative* effect). Because the coefficients for many individual tests were not reported, and because we primarily limited our coded outcome variables to three for any given study, we also tabulated the total number of tests conducted and the proportion of those tests that had significantly positive or significantly negative effects (as researchers typically reported significance and direction of effects even in the absence of coefficients). As indicated in Table 18.1, of 253 total tests (including studies that reported one or more multivariate effects), 54 (21%) demonstrated a significantly positive association and 7 (3%) a significantly negative association.

Potential Moderators. There were no statistically significant moderator effects of the expectancy–outcome association for any of the five potential moderators we evaluated. However, there was a trend for design type. The direction of this trend, though, is influenced by the inclusion or exclusion of the large sample outlier, thus

Table 18.1   Study Characteristics and Average Weighted Effects for Samples Included in the Meta-Analysis

Source	Treatment (Type/ Modality)	Expectancy Measure	Time	Primary outcomes	ES (r)	Study N	Total tests	Number significant (+, −)
Abouguendia et al. (2004)	Mixed/ Group	SS (multi)	B	General symptoms Grief symptoms Target objectives	0.27	107	3	2, 0
Barrios & Karoly (1983)	Mixed/ Individual	SS (multi)	B	Migraine Total headache Total disability	ns	30	7	0, 0
Basoglu et al. (1994)	CBT/ Individual	SS (single)	B	Global improvement Panic free	ns	154	2	0, 0
Bloch et al. (1976)	NR/Group	SS (multi)	B	Goal attainment Main problem change (therapist) Main problem change (rater)	0.31	27	3	1, 0
Borkovec & Costello (1993)	CBT/ Individual	CEQ	S1	HAM-A Assessor GAD severity PSWQ	0.26	66	10	5, 0
Borkovec et al. (2002)	CBT/ Individual	CEQ	S1	End state functioning	ns	76	1	0, 0
Buwalda & Bouman (2008)	O/Group	AS (single)	S1	GIAS	0.07	140	1	0, 0
Calsyn et al. (2003)	O/NR	SS (multi)	B	Psychotic symptoms Program satisfaction	0.14	65	1	0, 0
Chambless et al. (1997)	CBT/ Group	CEQ	S1	Anxious apprehension Anxiety & skill (patient) Anxiety & skill (rater)	0.17	64	5	5, 0
Clark et al. (1999)	CBT/ Individual	CEQ	S1	Panic/Anxiety	0.50	43	1	1, 0
Collins & Hyer (1986)	NR/NR	SS (multi)	S1	VETS global PARS global VETS improvement	0.09	4589	4	3, 0
Constantino et al. (2005)	Mixed/ Individual	SS (single)	S1	Purge frequency	0.13	220	1	0, 0
Crits-Christoph et al. (2004)	PD/ Individual	SS (single) SS (multi)	B B	HAM-A BAI PSWQ	0.10	68	6	2, 0
Dearing et al. (2005)	CBT/ Mixed	SS (multi)	B	CSQ	0.00	208	3	0, 0
Devilly & Borkovec (2000)– Study 2	CBT/NR	CEQ	S1	HAM-A PSWQ STAI	0.34	67	8	2, 0

(Continued)

Table 18.1   Continued

Source	Treatment (Type/ Modality)	Expectancy Measure	Time	Primary outcomes	ES (r)	Study N	Total tests	Number significant (+, −)
Devilly & Borkovec (2000)– Study 3	Mixed/ Individual	CEQ	S1	STAI BDI SCL-90-R global	0.06	22	18	1, 0
Gaudiano & Miller (2006)	O/Group	CEQ	B	Months in treatment HAM-D BRMS	0.16	61	2	0, 0
Ghosh et al. (1988)	CBT/ Individual	SS (single)	B	FQ phobic severity Help received	ns	84	2	0, 0
Goldstein (1960)	NR/ Individual	SS (multi)	B	Personality change	ns	15	1	0, 0
Goossens et al. (2005)	Mixed/ Individual	CEQ	B	Motor behavior Pain coping & control Negative effect	0.12	171	4	2, 0
Greer (1980)	NR/ Individual	PPEI	B, S1	DGWBS Social adjustment General outcome	−0.37	60	12	0, 7
Hardy et al. (1995)	Mixed/ Individual	CEQ	B, S1	BDI SCL-90-R IIP	0.15	117	8	7, 0
Joyce et al. (2003)	Mixed/ Individual	SS (multi)	B	Disturbance (patient) Disturbance (rater) Disturbance (therapist)	0.17	144	7	4, 0
Karzmark et al. (1983)	NR/NR	SS (multi)	S1	CSQ GAS	ns	110	1	0, 0
Lax et al. (1992)	CBT/ Individual	AS (NR)	B	Rituals Obsessive thoughts O-C checklist	0.20	55	40	4, 0
Lipkin (1954)	EXP/ Individual	SS (single)	B	TAT change	0.25	9	4	0, 0
Lorentzen & H glend (2004)	PD/Group	SS (single)	B	GAF SCL-90 IIP-C	0.16	69	5	1, 0
Martin et al. (1976)	NR/NR	PPEI	B	PEQ adjustment PEQ improvement	0.17	46	7	0, 0
Mathews et al. (1976)	CBT/ Individual	SS (multi) SS (single)	B B	Phobic severity	0.17	36	2	1, 0
McConaghy et al. (1985)	CBT/ Individual	SS (single)	S1	Anomalous urge Sexual urges Sexual behavior	0.41	20	6	1, 0

(Continued)

Table 18.1 Continued

Source	Treatment (Type/ Modality)	Expectancy Measure	Time	Primary outcomes	ES (r)	Study N	Total tests	Number significant (+, −)
Meyer et al. (2002)	Mixed/ Individual	AAE (single)	B	BDI/HAM-D	0.22	151	1	1, 0
Moene et al. (2003)	O/ Individual	AS (single)	B	VRS motor conversion Disability	0.27	24	2	0, 0
O'Malley et al. (1988)	INT/ Individual	SS (single)	B	Change SAS HAM-D	0.36	35	3	0, 0
Persson & Nordlund (1983)	Mixed/ Individual	SS (single)	B	Global disorder Free anxiety Ego restriction	0.13	71	18	3, 0
Price et al. (2008)	CBT/ Individual	CEQ	S1	QATF FFI	0.51	72	2	2, 0
Richert (1976)	NR/ Individual	AS (multi)	B	Self-satisfaction Complexity Permeability	0.11	26	3	1, 0
Schoenberger et al. (1997)	CBT/ Group	CEQ SS (multi)	S1 S1	PRCS FNE TBCL	0.11	56	10	0, 0
Shaw (1977)	CBT/ Group	SS (single)	B	FFQ	0.79	17	1	1, 0
Spinhoven & ter Kuile (2000)	Mixed/ Individual	SS (single)	B	Pain reduction	0.27	165	1	1, 0
Stern & Marks (1973)	CBT/ Individual	SS (multi)	B	Main phobia Panic Anxiety	ns	16	23	0, 0
ter Kuile et al. (1995)	CBT/ Individual	SS (single)	B	Headache	0.35	156	1	1, 0
Tollinton (1973)	NR/NR	SS (multi)	B	Distress	0.59	30	1	1, 0
Van Minnen et al. (2002)– Sample 1	CBT/ Individual	CEQ	S1	PTSD Symptom Scale	0.19	59	2	0, 0
Van Minnen et al. (2002)– Sample 2	CBT/ Individual	CEQ	S1	PTSD Symptom Scale	0.19	63	2	0, 0
Vannicelli & Becker (1981)	NR/ Combined	SS (single) SS (single)	B B	DASa DASb RFQ	0.06	100	3	0, 0

(Continued)

Table 18.1 **Continued**

Source	Treatment (Type/ Modality)	Expectancy Measure	Time	Primary outcomes	ES (r)	Study N	Total tests	Number significant (+, −)
Wenzel et al. (2008)	CBT/ Individual	AAE (single)	B	HAM-D SSI BDI-II	0.23	32	5	1, 0

Note: (alphabetized within sections). Treatment type: CBT = predominantly cognitive and/or behavioral therapy; EXP = predominantly humanistic/experiential therapy; INT = predominantly interpersonal/relational therapy; Mixed = different patients received different treatments (none predominant, or >60%); NR = not reported; O = predominantly other therapy; PD = predominantly psychodynamic therapy; *Treatment modality:* Combined = patients who received more than one treatment modality; Mixed = different patients received different modalities (none predominant, or >60%); NR = not reported; *Expectancy measure:* AAE (single) = Attitudes and Expectations Questionnaire single expectancy item; AS (multi) = author-specific expectancy measure with multiple items; AS (single) = author-specific expectancy measure with single item; CEQ = Credibility/Expectancy Questionnaire or modified version (including Borkovec & Nau's 1972 version); NR = not reported; PPEI = Patient Prognostic Expectancy Inventory; SS (multi) = study-specific expectancy measure with multiple items; SS (single) = study-specific expectancy measure with single item; *Expectancy assessment time:* B = baseline; S1 = postsession 1; *Primary outcomes:* BAI = Beck Anxiety Inventory; BDI = Beck Depression Inventory; BDI-II = Beck Depression Inventory–Second Edition; BRMS = Bech-Rafaelson Mania Scale; CSQ = Client Satisfaction Questionnaire; DASa = Drinking Abstinence Scale; DASb = Drinking Adjustment Scale; DGWBS = Dupuy General Well-Being Scale; FFI = Fear of Flying Inventory; FFQ = Flight Fear Questionnaire; FNE = Fear of Negative Evaluation; FQ = Fear Questionnaire; GAD = generalized anxiety disorder; GAF = Global Assessment of Functioning; GAS = Global Assessment Scale; GIAS = Groningen Illness Attitudes Scale; HAM-A = Hamilton Anxiety Rating Scale; HAM-D = Hamilton Rating Scale for Depression; IIP = Inventory of Interpersonal Problems; IIP-C = Inventory of Interpersonal Problems–Circumplex; O-C = obsessive-compulsive; PARS = Personal Adjustment and Role Skills Scale; PEQ = Psychotherapy Evaluation Questionnaire; PRCS = Personal Report of Confidence as a Speaker; PSWQ = Penn State Worry Questionnaire; QATF = Questionnaire on Attitudes Toward Flying; RFQ = Role-Functioning Questionnaire; SAS = Social Adjustment Scale; SCL-90-R Global = Symptom Checklist-90-Revised Global Distress; SSI = Scale for Suicidal Ideation; STAI–State-Trait Anxiety Inventory; TAT = Thematic Apperception Test; TBC = Timed Behavior Checklist; VETS Global = Veterans Adjustment Scale Global Adjustment Score; VETS Improvement = Veterans Adjustment Scale problem improvement item; VRS = Video Rating Scale; *ES* = effect size (coefficients coded such that positive *r*s reflect positive associations between outcome expectations and favorable outcome and negative *r*s a negative association); *ns* = nonsignificant; *Study N:* total initial study sample size; *Total tests:* total number of tests of an expectancy–symptom outcome association reported in the study, including those for which no coefficient was reported and/or a multivariate model was examined; *Number significant:* The number of significant positive and negative associations between expectancy and symptom outcome, including those for which no coefficient was reported and/or a multivariate model was examined.

rendering it problematic to interpret. The specific results were:

• Presenting diagnosis [$Q(3)$ = 2.00, p = 0.57], coded as mood (n = 4), anxiety (n = 17), substance abuse (n = 3), and other (n = 8)
• Treatment orientation [$Q(1)$ = 1.21, p = 0.27], coded as cognitive-behavioral (n = 22) or other (n = 24)
• Treatment modality [$Q(2)$ = 2.31, p = 0.31], coded as individual (n = 30), group (n = 7), or other (n = 3)
• Design type [$Q(2)$ = 5.63, p = 0.06], coded as comparative clinical trial (n = 23), open trial (n = 10), or naturalistic setting (n = 12)
• Publication date [$Q(1)$ = 0.13, p = 0.72], coded as before 2000 (n = 26) or from 2000 to 2009 (n = 20).

That is, the patient outcome expectation link to treatment outcome was fairly consistent across each of these variables.

Treatment Expectations

Many who have written about treatment expectations assume that they influence outcome; however, the research evidence does not strongly support this assumption. In early reviews (e.g., Duckro et al., 1979) and in our review of role expectation studies through the year 2000 (Arnkoff et al., 2002), the findings were equivocal (see also Noble et al., 2001). Arnkoff et al. identified 37 studies that addressed the relation between role expectations and/or role expectation disconfirmation and an outcome measure, with *disconfirmation* being defined as a discrepancy between patient and therapist role expectations and hypothesized to lead to a poor outcome (Goldstein, 1962). Nineteen studies demonstrated some evidence for a significant, positive association between role expectations/ absence of disconfirmation and either continuation in psychotherapy or patient, therapist, or independent clinician ratings of psychotherapy outcome. Twelve studies, however, had mixed results, while eight revealed no significant relationship between role expectancy and outcome (note that studies with more than one type of outcome measure could be counted more than once). The 19 positive, 12 mixed, and 8 nonsignificant results should be interpreted with caution in that many studies with positive results (especially the older ones) employed poor measurement of role expectations and/or outcome (e.g., interviews with no quantification or consensus analysis of qualitative data, dropout assessed by an arbitrary number of sessions attended). Particularly when the quality of measurement of expectations is taken into account, there was no outcome measure for which the significant findings outweighed the mixed and negative findings.

Subsequent research on the association of treatment expectations and psychotherapy outcome has shown additional positive findings. For example, Schneider and Klauer (2001) found that higher expectations of active involvement in psychotherapy were related to greater change in interpersonal functioning. In another study, treatment expectations in behavioral medicine treatment, specifically rejection of the treatment rationale, predicted program dropout (Davis & Addis, 2002). A study examining the relationship between patients' pretreatment role expectations and attrition found that individuals who scored outside of the normative range on the PEI-R total score were seven times more likely to terminate therapy prematurely (Aubuchon-Endsley & Callahan, 2009).

Another finding in the treatment expectations literature concerns the specific process expectation about treatment duration (Clarkin & Levy, 2004). Several studies have reported that the longer patients expect therapy to last, the longer they remain in treatment (e.g., Jenkins, Fuqua, & Blum, 1986; Mueller & Pekarik, 2000). However, several studies found that expectations for duration were either unrelated to actual duration (Hochberg, 1986) or showed significant, but small associations (Pekarik & Wierzbicki, 1986).

In sum, a dispassionate review of the extant research finds mostly positive but weak and mixed associations between treatment expectations and psychotherapy outcomes. Insufficient numbers of well-controlled studies exist to either conduct a meta-analysis (especially when carefully separating studies by specific type of treatment expectation) or to render a more definitive conclusion.

Mediators
Outcome Expectations
Although the correlational data (including in our own meta-analysis) suggest that outcome expectations show a small but significant association with treatment outcome, little is known about the specific mechanisms through which they operate (Arnkoff et al., 2002). Recently, however, several researchers have hypothesized that the expectancy–outcome association is mediated by the patient–therapist alliance. Several studies have provided partial support for this model in demonstrating that patients' outcome expectations are positively associated with alliance quality (a necessary step in demonstrating mediation) across various treatments for various conditions (e.g., Connolly Gibbons et al., 2003; Constantino et al., 2005).

We are aware of three studies that have *directly* investigated the putative mediator pathway. In research on patients with major depressive disorder receiving short-term individual psychotherapy or pharmaco-therapy (Meyer et al., 2002), patients with mixed diagnoses receiving short-term indi-vidual psychotherapy (Joyce et al., 2003), and group counseling for grief (Abouguendia, Joyce, Piper, & Ogrodniczuk, 2004), the therapeutic alliance was at least a partial mediator of patient expectancy effects on outcome, implicating the alliance as a robust mechanism. Meyer and associates drew on goal theory (e.g., Austin & Vancouver, 1996) to explain this finding, suggesting that people will only work toward a goal if they believe that they have a chance of achieving it. Thus, patients who have posi-tive outcome expectations (compared with more pessimistic beliefs) may be more likely to engage in a collaborative working rela-tionship with their therapist, which in turn may promote clinical improvement.

Several investigators (e.g., Bootzin & Lick, 1979; Higginbotham, 1977; Lick & Bootzin, 1975) have postulated that out-come expectations may produce change through promoting greater patient adher-ence to the treatment regimen. One study of cognitive-behavioral therapy for anxiety found preliminary support for this perspec-tive (Westra, Dozois, & Marcus, 2007). Early homework compliance mediated the association between baseline expectation of reducing one's anxiety and early symptom change.

Treatment Expectations
Similar to outcome expectations, formal examination of mediators of the association between treatment expectations and out-come has been limited. However, as with outcome expectations, there is some indi-rect evidence that the alliance might be a mediator. For example, Joyce and Piper (1998) found that patient expectations for the "typical session" were associated with better patient-rated alliance quality. In the same study, better alliance quality was also associated with less discrepancy between patients' expectations for the typical session and their actual experience of session use-fulness and comfort. In another study by the same investigators (Joyce, McCallum, Piper, & Ogrodniczuk, 2000), patients' base-line role behavior expectations interacted with their quality of object relations (QOR) to predict alliance quality. For patients with higher QOR, higher expectations of contributing to the treatment process was associated with negative change in alliance quality across short-term individual psy-chotherapy, suggesting that QOR may be an important moderator of the expectancy–alliance association. In a study of the asso-ciation between patients' pretreatment role expectations and early self-rated alliance quality, Patterson, Uhlin, and Anderson (2008) found that role expectations acco-unted for 31% of the variance in the goal dimension of the alliance, 30% in the patients' bond with the therapist, and 24% in the task dimension. Specific types of expectations were associated with the alli-ance; patients who were committed to therapy and expected to take responsibility for their work in therapy tended to report stronger alliances.

Patient Contributions
Although the clinical importance of patient outcome and treatment expectations has been well documented, we have a paltry understanding of factors that develop and maintain such beliefs. The available litera-ture suggests that diverse factors correlate with or determine patients' expectations.

Outcome Expectations
A study of CBT for fibromyalgia and chronic low back pain found that less fear

of reinjury and active pain-coping strategies were associated with higher pretreatment outcome expectations (Goossens, Vlaeyen, Hidding, Kole-Snijders, & Evers, 2005). These results are consistent with findings that less pain-related fear, more internal control of pain, and lower depression were associated with higher treatment outcome expectations for chronic low back pain sufferers (Smeets et al., 2008). The association between more severe presenting symptomatology and lower treatment outcome expectations has also been found with socially phobic patients (Safren et al., 1997). General hope might also be an important determinant of outcome expectations. For example, a study of students seeking mental health counseling found that patients who indicated more hopelessness had lower expectations of improvement (Goldfarb, 2002).

Treatment Expectations

Several cultural and demographic variables have emerged as correlates of patient treatment expectations. For example, Icelandic students expected their psychotherapists to have more expertise than did American students (Ægisdóttir & Gerstein, 2000). African-American and Latino/a college students have reported higher multicultural competence expectations of therapists compared to Asian-American, white-American, and biracial students (Constantine & Arorash, 2001).

Religion has also predicted treatment expectations. Highly religious married Christian couples (compared with low-to-moderately religious participants) were more likely to believe that a Christian marital therapist would be more effective than a non-Christian therapist (Ripley, Worthington, & Berry, 2001). Other research has found differences between evangelical and nonevangelical Christians, and highly and moderately conservative Christians, in their expectations about therapist directiveness and in-session religious behavior (Belaire & Young, 2002; Turton, 2004).

Intrapsychic and historical variables might also partially determine treatment expectations. For example, in a sample of undergraduate students, adaptive perfectionism, also known as healthy, positive striving, was associated with positive expectations toward both counseling process and outcome (Oliver, Hart, Ross, & Katz, 2001). For another example, group therapy patients who had previously been in therapy had higher expectations about the group treatment than patients without prior therapy experience (MacNair-Semands, 2002).

Limitations of the Research
Outcome Expectations

Several limitations characterize our meta-analysis on outcome expectations. First, because we decided to retain all studies that met our a priori criteria (in the service of comprehensiveness), the analysis contained studies of varying quality. However, to the extent that the more recent studies included improved measurement and methodology, it is interesting to note that publication year was not a moderator. Second, expectancy research has been plagued by poor measurement. In fact, of the 46 studies in our meta-analysis, we coded 31 (67.4%) as involving "poor" expectancy measurement. Problems included, but were not limited to, the use of 1-item scales, measures that confounded expectancy and another construct, scales that confounded outcome and treatment expectations, measures that used the same questions for both expected outcome and actual outcome, and the use of projective measures to assess outcome expectations. Third, the positive weighted effect may have been inflated by the imbalanced reporting of coefficients from only positive findings (i.e., a publication bias).

Finally, there could be a file drawer problem, especially with our excluding dissertations. However, because expectations were often not related to a primary, hypothesis-driven research question, we found that many authors openly reported negative or nonsignificant findings. This was supported by the symmetrical distribution of effect sizes across the studies included in our meta-analysis. Nevertheless, as previously noted, the relatively small fail-safe N suggests caution in our results.

In addition to these measurement and statistical limitations, other problems characterize the outcome expectancy literature. As reflected in our review, there are few data to support a direct causal relation between outcome expectations and favorable treatment outcomes. The most relevant experimental work relates to the use of pretreatment preparation to improve treatment response. In some of the earliest work, Frank and colleagues developed a pretreatment Role Induction Interview (RII) that addressed (a) the treatment rationale, (b) the importance of attendance, (c) patient and therapist expectations for role behavior, and (d) outcome expectations (Hoehn-Saric et al., 1964). In a controlled trial where patients either did or did not engage in the RII prior to treatment, RII patients achieved significantly greater improvement (on both therapist- and patient-rated measures), had better attendance levels, and engaged in more objectively coded favorable therapy behavior than the no-RII controls. However, most subsequent role induction studies have focused on socializing patients to treatment and on manipulating their expectations about how therapy will unfold and the role that they should expect to play. Manipulation studies specifically attempting to heighten patients' prognostic *outcome* expectations are virtually nonexistent.

Another limitation is that outcome expectations have tended to be viewed as a relatively static construct, often assessed at baseline or early treatment only. However, some studies have suggested that expectancies change as patients move beyond treatment's early stages. For example, Holt and Heimberg (1990) found that patients rated treatments as less credible, and expectations for improvement were lower when the RTQ was completed following Session 4 compared with the end of Session 1 in cognitive-behavioral group therapy. The authors concluded, "Credibility and outcome expectancy erode when exposed to treatment reality" (p. 214), perhaps as patients become more cynical before experiencing much progress. Others have suggested that prognostic expectaions might be too high and unrealistic at treatment's start, thus requiring time to rework their unrealistic nature (Greer, 1980). Whatever the case, it appears that expectations are malleable, thus limiting the empirical and clinical utility of static assessments of this construct.

Treatment Expectations
Unlike outcome expectations, there has been more experimental work on treatment expectations. Since the early RII work discussed above, there have been a variety of interventions used to manipulate patient treatment expectancies, and the research suggests that they are malleable (Dew & Bickman, 2005; Tinsley et al., 1988). In a comprehensive review of manipulation studies on adults involving audiotapes, videotapes, verbal instructions, printed materials, or counseling interviews, Tinsley and colleagues (1988) found significant changes in treatment expectancies in about 50% of the studies. One study found that presenting a credible treatment rationale helps to generate positive expectancies about the therapy, and that more positive expectancies are

found when the therapy is based on scientific research, tested in clinical trials, and new in relation to other therapies (Kazdin & Krouse, 1983). There have also been role induction studies using a pre-post control group design to try to enhance patient engagement and to address misperceptions about treatment, and many of these have been shown to improve retention and compliance (Dew & Bickman, 2005; Katz et al., 2004; Walitzer et al., 1999).

However, many manipulation studies are fraught with methodological problems, including lack of random assignment, use of analog participants in a laboratory setting, and the use of expectancy instruments with unknown or suspect psychometric properties (Tinsley et al., 1988). Moreover, most address treatment expectancies at one time only (often pretreatment).

Therapeutic Practices
Outcome Expectations

Although many therapies include elements that address various expectations, such strategies are rarely emphasized or explicit (Greenberg et al., 2006). We offer here several viable clinical strategies.

• Explicitly assess patients' prognostic expectations at the beginning of treatment. Depending on what is revealed (verbally or through a brief measure), therapists can verify and validate their patients' beliefs and consider behaving in a way that matches patients' level of optimism.

• Tread lightly and empathically in using strategies to enhance outcome expectations. Make a concerted effort to use hope-inspiring statements that neither too quickly threaten a patient's belief system or sense of self (Pinel & Constantino, 2003), nor promise an unrealistic degree or speed of change (Kirsch, 1990). Rather, such statements can be more general, such as "It makes sense that you sought treatment for your problems" or "Your problems are exactly the type for which this therapy can be of assistance" (Constantino, Klein, & Greenberg, 2006). The therapist can also express confidence and competence in such statements as, "I am confident that working together we can deal effectively with your depression," while maintaining a sense of understanding that the patient might not fully believe this statement at the outset.

• Personalize expectancy-enhancing statements based on patient experiences or strengths. For example, a therapist can state, "You have already conquered two major hurdles in admitting to yourself that you have a problem and in seeking help, which is not easy to do. This suggests a motivation and desire to change, despite any questions you might have about whether you *can* change." Or a clinician might convey, "You strike me as someone who can really accomplish things that you put your mind to."

• Offer a nontechnical review of the research findings on the intended treatment. For depressed patients, for example, a clinician could say, "Much research has shown that people in cognitive therapy for their depression tend to get significantly better than people who simply try to deal with their problems on their own."

• While articulating such outcome perspectives, do some foreshadowing about the *process* of change. Using the same example, the likelihood of small setbacks or fluctuations in mood can be normalized, highlighting that change is often gradual and nonlinear.

• Regularly check in on patients' outcome expectations and respond accordingly. For example, if a depressed patient has developed unrealistically high expectations after just a few sessions, the therapist should not only provide positive feedback to reinforce self-efficacy but also remind the patient that depression can be recurrent, thus bringing expectations more in line with the nature of the disorder. On the other hand, if a patient expresses diminished hope, the clinician could help him or her retrieve past successes to at least partially bolster future-oriented inspiration (in the context of empathy and validation of the current demoralization).

Treatment Expectations

• Heed the potential value of preparatory work and socialization to treatment, especially for patients who are inexperienced with therapy. Although certain treatment expectations could be diagnostic (e.g., "I expect my therapist to tell me exactly what to do because I am not able to do for myself"), others might simply reflect therapy naiveté. In the latter case, striving to shape or alter treatment expectations via socialization could be clinically indicated.

• When patients manifest treatment role or process expectations that are incompatible with the therapist's, investigate the patient's perspective, consider how these may reflect the patient's underlying dynamics, inform the patient of your own perspective, enter a process negotiation, and let the patient choose if the treatment seems appropriate (Van Audenhove & Vertommen, 2000).

• When the patient's expectations are not manifest, infer the type of role the patient wants by assessing activity level, deference toward the therapist, information presented or omitted, and responses to interventions calling for self-understanding and access to feelings

(Richert, 1983). These observations and subsequent negotiations might include trying to draw out a passive patient and giving a ballpark figure of the treatment length. The therapist can process decisions with the patient, thereby providing a rationale, and perhaps setting the foundation for a corrective experience.

References

Abouguendia, M., Joyce, A. S., Piper, W. E., & Ogrodniczuk, J. S. (2004). Alliance as a mediator of expectancy effects in short-term group psychotherapy. *Group Dynamics: Theory, Research, and Practice, 8,* 3–12.

Ægisdóttir, S., & Gerstein, L. (2000). Icelandic and American students' expectations about counseling. *Journal of Counseling & Development, 78,* 44–53.

Ægisdóttir, S., Gerstein, L., & Gridley, B. (2000). The factorial structure of the Expectations About Counseling Questionnaire-Brief Form: Some serious questions. *Measurement and Evaluation in Counseling and Development, 33,* 3–20.

Apfelbaum, B. (1958). *Dimensions of transference in psychotherapy.* Berkeley, CA: University of California Press.

Arnkoff, D. B., Glass, C. R., & Shapiro, S. J. (2002). Expectations and preferences. In J. C. Norcross (Ed.), *Psychotherapy relationships that work: Therapists contributions and responsiveness to patients* (pp. 325–46). New York: Oxford University Press.

Asch, S. E. (1946). Forming impressions of personality. *Journal of Abnormal and Social Psychology, 41,* 258–90.

Aubuchon-Endsley, N. L., & Callahan, J. L. (2009). The hour of departure: Predicting attrition in the training clinic from role expectancies. *Training and Education in Professional Psychology, 3,* 120–26.

Austin, J. T., & Vancouver, J. B. (1996). Goal constructs in psychology: Structure, process, and content. *Psychological Bulletin, 120,* 338–75.

Barrios, F. X., & Karoly, P. (1983). Treatment expectancy and therapeutic change in treatment of migraine headache: Are they related? *Psychological Reports, 52,* 59–68.

Basoglu, M., Marks, I. M., Swinson, R. P., Noshirvani, H., O'Sullivan, G., & Kuch, K. (1994).

Pre-treatment predictors of treatment outcome in panic disorder and agoraphobia treated with alprazolam and exposure. *Journal of Affective Disorders, 30*, 123–32.

Belaire, C., & Young, J. (2002). Conservative Christians' expectations of non-Christian counselors. *Counseling and Values, 46*, 175–87.

Berzins, J. I. (1971). *Revision of Psychotherapy Expectancy Inventory.* Unpublished manuscript, University of Kentucky, Lexington.

Bleyen, K., Vertommen, H., Vander Steene, G., & Van Audenhove, C. (2001). Psychometric properties of the Psychotherapy Expectancy Inventory—Revised (PEI-R). *Psychotherapy Research, 11*, 69–83.

Bloch, S., Bond, G., Qualls, B., Yalom, I., & Zimmerman, E. (1976). Patients' expectations of therapeutic improvement and their outcomes. *American Journal of Psychiatry, 133*, 1457–60.

Bootzin, R. R., & Lick, J. R. (1979). Expectancies in therapy research: Interpretive artifact or mediating mechanism? *Journal of Consulting and Clinical Psychology, 47*, 852–55.

Borkovec, T. D., & Costello, E. (1993). Efficacy of applied relaxation and cognitive-behavioral therapy in the treatment of generalized anxiety disorder. *Journal of Consulting and Clinical Psychology, 61*, 611–619.

Borkovec, T. D., & Nau, S. D. (1972). Credibility of analogue therapy rationales. *Journal of Behavior Therapy & Experimental Psychiatry, 3*, 257–60.

Borkovec, T. B., Newman, M. G., Pincus, A. L., & Lytle, R. (2002). A component analysis of cognitive-behavioral therapy for generalized anxiety disorder and the role of interpersonal problems. *Journal of Consulting and Clinical Psychology, 70*, 288–98.

Buwalda, F., & Bouman, T. (2008). Predicting the effect of psychoeducational group treatment for hypochondriasis. *Clinical Psychology & Psychotherapy, 15*, 396–403.

Calsyn, R., Morse, G., Yonker, R., Winter, J., Pierce, K., & Taylor, M. (2003). Client choice of treatment and client outcomes. *Journal of Community Psychology, 31*, 339–48.

Chambless, D. L., Tran, G. Q., & Glass, C. R. (1997). Predictors of response to cognitive-behavioral group therapy for social phobia. *Journal of Anxiety Disorders, 11*, 221–40.

Clark, D. M., Salkovskis, P. M., Hackmann, A., Wells, A., Ludgate, J., & Gelder, M. (1999). Brief cognitive therapy for panic disorder: A randomized controlled trial. *Journal of Consulting and Clinical Psychology, 67*, 583–89.

Clarkin, J. F., & Levy, K. N. (2004). The influence of client variables on psychotherapy. In M. J. Lambert (Ed.) *Bergin and Garfield's handbook of psychotherapy and behavior change* (5th ed., pp. 194–226). New York: John Wiley and Sons.

Cohen, J. (1988). *Statistical power analysis for the behavioral sciences* (2nd ed.). Mahwah, NJ: Erlbaum.

Collins, J. F., & Hyer, L. (1986). Treatment expectancy among psychiatric inpatients. *Journal of Clinical Psychology, 42*, 562–69.

Connolly Gibbons, M. B., Crits-Christoph, P., de la Cruz, C., Barber, J. P., Siqueland, L., & Gladis, M. (2003). Pretreatment expectations, interpersonal functioning, and symptoms in the prediction of the therapeutic alliance across supportive-expressive psychotherapy and cognitive therapy. *Psychotherapy Research, 13*, 59–76.

Constantine, M., & Arorash, T. (2001). Universal-diverse orientation and general expectations about counseling: Their relation to college students' multicultural counseling expectations. *Journal of College Student Development, 42*, 535–44.

Constantino, M. J., Arnow, B. A., Blasey, C., & Agras, W. S. (2005). The association between patient characteristics and the therapeutic alliance in cognitive-behavioral and interpersonal therapy for bulimia nervosa. *Journal of Consulting and Clinical Psychology, 73*, 203–211.

Constantino, M. J., Klein, R., & Greenberg, R. P. (2006). *Guidelines for enhancing patient expectations: A companion manual to cognitive therapy for depression.* Unpublished manuscript.

Crits-Christoph, P., Gibbons, M., Losardo, D., Narducci, J., Schamberger, M., & Gallop, R. (2004). Who benefits from brief psychodynamic therapy for generalized anxiety disorder? *Canadian Journal of Psychoanalysis, 12*, 301–24.

Davis, M., & Addis, M. (2002). Treatment expectations, experiences, and mental health functioning predict attrition status in behavioural medicine groups. *Irish Journal of Psychology, 23*, 37–51.

Dearing, R., Barrick, C., Dermen, K., & Walitzer, K. (2005). Indicators of client engagement: Influences on alcohol treatment satisfaction and outcomes. *Psychology of Addictive Behaviors, 19*, 71–78.

Devilly, G., & Borkovec, T. (2000). Psychometric properties of the credibility/expectancy questionnaire. *Journal of Behavior Therapy and Experimental Psychiatry, 31*, 73–86.

Dew, S. E., & Bickman, L. (2005). Client expectancies about therapy. *Mental Health Services Research, 7*, 21–33.

Duckro, P., Beal, D., & George, C. (1979). Research on the effects of disconfirmed client role expectations in psychotherapy: A critical review. *Psychological Bulletin, 86*, 260–75.

Evans, R. L., Smith, K. M., Halar, E. M., & Kiolet, C. L. (1985). Effect of expectation and level of adjustment on treatment outcome. *Psychological Reports, 57*(3, Pt. 1), 936–38.

Frank, J. D. (1961). *Persuasion and healing: A comparative study of psychotherapy.* Baltimore: The Johns Hopkins Press.

Garfield, S. L., & Wolpin, M. (1963). Expectations regarding psychotherapy. *Journal of Nervous and Mental Disease, 137*, 353–62.

Gaudiano, B., & Miller, I. (2006). Patients' expectancies, the alliance in pharmacotherapy, and treatment outcomes in bipolar disorder. *Journal of Consulting and Clinical Psychology, 74*, 671–76.

Ghosh, A., Marks, I. M., & Carr, A. C. (1988). Therapist contact and outcome of self-exposure treatment for phobias: A controlled study. *British Journal of Psychiatry, 152*, 234–38.

Goldfarb, D. (2002). College counseling center clients' expectations about counseling: How they relate to depression, hopelessness, and actual-ideal self-discrepancies. *Journal of College Counseling, 5*, 142–52.

Goldfried, M. R. (1980). Toward the delineation of therapeutic change principles. *American Psychologist, 35*, 991–99.

Goldstein, A. P. (1960). Therapist and client expectation of personality change in psychotherapy. *Journal of Counseling Psychology, 7*, 180–84.

Goldstein, A. P. (1962). *Therapist-patient expectancies in psychotherapy.* New York: Pergamon Press.

Goossens, M. E. J. B., Vlaeyen, J. W. S., Hidding, A., Kole-Snijders, A., & Evers, S. M. A. A. (2005). Treatment expectancy affects the outcome of cognitive-behavioral interventions in chronic pain. *Clinical Journal of Pain, 21*, 18–26.

Greenberg, R. P., Constantino, M. J., & Bruce, N. (2006). Are expectations still relevant for psychotherapy process and outcome? *Clinical Psychology Review, 26*, 657–78.

Greer, F. L. (1980). Prognostic expectations and outcome of brief therapy. *Psychological Reports, 46*, 973–74.

Hansson, L., & Berglund, M. (1987). Factors influencing treatment outcome and patient satisfaction in a short-term psychiatric ward: A path analysis study of the importance of patient involvement in treatment planning. *European Archives of Psychiatry & Neurological Sciences, 236*, 269–75.

Hardy, G. E., Barkham, M., Shapiro, D. A., Reynolds, S., Rees, A., & Stiles, W. B. (1995). Credibility and outcome of cognitive-behavioural and psychodynamic-interpersonal therapy. *British Journal of Clinical Psychology, 34*, 555–69.

Heckhausen, H., & Leppmann, P. (1991). *Motivation and action.* New York: Springer-Verlag Publishing.

Heine, R. W., & Trosman, H. (1960). Initial expectations of the doctor-patient interaction as a factor in continuance in psychotherapy. *Psychiatry, 23*, 275–78.

Higginbotham, H. N. (1977). Culture and the role of client expectancy in psychotherapy. In R.W. Brislin (Ed.), *Topics in culture learning* (Vol. 5, pp. 107–24). Honolulu, HI: East-West Center.

Hochberg, M. G. (1986). Client-therapist role expectations and psychotherapy duration. *Dissertation Abstracts International, 46*(10), 3595–3596B.

Hoehn-Saric, R., Frank, J., Imber, S., Nash, E., Stone, A., & Battle, C. (1964). Systematic preparation of patients for psychotherapy: I. Effects of therapy behavior and outcome. *Journal of Psychiatric Research, 2*, 267–81.

Holt, C. S., & Heimberg, R. G. (1990). The Reaction to Treatment Questionnaire: Measuring treatment credibility and outcome expectancies. *the Behavior Therapist, 13*, 213–214, 222.

Jenkins, S. J., Fuqua, D. R., & Blum, C. R. (1986). Factors related to duration of counseling in a university counseling center. *Psychological Reports, 58*, 467–72.

Joyce, A. S., McCallum, M., Piper, W. E., & Ogrodniczuk, J. S. (2000). Role behavior expectancies and alliance change in short-term individual psychotherapy. *Journal of Psychotherapy Practice and Research, 9*, 213–25.

Joyce, A. S., Ogrodniczuk, J. S., Piper, W. E., & McCallum, M. (2003). The alliance as mediator of expectancy effects in short-term individual therapy. *Journal of Consulting and Clinical Psychology, 71*, 672–79.

Joyce, A. S., & Piper, W. E. (1998). Expectancy, the therapeutic alliance, and treatment outcome in short-term individual psychotherapy. *Journal of Psychotherapy Practice and Research, 7*, 236–48.

Kamin, I., & Caughlan, J. (1963). Subjective experiences of outpatient psychotherapy. *American Journal of Psychotherapy, 17,* 660–68.

Karzmark, P., Greenfield, T., & Cross, H. (1983). The relationship between level of adjustment and expectations for therapy. *Journal of Clinical Psychology, 39,* 930–32.

Katz, E. C., Brown, B. S., Schwartz, R. P., Weintraub, E., Barksdale, W., & Robinson, R. (2004). Role induction: A method for enhancing early retention in outpatient drug-free treatment. *Journal of Consulting and Clinical Psychology, 72,* 227–34.

Kazdin, A. E., & Krouse, R. (1983). The impact of variations in treatment rationales on expectancies for therapeutic change. *Behavior Therapy, 14,* 657–71.

Kelley, H. H. (1950). Warm-cold variable in first impressions of persons. *Journal of Personality, 18,* 431–39.

Kirsch, I. (1985). Response expectancy as a determinant of experience and behavior. *American Psychologist, 40,* 1189–1202.

Kirsch, I. (1990). *Changing expectations: A key to effective psychotherapy.* Pacific Grove, CA: Brooks/Cole.

Lax, T., Basoglu, M., & Marks, I. M. (1992). Expectancy and compliance as predictors of outcome in obsessive-compulsive disorder. *Behavioural Psychotherapy, 20,* 257–66.

Lick, J., & Bootzin, R. (1975). Expectancy factors in the treatment of fear: Methodological and theoretical issues. *Psychological Bulletin, 82,* 917–31.

Lipkin, S. (1954). Clients' feelings and attitudes in relation to the outcome of client-centered therapy. *Psychological Monographs, 68*(1, No. 372), 1–30.

Lipsey, M. W., & Wilson, D. B. (2001). *Practical meta-analysis.* Thousand Oaks, CA: Sage Publications, Inc.

Lorentzen, S., & Høglend, P. (2004). Predictors of change during long-term analytic group psychotherapy. *Psychotherapy and Psychosomatics, 73,* 25–35.

MacNair-Semands, R. (2002). Predicting attendance and expectations for group therapy. *Group Dynamics: Theory, Research, and Practice, 6,* 219–228.

Martin, P. J., & Sterne, A. L. (1975). Prognostic expectations and treatment outcome. *Journal of Consulting and Clinical Psychology, 43,* 572–76.

Martin, P. J., Sterne, A. L., Claveaux, R., & Acree, N. J. (1976). Significant factors in the expectancy-improvement relationship: A second

look at an early study. *Research Communications in Psychology,* Psychiatry & Behavior, *1,* 367–379.

Mathews, A. M., Johnston, D. W., Lancashire, M., Munby, M., Shaw, P. M., & Gelder, M. G. (1976). Imaginal flooding and exposure to real phobic situations: Treatment outcome with agoraphobic patients. *British Journal of Psychiatry, 129,* 362–71.

McConaghy, N., Armstrong, M., & Blaszczynski, A. P. (1985). Expectancy, covert sensitization and imaginal desensitization in compulsive sexuality. *Acta Psychiatrica Scandinavica, 72,* 176–87.

Meyer, B., Pilkonis, P. A., Krupnick, J. L., Egan, M. K., Simmens, S. J., & Sotsky, S. M. (2002). Treatment expectancies, patient alliance, and outcome: Further analyses from the National Institute of Mental Health Treatment of Depression Collaborative Research Program. *Journal of Consulting and Clinical Psychology, 70,* 1051–55.

Moene, F., Spinhoven, P., Hoogduin, K., & Dyck, R. (2003). A randomized controlled clinical trial of a hypnosis-based treatment for patients with conversion disorder, motor type. *International Journal of Clinical and Experimental Hypnosis, 51,* 29–50.

Mueller, M., & Pekarik, G. (2000). Treatment duration prediction: Client accuracy and its relationship to dropout, outcome, and satisfaction. *Psychotherapy: Theory, Research, Practice, Training, 37,* 117–123.

Noble, L. M., Douglas, B. C., & Newman, S. P. (2001). What do patients expect of psychological services? A systematic and critical review of empirical studies. *Social Science & Medicine, 52,* 985–98.

Oliver, J., Hart, B., Ross, M., & Katz, B. (2001). Healthy perfectionism and positive expectations about counseling. *North American Journal of Psychology, 3,* 229–42.

O'Malley, S. S., Foley, S. H., Rounsaville, B. J., Watkins, J. T., Sotsky, S. M., Imber, S. D., et al. (1988). Therapist competence and patient outcome in interpersonal psychotherapy of depression. *Journal of Consulting and Clinical Psychology, 56,* 496–501.

Patterson, C. L., Uhlin, B., & Anderson, T. (2008). Clients' pretreatment counseling expectation as predictors of the working alliance. *Journal of Counseling Psychology, 55,* 528–34.

Pekarik, G., & Wierzbicki, M. (1986). The relationship between clients' expected and actual treatment duration. *Psychotherapy, 23,* 532–34.

Persson, G., & Nordlund, C. L. (1983). Expectations of improvement and attitudes to treatment processes in relation to outcome with four treatment methods for phobic disorders. *Acta Psychiatrica Scandinavica, 68,* 484–93.

Pinel, E. C., & Constantino, M. J. (2003). Putting self psychology to good use: When social psychologists and clinical psychologists unite. *Journal of Psychotherapy Integration, 13,* 9–32.

Price, M., Anderson, P., Henrich, C., & Rothbaum, B. (2008). Greater expectations: Using hierarchical linear modeling to examine expectancy for treatment outcome as a predictor of treatment response. *Behavior Therapy, 39,* 398–405.

Richert, A. (1983). Differential prescription for psychotherapy on the basis of client role preferences. *Psychotherapy: Theory, Research & Practice, 20,* 321–329.

Richert, A. J. (1976). Expectations, experiencing and change in psychotherapy. *Journal of Clinical Psychology, 32,* 438–44.

Rickers-Ovsiankina, M. A., Geller, J. D., Berzins, J. I., & Rogers, G. W. (1971). Patient's role expectancies in psychotherapy: A theoretical and measurement approach. *Psychotherapy: Theory, Research and Practice, 8,* 124–126.

Ripley, J., Worthington, E., & Berry, J. (2001). The effects of religiosity on preferences and expectations for marital therapy among married Christians. *American Journal of Family Therapy, 29,* 39–58.

Rosenthal, D., & Frank, J. D. (1956). Psychotherapy and the placebo effect. *Psychological Bulletin, 53,* 294–302.

Rosenzweig, S. (1936). Some implicit common factors in diverse methods of psychotherapy. *American Journal of Orthopsychiatry, 6,* 412–415.

Safren, S. A., Heimberg, R. G., & Juster, H. R. (1997). Clients' expectancies and their relationship to pretreatment symptomatology and outcome of cognitive-behavioral group treatment for social phobia. *Journal of Consulting and Clinical Psychology, 65,* 694–98.

Schneider, W., & Klauer, T. (2001). Symptom level, treatment motivation, and the effects of inpatient psychotherapy. *Psychotherapy Research, 11,* 153–67.

Schoenberger, N. E., Kirsch, I., Gearan, P., Montgomery, G., & Pastyrnak, S. L. (1997). Hypnotic enhancement of a cognitive behavioral treatment for public speaking anxiety. *Behavior Therapy, 28,* 127–40.

Schulte, D. (2008). Patients' outcome expectancies and their impression of suitability as predictors of treatment outcome. *Psychotherapy Research, 18,* 481–94.

Secord, P. F. (1958). Facial features and inference processes in interpersonal perception. In R. Taguiri & L. Petrillo (Eds.), *Person perception and interpersonal behavior* (pp. 300–315) Stanford, CA: Stanford University Press.

Shapiro, D. A. (1981). Comparative credibility of treatment rationales: Three tests of expectancy theory. *British Journal of Clinical Psychology, 21,* 111–22.

Shaw, H. (1977). A simple and effective treatment for flight phobia. *British Journal of Psychiatry, 130,* 229–32.

Smeets, R. J. E. M., Beelen, S., Goossens, M. E. J. B., Schouten, E. G. W., Knottnerus, A., & Vlaeyen, J. W. S. (2008) Treatment expectancy and credibility are associated with the outcome of both physical and cognitive-behavioral treatment in chronic low back pain. *Clinical Journal of Pain, 24,* 305–315.

Sotsky, S. M., Glass, D. E., Shea, M. T., Pilkonis, P. A., Collins, J. F., Elkin, I., et al. (1991). Patient predictors of response to psychotherapy and pharmacotherapy: Findings in the NIMH Treatment of Depression Collaborative Research Program. *American Journal of Psychiatry, 148,* 997–1008.

Spinhoven, P., & ter Kuile, M. (2000). Treatment outcome expectancies and hypnotic susceptibility as moderators of pain reduction in patients with chronic tension-type headache. *International Journal of Clinical and Experimental Hypnosis, 48,* 290–305.

Stern, R., & Marks, I. (1973). Brief and prolonged exposure: A comparison in agoraphobia patients. *Archives of General Psychiatry, 28,* 270–76.

ter Kuile, M. M., Spinhoven, P., & Linssen, C. G. (1995). Responders and nonresponders to autogenic training and cognitive self-hypnosis: Prediction of short- and long-term success in tension-type headache patients. *Headache: The Journal of Head and Face Pain, 35,* 630–36.

Tinsley, H. E. A, Bowman, S. L., & Barich, A. W. (1993). Counseling psychologists' perceptions of the occurrence and effects of unrealistic expectations about counseling and psychotherapy among their clients. *Journal of Counseling Psychology, 40,* 46–52.

Tinsely, H. E. A., Bowman, S. L., & Ray, S. B. (1988). Manipulation of expectancies about counseling and psychotherapy: Review and analysis of expectancy manipulation strategies and results. *Journal of Counseling Psychology, 35,* 99–108.

Tinsley, H. E. A., & Westcot, A. M. (1990). Analysis of the cognitions stimulated by the items on the Expectations About Counseling—Brief Form: An analysis of construct validity. *Journal of Counseling Psychology, 37*, 223–26.

Tinsley, H. E. A., Workman, K. R., & Kass, R. A. (1980). Factor analysis of the domain of client expectancies about counseling. *Journal of Counseling Psychology, 27*, 561–70.

Tollinton, H. (1973). Initial expectations and outcome. *British Journal of Medical Psychology, 46*, 251–57.

Turton, D. (2004). Expectations of counselling: A comparison between evangelical Christians and non-evangelical Christians. *Pastoral Psychology, 52*, 507–517.

Van Audenhove, C., & Vertommen, H. (2000). A negotiation approach to intake and treatment choice. *Journal of Psychotherapy Integration, 10*, 287–99.

Van Minnen, A., Arntz, A., & Keijsers, G. P. J. (2002). Prolonged exposure in patients with chronic PTSD: Predictors of treatment outcome and dropout. *Behaviour Research and Therapy, 40*, 439–57.

Vannicelli, M., & Becker, B. (1981). Prediction outcome in treatment of alcoholism: A study of staff and patients. *Journal of Studies on Alcohol, 42*, 938–50.

Walborn, F. S. (1996). *Process variables: Four common elements of counseling and psychotherapy.* Pacific Grove, CA: Brooks/Cole.

Walitzer, K. S., Dermen, K. H., & Conners, G. J. (1999). Strategies for preparing clients for treatment: A review. *Behavior Modification, 23*, 129–51.

Weinberger, J., & Eig, A. (1999). Expectancies: The ignored common factor in psychotherapy. In I. Kirsch (Ed.), *How expectancies shape experience* (pp. 357–82). Washington, DC: American Psychological Association.

Wenzel, A., Jeglic, E., Levy-Mack, H., Beck, A., & Brown, G. (2008). Treatment attitude and therapy outcome in patients with borderline personality disorder. *Journal of Cognitive Psychotherapy, 22*, 250–57.

Westra, H. A., Dozois, D. J., & Marcus, M. (2007). Expectancy, homework compliance, and initial change in cognitive-behavioral therapy for anxiety. *Journal of Consulting and Clinical Psychology, 75*, 363–73.

19 Attachment Style

Kenneth N. Levy, William D. Ellison, Lori N. Scott, *and* Samantha L. Bernecker

Attachment style or organization is a concept that derives from John Bowlby's attachment theory and refers to a person's characteristic ways of relating in intimate caregiving and receiving relationships, particularly with one's parents, children, and romantic partners. From an attachment perspective, these individuals are called attachment figures. The concept of attachment style involves one's confidence in the availability of the attachment figure so as to use that person as a *secure base* from which the individual can freely explore the world when not in distress, as well as the use of this attachment figure as a *safe haven* from which the individual seeks support, protection, and comfort in times of distress. Exploration of the world includes not only the physical world but also the examination of relationships with other people and the capacity for reflection on one's internal experience.

From its inception, John Bowlby (1982) conceptualized attachment theory as guiding clinical practice. Consistent with this idea, there has been increased interest in the application of an attachment theory perspective to psychotherapy (see Berant & Obegi, 2009; Levy & Kelly, 2009, for reviews). Bowlby not only suggested that the psychotherapist can become an attachment figure for the client, but he also thought it was important for the therapist

to become a reliable and trustworthy companion in the patient's exploration of his or her experiences. According to Bowlby (1988), secure attachment behaviors in psychotherapy include the use of the therapist as a secure base from which the individual can freely reflect on his or her experience, reflect on the possible contents of the minds of significant others, and explore the possibility of trying new experiences and engaging in novel behaviors. Additionally, Bowlby discussed patients turning to the therapist as a safe haven for comfort and support in times of distress. A number of clinical theorists have elaborated upon Bowlby's ideas about the function of attachment within the therapeutic relationship (e.g., Farber, Lippert, & Nevas, 1995; Farber & Metzger, 2009; Obegi, 2008).

The association between adult attachment and psychotherapy has been conceptualized and examined both with attachment as an outcome variable and attachment as a moderator of treatment outcome. Early findings from this body of research suggest that patient attachment status may be relevant to the course and outcome of psychotherapy and may also change as a result of psychotherapy. A recent review of this literature (Berant & Obegi, 2009) concluded that securely attached clients tend to benefit more from psychotherapy than insecurely attached clients. However, the findings across these studies have been variable, with some studies suggesting that securely attached clients may not necessarily show more improvement in treatment compared with insecurely attached clients (Cyranowski et al., 2002; Fonagy et al., 1996). In addition, the strength of the relation between attachment security and treatment outcome remains unclear.

This chapter will focus on what is known about the relation between clients' attachment styles and their success in psychotherapy. First, we will review definitions and measurement of attachment and provide clinical examples of attachment patterns in psychotherapy. Second, in order to draw an overall conclusion about the relation between attachment and treatment outcome, we will present an original meta-analysis of the research on the association between clients' pretreatment attachment style/organization and psychotherapy outcome. We conclude with limitations of the extant research and therapeutic practices based on the meta-analytic findings.

Definitions and Measures

In developing attachment theory, John Bowlby turned to a combination of scientific disciplines, including psychoanalysis, ethology, cognitive psychology, and developmental psychology, which provided an array of concepts that could explain affective bonding between infants and their caregivers. Bowlby's theory concerned both the short-term effects of this relationship for a sense of felt security and affect regulation and the long-term effects of early attachment experiences on personality development, relationship functioning, and psychopathology. He conceptualized human motivation in terms of *behavioral systems*, a concept borrowed from ethology, and noted that attachment-related behavior in infancy (e.g., clinging, crying,

smiling, monitoring caregivers, and developing a preference for a few reliable attachment figures) is part of a functional biological system that increases the likelihood of protection from dangers and predation, comfort during times of stress, and social learning. In fact, the fundamental survival gain of attachment lies not only in eliciting a protective caregiver response, but also in the experience of psychological containment of aversive affect states required for the development of a coherent and symbolizing self (Fonagy, 1999).

The caregiver's reliable and sensitive provision of loving care is believed to result in what Bowlby called a secure bond between the infant and the caregiver. This attachment security is conceptualized as deriving from repeated transactions with primary caregivers, through which the infant is believed to form internal working models (IWMs) of attachment relationships. These IWMs include expectations, beliefs, emotional appraisals, and rules for processing or excluding information. They can be partly conscious and partly unconscious and need not be completely consistent or coherent. IWMs are continually elaborated; with development, they organize personality and subsequently shape thoughts, feelings, and behaviors in future relationships. Thus, differences in caregiver behavior result in differences in infants' IWMs, which in turn are the basis for individual differences in the degree to which relationships are characterized by security.

Based on Bowlby's attachment theory, Ainsworth and her colleagues (Ainsworth et al., 1978) developed a laboratory method called the Strange Situation in order to evaluate individual differences in attachment security. The Strange Situation involves a series of short laboratory episodes staged in a playroom through which the infant, the caregiver, and a stranger interact in a comfortable setting and the behaviors of the infant are observed. Ainsworth and colleagues paid special attention to the infant's behavior upon reunion with the caregiver after a brief separation. Ainsworth (Ainsworth et al., 1978) identified three distinct patterns or styles of attachment that have since been termed *secure* (63% of the dyads tested), *anxious-resistant* or *ambivalent* (16%), and *avoidant* (21%).

In the Strange Situation, secure infants can find the brief separation from the caregiver and the entrance of the stranger to be upsetting, but they approach the caregiver upon his or her return for support, calm quickly upon the caregiver's return, are easily soothed by the caregiver's presence, and go back to exploration without fuss. In contrast, anxious-resistant infants tend to become extremely distressed upon the caregiver's departure, and they ambivalently approach the caregiver for attention and comfort upon the caregiver's return. They are clingy and dependent, often crying, but they also seem angry and resist their caregiver's efforts to soothe them. Avoidantly attached infants frequently act unfazed or unaware of the caregiver's departure and often avoid the caregiver upon reunion. Sometimes, these infants appear shut down and depressed, and at other times, indifferent and overinvested in play (although the play has a rote quality rather than a rich symbolic quality). Despite their outward appearance of calmness and unconcern, research has shown that avoidant infants are quite distressed in terms of physiological responding, similar to the anxious-resistant babies (Sroufe & Waters, 1977).

Despite the obvious resemblance of these patterns to temperament types (Kagan, 1998), and consistent with Bowlby's hypotheses, these attachment behaviors in the Strange Situation experiment are not simply a result of infant temperament (Belsky, Fish, & Isabella, 1991; see Levy, 2005; Vaughn &

Bost, 1999, for reviews). Temperament may affect the manner in which attachment security is expressed, but temperament does not affect the security of the attachment itself (Belsky & Rovine, 1987). For example, research has shown that both behaviorally inhibited and temperamentally fearful infants are frequently securely attached and engage in both secure-base and safe-haven behaviors (e.g., Gunnar et al., 1996; Stevenson-Hinde & Marshall, 1999). More importantly, Ainsworth's original work has been replicated and extended in hundreds of studies with thousands of infants and toddlers (see review by Fraley, 2002). Studies have found strong evidence for the influence of attachment patterns on later adaptation as well as remarkable continuity in attachment patterns over time.

A growing body of research (e.g., Grossmann, Grossmann, & Waters, 2005; Waters et al., 2000) examining attachment continuity suggests that patterns of attachment are both relatively stable over long periods of time *and* subject to change, influenced by a variety of factors including ongoing relationships with family members, new romantic relationships, traumatic life events, and possibly psychotherapy (Fraley, 2002; Ricks, 1985; Shaver, Hazan, & Bradshaw, 1988). These findings are consistent with Bowlby's (1982) idea that attachment theory was not limited to infant–parent relationships. He contended that the attachment system remains active throughout the life span, from the cradle to the grave.

Stemming from Bowlby's contention that the attachment system remains active throughout the life span, various investigators in the mid-1980s began to apply the tenets of attachment theory to the study of adult behavior and personality. Because these investigators worked independently, they often used slightly different terms for similar constructs or focused on different aspects of Bowlby and Ainsworth's writings.

Mary Main and her colleagues developed the Adult Attachment Interview (AAI; George, Kaplan, & Main, 1985; Main, Kaplan, & Cassidy, 1985), a 1-hour attachment history interview, noting that features in interviews with parents reliably predicted the Strange Situation behavior of their children. The interview inquires into "descriptions of early relationships and attachment and adult personality" by probing for both specific corroborative and contradictory memories of parents and the relationship with parents (Main et al., 1985, p. 98). Three major patterns of adult attachment were initially identified: *secure/autonomous*, *dismissing*, and *enmeshed/preoccupied*. More recently, two additional categories have been identified: *unresolved* and *cannot classify*. The first three categories parallel the attachment classifications originally identified in childhood of secure, avoidant, and anxious-resistant (Ainsworth, Blehar, Waters, & Wall, 1978), and the unresolved classification parallels a pattern Main later described in infants that she called *disorganized/disoriented* (Main & Solomon, 1986). A number of studies found that AAI classifications based on individuals' reports of interactions with their own parents could predict their children's Strange Situation classifications (see van IJzendoorn, 1995, for a review).

A 100-item Adult Attachment Q-set was derived from the AAI scoring system and has been applied to AAI transcripts (Kobak et al., 1993). This system identifies secure, preoccupied, and dismissing categories based on ratings of two dimensions: *security vs. anxiety* and *deactivation vs. hyperactivation*. Hyperactivating emotional strategies are typical of preoccupied individuals, whereas deactivitating strategies are typical of dismissing individuals. Scores are compared to a criterion or "ideal" prototype sort in order to identify the three organized attachment categories. One notable disadvantage of the Q-set is that there is no rating for a disorganized attachment dimension, nor can it identify the *cannot classify* category.

In contrast to Main's focus on relationships with parents, Hazan and Shaver (Hazan & Shaver, 1987, 1990; Shaver, Hazan, & Bradshaw, 1988), from a social-psychological perspective, extrapolated the childhood attachment paradigm to study attachment in adulthood by conceptualizing romantic love as an attachment process. They translated Ainsworth's secure, avoidant, and anxious-ambivalent attachment patterns into a paper-and-pencil prototype-matching measure of adult attachment styles (preferring the term anxious-ambivalent to anxious-resistant). Several other researchers have altered and extended the original Hazan and Shaver measure by breaking out the sentences in the prototypes into separate items. Factor analyses of these multi-item measures found a three-factor solution (desire for closeness, comfort with dependency, and anxiety about abandonment; Collins & Read, 1990) as well as a two-factor solution (desire for closeness and anxiety about abandonment; Simpson, 1990).

A number of empirical studies using Hazan and Shaver's (1987) measure or derivative measures of adult attachment have found that the distribution of adult attachment styles is similar to those found for infants. Approximately 55% of individuals are classified as secure, 25% as avoidant, and 20% as anxious (see reviews by Shaver & Clark, 1994, and Shaver & Hazan, 1993).

In an important development, Bartholomew (1990; Bartholomew & Horowitz, 1991) revised Hazan and Shaver's three-category classification scheme, proposing a four-category model that differentiated between two types of avoidant styles—fearful and dismissing. Bartholomew's key insight was an incongruity between Main's (Main & Goldwyn, 1998) and Hazan and Shaver's conceptions of avoidance. Main's prototype of the adult avoidant style (assessed in the context of parenting) is more defensive, denial oriented, and overtly unemotional than Hazan and Shaver's avoidant romantic attachment prototype, which seems more vulnerable, conscious of emotional pain, and "fearful." Thus, Main's avoidant style is predominantly dismissing, whereas Hazan and Shaver's avoidant style is predominantly fearful. Consistent with Bowlby's theory, Bartholomew's four categories could be arrayed in a two-dimensional space, with one dimension being *model of self* (positive vs. negative) and the other being *model of others* (positive vs. negative). For secure individuals, models of self and others are both generally positive. For preoccupied or anxious-ambivalent individuals, the model of others is positive (i.e., relationships are attractive) but the model of self is not. For dismissing individuals, the reverse is true: the somewhat defensively maintained model of self is positive, whereas the model of others is not (i.e., intimacy in relationships is regarded with caution or avoided). Fearful individuals have relatively negative models of both self and others. Bartholomew also developed an interview measure of attachment along with her self-report measure. The interview measure, initially referred to as the Bartholomew Attachment Interview (BAI) and later the Family Attachment Interview (FAI; Bartholomew & Horowitz, 1991), covers both relationships with parents (in line with the AAI) and relationships with close friends and romantic partners (in line with Shaver and Hazan's work).

In an effort to develop a more definitive measure of adult attachment and respond to the proliferation of attachment measures,

Brennan, Clark and Shaver (1998) created the Experiences in Close Relationships (ECR) scale, which was derived from a factor analysis of 60 attachment constructs representing 482 items extracted from a thorough literature search of measures used in and developed for previous attachment research. The ECR factor structure was consistent with Bartholomew and Horowitz's measure but showed stronger relations with other relevant constructs. Two short forms of the ECR have also been published (Fraley, Waller, & Brennan, 2000; Wei et al., 2007), with both highly related to the original ECR.

Measures Used in Studies in Our Meta-Analysis

Because research groups have approached the conceptualization and assessment of adult attachment patterns with emphasis on different aspects of Bowlby's writings, researchers have often identified slightly different patterns or used different names for the same dimensions. The measures described below are those used in the studies included in our meta-analysis.

Adult Attachment Prototype Rating (AAPR; Pilkonis, 1988) is a set of 88 items on which an interviewer rates an individual's attachment style. The rating system focuses on two dimensions, each with a number of facets. On the excessive dependency dimension, which corresponds to attachment anxiety, responders are compared to three prototypes: excessive dependency, borderline features, and compulsive caregiving. The prototypes on the excessive autonomy dimension, which corresponds to attachment avoidance, are defensive separation, antisocial features, and obsessive-compulsive features. A secure prototype was later added to the system (Strauss, Lobo-Drost, & Pilkonis, 1999).

Adult Attachment Scale (AAS; Collins & Read, 1990) is a self-report instrument developed by breaking Hazan and Shaver's (1987) prototype statements into 21 items. The number of items in the AAS was later shortened to 18 (Collins, 1996). Individuals rate these statements on a 5-point, Likert-type scale (1 = *not at all characteristic*; 5 = *very characteristic*). The subscales include comfort with closeness and intimacy (Close), comfort depending on others (Depend), and anxiety about abandonment (Anxiety). Responders can be categorized as follows: those with high Close and Depend scores and low Anxiety scores are Secure, those with high Anxiety scores and moderate Close and Depend scores are Anxious, and those with low scores on all three subscales are Avoidant. There is strong evidence throughout the literature for the scale's reliability and validity (Ravitz, Maunder, Hunter, Sthankiya, & Lancee, 2010).

Relationship Questionnaire (RQ; Bartholomew & Horowitz, 1991) is a self-report questionnaire based on Bartholomew's (1990) four-category model of attachment. The RQ consists of four paragraphs describing each of the attachment prototypes—secure, fearful, preoccupied, and dismissing. Participants rate how well each corresponds to their romantic relationship pattern, where 1 = *not at all like me* and 7 = *very much like me*. Participants then select the one paragraph that best describes them.

Relationship Style Questionnaire (RSQ; Bartholomew & Horowitz, 1991) contains 30 short statements drawn from three other attachment measures. Participants rate each question on a 5-point Likert scale to indicate the extent to which each statement best describes their characteristic style in close relationships. Five statements contribute to the secure and dismissing attachment patterns and four statements contribute to the fearful and preoccupied attachment patterns. Scores for each attachment pattern are calculated by taking the mean of the four or five items representing each attachment prototype. Two underlying dimensions can be derived either by conducting a factor analysis of the items or by using the scores from the four prototype items to create linear combinations representing the self- and other-model attachment dimensions.

Family Attachment Interview (FAI; Bartholomew & Horowitz, 1991) is a semistructured interview designed to assess adult attachment styles based on information about parents. The probes used in the interview are remarkably similar to those used in the Adult Attachment Interview, and as such, the FAI scoring system can be used with information generated from the AAI. The FAI scoring is similar to the AAI in that attachment ratings are based on content of reports as well as reporting style (e.g., defensive strategies that emerge during the interview, coherency of the report). However, the FAI codes people on four attachment styles (secure, fearful, preoccupied, and dismissing) rather than categorizing people into the AAI categories. The interviews are coded for each attachment pattern on a 9-point scale (1 = *no evidence of characteristics of the prototype*; 9 = *near perfect fit with the prototype*).

Attachment Style Questionnaire (ASQ; Feeney, Noller, & Hanrahan, 1994) is a 40-item self-report questionnaire rated on a 6-point, Likert-type scale. It includes subscales to measure Self-Confidence, Discomfort with Closeness, Need for Approval, Preoccupation, and Relationships as Secondary. The instrument has adequate reliability and has been found to converge with other attachment measures and to have predictive validity (Ravitz et al., 2010).

Reciprocal Attachment Questionnaire (RAQ; West & Sheldon-Keller, 1994) is a 43-item, 5-point, Likert-type self-report questionnaire designed to assess nine dimensions of adult attachment patterns with significant others. Four pattern subscales—Compulsive

Self-Reliance, Compulsive Care-Giving, Compulsive Care-Seeking, and Angry Withdrawal—assess dysfunctional patterns of adult attachment. There are also five attachment dimension subscales: Separation Protest, Feared Loss, Proximity Seeking, and Use and Perceived Availability of the attachment figure. The validity and reliability of the RAQ have been established in both clinical and nonclinical adult populations (West & Sheldon-Keller, 1994).

Avoidant Attachment Questionnaire (AAQ; West & Sheldon-Keller, 1994) is a 22-item, 5-point, Likert self-report questionnaire developed alongside the RAQ as an alternative for individuals who deny having a primary attachment figure. The questionnaire assesses four subscales: Maintains Distance in Relationships, High Priority on Self-Sufficiency, Attachment Relationship is a Threat to Security, and Desire for Close Affectional Bonds. There is a relative dearth of evidence on its reliability and validity, probably due to the infrequency of its use (Ravitz et al., 2010).

Experiences in Close Relationships (ECR; Brennan et al., 1998) is a 36-item, self-report questionnaire that assesses attachment security in close relationships by tapping two basic dimensions of attachment organization: anxiety and avoidance. These two dimensions underlie most measures of adult attachment style (Brennan et al., 1998) and parallel those identified by Ainsworth et al. (1978) as underlying patterns of behavior in the Strange Situation. Participants rate the extent to which each item is descriptive of their feelings in close relationships on a 7-point scale (1 = *not at all* to 7 = *very much*). Eighteen items assess attachment anxiety and 18 assess attachment avoidance. The reliability and validity of the scales have been demonstrated (Brennan et al., 1998).

Clinical Examples

In general, patients with secure attachment styles have been found to be more collaborative, receptive, and better able to utilize treatment. In contrast, those with dismissive styles have been found to be less engaged in treatment. Those with preoccupied states of mind with regard to attachment have been found to present as more needy in therapy but not necessarily compliant with treatment (e.g., Dozier, 1990; Riggs, Jacobovitz, & Hazen, 2002).

Secure Attachment

Given that secure individuals are more open to exploring their surroundings and relationships, it is not surprising that evidence suggests that persons with autonomous states of mind tend to be open, engaged, collaborative, compliant, committed, and proactive in treatment (Dozier, 1990; Korfmacher, Adam, Ogawa, & Egeland., 1997; Riggs et al., 2002). Although these individuals may enter treatment distressed, they tend to be trusting of therapists. Most importantly, they tend to be able to integrate and utilize their therapists' comments. Additionally, anecdotal evidence suggests that they can show more gratitude toward the therapist for providing treatment.

Preoccupied Attachment

Because preoccupied individuals can be so interpersonally engaged, they often initially appear to be easier to treat. Preoccupied individuals are often so distressed and interpersonally oriented that they are eager to discuss their worries and relationship difficulties as well as their own role in these problems (Dozier, 1990). Because the chaotic and contradictory representations of self and others of individuals classified as preoccupied are so rich, they may be more readily and vividly mentalized or represented by the therapist. However, both clinical and empirical evidence suggests that these individuals may be difficult to treat. In a number of papers, Slade (1999, 2004) has written about the unique challenges inherent to working clinically with preoccupied individuals. She warns that "Progress is… hard won" (Slade, 1999, p. 588) and that therapists must be prepared for the "slow creation of structures for the modulation of affect" (Slade, 1999, p. 586). She contends that change occurs over a long period of time from the therapist's long-term emotional availability and tolerance for chaos.

Clients with preoccupied attachment organization tend to present themselves as needy but are not more compliant with treatment plans than dismissing individuals (Dozier, 1990). Those classified as preoccupied, as compared with those classified as dismissive, tend to show less improvement (Fonagy et al., 1996). It is hypothesized that the preoccupied patients are more difficult to treat because their representational systems are intricately linked with emotions that are well-developed and elaborated by entrenched preoccupation with difficult events in their lives. This is also expressed in terms of their certainty about mental states and motivations for others' behaviors.

In our own work, we have found a number of difficult aspects related to working with preoccupied individuals that can be first identified in the narratives of AAIs. These include: (1) unmerited certainty about mental states; (2) rapid vacillations or oscillations between contradictory mental states; (3) current anger and confusion about time and people; (4) self-blame and derogations. Each of these issues, alone or in combination, may leave the therapist feeling confused and overwhelmed.

The following vignette contains aspects of all four of these issues. The patient was an unmarried 35-year-old woman of Southeast Asian descent. Despite being very attractive and highly intelligent, with an Ivy League education, she found herself unable to date and maintain employment. This was mainly because, though she was emotionally needy, she could not get along with others due to frequent angry outbursts. Even at 35, she was highly dependent on her parents, particularly for financial support, but also for emotional support. Her parents were at their wits' end with her and felt she was wasting her life away. Although they were traditional and perceived psychotherapy as a corrupt endeavour practiced by charlatans, they were willing to pay for psychotherapy.

The patient's relationship with her parents was anchored in two equally uncomfortable extremes that led her to vacillate between wanting to live at home and submit to their will, and wanting to break away from their control and become independent and self-reliant. At times, she would plead with the therapist in a loud pressured voice, "Dr. X, Dr. X, please, please tell me what to do! Should I try to work it out with my parents or should I just forget about them?" The patient rapidly flipped between desperately wanting to be close to her parents and feeling as if she could not live without them to wanting to have nothing to do with them. In each of these stances she would be adamant and inflexible about her position and then flip to the other. She would flip so quickly that when she was in one mental state she did not appear to recall the other mental state. However, when she would pose this question, both mental states were represented for a brief time.

In these moments the psychotherapist felt extremely pressured by the patient to provide her with an answer to her quandary. Any hesitation on the therapist's part was interpreted as withholding valuable information from the patient and was met with quick anger. The therapist felt backed into a corner with no good solution.

He did not feel he could simply give the patient advice. Besides, the solution was neither to submit to the parents nor to cut them off, but rather, to figure out how to have a mutually satisfying relationship with them. He also felt pressured because he realized that these moments where the patient had both sides of a conflict represented were rare and fleeting, and he wanted to make use of them, and yet, he was feeling pressured to answer a question that had no answer and would be both unsatisfying and infuriating to the patient.

Using his countertransference of being backed into a corner, the therapist commented to the patient that she must feel backed into a corner with no good option available. He continued by pointing out that if he told her to reconcile with her parents, he imagined that she might interpret this as if he felt she was wrong, they were right, and she should submit to their will and allow herself to be controlled by them. On the other hand, if he told her to resist their will, and leave them, she would feel as if the therapy was useless, and she would feel terribly abandoned by her parents and more dependent on the therapist. With both affective states acknowledged, validated in the patient, and tolerated by the therapist, the patient was able to refrain from her rapid oscillations long enough to have a productive discussion and develop a more integrated perspective on her situation vis-à-vis both her own and her parents' behaviors.

Dismissing Attachment
Dismissing patients are often resistant to treatment, have difficulty asking for help, and retreat from help when it is offered (Dozier, 1990). Indeed, dismissive patients often evoke countertransference feelings of being excluded from the patients' lives (Diamond et al., 1999, 2003). In our pilot study, a patient classified as dismissive came

into session one morning and announced, to her therapist's surprise, that she was getting married that afternoon. Although he had known of her engagement, it had been many months since she had brought up any aspect of her upcoming marriage. Additionally, dismissing individuals often become more distressed and confused when confronted with emotional issues in therapy (Dozier, Lomax, Tyrell, & Lee, 2001). Another dismissive patient, when reflecting on her experience in therapy, stated:

> He (the therapist) would start digging into things and find out why I was angry, and then I would realize something really made me mad, but I didn't want to be mad. With my parents, for example, I didn't want to be angry at them.

Finally, therapists working with dismissive patients may be pulled into enactments, where they find themselves in a situation analogous to a "chase and dodge" sequence with mothers and infants (Beebe & Lachmann, 1988), which leaves the patient feeling intruded upon only to withdraw further. Conversely, those with dismissing attachment may effectively curtail the therapist's capacity to engage with, visualize, or evoke the individual's representational world, or identify with the patient.

"Unresolved for Trauma or Loss" Attachment
An individual can be classified as unresolved on the Adult Attachment Interview for either loss or trauma experiences. This classification is unique in that it is given to an individual in addition to one of the organized attachment patterns (i.e., secure, preoccupied, or dismissing) and can be either primary or secondary, depending on a number of factors. Clinical writers have suggested that it can be very difficult to treat those patients who are unresolved for trauma or loss on the AAI.

In two studies it was found that between 32% and 60% of patients with borderline personality disorder (BPD) were classified as unresolved (Diamond et al., 2003; Levy et al., 2006). In a randomized clinical trial (Levy et al., 2006), we found a nonsignificant decrease from pretreatment to posttreatment in the number of patients classified as unresolved (32% vs. 22%). Unpublished data from this trial (Levy, Clarkin, & Kernberg, 2007) suggest that those BPD patients who were unresolved were more likely to drop out of treatment. However, in a small sample of women with childhood sexual and physical abuse-related posttraumatic stress disorder (PTSD), 62% of unresolved patients lost their unresolved status following treatment (Stovall-McClough & Cloitre, 2003).

Meta-Analytic Review

To characterize the relation between adult attachment and psychotherapy outcome, we conducted three separate meta-analyses. We hypothesized that attachment anxiety would be negatively related to outcome, that attachment avoidance would be negatively related to outcome, and that attachment security would be positively related to outcome. Because research on attachment is converging on the notion that the two dimensions of avoidance and attachment underlie adult attachment, we decided to focus on them instead of the individual attachment categories, which evidence more variability among assessment methods. In addition, we examined attachment security (which can be conceptualized as a blend of avoidance and anxiety dimensions) because it has often been the focus of psychotherapy research.

Inclusion Criteria and Search Strategy

Eligible studies were published reports of psychotherapy outcome in samples of treatment-seeking individuals. These studies were found first through articles reviewing the literature (e.g., Berant & Obegi, 2009) and second through a series of PsycINFO searches. These searches, conducted in December 2009, used the intersections of the terms *attachment, interpersonal style, relation* style*, or the name of an attachment measure with either *therap* outcome, psychotherap* outcome*, or *outcome*. The search initially returned 10,155 results. After foreign-language studies (531), dissertations (8), and studies that did not include treatment trials (9,448) were excluded, 168 articles remained. Many of these were irrelevant to the topic at hand; only studies that measured attachment and treatment outcome were included.

In order to be included in the meta-analyses, studies had to report statistics showing the relation between patients' pretreatment attachment security, anxiety, and/or avoidance to outcome posttreatment. In order to avoid confounding attachment with therapeutic alliance, reports were not included if the measure of attachment concerned client attachment to therapist. For many identified studies, statistics describing the relation between attachment and outcome were not directly available from the published report, in which cases the authors of the study were contacted via e-mail and asked to provide these statistics. The corresponding authors of 15 primary studies were contacted, of which 10 responded with suitable statistics. Our final pool of studies analyzed consisted of 14 studies, which contained 19 separate therapy samples with a combined N of 1,467. Table 19.1 lists the studies included in the meta-analysis along with relevant characteristics of their designs and samples.

Independence of ES Estimates

Effect sizes were considered independent if they described results from separate samples. In one case, relevant information from

Table 19.1 Summary of Studies Included in Meta-Analysis of Patient Attachment and Outcome

Study	Patients			Diagnosis	Attachment		Therapy		Outcome	
	N	% Female	Age (M)		Measure	Rater	Orientation	Duration (weeks)	Measure	Rater
Cyranowski et al. (2002)	162	100	37.6	MDD	RQ	C	D	14	HRSD	NT
Johnson & Talitman (1997)	34	0	42	Marital	AQ	C	D	12	DASsatis	C
Lawson & Brossart (2009)	49	0	31.73	IPV	AAS	C	I	17	Violence	C
									psyabuse	C
Levy et al. (2006)	22	95.5	32.27	BPD	ECR	C	D	52	GAF	NT
									BDI	C
									SCL-90-R	C
	15	93.3	32.53	BPD	ECR	C	CB	52	GAF	NT
									BDI	C
									SCL-90-R	C
	23	95.65	28.48	BPD	ECR	C	D	52	GAF	NT
									BDI	C
									SCL-90-R	C

(Continued)

Table 19.1 Continued

Study	Patients			Diagnosis	Attachment		Therapy		Outcome	
	N	% Female	Age (M)		Measure	Rater	Orientation	Duration (weeks)	Measure	Rater
Marmarosh et al. (2009)	31	71	24.6	Unspecified	ECR-S	C	E	15	SCL-90-R	C
McBride et al. (2006)	27	74.1	40.1	MDD	RSQ	C	D	17	BDI	C
									HAM-D	NT
	28	72.4	41	MDD	RSQ	C	CB	17	BDI	C
									HAM-D	NT
Meyer et al. (2001)	104	57	34.5	PDNOS	AAPR	T	E	14	GAF	NT
									HRSD	NT
									HAMA	NT
									SCL-90-R	C
Muller & Rosenkranz (2009)	101	64	42.8	PTSD	RSQ and RQ (combined)	C	D	8	SCL-90-R	C
Reis & Grenyer (2004)	58	58.6	45.98	MDD	RQ	C	D	16	TSC-40	C
									HRSD	NT

Study	N	% female	Age	Diagnosis	Attachment measure	Rater	Orientation	Sessions	Outcome measure	Rater
Saatsi et al. (2007)	82	72.7	34.92	MDD	Vignettes	C	CB	14	BDI	C
Stalker et al. (2005)	114	100	40.6	PTSD	RAQ	C	D	6	SCL-90-R	C
									MPSS-SR	C
	18	100	40.6	PTSD	AAQ	C	D	6	SCL-90-R	C
									MPSS-SR	C
Strauss et al. (2006)	476	70	34.4	PD	AAPR	NT	D	10	SCL-90-R	C
									IIP	C
Tasca et al. (2006)	33	100	42.75	BED	ASQ	C	CB	16	EDEbinge	NT
	33	100	42.75	BED	ASQ	C	D	16	EDEbinge	NT
Travis et al. (2001)	59	59	41	Unspecified	BARS	NT	D	21	SCL-90-R	C

Note: Raters: C = client, NT = nontreater, T = therapist

Orientations: CB = cognitive-behavioral, D = dynamic, E = eclectic, I = integrative

Diagnoses: BED = binge eating disorder, BPD = borderline personality disorder, IPV = intimate partner violence, MDD = major depressive disorder, PD = personality disorder, PDNOS = personality disorder not otherwise specified, PTSD = post-traumatic stress disorder

Attachment measures: AAPR = Adult Attachment Prototype Rating, AAI = Adult Attachment Interview, AAS = Adult Attachment Scale, AAQ = Avoidant Attachment Scale, AAQ = Adult Attachment Questionnaire, AQ = Attachment Questionnaire, ASQ = Attachment Style Questionnaire, BARS = Bartholomew Attachment Rating Scale, ECR/ECR-R = Experiences in Close Relationships scale/Experiences in Close Relationships–Revised, RAQ = Reciprocal Attachment Questionnaire, RSQ = Relationship Scales Questionnaire, RQ = Relationship Questionnaire

Outcome measures: BDI = Beck Depression Inventory, DASsatis = satisfaction subscale of the Dyadic Adjustment Scale, EDEbinge = Eating Disorder Examination assessment of days binged, GAF = Global Assessment of Functioning, HAMA = Hamilton Rating Scale for Anxiety, HAM-D = Six-Item Hamilton Depression Rating Scale, HRSD = Hamilton Rating Scale for Depression, IIP = Inventory of Interpersonal Problems, MPSS-SR = Modified PTSD Symptom Scale–Self-Report, psyabuse = psychological abuse subscale of the Conflict Tactics Scale, SCL-90-R = Symptom Checklist–90–Revised, TSC-40 = Trauma Symptom Checklist–40, violence = subscale of the Conflict Tactics Scale a single sample was available from multiple research reports (Kirchmann et al., 2009; Strauss et al., 2006), so only one statistic was drawn from these reports. In other cases, separate statistics from multiple samples (for example, different treatment groups) were presented in the same publication (Levy et al., 2006; McBride, Atkinson, Quilty, & Bagby, 2006; Stalker, Gebotys, & Harper, 2005; Tasca et al., 2006). For these studies, multiple effect size estimates were coded and treated as independent. Several studies provided statistics relating attachment to more than one outcome measure. These estimates were not considered independent because they were derived from the same sample and are thus likely to display substantial intercorrelation. Because we had no a priori reason to consider any one of these estimates representative of the study's "true" effect size, multiple effect size estimates from the same study were transformed to Z-scores (Hedges & Olkin, 1985), averaged together, and then back-transformed and treated as a single effect size.

Study Coding

Coding of the 14 studies was conducted by an advanced graduate student. Several patient characteristics were coded, including the proportion of the sample that was female, mean age of the sample, proportion of the sample that was White or Caucasian, and whether the primary diagnosis of the sample was an Axis I disorder (e.g., major depressive disorder) or an Axis II disorder (e.g., borderline personality disorder). The treatment characteristics coded included theoretical orientation (cognitive-behavioral or psychodynamic therapies) and length of treatment in weeks. Because the 19 samples included in the current study were offered 16 different types of psychotherapy, specific type of treatment was not formally coded. The operationalization of attachment was

coded for its degree of approximation to attachment avoidance and attachment anxiety, and attachment measures were coded for rater (client-rated or observer-rated attachment). Finally, the following therapist variables were coded: mean years of experience, proportion of therapists in the study that was female, and student status.

Effect Size Estimates

The effect size statistic used for the current meta-analysis was the Pearson product–moment correlation coefficient (r) describing the relation between attachment variables and posttreatment outcome measures. In some cases, statistics relating attachment to outcome took other forms, such as means and standard deviations for different attachment groups on outcome measures, t-tests of these values, or tables showing categories of outcome (e.g., how many individuals had achieved a certain symptom score) by attachment group. In these cases, statistics were transformed to r-values (using formulas presented in Lipsey & Wilson, 2001). Although it would be optimal to control for pretreatment correlations between attachment and symptom scales, this was not feasible because of inconsistent reporting among studies. Thus, all correlations used in the current analyses were zero-order correlations between pretreatment attachment and posttreatment outcome.

The 14 primary studies differed in a number of ways that could be expected to impart a systematic bias onto effect size estimates. Thus, we made two adjustments to the statistics reported in the published studies. Both of these adjustments pertain to the operationalization of attachment and outcome. First, each study was adjusted to account for differences in operationalization of attachment. Measures of attachment vary widely, and the 14 studies sampled in the current analysis used 11 separate measures. The current analysis focuses on attachment security and the underlying attachment dimensions of avoidance and anxiety, and when measures provide an imperfect assessment of these constructs, the resulting effect size estimate is attenuated (Schmidt, Le, & Oh, 2009). Therefore, each study was corrected to account for how closely its attachment measure approximated these dimensions of attachment. In order to do this, each observed effect size was divided by the correlation of the attachment measure used in the study with the ECR or ECR-R, which probably measures attachment anxiety and attachment avoidance with the most fidelity. These correlation values were culled from the available literature. Figure 19.1

shows the correlations between attachment measures used in the primary studies with attachment anxiety and avoidance from the ECR.

A second correction was applied to account for artificial dichotomization of attachment dimensions or dimensional outcome constructs, which also attenuates effect size estimates (Schmidt et al., 2009), especially if the dichotomy produces an uneven split between groups (Lipsey & Wilson, 2001). For example, if outcome is recovery based on a dimensional symptom score below a certain cutoff, effect size estimates based on the proportion of individuals in recovered, and nonrecovered groups are distorted when compared with estimates from dimensionally measured variables.

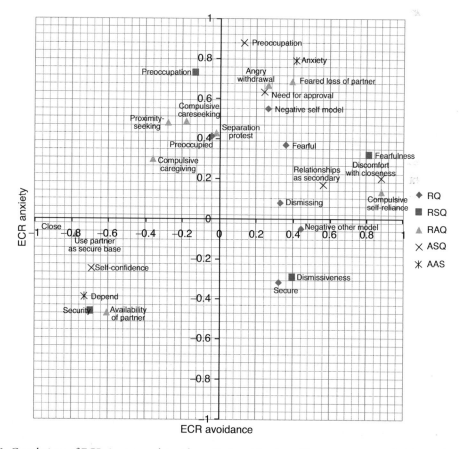

Fig. 19.1 Correlations of ECR Anxiety and Avoidance Scales with other self-report measures of adult attachment.
Note: AAS = Adult Attachment Scale (Collins & Read, 1990), ASQ = Attachment Style Questionnaire (Feeney et al., 1994), ECR = Experiences in Close Relationships scale (Brennan, Clark, & Shaver, 1998), RAQ = Reciprocal Attachment Questionnaire (West & Sheldon-Keller, 1994), RSQ = Relationship Scale Questionnaire (Griffin & Bartholomew, 1994)

Hunter and Schmidt's (1990) correction to these values was thus applied. To ensure that more valid estimates contributed more to the overall mean than estimates for which these two artifact corrections were large, each effect size estimate was weighted not only by sample size but was also assigned a weight based on the size of the two artifact corrections (Hunter & Schmidt, 2004; Schmidt et al., 2009).

The influence of outliers is also a concern because the present study involved a small but heterogeneous sample of primary studies. Outliers were detected by means of the sample-adjusted meta-analytic deviancy (SAMD; Huffcutt & Arthur, 1995) statistic, which takes into account the fact that smaller samples are more likely to produce deviant estimates of the population effect due to simple sampling error. The SAMD values associated with each of the primary studies were visually inspected in a scree plot to determine whether any values were substantially more deviant than would be expected.

Analyses

The mean effect size was computed as a weighted average of each independent sample's correlation coefficient. The weights were composed of two coefficients: the sample size, so that each study's contribution to the overall mean would be inversely proportional to sampling error, and a multiplier based on the artifact corrections made to each effect size, so that studies that more nearly approximated the constructs of interest were weighted more heavily (Hunter & Schmidt, 2004; Schmidt et al., 2009). Random-effects modeling was used for each analysis, given the multiple sources of variability between studies and the resultant implausibility of fixed-effects models (for which one fixed population of studies is assumed).

Several likely predictors of the relationship between attachment and outcome were tested as moderators of this effect. These variables (summarized under "Study Coding") were designated a priori and related to variance at several different levels, including sample variables, treatment descriptors, operationalization of attachment, and therapist variables. Moderation analyses were conducted via weighted least squares regression in which each effect size estimate was assigned a weight based on inverse variance (Lipsey & Wilson, 2001). Fisher's Z_r transformation (Hedges & Olkin, 1985) was used for each effect size estimate before regression analyses were conducted because of the problematic standard error formulation associated with correlation coefficients (Lipsey & Wilson, 2001). Effect size estimates used in the regression analyses were the attenuated (uncorrected) values; in order to control for the effects of measure unreliability and artificial dichotomization, the multiplier values representing these artifacts were used as covariates in each regression analysis (Borenstein, Hedges, Higgins, & Rothstein, 2009). Regression used random-effects modeling estimated via iterative maximum likelihood estimation (Wilson, 2005).

Results

The mean weighted r between attachment anxiety and psychotherapy outcome was −.224 (Cohen's weighted $d = -0.460$). Outcomes were coded so that higher numbers reflected better outcome. Thus, higher attachment anxiety predicted worse outcome after therapy. The 80% credibility interval around this estimate ranged from −.158 to −.291 ($d = -0.320$ to -0.608). Because a random-effects model was used, this range refers not to the distribution of estimates of a single parameter (r values), but to multiple population parameter (that is, rho) values. Thus, 80% of the parameter values describing the relation between attachment and anxiety lie in this interval.

The mean weighted r between attachment avoidance and treatment outcome was $-.014$ ($d = -0.028$), with an 80% credibility interval of $-.165$ to $.136$ ($d = -0.335$ to 0.275). This suggests that attachment avoidance had a negligible overall effect on outcomes in psychotherapy.

The mean weighted r between attachment security and outcome was $.182$ ($d = 0.370$), with an 80% credibility interval of $.042$ to $.321$ ($d = 0.084$ to 0.678). Thus, higher attachment security predicted more favorable outcomes in psychotherapy.

SAMD values were examined to check for the presence of outliers among the effect size estimates. No outliers could be identified among the primary studies' estimates of the relation between outcome and attachment anxiety, avoidance, or security. Therefore, all values were retained for further analyses.

Moderators and Mediators

For all three attachment dimensions, homogeneity of effect size estimates was tested by means of Hunter and Schmidt's (2004) 75% criterion, which estimates the amount of variance in effect sizes that is due to artifacts (such as imperfect validity or reliability of the measures used). If this value is more than 75% of the total variance, the authors suggest that a search for measureable moderators of the effect size may be unproductive because the remaining variance in effect sizes is comparatively small. This method was used because homogeneity tests based on a null hypothesis of homogeneity (such as the Q statistic) would likely have little power given the small sample of studies in the current meta-analyses. In the current study, a substantial portion of the variance in the corrected effect size estimates was indeed artifactual. The artifacts for which we corrected in the three meta-analyses accounted for 89%, 75%, and 82% of the variance in

attachment–outcome effect sizes for anxiety, avoidance, and security, respectively. Thus, the effect sizes that were combined in each of our meta-analyses could be considered fairly homogeneous after artifactual sources of variance are accounted for. Nevertheless, an exploratory analysis of potential moderators was conducted.

Unfortunately, for a number of the coded variables, the effects of moderator variables could not be estimated because data about them were not available from the primary studies, or because there was not enough variance among the primary studies on the moderator variable. For two examples, the moderating influence of sample ethnicity and therapist level of experience could not be estimated due to insufficient data or variability.

No moderators were found to influence the size of the relation between either attachment avoidance or attachment anxiety and treatment outcome. However, two sample-level moderators did significantly influence the effect of attachment security on outcome. Both the proportion of females ($Z = 2.78$, $p < .01$) and the mean age ($Z = 2.02$, $p < .05$) of the patients exerted an effect, such that the more female and older the sample, the smaller the observed relation between security and outcome. We suspect that the effect of gender can be explained by one study (Cyranowski et al., 2002), which included only women and found the weakest relation between security and outcome. In fact, running the analysis without including this study completely erased the significant gender effect, with a regression coefficient of nearly zero. Nonetheless, there are gender differences in attachment (i.e., studies suggest that more men than women demonstrate insecure and dismissing attachment styles; Bartholomew & Horowitz, 1991; Levy, Blatt, & Shaver, 1998; Levy & Kelly, 2010) that could potentially influence psychotherapy outcome, and this possibility might be further explored in future research.

Additionally, client age emerged as a significant moderator, such that the positive relation between attachment security and outcome was attenuated in samples that were older on average. This finding may be explained by cross-sectional research showing that older adults are more likely to be securely attached, and less likely to be fearfully attached, than younger adults (Diehl, Elnick, Bourbeau, & Labouvie-Vief, 1998; Mickelson, Kessler, & Shaver, 1997). If this is a developmental, rather than cohort-based, effect, this difference suggests that some preoccupied individuals become secure (perhaps by finding or creating an intimate relationship with a trustworthy other) as they age. Thus, it may be that there is a weaker relation between attachment and therapy outcome among older adults because there is less variability in their characteristic attachment styles.

Theoretical orientation was not a significant moderator of the effect sizes for anxiety or avoidance in our meta-analyses. However, our null findings for therapeutic orientation as a moderator may have been due to heterogeneity in the treatments that were grouped together into the same category. For example, in order to have enough studies of the same therapeutic orientation to combine in a meta-analysis, it was necessary to combine interpersonal with psychodynamic treatments, individual with group therapies, long-term and short-term treatments, and inpatient with outpatient treatments, although these are really quite different experiences of psychotherapy.

Nevertheless, the few studies that have examined the interaction between client attachment and treatment type in the prediction of outcome do suggest that clients respond differentially to different treatments based on their attachment style

(Bakermans-Kranenburg, Juffer, & van IJzendoorn, 1998; McBride et al., 2006; Tasca et al., 2006). There is preliminary evidence that dismissive/avoidant clients may benefit more from treatments that focus on cognitions and behaviors rather than emotionality and relationships, at least in short-term psychotherapy. For instance, one study examined two versions of a short-term treatment for promoting maternal sensitivity and found that insecure preoccupied mothers benefited more from an intervention that included both video feedback and discussion of childhood attachment experiences, whereas dismissive mothers benefited more from video feedback without such discussions (Bakermans-Kranenburg et al., 1998). In addition, a study examining short-term treatments for depression demonstrated that attachment avoidance was associated with more improvement with short-term cognitive-behavioral therapy (CBT) and less improvement with short-term interpersonal psychotherapy (IPT; McBride et al., 2006). Such findings parallel the early evidence that interpersonal and insight-oriented therapies tend to be slightly more effective among patients with internalizing coping styles, whereas symptom-focused and skill-building therapies tend to be more effective among externalizing patients (Beutler, Harwood, Kimpara, Verdirame, & Blau, this volume, Chapter 17).

Limitations of the Research

There are still relatively few empirical studies that have examined how client attachment influences psychotherapy outcome. In addition, there are few investigations regarding matching patients to treatments or therapists based on attachment patterns; so few, in fact, that we could not submit them to a meta-analysis.

Furthermore, in order to produce findings that are comparable to one another and that can be combined to yield meaningful and clinically relevant conclusions, it is important for investigators to use measures of attachment that are well validated and commonly used in the literature. Some studies have used attachment measures that do not correlate well with other measures of attachment, and that do not appear to converge with underlying dimensions of adult attachment (anxiety and avoidance).

Another limitation of our meta-analyses is that we could not control for the correlations between attachment and pretreatment functioning. The interpretation of posttreatment symptoms as outcome is potentially problematic because it does not consider baseline levels or actual change in symptoms as a function of treatment. Hence, any association between attachment and posttreatment functioning may, to some degree, reflect the relation between attachment and psychopathology. Although a number of studies that did control for the influence of pretreatment functioning on the association between attachment security and outcome have reported findings that are consistent with ours (e.g., Meyer, Pilkonis, Proietti, Heape, & Egan, 2001; Saatsi, Hardy, & Cahill, 2007; Strauss et al., 2006), the results of the current analyses should be interpreted with caution in that respect.

Therapeutic Practices

The estimated effect sizes for the association of both attachment security ($r = .18$) and attachment anxiety ($r = -.22$) with treatment outcomes are in the small-to-moderate range, but just below those found for the association of therapeutic alliance with outcome reported in this volume. Thus, in these 14 studies, clients' attachment style appears to contribute almost as much variance to psychotherapy outcome as does the alliance, a well-established and potent predictor of therapeutic change.

However, clients' attachment security also tends to be positively associated with therapeutic alliance, with an average effect size of $r = .17$ according to a recent meta-analysis (Diener, Hilsenroth, & Weinberger, 2009). Perhaps the capacity to develop a positive therapeutic alliance is enhanced by a client's level of attachment security. Conversely, the formation of a positive therapeutic alliance may serve as one mechanism by which a client's level of attachment security leads to better psychotherapy outcomes. Finally, an intriguing possibility is that both attachment security and therapeutic alliance predict unique aspects of psychotherapy outcome.

We derive several practice implications of the empirical research on attachment style and our meta-analysis that can guide psychotherapists:

• Assess the patient's attachment style. Attachment style or organization can influence the psychotherapy process, the responses of both patients and therapists, the quality of the therapeutic alliance, and the ultimate outcome of treatment. Thus, therapists should be attuned to indicators of a patient's attachment style. Formal interviewing or use of reliable self-report measures can be useful as part of the assessment process.

• Understanding a patient's attachment organization will provide important clues as to how the patient is likely to respond in treatment and to the therapist. Expect longer and more difficult treatment with anxiously attached patients but quicker and more positive outcomes with securely attached patients.

• Knowledge of the patient's attachment style can help the therapist anticipate how the patient may respond to the therapist's interventions and guide the therapist in calibrating to the patient's interpersonal style. That is, if the patient is dismissing in his or her attachment, the therapist may need to be more engaged. In contrast, if the patient is preoccupied in his or her attachment, the therapist should consider a stance designed to help the patient contain his or her emotional experience. This may include explicit articulations of the treatment frame, the provision of more structure to compensate for the patient's tendency to feel muddled, and efforts to avoid collusion with the patient who may pull the therapist to engage in more emotional/experiential techniques that only contribute to the patient feeling overwhelmed.

• At the same time, psychotherapists should not go too far in contrasting patients' attachment styles. Practice and research suggest that therapists titrate their interpersonal styles so as not to overwhelm dismissing patients or to appear disengaged, aloof, or uninterested to preoccupied patients.

• There is preliminary evidence that dismissing individuals do respond to cognitive or interpretive treatments slightly better than interpersonally focused treatments, at least in the context of short-term treatments. With regard to patients who score high on both the attachment anxiety and avoidance dimensions (fearful avoidant clients), it is especially important to attend to the structure of their internal working models, as findings suggest that there is much variation in this group's functioning in therapy and outcome.

• Attachment style can be modified during treatment, even in brief treatments and for patients with severe attachment difficulties, such as those suffering from borderline personality disorder. Therefore, change in attachment can be conceptualized as a proximal outcome, not just a predictive patient characteristic, and could be considered a goal of treatment.

Therapists might consider intervening with their patients in an effort to change attachment style. Early findings suggest that the focus on the relation between the therapist and patient and/or the use of interpretations may be the mechanisms by which change in attachment organization is achieved, at least for severely disturbed personality-disordered patients (Høglend et al., 2009; Levy et al., 2006). However, the early research also demonstrates that a range of treatments may be useful for achieving changes in attachment representations in less disturbed patients with neurotic-level or Axis I disorders.

References

References marked with an asterisk indicate studies included in the meta-analysis.

Ainsworth, M. S., Blehar, M. C., Waters, E., & Wall, S. (1978). *Patterns of attachment: A psychological study of the strange situation.* Oxford, UK: Lawrence Erlbaum.

Bakermans-Kranenburg, M. J., Juffer, F., & van Ijzendoorn, M. H. (1998). Interventions with video feedback and attachment discussions: Does type of maternal insecurity make a difference? *Infant Mental Health Journal, 19*(2), 202–219.

Bartholomew, K. (1990). Avoidance of intimacy: An attachment perspective. *Journal of Social and Personal Relationships, 7*(2), 147–78.

Bartholomew, K., & Horowitz, L. M. (1991). Attachment styles among young adults: A test of a four-category model. *Journal of Personality and Social Psychology, 61*(2), 226–44.

Beebe, B., & Lachmann, F. M. (1988). The contribution of mother-infant mutual influence to the origins of self- and object representations. *Psychoanalytic Psychology, 5*(4), 305–37.

Belsky, J., Fish, M., & Isabella, R. A. (1991). Continuity and discontinuity in infant negative and positive emotionality: Family antecedents and attachment consequences. Developmental Psychology, 27(3), 421–31.

Belsky, J., & Rovine, M. (1987). Temperament and attachment security in the strange situation: An empirical rapprochement. *Child Development, 58*(3), 787–95.

Berant, E., & Obegi, J. H. (2009). Attachment-informed psychotherapy research with adults.

In J. H. Obegi & E. Berant (Eds.), *Attachment theory and research in clinical work with adults* (pp. 461–69). New York: Guilford Press.

Bernier, A., & Dozier, M. (2002). The client-counselor match and the corrective emotional experience: Evidence from interpersonal and attachment research. *Psychotherapy: Theory, Research, Practice, Training, 39*(1), 32–43.

Borenstein, M., Hedges, L. V., Higgins, J. P. T., & Rothstein, H. R. (2009). *Introduction to meta-analysis.* Chichester, UK: Wiley.

Bowlby, J. (1978). Attachment theory and its therapeutic implications. *Adolescent Psychiatry, 6,* 5–33.

Bowlby, J. (1982). Attachment and loss: Retrospect and prospect. *American Journal of Orthopsychiatry, 52*(4), 664–78.

Bowlby, J. (1988). *A secure base: Parent-child attachment and healthy human development.* New York: Basic Books.

Brennan, K. A., Clark, C. L., & Shaver, P. R. (1998). Self-report measurement of adult attachment: An integrative overview. In J. A. Simpson and W. S. Rholes (Eds.), *Attachment theory and close relationships* (pp. 46–76). New York: Guilford Press.

Clarkin, J. F., & Levy, K. N. (2003). The influence of client variables on psychotherapy. In M. Lambert (Ed.), *Handbook of psychotherapy and behavior change* (5th ed., pp. 194–226). New York: Wiley & Sons.

Collins, N. L, & Read, S. J. (1990). Adult attachment, working models, and relationship quality in dating couples. *Journal of Personality and Social Psychology, 58*(4), 644–63.

Conradi, H. J., Gerisma, C., van Duijn, M., & de Jonge, P. (2006). Internal and external validity of the Experiences in Close Relationships questionnaire in an American and two Dutch samples. *European Journal of Psychiatry, 20*(4), 258–69.

*Cyranowski, J. M., Bookwala, J., Feske, U., Houck, P., Pilkonis, P., Kostelnik, B., et al. (2002). Adult attachment profiles, interpersonal difficulties, and response to interpersonal psychotherapy in women with recurrent major depression. *Journal of Social and Clinical Psychology, 21*(2), 191–217.

Diamond, D., Clarkin, J., Levine, H., Levy, K. N., Foelsch, P. & Yeomans, F. (1999). Borderline conditions and attachment: A preliminary report. *Psychoanalytic Inquiry, 19*(5), 831–84.

Diamond, D., Clarkin, J. F., Stovall-McClough, K. C., Levy, K. N., Foelsch, P. A., Levine, H., et al. (2003).

Patient-therapist attachment: Impact on the therapeutic process and outcome. In M. Cortina & M. Marrone (Eds.), *Attachment theory and the psychoanalytic process* (pp. 127–78). Philadelphia: Whurr Publishers.

Diehl, M., Elnick, A. B., Bourbeau, L. S., & Labouvie-Vief, G. (1998). Adult attachment styles: Their relations to family context and personality. *Journal of Personality and Social Psychology, 74*(6), 1656–69.

Diener, M. J., Hilsenroth, M. J., & Weinberger, J. (2009). A primer on meta-analysis of correlation coefficients: The relationship between patient-reported therapeutic alliance and adult attachment style as an illustration. *Psychotherapy Research, 19,* 519–26.

Dolan, R. T., Arnkoff, D. B., & Glass, C. R. (1993). Client attachment style and the psychotherapist's interpersonal stance. *Psychotherapy: Theory, Research, Practice, Training, 30*(3), 408–412.

Dozier, M. (1990). Attachment organization and treatment use for adults with serious psychopathological disorders. *Development and Psychopathology, 2*(1), 47–60.

Dozier, M., Lomax, L., Tyrrell, C. L., & Lee, S. W. (2001). The challenge of treatment for clients with dismissing states of mind. *Attachment & Human Development, 3*(1), 62–76.

Farber, B. A., Lippert, R. A., & Nevas, D. B. (1995). The therapist as attachment figure. *Psychotherapy: Theory, Research, Practice, Training, 32*(2), 204–212.

Farber, B. A., & Metzger, J. A. (2009). The therapist as secure base. In J. H. Obegi & E. Berant (Eds.), *Attachment theory and research in clinical work with adults* (pp.46–70). New York: Guilford Press.

Feeney, J. A., Noller, P., & Hanrahan, M. (1994). Assessing adult attachment. In M. B. Sperling & W. H. Berman (Eds.), *Attachment in adults: Clinical and developmental perspectives* (pp. 128–52). New York, NY: Guilford Press.

Fonagy, P. (1999). Attachment, the development of the self, and its pathology in personality disorders. In J. Derksen, C. Maffei, & H. Groen (Eds.), *Treatment of personality disorders* (pp. 53–68). Dordrecht, Netherlands: Kulwer Academic Publishers.

Fonagy, P., Leigh, T., Steele, M., Steele, H., Kennedy, R., Mattoon, G., et al. (1996). The relation of attachment status, psychiatric classification, and response to psychotherapy. *Journal of Consulting and Clinical Psychology, 64*(1), 22–31.

Fraley, R. C. (2002). Attachment stability from infancy to adulthood: Meta-analysis and dynamic modeling of developmental mechanisms. *Personality and Social Psychology*, 6(2), 123–51.

Fraley, R. C., Waller, N. G., & Brennan, K. A. (2000). An item response theory analysis of self-report measures of adult attachment. *Journal of Personality and Social Psychology*, 78(2), 350–65.

*Fuertes, J. N., Mislowack, A., Brown, S., Gur-Arie, S., Wilkinson, S., & Gelso, C. J. (2007). Correlates of the real relationship in psychotherapy: A study of dyads. *Psychotherapy Research*, 17(4), 423–30.

George, C., Kaplan, M., & Main, M. (1985). *Adult Attachment Interview*. Unpublished manuscript, Department of Psychology, University of California, Berkeley.

Griffin, D. W., & Bartholomew, K. (1994). Models of the self and other: Fundamental dimensions underlying measures of adult attachment. *Journal of Personality and Social Psychology*, 67(3), 430–445.

Grossmann, K. E., Grossmann, K., & Waters, E. (Eds.). (2005). *Attachment from infancy to adulthood: The major longitudinal studies*. New York: Guilford Publications.

Gunnar, M. R., Broderson, L., Nachmias, M., Buss, K., & Rigatuso, J. (1996). Stress reactivity and attachment security. *Developmental Psychobiology*, 29, 191–204.

Hardy, G. E., Stiles, W. B., Barkham, M., & Startup, M. (1998). Therapist responsiveness to client interpersonal styles during time-limited treatments for depression. *Journal of Consulting and Clinical Psychology*, 66(2), 304–312.

Hazan, C., & Shaver, P. R. (1987). Romantic love conceptualized as an attachment process. *Journal of Personality and Social Psychology*, 52(3), 511–24.

Hazan, C., & Shaver, P. R. (1990). Love and work: An attachment-theoretical perspective. *Journal of Personality and Social Psychology*, 59(2), 270–80.

Hedges, L. V., & Olkin, I. (1985). *Statistical methods for meta-analysis*. Orlando, FL: Academic Press.

Horowitz, L. M., Rosenberg, S. E., & Bartholomew, K. (1993). Interpersonal problems, attachment styles, and outcome in brief dynamic psychotherapy. *Journal of Consulting and Clinical Psychology*, 61(4), 549–60.

Huffcutt, A. I., & Arthur, W. (1995). Development of a new outlier statistic for meta-analytic data. *Journal of Applied Psychology*, 80, 327–34.

Hunter, J. E., & Schmidt, F. L. (1990). Dichotomization of continuous variables: The implications for meta-analysis. *Journal of Applied Psychology*, 75, 334–49.

Hunter, J. E., & Schmidt, F. L. (2000). Fixed effects vs. random effects meta-analysis models: Implications for cumulative research knowledge. *International Journal of Selection and Assessment*, 8(4), 275–92.

Hunter, J. E., & Schmidt, F. L. (2004). *Methods of meta-analysis: Correcting error and bias in research findings* (2nd ed.). Thousand Oaks, CA: Sage.

*Johnson, S. M, & Talitman, E. (1997). Predictors of success in emotionally focused marital therapy. *Journal of Marital & Family Therapy*, 23(2), 135–52.

Kagan, J. (1998). *Three seductive ideas*. Cambridge, MA: Harvard University Press.

Kilmann, P. R., Laughlin, J. E., Carranza, L. V., Downer, J. T., Major, S., & Parnell, M. M. (1999). Effects of an attachment-focused group preventive intervention on insecure women. *Group Dynamics: Theory, Research, and Practice*, 3(2), 138–47.

Kirchmann, H., Mestel, R., Schreiber-Willnow, K., Mattke, D., Seidler, K. P., Daudert, E., et al. (2009). Associations among attachment characteristics, patients' assessment of therapeutic factors, and treatment outcome following inpatient psychodynamic group psychotherapy. *Psychotherapy Research*, 19(2), 234–48.

Kivlighan, D. M., Patton, M. J., & Foote, D. (1998). Moderating effects of client attachment on the counselor experience–working alliance relationship. *Journal of Counseling Psychology*, 45(3), 274–78.

Kobak, R. R., Cole, H. E., Ferenz-Gillies, R., Fleming, W. S., & Gamble, W. (1993). Attachment and emotion regulation during mother-teen problem solving: A control theory analysis. *Child Development*, 64(1), 231–45.

Korfmacher, J., Adam, E., Ogawa, J., & Egeland, B. (1997). Adult attachment: Implications for the therapeutic process in a home visitation intervention. *Applied Developmental Science*, 1(1), 43–52.

*Lawson, D. M., & Brossart, D. F. (2009). Attachment, interpersonal problems, and treatment outcome in group therapy for intimate partner violence. *Psychology of Men & Masculinity*, 10(4), 288–301.

Levy, K. N. (2005). The implications of attachment theory and research for understanding borderline personality disorder. *Development and Psychopathology*, *17*, 959–86.

Levy, K. N., Beeney, J. E., Wasserman, R. H., & Clarkin, J. F. (2010). *Alliance at the borderline: The relationship between adult attachment and therapeutic alliance in borderline personality disorder*. Unpublished manuscript, Department of Psychology, Pennsylvania State University, University Park.

Levy, K. N., Blatt, S. J., & Shaver, P. R. (1998). Attachment styles and parental representations. *Journal of Personality and Social Psychology*, *74*(2), 407–419.

Levy, K. N., Clarkin, J. F., & Kernberg, O. F. (2007). *The relationship between unresolved attachment and therapy dropout in borderline personality disorder*. Unpublished manuscript, Department of Psychology, Pennsylvania State University, University Park.

Levy, K. N., & Kelly, K. M. (2009). Using interviews to assess adult attachment. In J. H. Obegi & E. Berant (Eds.), *Attachment theory and research in clinical work with adults* (pp. 121–52). New York: Guilford Press.

Levy, K. N., & Kelly, K. M. (2010). Sex differences in jealousy: A contribution from attachment theory. *Psychological Science. 21*, 168–73.

Levy, K. N., Meehan, K. B., Kelly, K. M., Reynoso, J. S., Clarkin, J. F., & Kernberg, O. F. (2006). Change in attachment patterns and reflective function in a randomized control trial of transference-focused psychotherapy for borderline personality disorder. *Journal of Consulting and Clinical Psychology*, *74*, 1027–40.

Levy, M. B., & Davis, K. E. (1988). Lovestyles and attachment styles compared: Their relations to each other and to various relationship characteristics. *Journal of Social and Personal Relationships*, *5*(4), 439–71.

Lipsey, M. W., & Wilson, D. B. (2001). *Practical meta-analysis*. Thousand Oaks, CA: Sage.

Main, M. (1995). Recent studies in attachment: Overview, with selected implications for clinical work. In S. Goldberg, R. Muir, & J. Kerr (Eds.), *Attachment theory: Social, developmental, and clinical perspectives* (pp. 407–74). Hillsdale, NJ: Analytic Press.

Main, M., & Goldwyn, R. (1998). *Adult attachment classification system*. Unpublished manuscript. University of California, Berkeley.

Main, M., Kaplan, N., & Cassidy, J. (1985). Security in infancy, childhood, and adulthood: A move to the level of representation. *Monographs of the Society for Research in Child Development*, *50*(1–2), 66–104.

Main, M., & Solomon, J. (1986). Discovery of an insecure-disorganized/disoriented attachment pattern. In T. B. Brazelton & M. W. Yogman (Eds.), *Affective development in infancy* (pp. 95–124). Westport, CT: Ablex Publishing.

Mallinckrodt, B., Porter, M. J., & Kivlighan, D. M. (2005). Client attachment to therapist, depth of in-session exploration, and object relations in brief psychotherapy. *Psychotherapy: Theory, Research, Practice, Training*, *42*(1), 85–100.

*Marmarosh, C. L., Gelso, C. J., Markin, R. D., Majors, R., Mallery, C., & Choi, J. (2009). The real relationship in psychotherapy: Relationships to adult attachments, working alliance, transference, and therapy outcome. *Journal of Counseling Psychology*, *56*(3), 337–50.

*McBride, C., Atkinson, L., Quilty, L. C., Bagby, R. M. (2006). Attachment as moderator of treatment outcome in major depression: A randomized control trial of interpersonal psychotherapy versus cognitive behavior therapy. *Journal of Consulting and Clinical Psychology*, *74*(6), 1041–54.

*Meyer, B., Pilkonis, P. A., Proietti, J. M., Heape, C. L., & Egan, M. (2001). Attachment styles and personality disorders as predictors of symptom course. *Journal of Personality Disorders*, *15*(5), 371–89.

Mickelson, K. D., Kessler, R. C., & Shaver, P. R. (1997). Adult attachment in a nationally representative sample. *Journal of Personality and Social Psychology*, *73*(5), 1092–1106.

*Muller, R. T., & Rosenkranz, S. E. (2009). Attachment and treatment response among adults in inpatient treatment for posttraumatic stress disorder. *Psychotherapy: Theory, Research, Practice, Training*, *46*(1), 82–96.

Obegi, J. H. (2008). The development of the client-therapist bond through the lens of attachment theory. *Psychotherapy: Theory, Research, Practice, Training*, *45*(4), 431–46.

Pilkonis, P. A. (1988). Personality prototypes among depressives: Themes of dependency and autonomy. *Journal of Personality Disorders*, *2*(2), 144–52.

Ravitz, P., Maunder, R. G., Hunter, J. A., Sthyankiya, B., & Lancee, W. J. (2010). Adult attachment measures: A 25-year review. *Journal of Psychosomatic Research*. Advance online publication. doi: 10.1016/j.jpsychores.2009.08.006

*Reis, S., & Grenyer, B. F. S. (2004). Fearful attachment, working alliance and treatment response for individuals with major depression. *Clinical Psychology & Psychotherapy, 11*(6), 414–24.

Ricks, M. H. (1985). The social transmission of parental behavior: Attachment across generations. *Monographs of the Society for Research in Child Development, 50*(1–2), 211–27.

Riggs, S. A., Jacobovitz, D., & Hazen, N. (2002). Adult attachment and history of psychotherapy in a normative sample. *Psychotherapy: Theory, Research, Practice, Training, 39*(4), 344–53.

Romano, V., Fitzpatrick, M., & Janzen, J. (2008). The secure-base hypothesis: Global attachment, attachment to counselor, and session exploration in psychotherapy. *Journal of Counseling Psychology, 55*(4), 495–504.

*Saatsi, S., Hardy, G. E., & Cahill, J. (2007). Predictors of outcome and completion status in cognitive therapy for depression. *Psychotherapy Research, 17*(2), 185–95.

Schmidt, F. L., Le, H., & Oh, I. S. (2009). Correcting for the distorting effects of study artifacts in meta-analysis. In H. Cooper, L. V. Hedges, & J. C. Valentine (Eds.), *The handbook of research synthesis and meta-analysis* (2nd ed.). New York: Sage.

Shaver, P. R., & Clark, C. L. (1994). The psychodynamics of adult romantic attachment. In J. M. Masling & R. F. Bornstein (Eds.), *Empirical perspectives on object relations theory* (pp. 105–56). Washington, DC: American Psychological Association.

Shaver, P. R., & Hazan, C. (1993). Adult romantic attachment: Theory and evidence. In D. Perlman & W. Jones (Eds.), *Advances in personal relationships* (Vol. 4, pp. 29–70). London, UK: Kingsley.

Shaver, P. R., Hazan, C., & Bradshaw, D. (1988). Love as attachment. In R. J. Sternberg & M. L. Barnes (Eds.), *The psychology of love* (pp. 68–99). New Haven, CT: Yale University Press.

Simpson, J. A. (1990). Influence of attachment style on romantic relationships. *Journal of Personality and Social Psychology, 59*(5), 971–80.

Slade, A. (1999). Attachment theory and research: Implications for the theory and practice of individual psychotherapy with adults. In J. Cassidy & P. R. Shaver (Eds.), *Handbook of attachment: Theory, research, and clinical applications* (pp. 575–94). New York: Guilford Press.

Slade, A. (2004). Two therapies: Attachment organization and the clinical process. In L. Atkinson & S. Goldberg (Eds.), *Attachment issues in*

psychopathology and intervention (pp. 181–206). Mawah, NJ: Lawrence Erlbaum Associates.

Sroufe, L. A., & Waters, E. (1977). Heart rate as a convergent measure in clinical and developmental research. *Merrill-Palmer Quarterly, 23*(1), 3–27.

*Stalker, C. A., Gebotys, R., & Harper, K. (2005). Insecure attachment as a predictor of outcome following inpatient trauma treatment for women survivors of childhood abuse. *Bulletin of the Menninger Clinic, 69*(2), 137–56.

Stevenson-Hinde, J., & Marshall, P. J. (1999). Behavioral inhibition, heart period, and respiratory sinus arrhythmia: An attachment perspective. *Child Development, 70*, 805–816.

Stovall-McClough, K. C., & Cloitre, M. (2003). Reorganization of unresolved childhood traumatic memories following exposure therapy. *Annals of the New York Academy of Sciences, 1008*, 297–99.

*Strauss, B. M., Kirchmann, H., Eckert, J., Lobo-Drost, A. J., Marquet, A., Papenhausen, R., et al. (2006). Attachment characteristics and treatment outcome following inpatient psychotherapy: Results of a multisite study. *Psychotherapy Research, 16*(5), 573–86.

Strauss, B. M., Lobo-Drost, A. J., & Pilkonis, P. A. (1999). Einschätzung von Bindungsstilen bei Erwachsenen: Erste Erfahrungen mit der deutschen Version einer Prototypenbeurteilung. [Evaluation of attachment styles in adults: First results with the German version of a prototype evaluation.] *Zeitschrift für Klinische Psychologie, Psychiatrie und Psychotherapie, 47*, 347–364.

*Tasca, G. A., Ritchie, K., Conrad, G., Balfour, L., Gayton, J., Lybanon, V., et al. (2006). Attachment scales predict outcome in a randomized controlled trial of two group therapies for binge eating disorder: An aptitude by treatment interaction. *Psychotherapy Research, 16*(1), 106–21.

*Travis, L. A., Bliwise, N. G., Binder, J. L., & Horne-Moyer, H. L. (2001). Changes in clients' attachment styles over the course of time-limited dynamic psychotherapy. *Psychotherapy: Theory, Research, Practice, Training, 38*(2), 149–59.

Ulberg, R., Marble, A., & Høglend, P. (2009). Do gender and level of relational functioning influence the long-term treatment response in dynamic psychotherapy? *Nordic Journal of Psychiatry, 63*(5), 412–419.

van Ijzendoorn, M. H. (1995). Adult attachment representations, parental responsiveness, and infant attachment: A meta-analysis on the predictive validity of the Adult Attachment Interview. *Psychological Bulletin, 117*(3), 387–403.

Vaughn, B. E., & Bost, K. K. (1999). Attachment and temperament: Redundant, independent, or interacting influences on interpersonal adaptation and personality development? In J. Cassidy & P. R. Shaver (Eds.), *Handbook of attachment: Theory, research, and clinical applications* (pp. 198–225). New York: Guilford Press.

Waters, E., Merrick, S., Treboux, D., Crowell, J., & Albersheim, L. (2000). Attachment security in infancy and early adulthood: A twenty-year longitudinal study. *Child Development, 71*(3), 684–89.

Wei, M., Russell, D. W., Mallinckrodt, B., & Vogel, D. L. (2007). The Experiences in Close Relationship Scale (ECR)-short form: Reliability, validity, and factor structure. *Journal of Personality Assessment, 88*(2), 187–204.

West, M. L., & Sheldon-Keller, A. E. (1994). *Patterns of relating: An adult attachment perspective.* New York: Guilford Press.

Wilson, D. B. (2005). Meta-analysis macros for SAS, SPSS, and Stata. Retrieved December 11, 2009, from http://mason.gmu.edu/~dwilsonb/ma.html

20 Religion and Spirituality

Everett L. Worthington, Jr., Joshua N. Hook, Don E. Davis, *and* Michael A. McDaniel

One relationship factor that can potentially affect the outcome of psychotherapy is the match or mismatch between a client's religious or spiritual (R/S) beliefs and the type of psychotherapy. Some R/S clients desire R/S-tailored or accommodated treatment. Others can comfortably accept a secular treatment. Even for those who do not request R/S treatment, some might benefit from the contextualization of treatment in their R/S framework.

There has been an increase in outcome studies examining psychotherapies that incorporate R/S beliefs (Hook et al., 2010; Pargament & Saunders, 2007; Post & Wade, 2009; Smith, Bartz, & Richards, 2007; Worthington & Aten, 2009). At the time of the first edition of *Psychotherapy Relationships That Work* (Norcross, 2002), there were only 11 outcome studies examining an R/S psychotherapy, making conclusions based on this set of studies necessarily tenuous (Worthington & Sandage, 2001). Furthermore, these studies were limited to mainly Christian or Muslim-accommodative cognitive-behavioral interventions. Thus, it was difficult to generalize to other types of R/S psychotherapies. As such, tailoring psychotherapy to the R/S beliefs of clients was judged to have promising empirical support, but it was suggested that more research on this topic was

needed (Norcross, 2002). The increase in number, variety, and rigor of outcome studies evaluating R/S psychotherapies allows for a far more rigorous evaluation of the effectiveness of tailoring psychotherapy to a patient's R/S convictions.

In this chapter, we first define R/S and discuss how these constructs are generally measured. Second, we offer clinical examples that illustrate how psychotherapy might be accommodated for one's R/S beliefs. Third, we present data from a meta-analysis examining the effectiveness of R/S psychotherapy. Fourth, we discuss patient contributions to the effectiveness of R/S psychotherapy. Fifth, we note several limitations of the present body of research. Finally, we give recommendations for therapists based on the present research evidence.

Definitions and Measures

Although the terms religion and spirituality have historically been closely linked (Sheldrake, 1992), current conceptualizations make important distinctions between religion and spirituality. *Religion* can be defined as adherence to a belief system and practices associated with a tradition and community in which there is agreement about what is believed and practiced (Hill et al., 2000). *Spirituality*, in contrast, can be defined as a more general feeling of closeness and connectedness to the sacred. What one views as sacred is often a socially influenced perception of either (a) a divine being or object or (b) a sense of ultimate reality or truth (Hill et al.). Many people experience their spirituality in the context of religion, but not all do.

Four types of spirituality have been identified on the basis of the type of sacred object (Davis, Hook, & Worthington, 2008; Worthington, 2009; Worthington & Aten, 2009). First, *religious spirituality* involves a sense of closeness and connection to the sacred as described by a specific religion (e.g., Christianity, Islam, Buddhism). This type of spirituality fosters a sense of closeness to a particular god or higher power. Second, *humanistic spirituality* involves a sense of closeness and connection to humankind. This type of spirituality develops a sense of connection to a general group of people, often involving feelings of love, altruism, or reflection. Third, *nature spirituality* involves a sense of closeness and connection to the environment or to nature. For example, one might experience wonder by witnessing a sunset or experiencing a natural wonder such as the Grand Canyon. Fourth, *cosmos spirituality* involves a sense of closeness and connection with the whole of creation. This type of spirituality might be experienced by meditating on the magnificence of creation, or by looking into the night sky and contemplating the vastness of the universe.

Psychotherapy has been defined as the "informed and intentional application of clinical methods and interpersonal stances derived from established psychological principles for the purpose of assisting people to modify their behaviors, cognitions, emotions, and/or other personal characteristics in directions which the participants deem desirable" (Norcross, 1990, p. 218). R/S psychotherapy shares many methods and goals as secular psychotherapy but also incorporates methods or goals that are R/S in nature. For example, in addition to using cognitive or behavioral techniques to alleviate depression, a clinician practicing R/S psychotherapy might conceptualize using an R/S framework and, within that framework, use methods such as prayer or religious imagery. Besides pursuing goals that are psychological, a client in R/S psychotherapy might also work toward spiritual goals, such as becoming more like Jesus Christ, or adhering more closely to the teachings of Buddha. R/S outcome variables, such as spiritual well-being, might be important in psychotherapy when clients' reasons for attending therapy and criteria for evaluating therapy include spiritual goals. Accordingly, the outcome measures used in the subsequent review and meta-analysis fall into two categories. First, almost all studies use a psychological outcome variable. A study examining R/S psychotherapy for depression, for example, might use the Beck Depression Inventory (BDI; Beck, Ward, Mendelson, Mock, & Erbaugh, 1961). Second, many studies also use a measure of spirituality. For example, a study examining R/S psychotherapy for unforgiveness might use not only a primary psychological measure of forgiveness but also a secondary measure of spiritual well-being (Ellison, 1983).

The majority of studies in the present review measured R/S beliefs simply by identification (i.e., the participant self-identified as Christian). Some studies used a measure of R/S beliefs or commitments (e.g., Religious Orientations Scale, Allport & Ross, 1967; Religious Commitment Inventory-10, Worthington et al., 2003) and employed a minimum cutoff score as a criterion for inclusion in the study. This ensured that the participants in the study were at least moderately engaged with their R/S beliefs. A few studies (e.g., Razali, Aminah, & Kahn, 2002) used a measure of R/S beliefs or commitments and also measured the extent to which R/S treatments had different effects for participants who were more (or less) committed.

Clinical Examples

We now provide several case examples of R/S psychotherapy from different theoretical and R/S perspectives.

Case Example 1:
Christian-Accommodative
Cognitive Therapy for Depression

The cognitive model of depression emphasizes the role of maladaptive cognition in both the causes and treatment of depression(Beck,1972).Christian-accommodative cognitive therapy for depression retains the main features of the secular theory yet places the psychotherapy in a religious context. For example, the rationale for psychotherapy, the homework assignments, and the challenging of negative automatic thoughts and core beliefs are integrated with and based on biblical teachings regarding the self, world, and future (Pecheur & Edwards, 1984).

Dana (age 31) was a Christian female who presented to psychotherapy with several symptoms of depression, including feelings of sadness, sleeping more than usual, low energy, weight gain, and loss of interest in everyday activities. As psychotherapy progressed, Dana explored negative beliefs about herself. Her most problematic core belief was that she was worthless and no one would ever love and accept her as she was. These beliefs seemed related to a difficult childhood. She had been physically abused by her mother, who eventually abandoned her. Dana was a committed Christian. At intake she stated that

she wanted to incorporate R/S issues in her psychotherapy. As Dana and her therapist explored and modified her negative core beliefs, they discussed how Dana thought God viewed her. Several passages of the Bible comforted Dana and helped her realize that, even though she viewed herself negatively, God and other people loved and accepted her as she was.

Case Example 2:
Spiritual Self-Schema
Therapy for Addiction

Spiritual self-schema therapy integrates cognitive-behavioral techniques with Buddhist psychological principles (Avants & Margolin, 2004). The goal of this psychotherapy is to modify a person's self-schema. When a self-schema is activated, beliefs about the self energize specific behaviors. This psychotherapy attempts to facilitate a shift from an "addict" self-schema to a "spiritual" self-schema that fosters mindfulness, compassion, and doing no harm to self or others (Margolin et al., 2007). Psychotherapy sessions focus on aspects of the Buddhist Noble Eightfold Path, which include training in mindfulness, morality, and wisdom.

Dave (age 47) did not ascribe to a religion. He considered himself to be spiritual. After he lost his job because he failed a drug test due to cocaine use, he checked into a rehabilitation facility. He had been dependent on drugs and alcohol on and off for 30 years. During psychotherapy, Dave was taught about the wandering nature of the mind, and how this contributed to his addict self-schema. If Dave did not work to control his mind, he usually thought of using drugs. Dave practiced a meditation technique called *anapanasati*, which involves sitting silently with eyes closed and focusing on the sensations experienced while breathing naturally. Dave improved his concentration and mindfulness with practice. Over time, he developed discipline over his maladaptive thoughts.

Case Example 3: Christian-Accommodative Forgiveness Therapy

REACH is a model of promoting forgiveness that involves five steps: recall the hurt, develop empathy toward the offender, give an altruistic gift of forgiveness, commit to forgive, and hold on to the forgiveness (Worthington, 1998). Christian versions of REACH actively encourage clients to access their religious beliefs while moving toward forgiveness (Lampton et al., 2005; Rye et al., 2005). Clients are encouraged to view forgiveness as a collaborative process with God and to consider prayer or use of Scripture in forgiving.

Lisa (age 20) was a Christian female who struggled to forgive her father. Her father had several extramarital affairs when Lisa was younger, which precipitated her parents' divorce when Lisa was 7. Lisa's father was unreliable when Lisa was growing up. He regularly broke promises, such as failing to attend birthday parties or soccer games. Lisa harbored resentment and anger toward her father. During her junior year of college, she concluded that her unforgiveness was a problem. Even though her father was not a part of her life, most days Lisa woke up actively angry, stressed, and upset toward her father. She attended a group psychoeducational workshop for people struggling with forgiveness. During the workshop, the group leader led Lisa and seven other people through the steps to promote forgiveness. Group members shared with each other how they had been hurt and worked toward developing empathy for their offender. The group also discussed God's role in forgiveness, which helped Lisa realize the extent that God and others had forgiven her. Lisa's gratitude to God for forgiving her helped her forgive her father.

Case Example 4: Muslim-Accommodative Cognitive Therapy for Anxiety

Similar to Christian-accommodative cognitive therapy for depression, Muslim-accommodative cognitive therapy for anxiety retains Beck's cognitive model (Beck, Rush, Shaw, & Emery, 1979), augmenting it with spiritual strategies and interventions. For example, psychotherapists work with clients to identify and challenge negative thoughts and beliefs using the Koran and Hadith (sayings and customs of the Prophet) as guidance (Razali, Aminah, & Khan, 2002). Clients are encouraged to cultivate feelings of closeness to Allah, pray regularly, and read the Koran.

Hasan (age 35) was a highly committed Muslim male, diagnosed with generalized anxiety disorder. He became worried every day, and his anxiety interfered with his marriage and job. In psychotherapy, Hasan acknowledged that he did not believe the world was a safe place, and he felt as if he had to worry or else something terrible might happen. The psychotherapist helped Hasan examine the evidence for and against his thoughts. Hasan and his psychotherapist worked together to develop religious coping strategies and discover religious truths to counteract his anxious thoughts. For example, it helped Hasan to remember that he believed that Allah was always in control, and that he could trust in Allah to be with him and comfort him.

Meta-Analytic Review

Past research assessing the efficacy and specificity of R/S psychotherapies has been mixed. McCullough (1999) evaluated the efficacy of Christian-accommodative psychotherapies for depression and concluded that the R/S psychotherapies worked as well, but not better than established secular therapies. Hook and colleagues (2010) reached a similar conclusion in their review of empirically supported R/S psychotherapies. They found some evidence for the efficacy of R/S psychotherapies. Thus, R/S psychotherapies performed better than control groups and equal to established secular psychotherapies. However, reviewers found little evidence for the specificity of R/S psychotherapies—that R/S psychotherapies consistently outperformed established secular psychotherapies. However, in a recent meta-analysis, Smith and associates (2007) found evidence for the positive effects of R/S psychotherapies even when compared with alternate treatments.

In the present meta-analytic study, we sought to determine the extent to which tailoring the psychotherapy relationship to the client's R/S faith is efficacious. We address this at three levels.

• First we compare outcomes of clients in R/S psychotherapy versus clients in no-treatment control groups. Studies using comparative designs control for possible confounding variables present in less rigorous designs. The use of control groups provides for credible inference concerning the efficacy of R/S psychotherapies.

• Second, we compare outcomes of clients in R/S psychotherapy versus clients in alternate psychotherapies. These types of studies not only control for possible confounding variables but also provide some evidence for the specificity of R/S psychotherapies.

• Third, we compare outcomes of clients in R/S psychotherapy versus clients in alternate psychotherapies that use a dismantling design. In these studies, the R/S psychotherapy and the comparison

treatment are equivalent in regard to theoretical orientation and duration of treatment but differ in whether they are accommodated to R/S clients. Comparison conditions may differ in strength, so these studies most rigorously test whether it is helpful to tailor psychotherapy to a client's R/S faith.

Method

Inclusion Criteria. Studies included in the present meta-analysis met a definition of psychotherapy (Norcross, 1990), and all studies explicitly integrated R/S considerations into psychotherapy. All studies included in the present review used random assignment and compared an R/S treatment with either (a) a no-treatment control condition or (b) an alternate treatment. We excluded studies of (a) 12-step groups such as Alcoholics Anonymous, (b) meditation or mindfulness interventions that were not explicitly R/S, (c) R/S interventions such as intercessory prayer that were not contextualized in a psychotherapy, and (d) one-session "workshop-type" interventions.

Literature Search. We conducted our literature search by (a) using two or more computer databases (listed in the next paragraph), (b) manually searching the references of previous meta-analyses and reviews, and (c) contacting relevant researchers for file-drawer studies. We included both published and unpublished studies. Effect sizes from published studies tend to be larger than effect sizes from unpublished studies, so limiting the review to published studies may exacerbate publication bias (Lipsey & Wilson, 2001).

First, we identified studies by searching the *PsychINFO*, *Social Sciences Citation Index*, and *Dissertation Abstracts International* databases up until December 1, 2009. The search used the key terms [*counseling* OR *therapy*] AND [*religio** OR *spiritu**] AND [*outcome*]. Second, we used previous reviews of the literature (Harris, Thoresen, McCullough, & Larson; Hodge, 2006; Hook et al., 2010; McCullough, 1999; Smith et al., 2007; Worthington, Kurusu, McCullough, & Sandage, 1996; Worthington & Sandage, 2001) to identify relevant studies. Third, we contacted the corresponding author from each study identified to inquire about studies we may have missed, including unpublished file-drawer studies.

Effect Size. The effect size used in this study was the standardized mean difference (d). The standardized mean difference is a standard deviation metric with zero indicating no mean group difference. The value of d summarizes the posttest difference between the R/S condition and the comparison condition. A positive d indicates that the R/S condition performed better, on average, than the comparison; a negative d indicates that the comparison condition performed better.

Missing Data. Some studies did not contain sufficient data for the calculation of effect sizes. For each study with insufficient data to calculate the effect size, we requested missing data from the corresponding author. If the necessary data could not be obtained, we excluded the study from the analysis.

Outcome of Search. Overall, a total of 51 samples from 46 separate studies evaluated R/S psychotherapy. Eleven samples employed both a control condition and an alternate treatment, resulting in 62 total comparisons. Of these comparisons, 5 did not have sufficient information to calculate the effect size, and 6 did not come from a study that employed random assignment to condition, leaving 51 valid comparisons for analysis. Of these comparisons, 22 compared R/S psychotherapy to a control condition, and 29 compared R/S psychotherapy to an alternate treatment. Of these 29 comparisons, 11 comparisons were identified that used a dismantling design in

which the R/S condition and the comparison condition were identical in theoretical orientation and duration of treatment.

Coding. The coding of studies included sample size, as well as information necessary to calculate the d and standard error of the d (e.g., means, standard deviations). Also coded were potential moderators including study design characteristics, treatment characteristics, and measurement characteristics. Study design characteristics coded involved source of data (published or unpublished). An effect for source of data would suggest that publication bias could be present, which might limit the conclusions that could be drawn from the meta-analysis. Treatment characteristics included treatment format (e.g., group, individual), problem rated (e.g., depression, anxiety), theoretical orientation (e.g., cognitive, behavioral), and type of R/S faith commitment (e.g., Christian, Muslim, general spirituality). Measurement characteristics involved type of measure (e.g., psychological, spiritual).

Data Analysis. Data analysis was conducted using Comprehensive Meta-Analysis Version 2.2 (Borenstein, Hedges, Higgins, & Rothstein, 2005). Random-effects models were used because we had no reason to believe that the population effect sizes were invariant. Consistent with random-effects models, studies were weighted by the sum of the inverse sampling variance plus tau-squared (Borenstein, Hedges, Higgins, & Rothstein, 2009). Separate analyses were conducted for psychological and spiritual outcomes. For studies that reported more than one effect size, we used the measure that best assessed the goal of the specific psychotherapy. For example, if a study purported to examine R/S cognitive-behavioral therapy for depression, a measure such as the Beck Depression Inventory was chosen and other measures, such as anxiety or general distress, were ignored. In addition, measures that had been subjected to peer review were chosen over non-peer-reviewed measures.

Results

The total number of participants from the 51 samples was 3,290 (1,524 from R/S psychotherapies, 921 from alternate psychotherapies, and 845 from no-treatment control conditions). Descriptive information for all studies is summarized in Table 20.1. R/S psychotherapies addressed problems in a variety of areas. A wide range of R/S perspectives were represented, although the most common perspectives were Christianity, Islam, and general spirituality. Many theoretical orientations were represented, although the most common theories were cognitive, cognitive-behavioral, and mind-body-spirit.

The meta-analytic results for psychological and spiritual outcomes are summarized in Table 20.2. The first column lists the level of comparison. Columns 2 through 6 list the posttest results. The second and third columns list the number of participants (N) and studies (k). The fourth and fifth columns list the mean d and 95% confidence interval for the observed d. The sixth column lists I^2, the ratio of true heterogeneity to total variation in observed effect sizes. Columns seven through eleven list the follow-up results using the same format.

Our first analysis examined whether patients in R/S psychotherapies showed greater improvement than would patients in no-treatment control conditions on both psychological and spiritual outcomes. This was largely the case (psychological d = 0.45; spiritual d = 0.51). Participants in R/S psychotherapies outperformed no-treatment control conditions on psychological and spiritual outcomes. These differences in outcomes were maintained at a smaller

magnitude at follow-up, although these results should be treated with caution because of the low number of studies reporting such data.

Our second analysis examined whether patients in R/S psychotherapies showed greater improvement than those in alternate psychotherapies on both psychological and spiritual outcomes. This was largely the case (psychological d = 0.26; spiritual d = 0.41). Participants in R/S psychotherapies outperformed alternate treatments on psychological and spiritual outcomes. These differences in outcomes were largely maintained at follow-up, although these results should be treated with caution because of the small number of studies reporting such data.

Our third analysis was limited to studies that used a dismantling design in which the R/S and alternate treatment had the same theoretical orientation and duration of treatment. For psychological outcomes, there was little difference between conditions (d = 0.13). For spiritual outcomes, participants in R/S psychotherapies outperformed participants in alternate psychotherapies at posttest (d = 0.33). This difference in outcome was maintained at follow-up, although this result should be treated with caution because of the low number of studies reporting such data.

In summary, the meta-analytic results present clear findings about the effectiveness of religious and spiritual tailoring. Consistent with Smith et al. (2007), there was some evidence that R/S psychotherapies outperformed alternate psychotherapies on both psychological and spiritual outcomes. However, this finding is difficult to interpret because comparison treatments varied in quality. When the analysis was limited to studies that used a dismantling design—studies in which the R/S condition and alternate condition utilized the same

Table 20.1 Descriptive Information for All Studies

Study	Published	Design	Random	N RS	N Alt	N Ctl	Belief	R/S	Problem	Theory	d (vs. Alt)	d (vs. Ctl)
Azhar & Varma (1995a)	Y	C	Y	15	15	NA	Muslim	R	Depression	Cognitive-behavioral	.75	NA
Azhar & Varma (1995b)	Y	C	Y	32	32	NA	Muslim	R	Depression	Cognitive-behavioral	.27	NA
Azhar et al. (1994)	Y	C	Y	31	31	NA	Muslim	R	Anxiety	Cognitive-behavioral	.28	NA
Baker (2000)	Y	C	Y	47	NA	47	General	S	Depression	Pastoral care	NA	NC
Barron (2007)	N	D	Y	20	19	NA	General	R	Depression	Cognitive-behavioral	.73	NA
Bay et al. (2008)	Y	C	Y	85	NA	85	General	S	Heart disease	Pastoral care	NA	.21
Bowland (2008)	N	C	Y	21	NA	22	General	S	Trauma	Spiritual	NA	.56
Byers et al. (in press)	Y	C	N	20	NA	19	Christian	R	Lack of hope	Installation of hope	NA	.10
Chan, Ho et al. (2006)	Y	C	Y	27	16	17	General	S	Breast cancer	Body-mind-spirit	.69	-.06
Chan, Ng et al. (2006)	Y	C	Y	69	NA	115	General	S	Anxiety	Body-mind-spirit	NA	NC
Cole (2005)	Y	C	Y	9	NA	7	General	S	Cancer	Spiritual	NA	-.52
Combs et al. (2000)	Y	C	Y	30	NA	32	Christian	R	Marital	Cognitive-behavioral	NA	.89
Gibbel (2010)	N	D	Y	24	19	22	General	S	Depression	Cognitive	.56	.61
Hart & Shapiro (2002)	N	C	Y	28	26	NA	General	S	Unforgiveness	12-step	.78	NA
Hawkins et al. (1999)	Y	D	N	18	11	NA	Christian	R	Depression	Cognitive-behavioral	.48	NA
Ho et al. (2009)	Y	C	Y	26	33	NA	General	S	Breast cancer	Body-mind-spirit	.09	NA
Hsiao et al. (2007)	Y	C	Y	14	12	NA	General	S	Depression	Body-mind-spirit	NC	NA

(Continued)

Table 20.1 Continued

Study	Published	Design	Random	N RS	N Alt	N Ctl	Belief	R/S	Problem	Theory	d (vs. Alt)	d (vs. Ctl)
Iler (2001)	Y	C	Y	25	NA	24	General	S	COPD	Pastoral care	NA	.61
Jackson (1999)	N	C	Y	14	NA	13	Christian	R	Unforgiveness	Promote empathy	NA	.91
Johnson et al. (1994)	Y	D	Y	13	16	NA	Christian	R	Depression	Rational-emotive	-.53	NA
Johnson & Ridley (1992)	Y	D	Y	5	5	NA	Christian	R	Depression	Rational-emotive	.32	NA
Lampton et al. (2005)	Y	C	N	42	NA	23	Christian	R	Unforgiveness	REACH	NA	.95
Lee et al. (2009)	Y	C	Y	69	NA	79	General	S	Colon cancer	Body-mind-spirit	NA	1.23
Liu et al. (2008)	Y	C	Y	12	NA	16	General	S	Breast cancer	Body-mind-spirit	NA	.66
Margolin et al. (2006)	Y	C	Y	30	30	NA	Buddhist	S	Drug use	Spiritual self-schema	.64	NA
Margolin et al. (2007)	Y	C	Y	14	11	NA	Buddhist	S	Drug use	Spiritual self-schema	.27	NA
McCain et al. (2008)	Y	C	Y	68	65	57	General	S	Stress, HIV	Spiritual growth	.24	-1.56
Miller et al. (2008)1	Y	C	Y	27	27	NA	General	S	Substance use	Spiritual guidance	-.41	NA
Miller et al. (2008)2	Y	C	N	31	34	NA	General	S	Substance use	Spiritual guidance	.17	NA
Nohr (2001)	N	D	Y	35	23	14	General	S	Stress	Cognitive-behavioral	.02	.30
Pecheur & Edwards (1984)	Y	D	Y	7	7	7	Christian	R	Depression	Cognitive	.57	2.06
Propst (1980)	Y	D	Y	7	10	11	Christian	R	Depression	Cognitive	NC	.95
Propst et al. (1992)1	Y	D	Y	10	9	11	Christian	R	Depression	Cognitive-behavioral	-.30	.93
Propst et al. (1992)2	Y	D	Y	9	10	11	Christian	R	Depression	Cognitive-behavioral	1.44	1.47
Razali et al. (2002)1	Y	C	Y	45	40	NA	Muslim	R	Anxiety	Cognitive	-.35	NA

(Continued)

Table 20.1 Continued

Study	Published	Design	Random	N RS	N Alt	N Ctl	Belief	R/S	Problem	Theory	d (vs. Alt)	d (vs. Ctl)
Razali et al. (2002)2	Y	C	Y	42	38	NA	Muslim	R	Anxiety	Cognitive	.13	NA
Razali et al. (1998)1	Y	C	Y	54	49	NA	Muslim	R	Anxiety	Cognitive	.31	NA
Razali et al. (1998)2	Y	C	Y	52	48	NA	Muslim	R	Depression	Cognitive	.32	NA
Richards et al. (2006)	Y	C	Y	43	35	NA	General	S	Eating disorders	Spiritual	.58	NA
Rosmarin et al. (2010)	N	C	Y	36	42	47	Jewish	R	Anxiety	Cognitive-behavioral	.23	.45
Rye & Pargament (2002)	Y	D	Y	19	20	19	Christian	R	Unforgiveness	REACH	.35	1.50
Rye et al. (2005)	Y	D	Y	50	49	50	Christian	R	Unforgiveness	REACH	-.03	.28
Scott (2001)	Y	D	N	15	3	NA	Christian	R	Breast cancer	Cognitive-behavioral	.21	NA
Stratton et al. (2008)	Y	C	N	22	NA	29	Christian	R	Unforgiveness	REACH	NA	.09
Targ & Levine (2002)	Y	C	Y	72	60	NA	General	S	Breast cancer	Body-mind-spirit	.14	NA
Toh & Tan (1997)	Y	C	Y	22	NA	24	Christian	R	Various	Lay counseling	NA	.71
Tonkin (2005)	Y	D	Y	9	9	NA	Christian	R	Eating disorders	Cognitive-behavioral	-2.00	NA
Trathen (1995)1	N	C	Y	23	NA	22	Christian	R	Premarital	PREP	NA	.05
Trathen (1995)2	N	C	Y	23	NA	22	Christian	R	Premarital	PREP	NA	.10
Yang et al. (2009)	Y	C	Y	17	19	NA	General	S	Depression	Body-mind-spirit	NC	NA
Zhang et al. (2002)	Y	C	Y	46	48	NA	Taoist	S	Anxiety	Cognitive	.85	NA

Note: RS = religious or spiritual psychotherapy; Alt = alternate psychotherapy; Ctl = control condition; Y = Yes; N = No; C = comparative design; D = dismantling design; NA = not applicable; R = religious; S = spiritual; NC = not able to calculate effect size.

Table 20.2 Overall Results for Psychological and Spiritual Outcomes

Comparison	Posttest					Follow-up				
	N	k	d	95% CI	I^2	N	k	d	95% CI	I^2
Psychological Outcomes										
Control	1,280	22	.45	0.15 to 0.75	83.84	602	8	.21	−0.43 to 0.86	92.62
Alternate	1,718	29	.26	0.10 to 0.41	57.47	610	13	.25	0.05 to 0.45	28.74
Dismantling	387	11	.13	−0.26 to 0.52	67.87	277	8	.22	−.09 to 0.52	30.34
Spiritual Outcomes										
Control	600	8	.51	0.19 to 0.84	71.18	317	4	.25	−.03 to 0.52	25.87
Alternate	707	14	.41	0.18 to 0.65	53.95	222	6	.32	−0.10 to 0.74	56.62
Dismantling	235	7	.33	0.07 to 0.59	0	126	4	.38	−0.16 to 0.91	51.96

Note: The symbol *N* is the sample size summed across studies. The *k* is the number of effect sizes summarized. The *d* is the weighted mean d across samples. The *95% CI* is the confidence interval for the mean *d*. The *I²* is the percentage of the observed variance that reflects real differences in effect sizes.

theoretical orientation and duration of psychotherapy—patients in R/S psychotherapies outperformed patients in alternate psychotherapies on spiritual outcomes but not on psychological outcomes. That is, participants in R/S psychotherapies showed similar reductions in psychological symptoms as did participants in similar alternate psychotherapies (e.g., similar reductions in depression) but showed better results on spiritual variables (e.g., greater increases in spiritual well-being).

Publication Bias

We conducted a series of analyses to determine whether our results were affected by publication bias. Publication bias refers to the tendency for studies available to the reviewer to be systematically different from studies that were unavailable such that conclusions may be biased. In our study, published studies had slightly higher effect sizes than unpublished studies (see Table 20.3), although in no case was this difference significant. Additionally, we used the trim and fill procedure (Duval & Tweedie, 2000) to estimate the effects of publication bias. The trim and fill procedure estimates the number of missing studies due to publication bias and statistically imputes these studies, recalculating the overall effect size. The effect sizes were somewhat reduced using this procedure, but the overall conclusions did not change (see Table 20.4). In summary, the results of the

Table 20.3 Comparison of Published and Unpublished Studies

Level of specificity	k published	d published	95% CI published	k unpublished	d unpublished	95% CI unpublished
Comparison with control	15	.49	.06 to 0.92	7	.41	.20 to 0.62
Comparison with alternate	23	.26	.10 to 0.41	6	.19	−.34 to 0.71
Comparison with alternate (dismantling)	7	.18	−.24 to 0.60	4	−.06	−.91 to 0.80

Note: The symbol *k* refers to the number of effect sizes summarized. The statistic *d* is the weighted mean standardized mean difference across samples. The *95% CI* is the confidence interval of the weighted mean standardized difference.

Table 20.4   Results for Trim and Fill Analyses

Comparison	Posttest		
	$K+$	d adj	95% CI
Psychological Outcomes			
Control	7	.15	−.13 to 0.44
Alternate	4	.17	.01 to 0.33
Dismantling	1	.03	−.37 to 0.43
Spiritual Outcomes			
Control	0	.51	.19 to 0.84
Alternate	3	.25	.03 to 0.51
Dismantling	1	.26	−.01 to 0.53

Note: The $K+$ is the number of the studies imputed by the trim and fill procedures. The symbol d adj is the weighted mean d of the distribution of d that contains both the observed and the imputed effects.

publication bias analyses indicate that it may be more difficult for studies on R/S psychotherapies with small magnitude or negative results to be published. These results should be taken with caution, as these analyses were conducted with a low number of studies.

Moderators

We tested three moderators of interest—treatment format (individual vs. group), target problem (psychological, forgiveness, or health), and type of R/S faith commitment (religious vs. spiritual). All moderator analyses were conducted on psychological outcomes at posttest. None of the moderators were statistically significant. That is, none of these variables accounted for appreciable variance in the effect size estimates in the reviewed studies.

Patient Contributions

The research reviewed in the present meta-analysis focused on the psychotherapist's contribution to the relationship. That is, analysis has addressed the question of whether it is helpful to tailor the psychotherapy to the client's religious and spiritual proclivities. However, characteristics of individual clients probably also affect tailoring.

One patient characteristic that might be especially pertinent is the client's R/S commitment. In the vast majority of studies, the participants have identified with a particular religion or spirituality under investigation; for instance, a study on Christian accommodative psychotherapy for depression would recruit only Christian participants. However, people differ in their level of R/S commitment. For some, R/S beliefs may be little more than a tradition or demographic characteristic, whereas for others R/S beliefs may be the driving force behind their core values, life goals, and everyday behaviors. Thus, religious commitment is likely more important than beliefs or a religious demographic identification (Worthington, 1988). We suggest that including R/S beliefs into psychotherapy may be more important for clients that are highly R/S committed than for clients who are less R/S committed. There is modest support for this hypothesis in a recent effectiveness—not randomized clinical trial—study (Wade, Worthington, & Vogel, 2007).

Unfortunately, this hypothesis has not been addressed frequently enough to be tested in the present review. The vast majority of studies have simply required that participants identify with the particular religion that is integrated with the psychotherapy or indicate that they are open to participate in a psychotherapy that includes spirituality. Two studies (Nohr, 2001; Razali, Aminah, & Khan, 2002) assessed the efficacy of R/S psychotherapies using clients with different levels of religious commitment. But their findings were mixed. Thus, there is not sufficient research on this patient factor to make viable conclusions or clinical recommendations.

Limitations of the Research

There are limitations of the research on R/S psychotherapies. First, although the quality of studies has improved in the past several years, some studies still suffered from less rigorous study designs and low power. In particular, there were relatively few comparisons ($n = 11$ with psychological effect sizes; $n = 7$ with spiritual effect sizes) that met the criteria for a dismantling design, meaning they compared R/S psychotherapy with an alternate psychotherapy that was the same in theoretical orientation and duration. These types of studies are especially important because they best answer the empirical question of whether it improves efficacy to incorporate R/S beliefs in an existing psychotherapy for R/S clients. Studies that compare R/S psychotherapy with a completely different type of psychotherapy can be rigorous as well. However, if participants in the R/S psychotherapy outperform participants in the alternate psychotherapy, it is difficult to discern whether this occurred because (a) the specific R/S elements caused the differential outcomes or (b) something else that was different between the two psychotherapies caused the differential outcomes.

Many studies with comparative designs used random assignment to conditions, but some did not. Random assignment to conditions is the gold standard of psychotherapy research, but it is sometimes difficult to accomplish in studies of R/S psychotherapy. Religion is an emotionally charged topic for many people, and thus, highly religious people may be less willing to be randomized to a secular treatment, and adamantly nonreligious people may not be willing to be randomized to a religious treatment.

Another limitation of this meta-analysis was publication bias. Our analyses indicated that some studies indicating negative or null findings for R/S psychotherapies may have been unpublished, literally sitting in a file-drawer somewhere. There are several possible reasons for publication bias in this literature. First, much of the research on R/S psychotherapy is conducted by researchers who have religious orientations. Author decisions may be a cause of the apparent publication bias. When the results of a study do not support the efficacy of R/S psychotherapy or yield an estimate of efficacy that is small, it may be that the authors tend not to submit the paper for publication. Second, when the research is published, some of the it has been published in religiously oriented journals. Editors and reviewers for journals with a religious theme may accept papers that are supportive of R/S psychotherapy more frequently than those that are not. Third, editors may be reluctant to publish comparative studies that report null findings because it is difficult to determine whether these results reflect (a) no true difference between conditions or (b) problems in the study design and implementation (e.g., low power).

Therapeutic Practices

To conclude, we offer several concrete applications for clinical practice based on the findings from our meta-analytic review.

• R/S psychotherapy works. The research evidence is consistent that R/S psychotherapies are efficacious at improving both psychological and spiritual outcomes, and there is some evidence that these gains are maintained at follow-up. Thus, R/S psychotherapies should be viewed as a valid alternative treatment option for R/S clients.

• The addition of R/S beliefs or practices to an established secular psychotherapy does not reliably improve psychological outcomes for R/S clients over and above the effects of the established secular psychotherapy alone. Although there was some evidence that R/S psychotherapies outperformed alternate psychotherapies, that difference was reduced when the analysis was limited to studies that used a dismantling design. Thus, at this time there is no empirical basis to recommend R/S psychotherapies over established secular psychotherapies when the primary or exclusive treatment outcome is symptom remission.

• R/S psychotherapies offer spiritual benefits to clients that are not present in secular psychotherapies. The meta-analytic results indicate that patients in R/S psychotherapies showed more improvement on spiritual outcomes than did patients in alternate psychotherapies, even when this analysis was limited to studies that used a dismantling design. Thus, for those patients and contexts in which spiritual outcomes are highly valued, R/S psychotherapy can be considered a treatment of choice.

• The incorporation of R/S beliefs or practices into psychotherapy should follow the desires and needs of the particular client. Psychotherapists are encouraged to ask about R/S beliefs and commitment as part of the intake process and to incorporate them into psychotherapy (a) as they feel comfortable and (b) in line with the preferences of the particular client. Research summarized elsewhere in this volume demonstrates that accommodating patient preferences modestly enhances treatment outcomes and decreases premature termination by a third (Swift, Callahan, & Vollmer, Chapter 15, this volume).

• We hypothesize that incorporating R/S beliefs or practices into psychotherapy might be more efficacious with clients who are highly religiously or spiritually committed. Few studies have addressed this hypothesis, but there is no research or clinical evidence to suggest that R/S psychotherapies produce *worse* outcomes than secular therapies for these patients. Thus, we recommend that practitioners consider offering R/S treatment to highly religious or spiritual patients.

References

An asterisk (*) indicates studies included in the meta-analysis.

Allport, G. W., & Ross, J. M. (1967). Personal religious orientation and prejudice. *Journal of Personality and Social Psychology, 5*, 432–33.

Avants, S. K., & Margolin, A. (2004). Development of Spiritual Self-Schema (3-S) therapy for the treatment of addictive and HIV risk behavior: A convergence of cognitive and Buddhist psychology. *Journal of Psychotherapy Integration, 14*(3), 253–289.

*Azhar, M. Z., & Varma, S. L. (1995a). Religious psychotherapy as management of bereavement. *Acta Psychiatrica Scandinavica, 91*, 233–35.

*Azhar, M. Z., & Varma, S. L. (1995b). Religious psychotherapy in depressive patients. *Psychotherapy and Psychosomatics, 63*, 165–73.

*Azhar, M. Z., Varma, S. L., & Dharap, A. S. (1994). Religious psychotherapy in anxiety disorder patients. *Acta Psychiatrica Scandinavica, 90*, 1–3.

*Baker, D. C. (2000). The investigation of pastoral care interventions as a treatment for depression among continuing care retirement community residents. *Journal of Religious Gerontology, 12*, 63–85.

*Barron, L. W. (2007). *Effect of religious coping skills training with group cognitive-behavioral therapy for treatment of depression.* Unpublished doctoral dissertation, Northcentral University, Prescott Valley, Arizona.

*Bay, P. S., Beckman, D., Trippi, J., Gunderman, R., & Terry, C. (2008). The effect of pastoral care services on anxiety, depression, hope, religious coping, and religious problem solving styles: A randomized controlled study. *Journal of Religious Health, 47*, 57–69.

Beck, A. T. (1972). *Depression: Causes and treatment.* Philadelphia: University of Pennsylvania Press.

Beck, A. T., Rush, A. J., Shaw, B. F., & Emery, G. (1979). *Cognitive therapy of depression.* New York: Guilford Press.

Beck, A. T., Ward, C. H., Mendelson, M., Mock, J., & Erbaugh, J. (1961). An inventory for measuring depression. *Archives of General Psychiatry, 4*, 561–71.

Borenstein, M., Hedges, L., Higgins, J., & Rothstein, H. R. (2005). *Comprehensive meta-analysis, Version 2.* Englewood, NJ: Biostat, Inc.

Borenstein, M., Hedges, L. V., Higgins, J. P. T., & Rothstein, H. R. (2009). Introduction to meta-analysis. Chichester, UK: Wiley.

*Bowland, S. E. (2008). *Evaluation of a psycho-social-spiritual intervention with older women survivors of interpersonal trauma.* Unpublished doctoral dissertation, Washington University in St. Louis, MO.

*Byers, A. B., Underwood, L. A., & Hardy, V. L. (in press). Spirituality group with female offenders: Impacting hope. *Journal of Correctional Health Care*, in press.

*Chan, C. L. W., Ho, R. T. H., Lee, P. W. H., Cheng, J. Y. Y., Leung, P. P. Y., Foo, W., et al. (2006). A randomized controlled trial of psychosocial interventions using the psychophysiological framework for Chinese breast cancer patients. *Journal of Psychosocial Oncology, 24*, 3–26.

*Chan, C. H. Y., Ng, E. H. Y., Chan, C. L. W., Ho, & Chan, T. H. Y. (2006). Effectiveness of psychosocial group intervention for reducing anxiety in women undergoing in vitro fertilization: A randomized controlled study. *Fertility and Sterility, 85*, 339–46.

*Cole, B. S. (2005). Spiritually-focused psychotherapy for people diagnosed with cancer: A pilot outcome study. *Mental Health, Religion, and Culture, 8*, 217–226.

*Combs, C. W., Bufford, R. K., Campbell, C. D., & Halter, L. L. (2000). Effects of cognitive-behavioral marriage enrichment: A controlled study. *Marriage and Family: A Christian Journal, 3*, 99–111.

Davis, D. E., Hook, J. N., & Worthington, E. L., Jr. (2008). Relational spirituality and forgiveness: The roles of attachment to God, religious coping, and viewing the transgression as a desecration. *Journal of Psychology and Christianity, 27*, 293–301.

Duval, S. J., & Tweedie, R. L. (2000). A nonparametric "trim and fill" method of accounting for publication bias in meta-analysis. *Journal of the American Statistical Association, 95*, 89–98.

Ellison, C. W. (1983). Spiritual well-being: Conceptualization and measurement. *Journal of Psychology and Theology, 11*, 330–40.

*Gibbel, M. R. (2010). *Evaluating a spiritually integrated intervention for depressed college students.* Unpublished doctoral dissertation, Bowling Green State University, OH.

Harris, A. H. S., Thoresen, C. E., McCullough, M. E., & Larson, D. B. (1999). Spiritually and religiously oriented health interventions. *Journal of Health Psychology, 4*, 413–33.

*Hart, K. E., & Shapiro, D. A. (2002, August). Secular and spiritual forgiveness interventions for recovering alcoholics harboring grudges. Paper presented at the Annual Convention of the American Psychological Association, Chicago.

*Hawkins, R. S., Tan, S., & Turk, A. A. (1999). Secular versus Christian inpatient cognitive-behavioral therapy programs: Impact on depression and spiritual well-being. *Journal of Psychology and Theology, 27*, 309–318.

Hill, P. C., Pargament, K. I., Hood, R. W., Jr., McCullough, M. E., Swyeres, J. P., Larson, D. B., et al. (2000). Conceptualizing religion and spirituality: Points of commonality, points of departure. *Journal for the Theory of Social Behavior, 30*, 51–77.

*Ho, T. H., Lo, P. H. Y., & Chan, C. L. W. (2009). The efficacy of the body-mind-spirit intervention and social support groups on chinese breast cancer patients. In Y. M. Lee, C. L. W. Chan, S. M. Ng, & P. P. Y. Leung.(Eds.), *Integrative Body-Mind-Spirit Social Work: An Empirically Based Approach to Assessment and Treatment* (pp. 217–34). New York: The Oxford University Press.

Hodge, D. R. (2006). Spiritually modified cognitive therapy: A review of the literature. *Social Work, 51*, 157–66.

Hook, J. N., Worthington, E. L., Jr., Davis, D. E., Jennings, D. J., II., Gartner, A. L., & Hook, J. P. (2010). Empirically supported religious and spiritual therapies. *Journal of Clinical Psychology, 66*, 46–72.

*Hsiao, F. H., Yang, T. T., Chen, C. C., Tsai, S. Y., Wang, K. C., Lai, Y. M., et al. (2007).

The comparison of effectiveness of two modalities of mental health nurse follow-up programmes for female outpatients with depression in Taipei, Taiwan. *Journal of Clinical Nursing, 16*, 1141–50.

*Iler, W. L. (2001). The impact of daily visits from chaplains on patients with chronic obstructive pulmonary disease (COPD): A pilot study. *Chaplaincy Today, 17*, 5–11.

*Jackson, R. E. (1999). *Reducing shame through forgiveness and empathy: A group therapy approach to promoting prosocial behavior.* Unpublished doctoral dissertation, Fuller Theological Seminary, Pasadena, CA.

*Johnson, W. B., DeVries, R., Ridley, C. R., Pettorini, D., & Peterson, D. R. (1994). The comparative efficacy of Christian and secular rational-emotive therapy with Christian clients. *Journal of Psychology and Theology, 22*, 130–40.

*Johnson, W. B., & Ridley, C. R. (1992). Brief Christian and non-Christian rational-emotive therapy with depressed Christian clients: An exploratory study. *Counseling and Values, 36*, 220–29.

*Lampton, C., Oliver, G. J., Worthington, E. L., Jr., & Berry, J. W. (2005). Helping Christian college students become more forgiving: An intervention study to promote forgiveness as part of a program to shape Christian character. *Journal of Psychology and Theology, 33*, 278–90.

*Lee, A. M., Chan, C. L. W., Ho, A. H. Y., Wang, C. N., Tang, V. Y. H., Lau S. S. M., et al. (2009). The efficacy of the body-mind-spirit intervention model on improving the quality of life and psychological well-being of chinese patients with colorectal cancer: A preliminary report. In Y. M. Lee, C. L. W. Chan, S. M., Ng, & P. P. Y. Leung (Eds.), *Integrative body-mind-spirit social work: An empirically based approach to assessment and treatment* (pp. 236–43). New York: The Oxford University Press.

Lipsey, M. W., & Wilson, D. B. (2001). *Practical meta-analysis.* Thousand Oaks, CA: Sage.

*Liu, C. J., Hsiung, P. C., Chang, K. J., Liu, Y. F., Want, K. C., Hsiao, F. H., et al. (2008). A study on the efficacy of body-mind-spirit group therapy for patients with breast cancer. *Journal of Clinical Nursing, 17*, 2539–49.

Luborsky, L., Diguer, L., Seligman, D. A., Rosenthal, R., Krause, E. D., Johnson, S., et al. (1999). The researcher's own therapy allegiances: A "wild card" in comparisons of treatment efficacy. *Clinical Psychology: Science and Practice, 6*, 95–106.

*Margolin, A., Beitel, M., Schuman-Olivier, Z., & Avants, S. K. (2006). A controlled study of a spirituality-focused intervention for increasing motivation for HIV prevention among drug users. *AIDS Education and Prevention, 18*, 311–22.

*Margolin, A., Schuman-Olivier, Z., Beitel, M., Arnold, R. M., Fulwiler, C. E., & Avants, S. K. (2007). *Journal of Clinical Psychology, 63*, 979–99.

*McCain, N. L., Gray, D. P., Elswick, R. K., Jr., Robins, J. W., Tuck, I., Walter, J. M., et al. (2008). A randomized clinical trial of alternative stress management interventions in persons with HIV infection. *Journal of Consulting and Clinical Psychology, 76*, 431–41.

McCullough, M. E. (1999). Research on religion-accommodative counseling: Review and meta-analysis. *Journal of Counseling Psychology, 46*, 92–98.

*Miller, W. R., Forcehimes, A., O'Leary, M. J., & LaNoue, M. D. (2008). Spiritual direction in addiction treatment: Two clinical trials. *Journal of Substance Abuse Treatment, 35*, 434–42.

*Nohr, R. W. (2001). *Outcome effects of receiving a spiritually informed vs. a standard cognitive-behavioral stress management workshop.* Unpublished doctoral dissertation, Marquette University, Milwaukee, WI.

Norcross, J. C. (1990). An eclectic definition of psychotherapy. In J. K. Zeig & W. M. Munion (Eds.), *What is psychotherapy? Contemporary perspectives* (pp. 218–20). San Francisco: Jossey-Bass.

Norcross, J. C. (Ed.). (2002). *Psychotherapy relationships that work: Therapist contributions and responsiveness to patients.* New York: Oxford University Press.

Pargament, K. I. (2007). *Spiritually integrated psychotherapy: Understanding and addressing the sacred.* New York: Guilford Press.

Pargament, K. I., & Saunders, S. M. (2007). Introduction to the special issue on spirituality and psychotherapy. *Journal of Clinical Psychology, 63*, 903–907.

*Pecheur, D. R., & Edwards, K. J. (1984). A comparison of secular and religious versions of cognitive therapy with depressed Christian college students. *Journal of Psychology and Theology, 12*, 45–54.

Post, B. C., & Wade, N. G. (2009). Religion and spirituality in psychotherapy: A practice-friendly review of research. *Journal of Clinical Psychology: In Session, 65*, 131–46.

*Propst, L. R. (1980). The comparative efficacy of religious and nonreligious imagery for the treatment of mild depression in religious individuals. *Cognitive Therapy and Research, 4*, 167–78.

*Propst, L. R., Ostrom, R., Watkins, P., Dean, T., & Mashburn, D. (1992). Comparative efficacy of religious and nonreligious cognitive-behavioral therapy for the treatment of clinical depression in religious individuals. *Journal of Consulting and Clinical Psychology, 60*, 94–103.

*Razali, S. M., Aminah, K., & Khan, U. A. (2002). Religious-cultural psychotherapy in the management of anxiety patients. *Transcultural Psychiatry, 39*, 130–36.

*Razali, S. M., Hasanah, C. I., Aminah, K., & Subramaniam, M. (1998). Religious-sociocultural psychotherapy in patients with anxiety and depression. *Australian and New Zealand Journal of Psychiatry, 32*, 867–72.

*Richards, P. S., Berrett, M. E., Hardman, R. K., & Eggett, D. L. (2006). Comparative efficacy of spirituality, cognitive, and emotional support groups for treating eating disorder inpatients. *Eating Disorders, 14*, 401–415.

*Rosmarin, D. H., Pargament, K. I., Pirutinsky, S., & Mahoney, A. (2010). *A randomized controlled evaluation of a spiritually-integrated cognitive-behavioral intervention for subclinical anxiety among religious Jews.* Unpublished manuscript, Bowling Green State University, OH.

*Rye, M. S., & Pargament, K. I. (2002). Forgiveness and romantic relationships in college: Can it heal the wounded heart? *Journal of Clinical Psychology, 58*, 419–41.

*Rye, M. S., Pargament, K. I., Pan, W., Yingling, D. W., Shogren, K. A., & Ito, M. (2005). Can group interventions facilitate forgiveness of an ex-spouse? A randomized clinical trial. *Journal of Consulting and Clinical Psychology, 73*, 880–92.

*Scott, S. (2001). *Faith supportive group therapy and symptom reduction in Christian breast cancer patients.* Unpublished doctoral dissertation, Regent University, Virginia Beach, VA.

Sheldrake, P. (1992). *Spirituality and history: Questions of interpretation and method.* New York: Crossroads.

Smith, T. B., Bartz, J., & Richards, P. S. (2007). Outcomes of religious and spiritual adaptations to psychotherapy: A meta-analytic review. *Psychotherapy Research, 17*, 643–55.

*Stratton, S. P., Dean, J. B., Nonneman, A. J., Bode, R. A., & Worthington, E. L., Jr. (2008).

Forgiveness interventions as spiritual development strategies: Comparing forgiveness workshop training, expressive writing about forgiveness, and retested controls. *Journal of Psychology and Christianity, 27*, 347–57.

*Targ, E. F., & Levine, E. G. (2002). The efficacy of a mind-body-spirit group for women with breast cancer: A randomized clinical trial. *General Hospital Psychiatry, 24*, 238–48.

*Toh, Y., & Tan, S. (1997). The effectiveness of church-based lay counselors: A controlled outcome study. *Journal of Psychology and Christianity, 16*, 260–67.

*Tonkin, K. M. (2005). *Obesity, bulimia, and binge-eating disorder: The use of a cognitive behavioral and spiritual intervention.* Unpublished doctoral dissertation, Bowling Green State University, OH.

*Trathen, D. W. (1995). *A comparison of the effectiveness of two Christian premarital counseling programs (skills and information-based) utilized by evangelical Protestant churches.* Unpublished doctoral dissertation, University of Denver, CO.

Wade, N. G., Worthington, E. L., Jr., & Vogul, D. L. (2007). Effectiveness of religiously tailored interventions in Christian therapy. *Psychotherapy Research, 17*, 91–105.

Worthington, E. L., Jr. (1988). Understanding the values of religious clients: A model and its application to counseling. *Journal of Counseling Psychology, 35*, 166–74.

Worthington, E. L., Jr. (1998). The pyramid model of forgiveness: Some interdisciplinary speculations about unforgiveness and the promotion of forgiveness. In E. Worthington (Ed.), *Dimensions of forgiveness: Psychological research and theological perspectives* (pp. 107–38). Philadelphia: Templeton Foundation Press.

Worthington, E. L., Jr. (2009). *A just forgiveness: Responsible healing without excusing injustice.* Downers Grove, IL: InterVarsity Press.

Worthington, E. L., Jr., & Aten, J. D. (2009). Psychotherapy with religious and spiritual clients: An introduction. *Journal of Clinical Psychology: In Session, 65*, 123–30.

Worthington, E. L., Jr., Kurusu, T. A., McCullough, M. E., & Sandage, S. J. (1996). Empirical research on religion and psychotherapeutic processes and outcomes: A 10-year review and research prospectus. *Psychological Bulletin, 119*, 448–87.

Worthington, E. L., Jr., & Sandage, S. J. (2001). Religion and spirituality. *Psychotherapy: Theory, Research, Practice, Training, 38*, 473–478.

Worthington, E. L., Jr., Wade, N. G., Hight, T. L., Ripley, J. S., McCullough, M. E., Berry, J. W., Schmitt, M. M., Berry, J. T., et al. (2003). The religious commitment inventory—10: Development, refinement, and validation of a brief scale for research and counseling. *Journal of Counseling Psychology, 50*, 84–96.

*Yang, T. T., Hsiao, F. H., Wang, K. C., Ng, S. M., Ho, R. T. H., Chan, C. L. W., et al. (2009). The effect of psychotherapy added to pharmacotherapy on cortisol responses. *Journal of Nervous and Mental Disease, 197*, 401–406.

*Zhang, Y., Young, D., Lee, S., Li, L., Zhang, H., Xiao, Z., et al. (2002). Chinese Taoist cognitive psychotherapy in the treatment of generalized anxiety disorder in contemporary China. *Transcultural Psychiatry, 39*, 115–29.

PART 4

Conclusions and Guidelines

Evidence-Based Therapy Relationships: Research Conclusions and Clinical Practices

John C. Norcross *and* Bruce E. Wampold

We shall not cease from exploration
And the end of all our exploring
Will be to arrive where we started
And know the place for the first time.
—T. S. Eliot ("Little Gidding" in *Four Quartets*)

Having traversed more than two dozen meta-analyses and arrived at the end of this book, we have the opportunity to present the interdivisional Task Force conclusions and to reflect on its work. Like the tireless traveler in Eliot's poem, we have rediscovered the therapy relationship and know it, again, for the first time.

This closing chapter presents the conclusions and recommendations of the second Task Force on Evidence-Based Therapy Relationships. These statements reaffirm and, in several instances, update those of the earlier Task Force (Norcross, 2001, 2002). We then offer some final thoughts on what works, what doesn't work, and clinical practice.

Conclusions of the Task Force

• The therapy relationship makes substantial and consistent contributions to psychotherapy outcome independent of the specific type of treatment.

• The therapy relationship accounts for why clients improve (or fail to improve) at least as much as the particular treatment method.

• Practice and treatment guidelines should explicitly address therapist behaviors and qualities that promote a facilitative therapy relationship.

• Efforts to promulgate best practices or evidence-based practices (EBPs) without including the relationship are seriously incomplete and potentially misleading.

• Adapting or tailoring the therapy relationship to specific patient characteristics (in addition to diagnosis) enhances the effectiveness of treatment.

• The therapy relationship acts in concert with treatment methods, patient characteristics, and practitioner qualities in determining effectiveness; a comprehensive understanding of effective (and ineffective) psychotherapy will consider all of these determinants and their optimal combinations.

• The following table summarizes the Task Force conclusions regarding the evidentiary strength of (a) elements of the therapy relationship primarily provided by the psychotherapist and (b) methods of adapting psychotherapy to particular patient characteristics.

• These conclusions do *not* by themselves constitute a set of practice standards but represent current scientific knowledge to be understood and applied in the context of all the clinical evidence available in each case.

	Elements of the relationship	Methods of adapting
Demonstrably effective	Alliance in individual psychotherapy	Reactance/Resistance level
	Alliance in youth psychotherapy	Preferences
	Alliance in family therapy	Culture
	Cohesion in group therapy	Religion and spirituality
	Empathy	
	Collecting client feedback	
Probably effective	Goal consensus	Stages of change
	Collaboration	Coping style
	Positive regard	
Promising but insufficient research to judge	Congruence/Genuineness	Expectations
	Repairing alliance ruptures	Attachment style
	Managing countertransference	

Recommendations of the Task Force
General Recommendations

1. We recommend that the results and conclusions of this second Task Force be widely disseminated in order to enhance awareness and use of what "works" in the therapy relationship.

2. Readers are encouraged to interpret these findings in the context of the acknowledged limitations of the Task Force's work.

3. We recommend that future Task Forces be established periodically to review these findings, include new elements of the relationship, incorporate the results of non-English language publications (where practical), and update these conclusions.

Practice Recommendations

4. Practitioners are encouraged to make the creation and cultivation of a therapy relationship, characterized by the elements found to be demonstrably and probably effective, a primary aim in the treatment of patients.

5. Practitioners are encouraged to adapt or tailor psychotherapy to those specific patient characteristics in ways found to be demonstrably and probably effective.

6. Practitioners are encouraged to routinely monitor patients' responses to the therapy relationship and ongoing treatment. Such monitoring leads to increased opportunities to reestablish collaboration, improve the relationship, modify technical strategies, and avoid premature termination.

7. Concurrent use of evidence-based therapy relationships *and* evidence-based treatments adapted to the patient is likely to generate the best outcomes.

Training Recommendations

8. Training and continuing education programs are encouraged to provide competency-based training in the demonstrably and probably effective elements of the therapy relationship.

9. Training and continuing education programs are encouraged to provide competency-based training in adapting

psychotherapy to the individual patient in ways that demonstrably and probably enhance treatment success.

10. Accreditation and certification bodies for mental health training programs should develop criteria for assessing the adequacy of training in evidence-based therapy relationships.

Research Recommendations

11. Researchers are encouraged to progress beyond correlational designs that associate the frequency of relationship behaviors with patient outcomes to methodologies capable of examining the complex associations among patient qualities, clinician behaviors, and treatment outcome. Of particular importance is disentangling the patient contributions and the therapist contributions to relationship elements and ultimately outcome.

12. Researchers are encouraged to examine the specific mediators and moderators of the links between the relationship elements and treatment outcome.

13. Researchers are encouraged to address the observational perspective (i.e., therapist, patient, or external rater) in future studies and reviews of "what works" in the therapy relationship. Agreement among observational perspectives provides a solid sense of established fact; divergence among perspectives holds important implications for practice.

Policy Recommendations

14. APA's Division of Psychotherapy, Division of Clinical Psychology, and other practice divisions are encouraged to educate its members on the benefits of evidence-based therapy relationships.

15. Mental health organizations as a whole are encouraged to educate their members about the improved outcomes associated with using evidence-based therapy relationships, as they frequently now do about evidence-based treatments.

16. We recommend that the American Psychological Association and other mental health organizations advocate for the research-substantiated benefits of a nurturing and responsive human relationship in psychotherapy.

17. Finally, administrators of mental health services are encouraged to attend to the relational features of those services. Attempts to improve the quality of care should account for treatment relationships and adaptations.

What Works

The process by which the preceding conclusions on which relationship elements and adaptation methods are effective requires some elaboration as these conclusions tend to be the most cited and controversial findings of the Task Force. These conclusions represent the consensus of expert panels composed of five judges who independently reviewed and rated the empirical evidence. They evaluated, for each relationship element or adaptation method, the previous research summary and the new meta-analysis according to the following criteria: number of empirical studies, consistency of empirical results, independence of supportive studies, magnitude of association between the relationship element and outcome, evidence for causal link between relationship element and outcome, and the ecological or external validity of research. Their respective ratings of demonstrably effective, probably effective, or promising but insufficient research to judge were then combined to render a consensus. In this way, we added a modicum of rigor and consensus to the process, which was admittedly less so in the first edition of the book.

The consensus deemed six of the relationship elements as demonstrably effective, three as probably effective, and three as promising but insufficient research to judge. The consensus of another panel deemed four adaptation methods as demonstrably effective, two as probably effective, and two as promising but insufficient research to judge. We were impressed by the skepticism and precision of the panelists (as scientists ought to be). At the same time, we were impressed by the disparate and perhaps elevated standards against which these relationship elements were evaluated.

Consider the evidentiary strength required for psychological treatments to be considered demonstrably efficacious in two influential compilations of evidence-based treatments. The Division of Clinical Psychology's Subcommittee on Research-Supported Treatments (www.div12.org/ PsychologicalTreatments/index.html) requires two between-group design experiments demonstrating that a psychological treatment is either (a) statistically superior to a pill or psychological placebo or to another treatment or (b) equivalent to an already established treatment in experiments with adequate sample sizes. The studies must have been conducted with treatment manuals and conducted by at least two different investigators. The typical effect size of those studies was often smaller than the effects for the relationship elements reported in this book. For listing in SAMHSA's National Registry of Evidence-based Programs and Practices (www.nrepp.samhsa.gov), only evidence of statistically significant behavioral outcomes demonstrated in at least one study, using an experimental or quasi-experimental design, that has been published in a peer-reviewed journal or comprehensive evaluation report is needed. The intervention

must be accompanied by implementation materials, training, and support resources that are ready to use by the public. By these standards, practically all of the relationship elements and adaptation methods in this volume would be considered demonstrably effective, if not for the requirement of a randomized clinical trial, which is neither clinically nor ethically feasible for the vast majority of the relationship elements.

In important ways, the criteria for relationship elements are more rigorous. Whereas the criteria for designating treatments as evidence based relies on only one or two studies, the evidence for relationship elements and adaptation methods discussed here are based on comprehensive meta-analyses of many studies (in excess of 50 in several cases), spanning various treatments and research groups. The studies used to establish evidence-based treatments are, however, clinical trials, which are often designated as the "gold standard" for establishing evidence. Nevertheless, these studies are often plagued by confounds such as researcher allegiance, cannot be blinded, and often contain bogus comparisons (Luborsky et al., 1999; Mohr et al., 2009; Wampold, 2001; Wampold et al., 2010). The point here is not to denigrate the criteria used to establish evidence-based treatments, but to underscore the robust scientific standards by which these relationship elements and adaptation methods have been evaluated.

A further research complication, but a clinical strength, concerns responsiveness. Research on the effectiveness of the psychotherapy relationship is constrained by therapist responsiveness—the ebb and flow of clinical interaction. Responsiveness refers to therapist behavior that is affected by emerging context, and occurs on many levels, including choice of a treatment method, case formulation, strategic use of the self, and then adjusting those to meet the emerging, evolving needs of the client in any given moment (Stiles, Honos-Webb, & Surko, 1998). Effective psychotherapists are responsive to the different needs of their clients, providing varying levels of relationship elements in different cases and, within the same case, at different moments. Successful responsiveness can confound attempts to find naturalistically observed linear relations of outcome with therapist behaviors (e.g., cohesion, positive regard). Because of such problems, the statistical relations between the relationship and outcome cannot always be trusted. By being clinically attuned and flexible, psychotherapists make it more difficult in research studies to discern what works.

In this volume, the relationship elements and adaptation methods are presented as separate, stand-alone practices. But as every seasoned psychotherapist knows, this is certainly never the case in clinical work. The alliance in individual therapy and cohesion in group therapy never act in isolation from other relationship behaviors, such as empathy or support. Nor does it seem humanly possible to cultivate a strong relationship with a patient without ascertaining his/her feedback on the therapeutic process and understanding the therapist's countertransference. Likewise, adapting treatment to a patient characteristic rarely occurs in isolation from other elements, such as forming a collaborative relationship with the patient. Stage of change, reactance level, culture, preferences, and the like all interconnect as we try to tailor therapy to the unique, complex individual. In short, while the relationship elements and adaptation methods featured in this book "work," they work together and interdependently.

What Doesn't Work

Translational research is both prescriptive and proscriptive; it tells us what works and what does not. In the following section, we highlight those therapist relational behaviors that are ineffective, perhaps even hurtful, in psychotherapy.

One means of identifying ineffective qualities of the therapeutic relationship is to simply reverse the effective behaviors. Thus, what do not work are poor alliances in individual psychotherapy, lack of cohesion in group therapy, and discordance in couple and family therapy. Paucity of empathy, collaboration, consensus, and positive regard predict treatment dropout and failure. The ineffective practitioner will neither seek nor respond to client feedback, will ignore alliance ruptures, and will not be aware of his/her countertransference. And less effective psychotherapists will rarely tailor or customize treatment to patient characteristics beyond diagnosis.

Another means of identifying ineffective qualities of the relationship is to scour the research literature and conduct polls of experts. Here are several behaviors to avoid according to that research (Duncan, Miller, Wampold, & Hubble, 2010) and a Delphi poll (Norcross, Koocher, & Garofalo, 2006):

• *Confrontations.* Controlled research trials, particularly in the addictions field, consistently find a confrontational style to be ineffective. In one review (Miller, Wilbourne, & Hettema, 2003), confrontation was ineffective in all 12 identified trials. By contrast, expressing empathy, rolling with resistance, developing discrepancy, and supporting self-efficacy, characteristic of Motivational Interviewing, have demonstrated large effects with a small number of sessions (Lundahl & Burke, 2009).

• *Negative Processes.* Client reports and research studies converge in warning therapists to avoid comments or behaviors that are hostile, pejorative, critical, rejecting, or blaming (Binder & Strupp, 1997; Lambert & Barley, 2002). Therapists who attack a client's dysfunctional thoughts or relational patterns need, repeatedly, to distinguish between attacking the person versus her behavior.

• *Assumptions.* Psychotherapists who assume or intuit their client's perceptions of relationship satisfaction and treatment success frequently misjudge these aspects. By contrast, therapists who specifically and respectfully inquire about their client's perceptions frequently enhance the alliance and prevent premature termination (Lambert & Shimokawa, this volume, Chapter 10).

• *Therapist Centricity.* A recurrent lesson from process-outcome research is that the client's observational perspective on the therapy relationship best predicts outcome (Orlinsky, Ronnestad, & Willutzki, 2004). Psychotherapy practice that relies on the therapist's observational perspective, while valuable, does not predict outcome as well. Therefore, privileging the client's experiences is central.

• *Rigidity.* By inflexibly and excessively structuring treatment, the therapist risks empathic failures and inattentiveness to clients' experiences. Such a therapist is likely to overlook a breach in the relationship and mistakenly assume she has not contributed to that breach. Dogmatic reliance on particular relational or therapy methods, incompatible with the client, imperils treatment (Ackerman & Hilsenroth, 2001).

• *Procrustean Bed.* As the field of psychotherapy has matured, using an identical therapy relationship (and treatment method) for all clients is now recognized as inappropriate and, in select cases, even unethical. The efficacy and applicability of psychotherapy will be enhanced by tailoring it to the unique needs of the client, not by imposing a Procrustean bed onto unwitting consumers of psychological services. We should all avoid the crimes of Procrustes, the legendary Greek innkeeper who would cut the long limbs of clients or stretch short limbs to fit his one-size bed.

• *Singularity.* In the quest to adapt psychotherapy, some psychotherapists become enamored of a single matching protocol and apply that match to virtually every patient who crosses their path. They are convinced that a single adaptation, be it the patient's reactance, diagnosis, culture, or stage of change, is the exclusive means of tailoring treatment to a successful outcome. However, the research appraised in this book convincingly demonstrates that many adaptations succeed. We must also guard against imposing the Procrustean bed when we adapt psychotherapy; one size, even in adaptation or tailoring, never works for all clients.

• *Flexibility without Fidelity.* The desire to be flexible and responsive with patients frequently gives rise to a clinical dilemma (Norcross, Hogan, & Koocher, 2008). Flexibility to the patient's preferences or culture offers the promise that it "fits" but not necessarily of research support for that preferred treatment. Fidelity to a research-supported treatment offers the promise that it "works" but not necessarily with that particular patient or population. Errors in either direction can portend clinical failure, but after half a book dedicated to the benefits of treatment adaptation, we should note the downside of ignoring brand-name therapies that possess considerable empirical evidence. Practitioners can become overly flexible when employing a treatment without any research evidence or when adapting a treatment in ways that markedly deviate from its established effectiveness. While the research supports adaptation in many cases, the research also recommends fidelity to treatments as found effective in controlled research. We need to balance flexibility with fidelity.

We can optimize therapy relationships by simultaneously using what works *and* studiously avoiding what does not work.

Concluding Thoughts

In the culture wars of psychotherapy that pit the therapy relationship against the treatment method (Norcross & Lambert, this volume, Chapter 1), it is easy to choose sides, ignore disconfirming research, and lose sight of our superordinate commitment to patient benefit. Instead, let us conclude, like T. S. Eliot, by "arriving where we started" and underscoring four incontrovertible but oft-neglected truths about psychotherapy relationships.

First, the interdivisional Task Force was commissioned in order to augment patient benefit. We continue to explore what works in the therapy relationship and what works when we adapt that relationship to (transdiagnostic) patient characteristics. That remains our collective aim: improving patient success, however measured and manifested in a given case.

Second, psychotherapists have always aimed to integrate the idiographic and the nomothetic, the particular and the general, in their craft. One means of doing so is to adapt psychotherapy to the *particulars* of the individual patient according to *generalities* identified by research. We can offer research-supported methods of individualizing psychotherapy to the entire person and his/her singular situation.

Third, psychotherapy is at root a human relationship. Even when "delivered" via distance or on a computer, psychotherapy is an irreducibly human encounter. Both parties bring themselves—their origins, cultures, personalities, psychopathology, expectations, biases, defenses, and strengths—to the human relationship. Some will judge that relationship to be a precondition of change and others a process of change, but all agree that it is a relational enterprise.

Fourth and final, how we create and cultivate that powerful human relationship can be guided by the fruits of research. As Carl Rogers (1980) compellingly demonstrated, there is no inherent tension between a relational approach and a scientific one. Science can and should inform us about what works in psychotherapy—be it a treatment method, an assessment measure, a patient behavior, an adaptation method, or yes, a therapy relationship.

References

Ackerman, S. J., & Hilsenroth, M. J. (2001). A review of therapist characteristics and techniques negatively impacting the therapeutic alliance. *Psychotherapy, 38,* 171–185.

Binder, J. L., & Strupp, H. H. (1997). "Negative process": A recurrently discovered and underestimated facet of therapeutic process and outcome in the individual psychotherapy of adults. *Clinical Psychology: Science and Practice, 4,* 121–139.

Duncan, B. L., Miller, S. D., Wampold, B. E., & Hubble, M. A. (Eds.) (2010). *Heart & soul of change in psychotherapy* (2nd ed.). Washington, DC: American Psychological Association.

Lambert, M. J., & Barley, D. E. (2002). Research summary on the therapeutic relationship and psychotherapy outcome. In J. C. Norcross (Ed.), *Psychotherapy relationships that work* (pp. 17–32). New York: Oxford.

Luborsky, L., Diguer, L., Seligman, D. A., Rosenthal, R., Krause, E. D., Johnson, S., et al. (1999). The researcher's own therapy allegiances: A "wild card" in comparisons of treatment efficacy. *Clinical Psychology: Science and Practice, 6,* 95–106.

Lundahl, B., & Burke, B. L. (2009). The effectiveness and applicability of motivational interviewing: A practice-friendly review of four meta-analyses. *Journal of Clinical Psychology: In Session, 11,* 1232–1245.

Miller, W. R., Wilbourne, P. L., & Hettema, J. E. (2003). What works? A summary of alcohol treatment outcome research. In R. K. Hester & W. R. Miller (Eds.), *Handbook of alcoholism treatment approaches: Effective alternatives* (3rd ed., pp. 13–63). Boston: Allyn & Bacon.

Mohr, D. C., Spring, B., Freedland, K. E., Beckner, V., Arean, P., Hollon, S. D., et al. (2009). The selection and design of control conditions for randomized controlled trials of psychological interventions. *Psychotherapy and Psychosomatics, 78*, 275–284.

Norcross, J. C. (Ed.). (2001). Empirically supported therapy relationships: Summary Report of the Division 29 Task Force. *Psychotherapy, 38*(4).

Norcross, J. C. (Ed.). (2002). *Psychotherapy relationships that work.* New York: Oxford University Press.

Norcross, J. C., Hogan, T. P., & Koocher, G. P. (2008). *Clinician's guide to evidence-based practices: Mental health and the addictions.* New York: Oxford University Press.

Norcross, J. C., Koocher, G. P., & Garofalo, A. (2006). Discredited psychological treatments and tests: A Delphi poll. *Professional Psychology: Research & Practice, 37*, 515–522.

Orlinsky, D. E., Ronnestad, M. H., & Willutzki, U. (2004). Fifty years of psychotherapy process-outcome research: Continuity and change. In M. J. Lambert (Ed.), *Handbook of psychotherapy and behavior change*, (5th ed.). New York: Wiley.

Rogers, C. R. (1980). *A way of being.* Boston: Houghton Mifflin.

Stiles, W. B., Honos-Webb, L., & Surko, M. (1998). Responsiveness in psychotherapy. *Clinical Psychology: Science and Practice, 5*, 439–458.

Wampold, B. E. (2001). *The great psychotherapy debate: Models, methods, and findings.* Mahwah, NJ: Lawrence Erlbaum.

Wampold, B. E., Imel, Z. E., Laska, K. M., Benish, S., Miller, S. D., Flückiger, C., et al. (2010). Determining what works in the treatment of PTSD. *Clinical Psychology Review, 8*, 923–933.

INDEX

moderators, 196–98
rating scales for, 193
research limitations, 198–99
research reports, 195t
Task Force conclusions about, 424f
therapeutic practices, 199–200
Global Assessment Scale (GAS), 42, 362t–365t
goal consensus, 41
client contribution, 163
clinical examples, 158–59
coding of study characteristics, 160–61
collaboration concept, 154t–157t, 157–58
definitions and measures, 153–58, 154t–156t
ES estimation, 161
file drawer analyses, 162–63
inclusion criteria and study selection, 159–60
meta-analysis, 161
meta-analytic findings, 161–62
moderators and mediators, 163
research limitations, 163–64
Task Force conclusions about, 424f
therapeutic practices, 164–65
Google Scholar, 77
Greenson, R. R., 26–27
Groningen Illness Attitudes Scale (GIAS), 362t–365t
Group Psychotherapy Interventions Rating Scale (GPIRS), 125, 125t–126t
group therapy
clinical examples, 115–17
coding and analysis, 117–18
correlations and range by outcome measure and cohesion, 122f
ES for cohesion-outcome relationship, 121f
group variables, 122–23
leader variables, 122
measures, 110–15, 111t–113t, 114t
member variables, 122
meta-analysis, 117
meta-analytic findings, 118, 129
moderators and mediators, 120–24
raters of outcome data, 121–22
research limitations, 124
search strategy, 117
study characteristics, 119t–120t, 121–22
Task Force conclusions about, 424f
therapeutic practices, 124–25
Guidelines for Providers of Psychological Services to Ethnic, Linguistic, and Culturally Diverse Populations, 316
Guidelines on Multicultural Education, Training, Research, Practice, and Organizational Change for Psychologists, 316

Halkides, G., 189
halo effect, 52–53, 52t
Hamilton Rating Scale for Anxiety (HRSA), 42, 362t–365t, 387t–389t
Hamilton Rating Scale for Depression (HRSD), 42, 387t–389t
Handelsman, J., 76
Hannover, W., 206
Hardy, G. E., 234–35
Harper, H., 234r
Harwood, M., 343
Hawley, K. M., 73
Hazan, C., 380–82
Hedges, L., 195, 213
Heimberg, R. G., 369
Helping Alliance Counting Signs (HAcs), 41
Helping Alliance Questionnaire-II (HAQ-II), 209
Helping Alliance Questionnaire-Self-Rated (HAq), 28, 41, 49–50
Helping Alliance Scale-Rated (HAr), 41
Helping Relationship Questionnaire (HRQ), 41
Henry, W. P., 7
Hilsenroth, M., 99–100
Holman, J., 343
Holt, C. S., 369
Hook, J. N., 406
Horan, F. P., 207
Horvath, A. C., 45
Howard, K., 207
Hunter, J. E., 99, 393
Hunter's & Schmidt's aggregation procedures, 47

IIP. See Inventory of Interpersonal Problems
Impact of Event Scale (IES), 42
individual psychotherapy
analysis methods, 46–47
clinical examples, 28, 42–45
concept attractiveness, 25
data sources, 45–46
definitions and reconceptualizations, 26–27
ES variability, 49
measures, 27, 51–52, 51f, 52t
meta-analytic findings, 47–49, 48f
patterns over time, 54–55
precursors of, 7–8
research limitations, 55
research reports, 29t–42t
sources-of-alliance assessment, 50–51
Task Force conclusions about, 424f
therapeutic practices, 56–57
time-of-alliance assessment, 50
types of treatments, 52
ineffective relational behaviors, 427–29
infant-parent relationship, 378–79
Inpatient Task and Goal Agreement (ITGA), 41

inpatient therapeutic alliance scales (ITAS), 41
institutional review board (IRB), 15
INT. See interpersonal/relational therapy
internalizing, 336–39
internalizing ratio (IR), 339
internal working models (IWMs), 378
interpersonal/relational therapy (INT), 362t–365t
attachment avoidance, 394
Interpersonal Variables Rating Scale (IVRS), 41
intimate partner violence (IPV), 387t–389t
Inventory of Interpersonal Problems (IIP), 209, 362t–365t, 387t–389t
Inventory of Interpersonal Problems-Circumplex (IIP-C), 362t–365t
IR. See internalizing ratio
IRB. See institutional review board

Jacobson, N. S., 213
Jolkovski, M. P., 252
Journal of Clinical Psychology, 344
Journal of Consulting and Clinical Psychology, 344
Journal of Counseling Psychology, 344
Jungbluth, N., 86

Kagan, J., 339, 349
Karver, M., 70, 75–76, 80–81, 86
Kaufman, N., 83
Kendall, P., 85
Kiesler, D., 190
Klauer, T., 366
Klein, D. N., 15
Kluger, A. N., 204
Kordy, H., 206
Kraus, D. R., 207

Lambert, M. J., 8, 213
leader, group therapy cohesion, 122, 126t
Lietaer, G., 188
limitations, of research. See research limitations
Lingiardi, V., 226
Llewelyn, S., 234–35
Luborsky, L., 26–27
Lunnen, K., 214

MAc meta-analysis package, 47
Main, Mary, 380
major depressive disorder (MDD), 387t–389t
McCullough, M. E., 405
mediators
affirmation, 178, 180, 181t
attachment styles, 393–94
child and adolescent psychotherapy, 80–81
client culture, 322, 325
client preference, 308–9